NONNUS OF NISIBIS, COMMENTARY ON THE GOSPEL OF SAINT JOHN

Society of Biblical Literature

Writings from the Islamic World

James T. Robinson, General Editor

Number 1

NONNUS OF NISIBIS, COMMENTARY ON THE GOSPEL OF SAINT JOHN

Translation of the Armenian Text

with Introduction and Commentary

by

Robert W. Thomson

SBL Press

Atlanta

Library of Congress Cataloging-in-Publication Data

Nonnus, of Nisibis, active 8th century, author.
    Commentary on the Gospel of Saint John / Nonnus of Nisibis ; translation of the Armenian text with introduction and commentary by Robert W. Thomson.
        p. cm. — (Society of Biblical Literature Writings from the Islamic World ; volume 1)
    ISBN 978-1-58983-987-8 (paper binding : alk. paper) — ISBN 978-1-58983-989-2 (electronic format) — ISBN 978-1-58983-988-5 (hardcover binding : alk. paper)
    1. Bible. John—Commentaries—Early works to 1800. I. Thomson, Robert W., 1934–II. Title.
    BS2615.53.N6513 2014
    226.5'07—dc23   2014010037

Cover images created by Craig S. Kaplan, University of Waterloo.
Cover design by Kathie Klein.

To Judith

Contents

The Commentary on the Gospel of Saint John by Nonnus, which dates to the mid-ninth century, is of interest for a variety of reasons: linguistic, historical, and theological. It is important linguistically because it is the first text translated from Arabic into Armenian; and it is notable as a Christian work, whereas the majority of texts translated from Arabic in later times were of a technical or secular origin.[1] It is a valuable historical source for relations of its original sponsor with the Muslim world of the ninth century. As a theological document it defends the miaphysite[2] position of the Armenian church in union with the western Syrian church against the Chalcedonian position of the Greek Byzantine church, and it exerted much influence on later Armenian commentators of the Bible.

Nonnus spent three years examining codices in Syrian monasteries in the course of preparing this commentary. Although he does not name any of his sources, it is possible to place his exegesis in the context of trends in Eastern Christian biblical exposition, primarily the Syrian tradition. In the translation that follows I have therefore placed emphasis on parallels in Syriac commentaries on the Gospel of John, noting also earlier Greek writers whose works were influential in Syria. In Armenian only the *Commentary on the Four Evangelists* by Step'annos of Siunik' predates this text, but that bears little relation to Nonnus's concerns.

The following translation, with my own commentary to the Armenian text, has been several years in the making. Over that time I have greatly profited from discussions with colleagues in the Oriental Institute and from comments to brief presentations at Armenian conferences. To all concerned I offer sincere thanks, especially to Sebastian Brock and David Taylor. I am also

---

1. The Arabic original, alas lost, is also of importance as an early example of Christian writing in that language. Nonnus's other writings were in Syriac.

2. The term "miaphysite" has recently become more popular than "monophysite," since it reflects more accurately Cyril of Alexandria's doctrine: "One nature [*mia physis*] of the Word incarnate."

grateful to the Director of the Matenadaran in Erevan for providing a disk with the text of their manuscript 5551.

The Oriental Institute
Robert W. Thomson
Oxford

Transcription

Armenian

ա բ գ դ ե զ է ը թ ժ ի լ խ ծ կ հ ձ ղ
a b g d e z ē ĕ t' ž i l x c k h j ł

ճ մ յ ն շ ո չ պ ջ ռ ս վ տ ր ց ւ փ ք
č m y n š o č' p ǰ ṙ s v t r c' w p' k'

Greek

α β γ δ ε ζ η θ ι κ λ μ ν
a b g d e z ē th i k l m n

ξ ο π ρ σ τ υ φ χ ψ ω ου
x o p r s t y ph ch ps ō ou

Syriac

ʾ b g d h w z ḥ ṭ y k
l m n s ʿ p ṣ q r š t

Series Editor's Foreword

In the Islamic world, from the ninth to the thirteenth century, there was a burgeoning of interest in the Bible. It was in Islamic Tiberias that the first critical edition of the Hebrew Bible—the Masoretic text—was produced, yet this is only one of many achievements during this extraordinarily productive era. In Iraq, Syria, Palestine, Yemen, Egypt, North Africa, and Spain Jews, Christians, and Samaritans produced multiple, often competing translations of the Bible into Arabic. They also penned hundreds of linear, verse-by-verse, word-by-word commentaries, written from multiple perspectives and representing different traditions. This focus on the Bible generated a large cognate literature as well, including lexicons and grammars, legal monographs and codes, systematic works of theology and philosophy, polemical tracts and heresiographies. Others also showed increasing awareness of and interest in the Bible, as exemplified by the Islamic "Legends of the Prophets" anthologies produced during the period and the appeal to biblical verses in Muslim and Zoroastrian anti-Jewish and anti-Christian polemics.

Despite growing awareness of the "Eastern" traditions of biblical studies, scholarship on medieval exegesis continues to be dominated by Western Europe: the Latin tradition, especially the school of St. Victor forward, and the Hebrew tradition, especially Rashi, Ibn Ezra, Nachmanides, and David Kimchi. These commentators have been written about again and again, their texts have been edited and translated, and a high degree of synthesis has been achieved. The Arabic tradition, in contrast, remains woefully understudied. Hundreds of works remain in manuscript, most of the texts that have been published have not been translated into European languages, and the few attempts at synthesis struggle to present conclusions based on 10 percent, at most, of the data.

To help create a foundation for the study of this, one of the last frontiers in the history of biblical studies, the Writings from the Islamic World (WIW) series makes available original sources from the Arabic tradition, including translations of the Bible and commentaries, as well as texts, translations, and studies related to the cognate literature. Texts in Arabic will be the primary focus, but works produced in other "Islamicate" languages will be included as well, especially Armenian, Hebrew, Persian, and Syriac. Volumes, which typically include an introduction, the original text with English translation, explanatory or textual notes, bibliography, and indices, are ideal for both scholars and students of religion, culture, and the history of exegesis during the medieval period.

We are proud to launch the WIW series with Robert Thomon's translation of Nonnus of Nisibis's *Commentary on the Gospel of Saint John*. Our sincere thanks go not only to Professor Thomson for proposing that SBL Press publish this important work but also to David Konstan and Johan Thom (former editors of the Writings from the Greco-Roman World series), who expertly managed the review and acceptance of the proposal and manuscript even before the WIW series existed.

James T. Robinson
The University of Chicago

Abbreviations

Primary Sources

Comm. Diat.	*Commentary on the Diatessaron* (attributed to Ephrem)
Comm. Jo.	Cyril of Alexandria, *Commentary on the Gospel of John*; Origen, *Commentary on John*
Gospels	Dionysius bar Salibi, *Commentary on the Gospels*
Hex.	Basil of Caesarea, *Hexaemeron*
Hist. eccl.	Eusebius, *Historia ecclesiastica* (*Ecclesiastical History*)
Hom. Jo.	John Chrysostom, *Homilies on John*
Jer	Jerusalem
John	Dionysius bar Salibi, *Commentary on John*
M	Mat 5551
Mat	Matenadaran
N	Ven 1630
Prologue	Philoxenus of Mabbug, *Commentary on the Johannine Prologue*
Teaching	*The Teaching of Saint Gregory* (= Agat'angełos, *History* 259–715)
V	Unspecified Venice manuscript
Ven	Venice
Z	Armenian Bible. *Astuacašunč' Matean hin ew nor Ktakaranac'*. Edited by Y. Zōhrapean. 1805. Reprint, Delmar, N.Y., 1984

Secondary Sources

AVANT	Treasures of the Armenian Christian Tradition, St. Nersess Armenian Seminary
CPG	*Clavis Patrum Graecorum*. Edited by M. Geerard. 5 vols. Turnhout, 1974–87
CSCO	Corpus Scriptorum Christianorum Orientalium
DOP	*Dumbarton Oaks Papers*

DOS	Dumbarton Oaks Studies
DSALL	Dutch Studies in Armenian Language and Literature
ECTT	Eastern Christian Texts in Translation
GCS	Die griechischen christlichen Schriftsteller
HA	*Handes Amsorya*
HATS	Harvard Armenian Texts and Studies
HUAS	Hebrew University Armenian Series
JCSSS	*Journal of the Canadian Society for Syriac Studies*
JTS	*Journal of Theological Studies*
LCE	Library of the Christian East
LOS	London Oriental Series
Mus	*Le Muséon: Revue d'études orientales*
NBHL	*Nor Baṙgirkʻ Haykazean Lezui*. Edited by G. Awetikean, X. Siwrmēlean, and M. Awgerean. 2 vols. 1836–37. Reprint, Erevan, 1979–81
NKGM	Nor Ktakarani Grkʻeri Meknutʻyunner
OCA	Orientalia Christiana Analecta
ODCC	*Oxford Dictionary of the Christian Church*. Edited by F. L. Cross and E. A. Livingstone. 3d rev. ed. Oxford, 2005
OECT	Oxford Early Christian Texts
OrChr	*Oriens Christianus*
ParOr	*Parole de l'Orient*
PG	Patrologia Graeca
PO	Patrologia Orientalis
REArm	*Revue des Études arméniennes*
SC	Sources chrétiennes
SD	Studies and Documents
SP	*Studia Patristica*
StCauc	*Studia Caucasica*
TM	*Travaux et Mémoires*

Introduction

Historical Background

By the year 800 the church in Armenia had long since broken communion with the Greek Byzantine church, primarily over the nature of Christ as defined by the Council of Chalcedon ("one person in two natures, human and divine"), and had forged its own independent identity in matters liturgical, doctrinal, canonical, and historiographical. Although the Council of Chalcedon—the fourth of the councils called ecumenical since they involved the whole empire, the *oikoumenē*—had been held back in 451, the Eastern Christian world remained in turmoil over its christological definition for more than two centuries thereafter. In Armenia the process of disentanglement from the Byzantine church in favor of the position of Cyril of Alexandria ("one nature of the Word incarnate") had not been straightforward. Not only were Armenians themselves divided on many of the issues, the Byzantines had wavered in the intensity of their desire to ensure theological unity in the areas formerly part of the Eastern Roman Empire. The last attempt to impose that unity by force, in the reign of Justinian II, had not been successful, and under the energetic leadership of Catholicos (Patriarch) John of Ojun, who presided over two councils (in 719 and 726, at Dvin and Manazkert), the Armenians had created their own, more or less unified, liturgical and doctrinal positions. John had also consolidated the Armenian tradition of canon law, based on the collection of Armenian councils and translations of early Greek ones. Furthermore, later in the eighth century the notion of Armenia as a coherent entity with its individual history stretching back to the most remote times had been successfully fashioned by Movsēs Xorenacʻi in his *History of Armenia*. Even though the country was now firmly under Muslim control, against the impositions of which the Armenian princes not infrequently rebelled, Armenian cultural activity had not been totally suppressed and was to revive in the ninth century.[1]

---

1. For the break with Byzantium, see Nina Garsoïan's epoch-making *L'église arménienne et le grand schisme d'Orient* (1999); for the development of Armenian theological and

Nonetheless, those of the Chalcedonian persuasion had not given up hope of bringing the Armenians into their fold. The events that brought Nonnus to Armenia from Nisibis and sparked the commission to write a commentary on the Gospel of John derive ultimately from the missionary interests in this regard of the rather obscure patriarch of Jerusalem, Thomas (807–21), and of the well-known polemicist Theodore Abū Qurrah (ca. 750–ca. 830). At some point between 811 and 813 Theodore, who had already gained fame as an apologist for the Chalcedonian cause and was one of the earliest Christian writers in Arabic,[2] was asked by Thomas to write an explanation of the Chalcedonian faith for the Armenian church. This was translated into Greek by the Syncellos of the Jerusalem patriarchate, Michael, who delivered it in Armenia when en route to Constantinople, in 813.[3] This *Epistle to the Armenians* does not actually mention the Armenians at all, nor is it directed specifically against Armenian ideas. Rather, it is a generic defense of Chalcedon, or perhaps part of a more comprehensive work, written before a copy was sent to Armenia.[4]

The *Epistle* was delivered to the prince of Taron, Ašot Bagratuni (775–826),[5] and in response Ašot invited Theodore Abū Qurrah to his court. In order to arrange a debate on the matter, Ašot also asked Abū Ra'ita to come and represent the miaphysite position. The latter had gained fame as an apologist writing in Syriac and Arabic.[6] Abū Ra'ita, however, did not come in person but sent the young deacon Nonnus of Nisibis with a brief treatise Abū Ra'ita had written to defend the miaphysite cause.[7] The debate was held before Ašot and his nobles in 817, and according to all later Armenian accounts

---

liturgical individuality, see Garsoïan 2012. Both books contain very full bibliographies. The date of the *History* by the unknown Movsēs remains controversial; see the introduction in Thomson's revised translation, and Garsoïan 2003–4.

2. For Theodore Abū Qurrah's use of Qur'anic language in his writing, see Swanson 2007 (esp. 117–23, "The Texts and the Islamic Environment").

3. The original Arabic is lost, but the Greek text survives; see PG 97:1504–21, translation in Lamoreaux 2005 (83–95). For Theodore Abū Qurrah, see also Griffith 2008 (esp. 60–63, for his debates with Muslims).

4. This treatise emphasizes that Christ is a single hypostasis: being both God and man, he has two natures, divine and human. The two natures are joined after the incarnation. Christ thus possesses two properties, two energies, and two wills.

5. Ašot, known as *Msaker*, "carnivorous," held the position of "prince of princes" from 806; see the genealogical table in Toumanoff 1990 (113). For a brief sketch of Armenia at this period, see Mahé and Mahé 2012 (ch. 4, "Caliphat (634–884)"); more detail in Ter-Ghewondyan 1976; Laurent 1980; Hovannisian 1997.

6. On Abū Ra'ita, see Griffith 1980. For his role in sending Nonnus to Armenia, see Griffith 2001 (esp. 49–53).

7. For this treatise, "Refutation of the Melchites concerning the Union," see Graf 1951, 65–72 of the Arabic text.

Nonnus prevailed.[8] Theodore was worsted and had to leave Armenia. From the theological point of view, therefore, the miaphysite position in Armenia was strengthened. This is neatly expressed by the thirteenth-century historian Vardan Arewelc'i: "The deacon Nanay came and disputed with Abu Qurra, defeating him by the power of the Holy Spirit. So the prince expelled him, and was confirmed even more in the faith of Saint Gregory."[9] As often happened, the later position of the Armenian church was defined as the faith of Saint Gregory the Illuminator.[10]

Following this debate, Nonnus was commissioned by Ašot's son Bagrat to prepare a commentary on the Gospel of John. The debate had no doubt been conducted in Arabic,[11] and when Nonnus presented his commentary to Bagrat some years later, it too was in Arabic. On the other hand, the sources used by Nonnus for his commentary were in Syriac.[12]

The Armenian translator of Nonnus's *Commentary* has left a preface describing the circumstances of the composition of the commentary and its translation.[13] He begins with the flourishes typical of Armenian authors as he describes his own inadequacy when faced by the commission of his noble patron, Smbat Bagratuni. Smbat, Bagrat's brother, had ordered a translation of the Arabic text into Armenian, though it was not completed for many years.[14] Like the earlier historian Agat'angełos, the translator refers to those who travel to the ends of India on a quest for the glittering topaz, those who dive for pearls, and those who seek to acquire the silk of royal purple that is produced by "nauseating worms" (*ordunk' zazrac'ealk'*). But he could not escape such a

---

8. This Nonnus, known in Armenian as Nanay the Syrian, is not to be confused with the fifth-century poet Nonnus of Panopolis in Egypt, who composed a paraphrase of the Gospel of John in Greek. (Baronian and Conybeare [1918] made this mistake in describing MS 74.) The references to "Nonnus" in Metzger 1975 are to the fifth-century writer's text of the Gospel of John, not to Nonnus of Nisibis's *Commentary*.

9. Vardan Arewelc'i, *Historical Compilation*, 78. He is the first historian to mention this debate.

10. For this trend to attribute later developments in the Armenian church to Gregory himself, see the introduction to Thomson 2010.

11. Although the copy of Theodore Abū Qurrah's treatise had been translated into Greek, Theodore himself spoke Arabic. Abū Ra'ita's contribution was in Arabic, and Nonnus knew Arabic, though most of his own writings are in Syriac. Syriac was a language known to ecclesiastical circles in Armenia but not used at court. For knowledge of Arabic in Armenia at this time, see Thomson, "Arabic in Armenia" (forthcoming).

12. The Arabic commentary is, of course, important as evidence for the adoption of Arabic by the Christians of Muslim Syria and Mesopotamia.

13. This is translated in full below, preceding the text of the commentary.

14. See further below, xxi.

sublime request. After four pages of similar rhetoric he comes to the point. A learned man by the name of Nanay (i.e., Nonnus), competent in Syrian literature and orthodox in faith, defeated a certain heretical philosopher and had him expelled from Armenia. This unnamed heretic, that is, Theodore Abū Qurrah, taught perversely by dividing into two the inseparable unity of Christ after the indivisible and unconfused unity. Nonnus reaffirmed the orthodox position: to confess one from two persons, the divine attributes by nature, but the lesser human characteristics by divine acceptance. And indeed, the *Commentary* is devoted to that position, a detailed exposition of Cyril of Alexandria's classic phrase: *mia physis tou Theou Logou sesarkōmenē.*

According to the preface, at some unstated time after the debate Nonnus was solicited by Bagrat Bagratuni to produce a commentary on the Gospel of John.[15] After rigorous fasts and prayers Nonnus undertook the task. He spent three years traveling through the deserts of Mesopotamia and composed a commentary, summarizing from many books, "one by one methodically, translating from the Syrian tongue into the Hagarene language." Alas, we are given no clues as to the identity of these Syriac sources, though there are several references to "other exemplars."[16] Bagrat was later captured by the Hagarenes (i.e., the Muslims). The author of the preface notes that when in prison, he sadly fell away from the divine faith and plunged into the pit of irreparable destruction, though the author also claims that in the depth of his heart Bagrat kept firm the profession of the true faith. By some chance, he continues, the book came into the hands of Smbat Bagratuni, Bagrat's brother, and it was Smbat who commanded it to be translated from Arabic. Meanwhile Nonnus himself had also been imprisoned, but he never abjured his faith, despite various temptations.[17] "After this had so happened," for the writer gives no dates, the book came to the princess of Siwnik', Marem Bagratuni, who repeated the command to have it translated. And if there are any blemishes in the ensuing result, the author of the preface begs his readers not to be critical. Finally, he describes the difference between John's Gospel and the three other (canonical) Gospels, with the circumstances of its original composition by the evangelist.

---

15. The spelling of Bagrat's name varies in the sources, often appearing as Bagarat. Bagrat is the usual form of this common name. For the Bagratuni family in the earlier period, see Garsoïan 1989 (362–63); and for stemmata of the various branches, see Toumanoff 1990.

16. See below, xxviii–xxix, for the references and their meaning.

17. For the imprisonment of Nonnus, see Mariès 1920–21 (276), and further below, xliii.

A few details may be added from other sources. Bagrat was arrested in 851 and imprisoned by the Muslim caliph in Samarra, where he apostatized.[18] T'ovma Arcruni notes: "The memory of his going astray ... remains from generation to generation for ever."[19] Bagrat died the next year in captivity.

The preface to the translation indicates that the Arabic text of the *Commentary on John* came into the hands of Bagrat's brother, Smbat, who commanded a translation to be made into Armenian; but in 855 he too was imprisoned in Samarra before that could be completed. Smbat died in prison without abjuring his faith, for which he gained the epithet of "the confessor." The book then came down to Smbat's granddaughter Marem, the wife of Vasak prince of Siunik'. It was she who finally had the translation completed, probably in the 880s.[20] The original Arabic text was not preserved, so we know the *Commentary* only in its Armenian form.

The translator ends the first half of the work with a colophon at the end of chapter 10. The wording seems to imply that he has finished his task; but it cannot mean that this was all that Smbat's command produced, since the translator names Smbat and Marem of Siwnik' together: "who commanded [pl.] this holy book to be translated." The second half of the commentary does not contain any personal comment by the original translator. So it remains unclear whether Smbat's original command for a translation resulted in a partial rendering, a preliminary draft, or nothing tangible.

MANUSCRIPTS AND PRINTED EDITION

One edition of Nonnus's *Commentary* exists, printed in 1920 in Venice. Its editor, Fr. K'erobē Č'rak'ean, used manuscript Ven 1630 (of the Mekhitarist collection at San Lazzaro in Venice), which was written in 1155 of our era in Amida (modern Diyarbekir).[21] He noted some variants in one modern manu-

---

18. See Garsoïan in Hovannisian 1997 (1:140).

19. The translator's preface to the Armenian text of the *Commentary* claims that Bagrat kept firm the profession of the true faith in the depth of his heart. According to T'ovma Arcruni, *History of the Arcrunik'*, 162, Bagrat himself had said that apostasy because of danger of suffering does no harm if one secretly keeps in one's heart the confession of faith. The phrasing of the passages in the translator's preface and in the historian is quite similar.

20. The exact date is not known, but Marem's father, Ašot, is called "prince of princes" in the translator's preface. Ašot acquired that title circa 862 but by 884 was officially "king." (He died in 890.) Ter-Łevondyan (1976, 235) indicates that he was called king in inscriptions as early as 874. Step'annos Orbelean, *History of Siwnik'*, ch. 37, gives information about Mariam's charitable work and her role in the foundation of the monastery of Sewan (for which see Pogossian 2012), but he does not mention Nonnus.

21. Ven 1630 contains only Nonnus's *Commentary*. It was written by Kirakos; for a full

script (which he fails to identify); there are indeed several nineteenth-century copies of the text in Venice.

The Matenadaran in Erevan kindly provided a disk of another manuscript, Mat 5551, also dated to 1155 but written in the monastery of Kamrjaǰor (south of Kars).[22] There are many differences between this manuscript and the printed edition in minor details, but the Matenadaran manuscript has generally a superior text, especially where Venice 1630 has omitted phrases.[23] These are the oldest dated manuscripts of the *Commentary*, though Mat 4134 also dates to the twelfth century, according to the catalogue. There are many other manuscripts dating from the thirteenth to the nineteenth centuries: at least twenty-seven in the Matenadaran, twelve in Jerusalem, and other examples in Paris, Vienna, Venice, and Oxford. The following list indicates the dates of these manuscripts and their places of writing, excluding those manuscripts that contain only extracts:

Date	Manuscript (Provenance)*
1155	Ven 1630 (Amida; = N); Mat 5551 (Kamrjaǰor; = M)
12th century	Mat 4134 (np)
1228	Jer 1295 (Skewra)
1286	Mat 10480 (not in catalogue)
13th century	Mat 5611 (np); Mat 6903 (np); Jer 1046 (np)
1306	Mat 2520 (Erzinjan? [commissioned by Yovhannēs Erznkac'i])
1322	Mat 1275 (Glajor?)
1347	Mat 1138 (Sis)
1363	Mat 2611 (Crimea)
1398	Jer 73 (Jerusalem)

---

description see Čemčemean 1998 (vol. 8, col. 509–14). Č'rak'ean (p. *lt'* [39]) notes some of the vagaries of its spelling.

22. Here I acknowledge the help of its director, Hratch Tamrazyan. Mat 5551 also contains the *Commentary on the Four Evangelists* by Step'annos of Siunik'; for a description, see Eganyan et al. 1970 (vol. 2, col. 131).

23. Mat 5551 is written in a variety of hands, and there are numerous colophons. Its history is clearly quite complicated and needs further elucidation.

14th century	Mat 1244 (np); Mat 1426 (np)
1414	Mat 1391 (np)
16th century	Mat 1350 (np)
1625	Mat 1278 (Xotanan [Siwnik'], Ējmiacin)
1634	Jer 633 (Jerusalem?)
1637	Jer 1113 (np)
1656	Mat 1449 (np)
1666	Mat 1390 (Nor Julfa)
17th century	Mat 4359 (np); Mat 1349 (np); Vienna 611 (np); Oxford 74
1725	Jer 675 (Jerusalem)
1729	Jer 68 (Caesarea)
1736	Jer 3196 (Jerusalem)
1737	Jer 154 (Jerusalem)
1786	Mat 1880 (Jerusalem)
18th century	Mat 6472 (np); Jer 3508
1809	Mat 2689 (Constantinople)
1822	Mat 7581 (Constantinople? [written by P. Polsec'i])
1825	Ven 1631, a copy of Ven 1630 (Venice)
1848	Mat 1348 (Samat'ia [Constantinople])
19th century	Ven 1632 (np); Ven 1633 (np); Mat 5705 (np); 7551 (np)
unclear	Jer 1759 (np; in *bologir*)

* np = provenance unknown

Many of the surviving manuscripts have no indication of their place of writing (at least, from descriptions in printed catalogues). Nonetheless, from the evidence it is clear that the Armenian version of this commentary by Nonnus had a wide circulation in historic Armenia. The oldest dated manuscripts, Mat 5551 and Ven 1630, were written at opposite ends of the country:

Mat 5551 in the northwest near Kars, Ven 1630 in the south on the Tigris at Amida. In 1228 a copy was made in Cilicia, at the monastery of Skewra, and in 1347 another copy at Sis, the capital of Armenian Cilicia. Far to the north in Crimea a copy was made in 1363. In central Armenia copies were made at Glajor (perhaps) in 1322, Ayrivank' (perhaps) in 1414, and Siwnik' and Ējmiacin in 1625. To the east a copy was written at Nor Julfa near Isfahan in 1666. To the west, in Anatolia copies were made at Erzinjan (perhaps) in 1306, and Caesarea in 1729. Numerous copies were made in Jerusalem: 1398, 1634, and four in the eighteenth century. In Constantinople copies were made only in the nineteenth century. A more detailed examination of the manuscripts than is presently available would enhance this picture. But of all later Armenian commentaries on John, only that by the late fourteenth-century Mattēos Jułayec'i circulated in a comparable number of copies.[24]

The translation of Nonnus below is based on the printed edition, which was made from Ven 1630 (= N), and is supplemented by the text in Mat 5551 (= M). The significant variants are indicated in the notes at the bottom of each page.[25] Wherever the editor Č'rak'ean notes a variant taken from his unspecified recent Venice manuscript, this is marked by "V." Sometimes this modern text is in agreement with M. Further corroboration of preferred readings comes from the numerous citations of this commentary in the *Commentary on John* by Grigor Tat'ewac'i, which is dated to 1409.[26]

Nonnus's *Commentary* is quite long, running to 445 printed pages in N and 222 folios in M (which lacks the preface and the text up to John 1:3).[27] Nonnus divides the Gospel text into longer or shorter sections. His commentary to each successive lemma also varies in length. At the end of chapter 10 there is a colophon by the translator recalling the sponsors Smbat Bagratuni and Marem princess of Siwnik', and chapter 11 begins with the title "Of the Same Holy Nanay." This indicates that the original work was divided into two sections. The printed edition provides four section breaks in the first four chapters.[28] Č'rak'ean suggests that these represent sections for public reading

---

24. See the descriptions in Petrosyan and Ter-Step'anyan 2002 (93–97).

25. By "significant" I mean any variants that would require a change in the English translation. Therefore variants of spelling of the same Armenian word are not noted.

26. Grigor begins this commentary by giving a résumé of the circumstances that led to the composition of Nonnus's text and explaining various terms.

27. Note that Č'rak'ean gives the page numbers of his manuscript (Ven 1630) in the margins to the text; these are the page numbers to which he refers in his introduction, not the page numbers of the book marked in the top corner.

28. At John 1:1; 1:18; 2:12; and 4:1.

or a sermon. They are not found in M and do not continue after the fourth, and thus they appear to be secondary divisions.

Since the Arabic text of the commentary has disappeared, we cannot check what changes, abbreviations, or expansions were introduced by the translator. The text of the commentary is expanded at various points by exhortations to the readers, and Č'rak'ean found parallels in some of these with other Armenian texts.[29] So it seems reasonable to suppose that they did not form part of Nonnus's original work but were added by the Armenian translator (or by a copyist before the manuscript tradition began to diverge). The passages in question all end with "Amen," but only some are marked as *yordorak*, "exhortation," by the editor of N or in M. These additions occur at the commentary on the following passages from John:

1:17: Exhortation to virtue.

2:11: A passage on Christ as the mystical groom at the end of the account of the wedding at Cana.

3:15: Following the reference to eternal life, an exhortation to avoid sin and perform good deeds in order to attain the supernal Jerusalem. Here M has *yor* (*yordorak*) in the margin, but N does not mark the passage.

6:59: A passage on the Eucharist as the food of life.

10:40–42: An exhortation to virtue. The editor of N marks this section as *yordorak*, but the scribe of M has no such indication. This is followed by a lengthy passage of praise for the church of Armenia, ending with a colophon by the translator and a reference to the patrons of the translation, Smbat Bagratuni and Marem princess of Siwnik'. Here ends Book I of the commentary.[30]

11:45–46: Praise for the resurrection of Lazarus, followed by exhortation to the readers. The editor of N marks the section as *yordorak*, but not the scribe of M.

12:50: Further exhortation to virtue. This is marked *yordorak* by the editor of N; the scribe of M has *Yk* (*yordorak*) in the margin.

19:37: Disparagement of the Old Israel and praise for the New.

21:25: Praise of the resurrection. This is marked as *yordorak* by the editor of N, but not by the scribe of M.

---

29. See notes to the commentary, ad loc.

30. After the "Exhortation," before the passage on the Armenian church, the scribe of M notes: "This book ends." So the division into two books dates at least to the twelfth century.

Translation and the Armenian Biblical Text

As the original Arabic is lost, the accuracy of the translator in rendering Non-nus's biblical text in the lemmata cannot be judged. The biblical passages in the two oldest dated manuscripts are often in disagreement with the standard Armenian biblical text, that is, with the text edited by Zōhrapean (= Z). That is not surprising, since the latter is based on the tradition of Armenian Cilicia, more than four hundred years after the commentary was translated.[31] In the notes to the lemmata in the translation below, the differences with Z are indicated; but in the absence of a critical edition of the Armenian Gospel of John, it is impossible to make any general comments about the relationship of the biblical text known to the ninth-century translator of the Arabic commentary with a more widely used ninth-century Armenian Bible.

Only a few verses of John's Gospel are omitted, the most obvious being the pericope of the woman taken in adultery (John 7:53–8:11), which is not found in the Old Syriac or in early Armenian Bibles.[32] John 5:4, regarding the angel who stirred the waters, is also missing; the commentary, however, does refer to the angel stirring the waters. Though printed in Z, this verse is not found in many early Armenian manuscripts. The lemma of 1:7b, "that all through him might believe," is omitted, though the commentary ends with a reference to "coming to faith." At 2:15 Nonnus also omits part of the lemma, "and he scattered the coins of the money changers and overthrew the tables," to which the commentary makes no reference. Nonnus does not include the lemma of 10:15b: "and I lay down my life for the sheep"; but the commentary following, to verse 17, picks up the theme. And at 18:8a the lemma omits Jesus's remark "I told you that," which appears in the repetition of the verse in the commentary. On the other hand, at 12:17–18 ("and the people who were with him testified … that he had performed those miracles"), the lemma may not be part of the original text; it interrupts the commentary to the previous verse, is not mentioned in the commentary, and is omitted in N.

Occasionally there is a minor variant between the lemma and the commentary, as at John 6:40, where "receives" appears in the lemma but "will receive" is found in the commentary. But the most curious discrepancy is that three times a reference to "Pharisees" in the lemma is changed to "Sadducees" in the commentary: at 1:24; 4:1–3; and 11:46.[33]

---

31. See Cox 1984.

32. See note to commentary on John 7:52 for this section as found in other commentaries.

33. See also commentary to John 12:12–13 for a reference to the Sadducees, where Pharisees have just been mentioned.

Nonnus makes only one serious mistake in identifying a biblical quotation. At John 16:25 he notes that John referred to Christ's postresurrection appearances also in the Catholic Epistles. His citation, on the other hand, is a direct quotation of Acts 1:3. Nonnus does not always identify the author quoted, but no other mistakes are made. He refers by name to the four evangelists and to Paul, Moses, Isaiah, and David. John is often called "the evangelist" or "the apostle"; "[Moses's] own history" refers to Genesis (at John 1:3); "Moses … prophesied" refers to Deuteronomy (at John 1:21b); "the law" refers to Deuteronomy (at John 3:15), as does "what Moses had said" (at 19:15a); the "book of Genesis" is so named at John 4:25, and "the Old Testament" at 4:26. There is a general reference to the "writings," *grealsn*, of Moses at 5:45.[34] "The earlier prophet" or "the prophetic voice" is Isaiah (at John 2:11; 11:9–10); "the prophecies" can refer to the Psalms or to Isaiah.[35]

More interestingly, in the commentary to Christ calling himself the "good shepherd" at John 10:11, the translator makes a reference to his own work in rendering the commentary from Arabic into Armenian. He discusses the meaning of the Armenian word used to translate "good": *kʿaǰ*. This he says means *bari*, "good," quoting Luke 18:19, where the Armenian biblical text does have *bari*. In the lemma for John 10:14, however, the translator uses *bari*, whereas the standard Armenian text (i.e., Z) repeats *kʿaǰ*. The basic meaning of *kʿaǰ* is "noble, valiant"; in John 10:11 and 14 the Greek is *kalos*; in the Greek of Luke 18:19 the adjective *agathos* is used. In Syriac *ṭbʾ* is used for both occurrences of "good."

Nonnus occasionally notes alternative readings for his biblical text:

1:28: "We have also found in a copy [*awrinak*] somewhere Betʾabra called Betʾania." This probably refers to a copy of the Bible, not a commentator. Although the commentators are indeed divided over the topic, the biblical manuscripts also diverge.[36] Here the lemma agrees with Z.

11:28: "We have found in some exemplars that the Lord commanded Mary to be summoned." Here the biblical text rather than a commentator seems to be involved, for Nonnus omits the second part of the verse in his lemma: "And she said, 'the teacher has come and summons you.'"[37] The phrase is found in Z, however, and in the wider biblical tradition.

---

34. Since *grealsn* is used, the meaning is not "books," which would be *girsn*.

35. There is one reference to the Holy Spirit prophesying (Ps 77), but it occurs in the "Exhortation" added to chapter 19, not in the commentary of Nonnus.

36. See note to the commentary, ad loc.

37. See note to the commentary, ad loc.

The translator appended to his introduction a brief description of the writing of their Gospels by the four evangelists.[38] Nonnus himself makes reference occasionally to the differences between John and the other evangelists. Thus at John 1:35 he states that John omitted what had been said by Matthew, Mark, and Luke concerning the temptation of Christ in the desert. At greater length he explains at 12:16 that John was not concerned to repeat what had been related by the other three evangelists but described what they had omitted, such as the wedding at Cana. Several times Nonnus distinguishes between different accounts of similar, but not necessarily identical, episodes: for example, the nobleman whose son was healed in John 4:46 and Matt 8; Jesus walking on the sea in John 6:18 and Matt 14; Mary anointing the Lord's feet in John 11:2 and in Matt 26 and Mark 14; the words of Jesus on the cross in John 19:30, compared to those in Matt 27 and Luke 23; and Mary coming first to the tomb in John 20:1 and Matt 28.

PARALLEL TEXTS IN SYRIAC AND GREEK

Nonnus spent three years combing Syrian monasteries in Mesopotamia. But neither the translator, in his preface, nor the author, in his text, gives any indication whatsoever as to the specific writers or works that Nonnus perused. In the commentary to the following verses, Nonnus does occasionally refer to another exemplar (*awrinak*), without identification, or to an author without naming him:

> 1:5a: "a certain other holy man," who "describes the various bodily movements of the passions[39] within us."
>
> 1:18: "to some this seems not to fit the context."
>
> 1:29: "someone from among the teachers says." This is a reference to a commentator; here John Chrysostom is intended.[40]
>
> 4:46–47: "to some it so seemed that this is the same person as Matthew described, but they did not understand correctly" (i.e., the nobleman whose son was ill in Capernaum).
>
> 5:15–16: "some of the commentators [*t'argmanič'k'*]," regarding the identity of the accounts by Matthew and John of the healing of the blind man.[41]

---

38. Translation below, 6–7.

39. Passions: *kirk'*; see the discussion of terms below, xxxviii.

40. See note to the commentary, ad loc.

41. John Chrysostom also noted various opinions; see note to the commentary, ad loc.

6:18–21: "some of the earlier [commentators] thought these [words] were what Matthew related" (i.e., Jesus walking on the sea).

7:4–5: "some have said," regarding the motives for Jesus's brothers urging him to go up to Jerusalem.

9:4–5: "we have found it in some examples," regarding the interpretation of "while it is daytime."

11:35–37: "we found also in some exemplars," regarding the interpretation of "Jesus wept."

12:20–21: "it is said somewhere," that is, by a commentator regarding the Gentiles who went up to the feast.

19:17b–18a: "we have found from the tradition of the ancients" (i.e., from apocryphal tales regarding the burial of Adam's skull at Golgotha). Nonbiblical sources were also used for the story of Christ's birth in a cave (at John 1:14b).

20:17a: "we have found from accurate examples," regarding Mary's thoughts concerning the risen Christ.

21:12: "we found from examples," regarding the disciples on seeing Jesus at the Lake of Tiberias.

In the notes to the following translation, parallels in other commentators to these passages have been adduced, but the precise texts to which Nonnus refers often remain unclear. Although Nonnus drew primarily on commentaries of the Syrian tradition, these included translations of Greek patristic writers. The direct origin of a comment in Nonnus is thus sometimes difficult to pin down.

The earliest writer in Syriac to be cited below is Ephrem Syrus (d. 373), a prolific author and composer of commentaries, though he did not write specifically on John.[42] The *Commentary on the Diatessaron* however, which is of interest for exegesis of John's Gospel, is from the circle of Ephrem, not the master himself. In any event, one can find in Nonnus a few parallels with that commentary, though it is not quoted directly.

More influential on Nonnus were the extensive *Homilies on John* by John Chrysostom; these were known in Syriac translation from the sixth century, and there are many parallels in the Armenian text of Nonnus's *Commentary*. Č'rak'ean gives parallels for three passages: at John 2:15, *xndreli ē…*; 4:6, *tes ew zvstakeloyn…*; and 11:43, *naew oč' ayloy…*.[43] He also indicates Chrysostom's

---

42. Curiously, the OT commentaries in Armenian attributed to him are much later compositions that derive from the tenth or eleventh century; see Mathews 1998, esp. the introduction.

43. See notes to the commentary, ad loc.

references to the "thieves and brigands" of 10:7–8, explained in the same fashion by Nonnus.[44] In fact, the parallels are far more extensive than that and can be found throughout the commentary, as indicated in the notes to the following translation. But since many other commentators also relied on Chrysostom, parallels between Chrysostom and Nonnus do not necessarily always derive from a *direct* reading by the latter of the former's *Homilies on John*. A passage from Chrysostom's *Hom. Jo.* 69, correctly ascribed to *Yova Oskeber*, has been added by a later scribe to the commentary following 11:42; it appears in M and V but not N.

Č'rak'ean notes two parallels with Severian of Gabbala, an opponent of John Chrysostom, at John 11:33 (*isk harc'aneln…*) and 11:41 (*ew zays aselov…*); both are passages from the story of Lazarus.[45] Many of Severian's homilies are in fact preserved under the name of Chrysostom. But he was little known in Syriac tradition.[46] If Nonnus did in fact read Severian—for other commentators also give similar interpretations to these passages—it is unclear whether he read him in Greek or in Syriac translation. In addition there are also numerous parallels with Cyril of Alexandria's *Commentary on the Gospel of John*, which was known in Syriac, though only fragments survive.[47]

After the fifth century the exegetical tradition begins to diverge between authors of the Western Syrian tradition and those from the church of the East, who were loyal to the school of Antioch. Of the first group, Philoxenus of Mabbug (d. 523) was a popular theologian in Armenia; quotations from his writings appear in the florilegia. Only fragments of his commentaries on the Gospels survive, but we do possess an extensive treatise on the prologue to the Gospel of John. This is a defense of a theological viewpoint shared by Nonnus[48] but is of little relevance for the general exposition of the whole Gospel. By far the most important Syriac commentary that has parallels in Nonnus is the one by Moše bar Kepha, who was much indebted

---

44. For other commentators with the same interpretation, see note to the commentary, ad loc.

45. The passages are from *Homily* 2 (Awgerean, 28, 34). This section of the homily (entitled *De incarnatione* in the Latin version, but without title in the Armenian text) deals with the resurrection of Lazarus. Other commentators give similar explanations; see the commentary below. This homily is by Severian, not Eusebius of Emesa; see Lehmann 1975 (171).

46. See references in *CPG*; Ortiz de Urbina 1965 (248): "inedita."

47. The parallels with Cyril are signaled in the notes to the commentary.

48. Defined by de Halleux, in his edition of Philoxenus's *Prologue*, as "un traité de polémique christologique" (p. xv). The fragments on John quoted by de Halleux (1963, 150–62) bear little relation to the exposition of Nonnus.

to John Chrysostom. Moše lived in the ninth century and died in 903, so he was obviously not a direct source for Nonnus. Nonetheless, he represents a tradition on which Nonnus drew, and parallels between his commentary and that of Nonnus abound.

Even later are the writings of Dionysius bar Salibi, known for his anti-Armenian attitude. He died in 1171, but two of his works are of importance for us: his general *Commentary on the Gospels*, and a separate work specifically on John. Parallels between these and Nonnus are frequent. Another reason for the importance of Dionysius is that he was familiar with Western Syriac as well as Eastern Syriac traditions, notably the *Commentary on John* by the early fifth-century Theodore of Mopsuestia, which was available in Syriac, and the *Commentary on the Gospels* by Išodad of Merv (d. c. 850) for the Eastern tradition. Parallels with the Syriac texts of Theodore and Išodad are also indicated in the notes to the following translation.

In the commentary by Nonnus one occasionally finds statements with no parallel in the Syriac tradition. In John 3, Jesus tells Nicodemus that unless someone is born again he cannot see the kingdom of God. Nonnus adds a description of our first, natural birth, the coming into being of a child from the elements of earth, water, air, and fire, with flesh and bones, sinews and tendons and ligaments, the stretching out of the skin, the hair, nails, membranes and fat, the five physical senses, and the four characteristics defined by the medical art, namely, phlegm, blood, and the two kinds of bile. These details of the human body are spelled out by John Chrysostom but are without parallel in the Syrian commentators.

On other occasions Nonnus agrees with all commentators, as in the explanation of John 8:33. The Jews said, "We are the seed of Abraham and have not ever been in servitude to anyone." Nonnus states: "How were they never in servitude to anyone, when they were slaves of Pharoah in Egypt for so long; after that they were kept captive in servitude in Babylon; and then to the Romans as well?" This is the line taken by everyone, with minor variations. John Chrysostom, Moše bar Kepha, Dionysius bar Salibi, Cyril of Alexandria, Theodore of Mopsuestia, Išodad, and, in Armenian, Taťewac'i all refer to Egyptians, Babylonians, and Romans, with some offering more detail than others. Step'annos of Siunik's *Commentary on the Four Evangelists* cites only a minority of the verses in John, and this passage is not among them.

On the other hand, there are explanations that do not appear earlier than Nonnus, or at least, the origin of which I have not traced. For example, in John 9 Jesus cures a man blind from birth. Nonnus says that this man was not just deprived of sight, but the places where his eyes should be were flat with his cheeks, destitute of all formed vessels. A similar description of the blind man is found in the later Dionysius bar Salibi, and Tat'ewac'i echoes Nonnus, but it seems not to appear earlier.[49]

Nonnus did not draw on earlier Armenian tradition, but it is interesting to note some differences of interpretation between his work and the eighth-century *Commentary on the Four Evangelists* by Step'annos of Siwnik'. The earliest Armenian attempts at biblical commentary are obscure, and controversy surrounds the dating of what survives from before Step'annos.[50] Before becoming the metropolitan of Siwnik', in the second decade of the eighth century Step'annos had spent several years in Constantinople translating Greek patristic works, notably the corpus of writings attributed to Dionysius the Areopagite.[51] His own *Commentary on the Four Evangelists* does not treat the Gospels in their entirety, or equally.[52] Therefore a full comparison with Nonnus is not possible. But it may be interesting to note the following interpretations by Step'annos of passages in John, interpretations that do not occur in the Syrian commentators to the same passages:

1:17: Christ's two shoes represent the incarnation and the descent to hell.

2:1–11: The groom and the bride at the wedding represent the Mosaic law and the soul, respectively, and the water and wine represent the teaching of the Mosaic law and the superior teaching (of Christ) "which makes souls rejoice."

2:14: The oxen, sheep, doves, and money changers in the temple represent various categories of people: those who only think of earthly things; those who pretend to have gentleness but do not; those who light-mindedly turn from one doctrine to another; and those who are not pure in heart.

9:2: Step'annos refers to philosophers outside the church who explain blindness and other blemishes, such as ill health, as the result of souls sinning before their incarnations in bodies.

---

49. See Nonnus, commentary to John 9:1.

50. For the earliest commentaries in Armenian and the activity of Step'annos, see Thomson 2006.

51. See the introduction to the Armenian text in Thomson 1987.

52. Of the 142 pages in the recent edition, the first 95 are devoted to Matthew. "The Gospel according to Mark," says Step'annos (1994, 111), "differs in no way from Matthew." The only passage he quotes is Mark 14:51–52, where he identifies the youth who fled naked with Mark himself. The Gospel of Luke takes up the next 22 pages, and another 23 cover the Gospel of John.

After Step'annos, no commentary on John was written in Armenian until the twelfth century. Sargis Kund, whose *Commentary on the Gospel of John* was composed in 1177, quotes numerous earlier writers, including Step'annos, Nanay (Nonnus), and various Armenian homelists, as well as Greek authors and Ephrem; but his work remains unpublished.[53] The commentary by Grigor Tat'ewac'i, written in 1409, luckily is available. As already mentioned above, this is valuable as a help to the elucidation of variants in the manuscript tradition of the Armenian rendering of Nonnus.[54] His comments have thus often been cited in the notes to the translation (though, admittedly, they shed no light on Nonnus's sources).

THEOLOGICAL EMPHASIS AND TECHNICAL VOCABULARY

Nonnus's *Commentary* does not deal exclusively with problems that have to be explained, either literally or allegorically. A good deal of the text is devoted to retelling the Gospel narrative in expanded form, a kind of midrash, in which the reader is sometimes addressed directly in the second person. Nonnus repeats the passage he is explicating, introducing it by saying: "In other words." And sometimes he ends with an exhortation, aimed at inculcating a reaction to the words of the Gospel.[55] Furthermore, he often refers to Old Testament predictions as an "example," *awrinak*, or "shadow," *stuer*, of the full revelation in Christ. This use of typology is widespread in early Armenian theologians.[56] Nonnus, however, generally confines his comparisons between the mystery of the Old Testament and the fulfillment in the New to biblical references to the law and the prophets and does not extend such comparisons to the interpretation of physical objects, as was common in Armenian commentators.[57]

It is also noticeable that Nonnus does not share the usual Armenian predilection for number symbolism. He passes over the six vessels, each containing two or three measures, at the marriage of Cana (John 2:5–6), and the five loaves and two fishes at the feeding of the five thousand (6:8–9). His only explanations of numbers are the following: the twelve baskets of remnants

---

53. See Petrosyan and Ter-Step'anyan 2002 (93) for the MSS.

54. See above, xxiv.

55. Č'rak'ean (introduction, p. *žt'* [19]) notes that compared to John Chrysostom, Nonnus rarely emphasizes the moral aspect of his commentary. He repeats earlier comments by Sargisean that Nonnus follows the Antiochene tradition of exegesis, the more literal explanatory style, not the allegorical.

56. See Thomson 2001, 21–23: "God's Eternal Plan and Biblical 'Types.'"

57. See, for example, the list of objects in the index to Thomson 2001 (264, s.v. "Types"). *Awrinak* has other meanings, such as "exemplar (of a book)," as above, xxviii.

(at John 6:12–13) and the twelve hours of the day (at 11:9–10) represent the twelve apostles; the sixth hour at the well of Samaria is parallel to the sixth age, in which faith will come to the world (at 4:26; see v. 6);[58] also parallel to the sixth age is the sixth day (when Adam departed from paradise and Christ died on the cross) (at 11:55). Nonnus also refers to the "mystery," *xorhurd*, of the number eight, representing the eighth age.[59] Various interpretations of the meaning of eight appear in Armenian writers, but the theme of the eighth as the final age is not common.[60] For Nonnus the 153 fish in the net represent baptism and the Trinity (at 21:13–14).

Nor is Nonnus greatly interested in the etymology of the various places mentioned in the Gospel. He explains *Bedhezda*, the Hebrew name for the *Propatikē* pool, as "descent" or "repose of mercy." "Descent of mercy" derives from John Chrysostom; the Syrian commentators suggest "house of mercy."[61] And in the description of the Samaritans he interprets the name either as derived from Mount Sameron or as meaning "guardians," *pahapank'*, correctly translating the stem *šmr* (at 4:21–22; see 3 Kgdms 16:24).

In his exposition Nonnus frequently uses the first person ("we must indicate," "I shall show you," "let us note," "let us examine," "it seems to me," "we must explain," and similar expressions) for his own views, as well as the first-person plural for exhortations ("let us flee from sin," etc.). He addresses the reader in the second person, often in the imperative, "see," or as a question, "did you see?"

Nonnus occasionally notes reasons for trusting the accuracy of the evangelist. These too have parallels in other commentators. Thus, he says, it is important to identify the place where events occur (e.g., regarding the place where John the Baptist was active); the same point is made by Cyril of Alexandria and Dionysius bar Salibi.[62] This is expanded at the beginning of Book II, at John 11:1: "It is customary for those who have undertaken to expound a history of things that occurred earlier both to make clear the event and also to explain the place, so that from both of these the account may be better validated." This idea is also expressed at the same place in their commentaries by Theodore of Mopsuestia and Cyril of Alexandria; and the Armenian homilist Mambrē in his second *Homily on the Resurrection of*

---

58. For the theme of six ages of the world, see note to commentary on John 12:50 .

59. See commentary to John 20:28, on the second appearance of Christ to the apostles in the upper room after the resurrection.

60. See Thomson 1976, 126, 129.

61. See commentary to John 5:1–3 and notes there.

62. See commentary to John 1:28 and note there.

Lazarus quotes this passage.[63] Nonnus also emphasizes personal testimony (e.g., at 3:31b–32: "It is a habit of human nature when [people] wish to make a statement more secure to confirm it with such [words as] *we have seen* and *we bear witness*"). This is confirmed by the closing words of John's Gospel, where Nonnus emphasizes the eyewitness testimony of the evangelist.

"Allegory" (*aṙak*, and once *aṙakabanut'iwn*)[64] is also important, not merely as a means to expound spiritual matters, but as a way to imprint their meaning on one's mind. Thus at John 4:35 Nonnus explains: "Allegorical matters are to be seriously investigated, whereas obvious things are not such. Also, when the allegorical becomes clear to the investigator, it remains more securely in his mind than something that passes through his ears once in a literal fashion."

Nonnus's prime concern, repeated again and again, is with the incarnation and the nature of Christ. The Fourth Gospel begins: "In the beginning was the Word." Throughout his commentary Nonnus is concerned with the Word— the incarnate Christ—and his relationship with the Father in the Trinity.

It is not possible to correlate the terminology used in the translation with the original Arabic, since that has not survived; but the Armenian text has close parallels with the terminology of other Armenian theological documents. Here follows a presentation of the main themes and key words, roughly in the order in which they appear in the commentary.

First, Nonnus emphasizes the "uncreatedness" of the Word (*anełut'iwn*, the abstract noun ending in *-ut'iwn* from *-eł*, the stem of the verb "to become," plus the negating prefix *an-*). This noun was not used in the very earliest original texts written in Armenian—Eznik or the *Teaching of Saint Gregory*, for example—but is often found in translations of the Hellenistic period; in the translation of Pseudo-Dionysius the Areopagite it renders *agenētos*. The base form plus adjectival ending in *-akan* is used for "created things," *ełakank'*.[65] In Nonnus's commentary to John 1:1 it is contrasted with the "coming into being" of creation, *linelut'iwn*, derived from the verb *linel*, an expression common in the *Teaching*.

---

63. See notes to Nonnus, commentary on John 11:1, below.

64. *Aṙak* is very common in Armenian, rendering *parabolē* in the NT; and the adjective *aṙakawor*, "allegorical," is found in many authors. But the abstract noun *aṙakabanut'iwn* (*-banut'iwn* rendering the Greek *-ologia*) is attested only in Nonnus, according to *NBHL*; see Nonnus, commentary to John 10:7–8.

65. Muradyan 2012, 231; Thomson 1997, 78.

Also stressed is the Word's "eternity," *anskzbnut'iwn*, the abstract noun derived from the adjective *anskizbn*, "without beginning," used of God by Eznik and the *Teaching*, and rendering *anarchos* in Pseudo-Dionysius.[66]

The Word is "inseparable" from the Father. *Ank'akut'iwn*, "without separation," is used for this, as in the *Teaching* or in Eznik for the relation of the three persons of the Trinity.[67] *Yarakc'ut'iwn*, "conjunction," and *anbažanut'iwn*, "indivisibility," are also used in the same sense.[68] In the *Teaching*, the similar expression *ank'ak aṙnel*, "to make inseparable," is found for Christ's joining humankind to his immortality.[69] The "essence," *ēut'iwn*, and the "will," *kamk'*, of Father and Son are one.[70] Several terms with the suffix *-kic'*, "sharing," are also used: *ēakic'*, "coessential";[71] *lcakic'* and *zugakic'*, "linked together," for the unity of Father and Son, both roots meaning "yoke"; *hawasar*, "equal," can be expanded to *hawasarakic'*, "coequal."[72] This suffix is very versatile, and *kamakic'* is used as frequently as *miakam*, "of one will." Frequent also are *patuakic'*, "of equal honor"; *p'aṙakic'*, "of equal glory, coglorious"; *gorcakic'*, "coworker."[73] In particular, to indicate the creative activity of the Son, *ararčakic'* ("cocreator") is used to explain John 1:3: "Everything was created through him."[74] The relationship with the Father is also described as one of "intimacy," *mtermut'iwn*.[75]

The incarnation of the Word is frequently described by the term *tnawrēnut'iwn*, or derivatives of it, an expression exactly rendering the Greek *oikonomia*.[76] This Grecism is not found in the earliest Armenian theologians but soon appears in translated texts and is then rapidly adopted.[77]

---

66. Eznik, §1; *Teaching* 263; Thomson 1997, 81.

67. *Teaching* 706; Eznik, §350.

68. On *anbažanut'iwn*, see also Thomson 1997 (77).

69. *Teaching* 385; cf. Lampe 1969, s.v. *atmētos*.

70. Nonnus, commentary to John 8:16b. For *ēut'iwn*, see further below, xxxix.

71. See Thomson 1997 (95), 2001 (16) for examples.

72. Nonnus, commentary to John 1:1, 2; 8:17. *Hawasar*, but not *hawasarakic'*, also appears in Pseudo-Dionysius (see Thomson 1997, 106).

73. *Gorcakic'* and *lcakic'* are found in numerous translations; see Muradyan 2012 (227); Thomson 1997 (ad loc.). For the abstract nouns *p'aṙakc'ut'iwn* and *gorcakc'ut'iwn*, see Nonnus, commentary to John 11:4. Cf. *yarakc'ut'iwn*, cited just above: *yar-a-k[i]c'-ut'iwn*.

74. See also Thomson 2001, 18.

75. See Nonnus, commentary to John 15:10b. The term is used in 2 Cor 8:8 to render *gnēsion*; see Lampe 1969 (s.v. *gnēsion*) for its use in patristic writers for the Father-Son relationship.

76. See also Nonnus, commentary to John 1:5, 27, 30; 4:3; 16:7; and elsewhere.

77. Muradyan 2012, 245; *NBHL*, s.v. *tnawrēnut'iwn*. The verb and adverb, *tnawrinem* and *tnawrinabar*, are found in Pseudo-Dionysius.

Tntesut'iwn is also found in the same sense.[78] They mean "regulation of a house" (*tnawrēnut'iwn*) and "oversight of a house" (*tntesut'iwn*), and the latter is common in the Armenian New Testament to render *oikonomia*.[79] The noun *matakararut'iwn*, "service, administration, dispensation" (e.g., at John 1:4, 29; 8:29) and the corresponding verb *matakararel* (e.g., at 1:29; 8:29) are also used in Nonnus's *Commentary* for Christ's earthly activity.

To render "incarnation" literally, the translator uses a variety of expressions. Two are based on *mard*, "man [i.e., human being]," and *marmin*, "body/ flesh": the verb *marmnanal*, "to become flesh" (e.g., at John 1:14; 4:3; 16:9, 33) with the cognate abstract noun *marmnaworut'iwn*, "incarnation" (e.g., at 20:6–8); and the verb *mardanal*, "to become man" (e.g., at 4:3; 5:15).[80] Related to the latter is the abstract noun, *mardełut'iwn* (at 1:27), not found in the earliest Armenian texts.[81] The "union" of the divine and human natures[82] is expressed by derivates of *mi*, "one": the verb *mianal*, "to be one, united," or the causative, *miac'uc'anel*, "to unite" (e.g., at 1:5); or the abstract nouns *miut'iwn*, "unity," and *miaworut'iwn*, "union" (e.g., at 1:5; 3:13). The verb *xarnel*, "to mix, join," is also used (e.g., at 3:13); this is an expression frequent in the *Teaching*, as is the verb *zgenum*, "to put on, clothe," where the body can be called a "garment," *patmučan*.[83] Once united the natures are "inseparable," *anoroš*, and "undivided," *anhat* (e.g., at 3:13; 8:16b).

The "essential," *ēakan*,[84] Word, the Son of God, became a son of man through his benevolence; the two natures are united in a single name, forming an indivisible unity (at John 3:13). "We do not profess the incarnation to be in two natures, but we confess the natures became one after the ineffable union" (at 14:9). Those who do not accept this union divide Christ into two, and if there are two natures, then there are two sons (at 5:18). Christ's nature

---

78. Nonnus, commentary to John 8:29.

79. For *oikonomia* in the sense of "incarnation," see Lampe 1969 (s.v. *oikonomia*).

80. On *marmnanal* and *mardanal*, see also Thomson 1997, 109. They are not found in the *Teaching* (see Thomson 2001, 26–32: "The Incarnation of Christ"), but Eznik uses *mardanal*. Armenian very rarely uses the term *mis*, "flesh," in the context of the incarnation; thus the distinction between *sarx* and *sōma* in Greek is rarely clear.

81. Composed of *mard* and *eł*, the stem of the verb "to be" (cf. *an-eł* above) plus the abstract ending *-ut'iwn*. It occurs in the *Homilies* attributed to Ełišē; see *NBHL*, s.v. *mardełut'iwn*.

82. This is usually described as "ineffable," *ančar*.

83. See Thomson 2001 (26–27) for other terms used in that text. In Nonnus, see commentary to John 6:57 (*zgenum*) and 19:23 (*zgenum patmučan*). For such terms, see also Brock 1982.

84. *Ēakan* is frequent in Eznik (e.g., §3) and Pseudo-Dionysius; Thomson 1997, 95; cf. *ēakic'* above as well as xl for the suffix *-akan*.

is divine, but he has "kinship," *azgakc'ut'iwn*, with our weakness in accordance with his "bodily condition," *marmnaworut'iwn* (at 11:21; 12:27a).[85] He has "bodily kinship," *azgakanut'iwn marmnaworut'ean*, with us from the Virgin (at 15:1).

The act of incarnation was one of "condescension," *zijanel*, or "emptying," *t'ap'umn*.[86] The human condition of the incarnate Word is rendered by several expressions, *karik'*, *kargk'*, and *kirk'*, all of which indicate those things that befall a human person in the sense of the Greek *pathē*, "experiences," often misleadingly translated as "passions."[87] These can be qualified: *tnawrinakan kargk'*, for example, of the incarnation; *ank'akut'ean kargk'*, for the state of inseparability; or *marmnakan kirk'*, bodily accidents.[88] This human condition was willingly accepted; and Nonnus frequently stresses the willingness of the Son to undergo his passion for the salvation of the world.

Nonnus stresses that the incarnation was real and not "apparent," *aṙ ačawk'*,[89] or "seeming," *erewut'eamb*, but Christ took a body "truly," *čšmartapēs* (at John 4:3, 6). On the other hand, it is always made clear that Christ was not overcome by human sufferings, like us; he allowed these failings of the human condition to affect him (at 4:6). Emotions could not really be active in him, in the way that they overcome us; when he wished he condescended to food and drink and sleep (at 11:33). Christ possesses his own will, though it is always in accordance with that of the Father (at 6:38), for Son and Father have *anjnišxanut'iwn*, "independence of will" (at 16:13b). Christ's body is not subject to death, like other bodies, because he is not subject to the consequences of sin. But death he accepted willingly because of his love for creation; for by his death creatures will receive immortal life (at 14:30).

Throughout the commentary Nonnus distinguishes between the "sublime," or "highest [aspects]," and the "humblest," in contrasting Christ's divinity and humanity: he uses the expressions *barjragoynk'* for the former, and

---

85. *Azgakc'ut'iwn* (i.e., *azg-a-k[i]c'-ut'iwn*) also appears in Pseudo-Dionysius; Thomson 1997, 75. *Azg* has a wide range of uses: "genus," "kind, people," "ethnic group, gender," or "sort."

86. *Zijanel*: e.g., at John 4:32, in the context of Christ eating; *t'ap'umn*: 10:11 (lit. "emptying"); his being weary, 4:6.

87. See, e.g., commentary to John 4:32–34: "He condescended to those things that derive from nature in order to confirm the dispensation of his incarnation, that he had a body not in appearance or as an illusion but truly." From the stem *kir*, the verb *krel* is used for "enduring, undergoing, suffering."

88. See, e.g., commentary to John 1:1, 26–27; 21:1; cf. *tnawrinakan xorhurd*, "the mystery of the incarnation," at 14:23; 17:4; 19:30.

89. *Aṙ ačawk'* is widely used to indicate a phantom; e.g., Matt 14:26; Mark 6:49, *phantasma*, of Christ walking on the water.

for the latter, *nuastagoynk'* or *xonarhagoynk'*. The sublime is not transformed into the humble, but these characteristics are shared by communication (at John 10:11). The human in Christ is composed of body and soul, which are both united with his divinity after the resurrection (at 10:17–18). The soul of a human can exist apart from the body, as in the case of Lazarus for the time he was in the tomb (at 11:43). In that case, Christ "wrested it from the Devil" and rejoined it to the body.

In the commentary to the first verse several other important terms appear that are common to all Armenian authors: *ēut'iwn* for "being," or "essence," to which the verb *goyanal* corresponds in the sense that the Word does not take his being from another.[90] To express equality of essence of Father and Son, *ēakic'* can be used; and *ēakan* is used for "essential."[91] *Bnut'iwn* is the term for "nature," the Greek *physis*. *Zawrut'iwn* is more ambiguous: the basic meaning is "force" or "power," but it is also used for "hypostasis."[92] "Person" is unambiguously rendered by *anjnaworut'iwn*, though *eresk'* (lit. "face") is also found (at John 8:30).[93] The Trinity is defined as *eṙanjean ew ezakay astuacut'iwn* (lit. "triple person and single Godhead").[94]

Nonnus is primarily concerned with the incarnate nature of the Word: "The Word was God and became man." Throughout his commentary the focus is on the relationship of the Father and Son; but the role of the Holy Spirit is not totally neglected. As explained at John 15:26, the Spirit proceeds from the Father and is thus distinguished from the angelic powers. There is no

---

90. See also above, n 84. The root *ē*, "being," occurs in the commentary to 3:13. *Ēut'iwn* is found in all Armenian authors. Its formation is unusual, in that *ē* is the third-person singular of the verb "to exist," whereas Armenian generally builds compounds from verbal stems or nouns; likewise from the third-person singular verb *goy* is derived *goyut'iwn*, "being." Cf. the Syriac abstract noun for "essence," *'ytut'*, derived from the verb form *'yt*. But see also Muradyan 2012 (121–22). For the stem *goy* and its derivatives, see Thomson 1997 (91), 2001 (16). *Iskut'iwn*, "essence," is found in Nonnus, commentary to John 1:18, but it is not common; cf. *Teaching* 383. In Pseudo-Dionysius it renders *tautotēs*; Thomson 1997 (99). It is noteworthy that it does not appear in the lexicon of technical terms compiled by Dorfmann-Lazarev (2004, 269–83) from the correspondence between Armenians and Byzantines in the ninth century.

91. See above, n. 84.

92. See Nonnus, commentary to John 1:1 (Č'rak'ean, 16): *patmołakan zawrut'ean hangamank'*, "the manner [or "circumstances"] of the historical hypostasis."

93. *Anjn* means "person" or "self"; e.g., John 5:18: he "made *himself* equal to God." *Anjnaworut'iwn* is the abstract noun from the adjectival form *anjn–awor*; this is not used in the Armenian Bible but is found in later writers, meaning "alive, having a *psychē*"; see examples in *NBHL*, s.v. *anjnaworut'iwn*.

94. In the translator's own addition to the "Exhortation" at the end of ch. 10 (Č'rak'ean, 242).

distinction regarding the nature of Father, Son, and Spirit: they are separate in "person," *anjaworut'iwn*, but united by "nature," *bnut'iwn* (at 16:13). The Spirit is "equal," *hawasarakic'*, in glory and nature (at 17:12).[95]

Purpose of the Commentary and Its Later Influence

On several occasions Nonnus refers to his opponents: those who do not understand the scriptures properly or who misinterpret the nature of Christ. In the former category he mocks the Jews as "thick-witted," *t'anjramit*, or "dim-witted," *karčamit*, because they are too literal in their understanding of the Old Testament. Since the Gospel of John prominently features debates between Christ and the Jews, according to Nonnus these attacks are directed against those who reject the divine nature of Christ and the Son of God. And because they are so frequent and deal only in general terms with those who fail to recognize Christ's divinity, it has been suggested that Nonnus, or perhaps his translator, had a more topical opponent in mind, namely, the Muslims who accepted Jesus as a prophet only and not as the Son of God.[96] To that we shall return.

More specific are the descriptions of those who are supposedly Christian but who misinterpret the sense of the incarnation and the nature of the incarnate Word. In his commentary to the very first verse, Nonnus refers to the Arians, who deny the eternity of the Son; and at John 14:9 he associates with Arius the name of Eunomius, who with his supporters confessed the Son to be created.[97] Such persons are called "Gentile tongues," *het'anosakan lezuk'*, who posit the Son as created and coming into being in time (at 1:2). The noun "schism," *herjuac*, is used to describe those who might think that the Son was less than the Spirit (at 16:13). And Nonnus refers to "schismatics," *herjuacołk'*, who deny that spiritual beings were created by the Word as "cocreator," *ararčakic'*, at the same time as the tangible creatures of this world (at 1:3).[98] The same term "schismatics" is also applied to those who claim that Christ possessed a body in the form of an apparition and not in reality (at

---

95. For *hawasarakic'*, see also above, xxxvi.

96. See Č'rak'ean's introduction, p. *žē* (18); he quotes Sargisean 1897 in support.

97. See also commentary to 8:57. Eunomius and Arius first appear together in Armenian in the version of the *Tome* of Proclus; see the *Book of Letters*; translation and commentary in Garsoïan 1999 (420–31).

98. The Syriac version of the *Hexaemeron* of Basil of Caesarea omits the section where Basil discusses the creation of angels prior to that of the world, hence the Armenian text (translated from Syriac) contains no reference to that debate. It was a topic that much interested Syrian theologians; see Thomson 2012 (n. 58 to *Homily* 1.4).

4:3).[99] Not all "opponents," *hakaṙakoł'*, are explicitly named. Some of them disputed that Christ could illuminate all who were to come into the world, as at 1:9, for there are obviously people who do not know Christ. In more general terms, the translator refers to the "unorthodoxy," *čarapaṙut'iwn*, of the schismatics in contrast to the "orthodoxy," *ułłapaṙut'iwn*, of the faith.[100]

Nonnus's main opponents, however, are those who claim that one can speak of two natures in the incarnate Christ. He claims that they interpret the actions of the human Christ as of a body separate and distinct from the Word; and if there are two natures, then there are two distinct and separate sons (at John 5:18).[101] Such persons are "dividers," *bažanołk'*, of the one Christ into two natures (at 6:62; 8:57). They are "dyophysites," *erkbnakk'*, and "schismatics," *herjuacołk'* (at 8:57; 20:28).[102] In addition to those who speak of two natures, those who propose two wills in Christ are equally attacked. They are "lovers of contrariness," *hakaṙakasērk'*, who interpret Christ's saying, "I descended from heaven, not to do my own will but the will of the one who sent me," as implying that Christ had two wills in opposition to each other (at 6:38). In this regard also, the commentary fits the general Armenian viewpoint that eventually rejected both the Chalcedonian formula of two natures and the seventh-century compromise of two wills.[103] As Garsoïan has pointed out, in the long run the Armenian Church pursued a course of moderate miaphysitism, more correctly defined as the theology of Cyril of Alexandria.[104]

A further group is attacked, "our opponents," *hakaṙakołk' mez*, who do not accept the Trisagion as sung in the Armenian fashion—that is, with the addition "who was crucified for us" directed to the Savior. The author claims that both John and Paul uphold his interpretation of Isaiah's vision.[105] The same interpretation of the Trisagion occurs in the "Exhortation" at the end of chapter 10. And in the extensive passage of exhortation added after the commentary to John 19:37, primarily a paean to the cross added by the translator,

---

99. Yovhannēs Ojnec'i also wrote against such heretics, called "Phantasiasts," *erewut'akank'*.

100. See the translator's addition to the "Exhortation" at the end of ch. 10 (Č'rak'ean, 244).

101. The argument that two natures implies two sons is forcefully pushed by those who adapted the Armenian translations of Athanasius; see Thomson 1965.

102. *Erk-b[u]n-ak* renders "dyo-phys-ite" literally.

103. This compromise, known as monothelitism (promoted by the emperor Heraclius, who had also earlier suggested the idea of one "activity" [*energeia*] in Christ), was rejected by the Council of Constantinople in 681.

104. Garsoïan 1999, 399.

105. Nonnus, commentary to John 12:41; see Isa 6:1–3.

the same idea is repeated: the six-winged seraphim sing their triple "holy" to the one on the cross.[106]

This commentary shows little trace of extreme Julianist ideas concerning the incorruptibility of Christ's body.[107] Only once does the author specifically state that Christ's body was incorruptible, and then only in the context of the dead body placed in the tomb after the crucifixion: "Nor in the tomb like our bodies was it corrupted and turned into its individual elements, but it remained always incorruptible and indissoluble [*anapakan ew anlucaneli*], united with the divine Word, who was pleased to become flesh, in accordance with the Gospel saying, for the salvation of mankind" (at John 19:23–24). Nonnus refers to our human nature as "corruptible" and sinful; but when the Word united it with his own (divine) nature it was rendered "luminous," and it burned with his divinity through the ineffable union (at 1:5). Elsewhere the term "incorruptible" is used in a liturgical context of Christ's body and blood (at 6:59; 9:35–37, 55), of heavenly rewards (at 6:27),[108] and of the "incorruptible" and "luminous" robe of which Adam and Eve were stripped in the garden of Eden (at 12:31a).[109] In the context of Christ's earthly activity, when he condescended to the human situation without his divine nature being compromised, the body was not distinct or separate from the Word (e.g., at 5:18); but the term "incorruptible" is not used.

The foregoing analysis of the terminology used in this *Commentary* indicates that the author's theology of the incarnation was in accordance with prior Armenian tradition and that the translator was familiar with Armenian usage. In his introduction, the editor of the printed edition comments on the compatibility of this theology with later Armenian expositions.[110] But the history of Armenian theology is not our present concern. The following annotation to the translation of the *Commentary on the Gospel of John* by Nonnus is an attempt to understand the background of the author's exegesis, rooted in earlier Syrian and Greek tradition.

---

106. The addition to the Trisagion by Peter the Fuller in the later fifth century was accepted by Syrian as well as Armenian miaphysites. For its use in Armenia, see Garitte 1952 (167–70).

107. For the influence in Armenia of ideas concerning the incorruptibility of Christ's body as propounded by Julian of Halicarnassus, see Garitte 1952 (117–30); Garsoïan 1999 (ch. 3); and Mathews and Sanjian 1991 (160).

108. Cf. the commentary to John 19:41, of our body raised to heavenly incorruption.

109. See also the "Exhortation" appended to ch. 10 (Č'rak'ean, 244). On the luminous robe, see Brock 1982.

110. See esp. Č'rak'ean, pp. *ie* (25) and *l* (30), where he gives parallels with the *Letter* of Vahan and with the twelfth-century theologians Nersēs Šnorhali and Nersēs of Lambron.

One further question remains, adumbrated above. Did Bagrat Bagratuni, who commissioned the *Commentary*, have a more topical opponent in mind, namely, the Muslims who accepted Jesus as a prophet only and not as the Son of God? The translator in his preface states: "He [Bagrat] always suffered no little zeal for Christ in order to admonish and reprove the ranks of the schismatics."[111] And the translator stresses that Nonnus himself, who was also imprisoned with his sons, was continually teaching and making opposition to the Muslims.[112] Are the emphasis in the *Commentary* on Christ's divine nature and the attacks on the Jews who refused to recognize it hidden attacks on the Muslim refusal to accept Christ's divinity? This was the suggestion of Barseł Sargisean, followed by the editor of the text and later writers on the subject.[113] Sargisean claims that Nonnus's eloquence was directed against the Islam of the ninth-century Muslims, when Armenian apostasies were only too frequent.

The Gospel of John, of course, puts much emphasis on Christ's divinity and uses dialogue with Jews as a rhetorical means to that effect. And in the context of the debate at Ašot Bagratuni's court, where the anti-Chalcedonian view concerning the person of Christ prevailed, John's Gospel makes an excellent starting point. Although there is no reference to Islam in this *Commentary*, which supports at length the miaphysite Armenian viewpoint of the ninth century, the translator does note that when in captivity Bagrat Bagratuni was particularly anxious to possess knowledge of the Christian faith.[114] In the near-contemporary debate between Patriarch Timothy I (Timotheos) of the Syrians and the Caliph Al-Mahdī, the Gospel of John is the biblical book most alluded to, though not the most quoted verbatim.[115] That disputation was also held in Arabic, but Timothy (patriarch 780–823) wrote the description of it as an apology in Syriac.

The original debate at Ašot Bagratuni's court between Theodore Abū Qurrah and Nonnus was prompted by internal Christian differences. His son Bagrat, however, saw the significance of John's Gospel, which would have been

---

111. Schismatics: *herjuacołk'*, for which see above. This is not the usual Armenian term for Muslims, which is "foreigners," *aylazgik'*, or "Hagarenes."

112. Nonnus was released in 862; see Vardan Arewelc'i, *Historical Compilation*; Kirakos Ganjakec'i, *History*, quoted just below.

113. Sargisean 1897 (26); Č'rak'ean (introduction, p. *žē* [18]); Mariès 1920–21 (292); Griffith 1991.

114. Admittedly, that was long after the commission to Nonnus. This commentary is not cited in Armenian attacks on the origin of Islam (see Thomson 1986), but its influence on later Armenian writers generally has yet to be properly studied.

115. See the introduction to Heimgartner's edition of Timotheos, *Disputation with Caliph Al-Mahdī*.

cited in the debate, in the wider context of discussions between Christians and Muslims concerning the person of Jesus Christ. His own personal interest lay more with the latter. *Habent sua fata libelli.* What began as an overt defense of orthodoxy as viewed by Nonnus and his tradition could well be used for other purposes, especially as the text was in Arabic. By the time it was translated into Armenian, its owner, the young princess Marem of Siwnik', had little interest in debates with Muslims. The Arabic was not preserved, and the Armenian text entered the mainstream of Armenian theological literature without any indication of its original Muslim connection.[116]

As noted above, Nonnus's *Commentary on the Gospel of John* was quoted by later Armenian writers on that Gospel. Outside of circles involved in biblical exegesis, however, direct references to Nonnus's *Commentary* are rare. Its wide circulation in manuscripts indicates that the text was known in monastic scriptoria from the twelfth century onward. Prior to that time, even historians fail to mention Nonnus, or Nanay, as he was known in Armenian, though they do mention Ašot *Msaker*, who hosted the debate between Theodore and Nonnus; his son Bagrat, who later apostatized; his brother Smbat, known as "the confessor"; and Marem, who had the text translated. However, memory of the debate resurfaces in the thirteenth century.

Kirakos Ganjakec'i refers briefly to the imprisonment of Nonnus, as mentioned by the translator in his preface. In his *History*, which concludes in 1265, Kirakos notes: "A certain Syrian deacon, Nanay by name, was arrested and brought before Jafr [the Caliph Djafar al-Mutawwakil, 847–61] because of his fame as a teacher. He boldly confessed Christ, though he was tortured and imprisoned for a long time. Later, by God's providence, he was released. He composed a *Commentary on the Gospel of John* in illuminating language."[117] Kirakos's contemporary Vardan Arewelc'i refers directly to the famous debate in his *Historical Compilation*, written soon after 1267. In somewhat garbled terms he states: "In those days [i.e., of Ašot Bagratuni] a bishop, Epikuṙa by name [Abū Qurrah], came to Ašot and tried to convert him to Chalcedon. When Buret [Abū Ra'ita] heard of this he dispatched the deacon Nanay, who came and disputed with Apikuṙa, defeating him by the power of the Holy Spirit. So the prince expelled him and was confirmed even more in the faith of Saint Gregory. Then Ašot died in his bed, and Smbat his son took the principality."[118]

---

116. Save for the translator's comments about Bagrat in his preface. In this context, cf. Accad 1998.

117. Kirakos Ganjakec'i, *History*, 79. For a brief description of the life and works of Kirakos, see Boisson-Chenorhokian 2005–7.

118. Vardan Arewelc'i, *Historical Compilation*, 78. Note the variation in the spelling of Epikuṙa.

This is echoed briefly in the chronicle of Mxit'ar Ayrivanec'i, which ends in 1328: "Epikuṙa attempted to make prince Ašot a Chalcedonian, but Buret vardapet sent his deacon Nanay, who vanquished Epikuṙa and wrote a commentary on [*mekneac'*] the Gospel of John."[119]

Vardan Arewelc'i, however, adds a further piece of information associating Nonnus with a much later event in Armenia, the Council of Širakavan in 862: "Photius, the patriarch of Constantinople, in the year 318 [869] sent the metropolitan of Nicaea Yohan to him [Ašot] bearing a letter for Zak'aria [Catholicos 855–877] in response to the question: 'Why was the fourth council held?' A council was convened in Širakavan, attended by the Syrian deacon Nanay. He had been brought close to death by Jap'r on account of the faith, but was released because of a fearful vision."[120] Vardan then proceeds to summarize the letter.

The correspondence between Photius and the Armenians has naturally attracted much attention, though in the long run it had little effect on the Armenians' theological position.[121] The council to which Vardan refers had been summoned to discuss the question of union of the two churches proposed in the letter from Photius, and the presence of Nonnus is attested in the introductory colophon to the Armenian text of the *Treatise of Vahan*, where he is called "a great deacon and a renowned philosopher [*sarkawag mec ew hṙčakeal p'ilisop'os*]." More significantly, the basic theology of Nonnus, "one Son from two natures," is echoed in that *Treatise*.[122]

The presence of Nonnus at Širakavan is certainly not impossible. He was a young deacon at the time of the debate before Ašot Bagratuni, when according to Michael the Syrian, Theodore refused to argue with such a young opponent.[123] The council took place less than fifty years later. What influence Nonnus personally had at that gathering is impossible to tell. The enthusiastic opinion of the Mekhitarist scholar Mik'ayēl Č'amčean, whose influential

---

119. Mxit'ar Ayrivanec'i, *History* (Patkanean, 67).

120. Vardan Arewelc'i, *Historical Compilation*, 82.

121. See recently Dorfmann-Lazarev 2004, with bibliography of previous scholarship. His interpretations have been challenged by Greenwood (2006), who gives a clear exposé of the extended correspondence and argues for the authenticity of Photius's *Letter*, known as the *Treatise of Vahan* (*Yohan* in Vardan) bishop of Nicaea, which had been denied by Garitte 1952 (370–75). See also the summary in Mahé 1993 (492–95); and for the council, Maksoudian 1988–89.

122. See the comparison of the texts in Dorfmann-Lazarev 2004 (153–54); translation of Vahan's treatise, ibid. (1–19).

123. See Maksoudian 1988–89 (336–37), referring to the Syriac text of Michael the Syrian's *Chronicle*; the Armenian version does not refer to Nonnus or the Council of Širakavan.

History of Armenia (*Patmut'iwn Hayoc'*) takes the story from creation down to 1784, that at Širakavan Nonnus united the Syrians and Armenians has no evidence to support it.[124] But if the person of Nonnus played little role in Armenian theological debates after his dramatic encounter with Theodore Abū Qurrah, and his name disappears until the thirteenth century, his influence continued to affect Armenian interpretations of the Gospel of John for many centuries.

To his *Commentary* and its background in Greek and Syrian exegesis we now turn, beginning with the unknown translator's own preface.

---

124. See Ananean, *Zak'aria Hayoc' Kat'ołikosi* 1995 (57), quoting from Č'amč'ean 1784–86 (2:687).

Nanay the Syrian Teacher:
Introduction to the Commentary on John the Evangelist

[by the Armenian Translator]

There is nothing more desirable than the fulfillment of friends' intense wishes, thereby to strengthen all the more the bond of divine love, and to draw into ourselves the immeasurable profit that derives from it, in accordance with the commandment: *Love hides a multitude of sins* (1 Pet 4:8). Now, if one undertakes a friend's request that is an impossible task, see what doubts and grief he raises even for his friend. If anyone indicates to his friend that he will travel to the ends of India on a quest for the glittering topaz, or will attempt the depths of the sea over such piled-up waves of dense and rough waters on a search for the valuable pearl,[1] [2] he longs for the natural places where the topaz is sought on account of the rocky planted slopes. And another, not possessing the skill of swimming in order to make the descent into the agitated waters of the sea, would he not then make no small effort to annul the blame of his friend, and through his firm love boldly provide excuses and not reveal his weakness, and withdrawing by noble agreement, save himself without any blame from an impossible quest?

So if in the search for material things or numerous necessities here below so much energetic labor is expended, why do you demand from me the quest for a heavenly, sublime, and unachievable object, from which not only the breadth of the earth and the depth of the sea divides [us], but which surpasses our physical nature? Nor can we with our thick minds comprehend it, or with our downward-dragging thoughts[2] contemplate or really explain it. Now, although these things are very hard for me and impossible, yet I shall be pleased to offer many praises [3] that you have found such talents in this

---

    1. Agat'angełos begins his *History* in a similar manner.
    2. **Downward-dragging thoughts**: cf. Basil of Caesarea, *Hex.* 9.2.

latter time for the profound investigation of wisdom, which has been called inscrutable by the most high-minded and celebrated persons,[3] not accessible to my impure understanding, it being very inappropriate for my impudence to penetrate to such sublime and heavenly realities.

But I have not found a way to disregard your pleasure, you who honor wisdom so highly that you are happy to seek it even from the poor and the lowly, like those who desire to acquire the royal purple and pursue profitable honor from various rustics, whereas others are enriched by weak nauseating worms from which silk is produced. I know your understanding is not ignorant of that, which in this world you possess overflowing with paternal splendor.

It would be not a little protracted to stretch to such a height for one totally incompetent, who is endowed with neither knowledgeable mind nor literary skill; nor is he worthy in accordance with the free gift of the Spirit (Rom 3:24), poured out with many streams of grace for the profit of us below; nor for someone lamentable in purity and entangled [4] in the chains of sin, who am not worthy to look up to the height of heaven or to speak of the one who dwells above heaven. For the weight of his sins, according to the prophet's saying, *is higher than my head* (Ps 37:5), and by it I stoop down, oppressed in worthy punishment.

But how shall I be helped by these to a discharge of the undertaking? For if through love alone I had come to such an impossible task, perhaps there would have been a means to escape and flee. But you have united your princely commands with the attributes of friendship. Therefore I found no way for me to make excuses as originally intended and to refuse and withdraw because of my weakness. For you have sincerely implored through your friendship in your divinely pleasing manner, O Lord Smbat Bagratuni.[4] Indeed, you imposed your immediate and princely commands, removing from me any means of escape, and you did not take into consideration my own weakness for such a sublime request. Nor again in my impurity did you reckon my insolence relevant for such a pure project, in order to remove a very heavy and oppressive weight for me. Behold, as I look to right and left no help is offered, according to the Gospel saying.[5] Therefore I direct many supplications to your Lordship to release me from such a lofty [5] undertaking, being unprofitable and useless for your merciful attention. Now I shall take

---

3. See references in *NBHL* to wisdom as *anhetazawteli*, notably in Basil and Gregory of Nazianzus; for the Greek, see Lampe 1969 (s.v. *anexichniastos*).

4. For Smbat, see further the introduction above, xix.

5. This is not a direct quotation from the Gospels. In the Psalms there are numerous requests for God to "look" and "help."

refuge in, and hold fast to, the grace of the Holy Spirit, *who grants liberally and does not censure.*[6]

Let us now set out the form of the demand. Perhaps through the prayers of the audience greater help will be forthcoming for me from the celestial grace. A certain archdeacon, by the name of Nanay,[7] very learned and competent in Syrian literature, possessor of many virtues, modest in life, pure regarding all bodily pleasures, received from the source, the Holy Spirit, the grace of teaching the orthodox faith in Christ. After censuring and defeating a certain heretic, a man eloquent and a philosopher, he had him expelled from the land of Armenia. He was teaching perversely, dividing into two the inseparable unity of Christ after the indivisible and unconfused unity.

He [Nanay] reaffirmed the orthodox profession in Christ: to confess one from two natures, the divine [attributes] by nature, but the lesser by willing acceptance.[8] He was solicited by the great Bagrat, who is from the house of the Bagratunik', a man who has acquired a very high repute and was even once named as "head of the princes" [6] by the barbarous nation of the Hagarenes, as if thereby they considered him worthy of greater honor, the circumstances of which we shall record briefly in their own place.[9] What, then, was the form of the request? To acquire for him a commentary on the holy Gospel of John.

With prompt zeal and through rigorous fasts and prayers, [Nanay] expended no little effort in going around for three years, traveling through the deserts in the land of Mesopotamia, where he hoped to find writings[10] of orthodox teaching. Having attained his quest by the guidance of heavenly providence, he composed the commentary of the holy Gospel of John in summary fashion, gathering from many [sources], one by one methodically, translating from the Syrian tongue into the Hagarene language.[11]

Now, when he was captured by the Hagarene nation, the great, noble, and high-minded prince of the Armenians was anxious to possess complete knowledge of the faith in Christ.[12] And he always suffered no little zeal

---

6. Jas 1:5, of God.

7. **Nanay**: the standard Armenian form for Nonnus, derived from the Syriac. For his life and works, see van Roey 1949.

8. For the theology of the commentary, see the introduction, xxxv–xl.

9. For Bagrat and this title, see Ter-Łevondyan 1976 (54); Canard, 406.

10. **Writings**: sg. N, pl. V.

11. The sources were written in Syriac, and Nonnus generally wrote in Syriac; see van Roey 1949. For the use of Arabic, see the introduction above, xix.

12. For Bagrat's imprisonment in Samarra, see T'ovma Arcruni, *History of the Arcrunik'*, 118, and Garsoïan in Hovannisiann 1997 (140); he died in 852.

for Christ in order to admonish and reprove the ranks of the schismatics.[13] However, thereafter he demonstrated no courageous bravery to match his grandeur but rapidly fell away from the divine faith that he possessed and immediately plunged into the pit of irreparable destruction. [7] Casting aside the emblem of the covenant of the true faith, he brought terrible grief on the whole land of Armenia, although he became an angel in our ears by keeping firm the profession of the true faith in the depth of his heart.[14]

At that time, through some chance the treasure of this book came to Lord Smbat Bagratuni. Receiving it with great joy he commanded it rapidly to be translated from the Hagarene into the Armenian language, not sparing my weakness. That great rhetor [Nanay], accomplished in arts and sciences, put such effort into it that he became exhausted. Who would not blame my audacity even to think of such a lofty plan? It is necessary not to leave without remembrance the virtue of that man that was accomplished thereafter but, as in a portrait, to indicate briefly his labor. Not as if in praise to eulogize him, for not even a great multitude of philosophers gathered in one place could compose a review worthy of him, but only in a few words to suggest this account for the edification of the audience.

He [Nanay] was captured in our time by the Hagarene nations because of his zeal for the glorious teaching and his continually making opposition, and he was imprisoned with his sons. [8] Through them they often made enticing propositions, with numerous gifts, but they did not humble his indomitable thoughts for Christ. They were also tempted by different means—by the threat of prison and bonds and various torments—but he never was frightened to abjure his great faith in Christ. He remained in prison for a long time,[15] not only keeping himself whole in his pure faith, but also becoming for many a cause of salvation. Fearlessly he took care of the prisoners in the jail, teaching and confirming them in the faith of the all-holy Trinity.

After this had so happened, the treasure of this book was brought to Marem Bagratuni, princess of Siwnik' through Ašot her father, the great and noble Bagratuni lord, prince of princes.[16] Then the blessed princess of Siwnik'

---

13. **Schismatics:** *herjuacołk'*. This term is used in the *Commentary* for non-"orthodox" Christians, rather than for Muslims; see the introduction above, xl.

14. For Bagrat's apostasy, see T'ovma Arcruni, *History of the Arcrunik'*, 158. According to T'ovma (162), "at the time of his apostasy Bagrat said that apostasy because of danger of suffering does no harm, if one secretly keeps in one's heart the confession of faith."

15. See van Roey 1949, 23–25: he was in captivity from 851 until 862; see also Yovhannēs Drasxanakertc'i, *History*, ch. 26. Kirakos Ganjakec'i, *History*, 79, also describes Nanay's sufferings in prison.

16. See the genealogical table in Toumanoff 1990 (table 16).

with zeal immediately commanded for a second time[17] that it be translated into the Armenian tongue, through the guidance of celestial providence. She arranged in abbreviated fashion the sublime divine faith, holding it as a priority in accordance with her sweet and most praiseworthy character, as she directed the care of her beloved holy mind uniformly toward all mankind. Especially her sincere faith in Christ [9] was preserved by celestial care untroubled for the assistance of her four children.[18] I am not ashamed to call her a lover of Christ and a living martyr[19] who for so long endured the long-suffering of the faith.

He [Nanay] was such a person that no one in this place could slander us as exaggerating, confusing our efforts with his, wishing to change or spoil anything. But lest the glory of a teacher be rendered incomplete or lacking by his pupil, let the audience pardon us a little. Just as wise doctors, who through the veins have learned the causes of illness and consequently find a means for a cure,[20] likewise we must with the eyes of the mind look to the exposition on which we have embarked, and if there be any blemish, heal it like spiritual limbs, and with unanimity of love bring succor in union of spiritual love and straightway lovingly remove poisonous and earthly rancor.

United by love in Christ let us hold to each other, both speakers and hearers, as light to the eyes and voice to the ears and smell to the nose. And if there may be any blemish of weakness of expression, with rhetorical art [we must] strengthen it and make it shine. Just as the warmth of fire expels cold from the body, and with liveliness clothes the color of the image, [10] likewise you, imbued with fervent love and the sparks of divine fire, fearlessly bring to us pure love in which there is no envy or hatred or reproach, *et cetera*.[21] And by the recollection of that love let us extinguish the multitude of sins, according to the commandment: *Love hides a multitude of sins* (1 Pet 4:8). And speakers and hearers, with united minds and thoughts let us approach the knowledge of this divine exposition, so that we may be equally assisted; so that the palates of our minds may be seasoned by the salt of the grace of the Holy Spirit

---

17. **A second time:** *erkic̕s angam*. Since only one version in Armenian is known, it would appear that Smbat's earlier command had not yet been fulfilled, rather than that this was a revision.

18. For Marem (Mariam) and her ancestry, see Toumanoff 1990 (table 43). For her charitable activities, see Pogossian 2012.

19. **Living martyr:** cf. the wives of the imprisoned nobles in Ełišē, *History of Vardan*, 202, called martyrs in their lifetime.

20. For doctors measuring the pulse of the veins, see Ełišē, *History of Vardan*, 172; for further references, see *NBHL* (s.v. *erak*).

21. Et cetera: *aylovk̕n handerj*. The translator does not complete his paraphrase of 1 Cor 13:4.

(Col 4:6), which flavors the discourse and purifies the soul and illuminates the mind.

Now if any of the critics cross our path and plot opposition, let us be unconcerned and voice opposition to them according to the commandment not to be rash, *et cetera*,[22] only to raise up praise freely to the Holy Spirit, who is the cause of the translation of words for those who take refuge in him, according to Paul's voice: *To another the interpretation of tongues* (1 Cor 12:10). Passing over the dangers, let us hasten to the task before us, for which reason we have undertaken this account.

Let us set down briefly the nature of the accounts of the evangelists, as much as our intellect is able, and journeying in that fashion [11] without straying, let us come to the explanation of the holy Gospel of John.

Concerning Matthew, Mark, and Luke, many have earlier spoken in each one's place. But concerning John, the subject of this discourse we have undertaken, let us say whatever is the most important.[23] He preached the gospel during the whole period of his apostleship without writing [it down]. But when the three Gospels had been set down and reached him in writing, as the account describes, they were acceptable to him, and he testified that they had been written truthfully, save that they lacked whatever had been done at the beginning of Christ's teaching. We are able to know that the three evangelists wrote down whatever was done by the Lord after the imprisonment of John the Baptist. It is indicated at the beginning of their accounts that after forty days, when the Lord fasted and overcame the chief tempter,[24] they began their story, according to Matthew's account: *When he heard that they had arrested John, he moved from Judea to Galilee* (Matt 4:12). Mark [says] that after John was betrayed, Jesus came to Galilee (Mark 1:14). And Luke had earlier written: *Herod, in addition to all the evils that he worked, furthermore arrested John and put him in prison* (Luke 3:19–20). Hence they begged John the apostle to give them a written account of the Lord's deeds during the period that was omitted by the other evangelists, [12] namely, the miracles done by Christ before the imprisonment of John. Which indeed John did write down: *This beginning of signs Jesus made in Cana of Galilee, and he revealed his glory* (John 2:11), indicating that that was his first miracle. Then John recorded in his own Gospel whatever had been done before John's imprisonment, whereas the

---

22. 1 Cor 13:5, of love.

23. For some Armenian views on the evangelists and the composition of their Gospels, see Thomson, "Armenian Traditions concerning the Writing of the Gospels" (forthcoming). Here the translator echoes information in Eusebius, *Hist. eccl.* 3.24.

24. **Chief tempter**: *p'orjapet*. For other titles given to Satan in Armenian, see *Teaching* 278–79.

three evangelists had written down whatever had been done by Christ after John's imprisonment.

Why, then, did John omit an account of our Savior's birth in the flesh? Because Matthew and Luke had previously written that down, therefore he began to write about his divinity. And being the fourth of the evangelists, it was not without a sublime mystery. For some said that in accordance with the four extremities of creation where it was necessary to spread the preaching of the gospel of the kingdom, of the same number should be the evangelists who were to preach the word of life across the whole world. Whereas to others it seemed appropriate that the irrigation of the world should be in accordance with the four ever-flowing rivers that streamed from the source in Eden; in a similar number these arose from the living source [13] in order to irrigate the thirsty minds of human nature.

Rightly this fourth evangelist, since the Spirit of God preserved him, made the following lofty mystery the beginning of his account, as the particular apostle who was called *son of thunder*[25] by the Lord, on account of his thundering heavenly things in order to arouse and open the minds of our human nature: *In the beginning was the word* (John 1:1).

---

25. Mark 3:17: the brothers James and John were both so named.

[15] Commentary on the Gospel of John [by] the Holy Nanay the Syrian Teacher

Book I

Chapter 1

I[1]

[1:1a] **In the beginning was the Word.**

At the beginning of our discourse we must indicate the exceeding wisdom of the evangelist, and the grace of the Holy Spirit, how in the introduction he expounds the uncreatedness[i] of the Son by saying in his preliminary words: *In the beginning*[ii] *was the Word.* What by this way did he reveal, save to show that the Word existed at the beginning of time, when God predetermined to create heaven and earth and the creatures in them; and not in accordance with the history of Moses, in the beginning creatures were to receive the origin of their existence and the Word come into being, but in order that the *was* might demonstrate the uncreatedness of the Word, and the Word might be established as superior to these created things?

Furthermore, one must inquire for what reason he calls the Son *Word*, save in order to give him a form in accordance with our weakness, because it was very necessary that we should recognize the eternity of the Son from the Father, lest we understand him as created like the Arians.[iii] [16] Therefore the evangelist names him *Word*. For just as a word has no existence from itself, nor its being from nothing, nor its birth from outside the mind, likewise the Son does not exist from himself, nor did he proceed from nothing. But just as a word takes its birth in the mind,[iv] so also the Son with the Father. See how

---

1. For this section heading, see the introduction, xxiv–xxv.

by a single word he introduced and secured the condition[v] of his uncreatedness and of his passionless birth, and of his inseparability and indissolubility.

The appellation of the word has also a further demonstration. Just as our speech is born from the mind and becomes perceptible to hearing through the word, and for listeners remains inseparable and indivisible in the mind, not partially separated through a voice but keeping its nature equally in both aspects,[vi] likewise the Word of God came to us in the flesh yet was not separated from the Father.[vii] But just as he is perfect with the Father, so [he is] perfect with us because of his indivisible nature.

Did you see the manner of the inseparability? I shall show you also the manner of the historical hypostasis.[viii] So the Son was called angel of the Father[ix] because of the difference [of] the Word from the Father to us.[x] Hence again he calls him *Word*, because just as we know the mind through a word, and we indicate the desires of the mind through a word, in like fashion we recognize the Father and his wishes through the Son. You heard Word; recognize also the mind of the Word. You saw the Son; recognize also the majesty of the Father testified by the Lord: *Who has seen me has seen the Father* (John 14:9), and *I and the Father are one* (10:30). You saw also the addition to the quotation. For he did not say, A word was in the beginning, but, *the Word*, in order to show [17] a word is distinguished not from many words but the Word, indicating the personality and the coexistence of the one who receives the Word. Not like a simple word, [which is] silent before being spoken and stops after being spoken,[xi] but being eternal remains in the glory of the divine essence.

Let us also note those who propose the opposite: Why was he called not Son but Word?[xii] It was necessary for our very weak minds to fall into much turbulence as to how he was born: after time or before time, without afflictions or with afflictions, without separation or being separated? Therefore he set down the word as a model, as we said above. Let us hear again the other contestations, those who say: Why was he named not Jesus or Christ but Word? These are appellations of the economy,[xiii] not of the particular divine essence. For Jesus has the meaning of salvation, since the name Savior indicates his saving us through the bodily [attributes]. But Christ, when he received the power of anointing according to his bodily condition, which was alienated from us because of Adam's transgressions, in this same way at the appropriate time he handed down to the apostles the name of sonship in their teaching all nations: *Baptize them in the name of the Father and of the Son and of the Holy Spirit* (Matt 28:19). Did you see how in each place the names are applied according to their suitability, and the equal honor linking the Son with the Father and the Holy Spirit, when he draws up the ranks of the holy disciples, raising them to the highest teaching? And because he expounded the unity of the Word and his passionless birth, to that he adds the following:

i. **Uncreatedness:** *anełut'iwn*. See the long discussion in Moše bar Kepha to John 1:2; Dionysius bar Salibi, *John*, 5; and Step'annos of Siwnik', 118; echoed by Tat'ewac'i, 55.

ii. **In the beginning:** *i skzbanē*. Timot'eos interprets this phrase in Gen 1:1 as *isk ban ē* (lit. "indeed, word, is"), as "Father, Son, Holy Spirit."

iii. Nonnus refers specifically to Arians only here, but they are often called heretics or schismatics. Step'annos of Siwnik', 118, to John 1:1, calls them schismatics.

iv. For a word being united to the mind, see also the commentary to John 14:7a. This idea is found in Moše bar Kepha; Dionysius bar Salibi, *John*, 6; and Tat'ewac'i, 45.

v. **Condition:** *kargk'*; for this term, see the introduction, xxxviii.

vi. For the production of speech from an image in the mind through the vocal organs, see Basil of Caesarea, *Hex.* 3.2 (Muradyan, 67), and Philoxenus, *Prologue* (de Halleux, 64 [§28]).

vii. This argument is emphasized in Philoxenus, *Prologue*.

viii. **Hypostasis:** *zawrut'iwn* (lit. "power"). See the introduction, xxxix.

ix. Cf. Isa 9:6; patristic references in Lampe 1969 (s.v. *angelos*, I B).

x. The text here is unclear and cannot be corrected from M, which begins at John 1:3.

xi. For the transient nature of a word, see *Comm. Diat.* 1.3; see also the commentary to John 5:36, below.

xii. For this question, see Moše bar Kepha, ad loc.

xiii. **Economy:** *tnawrinakan kargk'*. For the vocabulary, see the introduction, xxxviii. For the argument, cf. Dionysius bar Salibi, *John*, 7.

[18] [1:1b] The Word was with God.

Just as he indicates the conjunction[i] and eternity with the Father, he also sets down an indication of the personality, as person linked with person[ii] and naturally of equal honor, and not as partial with regard to perfect, or less compared to superior. Hence by pronouncing these [words], very clearly he introduces the essence of the Word.

i. **Conjunction:** *yarakc'ut'iwn*. For the vocabulary, see the introduction, xxxvi.

ii. **Person:** *anjnaworut'iwn*. See the long discussion in Moše bar Kepha, ad loc.; Dionysius bar Salibi, *John*, 10, refers to the *qnuma usyaya*. Tat'ewac'i, 49, gives a long definition of *anjn*.

[1:1c] And the Word was God.

He indicates that he is not in God, a created nature introduced and fashioned, but God all in all (1 Cor 15:28). For it is not possible for creatures to be linked with the uncreated, but the uncreated Word [is] the offspring of the uncreated Father.

[1:2] He was in the beginning with God.

Once more he indicates the conjunction of the Son with the Father. *He who is with God, who is,[i] always equally joined in harmony according to person, and a fenced wall[ii] to protect against the attacks of Gentile tongues, who posit the Son as created and younger than the Father, and coming into being in time. And he makes him totally ungraspable, especially through his theology.[iii]

   i. **He who … is:** *Ēn aṙ ēn astuac kaleal,* but *kayac̔eal* as quoted by Tat̔ewac̔i, 52. See Exod 3:14, and the use of *ē* discussed in Thomson 2001, 15–16).
   ii. **Fenced wall:** *c̔ank parspeal;* not an exact quotation, but many OT parallels.
   iii. **Theology:** *astuacabanut̔iwn.* The author of the Fourth Gospel is often known as the "theologian," *astuacaban;* see references in Lampe 1969 (s.v. *theologos,* B b).

[1:3a] Everything was created through him.

Since he had expounded in his theology the coexisting and uncreated existence of the Son, he consequently set down the manner of his being cocreator, indicating that all creatures received their being and existence through him, souls and bodies, breathing and not-breathing, all created things together. But because Moses did not speak in his own history about the coming into being of angels,[i] the evangelist [19] included their creation by the artisan the Word with that of other creatures[ii] and said:

   i. Here begins the text in M.
   ii. According to Basil of Caesarea (*Hex.* 1.5), angelic beings existed before the creation of the world. (The Syriac and Armenian versions of the *Hexaemeron* omit this passage.) But Moše bar Kepha states that John's "everything" covers all the details in Genesis, angels included. And Tat̔ewac̔i, 55, claims that angels are included in what Moses described.

[1:3b] Without him came into being nothing that came into being.[2]

He silenced the mouths of the schismatics[i] who divide the creative activity into two, indicating that there is nothing among things created, spiritual or tangible, which was not created by him and through him.[ii]

   i. Origen, *Comm. Jo.* 2.91 (Blanc, 265), states that the phrase "that came into being" was adopted by Chrysostom as an anti-Arian elucidation.
   ii. Theodore of Mopsuestia, 18, emphasizes the difference between spiritual and physical created things. Step̔annos of Siwnik̔, 118, discusses evil: it is not a created thing.

---

2. For the punctuation of vv. 3–4, see the discussion in Metzger 1975 (ad loc.).

[1:4a] **Through him was life.**

Because he explained that everything was created through him, therefore very splendidly he describes what follows by the administration of his providence: *Through him was life*, that is, by his[3] coming to us we received the original former state of immortal life, by recognizing our Creator,[i] from whom we had been separated and estranged by the deceit of the Devil and had fallen away from life. Did you see how he explains and exhorts [as follows]?

   i. Moše bar Kepha also defines life as recognizing God.

[1:4b] **The[4] life was the light of men.**

So he did not refer to that life in which we[5] live and move and are comparable to breathing and insensible things, because it was not appropriate to call that the light of mankind.[i] Rather, he desired to speak about faith and knowing the creator of creation, in accordance with [the saying]: *A people who sat in darkness saw a great light* (Isa 9:2; cf. Matt 4:16).

   i. The same argument is found in Moše bar Kepha, and Dionysius bar Salibi, *John*, 14. Cf. Tat'ewac'i, 59. Here Theodore of Mopsuestia, 19, emphasizes spiritual life.

[1:5a] **And the light was shining in the darkness.**

O what wonder, how immediately he repeats the circumstances of the light. Because he begins to show that through faith the race of mankind was illuminated, consequently he preached very clearly that *The light was[6] shining in the darkness*, in order to say that down below, where our human nature remained obscured in the blackness of gloom through devilish error, [20] the true light had descended from heaven and lit[7] its own body as a lamp for the world, and rendered us glorious and shining, we who once sat in the dark ignorance of sin, and brought us close to the rays of the divine and shadowless light. Furthermore, a certain other holy man describes the various bodily movements of the passions within us, which often darken the illuminating movements[8] of the mind,[i] so that with an allegorical word he informs us to

---

3. **His,** *nora*, M: *or*, N; *nora* in printed text.
4. **The,** NZ: om. M.
5. **We:** sg. M.
6. **Was,** *ēr*, NZ: "is," *ē*, M.
7. **Lit,** *eloyc'*, MV: "shown," *ec'oyc'*, N.
8. **Movements:** sg. M.

the effect that in the union of the Word of God with our nature, by mingling and uniting with his own nature this corruptible and sinful one he rendered it luminous, making it burn with his own divinity through the ineffable union.

i. Moše bar Kepha emphasizes the body as darkness. For Dionysius bar Salibi, *John*, 15, darkness is the world. On the other hand, the *Commentary on the Diatessaron* regards darkness as the period before the coming of Christ. The identity of the "other holy man" is not clear.

[1:5b] **And the darkness did not comprehend it.**

Although [the evangelist described] very clearly the Devil's remaining uncomprehending *regarding the mystery of carrying out the Dispensation,[9] yet on one occasion seeing him on the great heights he was terrified, and when he descended to the lower parts he was again in error and supposed him to be simply a man.[i] Yet it is appropriate to understand the same also concerning his saving passion, as I said above. This the prophet predicted from afar: *He did no sin, nor was deceit found in his mouth* (Isa 53:9).

i. Dionysius bar Salibi, *John*, 15, also refers here to Satan. Nonnus is describing the temptation of Christ (Matt 4:1–11; Mark 1:12–13; Luke 4:1–13).

[1:6] **There was a man sent from God; his name [was] John.**

Because he established such a lofty [saying] concerning Christ in the ears of the people, he placed next the name of the Baptist as a testimony for his own sayings and for the profitable succor of the crowds, since that man was very believable to the people. [21] See[10] again how he philosophizes by the grace of the Holy Spirit: he was *the man sent from God*. Now, if he was sent by God, then he spoke the words of God. And why are we distressed and indolent, as the words concern Christ? He also cites the name, because John was very well known and renowned for his prophetic grace,[i] having so close by his testimonies[11] and teachings.

i. **Grace:** *šnorh.* Tatʿewacʿi, 61, states that "John" means "grace," and in place of the standard Armenian for "Baptist," *mkrtičʿ*, he uses the term *karapet*. *Karapet* is not used of John in the Armenian Bible, but it renders *prodromos* at Heb 6:20, where it refers to Christ.

---

9. **Regarding … Dispensation:** "regarding the Dispensation and carrying out the mysteries" (or, "this mystery," *xorhurds*), M.
10. **See,** M: "did you see?" N.
11. **Testimonies:** sg. M.

[1:7a] **He came for a witness in order to bear witness about the light.**[12]

When he described that he had been sent by God, he set down next the reasons for which he had been sent by God: not that Christ had any need for him,[i] but for confirmation to the people and for an exhortation to those who might wish to come to faith[13] in the truth of Christ's gospel.

> i. Moše bar Kepha also indicates that the Word had no need of John.

[1:8] **He was not the light, but in order to bear witness concerning the light.**

Because the witness was[14] very much more trusted and honored among the Jews than the one about whom he testified, the evangelist announced that he was not the light that was shining but that he might bear witness concerning the light. *Although he seems to you more sublime and reliable, yet he possessed only the grace of testimony concerning the light.[15]

[1:9] **[He]**[16] **was the true light, which illuminated every man who was to come into the world.**

Because he demonstrated that John was not the light, he consequently described who the light is, showing that it is none other than Christ. Then he set down *was*, which contains an indication of his uncreatedness as not being created;[i] although in later times he shone upon the world, yet he was without beginning and uncreated. Not by a gift or by grace did he receive the light; *but from the being and essence of the Father he possessed the light[17] with which he illuminated everyone. And not as of old [did he illuminate] his own the true Israel, [22] because not in time does he possess the power of shining. Through the elements he is hidden and separated by a shadow like the light of the sun, but truly the light remains blazing in uncreatedness.

But what shall we say to the opponents, who say, How did he illuminate every man who was[18] to come into the world, for behold, we[19] see many not

---

12. The lemma in N and M omits v. 7b of Z: "that all through him might believe." But the commentary to this verse ends with an oblique reference to it.

13. **Faith**, *hawats*, N: "certain," *hawast*, M.

14. **Was**: om. M.

15. **Although … light**: om. N.

16. **[He]**: the subject is not expressed.

17. **But from … light**: om. N; "but from the being of the Father," V.

18. **Was**: "is," M.

19. **We**: sg. M.

illuminated by him and who do not even know him? To them we say, Not that he did not illuminate [them], but they did not wish to be enlightened like someone blind, or someone else who covers his eyes when looking at the delightful rays of the sun.[ii] So the sun was not the cause of their not being illuminated, because it shines[20] the beams of its rays uniformly and equally on all; but they were not illuminated, one by blindness and another by willingly closing his eyes against the vision of the sun's rays.

> i. This argument is echoed in Tat'ewac'i, 64.
> ii. There is a similar argument in Dionysius bar Salibi, *John*, 16.

[1:10a] **He was in the world.**

When he declared of the light that he was the true light,[i] he added to it, *This light was in the world*, indicating the profundity of the limitless and indivisible and unbounded divine nature. Lest some people, being dim-witted about the existence of the world, perversely suppose that it is created, he said:

> i. Theodore of Mopsuestia, 22, indicates that the light was in the world by nature and hypostasis. Here Dionysius bar Salibi, *John*, 17, emphasizes the Word was not created.

[1:10b] **The world was created through him.**

As if to say, although I said[21] he was in the world, yet he himself is the creator of the world.[i]

> i. Moše bar Kepha emphasizes this point.

[1:10c] **And the world did not know him.**

How necessary for the investigation of the truth of this saying are [these words]! Not about the whole world did he wish to speak, for behold, many even before the incarnation of the Word recognized him, like Abram, as is testified by the Lord: *Abraham desired to see my day.* [23] *He saw it and was glad* (John 8:56).[i] Unless he knew him,[22] why did he desire? See what he says regarding the prophets and the just ones: *Many prophets and just ones desired to see what you have seen, but did not see it* (Matt 13:17; Luke 10:24). Further-

---

20. **Shines:** "shone," M.
21. **Although I said:** om. M.
22. **Him:** om. M.

more, later many also believed in him. So he did not speak about the entire[23] human race but talked of carnal and worldly persons.

 i. Moše bar Kepha and Dionysius bar Salibi also refer to OT figures here.

[1:11] He came to his own, and his own did not receive him.

It seems to me that *his own* means the nation of the Jews,[i] because of his choosing them from among all nations and calling them his own people, and undertaking the birth according to the body from among them. He also testified that *I was sent nowhere else[24] save to the lost[25] sheep of the house of Israel* (Matt 15:24). Despite all this, they did not receive him, that is, did [not] believe. Once, he called them a vineyard, which he later explained in a parable, which they were to work: *This is the heir. Come, let us kill him* (Matt 21:38; Mark 12:7; Luke 20:14). Which indeed they did; taking him outside Jerusalem, they condemned him to death.

 i. The Jews: as John Chrysostom, *Hom. Jo.* 9.1, and Moše bar Kepha. Dionysius bar Salibi, *John*, 17, defines "his own" as all men, but more specifically (*qriḥya'ith*) the Jews.

[1:12] But to those who received him he gave authority to become sons of God, to those who believed in his name.

That is, those who believed in his name received him, whether from among Gentiles or other nations. To them he granted the lot of adoption in general (Gal 4:5; Eph 1:5),[i] according to Paul's saying: *There is no distinction, neither of Jew nor Gentile, neither of slave nor free, neither of male nor female; for you are all one in Christ[26] Jesus* (Gal 3:28).[ii] So these received the status of adoption through the birth of the holy font.

 i. Here Dionysius bar Salibi expands on the theme of God as Father.
 ii. Moše bar Kepha lists various categories of persons but does not quote Paul. The same theme is found in John Chrysostom, *Hom. Jo.* 10.2, without the quotation.

---

23. **Entire:** om. N.
24. **Sent nowhere else,** NZ: "not sent," M.
25. **Lost:** om. M.
26. **Christ:** om. M.

[1:13] Those who were born not from blood, nor from the will of the flesh, nor from the will of man, but from God.

[24] When he described the power of the grace whereby they were called sons of God, he next set down the cause of that grace, indicating that the sons of men were called sons of God, not through the transmission of blood[27] by the aggression of a man's will—by which the nations of mankind naturally receive their pattern of existence through descent[i]—but through the second birth at the descent of the Holy Spirit, which was wondrously worked upon us through the incarnation of the Son, as the following indicates:

i. Tat'ewac'i, 64, discusses at length the contrast between spiritual birth and physical birth; the latter involves blood from the mother and seed from the father.

[1:14a] The Word became flesh and dwelled among us.

When he said, *To those who received him he gave the authority to become sons of God*, and that *they were born from God*, he added thereto also the cause[28] through which they were raised so high: *The Word became flesh*, therefore the sons of men became sons of God.[i] Because the Son of God became a son of man, for that reason he was humbled so that he might raise us up, he was made poor so that he might render us illustrious, he was dishonored so that he might make us glorious. But just as we, although through the second birth we became sons of God by grace, yet we were not changed from our human nature; in the same fashion too, the Word, although he became flesh, yet he was not changed from his divine nature,[ii] nor by being humbled below was he diminished at all[29] from his divine glory, but he remains in the supernal glory of the Father's incomprehensibility.[30]

i. Dionysius bar Salibi, *John*, 18: God became a man (*breh de'naša*) in order to make us sons of God. This is the classic theme of Athanasius (e.g., *De incarnatione* 54): he became man that we might become divine.
ii. That Christ's divine nature was not changed by the incarnation is emphasized by Chrysostom, *Hom. Jo.* 11.1–2, and Step'annos of Siwnik', 120, as well as Moše bar Kepha and Dionysius bar Salibi.

---

27. **Of blood:** "by blood," N.
28. **Cause:** pl. M.
29. **At all:** om. M.
30. **Incomprehensibility,** M[corr]N; "divinity," MV.

[1:14b] And we saw his glory like the glory of the only begotten from the Father, full of grace and truth.

Although he was so humbled that he became flesh, yet the operations of his[31] divinity and glory did not remain hidden from creatures. He was born in the cave[i] but was worshiped by ranks of angels (Luke 2:13); **[25]** he was wrapped in swaddling bands (Luke 2:7, 12) but was offered gifts by the magi (Matt 2). He came to the temple as a child but released the elderly Simeon as one having authority over life and death (Luke 2). He was baptized by John but opened the heavens and was testified by the Father, *This is my beloved son,* and the Holy Spirit descended in the form of a dove (Matt 3:16–17; Mark 1:10–11; Luke 3:22; cf. John 1:32).[ii] He came humbly to the cross, but he darkened the sun above and split the veil of the temple. The rocks were rent, and the dead arose in reproof of the Jews (Matt 27:51–52; Mark 15:38; Luke 23:45), *and various other wonders occurred.[32] Truly the evangelist set down: *We have seen his glory, the glory as of the only begotten[33] from the Father.* Not by gift or grace bestowed were the wonders [performed], as for the saints; but the Son naturally and equally possessed the honor of the Father's divinity.

i. For the birth of Christ in a cave, see *Protevangelium of James* 18; Terian 2008a (ch. 8; in his introduction Terian gives the complicated history of the recensions). Patristic references to Justin and Origen are given in Lampe 1969 (s.v. *spēlaion*). For further Armenian references, see *The Discourse on the Epiphany* by Anania of Širak, translated in Terian 2008b (app. 1, p. 18), with references to Cyril of Jerusalem and the Armenian Lectionary.

ii. Moše bar Kepha lists similar aspects of the life of Christ.

[1:15a] John bore witness concerning him; he cried out and said:

Concerning this same one whom I preach to you, says [the evangelist], John loudly cried out in front of the nations, who is superior to all viewers, who also saw the one who had been prophesied. It is also a custom for the evangelists to summon the prophets for testimony when they wrote[34] their Gospel accounts about Christ.[i] Just as Matthew cites Isaiah for testimony of the birth of Christ (Matt 1:22–23; cf. Isa 7:14), and Jeremiah for the children of Bethlehem (Matt 2:17–18; cf. Jer 31:15), and the Lord's return from Egypt, *From Egypt my son will be called*[ii] (Matt 2:15; cf. Hos 11:1), likewise too John [cites] the testimonies of the Baptist.

---

31. **His:** om. N.

32. **And various … occurred,** MV: om. N.

33. The printed text adds *li,* "full."

34. **Wrote:** "write," MV.

  i. Moše bar Kepha states the same.
  ii. **My son will be called:** "I shall call my son," M (as Z).

[1:15b] This is the one about whom I spoke: he who is[35] **to come after me was before me, because he was prior to me.**

John previously mentioned the same, **[26]** as when he said: *I baptize you with water, but who will come after me is more powerful than I* (John 1:26–27; cf. Matt 3:11; Luke 3:16; Mark 1:7–8). But do not be distressed at all that, when [although] after him you hear his coming[36] to be prior to him. But because John was known previously to the people and was very clear concerning his prophecy, therefore he said, *Who*[37] *is to come after me*. See further what he said: *He was before me*. He indicates here his having no beginning, and his existence in the later time.

[1:16a] For from his fullness we have all received grace.

He demonstrated also the infinitude of the divine grace. He does not possess any acquired grace but fullness in divine fashion in accordance with the Father's essence, whence he pours out on us grace without separation or any diminution from himself,[i] but he remains always completely in fullness,[38] and on us he pours out inexhaustibly as from a fountain the gifts of his grace.

  i. Moše bar Kepha and Dionysius bar Salibi (*John*, 29) emphasize "no diminution," and Step'annos of Siwnik', 120, that there was no change or alteration of the nature of God the Word into the nature of flesh, "as when we say that water freezes."

[1:16b] Grace for grace.

He says something other than what was given of old to the Israelites. We have received grace,[i] because that [was] a shadow and this is truth; that temporal, and this permanent; that partial, and this perfect.[39]

  i. Moše bar Kepha contrasts what Jesus received with what we received.

---

35. **Is**, N: "was," MZ.

36. **Coming**, *zgalustn*, N: "is to come," *zgaloc'n*, M.

37. **He said, Who**, *asē or*, N: "he said," *asēr*, M.

38. **Completely in fullness**, *i lrman katarelapēs*, N: "in complete fullness," *i lrman katareluťean*, M.

39. Plural pronouns, "this, that," for "grace," the plural noun *šnorhk'*.

[1:17] For the law was given through Moses; grace and truth were through Jesus Christ.[40]

Because he stated that we received *grace for grace*, he indicated the incomparable comparison[i] of the two graces, contrasting[ii] Moses to the Savior, and the law of Moses to the gospel of Christ, instructing us that all that [27] was a shadow[iii] of the truth of the gospel that through Christ wondrously was worked[41] among us. For there a lamb was sacrificed, but here the true lamb of God is offered (Exod 12; cf. John 1:29; 1 Pet 1:19); there the sign of the cross was once[42] the rod of Moses (Exod 4) and the stretching out of his hands whereby Amalek was defeated (Exod 17), but here the Savior stretches out his arms on the life-giving cross. There the committing of sins is forbidden, but here he causes renunciation from thoughts [of sin]. There an eye for an eye and a death for a death is the law (Exod 24), but here through the grace of repentance he saves everyone. There the earth announced confession with marvelous[43] gifts, here the supernal Jerusalem with its ineffable and inseparable gifts. Did you see the superiority of the second grace and the gifts[44] of unparalleled beneficence?

So let us be respectful and not be disheartened, let us strive for our salvation and not be separated from or deprived of the exceeding grace. For if of old and under the law the obstinacy of Israel was so punished and condemned, of what sort of pardon will we be worthy when in laziness we deprive ourselves of grace? The son of God became man, and even accepted to condescend[45] to our humble estate, in order that he might raise us up. In particular, he bought [us] with his own honorable blood (Gal 3:13; Eph 1:7; Col 1:14; Rev 5:9) and rendered us worthy again of immortal life and eternal glory. Therefore let us hasten to reform ourselves and inherit the promised blessings in Christ Jesus our[46] Lord, with whom to the Father and also to the Holy Spirit are fitting glory and power and honor, now and always and forever and ever.[47] Amen.[iv]

   i. **Comparison:** *kšrut'iwn* (lit. "balance"); here "equivalence" seems inappropriate.

---

40. **Christ,** NZ: om. M.

41. **Was worked:** pl. M.

42. **Once,** *erbemn*: om. M.

43. **Marvelous,** *sk'ančeli*: "weak," *lk'aneli*, M.

44. **Gifts,** *zjirs*: "acts," *zirs*, N.

45. **Condescend,** *zijanel*, MN: "descend," *ijanel*, V.

46. **Our:** om. N.

47. Here the scribe of M adds a colophon: "I beg that you remember in your prayers Kirakos the holy vardapet and the patron of this holy book. Also do not forget Romanos a scribe for the Lord's sake."

ii. **Contrasting:** *awrinakelov* (lit. "making an example"). *Awrinak* is the standard term for "type" or "model."

iii. The law of Moses as a "shadow" (*stuer*), as Heb 10:1; the same term is used by Step'annos of Siwnik', 120. Moše bar Kepha and Dionysius bar Salibi (*John*, 27) use the expression *typos*, and Tat'ewac'i, 81, refers to *awrinak*. Dionysius (*John*, 27) gives the same parallels.

iv. For such exhortations to the reader, which all end with "Amen," see the introduction, xxv.

[28] II⁴⁸

[1:18] **No one has ever seen God, save only the only begotten Son, who [is] in the bosom of the Father, he has declared [him] to us.**

To some this[49] seems not to fit the context according to what had been said earlier, for up to this point he described the second of the graces that he poured out on us, yet now he says: *No one has ever seen God.*[i] But they did not understand it well, because this saying is set out very suitably. When he spoke about the grace of the gifts that we received in place of the grace of Moses, he then added to the same what concerns the sublime and incomprehensible essence, as if to say that the bestower of this grace is the only begotten Son, who alone sees the Father in essence and nature, and not like Moses. For although he [Moses], through whom Israel received the first grace, received the words from the hand of God, yet he did not ever see God totally but rather in some bodily form,[ii] as he once said, *This vision I multiplied*[iii] *for you* (Hos 12:10), just as in varied appearances he was revealed to the holy prophets in their respective times.[iv] Let us see again the status of adoption regarding the Father of the one called only begotten, as he possesses the original status of birth from the Father alone, and not from a mother, like that of other births. Now *the bosom of the Father* indicates his having his essential hypostasis by substance[v] and indivisibility. [29] Furthermore *bosom* metaphorically has the indication of a veil, the why and how of the essence and birth remaining hidden from us.

i. Moše bar Kepha also notes that the evangelist does not seem to accord with the OT.

ii. **Form:** *awrinak*, "example, model"; see above, commentary to v. 17.

iii. **I multiplied:** "I shall multiply," in M (as Z).

iv. Cyril of Alexandria gives a long list of God's appearances in the books of Isaiah and Ezekiel. Dionysius bar Salibi, *John*, 28, notes that men cannot see God in his nature,

---

48. For this heading, see the introduction, xxiv–xxv.

49. **This:** "thus," M.

kyana, not even angels, but he appeared in many forms. Tat'ewac'i, 82–83, explains that no created person or angel could grasp the divine "essence," *ēut'iwn*, except the Son who is "coexistent," *ēakic'*, with the Father; he lists appearances to Moses, Elias, Daniel, Ezekiel, Isaiah.

v. **Essential:** gen. of the noun *ēut'iwn*; **hypostasis:** *anjnaworut'iwn*; **substance:** *iskut'iwn*. For the terms, see the introduction, xxxv–xl. John Chrysostom, *Hom. Jo.* 15.2, emphasizes the equality of essence of the Word and Father. Tat'ewac'i, 86, states that the Son has a different *anjnaworut'iwn* from the Father, but the same "nature," *bnut'iwn*.

[1:19] And this is the testimony of John, when the Jews sent priests and Levites to him from Jerusalem to ask: Who are you?

Again the evangelist sets down the testimony of John, as he had previously described the bounty of the grace that flowed upon us through Christ, in order to reprove the obstinacy[50] of the Jews and their deceitfully sending and questioning John. For[51] they were making that inquiry not out of true faith, but [they] were hoping something like this might occur: that if he were to say, I am the Christ, we shall oppose and admonish him, and prevent him from baptizing.[i] Since he never previously spoke thus about himself, therefore those sent to him were baptized by him, as Matthew and Mark clearly relate about them (Matt 3:5–6; Mark 1:5).[ii] Furthermore, they did not send anyone from among the vulgar people, but from the priestly tribe of the Levites,[iii] so that perchance by their deceitful arguments they might be able to find some words from John.

i. As Moše bar Kepha, and Dionysius bar Salibi, *John*, 30.

ii. Theodore of Mopsuestia, 28, notes that Jesus did not say he was Elias or a prophet, as expected.

iii. John 1:24 states that they were from among the Pharisees. Cf. the change from Pharisees to Sadducees elsewhere (see the introduction, xxvi).

[1:20–21a] He confessed and did not deny; he confessed: I am not the Christ. And they asked him: Are you Elias?[52] And he said: I am not.

These [words are] of very clear understanding and have no profundity. But we must explain their deceitfulness. If he were to say, I am the Christ, they would show the falsehood and restrain him from baptizing, as we said above.

---

50. **Obstinacy:** pl. M.

51. **For:** om. NV.

52. **Are you Elias?** M: "Who are you?" N.

But [they decided] to ask, *Are you Elias?* because they had knowledge from the scriptures that Elias would come before Christ (Mal 4:5).[i]

> i. That Elias came before Christ is stressed by Dionysius bar Salibi, *John*, 31. This passage is elaborated by Theodore of Mopsuestia and Step'annos of Siwnik'.

[30] [1:21b] **Are you the prophet?**

They asked about this prophet, whom Moses had prophesied: *The Lord God will raise up a prophet for you from among your brothers like me; heed him* (Deut 18:15).[i]

> i. Step'annos of Siwnik', Moše bar Kepha, and Dionysius bar Salibi (*John*, 31) also refer to Moses and give this quotation.

[1:22–23] **So tell us who you are, so that we may give a response to those who sent us. What do you say about yourself? He said: I am a voice of a cry in the desert: *Prepare the ways of the Lord, and make straight the paths**[53] **of our God.**[54]

Because you have entered into such artful investigation[55] about me with fraud and deceitful words, I shall tell you precisely who I am. I am the one of whom Isaiah earlier prophesied to be *a voice of a cry in the desert.* Is not a word clear through a voice?[i] So then, I am the voice of the Word, and a forerunner[ii] of him, to preach to the world to *prepare the ways of the Lord* and to *make straight the paths of our God.*

> i. A word is known through a voice, as noted by Dionysius bar Salibi, *John*, 32. Tat'ewac'i, 90, notes that John is the "voice," *jayn*, and Christ the word; he uses here *barbaṙ* for "word," i.e., the "cry" of Isaiah, not the *ban* of Nonnus and John 1:1.
> ii. **Forerunner:** *karapet*; see above, note to commentary on v. 6.

[1:24] **And those who were sent were from among the Pharisees.**

We previously mentioned the Levites and the reasons for which they had been sent; let us now talk about the Sadducees.[i] Since they were very cunning

---

53. **Paths,** N: "path," MZ.
54. **Prepare … God:** "Make straight the way of the Lord," Z. Nonnus quotes Isa 40:3 directly in preference to the allusion in John 1:23.
55. **Investigation:** + "to speak," M.

and clever speakers,[ii] therefore they hoped through each other to find words from John.

    i. Nonnus also refers to Pharisees as Sadducees in the commentary to John 4:1 and 11:46; see the introduction, xxvi.
    ii. **Clever speakers**: *čartaraxaws*, often used of rhetoricians, but here not in a flattering sense.

[1:25] They asked him and said: Why do you baptize, if you are not the Christ, nor Elias, nor the prophet?

Did you see how obviously their wickedness was veiled? So truly we said that they were seeking reasons to prevent him from baptizing.

[1:26–27] John replied to them and said: I baptize you with water. Among you there is one whom you do not know, who is to come after me, of whom I am unworthy to loosen the laces of his shoes.

[31] Why did he say: *I baptize you with water*? So that thereby he might prepare them for the baptism of Christ; and he demonstrates that he would in no way hinder the latter's baptism. He emphasizes the reference to him, that *he would come after him*, so that thereby he might satisfy their minds and draw [them] to Christ as the giver of the greatest grace. For this was the baptism[56] of confession and repentance, whereas his was of freedom and total purity.[i] But what is: *I am unworthy to loosen the laces of his shoes*? He indicates the degree of his own immeasurable humility with regard to the other's incomparable majesty, that I am not even worthy to serve his feet.[ii] He also indicates the divinity of Christ and his own servile nature, as if to say that I am unable to understand or to describe even partially the nature of his dispensation[iii] and incarnation.

    i. Step'annos of Siwnik', 122, emphasizes that John's baptism was only a bodily one. Dionysius bar Salibi, *John*, 33, 37, states that John's baptism was a baptism of repentance and a shadow of Christ's.
    ii. Step'annos of Siwnik', 122, interprets the two shoes as the incarnation and the descent to hell, as also on p. 8, to Matt 3:11. Tat'ewac'i, 92–93, notes that Christ did not wear shoes.
    iii. **Dispensation**: *tnawrinakan kargk'*; for the terminology, see the introduction, xxxvi–xxxvii. Dionysius bar Salibi, *John*, 34, refers to John's inability to understand the least mysteries of the dispensation in the flesh.

---

56. **The baptism**: om. NV.

[1:28] This took place in Bet'abra, beyond the Jordan, where John was and was baptizing.

The evangelist also reveals the name of the place where John was baptizing,[i] because the people were acquainted and familiar with that place and had close knowledge of the things being done there by John. We have also found in a copy[ii] somewhere Bet'abra called Bet'ania, the village of Lazarus that is[57] close to Jerusalem.

i. Cyril of Alexandria notes that the evangelist gives the name in order to render his account more accurate, *akribēs*: "We are accustomed to record the places in which important events occurred." Dionysius bar Salibi indicates the same; see also the introduction, xxxiv. Nonnus, in the commentary to John 11:1, elaborates on the same point, in his discussion of Bethany, the village of Lazarus.

ii. **Copy**: *awrinak*, "exemplar." Nonnus occasionally refers to "other exemplars," usually meaning a different commentator; see the introduction, xxviii–xxix. But here a copy of the biblical text might be intended. John Chrysostom, *Hom. Jo.* 17.1, notes that Bethany is near Jerusalem, not across the Jordan. Moše bar Kepha does not discuss the place name; Dionysius bar Salibi, *John*, 34, has Bethany in the lemma but explains that "in accurate copies" Bethabra is written, because Bethany is not in the desert. Origen indicates that Bethany is found in most copies but should be changed to Bethabra, since Bethany is very close to Jerusalem. Tat'ewac'i, 93, referring to Origen's correction of the error, indicates that the village of Lazarus was not intended. Cyril of Alexandria and Theodore of Mopsuestia give Bethany in the lemma, without comment. Išodad explains the location of Bethany and notes a variant text giving Bet'abara. Step'annos of Siwnik', 123, refers to Bet'arbay in both lemma and commentary and explains the meaning as "house of wisdom." On the biblical text, see Metzger 1975 (ad loc.).

[1:29] The next day he saw[58] Jesus coming to him, and he said: Behold the lamb of God who removes the sins of the world.

Someone from among the teachers[i] says that [32] these things were said about the day of [his] baptism, when he came to John. But to us it seems better to understand it as a second coming of the Lord after the baptism, because Matthew described the day of the baptism (Matt 3:13–17). Now, the saying *Behold the lamb of God* means this is the one for whom we have been waiting according to the distant predictions of Isaiah: *He removes our sins and for our sake is tormented* (Isa 53:4). This mystery Moses also unerringly represented of old allegorically by the slaughter of the lamb in Egypt, whereby he saved the first-born of Israel. *This is the one who removes the sins of the world*, and as it were

---

57. **Is**: "was," M.
58. **Saw**: "sees," NZ.

by this he teaches and admonishes the people[59] that if he removes the sins of the world, does he not then need repentance and purity through the baptism, like you? For how is the purity of the world effected by me? But these things are now veiled from you[60] as a mystery of his dispensation.

Furthermore, he did not say that he removes specifically the sins of Israel, like the sacrifices of old, but those of the whole world, showing that he is Savior of the whole world and not of Israel alone. But what [does it mean] to say, *he removes*, and not, *he removed*? For those things would happen through the cross. Now he does not say[ii] he is intending to[iii] remove, because of his always removing [them] as he perpetually distributes his body and blood for the propitiation of the sins of the world. He is called a lamb because he would be sacrificed, not for himself but for the salvation of others, in accordance with Paul's saying, *He slew our sins in the body* (1 Pet 2:24), and *He nailed [them] to the wood of the cross* (Col 2:14).[iv] He is also rightly understood to be a lamb for the believers, by feeding us regularly with his own body. And he is a garment for us in accordance with Paul's saying: *We who have been baptized[61] in Christ have put on Christ* (Gal 3:27).

i. **Teachers:** *vardapetk'*. For this rank of Armenian scholars, see Thomson 1962, 2000 (43–46). The reference is to John Chrysostom, *Hom. Jo.* 17.1.

ii. **He does not say:** rendering the infinitive *aseln*.

iii. **He is intending to:** *handerjeal ē*, or "he is about to," or "will [remove]." Dionysius bar Salibi, *John*, 36, states that he was about to (*'thid*) remove sin by his death. Step'annos of Siwnik', 123, notes that he removes sins up to the end of the world—therefore "removed" and "will remove" are not appropriate.

iv. Note that Nonnus combines a quotation from 1 Peter with one from Colossians as "Paul's" saying; cf. introduction, xxvii.

[33] [1:30] This is he of whom I said: After me comes a man[62] who was before me, because he was prior to me.

See how he repeats the coming after himself, predicting later knowledge rather than himself. *He was before me* [indicates] the dispensation in the womb, *whom from the womb to the womb he worshiped (Luke 1:41)[63]; but *he was prior to me* indicates his being without beginning and his uncreatedness.[i]

i. Dionysius bar Salibi, *John*, 36–37, notes that "before me" refers to Christ's divinity,

---

59. **People:** pl. NV.

60. **From you,** *i jēnǰ*: "through," *i jeṙn*, M.

61. **Baptized,** N (= Z): "believed," M.

62. NV = Z: "who came," M.

63. **Whom … worshiped,** MV: om. N.

and "after me" to his humanity; but he is one and not divided. Theodore of Mopsuestia, 30, states that it is the view of heretics that "after me … before me" refers to the divine hypostasis.

[1:31] And I did not know him, save that he may be revealed to Israel; therefore[64] I came to baptize with water.

Let us examine[65] the meaning of this saying, how he did not recognize [Jesus], he who worshiped from the womb to the womb[66].[i] It was so that he might remove the suspicions of those who said that he did this because he had prior knowledge, or in accordance with the close relationship of Elisabeth with Mary, for these things were clear to the people. But do you, my friend, examine these matters: why did he not say, I do not recognize him, but rather, *I did not know him*? It was as if to say that I recognized the essence of his being but did not know the circumstances of the nature of his incarnation. Now his saying, *He may be[67] revealed to Israel, therefore I came to baptize with water*, is as if to say, For that reason I baptize with water, so that everyone[68] may be zealous to come to me; and as the people accumulated, his preaching concerning Christ might become appropriate to make ready his ways. But by my being in cities and in villages many are troubled at being deprived of the distribution of grace. We earlier mentioned these as not interpreting correctly what was said by us, but they think they were introduced by us as a justification of prior knowledge and relationship.[ii] Also by its habitual familiarity he draws them through his own baptism to the true baptism of Christ.

i. Step'annos of Siwnik', 124, explains that when Elisabeth met Mary (Luke 1:41), John knew that Mary's child was the Christ, but not that it is he who baptizes with Spirit and fire. Tat'ewac'i, 96, quotes Nanay (Nonnus) and adds that John did not know the form (*dēmk'*, "face, person, hypostasis") of Christ's incarnate body.

ii. The grammar of this sentence is unclear.

[1:32–33] And he said: [34] I saw the Spirit[69] like a dove descending from heaven, and it rested on him. And I did not know him, save the one who had

---

64. **Therefore**, *vasn aynorik*, MZ: *vasn aysorik*, N.

65. **Examine**, *ditescuk'*: "know," *gitescuk'*, M.

66. **To the womb**: om. M.

67. **May be**, M (= lemma): "is," N.

68. **Everyone**: "you all," M.

69. **Spirit**, NZ: "Holy Spirit," M.

sent me to baptize with water, he told me: On whom you will see the Spirit descending and resting, that is he who baptizes with the Holy Spirit.

What divinely inspired conceptions! Gradually he explains the allegorical mystery and expounds it concerning the true baptism of Christ being with the Spirit but not with water. Also the descent of the Holy Spirit and his resting on him he reveals to be not for any need of Christ's but for testimony and an indicative sign that this is the son of God, the Christ, who would come into the world. Furthermore he teaches us that as on him, so also on us will rest at baptism he who in the beginning was removed from us by Adam's transgressions.[i]

i. Tat'ewac'i, 97, makes it explicit that the Spirit was removed from Adam. Dionysius bar Salibi, *John*, 128–29, emphasizes that John prepared the Jews for penitence.

[1:34] **And I saw and testified that this is the Son of God.**

He indicates that my testimonies concerning Christ are very true, because I saw in front of my eyes the descent of the Holy Spirit from heaven, just as some others from among the prophets, like Moses and Ezekiel and Isaiah, were made worthy to see God. But what is:[70] *He who sent me to baptize, he told me, On whom you will see the Spirit descending, he it is?*[71] That is, this sign was given me in the desert while I was alone, to which I was later a witness. See also what he said: *This is the Son of God.* Not that he is[72] a son of God, but the Son of God,[73] so that by the addition of the article,[i] he might demonstrate the only begotten, the true, the coexisting, to be superior [35] to those who were called sons of God at various times by grace.

i. **Article:** *tar*, referring to the demonstrative suffix -*n*.

[1:35–36] **The next day John was standing, and two of his disciples; and seeing Jesus coming, he said: Behold, Christ, the lamb of God.**

We must know that this day was not in succession to the two days previously mentioned,[i] but this was after his return from the desert, when he fasted for forty days and overcame the chief tempter,[ii] which Matthew, Mark, and Luke had previously described in each of their own accounts (Matt 4; Mark

---

70. **Is,** *ē*: "might be," *icē*, M.
71. **He it is:** om. N.
72. **Not that he is:** "not yet," M.
73. **Of God:** om. N.

1:13; Luke 4). Therefore John omitted what had been related by them. Whence is this clear? Because it was not appropriate to be the third day[74] after the two days that he had recorded. For if it were the third day, then how could the marriage be said to occur on the third? But it would be appropriate to say it was on the fifth.[iii] So then, the first day is understood as that on which he went to the Pharisees and Sadducees; and the second, when John saw Jesus coming, and said, *This is the Son of God*; and the third, when John was standing and two of his disciples; and the fourth, when he wished to go to Galilee and saw Philip; and the fifth, the marriage in Cana of Galilee. That is adequate for the confirmation of the words, his saying on that day to his disciples: *Behold the lamb of God.* For they would be superfluous if he had spoken them on the previous day. So the passage indicates that they were waiting for him, as if he had delayed and they were continually looking out. When John saw him, he said, *Behold the lamb of God*, as if to say, Behold[75] [the one] for whom you were waiting and continually looking and asking about.

Furthermore, if [36] any of the disciples were with him in the desert, why do we say he was alone? See how Mark makes it clear: when he describes the baptism of Christ, he places next and immediately following that Jesus was led by the Spirit into the desert to be tempted by Satan (Mark 1:12–13).

i. Theodore of Mopsuestia, 33, notes that John baptized over many days, so here "the next day" means "one day." Step'annos of Siwnik' accepts that this was the third day from when the Pharisees asked Jesus who he was (vv. 19–24, above).

ii. **Chief tempter:** *p'orjapet*, as also at v. 43. The term is not used in the Bible, but see *Teaching* 278–79 for various names given to Satan.

iii. As Nonnus notes in his commentary to John 2:1–2; see also Tat'ewac'i, 98. Dionysius bar Salibi, *John*, 39–40, gives a list of events for each day and states that this was the third after the return from the desert.

[1:37] **Two of the disciples heard him speaking, and they followed Jesus.**

For when they heard their teacher say,[76] *Behold[77] the lamb of God, who takes away the sins of the world*, thenceforth they remained no more with him, but they followed the superior and higher one, who was so pleasing to their teacher John. Why two,[i] and not less or more? It is an indication of the two

---

74. **Day:** om. N.
75. **Behold:** om. N.
76. **Say:** om. N.
77. **Behold:** + "Christ," M.

nations, the Jews and Gentiles, who would abandon their old traditions[78] and follow the gospel of life, of the preaching of which John was the forerunner.[ii]

i. According to Dionysius bar Salibi, *John*, 42, one of the two was Andrew (see v. 40), the other John the evangelist, who did not reveal his name, out of humility.
ii. Forerunner: *karapet*; see above, note to commentary on v. 6.

[1:38a] When Jesus turned, he saw them and said to them: What do you seek?

Now why did he ask that? Behold, he knew what they were seeking. But because the two disciples so honored Christ, when they heard their teacher [say] that he was the lamb of God and the purity of the world, they were so bashful as to refrain from questioning thereafter. Therefore he gave them boldness[i] and an opportunity for questions and conversation, as the following indicates.

i. Dionysius bar Salibi, *John*, 41, states that Christ asked, although he knows everything before it happens, in order to provide boldness, *parrēsia* (in Syriac transliteration).

[1:38b–39] They said to him: Rabbi—which translated means "teacher"—where are your lodgings? He[79] said to them: Come and see. They came and saw where his lodgings were; *and they dwelled with him that day,[80] because it was about the tenth hour.

[37] Why did he not indicate the place but only call [on them] to follow him? Because knowledge of the place was of no advantage to them, except only following him, so that it might be an example to us not idly to investigate places and tardily do virtuous works, but unhesitatingly and zealously to take up the cross and follow Christ (Mark 8:34; cf. Matt 16:24; Luke 9:23), whereby we unfailingly encounter his lodging. And why did the evangelist introduce the hour, [saying], *It was about the tenth hour*, save to show the zeal of the men toward the faith? They did not remain at dawn, but in the evening at a late time they urged themselves on toward the faith. This was a sign to the Jews and Gentiles after them, who at the end of time would abandon their own traditions[81] and follow the gospel of Christ.

---

78. **Their old traditions:** "the old tradition," N.
79. **He,** NZ: "Jesus," M.
80. **And they dwelled ... day:** om. M.
81. **Traditions:** sg. N.

[1:40–41] Andrew, brother of Simon the rock, was one of the two who heard John[82] and followed him.[83] He first found his brother Simon and said to him: We have found the Messiah, which is translated "Christ."

He testified here to the eagerness of their minds, how they had always desired his manifestation and they were waiting to encounter [him]. On meeting him, they rapidly recognized him that he was the Christ. *We have found* indicates them as continually inquiring and seeking the truth.

[1:42] He brought him to Jesus. Looking at him, Jesus said: You are Simon son of Jona; you shall be called Kephas, which means "Peter."

In showing and revealing the all-seeing and all-comprehending knowledge of his divinity through citing both names, thereby he confirmed them even more in their saying: *We have found the Messiah.* But one must inquire why he named Simon as *Kephas, which means "Peter."*[i] **[38]** He was revealing the authority of his lordly rule, that he is the same who of old changed Abram to Abraham, and Jacob to Israel (Gen 17:5; 32:28).[ii]

 i. **Peter:** *Petros*, as in the lemma.
 ii. These changes of names are also cited by John Chrysostom, *Hom. Jo.* 19; Moše bar Kepha; and Dionysius bar Salibi, *John*, 44.

[1:43–44] On the next day he wished to go out to Galilee. He found Philip and said to him: Follow me. Philip was from Bethsaida, from the city of Andrew and Peter.

This is the second[i] day after his returning from the desert, when he overcame the chief tempter.[ii] Why did he go first to Galilee,[84] except for the naming or choice of the disciples, in order to fulfill the saying of Isaiah: *The land of Zabulon and the land of Nep'talim, Galilee of the Gentiles, a people who sat in darkness saw a great light* (Isa 9:1–2; cf. Matt 4:15–16)? When the evangelist [mentioned] first Philip from Bethsaida, from the city of Andrew and Peter, he did not thereby demonstrate his[85] superiority to them according to family or place, but it was to show the greater lowliness of the apostles: that Christ chose them not from among the wise and honorable but from some insignifi-

---

82. **John,** MZ: om. N.
83. **Him,** NZ: "Jesus," M.
84. **Galilee:** + "after returning," M.
85. **Demonstrate his,** *znora c'uc'anē*, M: *i nosa*, N (*sic*).

cant and unlearned[86] and obscure people. Therefore the evangelist indicates their names and places.

    i. **Second**: Tat'ewac'i, 105, explains this as the third (variant: "second") day after the calling of the apostles.
    ii. **Chief tempter**: see above, note to commentary on vv. 35–36.

[1:45–46] Philip found Nathaniel and said to him: We have found the one of whom Moses wrote in the law,[87] and the prophets,[88] Jesus son of Joseph in Galilee. Nathaniel said to him: Out of Nazareth can anything good occur? Philip said to him: Come and see.

It seems to me that the man was very wise and informed[89] and learned in the commandments of God, as is clear from the saying *From Nazareth can[90] anything good occur*, that is, that Jesus is to be revealed from Bethlehem, **[39]** from the village of David, according to the testimony of the prophets, and not from Nazareth.[i] Consider[91] here for me the man's love of truth;[92] because although according to the writings of the prophets the birth of Christ was expected, not from Nazareth but only from Bethlehem, yet he did not hesitate to follow Philip when he said, *Come and see.*

    i. Moše bar Kepha quotes Mic 5:2. According to Theodore of Mopsuestia, 36, the people of Nazareth were *pagani* (*dmn 'mm'*). So nothing good was to be expected.

[1:47] When Jesus saw Nathaniel coming toward him, he said about him: Behold, a man[93] truly an Israelite, in whom there is no deceit.

In order to show the firmness of the man's mind regarding the predictions of the holy prophets, he was not in any way deceived by Philip's words, but he hastened to become an eyewitness.

---

86. **And unlearned**: om. NV.

87. Deut 18:15, etc.

88. **The prophets** (nom.): "in the prophets," Theodore of Mopsuestia and Dionysius bar Salibi, *John*, 44, follow the Syriac text of the NT.

89. **And informed**: om. NV.

90. **Can**, *mart' icē*: "must," *part icē*, NV (*sic*).

91. **Consider**, *ditea*: "know," *giteay*, M.

92. **Love of truth**: "truth," N.

93. **A man**: om. MZ.

[1:48] Nathaniel said to him: Whence do you know me? Jesus[94] **replied and said to him: Before Philip called [you], while you were under the fig tree, I saw you.**

Here again the discernment of the man is revealed, who did not return any thanks to the Lord for his praises[i] but merely stated, *Whence do you know me?* so that if there be in you any power of knowledge of the thoughts of men, let it be revealed. Therefore he was made worthy of the higher teaching. So the Lord did not state in accordance with his words to Philip that he was from Bethlehem and not from Nazareth, because it was not appropriate to acknowledge that regarding himself. Therefore, passing over it, he described things that were very much more profitable and advantageous,[95] revealing to him his all-seeing and all-comprehending power.[ii] Thus he showed him the place where **[40]** Philip had met him and also mentioned the name of the fig tree.[iii] Astonished at that, Nathaniel said:

> i. Moše bar Kepha has the same argument.
> ii. Theodore of Mopsuestia, 36, emphasizes the same point.
> iii. Dionysius bar Salibi, *John*, 45, notes the importance of naming the place and the tree; cf. above, note to commentary on v. 28.

[1:49] Rabbi, you are the Christ, the[96] **Son of God; you are the king of Israel.**

Although these things were spoken thus by Nathaniel, yet not with sincere and firm faith like Peter, saying, *You are the Christ, the Son of God* (Matt 16:16),[i] but in supposition and with doubtful understanding. Therefore he first states that he was *the teacher*,[ii] and then *king of Israel*. Because if his naming him Son of God was without supposition,[iii] he would not have said he was king of Israel only but also[97] of all creatures.[iv] Therefore Christ made him informed gradually, and he drew him to higher things, as the following makes clear.

> i. John Chrysostom, *Hom. Jo.* 21, states that Nathaniel only recognized Jesus as a man.
> ii. **Teacher:** *vardapet*, rendering "rabbi"; for the term, see above, note to commentary on v. 29.
> iii. **Without supposition:** *aranc' karceac'*; or "not hypothetical." Cf. "in supposition," *karceawk'*, just above.

---

94. **Jesus**, MZ: "He," NV.
95. **And advantageous**: om. NV.
96. **The**: om. MZ.
97. **Also**: om. NV.

iv. Dionysius bar Salibi, *John*, 46, makes the same argument.

[1:50–51] Jesus answered him and said: In return for my saying that I saw you[98] under the fig tree, do you believe? You will see greater things than this. Amen, amen, I say to you: You will see the heavens opened and angels ascending and descending on the son of man.[99]

Do you see how he related the most luminous things and drew him to more perfect knowledge? Since you have believed through the place and the fig tree that I declared to you regarding Philip's conversation, in order to indicate to you my[100] all-seeing power, consequently understand even more perfect things about me: to call me not only *king of Israel* but [king] of all the earth, and of heaven, and of the angels. Therefore he said: *You will see the heavens opened, and angels of God ascending and descending[i] on the son of man.*[101] Through the ministrations[102] of the angels he indicated to him[103] his kingship over all creation, on the cross and at the resurrection, and before that[104] his being born in the cave;[ii] although Nathaniel understood all this later.

i. Step'annos of Siwnik', 124, states that heaven being opened and the angels descending refer to the second coming of Christ, and that more mystically, *xorhrdagoyn*, the passage refers to the hidden treasures of wisdom and knowledge of God. Tat'ewac'i, 110, specifically refers to the angels on Jacob's ladder.

ii. For Christ's birth in a cave, see above, commentary to v. 14.

---

98. **You:** om. MZ.
99. Cf. Gen 28:12.
100. **My,** *im:* om. NV.
101. **The son of man:** "him," NV.
102. **Ministrations:** sg. NV.
103. **Him:** "them," NV.
104. **That:** "these," M.

[2:1–2] **And on the third day there was a wedding in Cana of Galilee. And the mother of Jesus was there. Jesus was also invited and his disciples to the wedding.**

These things we described previously, the third day not being placed in proper order, but as the fifth.[i] But because the other evangelists described it remembering the days, and John explains the reasons omitted by them of the individual days, we have placed it a little earlier. *The mother of Jesus was there,* so that she might show that the summons to the wedding was not a haphazard event but one of God's[1] providential administration. The going to the wedding is an indication of such humility that the high-minded never show to their servants. But [it was] in order to show that he who united Adam and Eve in the garden and blessed the increase of their offspring, the same now honors the wedding and cares for and blesses the status of legal marriage.[ii]

i. The chronology of events concerns all the commentators; cf. commentary to John 1:35 for the day involved. Step'annos of Siwnik', 125–26, gives biblical parallels for the third day, and then a long allegorical explanation comparing the groom to the Mosiac law and the bride to the soul. He does, however, admit that the wedding was a human one, and the occasion real. Cyril of Alexandria refers to the third day as the end of time. Dionysius bar Salibi, *John*, 47, gives a long discussion, quoting Moše bar Kepha; he quotes Severus to the effect that the groom was Nicodemus and the master of ceremonies was Lazarus; Tat'ewac'i, 120, also discusses different views concerning the identity of the master of ceremonies. Dionysius states that this was the fourth day from the baptism, whereas Theodore of Mopsuestia and Tat'ewac'i, 114, indicate that it was the third.

ii. Moše bar Kepha gives a similar comment, and Dionysius bar Salibi, *John*, 49, indicates that marriage is pure. Tat'ewac'i, 115, repeats Nonnus's argument and adds others to justify the presence of Jesus and his mother at such unseemly (*anvayeluč'*) celebrations.

---

1. **God's**: om. NV.

[2:3–4] And when the wine ran out, his mother said to Jesus: They do not have wine. He[2] said to her: What have I and you, woman? My time has not arrived.

First one must inquire why Mary hoped the signs[3] to occur. Not before this does Christ appear to have worked miracles according to the evangelist's account: *This beginning of signs did Jesus make in Cana of Galilee, and he revealed his glory* (John 2:11).[i] But because she had seen the great signs and miracles that were accomplished over him at the time of his baptism, and after that[4] he had revealed himself and gathered the ranks of disciples, consequently she hoped for signs and miracles[5] to be worked by him.[ii] But why did the Lord respond as if in rebuke: [42] *What have I and you, woman?* Behold, the evangelist testified concerning him that he was obedient to Joseph and Mary (Luke 2:51).[iii] But[6] because Mary requested signs for acquiring glory[iv] and for a demonstration to the onlookers, which would have been no small boast for herself, therefore he gave a very stern response.

See also the sequel, and you will not be at all distressed that he was not yet able to perform signs.[v] Was he himself not Lord and creator of hours and times? But in order to demonstrate that he would do nothing for show or for a personal boast, save for the profit and advantage of many, therefore he pardoned somewhat the lack of wine in order that the sign might be very clear to everyone. For not all those summoned to the wedding yet knew the lack of wine; and when the need was revealed the request would be urgent for everyone, and to everyone[7] the operation of the miracle[8] would be clearly revealed, and the believers would be altogether helped, since for that reason I came to this place.

i. Dionysius bar Salibi quotes John Chrysostom to the effect that this was the first miracle after the baptism (see *Hom. Jo.* 23.1). Dionysius adds that the very first miracle was performed by Jesus in the temple when he was twelve years old; see Luke 2:41–52.

ii. That Mary hoped for a miracle is noted by Moše bar Kepha, quoting Jacob of Sarug; also Theodore of Mopsuestia; Dionysius bar Salibi, *John*, 50; and Tat'ewac'i, 115.

iii. This is stressed by John Chrysostom, *Hom. Jo.* 21.

iv. **Glory:** *parcank'*, or "a boast." *Comm. Diat.* 5.1 notes Mary's impatience and gives

2. **He,** NV: "Jesus," MZ.

3. **Signs:** sg. M.

4. **That,** *ainm*: "now," *aižm*, NV.

5. **Miracles:** sg. NV.

6. **But:** om. NV.

7. **And to everyone,** *ew amenec'un*, M: *amenerew*, NV.

8. **Miracle:** pl. M.

several explanations of Jesus's reprimand. Tat'ewac'i, 116, gives ten reasons for it, in accordance with his penchant for lists.

v. Nonnus does not here explain "My time has not yet arrived," but Dionysius bar Salibi, *John*, 51–52, and Tat'ewac'i, 117–18, give extended discussion to the topic.

[2:5–6] His mother said to the servants: Do whatever he tells you. There were there six marble vessels in accordance with the purity of the Jews. Each one of them held two or three measures.

Why was Mary sensible? Not for the sake of separating the time from the signs, but since the lack of wine would be clear to everyone, therefore she commanded the servants to be ready for his commands. One should inquire why the evangelist indicated the marble[i] vessels were for the purity of the Jews. It was so that he might totally remove the suspicion of those who were troubled there was wine in them. But those vessels were never receptacles[9] for wine, because for the sake of the Jews' purity they were set aside for washing.[ii] [**43**] For Palestine has little water in the courses of the rivers or from the flowing of fountains.[iii]

i. **Marble:** *kčeay*, as in the lemma, which Tat'ewac'i, 119, explains as meaning *marmar*. Step'annos of Siwnik', 127, states that the vessels were made of "stone," *k'arełēn*, and gives numerous biblical references to stone and its uses. For Step'annos six, with factors of two and three, is a perfect number. Dionysius bar Salibi, *John*, 54, also expands on the symbolism of the numbers two and three. Tat'ewac'i, 123–24, devotes a long passage to number symbolism; he also explains (ibid., 119) the "measure," *mar*, and calculates the total content of the six vessels. Moše bar Kepha refers to a variety of different measures and states that here the standard Edessene one was intended.

ii. John Chrysostom, *Hom. Jo.* 20, indicates that the vessels were not used for wine; and Theodore of Mopsuestia states that all houses had such vessels for ritual washing.

iii. The lack of water in Palestine is noted by Moše bar Kepha; Dionysius bar Salibi, *John*, 54; and Tat'ewac'i, 119.

[2:7] Jesus said to them: Fill the vessels with water. And they filled them to the top.

Again by this the evangelist[10] annuls the suspicion of those summoned to the wedding, that there was no mixture of wine with the water, but the vessels[11] were indeed filled with water to the top.[i]

---

9. **Receptacles:** sg. NV.
10. **The evangelist:** om. NV.
11. **The vessels:** om. NV.

i. Moše bar Kepha. Dionysius bar Salibi, *John*, 54–55, and Theodore of Mopsuestia, 40, also refer to this suspicion. Step'annos of Siwnik', 128, interprets the water as the teaching of the Mosaic law, and the wine as the superior teaching.

[2:8–9a] Jesus said to them:[12] **Now**[13] **take [some] and carry it to the master of ceremonies. And they took it. And when the master of ceremonies tasted the water, it had become**[14] **wine.**

We must not be unconcerned as to what need there was of the water. He would have been able through a command to fill the vessels; but it was in order to show that not for his own power did he work miracles but for our advantage. For he would have been able, just as in the desert by a command he multiplied the bread and fish for the sons of Israel, and he rained down manna from heaven, and summoned the quail from the sea.[i] But because this was the beginning of signs, therefore he arranged it very securely and very clearly, so that by believing in this sign[15] they might more easily believe in the other signs and miracles of which he would render them personal witnesses. For if they were to deny [them], their own hands would reprove them,[ii] and also their feet that had carried the vessels until they had filled them to the top.[16]

i. Matt 14; 15; par.; Exod 16:15, etc.; Wis 19:12; Exod 16:13.

ii. Dionysius bar Salibi, *John*, 55, and Tat'ewac'i, 120, present similar arguments. See also Nonnus's commentary to John 11:39, below, regarding the rolling away of the stone from Lazarus's tomb.

[2:9b–10] The master of ceremonies did not know whence it was, but the servants who had poured the water knew. The master of ceremonies spoke with the bridegroom and said: Everyone first offers sweet wine, and when they have drunk, then the bad.[17] **But you have kept the sweet wine until now.**

The master of ceremonies[18] not knowing contains nothing profound, because he was not aware in advance of the unprecedented miracles, but it was appropriate for the servants [44] to know, who had brought the water and

12. **To them:** om. M.

13. **Now,** MZ: om. NV.

14. **Become:** + "into," NV.

15. **Sign:** pl. M.

16. **To the top:** om. NV.

17. **Sweet, bad,** *anoyš, yori,* MNZ: "good," "worse," in Greek and Syriac.

18. **The master of ceremonies:** om. NV.

filled the vessels. Rightly he then[19] urged Mary to wait for the time when the master of ceremonies had realized the lack of wine, hence in astonishment he said: *You have kept the sweet wine.* By a truly divine command he changed the water into wine, causing the master of ceremonies to praise it, calling it sweet.[i]

i. Tat'ewac'i, 120, notes that "sweet," *anoyš,* was used in his time as a toast.

[2:11] **This beginning of signs Jesus did in Cana of Galilee; and he revealed his glory.**[20]

The evangelist indicated this was the beginning of signs and miracles by Christ, as the groom told the master of ceremonies.[i] And the report of the miracle[21] went out and spread among everyone (Matt 9:26; Luke 4:14), and many in astonishment believed in the unprecedented miracle that he had performed at the wedding. Therefore the evangelist introduced the name of the place, because it was[22] very well known to all, also from here the nations would follow, which he foretold through the earlier prophet: *The land of Zabulon and the land of Nep'talim, Galilee of the Gentiles, a people that sat in darkness saw a great*[23] *light* (Isa 9:1–2; Matt 4:15–16).

But why did he first perform miracles at the wedding, where the groom and bride [were present]? Because they were to become one flesh (Matt 19:5), and where [there would be] greater joy, so that it might be an allegorical example of the things to be performed among us. For he himself was the groom of the church, as the evangelist indicates: *He who has the bride, he is the groom.*[ii] And because the souls of the believers are like brides, dear[24] and beautiful in his hands. United with them through the grace of baptism, being their garment[iii] and uniting them to himself through the dispensation of his life-bringing body and blood,[iv] he made them worthy to be his limbs. Hence they continually rejoice in his bridal chamber and are joyful in the nuptial couch that passes not away. He also indicates that it is not necessary for the youths of the bride chamber to fast while the groom is still with them (Mark 2:19; cf. Matt 9:15; Luke 5:34).

One should also ask why he performed the beginning of signs by changing [45] water into wine.[v] This was for an allegory[vi] to us, so that he might

19. Then: om. NV.
20. Nonnus omits the end of the lemma: "And his disciples believed in him."
21. **Miracle:** pl. M.
22. **Was:** om. NV.
23. **Great:** om. NV.
24. **Dear,** *siruns:* om. NV.

demonstrate the cold and loose and soft[25] mind of human nature through the nature of water and might change and attach those weakened regarding knowledge of the divinity by the impurity of wicked sin to the more pleasant and warm and solid nature, so that it might possess thenceforth a desire for the undertaking of virtues, whereby it encounters divine knowledge in accordance with the nature of wine, to animate weakened human nature and strengthen it to desire food.

Did you see the intention of this mystery, how he draws up those raised from the lower life to the heights where Christ sits, where the choirs of angels are[vii] and the companies[viii] of saints. He invites them to the heavenly nuptial couch, to enter the heavenly groom's bridal chamber, to rejoice with the incorporeal hosts, to dance with the ranks of saints, to inherit unending life, joy without sadness, light without shadow, the ineffable blessings. Therefore, *being sober while it is still day*,[ix] let us join ourselves [to them], lest perchance the nuptial couch will be closed to us with the foolish virgins as the groom reckons us unknown (Matt 25:12); whence the sending forth is understood to be to the inextinguishable fire, to the unsleeping worm (Mark 9:48), to the gloomy darkness in restless torments. From that may we be freed and delivered, through the grace and benevolence of our Lord and Savior Jesus Christ, to whom with the Father and also the Holy Spirit be glory, power and honor, now and always and forever and ever. Amen.[x]

i. For the legend that the master of ceremonies was Lazarus, see also note to commentary on vv. 1–2, above.

ii. John 3:29 = Z.

iii. **Garment**: see the quotation from Gal 3:27 in the commentary to John 1:29, above.

iv. For the wedding at Cana as a type of the Eucharist in Armenian commentators, see Mathews and Sanjian 1991 (148–49).

v. **Water into wine**: lit. "wine from water."

vi. **Allegory**: *tarac'oyc'*. Nonnus more usually employs *awrinak* or *aṙak*.

vii. **Are**: *imanin* (lit. "are understood, perceived").

viii. **Companies**: *xoranadasut'iwnk'*, M; *xoradasut'iwnik'*, N; *xmbakc'ut'iwnk'*, V.

ix. Rom 13:13 (not quoted exactly).

x. For this paragraph, see introduction, xxv.

---

25. **And soft**: om. NV.

[46] III[26]

[2:12–13] **After this Jesus went down to Capernaum, he and his mother and his[27] brothers; and they were there not many days. And the Passover of the Jews was close, and Jesus went up to Jerusalem.**

After being baptized by John and acquiring[28] the disciples, then he conducted his teaching[29] everywhere and worked miracles in both the hearing and the sight of the people, and for the summons of the gospel of life. With many signs and with power Christ[30] continually strove for their salvation and correction. His leaving his mother and brothers there and going up to Jerusalem [were] in order that the evangelist might indicate how much zeal he had in himself only for the business of preaching the gospel and calling the nations. When in Capernaum he showed no few miracles[31] and signs, although the evangelist said nothing about that here. From there he went up to Jerusalem on the Feast of Passover because of the multitude[32] and nations who had come to the feast, so that he might teach in the presence of the people and reveal himself.

[2:14] **He found in the temple those selling oxen and sheep and doves, and the money changers sitting [there].**

Why did all this go on in the temple?[i] Because the high priests were avaricious, they did all this[33] in the temple for their own profit,[ii] so that the necessities for the offering of sacrifices might be found at hand, especially for those coming from elsewhere to the temple in order to carry out each one's vows and offerings.

i. Step'annos of Siwnik', 128, draws parallels between the various animals and categories of men: oxen are earthly people, sheep are mindless souls, doves are the light-minded.

ii. Tat'ewac'i, 126, explains that this went on, not in the inner court, but in the outer, as in "our" *žamatun*, where the people pray and the *vardapets* teach.

---

26. The section number is omitted by M. For its significance, see the introduction, xxiv.

27. **His, MZ:** om. NV.

28. **Acquiring,** *stanaloyn:* "nurturing," *snanaloyn,* NV.

29. **Teaching:** pl. M.

30. **Christ:** om. NV.

31. **Miracles:** sg. NV.

32. **Multitude:** "peoples," NV.

33. **They did all this:** "all this [acc.] occurred," NV.

[47] [2:15] He made a whip of cord and drove them all from the temple, the oxen and the sheep, and scattered the copper coins of the money changers.[34]

This passage raises the question why he was so angry as to make a whip and expel them very violently. The Lord[35] never seems to have acted like that when they called him a Samaritan, with other [insults], and mocked him on the cross, when he made no response *but replied very softly and gently.[36] Furthermore, he himself was lord of the temple, but he was not at all a defender of himself in this way as [he was] for the house. But because he was intending to perform healings on the Sabbath, for which the Jews slandered him as being opposed to God and a suppressor of the law, therefore he carried this out for their correction and to cut short the reasons for their slanders. For if he had been opposed to God, why would he have been angry or borne a grudge concerning the Father's temple when he saw it as a house of commerce, but rather sought vengeance and expelled them, [saying,] *Do not make the house of my Father a house of commerce,* in order to indicate that such words and deeds are not those of an opponent, but of one with the same will and mind by nature, as is appropriate for a son to behave toward a father?

Furthermore, he extended to us his teaching through this example, that we should always have zeal for God, and never[37] forgive it if we see what is not appropriate in the temple of his holiness. But we should be defenders of the truth like him and never pardon such outrages in his holy house: not to seek vengeance ourselves through patience, but to endure mildly like our Lord and teacher. The expelling from the temple of [48] the oxen and the sheep has another meaningful indication, in order that he might demonstrate that the offerings would cease and sacrifices be stopped.[i] Such sacrifices would not be offered in the temple after his coming into the world, but from then on all nations would follow the preaching of the gospel, whose shadow were the law and the sacrifices.

i. Moše bar Kepha and Dionysius bar Salibi (*John*, 58) offer the same argument.

---

34. Nonnus omits: "and overthrew the tables"; cf. Mathews and Sanjian 1991, 104.
35. **The Lord:** "he," NV.
36. **But replied … gently:** as MN[corr].
37. **Never,** *oč' erbek':* erbek', NV.

[2:16–17][38] **Do not make the house of my Father a house of commerce. Then his[39] disciples remembered that it was written[40]: Zeal of your house will eat[41] me up.**[42]

Why did he say this, save to mean: *The house of my Father should be called*[43] *a house of prayer for all nations, yet you have made it a den of thieves* (Matt 21:13; Mark 11:17)? The deceits and falsehoods in the temple were like those of thieves, he said, in buying and selling, which is appropriate to do in the dens of thieves rather than in the house of my Father.

[2:18] **The Jews replied and said to Jesus: What sign do you show us[44], because you do this?**

Did you see the zeal of their fury and alienation?[45] When they should have rejoiced and been glad for the sake of being zealous for the house of God, and for making it a place of holiness and prayer but not for buying and selling, then they introduced some other calumnies and false accusations.

[2:19] **Jesus replied to them and said: Destroy this temple, and in three days I shall raise it up.**

This was not pertinent to their questions.[i] But because he knew with his all-seeing power that they would not be at all helped by signs or accept them but they only said that out of deceit,[ii] therefore he turned the saying around by another example, which although they did not understand it at that time, yet when it would occur, then they would realize his foreknowledge. [49] This can be seen elsewhere. They sought from him to see a sign from heaven: *This nation asks to see a sign, but a sign will not be given them, save the sign of Jonah the prophet. For just as he was in the belly of the whale for three days and three nights, likewise the son of man must be in the heart of the earth for three days and three nights* (Matt 12:39–40; cf. Matt 16:4; Jonah 1:17).[iii] Did you see how

---

38. Nonnus omits: "And those who sold doves, he said to them."
39. **His**, NVZ: om. M.
40. **It was written**, MZ: om. NV.
41. **Will eat**, M (= Z): "has eaten," NV.
42. Ps 68:10 = Z.
43. **Should be called**: "is," M.
44. **Us**, MZ: om. NV.
45. **Alienation**: pl. NV.

far he extended his replies,[46] which here also he fashioned like the former: *Destroy this temple, and in three days I shall raise it up*? Because they sought the sign so that they might believe, it was a matter of fraud, as for those who had not previously seen signs or miracles from him. Yet they very frequently had seen and heard his wonder-working but being totally jealous said that was only seemingly, but not divinely, done as [by] the Son of God but [rather done by] an opponent of God and suppressor of the law. Therefore to cast and expel you from the temple was to reprove your suspicion that I am an opponent of God, and for a presage of the ceasing of the law and sacrifices.[iv]

Now, the sign that you seek from heaven, when you will destroy the temple of this body[v] through torments on the cross, when I shall willingly undergo death, when I shall dwell for three days in the heart of the earth, when you shall boast and suppose that you have conquered and your wicked plots have been accomplished; then fearsome signs[47] will appear to you from heaven. The heavens above will cry out shaking and quaking, and the sun will darken and the moon not give light, angels will descend from heaven[48] to earth, the earth will shake and the rocks split, the veil will be rent, the dead will come forth from their tombs, and everywhere [they] shall pronounce me Son of God (Matt 27:51–54). Then [50] that sign will be given to you that you now seek, as a reproach to you and a reprimand. But not now, because you do not believe and will not be profited.

    i. Moše bar Kepha indicates the same.

    ii. Dionysius bar Salibi, *John*, 59, also stresses the deceit and mocking.

    iii. Moše bar Kepha and Dionysius bar Salibi (*John*, 60) cite Jonah as foretelling the death and resurrection.

    iv. The ceasing of sacrifices is here stressed by Theodore of Mopsuestia.

    v. **This body**: see commentary to vv. 20–22, below.

[2:20–22] **The Jews said to him: For forty-six years this temple was being built, and you will set it up in three days? But he was speaking about the temple of his body. Then when he had risen from the dead, his disciples remembered that this was what he[49] had said, and they believed in the scripture and in the word that Jesus had spoken.[50]**

Did you see how the meaning of this saying became totally clear? For they

---

46. **Replies**: sg. NV.

47. **Signs**: sg. NV.

48. **From heaven**: om. NV.

49. **He**, NVZ: "Jesus," M.

50. **That Jesus had spoken**, NVZ: om. M.

understood the meaning of the saying to concern the temple, because they were thick-witted and they did not have a complete understanding of things to come.[i] But he was speaking about the temple of his own body.[ii] After he rose from the tomb on the third day, the disciples remembered what had once been said by the Lord. And seeing the heavenly and earthly signs at the time of the cross, they came to their senses and understood what had been previously said. Then they acquired no little profit for themselves, when such a long time earlier he had informed them about everything that would happen, which was not appropriate for anyone else save only God.

    i. Step'annos of Siwnik', 129, explains that Solomon's temple was burned in the days of Nebuchadnezzar; it was rebuilt in forty-six years but then razed by Antiochus. It was rebuilt and then knocked down and built again by Herod, "as Josephus describes." Theodore of Mopsuestia, 43, notes that the long delay of forty-six years after the return from Babylon is explained "in the historical books," and Išodad also explains the delay. Tat'ewac'i, 131, gives a lengthy description of the building of the temple over forty-six years from the reign of Cyrus to Darius and adds various symbolic interpretations of the number forty-six.

    ii. Moše bar Kepha expands at length on Christ's body in opposition to the "heretical Nestorians," and Dionysius bar Salibi, *John*, 60–65, gives a lengthy discourse on the temple and the incarnation.

[2:23–24a] **And when he was in Jerusalem at the Feast of Passover, many believed in his name, because they saw the signs that he performed. But Jesus himself did not entrust himself to them.**

Why did he not entrust himself to them, though behold, they believed in him? But because they did not have faith with all their heart and[51] truly, but were only reproved and won over by signs, therefore the evangelist[52] said, *Jesus himself*[53] *did not entrust himself to them*, [51] as not being true believers[54] but as partial believers by wonderful signs and not real followers of the truth.[i] For they bore not a little deceit in themselves, waiting for the opportune time when they might find means to trick him.

    i. Dionysius bar Salibi, *John*, 65, also emphasizes that they were mistrustful and not true believers.

---

51. **And**: om. NV.
52. **The evangelist**: om. NV.
53. **Jesus himself**, MZ: om. NV.
54. MN repeat "he entrusted himself to them."

[2:24b–25] Because he knew all. And it was not necessary that anyone[55] should testify about man, because he himself knew what was in man.

This is to be understood in accordance with the preceding words. Although in word they believed in him openly, yet he was not at all thereby deceived by their trickery, as our human nature through ignorance is often deceived and tricked. But he, *the knower of hearts* (Acts 1:24; 15:8), veiled his thoughts from them and understood, as was indeed appropriate for God, *who searches hearts and reins.*[i]

i. Ps 7:10, also cited here by Cyril of Alexandria; Moše bar Kepha cites Ps 43:22.

---

55. **Anyone,** MZ: "he," NV.

[3:1–2a] **There was a man from among the Pharisees whose name was Nicodemus, a prince of the Jews. He came to him by night.**

He indicates his coming to Jerusalem. This is the one who offered so much myrrh and aloes at the time of the burial for the care of Christ's body.[i] Now his coming at night was because of fear of the Jews.

i. John 19:39, where this episode is referred to.

[3:2b–3] **He said: Rabbi, we know that you have come as a teacher from God, because no one could perform these signs that you do unless God were with him. Jesus replied and said to him: Amen, amen,[1] I say to you, unless one be born again, he cannot see the kingdom of God.**

If you confess me, he says, as a true teacher and instructor sent from God and a teacher,[i] as you say, and for that reason you came so that I might make the truth known to you, whereby you will be able to approach God, it is necessary for you to learn as follows: that you must confess me as other than as you think [52] me to be, a simple man like one of the prophets, because those separate you very far from the truth. But search whereby you may be rendered worthy of the kingdom of heaven. For Nicodemus was not only *a prince of the Jews* but also a teacher. And because he came to the Lord to learn from him and follow the truth, therefore he imparted the most perfect knowledge to him: for what reason the Lord himself had come into the world, and that all the things in the law were examples and shadows of the revelation of the gospel. Therefore he said, *Whoever is not born again*—that is, he means not an earthly but a heavenly birth through the font[ii]—*will not enter the kingdom of heaven.* For the road that leads to the kingdom of the truth is faith in

1. **Amen, amen**, MZ: "Amen," N.

the Father and in the Son and in the Holy Spirit, which they were to receive through the font and inherit the kingdom of God.

    i. **Teacher**: *vardapet*; see above, note to commentary on John 1:29, for this rank in the Armenian hierarchy.
    ii. Nonnus anticipates v. 5.

[3:4] Nicodemus said to him: How can a man be born who has been born?[2] Surely it is not possible to enter his mother's womb a second time and be born?

When he said, *I know you have come as a teacher from God*, and he confessed that so many workings of miracles and signs had been revealed by him that he said he had come from God, he should not have reckoned that what he had said was impossible but should have sought a solution to the declaration. He did not do that through any[3] deceit but because, being weak in knowledge, he had not understood the birth as anything other than what occurs in accordance with the succession of the flesh. Therefore he said, *How can one who has been born[i] be born again?[ii]*

    i. **Who has been born**: "who is old," M; see note to lemma.
    ii. **Again**: *verstin*, but *krkin* in lemma.

[3:5] Jesus replied and said: Amen, amen, I say to you: unless someone will be born by water and Spirit, he cannot enter the kingdom of God.

[53] This rebirth that I have mentioned to you will be not according to the flesh and from a womb, as you supposed, but a spiritual and heavenly one from water and the Spirit. *By water and Spirit* he also recalls the other wonderful creation, because of the man's knowledge and learning in the old commandments. By water [he means] the later birth that originally was understood of Adam, when dust was mingled with it[i] (Gen 2:7); but by the Spirit, because being created from dust and water, through the Spirit he received life. And also that he might understand that the one who fashioned this first birth, he is the one who created this later birth from water and dust, just as the first birth is superior to the creation of our understanding. For incomprehensible to us is the coming into being from earth and water,

---

    2. **Who has been born**, *or cnealn icē*, NZ: "who is an old man," *or cern ē*, M. The variant is noted in Z.
    3. **Any**: om. N.

air and fire,[4] of flesh and bones, sinews and tendons and ligaments, and the stretching out of the skin and hair, and nails and membranes and fat, and the five conjoined senses, and the other four differences according to the medical arts, like the two biles and phlegm and blood.[ii] All this knowledge we have received by faith, but we have not comprehended by the guidance of the mind that God is able in everything to do what he wishes, and there is no weakness in him.

Thus this second birth, although it remains beyond our minds, yet we must accept it by faith, especially because of the one who narrates it to us; he indicates the trustworthiness and power of the one whose are the signs and miracles that he performs. Furthermore, we had no little need of this second birth, because at[5] the prior creation from water and dust, when by the breath of the Spirit we were made alive and received paradise as habitation, [54] we inherited the life of incorruptibility and immortality; but through the breaking of the commandment we were cast out of paradise and from immortality, so there was all the more need of re-creation for the renewal of the first birth through the rebirth by the Spirit and water back to the former life of immortality and place of habitation. For that very reason the Son of God came into the world.

He previously gave in old times this example of rebirth by water, as when the Jews through water purified themselves and became holy when they were about to enter the Holy of Holies (e.g., Exod 29:4); and as in the Jordan when Naaman the Syrian was purified of leprosy (4 Kgdms 5:14; Luke 4:27), or like Siloam that granted the healing of various diseases (John 9:7). These typified[iii] in themselves the grace of the font; for as they were examples they gave healing only to the body but not to the spirit, which they do not typify. So it was necessary[6] for the truth to be completed.

i. It: pl. *aynok'iwk* (*sic*, for *aynok'iwk'*).

ii. This passage on the constitution of the human body comes from John Chrysostom, *Hom. Jo.* 25.1. It appears in the Armenian version (1717 ed., as *Hom. Jo.* 24), which was translated from Syriac in the twelfth century; see Mathews 2010 (26). However, it is not repeated in the Syrian commentators.

iii. **Typified:** *awrinakēin*, from the noun *awrinak*, "example." John Chrysostom, *Hom. Jo.* 26.2, refers to Naaman as a *typos* of baptism, as does Tat'ewac'i, 141, who also refers to Siloam. The same examples are quoted by Dionysius bar Salibi, *John*, 71.

---

4. **And fire:** om. M.

5. **At:** om. N.

6. **Necessary:** *part*, N; *hark*, M.

[3:6] For what is born of flesh is flesh, and what is born of the Spirit, spirit.

For this birth of water and spirit is a spiritual and not a bodily birth, as you supposed; just as our bodies are born as flesh, likewise our spirit as spirit.[i]

i. Dionysius bar Salibi, *Gospels*, 78, and *John*, 69, applies this verse to the body of Christ.

[3:7–8a] Do not be surprised that I said to you: It is necessary to be born again. For the wind blows where it wishes; and[7] you hear its sound, but you do not know whence it comes or whither it is going.

Because these sayings appeared incomprehensible to him and very implausible, the birth from spirit not able to be spirit, like flesh from flesh, therefore he gave this[8] lesser example whereby he might be able to comprehend a little the example of spirit: *The wind blows where it wishes; and[9] you hear its sound, but you do not know whence it comes* [55] *or whither it goes.* If the wind, which is perceptible to hearing and when it blows is knowable to the discernment of the whole personality, by being hot or freezing,[i] yet it is not consequently[10] known to you whence it comes or whither it goes because of its subtlety, and is for you created and a fellow servant, why do you wish to know the character of the Spirit of God, which is not understandable to the senses or graspable by the mind?[ii] Furthermore, he said, *The wind blows where it wishes, and[11] you hear its sound,* because he made the wind an example of the descent of the Holy Spirit, which was to descend on the upper room according to the example of wind, just as *there was a noise from heaven as of violent wind, and it filled the whole house in which they were sitting* (Acts 2:2).[iii]

i. John Chrysostom, *Hom. Jo.* 26.2, explains that wind is a body, *sōma*.

ii. Dionysius bar Salibi, *John*, 70, explains that wind is a movement of air, but you cannot understand the Spirit of God.

iii. Moše bar Kepha and others give the same parallel. Theodore of Mopsuestia emphasizes the sound at the descent of the Spirit.

---

7. **And**, MZ: om. N.
8. **This**: om. N.
9. **And**: om. N (see lemma).
10. **Consequently**: om. N.
11. **And**: om. N (see lemma).

[3:8b] Likewise everyone born[12] by the Spirit.

Just like the wind, although we hear its sound, yet it is invisible and ungraspable as to whence the blowing derives or where it is going, likewise the birth of the Spirit is not seen by bodily eyes or comprehended by the understanding. For the wind, although it has subtlety in itself because of not being subject to vision, yet we are not unaware of its nature. But the being and coming of the Spirit remains superior to human understanding.

[3:9–10] Nicodemus replied and said: How it is possible for this to be? Jesus responded and said to him:[13] You are a teacher of Israel, and you do not know that?

Because Nicodemus still thought what Jesus had said was so impossible, he said: *How can this be?* This the man had read many times from the commandments, but being still thick-witted in his Jewishness he was unable [56] to observe what he had often read from the sayings. Therefore the Savior said: *You are a teacher of Israel, and you do not know that?* As to what you declared, are there not previous examples for you of what has been said by me concerning water and the waters with which you always wash, when you plan to be cleansed of the impurities that prevent you from entering the house of God? And as elsewhere bodily diseases are cured at Siloam, which foretells the power of the font, or the Jordan, which purified Naaman the Syrian of his leprosy.[i]

Now, concerning the Holy Spirit hear from the prophets, which you accept to read, being a teacher of Israel. What did David say? *Renew aright the spirit in my belly* (Ps 50:12), *and *Let your good spirit lead me to the right land* (142:10),[14] and *Do not remove from me your holy spirit* (50:13). And many more are the sayings from the prophets concerning the Holy Spirit that you read. But there is still a veil over your hearts; as you reflect on the examples, you do not hasten toward the truth. And being a teacher of Israel, why did you understand the begetting of human nature according to a single example, yet behold, you read that many are born through other examples?

So Adam the first-created was born not from a womb or by seed and the will of a man but from dust according to God's command; likewise Eve, only from his rib but not from a man and woman (Gen 2:7, 21–22). Now

---

12. **Everyone born,** *amenayn cnealn* (sg.), NZ: *amenayn cnealk'n* (pl.), M.

13. **To him,** MZ: om. N.

14. **And let … land:** om. N.

although Isaac was born not from dust nor only from a rib but from a father and mother, yet he was born from a barren womb and from a father weak in bodily desire, as Sarah testified, *How can this happen to me?* and *My master has become old* (Gen 18:12). Furthermore, Aaron's rod, not being green by nature, how could it raise up in itself leaves and flowers and fruits (Num 17:8; Heb 9:4)?[ii] [57] Or just as I believed in the previous signs that were worthy of great wonder: like the rod making the rock a source for so many streams of water (Num 20:11); or when the people[15] were going around Jericho with the ark,[16] the walls and ramparts of the impregnable city collapsed (Josh 6:20); or causing[17] the stopping of the sun and moon for such a long time, which had never happened [before] (Josh 10:13). And you hand down other such events hard to credit and impossible for you to believe: like the splitting of the sea (Exod 14:21) with other wonders in the desert.[18] These in no way [demonstrate] the weakness of God. So being amazed at these things, do you doubt that what I have said is not possible, yet you confess me to be a teacher and to come from God?

    i. See commentary to v. 5, above.
    ii. Tat'ewac'i, 145, repeats the examples of Adam and Eve, Isaac, and Aaron's rod.

[3:11] **Amen, amen, I say to you, that we say what we know, and we bear witness to what we have seen, yet you do not accept our testimony.**

How do you, and many of you teachers of the Jews, teach your people what you have never seen or been near to? They are amazing and difficult to believe, but through faith they are accepted and taught by you. Yet you do not accept my instruction and testimony that I teach, which I do not possess through hearsay, like your teachings,[19] but what I have indeed seen, especially those wonders worked through me. By saying furthermore, *We speak and know and bear witness,*[i] he taught about the Father and himself and the Holy Spirit. Although at that time Nicodemus did not understand anything, yet later he profited from it not a little, when he attained complete knowledge.

    i. Theodore of Mopsuestia states that the plural "we" indicates Christ's divine nature. Moše bar Kepha suggests that the plural form either implies a singular or involves the Father.

---

15. **People:** pl. M.
16. **With the ark:** om. N.
17. **Causing:** om. N.
18. **In the desert:** om. N.
19. **Teachings:** sg. N.

[3:12] So if I spoke earthly things to you, and you do not believe,[20] how will you believe if I shall speak heavenly things?[21]

After he mentioned the rebirth, baptism through water and the Spirit, and he drew Nicodemus closer to the faith through the examples [58] that he illustrated by the blowing of the wind and the operation of water, and through other signs of which not only Nicodemus but also all teachers of the Jews possessed knowledge, then he offered further higher and more perfect knowledge: *If I spoke earthly things to you, and you do not believe*—the birth of the font, he means, which although it is spiritual and heavenly yet occurs on earth and in the world—*how, if I shall speak heavenly things, will you believe?* If you do not believe in this, which has so many examples of occurring on earth and in the world, even if I declare[22] what is very difficult and incomprehensible to you, which is the true faith—my heavenly birth, my sonship from the Father, my being uncreated and without beginning, eternal and without end, indivisible and inseparable in unity—how will you believe those things? He also stated: *How will you believe if I speak heavenly things?* He did not say: Will you understand? And by showing them that in accordance with the very wonderful signs that I am continually performing as assurance for you, not merely in your minds do you not understand that nobody would be able to do that except the Son of God, but you do not believe, he reproved their willful denial and wickedness.[23]

[3:13] No one has ascended to heaven, except he who came down from heaven, the son of man, who is in heaven.

When he said, *We speak what we know, and we bear witness to what we have seen, and you do not accept our testimony,* and *If I shall speak heavenly things,[24] how will you believe?* he did not then omit what they wished to ask: How do you, being a man on earth among us, say that you speak what you heard and bear witness to what you saw, and relate heavenly matters? Therefore he said, *No one ascended* [59] *to heaven,* that is, no prophet nor anyone else of mankind, among whom you reckoned me similar to them, by calling [me] a teacher and from God, unless he descended from heaven, as

---

20. **Believe:** + "me," N.

21. **Things:** + "to you," N (see quotation in commentary).

22. **Declare:** + "to you," M.

23. **Wickedness:** pl. M.

24. **Things:** + "to you," M.

I truly have, being[25] the son of man according to the likeness of mankind. Although I said, *He ascended to heaven*, and also, *he descended from heaven*, yet he is always in heaven. And I did not [say] he was in heaven only before his descending, and again after his ascending he was in heaven; because his descent is only his revelation and being humbled but not a change from place to place. Furthermore, his ascension is not a cutting off and separation from the world but simply a remaining invisible from worldly natures. Therefore he said, *The son of man, who is in heaven.*

These things truly are clear for a testimony to you that *son of man*[i] signified the Son of God, the essential[ii] Word in heaven, who became a son of man through his benevolence. And because of his eternity he said, *Who is* [ē] *in heaven*, but did not say, Who occurs [*lini*] in heaven, in order to reveal his indivisible nature.[iii] What, then, do your sayings mean, except the unity and inseparability of the two natures?[iv] Hence by saying, *son of man*, he described the two natures united with a single name. So ascribing the divine [attributes] to the body and the bodily ones to the divinity, therefore he said the son of man is in heaven. Now if the properties were separated and differentiated from the natures, how with a human name could he silence and suppress the name of the divinity? He indicated that he, who taking [a body] from Mary was called son of David, is always in heaven. And when was the one born son of man[26] from the Virgin, in heaven before the ascension? So then from the words of the Savior himself we must profess without doubting the indivisible unity. [**60**]

Because with so many examples he taught him the pattern of baptism and the grace that derives therefrom, yet he being still thick-witted did not at all perfectly understand that the grace that he taught about was invisible. Consequently he spoke a little about the setting up of the cross that would take place for the sake of our salvation, and his hanging [on it], and his death whereby he would grant us immortality, explaining with a few examples because of the man's being too ignorant and weak for such a high mystery. However, he gave him a modest indication to be a record for when that would become the cause of his faith, just as indeed happened. For just as through baptism one recognizes the Savior in accordance with Paul's saying, *We*[v] *who have been baptized in Christ have put on Christ* (Gal 3:27), likewise through the sufferings of the cross one believes and recognizes the power of baptism. Therefore just as he explained the power and grace of baptism through an example in a hidden

---

25. **Being:** om. N.
26. **Son of man:** om. N.

fashion appropriately to their weakness, so also he gave a brief example of the torments of the cross in a veiled manner, saying:

i. **Son of man:** John Chrysostom, *Hom. Jo.* 27.1, states that "son of man" does not refer to the flesh but is used figuratively for the whole (*apo tēs ellatonos ousias holon heauton*). This is explained by Išodad as "a general expression." Theodore of Mopsuestia, 50, states that the ascending and descending refer to Christ's human nature; but Moše bar Kepha attacks Theodore for taking this to mean Christ is a natural man. Dionysius bar Salibi, *John*, 73, cites Moše and John Chrysostom. He adds that it is a custom of scripture to speak as often of his divinity as of his humanity.

ii. **Essential:** *ēakan*. For the term, see the introduction, xxxvii, and the next note.

iii. Nonnus distinguishes the verb *ē*, referring to one's essential nature, from the verb *lini*, referring to becoming. See the introduction above, xxxv. For the difference between the derived nouns *ēut'iwn* and *linelut'iwn*, see Thomson 2001 (15–17).

iv. Moše bar Kepha here refers to John Chrysostom as cited in n. i above. The editor Č'rak'ean (p. *l* [30]) notes a parallel with a *Letter to Those in Mesopotamia* by Nersēs Šnorhali (1871 ed., 248) but it is not a direct quotation save for the citation of John 3:13.

v. **We:** as MN; the editor changes the text of N to conform to Z and the Greek, which have verbs in the second-person plural.

[3:14] As Moses raised up the serpent in the desert,[27] so the son of man must be raised up.

So he declares that the mystery of the old and new commandments is one, and all the former were examples and shadows[i] of the latter. And if this were so, it is necessary for the son of man to be raised up. He says to be raised up willingly, and not to endure[28] that by being forced by someone, as the Jews might suppose.[29] Now, what does the following mean?

i. **Examples and shadows:** echoed by Dionysius bar Salibi, *John*, 81, and Tat'ewac'i, 151. Moše bar Kepha expands on the typology of the serpent and the cross, the theme of Nonnus's commentary to the next verse. Moše is much concerned with Nestorius and his party, especially Theodore of Mopsuestia.

[3:15] Whoever believes in him will receive everlasting life.

The people of Moses did not believe in the declarations of God but turned away their faces and did not look on the bronze serpent. [61] In their unbelief

---

27. Num 21:9.

28. **To endure,** *krel*, M: "he endures," *krē*, N.

29. **Might suppose,** *karcic'en*, M: "supposed," *kardec'in*, N.

that it would be of no help against the poisonous bites[30] of stinging snakes, they were consequently killed; but when they believed in the words of God without any doubts and looked on the bronze serpent, they were saved from the poisonous snakes (Num 21). In the same way, those who will disbelieve when the son of man will be raised up on the cross, confessing him to be a simple man, will endure eternal death. Those who believe in this divine teaching that I have often delivered, in the torments of the cross, and looking on with faith have confessed the Son of God upon the cross, these store up for themselves the eternal life of immortality. Now, if anyone of the enemy opposes us and says, How do those who confess someone crucified and dead have life? let us silence them with that example. And if [they say], How is a cure from the attack of poisonous serpents granted to those who look upon the bronze serpent with faith? Or if, turning to another example, they were to say, How does the cursed one cure and grant life? Behold, it is said in the law: *Cursed is everyone*[31] *who will be hung on a tree* (Deut 21:23).

Here again[32] by the same example let us reprove them and put them to shame, just as the serpent was cursed, especially that one first cursed by God according to the saying: *Be cursed among all animals and beasts of the earth;*[33] *and on your flanks and belly you shall go, and you will eat dust all the days of your life; and I shall place enmity between you and the woman, and between your offspring and her offspring;* *and it shall watch your head, and you shall watch its heel* (Gen 3:14–15). However,[34] that one was the cause of life and salvation for them from the mortal bites of the stinging serpents, and it did not prevent the people of Moses from believing in the divine sayings and looking on the bronze serpent [62] because of the earlier curse in paradise. In the same way, whoever believes in him, that he put on the body of our curses and hung from a tree for our salvation, is saved and inherits eternal life. Not as they there received for a short time respite through the bronze serpent, and then again a second death, because there faith in the bronze serpent merely provided recovery for the body from the strikes of very visible poisonous serpents. But to those[35] who believe in this one who was called son of man, who is in heaven, he grants the eternal life of the Spirit from the bite of the hidden serpent; and after that, death can control [them] no more. Furthermore, just as the bronze serpent was hung on wood, freeing [them] from the poison of biting serpents,

---

30. **Bites:** "attacks," N.

31. **Everyone,** MZ: om. N.

32. **Here again:** om. N.

33. **Be cursed ... earth:** om. N.

34. **And it shall watch ... However:** om. N.

35. **Those:** sg. N.

through which was appropriately provided a cure for those[36] bitten by poisonous serpents; in the same fashion this one called the son of man who was hanging on the cross, being free of the condition of sin, which was the cause of death, cured us from the poison of the mortal serpent, and *abolishing the death of sin within us, granted everlasting immortality* (2 Tim 1:10).

Consequently,[i] beloved, let us flee from sin lest perchance once more the snake bites us and we perish. For if we were healed by the Son of God, who for our sake hung on the tree, let us preserve that healthy state within us, keeping ourselves in order and fortifying our heels, lest once again it strike us and we suffer eternal death. Let us be zealous to tread on the head of the dragon,[ii] so that we may extinguish the flaming furnace of passion.[37] And as for your saying:[38] What will be our armor with which we trample on the dragon and extinguish Gehenna? To keep your whole self from immorality, your mouth from perjury and from false words, to bridle your tongue from speaking evil, to shut your ears to harmful pornographic conversations, to purify your eyes from disgraceful and lascivious sights, [63] to restrain your taste from greed and gluttony, to close your nose to the stench of voluptuous aromas, to straighten your heart away from harmful[39] thoughts that are the repository of all wicked intentions. For behold, these are all things that enslave the soul on the path to hell.

But *serve the Lord with fear* (Ps 2:11), instructed by the prophet David;[40] clothe the naked, feed the hungry, receive the homeless,[41] relieve the oppressed, assist the weak, attend to the sick, help the imprisoned, forgive debtors' debts, stretch out your hand to the needy. Tire yourself continually with fasts and prayers and holiness, for behold, this is the road that brings you to the desired city, to the supernal Jerusalem, to blessings that do not pass and riches that cannot be stolen, which may we all[42] enjoy through the grace and benevolence of our Lord and Savior[43] Jesus Christ, with whom to the omnipotent Father and the Holy Spirit be glory, honor, and praise, now and always, and forever and ever. Amen.[44]

---

36. Those: sg. N.

37. **Passion,** *axti*, M: "the world to come," *anti* (lit. "there"), N.

38. **As for your saying,** *or asesd*, N: "who says," M.

39. **Harmful:** "evil," N.

40. **David:** om. N.

41. **Receive the homeless:** om. N.

42. **All:** om. N.

43. **And Savior:** om. N.

44. Scribal colophon in N: "Lord God, have mercy on the priest Luke who granted the exemplar. Amen."

i. Here M notes in the margin *yor* (i.e., *yordorak*, "exhortation"). For these sections, not original to Nonnus's Arabic version, see the introduction, xxv.

ii. **Dragon:** *višap*; cf. Ps 9:3. Although the word is often used of a snake, it does not occur in the Armenian text of Genesis.

[64] [3:16] For God so loved the world that he gave his own only begotten Son, so that everyone who believes in him may not perish.

Because he earlier described the salvation and life that he was intending to bestow through the crucified one, which we inherited through his torments and death, he set down next the reasons. He made it clear that he did not suffer that[45] because of his own weakness and the violence of the crucifiers but of his own free will, and not only by his own will, but also by the will of the Father,[i] because the Father so loved the world—that is, those who believe in him who are now in the world[ii]—that he gave his only begotten Son. He means the coexistent,[iii] equally glorious, and uncreated one, not like[46] anyone of mankind who had acquired [that] through grace, like someone among the prophets or the saints or one of the angels. And why was this so? So that mankind might not always remain in the darkness of the ignorance of sin through unbelief.

i. Dionysius bar Salibi, *John*, 82, also emphasizes the will of the Father.

ii. This is echoed by Taťewac'i, 154.

iii. **Coexistent:** *ēakic'*; for the term, see the introduction, xxxvi.

[3:17–18] For God did not send his Son into the world to judge the world, but so that the world might be saved through him. Whoever believes in him will not be condemned; and whoever does not believe in him is already condemned, because he did not believe in the name of the only begotten Son of God.

Because first he declared, *God so loved the world that he gave his only begotten Son, so that everyone who believes in him may not perish*, after that he also indicates the reason:[47] since we are not worthy of [his] love, he says, therefore he so loved us that he gave his only begotten Son. Thereby he reveals his immeasurable mercy for us and his providence; hence he adds: *God did not send his Son into the world that the world might be judged through him.* * So the world deserved great judgments and punishments for so many varied wicked

---

45. **That:** om. N.

46. **Like:** om. N.

47. **Also indicates the reason,** *zpatčarn ews c'uc'anē*, N: "also reveals the reasons," *zpatčarsn erewec'uc'anē*, M.

deeds.[48] But when he was among us he did not [65] demand any vengeance from us or condemn us with punishments and judgments. But he passed over our evil deeds, and healed our diseases, and benevolently forgave our sins many times, and summoned us to knowledge of his divinity in order to save us from the worship of demons, through which we were guilty of judgments and punishments.

Let us also investigate this: *Whoever does not believe in him has already been condemned*. He did not say, condemned at the present time, but [means] the unerring judgments that they will encounter.[i] For just as he said to Adam, *On the day you will eat from the tree you will die by death* (Gen 2:17), he did not at that very time die, but by his becoming mortal, death reigned over him. Although he suffered death at a distant time,[ii] yet being mortal from then on he was reckoned in the number of mortals. In the same way too those who deny the Son of God, although they are not already condemned, yet because of the real condemnation that lies before them [they] are said to be condemned already.

i. Here Tat'ewac'i, 154, introduces the question of purgatory. This Western concept first entered Armenia in the thirteenth century.

ii. Tat'ewac'i, 155, notes that Adam lived for 930 years; see Gen 5:5.

[3:19a] And this is the judgment, that the light came into the world, and men loved darkness more than light.

Therefore they suffered great judgments and retributions. *The Father so loved them that he sent his own Son into the world*, related to them, in order to endure for their sake all human conditions[i] save for sin, but they did not regard him at all as from the Father for their own salvation. However, by perpetually exercising providence for that end, I contrived their salvation, being light for *those who sit in the darkness* of sin;[ii] and I work divine signs and miracles [66] so that they might believe in the truth. But they, by remaining always opposed and resistant to the truth, are like those who love the darkness more than the light.[iii] And after he had made these things clear, he then indicates the causes whereby they chose the darkness rather than the light. He says:

i. **Conditions:** *kirk'*; for the term, see the introduction, xxxviii.

ii. Many parallels (e.g., Matt 4:16).

iii. Dionysius bar Salibi, *John*, 83, equates "the world" with humankind, "judgment" with punishment, "light" with the soul, and "darkness" with sin.

---

48. **So the world ... deeds:** om. N.

[3:19b–21] Because their deeds were evil. For everyone who works evil hates the light and does not come to the light lest his deeds be reproved. But whoever does the truth comes to the light, so that his deeds may be revealed, that they were done through God.

When he declared that they had chosen darkness rather than light—and that is no small foolishness to hate light and love darkness—he then sets down the reason for which they chose darkness rather than light:[i] *Because their deeds were evil.* Just as everyone who works evil does not desire the light lest he be reprimanded for what he has done, likewise, as for those who have not believed in[49] me because of loving their evil deeds, I did not bring judgments and punishments upon them in the likeness of the light when it reprimands, although they thought so. Did I not eat and drink with tax gatherers and sinners, and grant the yoke of repentance to be light and mild, not an eye for an eye, and a tooth for a tooth, and death for death? For I am[50] not, as they say, a Samaritan and son of Joseph but heavenly and the Son of God, shining light on those in the world who were sitting in the shadows of sin and death.[51] But they did not at all accept [me], *because their deeds were evil,* and therefore they followed darkness, choosing darkness[52] rather than light.

i. **Darkness, light:** Dionysius bar Salibi, *John,* 84, here quotes John Chrysostom with reference to Jews and pagans; see Chrysostom, *Hom. Jo.* 28.3.

[3:22a] **After this Jesus and his disciples came to the land of Judea.**

[**67**] Why did he come to the land of Judea, save because he was spreading everywhere the preaching of the gospel and revealing signs and wonders, so that he might convert them from the law to the gospel, to a confession and knowledge of the perfect faith in the Holy Trinity?

[3:22b] **And there he went around with them and baptized.**

The Savior himself did not baptize, although the evangelist shaped his narrative in that way, but to him he ascribed the baptizing by the disciples because of his commanding them. What the evangelist clearly declared later testifies to these sayings: *Jesus himself did not baptize, but his disciples* (John

---

49. **Believed in:** "followed," M.
50. **I am:** "He is," M.
51. **Sin and death:** "the death of sin," M.
52. **Darkness:** om. N.

4:2).[i] And why was that? Because it was not yet the time for the baptism of the Holy Spirit. This John had said: *He will baptize you with the Spirit* (Mark 1:8).[ii] For the baptism of the disciples was like that of John the Baptist,[iii] not like that when they baptized later, after the resurrection of Christ[53] from the dead and his giving such power and honor, when they recognized him truly to be the Son of God. Therefore the latter were baptisms of forgiveness and renewal; but those before the cross, of confession and repentance.[iv]

i. John Chrysostom, *Hom. Jo.* 29, states that Jesus refrained from baptizing in order not to put his own disciples into greater envy and contention; see further the commentary to v. 25, below.
ii. M adds: "into the Holy Spirit and fire"; see Matt 3:11; Luke 3:16.
iii. Moše bar Kepha stresses this point.
iv. Tat'ewac'i, 160, echoes Nonnus here.

[3:23–24] **John also was baptizing in Aenon, near to Saɫim, because there were many waters there; and they came and were baptized. For they[54] had not yet thrown John into prison.**

Before these things the evangelist described John baptizing the people[55] nowhere other than [in] the Jordan. Why did he move to this other place[56] save in order to spread his testimony[57] concerning Christ, for which reason he had been sent, and to carry out his service everywhere, just as he had been called a loud voice (John 1:23)? But what does this mean: *They had not yet thrown John into prison?*[i] It is to show us that not as a consequence of that did the Savior prevent him from baptizing, when the disciples of Christ baptized, because by preventing him no small schism and [68] hatred would have occurred among the disciples toward John. Therefore he allowed them equally to conduct the baptism of repentance. By that he revealed even more the nature of the united[ii] plan, whereby the people would become familiar and rapidly bring themselves to the superior baptism of renewal of the nation, which they were to baptize afterward in the name of the Father and the Son and the Holy Spirit.

i. Nonnus himself frequently notes that John provides details omitted by the other evangelists. Here Moše bar Kepha and Dionysius bar Salibi (*John*, 86) note the same.

---

53. **Of Christ:** om. N.
54. **They:** The unexpressed subject, John being in the accusative case, as Z.
55. **People:** pl. M.
56. **This other place,** *yayl teɫis:* or "to other places."
57. **Testimony:** pl. M.

ii. **United**: *miakan*, N; "of one will," *miakam*, M. Nonnus often stresses the unity of will between Father and Son; see the introduction, xxxvi.

[3:25] There was a question between the disciples of John and a Jew concerning purity.[58]

What, then, would it mean that he said, *There was a question between the disciples of John*[59] *and a Jew*, and he did not say, between a Jew and the disciple[60] of John? It was to demonstrate that the beginning of the dispute occurred from the disciple[i] and not from the Jew, because the disciples of John were envious for their teacher when they saw the Savior's disciples perpetually baptizing the people.[ii] Whence is this clear? When they came to the Lord and said: *Why do we and the Pharisees fast, and your disciples do not fast?* (Matt 9:14; Mark 2:18). These are clearly words of jealousy spoken by them. Why should that be? Because his disciples considered John's baptism superior to that of the disciples of Christ; but the Jew reckoned[61] that of Christ's disciples superior because of so many more signs being worked by Christ than by John, and [because of] the testimonies of John concerning Jesus, when he said, *I am not the Christ, but I have been sent before him* (John 3:28), and *I am not worthy to loose the fastenings of his shoes* (John 1:27).

i. **The disciple**: sg. in MN, but note the pl. in M just above. Nonnus's commentary here seems to reflect the Syriac tradition noted in the lemma.

ii. For the envy of John's disciples, see John Chrysostom, *Hom. Jo.* 29.2, who is followed by Dionysius bar Salibi, *John*, 87. Moše bar Kepha refers to Philoxenus on this dispute.

[3:26] They came to John and said to him: Rabbi,[62] **the one who was with you beyond the Jordan, to whom you bore witness, behold, he**[63] **is baptizing and all come to him.**

Behold, the meaning of this saying that we mentioned above has been made totally clear. They had envy of the Lord's disciples, and because they had not fixed in their minds [**69**] as always unforgettable the testimonies by their own teacher concerning the Savior, who bore such superior witness about

---

58. The lemma in MN = Z. In Theodore of Mopsuestia and the Peshitta the lemma reads: "Between one of John's disciples and a certain Jew."

59. **Of John**: "his," N.

60. **Disciple**: pl. M.

61. **The Jew reckoned**: pl. N.

62. **Rabbi**, MZ: om. N.

63. **He**, NZ: "he too," M.

him[64] and their own very humble station, just as we have often said. And they had not heard the voice coming from the heights: *This is my beloved Son* (Matt 3:17 par.). Therefore it introduced some envy for John's [disciples].[i] *Who was beyond the Jordan, to whom you bore witness, behold, he is baptizing and all come to him.* Perhaps by this in accordance with their envy they would be able to extract some words from him on whom they depended and contrive some other words of envy.

    i. This phrase is unclear. The verb, *arkanelov*, has no subject; "John," *Yovhannu*, could be gen. or dat.

[3:27] John replied to them and said: A son of man cannot receive anything from himself, unless it has been given him from heaven above.

What, then, did he respond to them except the opposite to what they hoped? But that gently and in a hidden fashion, because they hoped in themselves that John would say something superior about himself rather than about Christ. But he did not teach clearly because of their ignorance; as later when he was in prison he sent the same disciples to ask: *Are you the Christ, or should we await another?* Not because of having any doubts, for behold, he himself was crying out to the world, **Behold the lamb of God, who removes the sins of the world,*[65] and saying many things about his immeasurable majesty; but so that when his disciples went they might recognize **the power of his immeasurable majesty*[66] from the signs that the Lord performed.[67] He said: *Go, tell John what you have seen and heard. The blind see, the lame walk, lepers are cleansed, the deaf hear, the dead arise,* with the other things. And: *Blessed is he who will not stumble in me.* He was reproving their stumbling (Matt 11:2–6; Luke 7:18–23).

But what could this be: *A man cannot receive anything from himself, unless it is given him from above?* As if to say, if no one can receive[68] spiritual and necessary things unless they are granted him from above, then my testimony that I bore about him, [70] and the deeds that I perform, have been granted from above. So if you receive my words, you must believe my testimony that I bore concerning him before his coming to me for baptism, and afterward

---

64. **Him:** "himself," M.

65. **Behold ... world:** om. N.

66. **The power ... majesty:** "the measure of his majesty," M.

67. **Performed:** + "He healed many sick and," M.

68. **Receive:** "do," M (i.e., confusion between *aṙnel* and *aṙnul*).

that he is so much superior to me, whose shoes even I am not worthy to serve (Mark 1:7; Luke 3:16).

[3:28] You yourselves bear me witness that I said: I am not the Christ, but I have been sent before him.

If you confess me[69] as your teacher, and that I said, *A man cannot[70] receive of himself unless it be given him from above*, sufficient for you is what you heard from me: *I am not the Christ but have been sent before him*, having from God this testimony that was given to me from the heights concerning him,[i] being sent before him and a voice of a cry to inform the world that he is the Son of God.

   i. Dionysius bar Salibi, *John*, 89, stresses that John was sent by the Father.

[3:29a] He who has the bride[71] is the bridegroom. Now the friend of the groom, who stands and hears him, rejoices gladly at the voice of the groom.

Whom, then, did he call the groom, if not Christ? Now the bride [is] those who believe[72] in him. For just as there is no love greater than that of the groom and bride, the greatness of which love even Adam through his first creation by grace prophesied by saying, *For that reason a man will leave his father and mother and follow his wife, and the two will become one flesh* (Gen 2:24; cf. Matt 9:5 par.),[i] likewise there is no love greater than Christ's love for those who believe in him. Whence is this clear? From his laying down his life for their sake, as he testified about his love: *Greater love than this will no one have, that he lay down his life for his friends* (John 15:13).

[71] Furthermore, we have put him on through baptism according to Paul's saying (Gal 3:27), and we have communicated in his body and blood. Therefore Paul says, when he recalls the commandment about a man and a woman in accordance with the first-created Adam, *But I speak to Christ and the church* (Eph 5:31–32), demonstrating that just as those were bodily, so are these spiritual. But why here did he call himself the friend of the groom, yet once had said: *I am not worthy even to loose the latchets of his shoes* (Mark 1:7; John 1:27)? He reveals[73] the superiority of his immeasurable love to that of the

---

69. **Me:** om. M.

70. **Cannot:** "can," N ("not" added by editor).

71. **Bride:** om. M.

72. **Believe:** "will believe," N.

73. **He reveals:** om. N.

others for Christ. For[74] just as the friend of the groom is more joyful than the other servants when he hears his rejoicing, so I also.[ii]

And what is this: *The friend of the groom who stands and hears him rejoices gladly*? It is as if to say that my testimonies concerning him were fulfilled. He has no need for this, save because the world did not recognize him. Therefore I was sent to be the voice of a cry and to preach to the world his coming. But now it is necessary for me, like one of the servants, to stand and hear his secret mysteries that are to be fulfilled, as I now hear announced in a very loud voice.

i. John Chrysostom, *Hom. Jo.* 29.3, refers here to the marriage of God and the church, but Moše bar Kepha refers to that of Christ with the church; this is echoed by Dionysius bar Salibi, *Gospels*, 19, and *John*, 89. Moše quotes Eph 5:32, to which Nonnus refers in the next paragraph. On the other hand, Cyril of Alexandria refers to the bride as Christ's humanity; and Theodore of Mopsuestia also discusses the incarnation of Christ.

ii. Moše bar Kepha notes that the voice of the groom is the teaching of the church.

[3:29b] **So this[75] joy that is mine has been fulfilled.**

My joy has been fulfilled, he says, because of the completion of the preaching concerning him for which I was sent. For behold, all nations hasten to the faith and to recognize[76] him to be the Son of God. This was my joy that has now been fulfilled. Furthermore, by saying, *this joy of mine[77] has been fulfilled*, he separates his disciples from experiencing anything similar concerning Christ, especially from asking him anything similar.[i]

i. The sense of this last sentence is unclear.

[3:30] **He must increase, and I diminish.**

[72] This is as if to say that he is the true one to be recognized by mankind as very superior and higher; but not according to nature did he acquire that majesty, because he perpetually possesses divine nature. *For me to diminish*, so that the whole world[78] and you might know that I have been sent before him as servant and retainer. Now my role took a short time to accomplish, but his[79] increases through the preaching of the gospel and remains forever.

---

74. **For:** om. N.

75. This: om. M.

76. **To recognize:** "they recognize," N.

77. **Of mine:** om. N.

78. **World:** pl. N.

79. **His,** *norayn*, M: "he," *nora*, N.

[3:31a] **Who comes from above is above all; who is from earth is from the earth and speaks from the earth.**

Because he first declared,[80] *He must increase, and I diminish,* he then set down the gulf between the two: the former's immeasurable highness and his own great humility, in accordance with the two fellow servants of whom the one acquired wealth from the king and had honor, being higher than his companion (Matt 18:23–34). But the great disparity [is] like that of the creator and creation. See what he said: *Whoever comes from above is above all; whoever is from earth is from the earth*[81] *and speaks from the earth.* The coming[82] from above clearly declares the descent of the divine nature, but what is: *He is above all?* It shows that although the angels are in heaven, yet he is superior to them because they are servants to him.

Now as for his saying about himself, *Whoever is from earth speaks from earth,* he does not say that in accordance with any[83] heavenly understanding of his words, because behold, even in the womb of[84] Elisabeth he was filled with the Holy Spirit (Luke 1:15). But just as he distinguished the opinion of his nature from his own disciples by saying that he was God[85] from heaven, but he himself was a servant[86] from earth, so also as regards the teaching of the Savior he said his own was from earth, but that of the former from heaven. This our Savior also said to Nicodemus: *If I spoke*[87] *earthly things to you and you do not believe, how if I shall speak heavenly things, will you believe?* (John 3:12). Not that the rebirth was something earthly, [73] but he said, *earthly,* in comparison with[88] his own uncreated and timeless heavenly birth from the Father.[i] Likewise John fashioned his speech for his own disciples regarding Christ.

    i. Moše bar Kepha here emphasizes the birth from the Father.

---

    80. **Declared,** *čaṙeac'*: "related," *patmeac'*, N.

    81. **Is from the earth:** om. MN.

    82. **The coming,** *galn*: *zgaln,* N (*sic*).

    83. **Any:** om. N.

    84. **Of:** om. N (cf. Luke 1:41).

    85. **God:** om. N.

    86. **A servant:** om. N.

    87. **Spoke,** MZ: "were to speak," N.

    88. **In comparison with,** *ěst hamemateloyn*: "in accordance with his incomparable," *ěst anhamemateloyn,* M.

[3:31b–32] **Whoever comes from heaven testifies to what he has seen and heard. Yet no one receives his testimony.**

Do not be astonished at his saying, *He testifies to what he has seen and heard*, by thinking that he had some need in this to see or to hear, for behold, God had predicted it by saying, *Whoever comes from heaven is above all*; but he condescended to the disciples in this. For it is a habit of human nature when [people] wish to make a statement more secure to confirm it with such [words as] *we have seen* and *we bear witness* (cf. John 3:11). Because the hearers could not yet bear superior teaching, therefore he drew them to the higher knowledge through an accustomed and familiar example. Teachers are continually accustomed to do this for their pupils; for they teach them the highest knowledge not in accordance with their ability but in accordance with the students' comprehension, which Paul did, saying: *I was not able to speak with you as with spiritual ones, but as with bodily ones* (1 Cor 3:1). Not that Paul was unable to speak spiritual [words], but his hearers were not yet able to receive spiritual things.

Now, what is this: *No one accepts his testimony?* Not that he said everyone was incapable of receiving his testimonies,[i] because he next said: *Whoever receives his testimony has sealed that God is true.* Furthermore, John's own disciples were those who received it. But he said this concerning those who do not receive, [74] who followed the denial of the Jews. To this the evangelist bears witness, for he says:[89] *He came to his own, and his own did not receive him* (John 1:11). He did not speak about all the Jews but of those who did not receive [him], for there were many of the Jews who did receive him. Hereby he also urges his own disciples to a better reception and warns them not to be among those who do not receive him.

i. John Chrysostom, *Hom. Jo.* 30.2, states that here "no one" means only a few; Moše bar Kepha agrees.

[3:33] **Whoever receives his testimony has sealed that God is true. For he whom God sent speaks the words of God.**

Hereby he further encourages them to the faith, as if to say that he who receives his testimony and believes in him has born witness that God is true, believing the testimonies that have come from heaven; *for who has seen and

---

89. **For he says:** om. N.

heard that in heaven has testified.[90] But whoever does not believe in him,[91] neither does he confess[92] God to be true, because if his witness is the testimony of God, then absolutely he is God. But those who do not receive the testimony, they do not accept him to be God.

[3:34] For God does not give the Spirit by measure.

These sayings referring to the Savior were for the sake of his own disciples. Perhaps John was attempting to bring them to rectitude in every way. *He does not give the Spirit by measure.* Although many are the divisions of the Spirit and the [varieties of] grace[i] that he granted and bestowed on the prophets and the holy ones, yet it does not compare to this. For there according to each one's ability, but here he grants it totally because of his own humbling from heaven and relating the things seen and heard there. He did not wish to speak about the personality of the Holy Spirit but about the distribution of the [varieties of] grace that derive from the Lord.

    i. [**Varieties of**] **grace**: *šnorhk'* (pl.). Although this noun is generally in a plural form, here varieties of grace are intended.

[75] [3:35] The Father loves the Son and gave everything into his hands.

Because he previously said, *God does not give the Spirit by measure,* as we have related, and earlier had said, *God sent [him],* and these were very modest [words] for the sake of the weakness of the listeners, consequently those who heard did not suppose anything else other than that he was a creature because of his being sent by God and what he said about the Spirit. Therefore he raised his discourse to a higher plane in order to inform them of his divine nature and to remove the doubts that they harbored. For that reason he said, *The Father loves the Son and gave everything into his hands,* as if to say, let not these sayings harm you, that he was sent and that he received Spirit; these words are not[93] about a creature but about the Son. And God, who sent him, is his Father but not creator. And he did not give the grace partially, as of old to the prophets, but he possesses in his essence totally all grace and power.

---

90. **For … testified**: om. N.

91. **In him**: om. M.

92. **Does he confess**: "has he confessed," M.

93. **Not**: om. M.

[3:36a] Whoever believes in the Son receives eternal life.

See how he drew them little by little to perfect knowledge and clearly expounded the unified nature[i] and being that he possesses with regard to the Father. *Whoever believes in the Son receives eternal life.* And how would he grant eternal life, unless he were by nature God? For if he were a creature, as you suppose, he would not have authority to grant eternal life. But if he is lord of eternal life, then he is God of all created beings.[ii]

    i. **Unified nature**, *miakan bnut'iwnn*, N: "unity," *miasnakanut'iwnn*, M. For such terminology, see the introduction, xxxvi.
    ii. **Created beings**: *ełakank'*, from *ełanim*, "to come into being"; cf. *eł*, introduction, xxxv.

[3:36b] And whoever does not obey the Son will not see life, but the anger of God remains on him.

[76] When he had expounded the recompenses of the faith, *that those who believe receive eternal life,[94] he then set down the destruction of those who do not believe: *The anger of God remains on them.*[95] Just as eternal life is granted to the believers, so eternal torments are prepared for the unbelievers (cf. Matt 25:46; John 5:29).

---

94. That … life: om. N.
95. Them: "him," N.

[76] CHAPTER 4[1]

[4:1–2] **Now,[2] when Jesus knew that the Pharisees had heard that Jesus was creating and baptizing more disciples than John, for Jesus himself did not baptize, but his disciples.**

He said this concerning the calumniating[3] Jews, who continually tried to fabricate some charges against him and to move the Sadducees[i] and all the people to hatred of the Savior, just as later they came and offered false witness.

i. **Sadducees**: Nonnus makes the same change from Pharisees elsewhere; see the introduction, xxvi. Dionysius bar Salibi, *John*, 94, refers to the envy of the Pharisees.

[4:3] **He left the land[4] of Judea and came again to Galilee.**

Why did he leave Judea? Not through fear of the Sadducees; for unless he himself had wished, they would never have been able to harm him. It is clear that he often passed through the midst of those who planned to lay hands on him, and he was able to do the same here. But see how he arranges everything to abbreviate the causes of many things. For when he heard that the Sadducees and Jews wished to lay hands on him, he did not act in the same manner. For if he had always shown himself to be such, he would then have provided no little[5] suspicion to his enemies that he possessed a body somewhat in the form of some apparition, but not in reality and [77] truly.[i] Also many among the schismatics even after so many revelations still declare that he had a body not truly but apparently, for which reason the Savior proved the genuineness of his body as much as of his divinity.

------

1. **4**, *D*, N: om. M; see introduction, xxiv.
2. **Now**, *isk*: om. MZ.
3. **Calumniating**: "the calumniators among," M.
4. **Land**, *ašxarh*, N: *erkir*, MVZ.
5. **No little**: om. M.

Why was this? Because through the economy[ii] of the body we were to receive in us great grace when we understood these things truly, that for our sake and for our salvation he was incarnate and made man, being related to us and an example for the better, and always journeying along the same path as us to virtue,[6] when travails and oppression are inflicted by enemies. But what means: *He came again to Galilee*? For when he went into the desert[7] to be tempted by Satan, he went there after his return, and this is the second time he went into Galilee (Luke 4:14). Therefore he said: *He came again to Galilee.*

i. Here John Chrysostom, *Hom. Jo.* 31.1, discusses the reality of Christ's body; this is quoted by Tat'ewac'i, 178.

ii. **Economy:** *tnawrinut'iwn*; see the introduction, xxxvi–xxxviii, for the terms used in this paragraph to describe the incarnation.

[4:4] **And he needed to pass through Samaria.**

And what was his passing through, except that because he previously knew through the foresight of his divinity the advantages that would occur there, and the faith of the Samaritans in him through the Samaritan woman, therefore he passed through Samaria?[i] But he did not stay there. Why? Lest the Jews fabricate[8] reasons along the pattern of: Why do you do this? And behold, it is not right to mingle with Samaritans.[9] This he[10] also commanded his disciples: *Do not enter the cities of the Samaritans* (Matt 10:5).

i. Here Dionysius bar Salibi, *John*, 95–96, discusses the origin of the name Samaria and gives its ancient history. He notes that the Samaritans accept only the books of Moses and call Abraham their father. Tat'ewac'i, 179, also expands on the history of Samaria. For Nonnus's own description and etymology, see below, commentary to vv. 21–22.

[4:5–6a] **He came to a city of the Samaritans that is called Sēk'ar, near to the village that Jacob gave to his son Joseph. And there was a well of Jacob's there.**

He said, *near to the village*,[11] because the city that he said Jesus came to, which was called Sēk'ar,[i] [78] was the village of Jacob that he gave to his son

---

6. **Virtue:** + "and endurance," M.

7. **Desert:** + "for forty days," M.

8. **Fabricate:** + "some," M.

9. **Samaritans:** + "as the laws warn," M.

10. **He:** + "himself," M.

11. **Village:** + "he did not say some city near to the village," M.

Joseph. Now, when he declared that he came to the city, he indicated that he had not yet entered the city but sat down near the city.

i. John Chrysostom, *Hom. Jo.* 31.5–6, discusses the connection of Sēk'ar with Jacob. Here Moše bar Kepha, 311, refers to Dinah, Jacob's daughter, and Tat'ewac'i, 180, repeats the story of Dinah from Gen 33:18–34:2.

[4:6b] And Jesus, being weary from the journey, sat down.

See[12] the example of being weary that he described[13] in order to mark his immeasurable humility in walking on foot and not acquiring horses.[i] Thereby he also notes something else—the reality of his body—so that through that we might realize and understand that he took a body not in appearance but truly.[ii] For although he was not in fact overcome by human conditions[iii] like us, yet when he allowed his nature to endure its own [natural conditions], he endured them truly; and when he wished he raised himself above those things that are in nature.[iv] And when he willingly bore them, he was comparable to us in accordance with his relationship of the body.

i. Tat'ewac'i, 180, repeats the comment on riding horses, but it does not appear in non-Armenian commentators.

ii. Moše bar Kepha and Dionysius bar Salibi emphasize this point.

iii. **Human conditions:** *kirk'*; for this and similar terms, see the introduction, xxxviii.

iv. Moše bar Kepha stresses the willingness of Christ in taking on the human condition, and Tat'ewac'i, 181, expands on the human characteristics of hunger, thirst, tiredness, sweat, and so on.

[4:6c–7] He sat down at the fountain, and it was about the sixth hour. A woman came from Samaria to draw water. Jesus said to her: Give me to drink.

So do not think that his asking for water was through having some need.[14] Whence is this clear? For afterward he did not have such eagerness to drink water,[i] but he asked [for] water for the journey in order to prepare the woman for conversation, in accordance with his foreknowledge that good things would happen through the woman. Now by saying, *fountain,*[ii] he indicated the well.[iii]

---

12. **See:** "Did you see?" M.

13. **Described:** + "to us," M.

14. **Need:** + "for water by necessity," M.

i. Tat'ewac'i, 181, notes that in fact Jesus did not drink; his asking the woman was in order to lead her to faith.

ii. **Fountain:** *ałbiwr*, "source," as Z and v. 6.

iii. **Well:** *jrhor*, in John only in vv. 11–12. Dionysius bar Salibi, *John*, 97, states that Jesus sat on the ground.

[4:8] For his disciples had gone to the city in order to buy food.

He indicated again by this his immeasurable humility, in that not a single one of the disciples had bothered to stay with him, but he was sitting alone. Furthermore, the disciples did not take the trouble always to carry a little food with them for any pressing needs.

[4:9] The Samaritan woman said to him: You are a Jew. [79] Why do you ask to drink from me, a Samaritan woman, because the Jews never mingle with Samaritans?

How did the woman know that he was from among the Jews? She noticed it through his conversation and likeness.[i] Now, what does it mean: *The Jews never mingle with Samaritans*? It shows that the Jews are the ones who separate from the Samaritans, not Samaritans from the Jews.[ii] Therefore he put them earlier in his account. Let us not leave this further remark of his without investigation: *Why do you who are a Jew seek to drink from me?* It was spoken very wisely and inscrutably, as if to say either that you are ignorant of the law, for behold, it forbids Jews to mingle with Samaritans, or you despise the law.

i. Moše bar Kepha; Dionysius bar Salibi, *John*, 98; and Tat'ewac'i, 182, note that Jesus was recognized through his accent and clothing.

ii. John Chrysostom, *Hom. Jo.* 31.4, indicates that the schism was caused by the Jews, as does Moše bar Kepha. Tat'ewac'i, 182, notes that the Jews abhorred the Samaritans, not vice versa, just as "now" Christians abhor the Muslims (*aylazgik'*), rather than vice versa.

[4:10] Jesus replied and said: If you knew the gifts of God and who it is that asks you, Give me to drink, then you would ask him, and he would give you living water.

What, then, did he teach the woman? He said that if you knew the great grace that will come upon you, and the reason for my conversation with you— in that not for any need do I ask water from you but so that I may give you living water to drink—then you would have hastened to [fulfill] the request.[i] Not as you see me do you need to know, but when you will know, the living water will be granted to you that always brings you refreshment for the thirst superior to bodily understanding.

i. Edwards (2004, 55) notes that "gift," as in the lemma, was a rabbinic appellation for the Torah. Theodore of Mopsuestia refers to the precepts of the law; but Tat'ewac'i, 183, refers to the grace of the Holy Spirit; cf. Ps 35:10.

[4:11] The woman said to him: Lord, because you do not have a pail and the well is deep, whence will you be able to give me living water?

Why did the Lord encourage her, save because she thought he was superior to what she had earlier supposed, although not yet did she fully [80] understand about the living water that he said he would grant her? Since she understood what he said literally, she did not comprehend any of its hidden meaning because of her weakness. Whence is this clear? He did not respond as would have been appropriate for what he heard. What, then, is that? It would have been appropriate for the woman to say: If you had living water, it would have been necessary first to refresh your own thirst.[i]

i. Moše bar Kepha makes the same point.

[4:12] Surely you are not someone greater than our father Jacob who gave us this well, and he himself drank from it, and his children and his flocks.

As if to say, if you really had a pail with you, I would have hoped you would draw from this same well and give me the water of which you speak; or if the well did not have such a depth,[i] perhaps you would have been able to devise something. But as you do not have a pail, and the well has such a depth, how will you be able to give me the living water you mention? Surely you are not greater than our father Jacob, who did not drink from elsewhere than hence, he himself and his sons and his flocks. If he had had another spring other than this, as you say, perhaps he would have drunk from it.

Why did the woman refer to Jacob so much? Because in her knowledge she thought him to be very great, whereas as yet she did not know the greater superiority of Christ; therefore she repeated: *Surely you are not greater than our father Jacob?* But why does she call Jacob her father, being a Samaritan and not a Jew? Because the Samaritans took their inheritance from Jethro, but Abraham was from Chaldea,[15] they being bordering neighbors to each other. Also through another example she adduces a reason for relationship with Jacob, because of having their law and circumcision. Therefore she extended the relationship to Abraham and his sons.

---

15. **From Chaldea**, *i K'aldeay*, N: "in the city," *i kalak'in*, M.

i. The Syrian commentators do not speculate on the depth of the well. Edwards (2004, 56) notes a reference to its being 75 feet deep.

[81] [4:13–14] **Jesus responded and said to her: Everyone who drinks from this water will thirst again. But whoever drinks the water that I shall give him will never thirst. *The water that I shall give him will be a spring of water flowing for eternal life.**[16]

The Savior turns his responses into another example and does not make his reply in accordance with the woman's words. Why was that? Because it was not appropriate for him to bear witness about himself that he was greater than Jacob, since the woman had not yet seen in him the superior signs whereby she would have assented to his words, and she confirmed in her mind Jacob to be greater. Therefore he turned his words to what was more profitable and useful. He repeated the reference to water, which indicated the grace and power[17] of the Holy Spirit, as he once said, *Whoever believes in me, from his stomach will flow rivers of living waters,* which the evangelist very clearly explained (John 7:38–39).[i] He said this, he said, concerning the Spirit that they would receive.

But why does he model the grace and power of the Holy[18] Spirit through water, condescending to the weakness of the woman through a thing familiar and very well known? Just as water refreshes thirst, and purifies from filth, and extinguishes the heat[19] and prevents[20] the burning of fire, and makes needful seeds grow and renders them fruitful,[ii] likewise the Holy Spirit operates on whomever he dwells in accordance with spiritual considerations. Also through another example we know the workings and power[21] of the Holy Spirit, in the model of fire according to John the Baptist, which he taught regarding Christ: *He will baptize you in the Holy*[22] *Spirit and in fire* (Matt 3:11; Luke 3:16), so that you may recognize the power of the Holy Spirit with a view to the burning up and destruction of the habits of sin within us, and rendering luminous those in whom he dwells.

[82] Furthermore, through mentioning water, as we said above, he informs the woman about a thing well known, which by reading the prophet we always have in ourselves: *My soul thirsts for you, God* (Ps 41:3).[iii] Also the

---

16. **The water … life:** om. M.
17. **Power:** pl. M.
18. **Holy:** om. M.
19. **Filth, heat:** pl. M.
20. **Prevents:** om. N.
21. **And power:** om. N.
22. **Holy, as Z:** om. M.

saying *Whoever drinks the water that I shall give will never thirst* does not at all mean that it removes the thirst of the body as long as it is alive; but by drinking once the life-giving water, no more thereafter will thirst control him, that need that the prophet mentions, *My soul thirsts for you, God*, indicating openly the grace of the font.

    i. Moše bar Kepha refers here to John Chrysostom regarding the water as the Spirit, noting that the Spirit in scripture is called water, fire, and other names; see John Chrysostom, *Hom. Jo.* 32.1, for water as Spirit.

    ii. Moše bar Kepha notes that water makes things grow, and Dionysius bar Salibi, *John*, 100, develops the model of fire.

    iii. Tat'ewac'i, 187–88, also quotes this psalm and equates the water with baptism.

[4:15] The woman said to him: Lord, give me that water, so that I may not thirst nor come here to draw water.

See the woman's rapid pursuit of the truth and her desire to drink the water of which she heard, believing what he said: *Whoever drinks of the water that I shall give will never thirst*. Therefore she asked, saying: *Give me that water so that I may not thirst*. Also the woman reckoned him superior to Jacob,[i] although she[23] did not yet completely understand about the Savior what sort of person he was.

    i. Moše bar Kepha and Dionysius bar Salibi (*John*, 100) also state that the woman reckoned Christ greater than Jacob.

[4:16–18] Jesus said to her: Go and summon your husband, and come here. The woman replied to him and said: I do not have a husband. Jesus said to her: You said well, that I do not have a husband, for you have changed five husbands, and the one you now have is not your husband. That you rightly said.

After he had imparted so much instruction to her that he drew the woman to trust in his words, that he would give her the water for which hereafter she would not thirst, then he taught her something else even higher whereby he could draw the woman closer to the faith, revealing a secret of the woman about her husband [83] that the woman had denied, saying: *I do not have a husband*. Yet she still had a husband as people thought, because the woman's affairs were secret. But let us see what the Savior said: *You said well that I do not have a husband*, as if [to say] that because she did not wish to give up his

---

    23. **She:** "the woman," N.

teaching, you accepted it so happily that you pretended, *I have no husband.*[24]
For in fact you do not have a husband. Although in name you[25] have the repu-
tation of widowhood[26] in order to make people so think, yet you do not have
a real husband.

What could this mean? Because widows, and women[27] without husbands
for whatever reason, were despised and disdained by the Jews and Samaritans, and because the woman[28] had changed five husbands, therefore they
ostracized the woman, and nobody was anxious to marry her.[i] Therefore the
woman in her wisdom sought means to keep it secret, because of the disdain
we mentioned above, and only in name did she link that husband to her in
order to make the citizens so think.[ii] But she did not have the status of marriage in accordance with husband and wife.

i. Dionysius bar Salibi, *John,* 101, gives various views including that of Ephrem, that
the woman's husbands had died one after the other. Išodad elaborates on this.

ii. Moše bar Kepha has a similar argument.

[4:19–20] **The woman said to him: Lord,[29] it seems that you are[30] some
prophet. Our father worshiped on this mountain; yet you say that only in
Jerusalem is the place where one should worship.**

Be amazed[31] here at the woman's love of truth, how she did not wish to
take her leave, being ashamed when he openly revealed her greatest[32] secrets.
Furthermore, she did not seek anything else of bodily needs from him, but[33]
she thought discovery of the faith to be of greater profit than anything of
worldly concerns. Therefore she asked to learn the place where worship was
truly to be conducted. [84] And what means: *Our fathers worshiped on this
mountain?* The woman knew that only there her fathers conducted worship;
but she[34] did not know truly the reasons, although she had heard from the
tradition of the elders that Abraham had brought Isaac to that mountain as

24. **Husband:** + "but you well said that I do not have a husband," M.
25. **You:** "she," M.
26. **Widowhood:** + "for you but only," M.
27. **Women,** M: "those," N.
28. **The woman,** M: "she," N.
29. **Lord,** NZ: om. M.
30. **You are,** *es du,* NZ: om. *du,* M.
31. **Be amazed,** *sk'ančac'ir,* M: "amazed," *sk'ančac'eal,* N.
32. **Greatest:** om. M.
33. **But,** N: "save the greatest profit, because," M.
34. **She:** "they," MV.

a sacrifice,[i] when he was saved by a warning from above to substitute a ram for him.[35]

i. Gen 22, on Mt. Moriah. Here *Comm. Diat.* 12.20 notes that the Samaritans worshiped on Mt. Sechem, or at Bethel, or Mt. Gerizim. Moše bar Kepha also refers to Abraham and Isaac. Dionysius bar Salibi, *John*, 102, names the mountain Gerezim, as does Tat'ewac'i, 193.

[4:21a] **Jesus said to her: Woman, believe in me, because the time will come when they shall worship the Father neither on this mountain nor in Jerusalem.**

After he had convinced the woman through his teaching, so that she knew that he truly knew all secrets and she thought the Lord was some prophet, then he said to the woman, *Believe in me*, so that thereby he might bring her to even higher knowledge.[i] As he had done for Nicodemus, who was the teacher of the Jews (John 3), so here also, because the Lord was accustomed in this way to draw us to better things through his very profitable teachings and gradually to make us useful, which one can see here. For he did not respond in accordance with the woman's words,[36] but leaving that aside, he hastened to another argument. He did not say to the woman, Why did the Samaritans worship on that mountain, or the Jews in Jerusalem? But he drew her to further profitable and valuable understanding, which was of no little advantage, not merely for the woman, but also[37] for everyone. He said:

i. Tat'ewac'i, 195, explains "the time will come," in the lemma, as the time when the gospel has been preached in all places, forty years after the crucifixion.

[4:21b–22] **The time will come that they shall not worship on this mountain, like you, nor in Jerusalem like the Jews.[38] You worship whom [85] you know not. We worship whom we know, because salvation is from the Jews.**

When he described the abolition of both worships, of the Jews and of the Samaritans, indicating that they had no stability in themselves but were[39] temporary, then he explained to the woman the haughtiness and boasting of the Jews that they possessed concerning their temple and city; not that he was

---

35. **For him:** om. M.
36. **Words:** *banic'*, N; *xawsic'*, MV.
37. **Also:** om. N.
38. Note the repetition of v. 21 in different words.
39. **Were:** "are," M.

an advocate for them, as the woman supposed he was thinking about the Jews, but he predicted the cessation of both. But see what he set down next, and he praises the Jews a little more than them. *You worship whom you do not know; we worship whom we know.* What does this mean? It is as if to say: *you worship whom you do not know,* as the woman was ignorant that idols had been buried on that mountain at some time by her own ancestors, when they had been sent by the Israelites away from King Nebuchadnezzar for the preservation of the city of Jerusalem after the captivity. And when wild beasts had chewed them, they raised a complaint to the king. He learned from some people that no one is able to dwell in that city, save only those who possess the gift of the laws of God. At his command one of the priests set out, whose name was Ezra, bringing with him the laws and the prophets, and bearing the command to break up the idols. When the Samaritans who lived in Jerusalem learned of this—they were called[40] Samaritans, which is translated as guardians[i] or according to the mountain Sameron—they rapidly buried their gods in that mountain, and through tradition the woman preserved their worship on the mountain, but she did not know the reasons.[ii] Therefore the Lord[41] said: *You worship whom you do not know.*

But what does what he said[42] mean regarding the Jews: *They worship whom they know?* It is as if to say [86] that they recognize God to be creator and cause of existing things, although they do not[43] fully recognize him. Let us look at this also, why he placed himself with the Jews. He condescended to the woman's weakness, just as she thought he was from among the Jews in saying: *You, who are a Jew, why do you seek drink from me, a Samaritan woman?* Furthermore, in accordance with the virgin from whom he put on flesh, it would have been in no way inappropriate to say the same as Paul said: *From whom is also Christ according to the flesh, *who is God blessed forever* (Rom 9:5).[44] Through that allegorical saying he informed the woman that he was Savior, saying that salvation is from the Jews, that is, his receiving flesh from them whereby he redeemed the nations of mankind.

    i. **Guardians:** *pahapank'.* The Hebrew stem *šmr* means to "keep, preserve, be on guard." In the Hebrew of 3 Kgdms 16:24 the name Šameron is derived from the owner Šemer. In the Armenian version, which derives from the LXX, the names become Sameron and Samer.

---

    40. **They were called:** om. N.
    41. **The Lord:** "he," N.
    42. **What he said:** om. N.
    43. **Not:** "no longer," M.
    44. **Who is … forever:** om. N.

ii. The Syrian commentators do not reproduce this tale about the idols. Parallels to the remarks in Nonnus may be found in Epiphanius, *De gemmis* (see Pummer 2002; I am grateful to Sebastian Brock for this reference). A complete Syriac version of this is no longer extant. For the idols, Ezra, the etymology of Samaritans as "guardians," the bowing down toward Gerizim from every direction, with many further details not given here, see the Georgian version (Blake and De Vis, 189–92). The fragmentary Armenian version (Stone 1989) does not contain this information. Tat'ewac'i, 195, expands on the directions that various cults face for worship, including Jews and Samaritans, and notes that the Muslims (*aylazgik'*) worship facing the Kaaba, "which they call K'ahba and Łbla [*qibla*]."

[4:23a] **But the time will come, and now indeed is, when the true worshipers shall worship the Father in Spirit and in truth.**

Mark for me the teachings in wisdom. Although I said: *The Jews worship whom they know, yet a time will come, and now indeed is,* that this will be abolished. What means: *Now indeed is*? It is as if to say that the time has indeed[45] arrived. And what means: *The true worshipers shall worship the Father in Spirit and in truth*? He says, not like you, and not like the Jews, but those who will worship the Father in Spirit and in truth. *They shall worship in Spirit*—the knowledge of the Holy Spirit; *and in truth*—in knowledge of himself, for he himself indeed[46] was truth and life (John 14:6). But why did he place the Spirit before himself in teaching the woman? Because through the guidance of the Holy Spirit one can recognize the Son, as Paul bears witness, saying: *God sent the Spirit of his Son into our hearts* (Gal 4:6). And the Lord bore witness concerning the Holy Spirit: *He will come and testify about me and will teach you everything* (John 14:26).

Where, then, would these worshipers be, save in the church of God,[i] who are worshipers through the holy font, [87] and knowing the all-holy Trinity always worship in Spirit and in truth? *In Spirit and in truth* has yet another meaning: no longer in accordance with the law, like the Jews, nor in ignorance, like the Samaritans, but being perfect in truth and recognizing in truth the one nature[47] and the three persons.

i. Moše bar Kepha emphasizes that the true worshipers are Christians, but he has no reference here to the Trinity. Tat'ewac'i, 197, refers to the abolition of the Jewish law and to the Samaritans.

---

45. **Indeed**: om. M.
46. **Indeed**: om. M.
47. **One nature**: "unity," N.

[4:23b–24] Because the Father seeks such worshipers of his.[48] God is Spirit, and his worshipers must worship him in Spirit and in truth.

After he had informed the woman about the truth of the worshipers, then appropriately he set out the following teaching. Therefore he said that *the Father seeks such worshipers, who worship in Spirit and truth*, not like the Jews and Samaritans. Why? Because *God is Spirit*, that is, not corporeal. *And if [he is] not corporeal,[49] then it is necessary for his worshipers to worship and praise and serve him, not corporeally like the Jews and Samaritans, but as is right for the incorporeal Godhead. What, then, would this be? He says one must worship with a pure soul,[i] and in truth, as if to say not through the law, like the Jews and you who worship in circumcision, which is a shadow of baptism,[ii] and through sacrifices, which are a sign of the sacrifice of the Son of God.

i. **Soul:** *hogi*, the same term as is used for "spirit."
ii. Circumcision as a shadow of baptism is repeated by Tat'ewac'i, 197–98, but is not mentioned here by the Syrian commentators. For the theme, see Lampe 1969 (s.v. *peritomē*, II A 12).

[4:25] The woman said to him: I know that Messiah comes, called Christ. When he will come, he will tell us everything.

The woman was weak with regard to the nature of the worshipers that the Lord had taught, and she was unable to understand truly. For that reason he changed his argument to another strategem. *We know that Mesia comes,* **[88]** and thereby she created another reason for conversation, because very happily she wished to listen to him. Now if someone were to say, how did the woman know that Mesia is coming, since she was a Samaritan and not a Jew, we would say to them: From the book of[50] Genesis and from the prophets that they continually read, and through examples and prophecies they were aware and understood about Christ.[i]

i. Here John Chrysostom, *Hom. Jo.* 33.2, gives a long list of OT examples, as also Tat'ewac'i, 199.

---

48. **Of his,** *iwr*, MZ: om. N.
49. **And if … corporeal:** om. N.
50. **The book of:** om. N.

[4:26] Jesus said to her: I who speak with you am he.

Why so rapidly did he inform the woman, when he did not grant the same to the Jews when they said: *How long will you tire our souls? If you are the Christ, tell us freely* (John 10:24). But he said nothing like that about himself. What, then, was the reason? Because through his foreseeing[51] and prescient power he saw the faith and fearless acceptance in the woman that he was the[52] Christ, therefore he informed her.[i] But recognizing the malignity and merciless denial of the Jews, that in no way would they accept him or be helped, therefore he refrained from telling them that he himself was Christ.

Since through the guidance of the Holy Spirit we have employed these words, undertaking the execution of such an incomprehensible topic but hoping in the gift of grace from above, let us set down briefly the most secret things that the evangelist related: *He left Judea and came to Galilee.* What, then, would this signify, to leave the Jews[53] and move to the Gentiles? Indeed, Galilee is called the dwelling of Gentiles according to Isaiah's prophecy: *The other side of the Jordan, Galilee of the Gentiles* (Isa 9:1). See another example of the truth. For just as the Jews, envious of the disciples regarding baptism, plotted evil, for which reason he had come to Judea, likewise too[54] when the Jews will hate and persecute the disciples because of the preaching of the gospel, [89] the invocation of[55] the divine grace will then move to the Gentiles.

But this also one must not omit. Why, when he was weary, did he take his rest near to the village of Joseph that Jacob had given to his son? It is very necessary to examine the faith caused there through a woman but not a man. For the destruction of that place and the ruin and extermination of the people in it was brought about by a woman, that is, Dinah daughter of Jacob, as the Old Testament relates (Gen 34). Therefore through a woman he makes the renewal.[ii] Also, because by bodily desire such destruction occurred through a woman, who was from among the daughters of Abraham, it was thus appropriate through a woman for spiritual desires to be renewed in her who according to bodily relationship was descended from Abraham. Just as renewal and salvation *for that people occurred through the well, so too salvation[56] and renewal of the race of mankind was to be made through the grace of the font;[iii]

---

51. **Foreseeing:** om. N.

52. **The:** om. N.

53. **The Jews,** M: "Judea," N.

54. **Too:** om. N.

55. **The invocation of,** *koč'umnn*: om. N.

56. **For that … salvation:** om. N.

and just as their faith occurred at the sixth hour of the day, likewise the faith of the whole world would come about at the sixth hour (John 4:6; 19:14).[iv]

Just as when he traveled on his journey wearied in the body, because of the harshness of the Jews that they plotted at that hour due to envy at the baptism of the disciples, he rested nowhere else save at the well near to the city of the Samarians, likewise, sated with the Jews when he endured so much effort but they were not at all profited, as he said through the prophecy, *I am sated with your sacrifices* (Isa 1:11), he was intending to move to the church of the Gentiles in accordance with what the Holy Spirit says through the prophet: *This is my rest forever; and forever I shall reside in it, because I am pleased with it. Those whom he blessed I shall bless, and his poor I shall fill with bread* (Ps 131:14–15). He means, to bless the souls of those baptized with such blessings as will never fail, and to fill[57] them with bread through the grace of his body.

i. *Comm. Diat.* 12.18 notes the progressive nature of Jesus's revelation to the woman: as Jew, as prophet, as Christ.

ii. Tat'ewac'i, 201, echoes Nonnus, but the Syrian commentators do not here refer to Dinah. Nor does Nonnus mention her again.

iii. For the comparison of the well and baptism, see Mathews and Sanjian 1991 (149–50).

iv. For the six ages, see the introduction, xxxv, with further references. It is a major theme in the *Teaching of Saint Gregory* (see esp. 670–71).

[4:27] **At that point his disciples arrived, and [90] they were amazed that he was speaking with a woman.[58] But none of them said, What do you seek? or, What are you talking about with her?**

Why, then, were they astonished, save at the immeasurable humility of the teacher when they saw him so meek as to be speaking at length with the woman?[i] Not with some important person, but one so insignificant that she herself had undertaken the task of going to the well to draw water. That did not indicate grandeur but great lack of dignity and poverty. What does it mean: *None of them asked, What do you seek, or, What are you speaking about with her?* It is as if they were respectful of their teacher and did not dare to investigate. This is clear when Peter nodded to John to ask who it might it be who would betray him (John 21:20).

i. John Chrysostom, *Hom. Jo.* 33.3, also stresses here Christ's humility.

---

57. **To fill:** "he filled," N.

58. **A woman,** N (and the Greek): "the woman," MZ.

[4:28a] **The woman left her pot.**

That was not a small indication of the Lord's foresight, her eager willingness and zeal for the faith. Therefore he sat at the well, awaiting her return; in accordance with his prescient power he saw the multiple profit that would accrue to the woman. Likewise, the woman leaving her pot and going into the city indicates the great zeal of the woman, that she had come because of lack of water in order to bring [some] home, but not that the woman was thirsty. It would raise her to spiritual wisdom in accordance with the Lord's saying: *I have come to cast fire on the earth* (Luke 12:49). In this way the woman, who had never undertaken any occupation, very rapidly brought an example for a description of a female teacher.[i]

i. **Female teacher**: *vardapetuhi*, a rare feminine form of *vardapet*, for which see note to commentary on John 1:29, above. Movsēs Xorenac'i, *History*, 2:91, so describes Nunē who converted the Georgians.

[4:28b–30] **She went to the city and said to the men: Come, see a man who told me everything that I have done. Is he not the Christ? They went out of the city and came to him.**

[**91**] Note for me here the wisdom and intelligence of the woman, because she did not leave her pot for some other words of instruction. But when she heard from him, *I am the Christ*, knowing that [these words] would not appear so reliable and acceptable to anyone, she said: *Come, see a man who told me everything that I have done. Is he not the Christ?* Therefore those [words] were more acceptable and appropriate to bring them eagerly to see the man who knows secrets. I also find another testimony of the woman's wisdom and sagacity, because the Lord spoke only one secret of hers, which concerned a husband. But she said: *He told [me] everything that I have done.* Surely not as a lie or stupidly did she report that. God forbid! But through the one[59] secret thing that the Lord told her, the woman understood the whole, that he knew all the secrets of mankind.

---

59. **The one**, *miovn*: "the other," *miwsovn*, M.

[4:31] And before they had come, the disciples begged him and said: Rabbi, eat bread.

Because when they saw him weary and sitting down, they accordingly supposed that he was hungry, and that perhaps as someone weary he needed to rest and likewise to eat. For that reason they begged him: *Rabbi, eat bread.*

[4:32–34] He said to them: I have food to eat that you do not know. The disciples said to each other: Did anyone bring him something to eat? Jesus said to them: My food is this, that I shall do the will of the one who sent me, and I shall accomplish his deeds.

The meaning of these sayings needs investigating. *I have food that you do not know* is to indicate that he did not have any need in himself for food, like us, because hunger did not really act upon him in the way that it overcomes us. But when he wished, [92] he condescended to those things that derive from nature in order to confirm the dispensation of his incarnation,[i] that he had a body not in appearance or as an illusion but truly. The saying *I have food that you do not know* also has another meaning, as if to say that just as human nature has no small desire for the taste of food, likewise I have no small desire for the salvation of the world that will occur through faith.[ii] This he declared openly: *This is the will of my Father that I accomplish his deeds.* This is no small indication of the nature with a single will,[iii] for which reason he had been sent by the Father for the salvation of the world.

i. **Dispensation of his incarnation:** *zmarmnaworutʿeann tnawrinakansn.* For these terms, see the introduction, xxxvi–xxxvii; and for condescension to the natural things that affect us humans, see xxxviii.

ii. Theodore of Mopsuestia, 66; Moše bar Kepha; and Dionysius bar Salibi, *John,* 104, all refer to the conversion of the world as Christ's food. Origen, *Comm. Jo.* 13.34, interprets the food as knowledge of God and has a long discussion of the parables that involve meals. See also John Chrysostom, *Hom. Jo.* 34.1, for Christ's hunger.

iii. **Single will:** *miakam.* Nonnus frequently stresses the unity of the Father and Son; see the introduction, xxxvi.

[4:35] **Do you not say that there are still four months and the harvest takes place? Behold, I say to you:**[60] **Raise up your eyes and see, the fields have turned white and are ready for harvest.**

This saying is allegorical. What, then, does it reveal? *You say the harvest will take place in four months*; but I now show you a different harvest already present.[i] What would that be? [By] the coming of the Samaritans rapidly to me from the city through their new faith, understand the harvest of the other nations.[ii] *Raise up your eyes*. Now he says, You see already the multitudes coming rapidly from the city. He also told them to look with the eye of the Spirit at the hidden mystery that would take place. By saying, *The fields have turned white*, he means their purity in faith in himself that would now occur; and from the black gloomy darkness of sin they would become white through their faith. And let us not omit the question why he spoke these things allegorically. Allegorical matters are to be seriously investigated, whereas obvious things are not such. Also, when the allegorical becomes clear to the investigator, it remains more securely in **[93]** his mind than something that passes through his ears once in a literal fashion.[iii]

i. Nonnus shows little interest in the symbolism of numbers. The Syrian commentators do not explain the meaning of four here, but Origen, *Comm. Jo.* 13.40, refers to the four elements and the four spheres of the cosmos. Tat'ewac'i, 206, calculates four months from Passover to the June harvest, with other meanings.

ii. Moše bar Kepha; Dionysius bar Salibi, *John*, 105; and Theodore of Mopsuestia indicate that Christ is referring to the conversion of the Samaritans and Gentiles.

iii. **In a literal fashion**: *parzaguniw*. Tat'ewac'i, 207, also notes that allegory remains more firmly in the mind.

[4:36a] **And he who reaps receives wages and gathers fruit for eternal life.**

By reapers he meant his disciples,[i] because by drawing the race[61] of mankind to knowledge of God they plucked them away from evil deeds. And this fruit is not an earthly temporary one but the cause of eternal life.

i. **Disciples**, *zašakertac'n*: "angels," *hreštakac'n*, V (!). Theodore of Mopsuestia, 67, and Tat'ewac'i, 208, here refer to the apostles; see commentary to v. 36b.

60. **I say to you**, NZ: "I send you," M; cf. Matt 10:16; Luke 10:3; John 20:21.
61. **Race**, *azg*, M: pl. N.

[4:36b] **And he who sows and he who reaps, together they will rejoice.**

By sowers he means the ranks of prophets, and by reapers the crowds of apostles.[i] Why should this be? The prophets sowed the word of faith in men's minds through their divine messages, whereas the disciples reaped by them the complete faith. Hence it is clear that the law and the prophets were examples and shadows of this gospel, as the giver of both commandments is one. The saying *The sower and the reaper will rejoice together* also contains another example. It indicates that not according to a worldly model did he say, *The reaper rejoices when he reaps what he has not sown*, but the sower is very distressed when he does not reap what he has sown, and someone else usurps his seeds and reaps them. But the joy of the prophets and of the apostles will be theirs in common.

    i. Moše bar Kepha and Dionysius bar Salibi (*John*, 105) give the same interpretation. But Nonnus refers to "disciples" again in the comments that follow.

[4:37] **In this is the word true,[62] that it is one who sows and it is[63] another who reaps.**

Again he verifies the saying by repeating it to confirm the disciples, as if to say [94] that in accordance with the habit of mankind those who are fatigued and weary sow and reap and gather the produce, but someone else steals what they have gathered into barns. There exist such examples among mankind. Now, if this so happens sometimes[64] in bodily matters, then the saying is true that he[65] spoke concerning the sower and reaper.

[4:38] **And I sent you to reap what you had not sown. Others had labored, and you entered into their labors.**

Because he expounded to them the example of the harvest, that you are the reapers, and he said that the wages were equal for them and the prophets, consequently the disciples were pondering about themselves, reckoning the saying very significant.[i] For they were thinking something like this, that perhaps the prophets had been sent nowhere else save specifically to the Jews, whereas he was intending to send us through the whole world. Whence would

---

62. **Is the word true,** MZ: "the word is true," N.

63. **It is,** MZ: om. N.

64. **Sometimes:** om. N.

65. **He:** "I," M.

they have supposed this? From when he said, *I have sent you to reap what you have not sown,* that is, all nations among whom none of the prophets had sown. For although the prophets were different from the apostles, yet as their preaching is one, here that of the former is said of the latter, and vice versa, in accordance with his saying: *Whoever sows and whoever reaps, together they will rejoice.*

   i. For John Chrysostom, *Hom. Jo.* 34.2; Moše bar Kepha; and Dionysius bar Salibi, *John*, 106, "the others" of the lemma are the prophets. Theodore of Mopsuestia refers to the both the prophets and the just.

[4:39] And many of the Samaritans from that city believed in him because of the word of the woman testifying:[66] He told me everything that I have done.

See the wisdom of the evangelist, why he set down those remarks. First to verify what the Lord had earlier said: *Raise up your eyes and see, the fields have turned white *and are ready for harvest.*[67] He showed that the sayings had borne fruit. And he said[68] also **[95]** that many of the Samaritans had believed in him because of the woman's word to indicate the accusation[i] and the great separation of the two nations, Jews and Samaritans. As if to say of the Jews, *who had seen so many signs and miracles [performed] by the Savior, and were always running from the law and the prophets, and knew the testimonies concerning him,[69] that they did not believe at all, but plotted so much wickedness against him, as they indeed carried out. But the Samaritans, through the simple words of a single woman, believed and followed the truth.

Furthermore, the woman did not relate the highest things, that he was the Christ, but only: *He told me everything that I had done. Would he not be the Christ?* Who would not be astonished at these sayings? The Samaritans, despite being enemies, through the modest words of a single woman were so rapid to the faith; but the Jews, despite being related and possessing so many testimonies about him from their own commandments, and being eyewitnesses of innumerable signs, not only denied [him] but even plotted to lay hands on him and hang him from a cross.[ii]

   i. **Accusation:** *ambastanut'iwn* (i.e., the charges against each other). Moše bar Kepha also refers here to the separation of Jews and Samaritans.
   ii. **Cross:** *p'ayt* (lit. "wood").

---

   66. **Woman testifying,** MZ: "woman's testimonies," N.
   67. **And are…harvest:** om. M.
   68. **He said:** om. N.
   69. **Who had seen…him:** "knew so many signs and wonders about him," N.

[4:40–42] **Now, when the Samaritans came to him, they begged him to stay with them; and he was there two days. And many more believed in him because of his words. And they said to the woman: Henceforth no more do we believe because of your declarations but because we ourselves have heard him, and we know that he is the true Savior of the worlds.**

Why does the evangelist repeat concerning the Samaritans that many believed in him, except in order to show that these were not the ones who previously left the city and believed through the woman, but those who believed after his entry into the city and after hearing his teaching knew that he is the true Savior of the worlds?[i] And what is *Savior of the world*? It is as if to say, not specifically of the Jews, **[96]** but of the whole world.[ii] Furthermore, the evangelist did not report anything of what the Savior taught the Samaritans in the city or the signs and miracles he demonstrated. Hence it is clear that very many [examples of] the signs and teaching of the Savior were not written down, as this same evangelist indicated: *There are many other things that Jesus did that are not written in this book, which this world would not be sufficient to contain the books if they were written* (John 21:25).

i. **Worlds:** pl., as in the lemma; but sg. just below.

ii. Dionysius bar Salibi, *John*, 107, notes that Christ was Savior not of his own, like one of the prophets, but of all who died in sin.

[4:43–44] **And after two days he left there and went to Galilee, for Jesus himself testified: A prophet does not have honor in his own land.**

What means his saying: *A prophet does not have honor in his own land*? For he left Judea and came to Galilee, and did not enter into Capernaum; but he came to Galilee and called Capernaum his habitation.[i] Why did he not go[70] into Capernaum? Because he frequently performed signs there, but they accepted nothing and did not follow his teaching, for this reason he said: *A prophet does not have honor in his own land.*[71]

i. Dionysius bar Salibi, *John*, 107, notes that Jesus called Capernaum his city, and Moše bar Kepha indicates that Capernaum did not receive him.

---

70. **Go:** "come," M.

71. **Land:** "city," M.

[4:45] **But when he came to Galilee, the Galileans received him because they had seen all the signs that he did in Jerusalem at the feast, since they too had come to the feast.**

Why, then, did the evangelist employ that [expression], except to make clear concerning the Galileans that they also were despised by the Jews, as Nathaniel, who was a teacher of the Jews, also[72] declared when he said: *Can anything good be done in Galilee?*[i] The Jews also said something similar to Nicodemus: *Investigate and see that a prophet does not arise from Galilee* (John 7:52). Therefore the evangelist demonstrates that they are even more honorable than the Jews vaunting [97] in themselves, who said they did nothing outside the commandment, and always despised them.

The evangelist also sets down that the Galileans received him because of the signs that they saw in Jerusalem. Why does he recall this? In order to show us that he did not perform any signs among them when he came to Galilee, but they believed in him only through the signs that they saw in Jerusalem. Through this he reveals their honor to be greater than that of the Jews. For the Jews did not believe, although they were always seeing the signs among themselves, whereas the former believed what they once saw elsewhere. But although the former were found to be more praiseworthy than the Jews, even more praiseworthy than them were the Samaritans; for they were instructed by himself, but the Samaritans by a woman before seeing any signs.[ii]

    i. John 1:46 (but there "Nazareth" rather than "Galilee").
    ii. Moše bar Kepha ranks (1) Samaritans, (2) Galileans, (3) Jews.

[4:46–47] **He came again to Cana of Galilee, where he had made the water into[73] wine. And there was a nobleman there whose son was ill in Capernaum. When he heard that Jesus had come from Judea to Galilee, he came to him and begged that he would come down and heal his son, because he was close to dying.**

To some it so seemed that this is the same person as Matthew described (Matt 8:5–13), but they did not understand correctly. Whence is this clear? The former strongly refused when he heard the Savior would go to his house, but this one only asked him to go, yet he did not go. The former met our Savior when he entered Capernaum on descending from the mountain, and

---

    72. **Also:** om. N.
    73. **Into:** om. MZ.

the latter met him when he returned from the Samaritans and was going to
Galilee. The former's son was a paralytic, but this one's had a fever.[i]

i. John Chrysostom, *Hom. Jo.* 35.2, points out that the two healings were different.
Moše bar Kepha quotes him ("Mar Yohannes") and points out that the occasions are different. Dionysius bar Salibi, *John*, 109, also gives the differences between Matthew and
John. Tat'ewac'i, 214, gives three similarities between the stories, and six differences (in
accordance with his love of lists).

[4:48] **Jesus said to him:[74] Unless you were to see[75] some signs and miracles,
you would not believe.**

Why did the Lord say: *Unless you were to see[76] some[77] signs and miracles,
you would not believe?* The man went for the reason that he believed that he
was able to heal his son. But although he went and asked for [98] healing, yet
he did not have strong faith in himself that he was the Christ, but he acted as
if he so thought. Likewise, someone who is caught in trouble will often go to
those whom he does not know well in order to find the solution and because
of his need seizes every [chance]. *The report of his servants is also clear,[78]
when they came to meet him and gave news about his son's life. He did not
pronounce any word about belief but merely asked for the hour. I can clarify
this with another example. His urging the Savior before his son died, this too
was a sign of lack of belief, and not as the other [evangelist] says: *Say the word,
and my child will be healed* (Matt 8:8).

[4:49–54] **The nobleman said to him: Lord, come down before my child dies.
Jesus said to him: Go, your son is alive. And the man believed the word that
Jesus spoke to him and went. And while he was going down, his servants
came to meet him. They gave news and said that his child was alive. He
asked them about the hour at which he had recovered, and they said: Yesterday at the seventh hour the fever left him. His father knew that [it was] at
that hour in which Jesus had said: Go, your son lives. And he believed and**

74. **To him**: om. M.
75. **Were to see**: "see," MZ.
76. **Were to see**: "see," M.
77. **Some**: om. M.
78. **The report … clear**: "It is also clear from the servants," M.

all his house. This second sign again Jesus did, when he came from Judea to Galilee.

We said earlier, although in accordance with the supposition that the man had asked for healing, and he did not have such strong faith as the other one who said, *I am not worthy that you should enter under my roof* (Matt 8:8), yet the Lord did not withhold his gift from him. Why? Because the faith that afterward was to come to him and to his house, he *had seen through his prescient power.[79] And this is clear in the evangelist's saying: [99] *The man believed the word that Jesus had spoken to him.* But see the meaning of the statement that the servants delivered: *Yesterday at the seventh hour the fever left him.* Do not think the fever left him, as if the onlookers suspected the illness might return again to him, but as follows: a sign of complete health unexpectedly appeared in the child. Not like the arts of doctors, who gradually restore strength after the disease has been cured;[i] but at his command the body was completely strengthened again, so *the miraculous activity of that divine power[80] would be obvious to the onlookers.

   i. For natural recovery, see the commentary to John 5:8, below.

---

79. **Had seen…power:** "his prescient power had seen," M.
80. **The miraculous…power:** "that miraculous activity of the divine power," M.

[5:1–3] **After this there was a feast of the Jews, and Jesus went up to Jerusalem. There were in Jerusalem at the *Propatikē* pool, which was called
in Hebrew *Bedhezda*, five porticos, in which lay a great multitude of sick,
blind, lame,**[1] **withered, who were waiting for the agitation of the waters.**

Which feast would this be, save the one after Passover, when they ate the
lamb, that they celebrated after ten days, that was called Feast of Tabernacles?[i]
It is clear that the evangelist mentioned that feast also on which they sacrificed
the lamb, which they always celebrated in accordance with the Egyptian command. Why, then, did the Savior go up to Jerusalem for the feasts? Because
of the nations that gathered for the feast, so that there he might carry out his
teaching[2] and signs in front of all the nations[ii] and reprimand the calumny of
the Jews who said that he was an opponent of God and a breaker of the law.

Now, what does *Bedhezda* mean? "Descent" or "repose of mercy."[iii] And
why were the waters agitated? Because in accordance with the command of
God an angel of the Lord descended and stirred the waters for the healing
[100] of bodily diseases,[iv] which presaged the purity of souls[3] through the
font, because the *Propatikē* was an example of the holy font. Just as there healing of diseases [occurred], so too here the obliteration of sins would occur.[v]
And just as there it was not the power of the water[4] that gave health to the diseased but the descent of the angel, likewise also here the water does not grant
forgiveness of sins but the descent of the Holy Spirit to the font.[vi]

    i. **Tabernacles:** *Taławaraharac'*. Moše bar Kepha and Dionysius bar Salibi (*John*, 110)
refer to the Feast of Pentecost.
    ii. Moše bar Kepha also states that Jesus went up to teach because of the crowds.
    iii. Dionysius bar Salibi, *John*, 111, gives the etymology as "house of mercy" (*byt ḥsd'*)

---

    1. **Blind, lame,** MZ: tr. N.
    2. **Teaching:** pl. M.
    3. **Of souls,** *ogwoc'n*, N: "of the Spirit," *hogwoyn*, M.
    4. **Water:** pl. M.

or "house of insult" (*byt ṣ'r*') but notes that "others say, 'house of mercy.'" Tat'ewac'i, 221, interprets *Bet'hezda* (with a *t'*) as "house of sheep" but notes that John Chrysostom interprets it as "descent of mercy." Chrysostom, *Hom. Jo.* 36.1, interprets the pool in terms of baptism but does not there explicitly give the etymology.

iv. Išodad names the angel as Michael. Theodore of Mopsuestia stresses that only the first to enter the pool is healed, though he does not cite v. 4.

v. The parallel between diseases and sins is also made by Dionysius bar Salibi, *John*, 112, and echoed by Tat'ewac'i, 224.

vi. Nonnus omits v. 4 as a lemma but refers in his commentary to the descent of the angel. John Chrysostom does not cite v. 4 in his *Homilies on John*. This whole episode is not included in the *Commentary* of Step'annos of Siwnik'. Tat'ewac'i, 222–23, does discuss the verse but omits it as a lemma. For the text of v. 4, which is found in Z, see the variant readings discussed in Metzger 1975 (ad loc.) and the accompanying Greek text. Dionysius bar Salibi, *John*, 110, discusses the number of dippings: he states that the Theologos (Gregory of Nazianzus) refers to five, and Moše bar Kepha to six, but "we say" nine.

[5:5–7] **And there was there a man whose illness had lasted for thirty-eight years. When Jesus saw him lying there and knew that it had been a long time since, he said to him: Do you wish to be healthy? The sick one replied to him:[5] Lord, I have no one to put me in the pool when the waters are agitated. And while I am tottering, someone else descends before me.**

The Lord was not ignorant of the reason[6] for the diseased one that he heard from him, because it was clear to everyone that the afflicted who were lying[7] and lingering there were waiting for healing.[i] *But he did this to provide for him an opportunity to him for conversation[8] and to awaken him to the faith.[ii] See[9] the man's response: *Lord, I have no one to put me into the pool when the waters are agitated,* as if to say that my remaining here for so long is not because of my not being eager for healing but because of the immeasurable weakness of my person. For *while I am tottering, others precede me.* See how he set before the Savior the pitiable weakness of his own body.

i. Nonnus does not comment on the thirty-eight years. Cyril of Alexandria discusses the significance of the number, noting that it is not yet forty, which was an important number. Tat'ewac'i, 225, notes that "some say Job was tested [*i p'orjut'ean*] for thirty-eight years."

ii. The passage omitted by N in this sentence (see the footnote) is found in Tat'ewac'i,

---

5. **To him,** MZ: om. N.

6. **Reason:** pl. N.

7. **Were lying,** MV: "had come," N.

8. **But … conversation:** om. N.

9. **See,** *tes,* N: "did you see," *teser,* M.

though he does not cite Nonnus by name. This demonstrates the value of his later commentary as a textual witness; see the introduction, xxiv.

[5:8–9a] Jesus said to him: Arise, take your bed, and go. And the man was healed, and got up, took his bed, and went about.

When he fashioned for him a way to the faith [101] by questioning him, and then commanded him to take his bed and go, see the man's faith, that he did not at all hesitate by reflecting that if he had been so long in such weakness that he was not even able to descend into the pool, how through one word not only could he undertake to rise up, but also even lift his bed; but he arose promptly and immediately. Why did he also command him to take up his bed? So that the command would appear to the hearers not without result and power.[i] It also shows that he brought him to perfect health by the single divine word, and there was no need, as with the custom of doctors, after the cure to remain waiting for the strength of his person [to recover] in accordance with human nature.[ii] These things the Lord frequently commanded, as when raising the dead [girl] he ordered her to eat, demonstrating that he had restored her nature to its previous health before the onslaught of the disease (Luke 8:55).[iii]

i. *Comm. Diat.* 13.2 states that even if the paralytic had remained silent, the bed would proclaim the miracle.

ii. For human nature taking time to recover, see also above, commentary to John 4:54. For doctors, see also the commentary to John 9:32.

iii. John Chrysostom, *Hom. Jo.* 37.1, cites the same example.

[5:9b–10] And it was the Sabbath on that day. The Jews said to the one healed: It is the Sabbath, and it is not right for your to lift up your bed.

What would this be other than to be a sign of the hatred and calumny that they bore in themselves against him,[10] when it was necessary to be amazed and believe and give praise for such wonderful signs and blessings, and that he was the true Christ for whom they were waiting according to the law and the prophets? Passing over all this, they tried to find the Sabbath an excuse for their blame and hatred, and thereby to disparage the amazing working of miracles.

---

10. **Him:** "them," M.

[5:11] He answered them and said: The one who healed me, he told me, Take up your bed and go.

Wisely did the healed one give his response, as if to say that the one who healed me **[102]** knows better than you what is right, whether it was allowed on that day to lift up the bed or not. It was also as if he said that it is more appropriate to obey him[11] than you.

[5:12–13a] They questioned him and said: Who was the man who said to you,[12] Take up your bed and go about? And the healed one did not know who it was.

See their immeasurable cunning and veiled wickedness! They did not ask who it was who cured you but who was the one who said to you: *Take up your bed and go about.*[i] For they did not wish even by a single word to refer to the blessings and miracles, but they rather declared the excuses for their hatred and wickedness, namely, the Sabbath.

    i. Dionysius bar Salibi, *John*, 114, also emphasizes this interpretation.

[5:13b] For he had avoided that place because of the crowd.

By his being distant the testimony[13] concerning the sign that he had done was further confirmed.[i] By his being nearby [there would have been] nothing other than opposition and the fabrication of excuses and the purloining of what had happened. As we said above, by abandoning the question of the healing, they asked about only the affair of the bed. Now after his withdrawal, thereafter there was no little inquiry and astonishment among them over the miracle, although they did not accept it truly.

    i. John Chrysostom, *Hom. Jo.* 37.2, makes the same argument.

[5:14] After this Jesus found him in the temple and said to him: Behold, you have been restored to health. But sin no more, lest further evil befall you.

Why did he make himself known to him not before he healed him but only now? It seems to me for two reasons. First, that the one healed might

---

11. **Him:** "me," M.
12. **To you,** MZ: om. N.
13. **Testimony:** pl. N.

recognize his physician, and not only offer thanks for such great blessings, but also believe in him with his whole heart. Secondly, for a reproach of the Jews for expropriating the miracles, remaining ignorant, and asking [103] him: *Who is it who said to you, take your bed and go about?*

We must also investigate what the Lord[14] said: *Behold, you have been restored to health, but sin no more.* It shows that sin was the reason for the man's illness,[i] and so that he might not regard the gift and blessing of healing as something insignificant and come to forget it as the Jews wished. It gives us also perhaps another example, that when we sin once or twice, he pardons and is silent;[15] and when dangers overcome us, he provides and saves, lest we be incited again to the same. And then, perchance, when temptations once more come upon us, he may have no concern for our salvation, and we perish. Furthermore, by this he gives us another example of future judgments, that by curing us once of the diseases of our sins through the grace of the holy font,[ii] that we do not repeat the same and some worse evil befall us, when we shall be handed over to the fearful judgment of unending torments.

i. As Moše bar Kepha, and Dionysius bar Salibi, *John*, 115. Step'annos of Siwnik', 131, also notes that sin may cause illness.

ii. **Font**: see commentary to v. 3, above; further interpretations of this episode are discussed in Mathews and Sanjian 1991 (151–52).

[5:15–16] **The man went and told the Jews that it was Jesus who healed *me. Therefore the Jews persecuted Jesus, because he did that on the Sabbath.**[16]

Let no one suppose that through some calumny[17] the man said that to the Jews in order to betray him, but it was a demonstration of great love, as if he wished to explain the blessings and miracles to them, who had not asked him that question but about the bed as to who commanded [him] to lift it up. But he left aside the matter of the bed and talked about the healing in order to reprimand them. Some of the commentators[i] said that what he did is the same as Matthew related, but that is not at all appropriate, because [Matthew] has the one he healed in Capernaum come before him with his bed, whereas this was in Jerusalem near to Siloam. Furthermore, this took place at Passover on the day of the Sabbath, whereas the former was not at Passover nor on the Sabbath day. And behold, he ordered this one to take up his bed, and after a few

---

14. The Lord: om. N.

15. **Is silent**, *lṙē*, M: "listens," *lsē*, N.

16. **Me…Sabbath**: om. M.

17. **Calumny**, *čaraxawsut'iwn*, M: "wickedness," *čarut'iwn*, N.

days he met him [104] in the temple and said, *Behold, you have been restored to health, but sin no more*, whereas nothing similar is ever related concerning the former.[ii]

See also that he always conducted his teaching through miracles in order to assist them; for when he was about to teach them something in order to demonstrate that he was God incarnate[iii] and not a mere man, he did not utter any strange and elevated things about himself in apparent fraud like many deceivers, of whom he said: *Those who came before me were thieves and robbers* (John 10:8); but he worked astonishing and amazing signs and then afterward introduced his instruction, so that his teachings might be trustworthy through the miracles. First he expounded his teachings, and then next set down the signs, so that as the teachings might be verified through the signs, in the same way through his teachings the miracles might be confirmed.

Let us make what has been said very clear to you listeners.[18] See what he did when he wished to teach about his body: *I am the bread[iv] that came down from heaven* (John 6:41, 58). First he showed signs by the five loaves and two fishes, satisfying the five thousand, disregarding the remnants after they were sated with food (Matt 14:15–21; Mark 6:35–44; Luke 9:12–17); then he taught: *I am the bread of life that came down from heaven*. In addition, there was an occasion when first he set out his teachings, as we said above, and then introduced the miracles, as when he said, *Before Abraham came into being, I am* (John 8:58; 9:1–7), and then cured the blind one, who did not have his blindness by some chance or accident but from the very womb. Therefore he made clay[v] and applied it as plaster to his eyes, demonstrating *the lack in nature, for which reason he filled it[19] from the original matter of which Adam was created; and thereby he confirmed what he had said, *Before Abraham came into being, I am*, so as to show that he was the creator of Adam.

So here, when first he [105] revealed[20] wonders, and the Jews contrived an excuse on the pretext of the Sabbath in order to disparage the power of the signs, he consequently taught few words, whereby he indicated his complete divinity. See what he said: Like the Father, who forbade you[21] from working on the Sabbath day (Deut 5:12–14; Jer 17:21; etc.), he himself is always working, whereby he provides for the race of mankind; likewise I too.

---

18. **You listeners,** *lsawłac'd* (voc.), M: "those listening," *lsawłac'n*, N.

19. **The lack … it:** "that he fills this lack in nature," N.

20. **Revealed,** *erewec'oyc'*, M: "demonstrated," *ec'oyc'*, N.

21. **You,** N: "us," M.

i. **Commentators:** *t'argmanič'k'* (lit. "interpreters"); see the introduction, xxviii–xxix, for this term used by Nonnus to refer to his sources. Tat'ewac'i (passim) refers to Nanay (Nonnus) as *meknič'*; cf. *meknut'iwn*, "commentary, explanation."

ii. See Matt 9:1–8, and Mark 2:1–12, where Capernaum is specifically mentioned. John Chrysostom, *Hom. Jo.* 37.1, states that "some," *tines*, think the two episodes are identical, but he gives a long explanation of the differences.

iii. **Incarnate:** *mardac'eal*, "made man." For the terminology, see the introduction, xxxvii.

iv. **Bread:** "bread of life" in M; see John 6:35, 48.

v. **Clay:** *kaw*, but *hoł* in Gen 2:7. For the link between this episode and creation, see Mathews and Sanjian 1991 (151–52).

[5:17] *And Jesus responded and said:[22] My Father is working until now, and I work.

Did you understand what I said,[23] or should we repeat it? Just as the Father, he said, forbade you to do any work on the day[24] of the Sabbath, yet he himself works and provides for creatures, because he makes the sun rise over the earth also on the Sabbath,[25] and the moon and the stars, and he scatters the winds and makes the rivers run, he causes the fountains to flow and the winds to blow, he makes the rains fall and the plants to blossom and grow, and he nourishes the fruits, feeds living things,[i] fashions bodies in the womb and joins souls [to them] and makes them increase.[ii] In the same fashion too I have authority on the Sabbath to provide for the race of mankind and to heal them from their diseases.

i. **Living things:** *šnč'awors* (lit. those with *šunč'*, "breath" or "soul"). In the following phrase "soul" renders *hogi*.

ii. A similar list of activities on the Sabbath is found in most commentators: John Chrysostom, *Hom. Jo.* 38.2; Moše bar Kepha; Dionysius bar Salibi, *John*, 117–18; Išodad; and more briefly, Cyril of Alexandria. The *Commentary on the Diatessaron* lists angels, luminaries, rivers, rain, and dew.

---

22. **And Jesus … said:** om. M.

23. **I said,** *asac'is*, M: *asac'in*, N (not "they said"; the *-s* and *-n* are the required demonstratives following the relative pronoun).

24. **Day:** pl. M.

25. **Sabbath:** pl. M.

[5:18] Therefore the Jews[26] sought all the more to kill him, because not only did he destroy the Sabbaths, but he also[27] called God his Father and made himself equal to God.

These among the Jews did not understand in accordance with the calumnies of others about the Lord that he made himself equal with God, but the Savior himself testified about himself, *I in the Father and the Father in me* (John 14:10), and *I and my[28] Father are one* (John 10:30). Likewise too are the sayings about the Sabbaths in accordance with the frequent[29] healings that occurred on them. For if the Jews had said these things differently, the evangelist would have explained their meaning, as he made clear elsewhere. As when the Savior said, *Destroy this temple, and in three days I shall raise it up,* **[106]** which they thought concerned their own temple. But the evangelist explained the meaning of this saying: *Christ was speaking about the temple of his own body* (John 2:19, 21), and not as the Jews supposed.

Luke demonstrates likewise when the Lord[30] commanded to beware of the leaven of the Pharisees, the meaning of which they understood literally but which Luke explained, as is very clear.[i] Why, then, did we introduce this, save for some other significant need? For if the Jews, being hostile to the Savior, yet in the[31] Savior's words thought him equal to the Father and did not consider there to be any difference regarding the natures, although they denied his nature yet they did not divide him into two—what would we say to such foolish and mentally blind people who call themselves Christians yet divide the one Christ into two,[ii] especially as they do not look wisely on the miracles that he did on the Sabbath? For to spit on the ground and fashion clay with his life-bringing hands (John 9:6) are clearly both to be understood of the body. But the working of miracles through that same body indicates his essence and equality, by his saying: *My Father works until now, and I work.* Surely they do not deny the spit and the hand of the body alone to be what cured the blind man, or his speaking to the condition of equality? How are these to be verified if the body is separate and distinct from the Word, and corruptible and unmingled, and the specific operations of the body according to their understanding are to be ascribed[32] to the Word, and he is to be drawn

---

26. **The Jews**, MZ: "they," N.

27. **Also**, MZ: om. N.

28. **My**: om. N.

29. **Frequent**, *bazum angam*, M: "many," *bazum*, N.

30. **The Lord**, M: "of the Lord," N (*sic*).

31. **Savior, yet in the**: om. N.

32. **Ascribed**, *hramayel*, M: "reckoned," *hamarel*, N.

to equality with the Father? Let them be ashamed at the unintelligent words they babble. Perhaps they would be put to shame by his enemies, who sought to kill him for the reason that he made himself equal to God, and they did not adduce any explanation of the division and distinction according to the flesh.

But let us return to their reason that is even weaker than a spider's web, which they pronounce in a different argument. [107] His saying *My*[33] *Father works until now, and I work*, they[34] claim he declared of his divine nature.[iii] But the saying *The Son cannot do anything of himself unless he sees the Father doing it* (John 5:19) *he pronounced regarding his weak human nature.[35] So then, the latter being opposed to the former, it indicates and reveals the two natures. If that were not the case, they say, how would it be appropriate to say regarding the divine nature that he cannot of himself act, unless he were to see the Father acting? Let us say this to them, that the Son did not say he could not act of himself unless he were to see the Father acting. If he is the only begotten Son from the Father before ages, what they suppose is false, that he said that regarding the human nature. But if the one born from Mary, by distinction the son of man, is the speaker of these things, not only are there two[36] natures in Christ, but two distinct and separate sons. So let us abandon their foolish suppositions full of falsehood and implausibility,[37] and let us bestir ourselves to the task ahead, which confirms even more the orthodox testimonies.[iv]

i. Luke 12:1: it is "hypocrisy," *kełcaworut'iwn'*; cf. Matt 16:6; Mark 8:15.

ii. In his commentary to John 8:57, Nonnus names the "dyophysites" (*erkabnakk'*); see the introduction, xli. Here Tat'ewac'i, 232, explicitly refers to Chalcedonians and Nestorians.

iii. Here Cyril of Alexandria, *Comm. Jo.* 2.6, emphasizes the identity of the essence (*tautotēs tēs ousias*) of the Son and Father.

iv. The grammar of the last two paragraphs is unclear, and the argument obscure.

[5:19] Jesus replied and said to them: Amen, amen, I say to you, the son of man could not do anything of himself, unless he were to see the Father doing it.

Because he earlier said, *What the Father works, I also work*,[i] and therefore they sought to kill him[38] because he made himself equal to God and destroyed

---

33. **My:** om. M.

34. **They:** sg. N.

35. **He pronounced … nature:** "regarding his human weakness," N.

36. **Two,** M: om. N (added by editor).

37. **And implausibility:** om. N.

38. **Him:** om. N.

the Sabbaths, for that reason he quenched somewhat their heat and condescended with a humbler expression than before, although its meaning is not far from the former.[39] [108] How does the latter cause the more perfect to stumble? Surely the Son was not unable to do anything except what he saw the Father doing previously? Did he cure the paralytic for the reason that he saw at that time the Father also healing some paralytic (Matt 9:2)? Or did he turn the water into wine in Galilee at the very time when the Father did something similar (John 2:1–11)? Also when he joined in and slept at feasts and parties, and innumerable other such occasions, did he see the Father also indulging in all the same activities, and for that reason did so himself? And where would they place his saying about power: *I have the power to lay down my life, and I have the power to take it up again* (John 10:17–18)? Or his saying: *I departed from the Father and came to the world*; and again:[40] *I shall abandon this world and go to the Father* (John 16:28)?

O foolish ones! How is the Son not able to do anything of himself? Do not the angels and demons and nations of mankind, having freewill, do what they wish and turn away from what they do not like? So the angels of their own volition remained always in their majestic stations and in glory, while Satan of his own free will rebelled, and falling down below became darkness. Likewise Adam, not by force but by his independent will, transgressed the commandment. How is the Son unable to do anything by himself? This is sufficient to reprehend those who calumniate the Son by attributing weakness to him.

Let them be ashamed and shut their mouths regarding his saying, *Whatever the Father works, I work also* (John 5:19), and *As the Father raises up and makes alive, so also the Son* (5:21). So then these are sayings of dispensation for the needs of the occasion and not of weakness. I must also mention other examples of inability, for not with a literal meaning can one understand the saying. As when he said: [109] *A city cannot be hidden that stands on a hill* (Matt 5:14).[ii] He said this not of some weakness but of the impossibility because of its size. Nor can bridal attendants fast, because of its unsuitability (Mark 2:19; Luke 5:34). Nor can a cub fight with a lion, because of its weakness. And there are many other such [examples]. But for us let these be sufficient.

i. A repetition of v. 17 with a direct object.

ii. This example is also found in Dionysius bar Salibi, *John*, 120, and in a list of impossibilities in Išodad.

---

39. **Former:** sg. N, pl. M.
40. **And again:** om. N.

[5:20] The Father loves the Son and shows him everything that he himself does. And he will show him even greater works than these[41] at which you marvel.

These are words of no small service. Just as when he said, *My Father works until now, and I work,* and the Jews were so vexed that they wished to kill him, so he put this down next, *The Son is not able to do [anything] of himself,* and thereby calmed their passion; the same one can also see here, because first he said: What the Father does, the Son works the same like him. And this is not at all different from the former statement, when he made himself equal to the Father, but is very comparable to it. Therefore in the same fashion he again condescends a little and says: *The Father loves the Son and shows him everything.*[i] The saying is clear from the third word,[ii] because again he draws the argument to the same sublime significance. *As the Father raises the dead and makes them alive, likewise the Son makes alive whom he wishes.*[iii] These words do not indicate anything such as that he needed continually to look and learn and then act. For if he worked nothing save only what he saw from the Father, he would have been no superior to his disciples, because he taught them some such thing: *When the Holy Spirit will come, he will teach you everything* (John 14:26; cf. Luke 12:12). So about this matter let this much be sufficient.

It behooves us also, when [110] we undertake to explain the meaning of our Savior's words individually and precisely,[iv] not to omit the reason[42] for his teaching and the meaning of the Sabbath. This is because when he healed the paralytic on the Sabbath and ordered him to take up his bed, for that reason they said a dissolution of the Sabbath was being created, because on it he ordered [him] to take up his bed, and the keeping of the divine commandment among the Jews was being destroyed; and[43] in their minds they always bore an excuse that he was opposed to God. Consequently, when they saw such a marvelous sign they should have considered something different: that it was not an opponent of God who was doing such things but God. And if Christ spoke truly, as we continually read from our scriptures, if he were against God and an opponent, God would never be for him a coworker; but indeed God was with him, as when Nicodemus so said and many others (John 3:2), when they saw such a thing.

---

41. **These,** MZ (and in commentary): "this," N.
42. **Reason:** pl. N.
43. **And:** om. N.

Therefore in this way the Savior arranged suitably and appropriately the operation of his signs, not as if by God's command such miracles were performed, but as a coworker of God and having equal power. For that reason we said above that when he was about to teach anything first he performed signs, and after teaching he multiplied the miracles so that the signs of his teaching might be a witness that he was not opposed to God. Therefore he said, *The Son cannot do anything of himself, unless he sees the Father doing it*, and *The Father loves the Son and shows him everything that he does himself.* And if the Father shows him everything that he himself does, then by annulling the Sabbaths he is not opposed to God.

Let us also see what he said: *Even greater works than these he will show him, at which you marvel.*^v [111] What, then, would this be? It means he will demonstrate that you are about to see further great miracles and signs, much superior to the one at which you now marvel involving the paralytic and of his power to lift up the bed and annul the Sabbath.[44]

 i. The editor prints this reprise of the first part of the lemma as a separate lemma.
 ii. **Third word**: The Father/loves/*the Son.*
 iii. Nonnus refers to v. 21, the following lemma.
 iv. **Precisely**: *očov*, or "methodically."
 v. The editor prints this reprise of the lemma as a separate lemma.

[5:21] **For as the Father raises the dead and makes them alive, likewise the Son makes alive whom he wishes.**

Because he first said that he would show works even greater than these, he then next[45] sets out the meaning of the saying, which is much more glorious than the healing of the paralytic at which they marveled. And what is that? To raise the dead, whom he might wish. For if the sayings are true and clear in their understanding, that *the Son cannot do anything of himself*, just as the dim-witted supposed, how then did he say: *As the Father raises the dead and makes them alive, likewise the Son whom he wishes*?

[5:22] **And the Father does not judge anyone, but he gave all judgment to his Son.**

Did you see what he said, that *he would show him greater works than these*? And because he first spoke about the resurrection, that *he would raise*

---

44. **Sabbath**: pl. N.
45. **Next**: om. N.

the dead, he then set down the judgment that occurs after the resurrection, showing that the judgment too is his and not the Father's. For the Son is judge, although there is one will,[i] so that he might make them more versed in the understanding of providence and the dispensation, by the humbler things removing the suspicions of opposition, and by the higher to make known the condition of his authoritative power. But what is: *The Father does not judge anyone?* The saying deserves strict examination. It is as if to say, being invisible by nature,[ii] because of not having a body, [112] as he said, *No one has seen God* (John 1:18), and *God is spirit* (4:24), so then it is necessary that the one who judges bodily beings definitely be visible to bodily beings.

I have a further reason[46] to expound, in no way dishonorable. Since he himself was humbled to earth, he endured in himself such humility for the sake of our salvation that he dwelled for nine months in the womb and was suckled, and endured every condition[iii] except sin, and demonstrated his teachings and innumerable signs and healings; he also endured torments and death for the sake of giving us life. So the same one undoubtedly judges his deniers and enemies and those who do not heed[47] the preaching of his gospel. For they cannot there fabricate some excuse against him and pretend, as he said, *Unless I had come and spoken with them they would have had no sin* (John 15:22), but now they have nothing to say on the day of judgment.

i. The equality of Son and Father is here stressed by John Chrysostom, *Hom. Jo.* 39.1, and Cyril of Alexandria, *Comm. Jo.* 2.8. Tat'ewac'i, 237, refers to a single activity (*mi nergorcut'iwn*).

ii. As emphasized by Theodore of Mopsuestia, 82, 83.

iii. **Condition:** *kirk'*; see the introduction, xxxviii.

[5:23] So that all may honor the Son, as they honor the Father. Whoever does not honor the Son does not honor the Father, his creator.

See what he taught very gently for their profit and assistance. For if he is the same who will raise the dead and judge the nations of mankind, then they must honor him as they honor the Father. And if he is equal in honor to the Father,[i] why do you always in opposition falsify the truth and remove his power[48] and deny the signs of equality, and even seek to kill him? For if the Father sent me, then I am not opposed to him for annulling the Sabbaths, as you suppose.

---

46. **Reason:** pl. M.

47. **Heed:** "follow," N.

48. **Power:** pl. M.

i. Equality of honor (*to homotimon*) is stressed by John Chrysostom, *Hom. Jo.* 39.1, and Theodore of Mopsuestia. Moše bar Kepha refers to one will, one power, one activity.

[5:24] **Amen, amen, I say to you, that whoever hears my word and believes in the one who sent me receives life everlasting. And he does not enter into judgment but was removed from death to life.**[49]

Mark for me here this saying,[50] how [113] he removes their supposition in that they continually said he was opposed [to the Father]: *Whoever hears my word and*[51] *believes in the one who sent me.* And what is this: *He honors me who hears my word?*[i] By hearing, he means to receive with faith and not simply listening. And what is my word that I demand from you? To hear and believe in him who sent me. Not as you suppose by turning you away from the Father. To believe in him is nothing other than [to believe] in speakers of ordinary things.[ii] Did you not hear when I[52] said: *As they honor the Father, likewise they may honor the Son?* Now, what is that? If anyone believes in him, he will not enter into judgment,[53] because he believed in the Son of God. So he is separated from the judgment of the deniers, those who are examined according to their faith. But these enter into judgment only according to their deeds and manner of life, and if there is any righteousness in them equal to their faith, then they will receive very great gifts of compensation.[54]

i. Based on vv. 23–24.
ii. **Speakers of ordinary things:** the meaning of *yasawɫs hasarakac'* is not clear.

[5:25] **Amen, amen, I say to you, that the time is coming and indeed now is, when the dead shall hear the voice of the Son of God, and those who hear shall live.**

Because he previously said, *As the Father raises and makes alive, likewise also the Son*[55] *makes alive whom he wishes,* and these words without the testimony of any events occurring did not seem true to those listening, and the Jews entertained no little disbelief, therefore he said, *The time is coming.* He

---

49. Taťewac'i omits vv. 24–30.

50. **This saying,** *zbans:* om. N.

51. **Word and:** "words," M.

52. **I:** "he," N.

53. **Judgment:** + "he means judgment concerning the faith, into that he will not enter," M.

54. **Of compensation:** "and compensation," M.

55. **Son:** + "raises and," M.

referred to the resurrection when the dead will rise. And because the resurrection will occur in a future time, he then verified the potency of his own authority and power that he had expounded, which after a short time he was to operate, by saying, *It now is*, which he[56] said is to raise those I wish from the dead. And what is this? It is as if to say that when [114] you will see me raising[57] the dead—not through supplications but with a voice and authoritative command, as he summoned Lazarus from the tomb (John 11:43),[58] and [he said], *I say to you, girl, arise* (Mark 5:41),[i] and many[59] other such [occasions]—then you will realize and know that the same voice and power will raise from the tombs and vivify all nations of mankind.

i. Here John Chrysostom, *Hom. Jo.* 39.3; Theodore of Mopsuestia, 84; Cyril of Alexandria, *Comm. Jo.* 2.8; and Moše bar Kepha all give the example of Lazarus but not that of the girl.

[5:26–27a] **For as the Father has life in himself, likewise he gave also to the Son to have life in himself. And he gave him authority to make judgment.**

Because he had told them that he himself was the one who raises[60] the dead from their tombs on the day of resurrection, he gave them another sign to confirm the sayings, and lest they be any further troubled so as to say in their minds, Although now he raises the dead, yet that is[61] no indication regarding the resurrection that he will do something similar then; for Elias and his disciple did such things, but at the resurrection those who will be in tombs cannot be causes of resurrection—therefore he said: *Just as the Father has life in himself, likewise he gave also to the Son to have life in himself.* That is, not by grace does he have some acquired powers of signs concerning resurrection, as you comparably think about Elias and some others, who had acquired that [power] as a reward of their virtue; but *as the Father has life in himself,* that is, to do that by nature, likewise he gave also to the Son to have it.

Do not be amazed at his giving, because he did these things for the sake of removing the opposition, as they always said he was opposed to God. Therefore he declares that he works the miracles by the Father, not in accordance with a command but by agreement. For on one occasion he says he received,

---

56. **He:** "they," M.

57. **You will see me raising:** "I raise," N.

58. **Tomb:** pl. M.

59. **Many:** om. N.

60. **Raises:** + *i*, N (*sic*).

61. **Is:** "will be," N.

and on another he acted by himself, as when he said: *As the Father raises and makes alive, likewise* [115] *the Son too.*[62] In this way you should understand that he gave him authority to make judgment.

[5:27b–29a] **And because he is son of man, why do you marvel at that? For the time will come in which all who will be in tombs will hear his voice, and they will come forth.**

Because the Jews and those like them from the among the Gentiles and other nations were offended at our Savior for the fact that he submitted to bodily humiliations, when they heard such words they seemed to them very astonishing and terrible. Although they were words of dispensation,[i] yet the sayings were not appropriate save to God alone. Therefore the Savior said: *Because he is son of man, why do you marvel at that?* As if to say, do not be offended at that or let the sayings[63] seem difficult to you, since you see me in the humble condition of humanity. For *there will come a time that all who will be*[64] *in tombs*, through the one whom you call *son of man will come forth* from their tombs, and at that time you will recognize me to be[65] God and the Son of God. For not as now, when you are thick-minded and suppose me to be a mere man, will you be offended at these sayings.

 i. **Dispensation:** *matakararut'iwn* (lit. "service, economy"); see the introduction, xxxvii.

[5:29b] **Those who have done good things, to the resurrection of life; and those who have done wicked things, to the resurrection of judgments.**

Because a little earlier he had said, *Whoever hears*[66] *my words and believes in the one who sent me receives life everlasting and does not enter into judgment,* he then reveals the details of the task concerning the faith, and that through him on the day of judgment there will be compensations of gifts and punishments.

---

62. **The Father:** "he," N. **The Son too:** om. N. The editor adds: "The Son too makes alive whom he wishes." Cf. v. 21 above.

63. **The sayings:** om. N.

64. **Will be,** *ic̔en,* N (but lemma, *kayc̔en*): "are," *en,* M.

65. **Me to be:** om. N.

66. **Hears:** "will hear," N.

[5:30a] **I cannot do anything by myself, but as I hear, I judge; and my judgment is just.**

See how he always conducts his teaching according to necessity and appropriateness. [**116**] First he said, *The Father judges no one*, and ascribed to himself the retributions of judgment, at which the Jews were much vexed; for the prophets stated judgment to belong to God,[i] and they did not confess the Son as God but the Father only. Therefore he again condescends for them and says, *The Son*[67] *cannot make judgment by himself, but as I hear, I judge*, indicating that that belongs to the Father, in order to remove their wicked error. And he shows that his will and that of the Father are one; and the same is an allegory[ii] of the equality of the nature and authority,[iii] which the following also reveals.

> i. Deut 32:35, and many parallels, some quoted by Tat'ewac'i, 238.
> ii. **Allegory**: *tarac'oyc'*.
> iii. Theodore of Mopsuestia also refers here to the equality of Son and Father.

[5:30b] **For I seek not my will but the will of the one who sent me.**

Because he spoke previously about himself, *My judgment is just, for as I hear from the Father, so I judge*, just as he said, *As I hear I judge*, therefore he said, *I seek not my will but the will of the one who sent me*. By that he reprimanded their presumption, as if to say: I do not judge in judgment[68] according to my will, and I shall work no other deeds save by the will of the Father who sent me. So then, what I did on the Sabbath day, at which you are so angered, I did not do of myself against God, as you suppose, but by the Father's will. By these [words] he condemns the reason for their wicked error, that they wished in this way always to contrive and invent. But he did not make it clear that his will is one thing, and another that of the Father,[i] but so that he might totally confirm their united will in order to predict for them the equality of their nature and power.

> i. Moše bar Kepha emphasizes the distinction.

---

67. **The Son**: om. N.
68. **In judgment**: "judgment" (acc.), N.

[117] [5:31] If I bear witness about myself, my testimony is not true.

When he said, *It is the same who will raise the dead and who judges after raising them*, and *Whoever hears his word*[69] *and receives does not enter into judgment*, and *His judgment is true*, and other such things, which, although he attributed the cause to the Father, yet seemed among the Jews to be very horrifying and amazing, and also not acceptable as being above the one who uttered them—for that reason the thoughts in their minds remained restless and agitated. Hence they planned nothing less than to lay hands on him, being vexed at his always saying such extreme things about himself. Such wondrous sayings were appropriate to none from among mankind, not even for a king or powerful ruler to say what he pleased. Therefore the Savior said: *If I bear witness about myself, my testimony is not true.* That is, in that you think in disbelief, neither following any signs nor being attentive to [his] teaching, therefore he arranged three testimonies to reprove their stubbornness: the miracles of the signs; the saying by the Father, *This is my beloved Son*; the frequent testimonies from John.[i] And first he set down that of John concerning him, the beginning of his testimonies, and said:

i. The same three testimonies are cited by John Chrysostom, *Hom. Jo.* 40.1, and in a different order by Moše bar Kepha, and Dionysius bar Salibi, *John*, 130. Tat'ewac'i, 239–40, adds a fourth: the prophets.

[5:32] There is another who bears witness concerning me, and you know that[70] his[71] testimony that he testified about me is true.

What is: *His testimony is true*? He means the testimony of John. And because he previously said, *If I bear witness about myself,*[72] *my testimony is not true*, therefore he introduced[73] John, in whom they had so much faith that they were continually [118] going to him and considered him to be a famous and notable man.

---

69. **Word**, N: "words," M.
70. **That**, *etē*, NZ: "only," *ewet'*, M.
71. **His**, NM: "the," Z.
72. **About myself**: om. M.
73. **Introduced**, *yaṙaǰ berē*, VM: "puts next," *yaǰordē*, N.

[5:33] **You sent to John, and he bore witness to the truth.**

What means: *You sent to John*? Did he not earlier depose testimony concerning me? Perhaps thereby you fabricated some excuses. Furthermore, you did not ask about me when you sent [to him] but about himself: *If you are the Christ, tell us.*[i] Now, if he seems reliable to you, as you once indicated, you must believe what you asked about. For if he had indeed testified about himself, although to you it seemed little appropriate to entertain those thoughts, yet now you must believe in the man's truthfulness. But if he did not testify about himself, but he attributed the testimony[74] to someone else, without any compulsion, why do you not believe?

i. This precise question was posed to Jesus: Luke 22:67; John 10:24. John declared, "I am not the Christ" (John 1:20; 3:28; cf. Luke 3:15).

[5:34a] **But I do not receive testimony from mankind.**

In order to show the superiority of his nature, although John bore witness about me, yet for that I have no need. And lest they say about that, Why did you recall the man's testimony, yet you have no need of it? he said:

[5:34b] **I say this so that you may be saved.**

That man was a great prophet among you, he said, and very trustworthy; therefore you were baptized by him, and you followed [him] into deserts and [other] places, and his testimony was [accepted] as true among you. For that reason I mentioned him. Perhaps believing through that, you will be saved from judgment. Not because of my having any need was I concerned to recall his testimony.

[5:35] **He was the lamp that was lit and shining, and you wished for a time to rejoice in his light.**

[**119**] This passage is allegorical and contains no insignificant reprimand[75] of them. First he said, *I do not receive testimony*[76] *from mankind,*

---

74. **Testimony:** pl. M.
75. **Reprimand:** pl. M.
76. **Testimony** (*vkayut'iwn*, v. 34a): *vkayut'iwns*, NM, either plural, or possessive suffix, "my testimony."

indicating[77] John, therefore the measure of the honor that belongs to John he set down with an allegorical expression. And what he said is true,[78] that he has no need of testimony from mankind. And what means: *He was the lamp that was lit and shining*? It is as if to say that as a lamp is needed at the evening hour[79] because of the gloomy shadow, but when the sun shines, then it is not able to show the weak rays of its light, and there will be no further need of it.[i] You must understand some such disproportion between myself and John. So then what I said above was true, that I had no need for his testimony about myself. Because you saw so many signs and miracles done by me, thereby you would have known him to be much less significant in comparison with me, as a lamp compared to the sun. For John in his own time when he was baptizing and teaching[80] was a light, and his testimonies concerning me shone out like a lamp in your darkened minds. But now has arrived [the time of] my divine signs and miracles, in comparison with which those worked by John are less, to which applies the example of a lamp compared to the sun. And if this is so, then I have no need for his testimonies, just as the sun does not require a lamp for testimony concerning its illumination.

Furthermore, with a different example he called John by the name of a lamp, in order to show that just as a lamp does not have light united with itself by nature *but acquires it from fire,[81] so also John did not possess by nature what he performed, but by gifts of supernal grace. Now the sun always has its light by nature, [120] united to it indissolubly and inseparably, and perpetually shining it fills all creation with light through its rays. But let us not omit what he said: *You wished to rejoice for a time in his light*. These were words of great mocking and contempt for them, as if to say that you thought John a great prophet, and I called him light, yet you did not receive him for more than a short time. But later through envy, him too you hated.

i. The same simile is found in Theodore of Mopsuestia, 88; Dionysius bar Salibi, *John*, 130; and Taťewacʻi, 242. Stepʻannos of Siwnikʻ, 133, notes: "Christ is light, but John said a lamp."

---

77. **Indicating**, M^corrN: "witnessing," M.
78. **What he said is true**, N: "he verified what he said," M.
79. **Hour**: "time," N.
80. **And teaching**: om. N.
81. **But acquires … fire**: om. N.

[5:36] **But I have a testimony greater than that of John; the deeds that the Father gave me[82] to carry out, these same deeds will bear witness concerning me, that the Father sent me.**

See how completely he set out the truth and tried to correct their lack of belief. John, he said, through words applied his testimonies to me, which you are able to contradict, as you indeed are intending. But what means will you find [to deny] the deeds, the signs and miracles that you saw, like what you saw happen to the paralytic? There is no way to deny these or contradict them, because deeds are publicly visible and are not words briefly expressed[83] in the hearing of some and then dissolved.[i] Now, what means: *The Father sent me*? It is as if to say that the deeds and miracles will be witnesses that I am not opposed to the Father, as you say, but the Father sent me.

i. For the transient nature of a word, see commentary to John 1:1, at n. xi.

[5:37a] **And the Father who sent me, he testified concerning me.**

He set down another firm prediction for their correction, that [the testimony] concerning the signs and working of miracles is superior to the witness of John: *And the Father also testified.* When would that be? In the presence of all of you, he said, he testified concerning me. When I was baptized in the Jordan [121] a loud voice sounded from the heights in the hearing of you all: *This is my beloved Son, in whom I am pleased* (Matt 3:17; Mark 1:11; Luke 3:22). This is the third testimony that we once said that he arranged,[i] when they did not believe in him when he declared such sublime things about himself.

i. Moše bar Kepha refers to these three testimonies, for which see the commentary to v. 31, above.

[5:37b] **You did not hear his voice, nor did you see his appearance.**

It is necessary for you to be satisfied with these testimonies and not to have any need of further testimonies[84] in order to strengthen your tottering minds and thoughts, and to believe without doubt in me that I am the Son of God truly by nature, and not by grace, for *you never heard his voice, nor did*

---

82. **Me,** *zis,* NZ: "to me," *inj,* M.
83. **Expressed:** *kočecʿealkʿ,* N; *hnčecʿealkʿ,* M.
84. **Testimonies:** sg. M.

you see his appearance. As at the Jordan he says that you heard his voice when he testified concerning me, *This is my beloved son,* you also saw his appearance when the Holy Spirit descended in the form of a dove and rested upon me, in confirmation of the same testimony, the like of which you have never or elsewhere heard or seen.

[5:38] **And you do not have his word dwelling in you, since you do not believe in the one whom he sent.**

See how totally he is concerned with their correction and proves and confirms the truth, so that perchance they may gain some profit and become better. If you heard his voice and saw his appearance, as I said above, and the predictions of the prophetic words about him you say are with you, why do you not sincerely possess the faith?

[5:39] **Examine the scriptures, because you reckon that through them you have eternal life; and they are the ones that testify about me.**

Very fine are these words and most worthy to be investigated. For first he sets down the testimonies of John, and then his own working of miracles, [122] and after that the Father's testimonies at his going down into the Jordan and the descent of the Holy Spirit. After all that he turns them to the holy scriptures. But he does not say, Read the scriptures, because they had often read them, but *Examine.*[i] And what means that? As for the scandal concerning me you have in yourselves, examine from scripture, because you will find frequent prophecies and examples[ii] that I am Savior and Son of God,[iii] and not opposed to God as you always proclaim.

   i. Moše bar Kepha also emphasizes this point.
   ii. **Examples:** *awrinaks*; see the introduction, xxxiii.
   iii. Tat'ewac'i, 248–49, cites numerous OT prophecies.

[5:40] **And you do not wish to come to me, so that you may have life.**

By this he reproves even more their impieties, as if to say: When you examine the scriptures you find many testimonies concerning me clearly expressed, and signs and examples, yet you do not believe in me—not because you do not find the testimonies, but because you do not wish to believe in me.

[5:41–42] I do not receive glory from mankind, but I know that you do not have the love of God in yourselves.

Not for the testimonies of John concerning me, and my miracles, and the testimony of the Father, and the descent of the Holy Spirit, and the testimonies that you will find from the scriptures when you examine them, not for that reason do I wish to receive glory from you, but so that I may inform you and reprove you; that not for the sake of loving God and his being guarantor or his law—as you seek excuses to contradict me and plot to kill me—but because the love of God is not in you, for that reason you remain stubborn in such wicked intentions.

[5:43] I came in the name of my Father, and you do not receive me. But if someone else were to come in his own name, him you would receive.

[123] This introduces even better the details of the reproof. Whence is this clear? From his saying, *I came in the name of my Father*, to indicate that he attributes the cause of all[85] the signs and teachings to the Father in order to quash the reason that you allege, my being opposed to the Father. But what means: *If anyone else were to come in his own name, him you would receive*? He means[86] the Antichrist, the *Ner̄n*, who pronounces himself God and does not attribute the cause to the Father like me.[i] These [sayings] furthermore testify that you do not have the love of God in you; for if you had in you the love of God, you would then assuredly love the one who said the Father was the cause of his miracles and signs and sent him into the world. Him you would receive, and in him you would believe, and you would hate and deny the one who intends to come in his own name.

i. The Armenian text reads: *derakr'istosn, Ner̄n. Ner̄n* is standard Armenian for "Antichrist," as at 1 John 2:18 (etc.). The calque *derak'ristos* (*der* = "in place of") is not found in the earliest Armenian texts; see the references in *NBHL*. Here John Chrysostom, *Hom. Jo.* 41.1, refers to the Antichrist, as do Theodore of Mopsuestia, Dionysius bar Salibi (*John*, 132), and Step'annos of Siwnik', but not Moše bar Kepha or Cyril of Alexandria. Tat'ewac'i, 251, does not mention the Antichrist but mentions Judas and Theudas, to whom Nonnus refers in his commentary to John 10:7–8, below.

---

85. **All:** om. M.
86. **He means:** om. N.

[5:44a] How are you[87] able to believe, since you take glory from each other?

For the following reason, he says, you do not believe in me or follow, because you love the world and delight in glory from mankind. But my instruction teaches[88] the opposite of that: separation from love of the world and pride of the glory in it.[i] Whereas you do not receive [me] because you reckon praise and glory from mankind more important than *what belongs to God*[89] *alone*.[ii]

> i. Moše bar Kepha presents a similar argument.
> ii. Nonnus omits v. 44b as a lemma but here echoes its theme.

[5:45] Do not think that I shall accuse you to the Father. Your accuser exists, Moses in whom you hoped.

Let us learn the meaning of this saying, beloved, how in every way he cuts off their vain hope and false excuses and takes so much effort upon himself for their correction. For this reason the Jews were vexed and plotted to lay hands on him and kill him,[90] reckoning themselves to be defenders[91] of Moses, so that they counted the Savior a subverter of the law of Moses and an opponent [124] and a destroyer of the Sabbath. Therefore he says, *Moses in whom you hoped*, thinking me an opponent of his [laws], he is the one who will accuse you. What does this mean? Moses, he says, wrote and commanded about me,[i] and if you were to examine his writings and wish to believe in me, that would be sufficient for you with regard to faith and correction. But out of your envy and wickedness, since you do not wish to believe in me nor do you comprehend the writings of Moses, therefore he, *in whom you hoped*, will be your accuser to the Father. For through his prophetic grace, right from the beginning he prophesied about you, which now you justify: *You will see your lives hanging from a tree, and you will not believe in your lives*.[ii]

> i. Here *Comm. Diat.* 13.11 and John Chrysostom, *Hom. Jo.* 41.2, refer to Deut 1–3.
> ii. Deut 28:66 (not Z).

---

87. **You**, *duk'*, NZ: om. M.
88. **Teaches**: fut. N.
89. **God**: om. M.
90. **And kill him**: om. N.
91. **Defenders**: sg. N.

[5:46–47] **For if you believed in Moses, then you would believe also in me, because he wrote about me. For if you do not believe in his writing,**[92] **how will you believe in my words?**

Do not be at all vexed in your mind at the Savior saying, *If you do not believe in his words,*[i] *how will you believe in my words?* Moses was certainly not[93] more worthy of being heard than he, or more reliable, or greater, but he condescended to these [words] for the Jews, as if to say: In whom you had such belief, on whom indeed you depend and through whom you reckon you have knowledge, and whose benefits you have always in your minds, and whom you also reckon as a very great and incomparable man—*if, then, you do not believe in his writings,* whom you hold in such honor and respect and without whom you do nothing, *how will you believe in my words,* whom you call a Samaritan (John 8:48) and son of Joseph (John 6:42) and even a madman[ii] (John 10:21)?

i. Note the change from the lemma.
ii. **Madman:** *diwahar.*

---

92. **Writing:** *groyn* (sg.), MN; *groc'n* (pl.), Z.
93. **Certainly not,** *oč' etē*, N: "if," *etē*, M.

[6:1–2] **After this Jesus went to the other side of the Sea of Galilee of Tiberias. And a great crowd followed him, [125] because they saw the miracles that he was performing on the sick.**

Why did the evangelist relate this, save to illustrate his going for the second time from Jerusalem to Galilee of Tiberias in order to perform there frequent signs and miracles; and because the going of such a multitude of people from Jerusalem was not for the sake of the faith and following the truth but merely to be amazed at the sight of the miracles? People are accustomed to rush when they hear that some novel[1] working of miracles occurs somewhere. But they did not follow [him] for the sake of faith or following the truth.

[6:3] **Jesus ascended a mountain and there sat with his disciples.**

These [words] were related by the evangelist in order to instruct us, showing the Savior ascending a mountain by himself with the disciples only, so that we too,[2] when we often exert ourselves for the correction of many, will consequently also be by ourselves and act zealously for the correction of ourselves and those very close to us.[i] For all the ministrations of the Savior were not for some need of his own but were carried out for our correction and salvation.[3]

    i. Moše bar Kepha here refers to seeking quiet and silence for prayer.

[6:4–7] **And the feast of the Jews was near. Jesus lifted up[4] his eyes and saw a great crowd coming to him. He[5] said to Philip: Whence shall we buy bread**

---

1. **Novel:** "of new form," *norajew*, N; "newly worked," *noragorc*, M.
2. **Too:** om. N.
3. **And salvation:** om. N.
4. **Lifted up:** *ambarj*, N; *barj*, M (*barj i ver*, Z).
5. **He:** + *na*, M.

so that these may eat? He said this, testing him,[6] **but he himself knew what he was going to do. Philip replied: Two hundred** dahekans **of bread would not be sufficient for them, even if each one were to take**[7] **a little.**

Why did the Omniscient[8] ask Philip this?[i] Perhaps for his correction, because he had great need for that. And it is clear from what he said later[9] to the Lord, *Show us the Father, and it will be enough for us* (John 14:8),[ii] because these were words of one estimating the Father higher than him. But what means what the evangelist said: [**126**] *He questioned Philip, testing him*? It was to show that he did not question Philip about that, namely, that he did not know what he would do next, but in order to advise him and awaken his mind to the power of the marvelous miracle[10] that he was about to perform.

Would you like me to show you an example of old similar to these sayings? See what he said to Moses: *What is that*[11] *in your hand*, before he made it[iii] a serpent (Exod 4:2).[iv] So the questions were asked not in ignorance but so that he would be even more amazed and terrified by the reference to the rod of Moses and throwing it to the ground when it would turn into the form of a snake. Likewise here too, first he asked the question, so that when Philip would say that two hundred *dahekans*[v] of bread would not suffice for such a multitude, he would be even more astonished and[12] believe in the divine miracles,[vi] when he would see such multitudes[13] fed to satiety from five barley loaves and two fishes.

   i. **Omniscient:** *amenagēt*; in the Armenian Bible only at 2 Macc 5:35.
   ii. Cyril of Alexandria, *Comm. Jo.* 3, indicates that Philip had greater need of instruction than the others; also Moše bar Kepha, and Dionysius bar Salibi, *John*, 134.
   iii. **He made it:** the text in N (*zaṙnel zna*) emphasizes "it"; that in M (*zaṙnel nora*), "he."
   iv. John Chrysostom, *Hom. Jo.* 40.1, and Moše bar Kepha cite the same example.
   v. *Dahekan* renders a variety of foreign terms for units of money (see Hübschmann 1897, 133).
   vi. Theodore of Mopsuestia also refers to the increase in Philip's faith.

---

   6. **Him,** NZ: "them," M.
   7. **Were to take:** sg. NZ, pl. M.
   8. **The Omniscient:** om. N.
   9. **Later:** om. N.
   10. **Miracle:** pl. N.
   11. **That:** *ayd*, MZ; om. N.
   12. **And:** om. N.
   13. **Multitudes:** "a multitude," N.

[6:8–9] One of his disciples, Andrew brother of Simon the Rock, said to him: There is here a youth who has five barley loaves and two fishes, but[14] what is that for so many people?

Andrew was certainly not ignorant that such little food would be of no help for such a multitude,[i] for he said, *What is that for such a multitude?*[ii] because he did not wish to hide anything from his teacher, since to hide those things would not be praiseworthy when the teacher asked. It was[15] a further sign of satiety, lest he not reveal his preparing them.[iii]

i. Nonnus does not comment on the numbers two and five, though in v. 13 he interprets twelve; see further the introduction, xxxiii–xxxiv. Cyril of Alexandria interprets the five loaves as the five books of Moses and the two fishes as the *apostolikon kai euangelikon kērygma*. Tat'ewac'i, 267, also refers to the five books of Moses and interprets the two as the prophetic and historical books of scripture. Dionysius bar Salibi recalls Elisha, who filled thousands; but 2 Kgdms 4:43 refers to one hundred feeding off twenty loaves!

ii. **A multitude**: note the change from the lemma.

iii. The meaning of the last sentence is unclear.

[6:10] Jesus said: Have the people sit down. And there was much grass in that place. And the people sat down, in number about five thousand.

Why before preparing the food did he order them to make them sit down? So that in creating previously among them confidence in the miracle that he was about to perform, **[127]** they might consequently realize in their minds that he was able to feed them. Therefore he made them sit down, although they knew that no one among the crowds possessed any food. And by waiting for the food, they might carry in themselves belief in the same, whereby they would be made worthy of grace. And by waiting again for the miracle, when it occurred he might appear more trustworthy and more reliable.[i]

i. Cyril of Alexandria, *Comm. Jo.* 3, points out that in Greek only men are numbered, the women and children not being counted; this follows "custom," *synētheia*. A similar statement is found in Moše bar Kepha. Tat'ewac'i, 259, says that it was a Hebrew custom to count only men, and he refers to the account of the miracle in Matt 14:21.

---

14. **But**, NZ: om. M.

15. **Was**, *ēr*, N: "appeared," *erewēr*, M.

[6:11] And Jesus took the bread and gave thanks, and he distributed it to those sitting; likewise from among the fishes, as much as they desired.

We must investigate the reasons[16] why, when he took the bread, here first he gave thanks and then distributed it. For we know that he often did even superior miracles to this, but he did not first pray: as when he rebuked the sea (Matt 8:26), or his healing the blind one (John 9), or saying to the paralytic, *Arise, take your bed, and go* (John 5:8). But [he did this] in order thereby to counsel the disciples and them all, before[17] approaching food to pray and give thanks, and then to taste.[i] I also have another reason to offer: because such a large crowd of Jews was nearby, it was in order to show and indicate by thanking the Father that he was not opposed to the Father, as they supposed, but was always of the same will and counsel.[ii] This was no small indication of their power being one.

i. That Jesus prayed here in order to instruct us to pray before eating is echoed in many commentators: John Chrysostom; Theodore of Mopsuestia; and Dionysius bar Salibi, *John,* 136. Tat'ewac'i, 261, quotes Chrysostom.
ii. Moše bar Kepha offers the same interpretation; see also Tat'ewac'i, 261.

[6:12–13] And when they were sated, he said to his disciples: Collect the remaining remnants, lest anything be lost. They collected them and filled twelve baskets of remnants from the five barley loaves that were left over from those who ate.

This was a second sign and wonder, that there were no more than twelve baskets and no less, but it accorded with the number of the disciples who had served the food.[i] Since they received it from his life-giving hands and distributed it to those sitting, therefore by the twelve baskets of remnants of food [128] it showed them also to be participating in his power. But if [you ask] why all the remnants were fragments, it was to show that from nowhere else was there a superfluity of bread that someone brought with him, or bought anywhere, but the five loaves that he himself broke up and[18] distributed, from them came the increase and abundance.[ii]

i. All commentators explain twelve in this manner: John Chrysostom, Cyril of Alexandria, Theodore of Mopsuestia, Moše bar Kepha, Dionysius bar Salibi, and Tat'ewac'i.

---

16. **Reasons:** sg. N.
17. **Before:** "first when," N.
18. **Broke up and:** om. N.

ii. Theodore of Mopsuestia, 95, states that the fragments illustrate that Christ performed this miracle not out of necessity, like prophets, but in accordance with his excellence of power.

[6:14] Now, when the people saw the signs that he performed, they said: This is the true prophet who was to come to the world.

See how much they reprove themselves on one occasion, and again on another they deny it. When for their profit they saw the signs, they did not hide what they knew. For unless they accurately knew from scripture that he[19] was to come, they would not have said that. And who would the prophet be, whom they mentioned separately from the other prophets, as Moses described: *God will raise up a prophet for you*[20]?[i] And why did he foretell only about the one, yet behold, there were many prophets to come after Moses? So he meant Christ, who was to teach even superior and more wonderful things.

But why does he call him by the name of a prophet? It was because of the unbelief and weak faith of the nation, so that perhaps through the name of the prophet[21] they would receive him according to custom and join him, and they would attain perfect knowledge from the signs and miracles. See what he makes clear through what follows: *Whoever does not heed that prophet will be destroyed from Israel,*[ii] just as happened to the crucifiers. After the ascension of the Savior the nation of the Jews was destroyed by the sword in Jerusalem through the Romans, more than three hundred thousand myriad ranks.[iii]

i. Deut 18:15, also cited by Tat'ewac'i, 266, without the addition in M.
ii. Not a direct quotation of Deut 18:19.
iii. Cyril of Alexandria refers to the Jews being removed from Jerusalem but gives no number. Tat'ewac'i, 266, refers to the attack on Jerusalem by Titus and Vespasian: they killed by the sword 360,000 and made 500,000 captive. Tat'ewac'i also refers to the end of the world and the apocalyptic story of Agadron; for which, see Sanjian 1966.

[6:15] When Jesus knew that they were about to come to seize him so that they might make him king, he went again to the mountain alone.

What means what he said, save that he might show that despite always having so many signs, they never believed in him? But when he had sated them, they wished to make [**129**] him[22] their king, for a testimony that they

19. **He:** "the Christ," M.
20. **You:** + "from among your brothers like myself; heed him," M.
21. **Of the prophet:** *margarēin*, N; "prophetic," *margarēakan*, M.
22. **Him:** om. N.

were only slaves to their stomachs and to ridiculous gluttony[i] but had no zeal
in themselves for the truth.

i. Moše bar Kepha here refers to their stomachs being full; cf. Phil 3:19.

[6:16–17] **And when it was evening, his disciples went down to the shore.
And entering a ship they went to the other side of the sea, to Capernaum.
And when it became dark, Jesus had not yet come to them.**

Concerning *When it had become dark, Jesus had not yet come to them*, it
seems to me appropriate to say that it was to indicate that up to then they were
awaiting his arrival; and when he did not come to them, they therefore went
into the ship and went to Capernaum, where they would join [him],[23] as if
they were hoping to meet him there, or that they would find him somewhere
near to Capernaum.[i]

i. John Chrysostom, *Hom. Jo.* 43.1, indicates that it was the disciples' decision to go to
Capernaum, which is echoed in Dionysius bar Salibi, and Tat'ewac'i, 270. Cyril of Alexandria, however, states that Jesus had commanded them to go.

[6:18–21] **And the sea was disturbed by the blowing of a violent wind. And
after they had traveled twenty-five or thirty stadia, they saw Jesus walking
on the sea and near to the ship, and they were greatly terrified. And he said
to them: It is I; do not fear. And they wished to receive him into the ship,[24]
and immediately the ship arrived at the land to which they were going.**

Some of the earlier [commentators] thought these [words] were what
Matthew related (Matt 14:24–34),[i] but they did not understand truly. Whence
is this clear? For there Peter asked him to command him to come to him,
but here the sea was agitated in confusion. Also here the Lord encouraged
them and said, *Do not fear*; but there he did not speak similarly.[25] So let us
review the miracles performed in this [account], not just a single one, but
a triple working of miracles in a single moment; and let us be amazed at his
inscrutable operation. The first,[26] is that he himself walked on the sea; [130]
the second, that the disturbance of the raging waves was suddenly calmed
in its fearful roaring; the third, that when he said, *Do not fear*, he brought

---

23. **They would join [him]:** "he would join [them]," M.
24. **Into the ship:** M = Z; om. N.
25. **Speak similarly:** "say the same," N.
26. **The first:** om. N (but printed by the editor in place of "and" in his manuscript).

them rapidly to the place to which they wished to go. To whom, then, does such working of miracles pertain, or who would be capable of such elevated powers, except the one and only Word God, the only begotten Son, the one equal in essence and glory to the Father?

i. John Chrysostom, *Hom. Jo.* 43.1, discusses the differences in Matthew's account. Moše bar Kepha and Dionysius bar Salibi also indicate that this was a different occasion. But Tatʿewacʿi, 271, states that it was the same occasion, although "some say" that it was different from Matthew's account.

[6:22] **The next day the people who were on the other side of the sea saw that there was no other ship there, except only the single one into which the disciples of Jesus had entered. And Jesus had not entered into that ship with his disciples, but only his disciples had gone.**

Who, then, were those people that were on the other side of the sea, except those whose hunger he had filled from the five loaves and two fishes? They had wished to seize him and make him their king, because that miracle was reckoned so pleasing to them that it could not be compared to the other signs. And why was that, except because they were servants and slaves to their stomachs,[i] and not seekers of the truth?

i. John Chrysostom, *Hom. Jo.* 43.1, emphasizes their desire for food. Dionysius bar Salibi, *John*, 139, also calls them "servants to the stomachs."

[6:23–25] **And when other ships came from Tiberias close to that place where they had eaten bread, and when the people saw that Jesus was not there, nor his disciples, they took the ships and came to Capernaum to seek out Jesus.[27] When they found him on the other side of the sea, they said to him: Rabbi, when did you come here?**

Note here, too,[28] their perfidious words, because they did indeed know that he had not entered the ship with them. Therefore the evangelist said, *The people saw that there was no other ship there, except only the single[29] one into which Jesus's disciples had entered*, whereas Jesus had not entered the ship with his disciples. This [131] they truly knew, yet asked: *Rabbi, when did you come here?* Why was that?[30] It was in accordance with their deceit and treachery. For

---

27. **Jesus**, M^corrNZ: "him," M.

28. **Too:** om. N.

29. **The single**, MZ: om. N.

30. **Why was that?:** om. M.

they had seen so many signs when he sated such a multitude on the mountain from such a small amount of food, yet he himself pardoned their denial. They did not ask how or why[31] he had come here, when behold, there was no other ship, but they hid that because it was the stuff of miracles to come to that city without a ship; so they asked him: *When did you come here?*

[6:26] **Jesus replied to them and said: Amen, amen, I say to you, you seek me, not that you saw any signs, but because you ate of the bread and were sated.**

To what purpose, then, did the Lord[32] give them this response? It was to show that I am not at all unaware why you have followed me now: not because of any faith in the signs, nor in order to request other signs now for confirmation in the faith. For if they had entertained such thoughts, they should have investigated that one alone, namely, how without sailing across the sea you reached this city. But they passed over any discussion of signs and miracles, and only asked: *When did you arrive here?*

[6:27a] **Go, work, not for perishable food, but [for] *the food that remains for eternal life,[33] which the son of man will give you.**

Because they were so pleased with the miracles that occurred from the bread and did not in any way pursue the spiritual advantages, therefore he reproved them, as if to say: Why do you always labor and toil for the desire of food that is corruptible and does not last at all, yet make no effort for spiritual and profitable and enduring nourishment, whereby your souls would be fattened and helped and delighted, and whose rewards would always remain indissoluble? But you [132] follow me only for the sake of bodily corruptible food. Consequently, change to other kinds of more advantageous[34] and longer-lasting food, and from now on work for that. Concerning it I have continually taught you and placed before you demonstrations of the miracles, so that you might believe in the truth. This is the food that the son of man will give you through faith—his body and blood.[i]

i. The body and blood are not specified in John Chrysostom's general description of spiritual food (*Hom. Jo.* 44), nor in Cyril of Alexandria's discussion of *mystikē* and *pneumatikē trophē*.

---

31. **How or why**, N: tr. M.
32. **The Lord**: om. N.
33. **The food…life**: om. M.
34. **More advantageous**, *awgtakaragoyn*, M: "advantage," *awgtakarut'iwn*, N.

[6:27b] **For God the Father sealed him.**

Do not think [he] is in any way damaged by these words, that he received later as a gift the sealing from the Father to be God.[i] Because he first said that the one whom you call the son of man, he it is who will grant you the spiritual food—by which he[35] prefigures the faith that was the cause for them of eternal life—such sayings seemed to them very extreme. Therefore according to his custom he moderated his saying a little, as if to say: Whom you call the son of man, him the Father in the hearing of all of you sealed as God. And when was that? When he testified at the Jordan: *This is my beloved Son* (Matt 3:17 par.). Not only did he call him specifically Son, lest you understand it according to grace, but he also added *beloved*. Thereby he indicated his essence and birth from himself. If he is coessential with the Father, then he is also equal; and if equal,[36] then in every way also God. This is the sealing, the revealing and making known to the world through his testimony.

i. In Armenian (unlike the Greek) the lemma is ambiguous: *zna hayr knkʻeacʻ astuac*; for "God" could agree with "Father" or be a predicate: "The Father sealed him as God." The commentators render the lemma as translated above. Theodore of Mopsuestia notes that Christ is often named God, and Cyril of Alexandria states that Christ was sealed as an *eikōn* of God the Father. Dionysius bar Salibi, *John*, 140, notes that the Father testified and confirmed that he is God, "whom you saw as a man"; cf. Nonnus just below.

[6:28] **They said to him:[37] What should we do so that we may work the works of God?**

See the deceitful treachery of their words: *What should we do so that we may work the works of God?* They did not ask that they might learn the works that pertain to God, but with cunning and deceit, as if they were waiting to acquire again from him a surfeit of food like they had seen [before]. For nothing other than this appeared desirable to them.

[133] [6:29] **Jesus replied[38] and said to them: This is the work of God, that you believe in the one who sent me.**

See how he gradually revealed the truth to them, condescending to their weakness. Because they asked, What is the work of God? he then revealed it to

---

35. **By which he**, *orov*, M: "which," *or*, N.
36. **And if equal**: om. N.
37. **To him**, MZ: om. N.
38. **Replied**, MZ: + "to them," N.

be belief in the one who sent him. Why did he not simply say, Believe in me, except that because they would not receive him, therefore he found a means in accordance with their impiety: Lest you think that faith arises from works, therefore he said that; because faith is different from works, just as works are different from faith. But because they asked only, *What is the work of God that we should do?* for that reason he clearly indicated that the work of God, by which you asked God would be pleased,[39] is the confession of faith. And if you were to make that [confession], the necessary works would follow from it.

[6:30] They said to him:[40] What signs[41] do you show,[42] so that we may see and believe? What are you doing?

So who are these who utter this calumny and seek pretexts? Do not suppose that they were only those who saw his signs but also those who ate the bread, who were sated and saw more than twelve baskets of remnants of the fragments from five barley loaves and two fishes. What worse denial and impiety than that could there be, when rapidly denying such wonderful signs they forgot them, as if they had never seen them? Rightly did we say earlier that they were questioning the Savior about this, *What is the work of God*, not in order to learn and do it but only out of treachery and deceit.

[134] [6:31] Our fathers ate the manna in the desert, as it is also written: He gave them the bread of heaven to eat.[43]

One must be amazed at their foolish impiety and veiled wickedness. They did not say, God or Moses fed our fathers with manna in the desert,[i] but, *What are you doing?* lest they implicate him in some honor thereby. And, *Our fathers ate the manna in the desert*, so that thereby they might greatly disparage the blessings of the bread and of the miracles,[ii] not making the bread at all comparable to the manna, as if in that way they might all the more anger and provoke him to the continual miraculous working of such food[44] for them. They paid not the slightest attention to his responses to their asking, *What signs do you do?* lest by his recalling the signs of the bread he reprove them.

---

39. **Would be pleased:** "is pleased," N.
40. **To him,** MZ: om. N.
41. **Signs:** sg. Z.
42. **Show,** MN: "do," Z.
43. **To eat,** NZ: om. M, as Ps 77:24.
44. **Food,** MV: om. N.

They were dependent on another reason through their deceit—the manna, in that they could not find a means through envy of the manna to induce him to the continuous preparation of food. Why did they not remember the other sublime signs that occurred in the time of their fathers, like their being led by the pillar of fire (Exod 14:24), and the splitting of the sea (14:21), and the rock producing a spring (17:6),[iii] and frequent other such miracles, but only the manna? So the sayings are true, that because of their subtle deceit they were contemplating the same desire for food.

i. Moše bar Kepha makes the same argument.
ii. Išodad also refers to their disparaging the bread.
iii. John Chrysostom, *Hom. Jo.* 45.1, refers to Moses's rod, and Išodad to the rock producing water.

[6:32] **Jesus said to them: Amen, amen, I say to you, that Moses did not give you the bread from heaven, *but my Father gives[45] you the true bread from heaven.[46]**

See the meaning of the responses. Since the Jews took it only as a boast for themselves that *our fathers ate the manna in the desert*, so that they might show by mentioning the manna that the miracles of the bread were much less significant, [135] therefore the Lord stopped reproving them by the reference he had made to the bread, lest they were to say: Why did you introduce the bread instead of the manna, as if by that you inform us regarding yourself of things greater than and superior to[47] those of God? Therefore he set out a different response through the food, in order to show them that to you who boast through recalling such wonderful manna,[i] *Moses did not give* [it], *but my Father gives[48] you the bread from heaven*. And why did he not say he himself gives[49] the bread from heaven? Because they did not reckon him greater than Moses, therefore he ascribed the cause[50] to the Father. Thereby he prevented them from neglecting and despising what he was about to teach them next to this for their profit, but also for the advantage of the whole world, which he expressed as follows:

i. John Chrysostom, *Hom. Jo.* 45.1, indicates that manna was a *typos* of the true bread,

---

45. **Gives**, N: "will give," Z.
46. **But…heaven**: om. M.
47. **And superior to**: om. N.
48. **Gives**, M (= lemma): "will give," NZ.
49. **Say, gives**, *asē tal*, M: "to say," *asel*, N (*sic*).
50. **The cause**: om. N.

as also Moše bar Kepha. Cyril of Alexandria states that the manna was *hōs en skiais* ("as in shadows"); cf. introduction xxxi.

[6:33] **For the bread from God is he who descends from heaven**[51] **and gives life to the world.**

The bread that descends from God and gives life to the world is I myself, he says, who have been sent by the Father, who am also about to distribute my body[i] as food for the dissolution of the first corruption, which the tasting of the fruit brought about on the race of mankind. But what is *to the world*? Not, he says, especially to the Jews, as you think, but also to all nations.[ii] Likewise, not some bodily food, because that gives life to those who eat it only for a little time, and then again it is dissolved in the course of time, but spiritual food, indestructible and unending.

 i. Tat'ewac'i, 279, expands to refer to the holy body and blood.
 ii. The whole world is stressed by John Chrysostom, *Hom. Jo.* 45.1, and Theodore of Mopsuestia.

[6:34] **They said to him: Lord, at all times give us that bread.**

See how their plans for a surfeit of food were reproved, as we have often said. For it was never a custom for the Jews to call our Savior *our God* or *our Lord*. But when they hoped to gain something similar [**136**] to what they requested, *At all times give us that bread* that he had indicated to them, then they entitled him *lord* and asked him to give it them at all times.

[6:35] **Jesus said to them: I am the bread of life. Whoever comes to me will not hunger; and whoever believes in me will never thirst.**

From then on he removed the allegorical expressions and spoke clear words to them, in order to show that the bread that I told you is from the Father and descended from heaven, which also[52] gives life to the world and for which you asked, is I myself. Thereby he counseled them and brought them to correction, that it was superior to the thoughts that they entertained in accordance with bodily food. Also he described the bread of life that descended from heaven as pertaining not to a body but to his divinity.[i] For what descended from heaven was the divinity. Then, being united with the body, the body was

---

51. **From heaven:** om. M.
52. **Also:** om. N.

from then on the bread of life, not descended from heaven but united with the one who descended from heaven. This he made clear, saying: *The bread that I shall give is my body*. How, then, are we to understand this? Just as the body by union with the divine Word is said to have descended from heaven, likewise this special bread by the descent of the Holy Spirit is understood as the body of the Savior through undoubting faith.

i. Moše bar Kepha quotes "Mar Johannes" to the effect that the bread of life refers not to the Lord's body but to his divinity; see John Chrysostom, *Hom. Jo.* 45.2. Dionysius bar Salibi, *John*, 142, is of the same opinion.

[6:36] **But I said to you that you saw me, yet do not believe.**

Well did he set these [words] down, because previously he had said the same to them. *You seek me*, he said, *not because you have seen any signs, but because you ate from the bread and were sated* (John 6:26).[i] Hence it is clear that they were seeking him not for the sake of believing in him but for the sake of food with which he filled their hunger. *Truly*, he said, *you saw me and did not*[53] *believe*. [137] He also[54] said the same to Nicodemus: *We speak what we have heard, and we bear witness to what we have seen, and you do not receive our testimony* (John 3:11). This contains the same example, because those who did not receive the testimonies were never going to believe.

i. Dionysius bar Salibi, *John*, 143, here refers to the books of the prophets that prophesied about Jesus.

[6:37] **Everything that the Father gives me will come to me; and whoever comes to me I shall not cast out.**

First he set down *You saw me and did not*[55] *believe*, then introduces concerning himself another saying more appropriate and helpful: *Everything that the Father gives me will come to me*. What would this mean, except that he will ascribe the faith to the Father and thereby make them more receptive, in order to show that whoever believes in me, that is the will of God? This is what the giving indicates, and that the Father gives, namely, that he is very pleased and guides[56] those who will be inclined[57] to the faith. Whereas those who do

---

53. **Did not:** "will not," N ("do not," Z).
54. **Also:** om. N.
55. **Did not:** "will not," N; cf. the note to v. 36, above.
56. **Guides:** "will guide," N.
57. **Will be inclined:** "were inclined," M.

not believe in me do not accomplish the will of the Father but are found to be opponents of his will. And those who will not be opponents of his will and will come to me, I shall receive them and not expel them, even if they may be guilty and worthy of much punishment. This, then, is [the meaning of] *I shall not cast out.*

[6:38–39] **For I descended from heaven, not to do my own will but the will of the one who sent me. This is the will of my Father who sent me, that I should lose nothing of all that the Father gave me, but I should raise it up on the last day.**

The meaning of this declaration is unclear, hence those who love contrariness find some reasons for opposition to cast against us, concerning the saying: *I descended not to do my own will but the will of the one who sent me.* Hereby, as if acquiring two wills in opposition to each other, they contrive arguments. For which reason it is necessary to explain the meaning of this declaration.[i]

Not in the person of that one did he say he does not do his own will, [**138**] as if possessing a will in opposition to the Father, or not having a will but always acting in accordance with someone else's will. First let us see whether he has a will of his own or not. And he certainly does. This is clear from his saying: *I descended from heaven.* This indicates specifically his own will, because if it were not so, he should have said: I was sent from heaven. Now the saying *Not that I should do my own will but the will of the one who sent me* is in order to silence the Jews, who were always alleging that he opposed the will of God, and taught to do[58] the opposite of God's commandment, and was a destroyer of the law. Now, if I descended from heaven for the purpose of doing my Father's will, then I am not opposed to God. Furthermore, something else is to be made clear, that he taught the will of the Father. Therefore those who do not receive him are the ones opposed to the Father.

Then again what is: *I shall raise it*[ii] *on the last day*? It does not demonstrate that he will raise only those who believed in him, but he will also raise with them the nonbelievers. Rather, it was in order to make clear that he will raise those who believe in him to life everlasting, while the unbelievers [he will send] to eternal torments. It was not at all appropriate or helpful to express that openly, but he expounded only the best as concerns the former and omitted the latter. Furthermore, his saying, *I shall raise it on the last day,* clearly indicates he possesses will and authority and power in himself. Attributing all

---

58. **To do**: om. N.

the highest things to the Father was in order to suppress the impiety of those who said he was opposed to God, but not any indication of weakness.

i. Cyril of Alexandria, *Comm. Jo.* 4.1, states that this *logos* seems *dyscherēs*. He emphasizes the will of Christ in suffering and the unity of will in the Trinity.

ii. Since Armenian does not distinguish grammatical gender, *zna* in the lemma and here could mean "it" (as in the Greek) or "him/her."

[6:40] This is the will of my Father, that everyone who will see the Son and believe in him receives[59] eternal life; and I shall raise him up on the last day.

O his unlimited love of man, how **[139]** he kindles their childlike minds and brings them gradually to correction! First he said, *I descended from heaven, not to do the will of my Father[60] but the will of the one who sent me,* and *This is the will of my Father, that of what the Father gave me I should not lose [any] of them;[61]* then he reveals the meaning of the saying, because they did not understand at all what he said. Therefore he said: *This is the will of my Father, that everyone who will see the Son and believe in him will receive[62] eternal life.* That is, those who will see me and believe will not endure eternal death, which in accordance with sin rules over the race of mankind.

Why did he repeat so often the resurrection?[i] Because the Jews had accurate knowledge of the resurrection from the prophets, therefore by recalling the resurrection he stung them, always recalling and showing that there would be compensations for good deeds, and at the same time for wicked ones; and that if they had followed the faith they would have been saved on that fearful day from the unbearable torments. Furthermore, he said, *I shall raise him,* in order to presage for them that he was lord of life and death. And his sometimes attributing the cause to the Father was for the service and correction of the Jews, and the elimination of those who said he was always opposed to God.

Let us also investigate his not always expounding the highest things about himself nor continually the most humble. For what reason? If he had continuously expounded the highest things about himself, the Jews would have been no little hurt by that.[ii] For if while he was often attributing the highest things to the Father, and they were saying that he was opposed to the Father, how much more frequent would have been their impieties and wickedness

---

59. **Receives,** *ĕnduni,* MN: "will receive," *ĕnkalc'i,* Z.

60. **My Father:** "my," printed text.

61. **Of them:** *i noc'anē,* MN, whereas the lemma of v. 39 has the singular *i nmanē.*

62. **Will receive,** *ĕndunic'i,* M: "receives," *ĕnduni,* N; see note to the lemma.

[in saying] that he was imputing the highest things to himself! [140] Like-wise, the most humble things he did not always [attribute to himself], because if by his sometimes willingly condescending to the lowliest things they had been scandalized *and said he was a mere man,[63] what would they have been when he was continually expounding the most humble things about himself? But by sometimes teaching the highest things he indicated his divine nature, and by sometimes expounding the most humble about himself,[64] not only did he silence the wickedness of the Jews, but he also made clear his descent to human rank.[iii]

i. Theodore of Mopsuestia, 103, also draws attention to the repetition. John Chrysos-tom, *Hom. Jo.* 45.4, here expounds the resurrection and future judgment.

ii. Cyril of Alexandria does not discuss the Jews here but emphasizes the equality of nature of the Son and Father.

iii. **Rank:** *karg*, pl. M. For such vocabulary, see the introduction, xxxviii.

[6:41–42] **The Jews complained about him, because he said: I am the bread that descended from heaven; and they said: Is not this the son of Joseph, whose father we know?[65] So how does he say: I descended from heaven?**

Do not be astonished as to why they linked him with Joseph, calling him his son. Because these [words] concern his saying, *I am the bread of life who descended from heaven*, thereby they wished to obstruct[66] him, to contradict and remove those sayings. Whence is that clear? First when he fed such a multitude from five barley[67] loaves and two fishes, they there said: *This is the true prophet who was to come* (John 6:14). But now when they wished to raise objections, they called him *the son of Joseph*, whence it is even clearer that they were merely slaves to their stomachs[i] and had no concern at all for the truth. Let us also examine what the evangelist says: *The Jews complained about him.* By this an accusation is made against them, that those who so rapidly denied the signs and benefits, yet who so loved him that they even wished to seize him and make him their king, here after a short time denied his miracles and called him the *son of Joseph* and[68] *of the carpenter* (Matt 13:55; cf. Mark 6:3).

i. Here Moše bar Kepha cites Phil 3:19; see also above, commentary to v. 15.

---

63. **And said…man:** om. N.
64. **About himself:** om. M.
65. **We know,** *mek' gitemk'*, MZ: om. *mek'*, N.
66. **They wished to obstruct:** "they obstructed," N.
67. **Barley:** om. N.
68. **Of Joseph and:** om. N.

[6:43–44] **Jesus replied and said: Do not grumble among yourselves. No one can come to me unless the Father who sent me will draw him; and I shall raise him on the last day.**

[141] *It seems to me that the evangelist describes what the Savior said, *Do not grumble among yourselves*,[69] in order to show us that the Savior reproved them for speaking secretly among themselves, not that they contradicted[70] him according to their habit; nor did he concern himself with their blaming [him] and separate [from them] or contradict them that he was not the son of Joseph, as they said. But he passed over that and turned to a different argument from which he might provide[71] some help to them. He indicated with a gentle word that he was not the son of Joseph, as they thought, but had descended from heaven and [was] the Son of God.[72] And your grumbling among yourselves does not specifically concern me but also is about the Father and my descent from heaven[73] and my doing the will of the Father.

But what means: *No one can come to me unless the Father will draw*[74] *him*? By this he does not remove his independence; for unless the Jews were independent,[i] then they would not have been punished for their denial. But it is as if to say: If you had believed in the Father, then you would have received me, and by faith in him you would have been drawn to me, because he had sent the prophets to you concerning my coming and gave examples[ii] in advance. Now you profess to have faith in the Father, but in your minds you think the opposite. Because you have never considered the testimonies of the prophets and examples, therefore you are unable to come to me unless the Father will draw you—that is, unless you believe fully in the Father, faith in whom will draw you rapidly to me. This the next [verse] makes clear.

i. **Independent:** *anjnišxan* (i.e., freedom of will, a calque on *autexousios*). Man's "freedom of will," *anjnišxanut'iwn*, is the major theme of Eznik's treatise, misleadingly known as *Against the Sects*, or *On God*. See also the commentary to the following verse for *anjnišxan kamk'*, "independent will." Nonnus expands on the subject several times (see, e.g., the commentary to John 7:1).

ii. **Examples:** *awrinaks*, the standard term for "types" (i.e., the use of OT persons or events as foreshadowing Christ and his dispensation). See the introduction, xxxiii.

---

69. **It seems…yourselves:** om. N.

70. **Contradicted,** *hakačarēin*, M: "opposed," *hakarakēin*, N.

71. **Might provide:** "provided," M.

72. **And [was] the Son of God:** om. N.

73. **From heaven:** om. N.

74. **Will draw,** N (= lemma): "draws," M.

[6:45] It is written in the prophets: And they shall all be instructed by God.[75] **Everyone who listens to the Father and learns, comes to me.**

Because he first said, *No one is able to come to me unless the Father will draw him*, he put down next the testimony of Isaiah the prophet and thereby reprimands them and urges them to the faith. This also he expounds: *They shall all be instructed by God*, for **[142]** the confirmation of the previous sayings that we mentioned above, that he did not reject his independence. How is this done? If God's drawing to the faith occurs through the learning of his teaching, then the learning will not be other than with the readiness of independent will,[i] so the not being able is no other than what he said. But let us only pay heed to what he said: *[Everyone] who listens to the*[76] *Father and learns, comes to me*. He did not intend to say specifically listening, because the Jews did not only listen but also learned the testimonies from the Father about the Son through the prophets, yet they did not receive him; but by learning he means receiving, whereby they listened to the testimonies.

i. **Independent will:** *anjnišxan kamk'*; see note to the previous verse.

[6:46] No one has seen the Father, except the one who is from God, he has seen the Father.

Because he first said, *No one is able to come to me unless the Father will draw him*, and again, *[Everyone] who listens to the Father and learns, comes to me*,[77] consequently the Jews were vexed in their minds about the Father, when he expounded all this. In their thick-wittedness [they supposed] the Father to be tangible,[i] who was seen and heard by him, therefore he set down, *No one has seen the Father*, by which he informed them about the invisible nature of the Godhead, and he separated them from the bodily conceptions that they were supposing about the Father.

Now this must be investigated, what the Lord said:[78] *Whoever is from God, he has seen the Father*. Behold how he instructed them and with very mild words made it known that he was from the essence of God and not the son of Joseph, as they thought. But why, they said, did he not[79] always explain this in simple terms? We have often mentioned the reason: to put an end to

---

75. Isa 54:13; see also 1 Thess 4:9.
76. **The**, MZ (= lemma): "my," N.
77. **Comes to me:** om. M.
78. **What the Lord said:** om. N.
79. **Not:** om. N.

the fury of their wickedness, they who [143] were always saying that he was opposed to God. Therefore wisely he condescended to them.

i. **Tangible:** *zgali.* Here Cyril of Alexandria, *Comm. Jo.* 4.1, refers to the Jews supposing the nature of God to be visible.

[6:47–48] Amen, amen, I say to you, that whoever believes receives life everlasting. I am the bread of life.

See how he removes their excuse and cuts the root of their wicked thoughts by which they were always separated from the faith, merely alleging that he was opposed to God, by saying, *The Father sent me,* and *No one can come to me unless my Father will draw him to me.* Next he set down also a testimony from the prophet, after which he then said: *Amen, amen, I say to you, that whoever believes receives eternal life.* Do not suppose him to mean that he no more will endure the bodily death imposed upon us, but as if he were to say that through faith he remains always alive. And as, by being alive in the body, he has died the death of sin, likewise too by faith he is understood to be alive, although in the body he may have died.

Something further is also to be understood. For those who bear in themselves truly the faith and light of resurrection, no more thereafter is the death of their bodies called death. To this Paul also bears witness, calling death sleep, not removing the suspicion of death, but with regard to the true resurrection he calls it sleep, demonstrating that we shall wake up as if from sleep on the future day.[i] See also what follows. When he declared, *Whoever believes in me receives everlasting life,* he joins to the same: *I am the bread of life.* What does this mean except that he teaches in accordance with their thick-wittedness, as if to say that just as you say you have in you life for your bodies from bread, without which it is not possible to survive, likewise my body has become food for believers; it gives everlasting life, which is not food for the body, but for the soul?

i. Not a direct quotation; cf. Rom 13:1; 1 Cor 15:51; 1 Thess 4:15.

[144] [6:49–50] Your fathers ate manna in the desert and died. This is the bread that has come down from heaven, in order that whoever eats from it will not die.

We must investigate the reason for so many repetitions of the statements and teachings about the bread. When they saw the miracle of feeding such a multitude from five barley loaves and two fishes, these deeds seemed very pleasing to them. Therefore they were always expecting him to do the same and to have the needs of their hunger continuously provided by him without any labor.[80] And they were so desirous for the same that they even denied what had happened and said, *What signs do you show,*[81] *so that we may see and believe in you?* (John 6:30), so that perhaps thereby they might have a better means to spur him to do the same. Furthermore, see by what reminiscence they planned it: **Our fathers,* they said, *ate manna in the desert*[82] (John 6:31), so that thereby they might make themselves much more worthy of honor, as if it were necessary for you to do such a thing in order for them to believe in you.

Now, why did the Savior ignore their words after that and turn his teaching from bodily things to spiritual ones? He showed them how superior and lasting is the bread that he said he would give them compared to manna. Therefore he said: *Your fathers ate manna in the desert and died.* This indicates to them that the manna in which they gloried was not at all profitable; for it did not save them from death, nor did it bring them to the promised land that he had once promised them. But they died right there, stricken by the anger[i] of God, and the manna was of no support to them. Whereas the bread of life that has descended from heaven possesses a different power from manna, because it saves from the death that is the consequence of sin, [145] and it alone leads to the land, not the one bereft of promise, but to the supernal Jerusalem, to unending and eternal and sorrowless life.

i. **Anger:** *xṙovut'iwn* (lit. "trouble, confusion"). This noun and the related verb, *xṙovel,* do not occur in the Armenian OT with regard to manna; but in Gen 14:24 "God troubled the camp of the Egyptians." *Comm. Diat.* 12.11 notes that Moses's bread was given only to the Israelites, but Christ's gift is for the whole world; cf. the following verse.

[6:51–52a][83] I am the bread of life[84] that came down from heaven. If anyone eats of this bread, he will live forever.

He often repeats his teaching concerning the descent of the bread from heaven, and that for most valuable profit; because when the Jews recalled the manna that had been once given them from heaven, they thought that he would thereby be more spurred on for their own pleasure to encounter ready nourishment again like that he provided for them on the mountain,

---

80. **Labor:** pl. M.

81. **Show,** N (and v. 30, above): "do," MZ.

82. **Our fathers … desert:** om. M.

83. Z begins v. 52 at "If anyone." Hence from here to the end of the chapter the numbering is one verse behind the standard numbering of the Greek, making seventy-two verses instead of seventy-one.

84. **Of life,** *kenac':* om. M; "living," *kendani,* Z.

or he would cause manna to come down from heaven. Therefore the Savior frequently spoke about the bread of life[85] that descended from heaven. Why would this be? It was in order to inform them that this bread that I said was [bread] of life is not in the pattern of bread from earth; and it is not alive and does not possess a cause for life. And if it is not alive but preserves life sometimes in the bodies of men, being the natural[86] food of their nature, how much more[87] desirable will be the bread of life that possesses the power of immortality for their souls![88] And what, then, would be the pattern of eating it? With faith and hope.

[6:52b] **And the bread that I shall give is my body, which I shall give for the life of the world.**

Since at first he did not expound clearly the bread of life that descended from heaven, save through an allegorical expression, knowledge of it remained unclear to them. So after that he taught more straightforwardly, when he rendered his wording easily grasped, by saying: *The bread that I shall give is my body, which I shall give for the life of the world.*[i] When would this occur? *When I shall be raised up,* [146] he said, on the cross for the salvation of the world (John 12:32),[ii] then I shall distribute to the world my body for the forgiveness of sins and as a cause for eternal life.

    i. Here Cyril of Alexandria, *Comm. Jo.* 4.2, refers to the bread offered on the altar. Tat'ewac'i, 294, mentions explicitly the "liturgy," *patarag.*
    ii. Dionysius bar Salibi, *John*, 147, refers to the cross, as also Tat'ewac'i, 294.

[6:53] **The Jews disputed among themselves and said: How can he give us his body to eat?**

This too is no small indication of their unbelief and wickedness, that so rapidly they put aside the recollection of the miracles of the bread at which they had been so pleased. For if they had not in this way forgotten the benefits, here they would have easily given credence to the sayings and would have asked the Savior, How did you say this would happen? and they would not have disputed among themselves about it.[89]

---

    85. **Of life:** om. M (as in lemma).
    86. **Natural:** om. N.
    87. **More:** om. M.
    88. **Souls:** sg. M.
    89. **About it:** om. N.

[6:54] Jesus said to them: Amen, amen, I say to you, unless you eat the body of the son of man and drink his blood, you do not have life in yourselves.

As if to say, although you have been instructed so many times, yet it still seems impossible to you; but it is very possible to occur, that unless *you eat the body and drink the blood* of the one whom you call the *son of man, you do not have life in yourselves.* For just as no one can have life in himself according to the body without eating[90] and drinking, in the same way no one can receive the eternal life of the soul unless he eats this spiritual food, *the body and blood of the son of man.*[i] For he communicates in[ii] and is united with the divine nature and grants life and renewal to those who taste.

> i. Dionysius bar Salibi, *John*, 148, has the same argument. Tat'ewac'i, 296, again refers to the *patarag*, though not specifically to "the body and blood of the son of man."
> ii. As Išodad also explains.

[6:55] Whoever eats my body and drinks my blood has eternal life, and I shall raise him up on the last day.

Since he first set down, *Unless one eats the body of the son of man and drinks his blood, he does not have life,*[91] lest they think that the son of man whom he had mentioned was someone other than himself, he then made it clear that it was his own body and blood that he had spoken of. Now, what means: *I shall raise him up on the last day*? In order to cut short their responses, lest they say that [147] *Abraham and the prophets died* (John 8:52–53), yet you say that they did not die, he then mentioned the resurrection, in order to show that by saying, resurrection, he indicated that of the dead, and thereby it might be[92] clear to them that he was saying that not about the bodily life but about the eternal one that will follow the resurrection.

[6:56] For my body is true food, and my blood is[93] true drink.

This was in order to confirm what he had said to them, because being thus unbelieving in his words, they were saying, How does he give us[94] his body to be eaten? It seemed as if that would be some allegorical example,[i] or

---

90. **Eating:** "food," M.
91. **He does not have life:** om. N.
92. **Might be:** "is," M.
93. **Is, NZ:** om. M.
94. **Us:** om. N.

some other kind [of speech] that we do not yet[95] accurately know. Therefore he confirmed his declaration by saying: *My body is true food, and my blood true drink*, and not as you stumble. This also contains another true mystery.[ii] He said this would not be like some other nourishment, because this alone is true food for bestowing eternal life; but it is not that by which you are always nourished, which would be no help to you regarding such gifts.

 i. **Allegorical example:** *aṙak awrinaki*; for these terms, see the introduction, xxxiii–xxxv. Tatʻewacʻi, 299, indicates that Christ's body is not an *awrinak*, and he then attacks the Franks' mode of communion.
 ii. **Mystery:** *xorhurd*. For the use of this term, see Thomson 2001 (22).

[6:57] Whoever eats my body and drinks my blood will dwell[96] in me, and I in him.

These sayings are very important and necessary for the faith. For just as food, he says, and drink by being transformed into the body's nature are so united with and transformed into that nature that they are changed into body and blood and are united without distinction, so that they become part of that nature,[i] in the same fashion *whoever eats my body and drinks my blood* worthily is then mingled and united with me and is glorified in the resurrection, remaining similar **[148]** to this body that I have put on[ii] from your nature, just as the apostle testifies: *We shall become similar to him* (1 John 3:2).

 i. **Part of that nature:** *ĕnd bnutʻeann* (lit. "with that nature"). For the transformation, cf. Theodore of Mopsuestia, ad loc., 106.
 ii. **Put on:** *zgecʻay*. For expressions describing the incarnation, see the introduction, xxxvii.

[6:58] As the living Father sent me, I am living because of the Father; and whoever eats me, he too will live because of me.

See what he demonstrated and revealed concerning the tremendous advantage that would derive from that: *Whoever eats my body and drinks my blood will dwell in me, and I in him, and he will inherit eternal life.*[i] He then indicates the cause from which the life would come, saying, *Whoever eats me will live*, because of my dwelling in him, just as he said that *he was living because of the Father*. Not that he acquired life from him, but as possessing the same immortal nature.[ii]

---

95. **Yet:** om. N.
96. **Will dwell,** M^corrNZ: "dwells," M.

i. A conflation of vv. 55 and 57.

ii. Here Cyril of Alexandria, *Comm. Jo.* 4.3, also emphasizes the identical nature of the Trinity.

[6:59] This is the bread that descended from heaven. Not as your fathers ate manna in the desert and died; whoever eats this bread will live forever.

See how often he repeats the sayings concerning the bread and eternal life.[i] Because through this the faith would be consummated, therefore he came into the world. Furthermore, one cannot pass over so many references to the resurrection without inquiry, but [it was] in order to show that the eternal life, which he promised through the tasting of his body and blood, would occur after the resurrection. Because he is the origin and cause of unending life, hence the bands of the just are sent to perpetual and endless life. Also, just as Adam believed in Satan and hoped to receive what he promised through eating that food in which the power of death was secretly hidden, but did not die immediately following the transgression of the commandment, which the commandment made clear, [149] *God said: On the day on which you will eat from it*[97] *you will die by death* (Gen 2:17), yet he, although he did not die right then in the body but after much time—in the same way, those who believe in the Lord's promises receive hidden in themselves the power of eternal life, although in the body they endure the sentence of death.

Furthermore, just as Adam, although he did not truly die in the body save after nine hundred[98] years (Gen 5:5), yet death really was hidden in his nature and consequently made him mortal, and afterward he truly suffered death through the power of death hidden in him—in the same way, although we do not now possess visibly in us the promised power of eternal life, yet immortality truly lies hidden in our nature and is revealed on the day of resurrection by vivifying us with indissoluble life. For just as the food was the cause of the death of[99] the original man, likewise food became for us the cause of eternal life. And just as the food, although it became the cause of death, did not kill us for the reason that it was fatal by nature, but because Adam ate it believing in Satan's promises—in the same way this food grants eternal life, not by possessing naturally the power of immortality, but through faith in the Savior's promises and hope in his words. In this way through the opposites he destroys

---

97. **It**, NZ: "that tree," MV.

98. **900**, N: 930, MZ.

99. **The death of**: om. N.

our opposites, making life spring up in us who worthily communicate in the vivifying[100] body and blood of the Son of God.

Let us contemplate, brethren,[ii] the ineffable blessings that the Son of God has granted us. But although he so loved us that he distributed to us [150] his incorruptible body and blood as food and as a cause of eternal life, yet let us examine how much need there is of purity. Let us hear what the Savior himself said elsewhere: *When you offer the sacrifice, and you then remember that your brother may have some grievance concerning you, leave the sacrifice, and go first and be reconciled with the brother, and then come and offer the sacrifice* (Matt 5:23–24). See how much purity he demanded: he commanded not to complete the sacrifice that a little rancor or forgetfulness had interrupted but first to be purified through reconciliation. How much shameless audacity and arrogance would there be, when through rancor of the brother you still have evil fixed in you, yet you would dare[101] to approach the holy mystery!

Hear again Paul proclaiming: *Let a man test himself and then eat of the bread and drink from the cup* (1 Cor 11:28). And he does not merely stop here but also adds more frightening warnings: *For that reason there are many sick and afflicted among you, and even more are those who have fallen asleep* (1 Cor 11:30). O inconsolable afflictions and unrelieved mourning, when the medicine[iii] of eternal life becomes the cause of eternal death! See also what he said elsewhere similar to this: *To crucify afresh the Son of God *and put him again to shame*[102] (Heb 6:6). Truly such a person is comparable to those who, thinking him a mere man, condemned him to death—the one who dares to taste the body and blood as if it were of a simple man.

Let us be on our guard, lest we be found guilty of that, and let us heed the cry of the priest who says: Let none of the catechumens,[103] none of the unbelievers, and none of the unrepentant rashly[104] approach.[iv] Furthermore, [151] let us wisely examine the model of this ineffable mystery: once the seraph approached the burning coal with tongs.[v] But how shall we, by carrying unworthily the fire [of] God within us, not be burned up and perish, consumed by fire? So where now are those who through a wicked habit continually communicate without discernment? Whence will they be able to pretend and excuse their reasons for sin, if instead of repentance, you[vi] approach, communicate, and be purified. But let us separate ourselves from such wicked thoughts and not approach unworthily nor wickedly depart,[vii] because both

---

100. **Vivifying**, MV: om. N.

101. **Would dare**, N: "dare," M.

102. **And put … shame**, MZ: om. N.

103. **None of the catechumens**: om. N.

104. **Rashly**, *yandgneal*: om. N.

are most impious. But [let us] approach not in disgust, not indolently, *and not having any scruple in mind by which we are condemned,[105] but through pure behavior and pure thoughts and with pure minds,[106] aflame through instruction in the divine faith,[107] which the Lord himself came to provide, *ardent in the spirit and serving the Lord,*[108] according to Paul (Rom 12:11), in order to preserve in us the same purity also for the future and to approach the divine light without shame.

For this is the purity of humankind, this is the road that leads to the inalienable splendor of heaven, this is the ship that brings [us] to the secure harbor, this is the door that opens to the garden of delight, this is what makes us members of the fiery ranks, this is what makes us worthy of the sight of the incorporeal Trinity. Let us communicate in them with pure conduct and pure thoughts, become the body of Christ, and with him enter the heavenly bridal chamber, glorifying the thrice-holy majesty and single divinity,[109] to whom be glory, honor, and authority, now and always, and forever and ever. Amen.

i. The repetition is also noted by John Chrysostom, *Hom. Jo.* 47.1, and Tat'ewac'i, 302.

ii. This section of the commentary, ending with "Amen," is one of the additions to the original; see the introduction, xxv. The expanded version in Tat'ewac'i, 305–10, is titled *yordorak pataragi,* "exhortation on the liturgy."

iii. **Medicine:** *deł;* for this term as used of the Eucharist, see Lampe 1969 (s.v. *pharmakon*).

iv. This proclamation occurs immediately before the start of the Anaphora. The same three categories appear in the liturgy on which tenth-century Xosrov Anjewac'i wrote his *Commentary on the Liturgy* (see Cowe, §17).

v. Isa 6:1–8, which is quoted at greater length by Tat'ewac'i, 307.

vi. The author turns to the second-person singular.

vii. **Depart:** *i bac' hražarel,* or "abstain, separate oneself from."

[152] [6:60] This he spoke in the synagogue while he was teaching in Capernaum.

By marking the place the evangelist[110] indicated where he frequently performed signs and miracles, where also he had occasion to speak the most sublime words about himself after so many miracles and healings.

---

105. **And not having … condemned:** om. N.

106. **And with pure minds:** om. N.

107. **Faith:** om. N.

108. **And serving the Lord:** om. N.

109. **And single divinity:** om. M.

110. **The evangelist:** "he," N.

[6:61] **And many of the disciples, when they heard, said: This saying[111] is hard. Who will be able to heed it?**

What is hard? It means that what he declares about himself is exceedingly sublime. And who indeed among the listeners could believe?

[6:62–63] **When Jesus knew in himself that his disciples were complaining about that, he said to them: Does this cause you to stumble? But if you were to see the son of man ascend where he was before?**

Notice for me the evangelist's total wisdom by the grace of the Holy Spirit. He fully reveals the Savior's secret knowledge, which can also be seen here. *Jesus knew in himself*, he says; that is, he did not hear from anyone what they were complaining among themselves, but through his divine perceptive power he saw everything. Therefore he said: *Does this cause you to stumble*, that I said, *Whoever eats this bread will live forever?* (John 6:55 [54]). Now if these things seemed so sublime and impossible that you indeed did stumble, then what will you understand when *you see the son of man ascending where he was before*? See how he tries to make them firm and useful and imparts the most sublime knowledge, than which nothing is greater or more wonderful.

He said: *The son of man, where he was before, thither he will ascend*. The same he said to Nicodemus: **No one ascended to heaven except the son of man, who descended from heaven*[112] (John 3:13).[i] So why did he not say, the Son of God, [153] since from this he came down to a particularly humble expression? Now the son of man is the body that he put on from Mary, and his coming from heaven indicates the inseparable unity concerning the uniting of the son of man with the Son of God, who descended from heaven; by gathering the two into one inseparably in unity he called the son of God son of man.[ii] Where would be the dividers of the one Christ into two natures?[iii] These are the words of the Lord himself and not of any of the teachers. So then let them be silent and hold their tongues, because the Savior himself knows more than they.

i. The quotation is also given by Tat'ewac'i, 311.

ii. Dionysius bar Salibi, *Gospels*, 378, notes that Christ called himself "son of man," but not "a man" (i.e., son of the first man, Adam, the common father).

iii. Cyril of Alexandria, *Comm. Jo.* 4.3, makes the same reference to dyophysites. The

111. **This saying**: *ban-d*, N; *ban-d ayd*, MZ.
112. **No one … heaven**: om. N.

argument is similar to the commentary to John 3:13, where Č'rak'ean noted a parallel in Nersēs Šnorhali; see note ad loc.

[6:64–65a] **The Spirit is life-giving; the body is of no avail. The word that I spoke with you is spirit and life. But there are some of you who do not believe.**

See how much concern he has for their salvation, and [how] he tries to render them wise and useful. Since they did not believe concerning the bread that granted eternal life, nor in his ascending where he had been before, as he made clear by saying, *There are some of you who do not believe*, therefore he teaches something else: *The spirit is life-giving*. What does he indicate by that? Those who will look on these sayings with spiritual understanding and eyes, these receive the promised eternal life. *The body does not avail*.[i] Bodily understanding, he says, is of no help but is only a cause of stumbling, just as I see you now. For if you contemplate these sayings with the eye of the Spirit, there would be no stumbling in you concerning my descent from heaven and my body being true nourishment. But because you look with corporeal eyes and accordingly fashion your thoughts[113] in a bodily manner, therefore you stumble and roll, calling me a son of Joseph.[ii] [154] But if from the testimonies of the deeds and the miracles you had any sense, you would investigate these sayings with spiritual understanding, and the food that I said I would give you would provide you with life.

i. Here Moše bar Kepha, 467–75, has a long discussion against Theodore and the idea that the body does not avail.
ii. Dionysius bar Salibi, *John*, 151, refers back to vv. 41–42.

[6:64b] **The word that I spoke with you is spirit and life.**

He indicates the same thing again. *My word*, he says, *is spirit*, and if it is spirit, it must be understood through spiritual understanding. And if it is life, then it is not bodily, because bodies are mortal. So one must separate oneself from bodily thoughts and be raised up to higher things.

---

113. **Thoughts:** sg. N.

[6:65b] Because Jesus knew from the beginning who those were who did not believe, and who he was who would betray him.

Once more the evangelist reveals the power of the divine foresight: *He knew from the beginning who those were who did not receive [him],*[i] *and who it was who would betray him.* By *those who did not receive* he indicates the Jews, and by *betraying,* Judas Iscariot.[ii] This was to show that from the beginning until the end Jesus knew everything, because he himself was the creator of human nature.

    i. Nonnus refers back to John 5:43.
    ii. Moše bar Kepha makes the same identifications.

[6:65c–66] And he said: Therefore I told you that no one is able to come to me unless it has been given him from above.[114]

These sayings have no small need of investigation, because to the narrow-minded and the lovers of opposition it seems to remove independent will by his saying: *No one is able to come to me unless it has been given him from above.* However, lest these words expressed with this wisdom should cause us to stumble, therefore he said: *I told you;* that is, because of my having foreknowledge of what would be done by you, I spoke before it occurred. For when those who remain in denial will not receive me, you will believe what I now[115] said. [155] And when Judas will betray me, you will remember what I earlier said to you; and that will be no small reason for you to strengthen your faith. But what means: *No [one] is*[116] *able to come to me unless it has been given him from above*? It means the same as: No one is able to come to me, unless the Father has previously seen his faith; when he reckons him worthy[117] through his having in himself zeal for the faith and the compensation of eternal life, he will draw him to me.

---

114. **From above,** MN: "from my Father," Z and the lemma in Tat'ewac'i, 314.
115. **Now:** om. N.
116. **No [one] is:** "You are not," N.
117. **Worthy:** pl. N (*sic*).

[6:67] From then on many of his disciples went back and did not go around with him.

See the truth of the evangelist: for[118] he hides nothing of what is unpleasing but accurately reveals everything. Because of that saying that they had heard, *No one can come to me unless it has been given him from above*, many of the disciples, who unlike the twelve apostles were not strong in the faith,[i] separated from the faith; that is, they went back and thereafter no more heeded[119] his teaching with attentiveness.

i. All commentators stress that those who turned back were not among the Twelve; but see the next lemma.

[6:68] Jesus said to the twelve disciples: Do you also wish to go?

What immeasurable humility: *Do you also wish to go?*[i] It shows that he leads no one unwillingly to obedience, and that those who turned back also acted with independent will. Furthermore, not intending to offend the disciples did he say, *Do you also wish to go*, but he showed that I do not force you outside your own wishes. Thereby he does not only reproach them but also forewarns them by what the others did. Furthermore, regarding his saying, *No one is able to come to me unless it has been given him from above*,[120] not that it is given from above [156] to the latter, but not to the former; rather, in accordance with what we said above, the Father previously saw the strength of faith and zeal of the latter, in accordance with the prophet, *Your eyes saw my indolence* (Ps 138:16), and great gifts were given them. But when he saw the opposition of the former, which indeed they carried out, they were unable to inherit the great gifts because of not desiring and loving the faith.

i. **Do you wish:** *mitē ... kamik'*. The Armenian *mitē* implies a negative answer: "Surely you do not wish."

---

118. **For:** om. N.
119. **No more heeded:** "did not heed," M.
120. **From above:** om. N.

[6:69–70] Simon Peter replied and said: Lord, to whom would we go? You have the words of eternal life, and we[121] have believed and recognized that you are the Christ, son of the living[122] God.

Peter replied for himself and his companions, in order to show that we have done what you[123] instructed; that is his saying: *To whom shall we go?* In other words, if you once said, *Whoever does not love me more than father and mother,*[124] *brothers and all his kin, is not worthy of me,*[i] all this we have done, and now to whom would we go? This was as if to say, if there is anything else lacking from what you commanded, let us know so that we may complete it. But what means: *You have the words of eternal life?*[125] He revealed by this saying that we have believed truly in your sayings that you taught us: *Whoever believes in me receives eternal life, and I shall raise him up on the last day.*[ii] Now if we knew and believed that you are Christ the Son of God, we would not speak in accordance with the Jews who called you a son of Joseph; but from your miracles we recognized that you are the Christ. And from your promising eternal life, we have believed that you are the Son of God.

i. Based on Matt 10:37; 19:29.
ii. A combination of John 6:47 and 54.

[6:71–72] Jesus answered them and said: Did I not choose you twelve, and one of you is Satan? He spoke about Judas Iscariot [son] of Simeon, because he indeed was to betray him and was one of the Twelve.[126]

[157] Why did he reveal that to them at this point, save that because Peter had made that response only for himself and the other apostles, *We have believed and recognized that you are the Christ, the Son of God,* he consequently revealed what would be done by one of them. This was so that he might terrify the one who was to do it and bring him to prudence, although he was not to heed it at all, but totally removed the excuses. But why did he not introduce the name of the one who was to betray him? It was lest by that he bring him to greater presumption and insolence,[i] or if the disciples were vexed they might then reject him from their midst. That would have been for him

---

121. **We:** + *mek'*, MZ.
122. **Living:** om. MZ.
123. **You:** "we," M (*sic*).
124. **And mother,** NZ: om. M.
125. **Words of eternal life:** "word of life," N.
126. **And was one of the Twelve,** NZ: om. M.

no small cause of hatred and wickedness regarding the betrayal. Furthermore, it was so that he might indicate thereby to the disciples that he would willingly endure the torments that would be inflicted by the Jews through Judas's betrayal, which knowing in advance he did not fear.

Why did he call him Satan? Not only because he was like-minded with Satan, but in order that he might teach us never to hide by partiality the wickedness of evildoers, even if they are very closely related, but one should grasp the truth. For the prophet also once[127] declared: *Woe to whoever says*[ii] *the evil is good and the good evil* (Isa 5:20). See the impartiality of the evangelist, who did not hesitate to tell [the truth]. Also, because he was a fellow disciple he was known to the twelve apostles. But he [the evangelist] had no zeal for such things other than for the truth, for which reason he repeated the Savior's saying, *Did not I choose you twelve?* and *One of you is Satan.* And that is Judas Iscariot, [son] of Simeon.[128]

i. Dionysius bar Salibi, *John*, 154, also refers to the danger of increasing Judas's presumption. Moše bar Kepha discusses the question why Jesus did not name Judas.

ii. **Whoever says:** "those who say," Z.

127. **Once:** om. N.

128. **Simeon:** + "showing that the one who would betray him was among the Twelve and the disciples, and was Satan," M.

<h1 style="text-align:center">[158] Chapter 7</h1>

[7:1] And after this Jesus went around in Galilee, because he did not wish to go around in Judea, since the Jews were seeking to kill him.

Do not be distressed at such a thing,[1] that for fear of the Jews he did not wish to go around in Judea, because they were seeking to kill him. Why was he frightened, he who[2] many times when they had wished to arrest him had passed through their midst, being veiled from their eyes? And would not he who raised the dead and calmed the sea (Matt 8:26; Mark 4:39; Luke 8:22), have been able to save himself from them? It was not for that reason, but lest by saving himself from them by force, he might bring them to the faith against their wishes, removing their independent will. The same is to be seen among us. Never against our will does he turn us from our wicked sins, but merely by teaching us the truth and revealing what pleases him we are helped, and he leaves us to our own wishes. The same is to be understood here.

[7:2–3] And the Feast of Tabernacles of the Jews was close. His brothers said to him: Leave here, and go to Judea, so that your disciples also may see the works that you do.

Why did they make this request or were they called his brothers? Because they were the sons of Joseph[i] and reckoned that the marvelous signs were a source of pride to themselves, especially on this feast in which the whole nation of the Jews gathered at Jerusalem.[ii] But the disciples whom they mentioned were different, showing that those who had turned back and were not going around with him were other than the Twelve. For there were also others who went around following the Savior, although they were not comparable to the Twelve or of equal honor.[iii]

---

1. **Such a thing,** *aynpisi inč'*: "so," *aynpēs inč'*, N.
2. **He who,** *or:* "where," *ur*, N.

i. For the sons of Joseph, see John Chrysostom, *Hom. Jo.* 48.2. Cyril of Alexandria, *Comm. Jo.* 4.5, emphasizes that they were sons of Joseph and not of Mary. Moše bar Kepha and Dionysius bar Salibi (*John*, 154–55) give their names: Jacob, Iose, Simon, and Juda; see Mark 6:3. Tat'ewac'i, 320, gives the same names, noting that two were among the Twelve, and two among the seventy-two. In his commentary to vv. 40–44 below, Nonnus names James (Jacob) and John as brothers of Jesus.

ii. Moše bar Kepha explains the dates of the Feasts of Tabernacles (in Tišrin) and Passover (in Nisan), which are six months apart. Dionysius bar Salibi, *John*, 154–55, also notes that the festivals are six months apart. Tat'ewac'i, 320, explains the origin of the feast as the remembrance of the forty years in the desert.

iii. These are variously numbered as seventy or seventy-two.

[7:4–5] For there is no one who will do anything in secret, yet he seeks to be public. If you do this, reveal yourself to the world. For neither did his brothers believe in him.

[159] With allegorical wording his brothers spoke this, as if to say that every man who desires to hide himself never reveals [himself]; but who desires to be revealed never hides [himself].[i] What [things] you do are opposed to both sayings, because the signs that you perform never suggest you are hiding yourself, since the report of your fame vibrates throughout this whole land. So why do you not reveal yourself to the world? Because of the envy that they nurtured in themselves concerning him, it seems to us that these words were [spoken] treacherously and not as some have said, that to gain glory for themselves to be called his brothers they urged him to these [actions].[ii]

But it seemed better to us that their hurrying him to Jerusalem to demonstrate his signs there was in order to test his power when he would be among his enemies, for they knew that the Jews wished to kill him. To this the evangelist also testifies by saying: *His brothers did not believe in him.* O the man's love of the truth, who never avoids or omits the truth, but just as he accurately narrates what is good about the disciples, likewise he reveals the bad! For as above he described Judas, of whom the Savior said, *One of you is Satan* (John 6:70), so likewise here he made their unbelief clear.[iii]

i. The verbs are active, but no object is provided.

ii. John Chrysostom, *Hom. Jo.* 48.1, here refers to "vainglory" (*philodoxia*).

iii. Theodore of Mopsuestia also refers to Jesus's brothers' bad opinion of him.

[7:6] **Jesus said to them: My time has not[3] arrived. But your time is always ready.**

Because they were urging him to go up to Jerusalem to the feast and to perform signs there[4] and reveal himself, therefore he said: *My time* [160] *has not arrived.* The reason that I shall not go up to the feast in Jerusalem is not because of being afraid of the Jews, as you suppose, but because my time has not yet arrived.[i] What, then, would be his time? The torments of the cross,[ii] he means, through which I am going to endure death for the salvation of the world.[5] But what means: *Your time is always ready?* O incomprehensible teaching and inscrutable words with great wisdom! *What would be the meaning of these sayings?[6] It is as if to say, my time[7] has not arrived; that is, the time has not yet[8] come in which I am willingly going to endure death. But for you, by unwillingly enduring death because the power of death rules over you, at every time it is ready. From that it is clear that since from the beginning death ruled over us because of the transgression of the commandment, sometimes it occurs to us at the right time, sometimes at an inopportune time; also by accident it often befalls us. That is what the Savior[9] meant by *ready.*

i. Note the variation in quoting the lemma: "has not arrived," *čew ē haseal*; "has not yet arrived," *čew ews ē haseal.* See also v. 8: "My time has not yet been [*čew ews ē*] completed."

ii. John Chrysostom, *Hom. Jo.* 48.2, explains the time as the cross, as do Moše bar Kepha, and Dionysius bar Salibi, *John,* 156.

[7:7] **The world cannot hate you, but it hated me, because I bear witness concerning it that its works are evil.**

Be amazed at his unbounded wisdom,[10] how gently he reproves them for their unbelief, which the evangelist made clear, and because of which they urged him to attend the feast and to test the measure of his power when he would be among enemies. *The world cannot hate you,* he said. By this he blamed and reproved them. Why can it not? they said. Because through your unbelief you are now accomplices of those who love the world.[i] *But it hated*

---

3. **Not:** + "yet," *ews,* N.
4. **There:** om. M.
5. **For the salvation of the world,** MV: om. N.
6. **What would … sayings:** om. N.
7. **My time:** om. M.
8. **Yet:** om. N.
9. **The Savior:** "he," N.
10. **At his unbounded wisdom:** om. N.

me, because I testify to their wicked deeds. As if to say that I continually reprimand their unbelief and denial, **[161]** which they work through envy and love of the world.

    i. Cyril of Alexandria, *Comm. Jo.* 4.5, gives a similar argument.

[7:8] You go to that feast. I shall not go to that feast, because my time has not yet been completed.

Because he previously indicated that they do not hate you at all, since through unbelief you now share their thoughts, *you go to that feast* without hesitation. But *I shall not go to that feast*; that is, they seek to kill me, and *my time has not arrived* in which I shall willingly suffer death for the life of mankind.

[7:9–10a] When he had said that, he himself remained in Galilee. When his brothers had gone up, then he too went up to the feast.

Let no one say: Why did he first say, *I shall not go to that feast*, and later he went? Not at all did he refuse to go up to the feast, but first he introduced a distinction,[i] the plans for his own and for their going up. He indicated that he would not go up with them, for the reason previously mentioned by us, when in order to test him they urged him to present himself to his enemies. Do you wish that I show you an allegory very similar to this? When rebuking his mother in Cana of Galilee, he said: *What have I and you, woman? My time has not arrived* (John 2:4). Yet next he performed the miracle[11] that his mother requested, showing that I do not perform [it] according to your pleasure but in accordance with the profit of all, which here too can be seen. Not because his brothers summoned him did he go up to the feast but for the profit of all nations in common.

    i. **Distinction:** *xtroc'*, which could also mean "a gap of time."

[7:10b] Not openly, but as if in secret.

Do not then think the secret was some apprehension, because not out of fear did the Savior do that, but for the sake of some greater advantage he acted in that way. **[162]** And because the multitude was split into two, some being very pleased to hear from him and see some signs, but others never so, therefore *not openly but as it were in secret*, says the evangelist, in order

---

    11. **Miracle:** pl. N.

to announce the most secret things for their advantage to those who desired them, and in order to prevent the opposition of his enemies by not revealing himself to them even once.

[7:11] **And the Jews sought him at the feast and said: Where might he be?**

He speaks not about all the Jews but about the leaders and elders of the people. See the indication of the immeasurable hatred and wickedness[12] [of those] who did not even cite his name: [they did not say,] Where is the Christ? but, *Where might he be?* For they totally did not[13] wish to say any such thing about him that would predict something superior or worthy of love.[i]

    i. The meaning of the last phrase is unclear, "worthy" being in the plural.

[7:12–13] **And there was murmuring about him among the people.[14] Some said that he was good; others said: No, but he leads the people[15] astray. And no one openly spoke about him for fear of the Jews.**

A little earlier we said that the people were divided into two, which now the evangelist himself reveals by saying: *Some said he was good, but others said[16] that he was leading the people astray.* Who, then, were they who said he was good, who followed his signs and were amazed at his miracles? But those who totally did not wish to receive him were unable to adduce anything else in order to remove altogether his wonders, save to say that those were indications of deceit and error. That is, that he was not from God but was opposed to him, and everything that he did was [done] not in truth but in appearance. Who were those who said this? The high priests and elders of the people, as is clear from the evangelist saying that no one was able to speak about him openly. **[163]** He means the people [were fearful] of the nobles, but not the princes or the high priests of the rabble.[i]

    i. The meaning of the last sentence in Nonnus is unclear. The context and the corresponding passage in Tat'ewac'i, 324–25, indicate that the common people accepted Jesus, but the high priests and princes ("Pharisees" in Tat'ewac'i) did not. John Chrysostom, *Hom. Jo.* 49.1, contrasts the opinion of the multitude who thought Jesus good with that of the princes and priests. Similarly, Dionysius bar Salibi, *John*, 158, contrasts the opinion of the

------

    12. **And wickedness**: om. N.
    13. **Not**: om. N.
    14. **People**: pl. MNZ.
    15. **People, NZ**: pl. M.
    16. **Said**: om. M.

"simple crowd" (*knš' pšyt'*) with the opinion of the "others who said no," namely, the scribes, Pharisees, and priests.

[7:14–15] When the feast was in mid-course, Jesus went up to the temple and taught. The Jews were amazed and said: How does this one know letters, for he has not studied at all?

What does it mean: *When the feast was in mid-course?* Since they celebrated the feast for a few days one after the other, they were confused and agitated during those days. Now when that had passed,[i] then, he says, *Jesus went up to the temple*, indicating that when[17] for a brief while their errors and wicked agitations had ceased, at that time he went up to the temple to teach. And from then on[18] both sides heeded his teaching, some with pleasure as we said before, but others in order to find perchance some pretexts from his words. Whence is this clear? When they heard such lofty teachings,[19] they did not receive or believe them and question those who had remained[ii] but said to each other in amazement, *How does this one know letters, for he has not studied at all?* so that perhaps thereby they might set him at naught and show his teachings to be unacceptable as those of one not fully grasping what he was saying but teaching what little he had acquired through listening.

   i. Nonnus does not explain why the first few days of the feast would be agitated. Tat'ewac'i, 325, states that this was the fourth day of seven.
   ii. **Question those who had remained:** *zmnac'ealsn k'nnein.* There being no grammatical gender in Armenian, this might mean: "examine what remained."

[7:16] Jesus replied and said to them: My teaching is not mine but of the one who sent me.

Did you see the truth of the matter, how gently he reproved what they were saying and made it clear? And since they had made the pretext, *How does this one know letters, for he has not studied at all?* he declared: Not from letters alone do I have what I am teaching, which seemed something grand and wonderful to you, but it is[20] indeed from God. By that he cut short not only their words about his lack of learning but also their saying that he was[21] opposed to God. For if this is not my teaching **[164]** but that of the one who sent me,

---

17. **When:** om. N.
18. **From then on:** om. N.
19. **Teachings:** sg. N.
20. **It is,** *ē,* M: "if," *etē,* N.
21. **He was,** *gol:* om. N.

then I am not opposed to God, as you suppose, because I teach his teaching,[22] whereby it is clear that I am of the same will rather than opposed [to him].

[7:17] If anyone wishes to do his will, he shall know concerning my teaching[23] whether it is from God, or whether I speak from my own self.

What means: *If anyone wishes to do his will?* It is as if to say that if you cast from yourselves the envy and imputation and wickedness that you now possess, which is very hateful to God as you know from the commandment,[i] it would be easy for you to believe and accept that my teaching[ii] is from God, and not opposed to God, as you think.

    i. **Envy**: *naxanj*, perhaps a reference to Lev 18:18; **imputation**: *ambastanut'iwn*, or "accusation," is not used in the Law; **wickedness**: *čarut'iwn*. Since the text of the commentary is a translation, it is not clear what precise terms Nonnus may be referring to, and whether or not by "commandment" he means those of Moses.

    ii. **My teaching**: *vardapetut'iwns im*, here with the possessive pronoun; cf. the text of the lemma.

[7:18] Whoever speaks from himself seeks glory for himself. But whoever seeks glory for the one who sent him, he is true, and unrighteousness does not exist in him.

Because first he described his own teaching as not from himself but of the one who sent him, he then set down some testimonies to make his sayings easily acceptable. *Whoever speaks from himself seeks glory for himself* means that such a person may draw glory and praise to himself. But whoever will ascribe the sayings to another rather than to himself, then to him to whom the words have been applied is attached glory in all respects. Now if I continuously ascribe the working of the signs and the teachings to the Father, then it is clear that I do not seek my own glory but the glory of the Father who sent me. So you must follow my sayings and reject the scandals in which you say that I am opposed to the Father.

---

22. Teaching: pl. M.
23. **My teaching**: *vardpetut'eans*. The suffix *-s* has the nuance of "this" or "my."

[7:19–20a] Did not Moses give you the law, yet none of you keeps the law? Why do you seek to kill me?

Did we not mention previously the reason[24] **[165]** for which the Savior left Judea and came to Galilee? The evangelist explained that when he healed the paralytic on the Sabbath day, therefore the Jews were vexed and sought to kill him, because he destroyed the Sabbath and made himself equal to God (John 5:18).[i] Therefore once more he introduces the Sabbath and repeats that he said his teaching was not from himself but from the Father, lest they say: How do you say[25] you have your teaching from the Father, yet you destroy the Sabbaths that it was commanded to keep by the divinely bestowed laws? Therefore he next puts down Moses in order to excise the pretext for their wickedness concerning the Sabbath and his being equal to God. For that reason he said: *None of you keeps the law. Why do you seek to kill me?*

What does this mean? He says,[26] *I did not come to destroy*[27] the Mosaic [law] *but to complete it* (Matt 5:17),[ii] for it prevented the committing of sin, whereas I separate you from its very cause. For there he said not to commit adultery (Exod 20:14), whereas I prohibit looking with lust (Matt 5:28). He merely prevented swearing falsely (Exod 20:16), whereas I prohibit swearing at all[28] (Matt 5:34). He suppressed stealing (Exod 20:15), but I command the dissemination to the needy of lawfully acquired possessions (Luke 18:22). There an eye for an eye and a death for a death (Exod 21:12, 24), but I command to pray for enemies (Matt 5:44). So I do not destroy the laws of Moses but complete them. But you never keep the law, for although in many ways and examples (Heb 1:1) you have learned from the laws of Moses the testimonies that concern me, yet you have no zeal for that, but you seek to kill me.

i. Theodore of Mopsuestia, 112, also refers here to the healing of the paralytic; and Cyril of Alexandria, *Comm. Jo.* 4.5, refers to the condemnation of Christ for breaking the Sabbath.

ii. Here John Chrysostom, *Hom. Jo.* 49.1, specifies the law: *ou phoneueis* (Exod 20:15).

---

24. **Reason:** pl. N.
25. **You say:** om. M.
26. **He says:** om. M.
27. **Destroy,** *lucanel,* MZ: "abrogate," *xap'anel,* N.
28. **At all:** om. N.

[7:20b] The people replied: There is a demon in you. Who is it who seeks to kill you?

Who would not be astonished at their fury [166] and shameless arrogance? See the disrespectful insults, and the detestable wickedness of those who later became murderers!

[7:21] Jesus replied to them and said: I have done one work, and you are all amazed.

O unbounded benevolence and incomparable gentleness! He did not reply in accordance with their derision but turned his discourse to another subject by recalling again the healing of the paralytic at which they had once been astonished.[i] Thereby he brought their fury to calm. But what means: *You are amazed*? He says you were stirred up and confused about the sign [and said]: How does he do that and destroy the Sabbaths?

    i. All commentators define the "one work" as the healing of the paralytic.

[7:22] For that reason Moses gave you circumcision, for it was not from Moses but from the fathers; *and on the Sabbath you circumcise a man.[29]

Did you see how gently he reproved what they alleged regarding the Mosaic law?[i] The law that Moses commanded you is not the law of Moses, who has legislated something for you, but was created earlier than him. Abraham first acquired it (Gen 17:10),[ii] and this same law of Moses[iii] was annulled. How, then, could he be the annuller? Since you have the command to circumcise an infant at the age of eight days (Gen 17:12), and often the circumcision occurs on the Sabbath, by honoring the Sabbath you do not prevent the circumcision, but on that very Sabbath day you circumcise.[iv] So then it is clear that through the law of Abraham you annul the law of Moses, which you confess to observe indestructibly. If this is so, why are you angry with me, because it is far superior and more honorable to heal the whole man on the Sabbath than merely to circumcise?[v]

    i. **Law:** *awrēnk'*, a plural form throughout for the collective noun.
    ii. The priority of Abraham is stressed by Dionysius bar Salibi, *John*, 161, and Tat'ewac'i, 330.
    iii. **This same law of Moses:** or, "the law of this same Moses."

---

    29. **And … man:** om. M.

iv. Theodore of Mopsuestia states that Moses ordered circumcision on the Sabbath.
Išodad and Dionysius bar Salibi indicate that circumcision breaks the Sabbath rule.

v. Dionysius bar Salibi offers a similar argument.

[167] [7:23] Now, if a man receives circumcision on the Sabbath, lest the law of Moses be broken, are you angry with me because I have cured a man whole on the Sabbath?

Did you see how he silenced them? For if you, he says, on account of the Sabbath occurring on the eighth [day],[i] circumcise and break the Sabbath, which you have received the command to observe and on it to do nothing[ii] save the most insignificant things, then you break the law through the law, that is, the Sabbath by the circumcision, and not the circumcision by the Sabbath. You have become angry with me because once I healed on the Sabbath all the limbs of the man. So you should either observe the law concerning the Sabbath and refrain from circumcision on the Sabbath day, or not be angry with me because of the healing that [I performed] on the Sabbath. So if you annul the circumcision and become angry with me over the healing, then you testify about your own selves that you are very unjust and impious.

   i. **Eighth [day]:** i.e., the eighth day after the child's birth.
   ii. **To do nothing:** *datarkanal*, as 1 Esd 1:58 (Armenian version).

[7:24] Do not judge according to appearance, but carry out right judgment.

What, then, means what he said: *Do not judge according to appearance,* yet you ascribe the law to Moses, because he commanded you to annul the Sabbath by circumcision, which is very incomparable and unequal to my miracles? If the breaking of the Sabbath is blameworthy, then should you have blamed Moses, who destroyed the Sabbath through circumcision? But you passed over him and are angry at me. Let us also see what he says, that if it seemed good to Moses to make another's law superior to his own law, that is, the circumcision of Abraham [168] to his own Sabbaths,[i] then you are not possessors of the law but merely followers. You must conciliate and assent to Moses, who annulled the Sabbath by circumcision. So then you judge according to appearance and not rightly.

   i. In this discussion concerning the Sabbath, the word *šabat'* appears sometimes in the singular, sometimes in the plural (without variants in the MSS), for no clear reason.

[7:25–26] Some of the Jerusalemites said: Is not this the one whom they sought to kill? Behold, he speaks openly, yet they say nothing to him. Perhaps then the princes knew that this is the Christ.

Why did the evangelist reveal that the speakers were Jerusalemites? It was in order to show that those [words] were not spoken by people who had come from anywhere to the feast, but they were themselves Jerusalemites, and by this to indicate that they were worse and more filled with hate than the others.[i] They had seen so many signs and miracles by which they would have been more able to recognize that he was the Christ than those who had come to the feast for the occasion. But the latter were silent, and these were continually slandering [him].

    i. Moše bar Kepha indicates the same.

[7:27] But we know whence this one is. However, when the Christ will come, no one knows whence he will be.

Did you really understand what they said, how to know through ignorance and to be ignorant with knowledge? What would this mean? They said they knew the one whom they called the Galilean and son of Joseph; and they said they did not know the one whom they pointed out[i] to the magi and to Herod when they asked where the Christ would be born, and they said: *In Bethlehem of Judea* (Matt 2:5).[ii] This they had frequently learned from the prophets, and they indicated the place unerringly. Did you see how they perverted the truth and testify to their [own] falsehood?

    i. **Pointed out:** *matamb c'uc'anēin* (lit. "showed with a finger"). There is no reference to a "finger," *matn*, in the biblical account of the visit of the magi (Matt 2:1–12), though in illuminated manuscripts the magi are often portrayed pointing to the star. The related expression *matnac'oyc' aṙnel* is common, meaning "to indicate."
    ii. Here Moše bar Kepha, Dionysius bar Salibi, and Išodad cite Mic 5:2.

[7:28a] Jesus cried out in the temple; he taught and said: You both know me and you know whence I am. I have not come of myself, but the one who sent me is true.

[169] Because they first said, *When the*[30] *Christ will come no one knows, but we know this one*, consequently he teaches something different by saying,

---

    30. The: om. N.

You both know me and you know whence I am. If you are true in your speaking, you must know me as different than whom you said I was, son of Joseph and a Galilean;[i] [you must] know[31] me not thus but as Son of God, and by his will sent to earth from heaven, not from Galilee.[32] He truly is the one to whom he testified concerning me: *This is my beloved son, with whom I am pleased* (Matt 3:17; Mark 1:11; Luke 3:22).

    i. The grammar of this sentence is confused.

[7:28b–29] Whom you do not know; but I know him, because indeed I am from him, and he sent me.

By this he reproves them even more. Whom you do not recognize; that is, *if you recognized him,[33] then you would recognize me because of my coming[34] from him. But I know him, because I am indeed from him, and he sent me. Not, he says, like the prophets[35] who were sent from him do I know him, but perfectly, that is, by nature and essence.

[7:30] They sought to arrest him, *but he went from their hands,[36] and no one laid hands on him, because his hour had not yet come.

Why does the evangelist reveal that they sought to arrest him and he went from their hands? It was to indicate his power to us,[37] that he was willingly seized when he was seized, and he did not come to the torments of the cross by compulsion.[i]

    i. This is the argument in Cyril of Alexandria; Theodore of Mopsuestia; Moše bar Kepha; and Dionysius bar Salibi, *John*, 163.

[7:31–32] And many of the people believed in him and said: When the Christ will come, will he not perform more signs than this one does? And

---

31. **Know**, *gitel*, M: "to be," *linel*, N.
32. **Galilee**: + "but to Bethlehem, in the flesh from the house of David," M.
33. **If…him**: om. N.
34. **Coming**, *galoy*, N: "being," *goloy*, M.
35. **Prophets**: sg. N (but pl. verb).
36. **But…hands**: MNZ, but not in the Greek; cf. John 10:39.
37. **Us**: + "and," M.

the Pharisees heard the murmuring of the people, and the high priests and Pharisees sent servants to arrest him.

[170] Did you see the errors and envy of the Pharisees and high priests,[38] how they bore witness against themselves that they did not seek to kill him because of the Sabbath—since the discussion about the Sabbath had been concluded when he silenced and reprimanded them so much—but they only wished to kill him lest the people believe in him,[i] and by following him would despise their high priesthood?[39] But why did they not send [persons] from among the people to arrest him but from among the servants? It was because the servants perhaps were Romans, Pilate's soldiers possessed of royal authority.[ii] For that reason they dispatched them excited and full of anger to arrest him. But they had no confidence in the people; because of the signs that they were continually seeing [performed] by the Savior perhaps they would not lay hands on him, they who also said: *When the Christ will come, will he not perform more signs than this one does?* Whereby it is clear that for that reason they did not trust the people.

 i. Dionysius bar Salibi, *John*, 164, notes that the Pharisees and high priests acted out of envy, not because of the Sabbath.
 ii. Other commentators do not identify the servants with Pilate's Roman soldiers.

[7:33–34] **Jesus said: For a short time more[40] I am with you, and I go to him who sent me. You shall seek me and not find, and where I go you cannot come.**

O awesome spoken words, which they did not at all understand at the time! It is as if to say: You who now wish to seize me and are unable,[41] after a little time I shall willingly deliver myself into your hands. And although you will suppose me to have died after being tormented on the cross, yet I shall rapidly rise and ascend to heaven;[i] you will seek me so that I may show you the same signs, especially when the Roman bandits and their swords will come upon you,[ii] but you will not find me. And you will not be able to come to me, [171] because of my being from then onward in heaven. But now, for the short time as long as I am with you, I shall not allow the bandits and the great destruction to come upon you, because it is necessary to fulfill all the writings

---

38. **High priests**, MV: "priests," N.
39. **High priesthood**: pl. M.
40. **More**, MZ: om. N.
41. **And are unable**: om. M.

regarding service and support for the world, especially when fearsome signs and miracles will occur on the cross as a reprimand to you and for the preaching of my divinity.

i. Cyril of Alexandria and Dionysius bar Salibi (*John*, 164) here refer to the ascension.
ii. Moše bar Kepha and Dionysius bar Salibi (*John*, 165) here refer to the Roman attack in 70 CE under Titus.

[7:35–36] The Jews said: Whither then will he go, that we shall not find him? Will he go to the diaspora of the Gentiles and teach the Gentiles? What is that[42] saying that he pronounced: You will seek me and will not find, and where I go, you cannot come?

It is a [cause of] wonder whither he would go. Yet [the words] have no profundity, even though they did not understand the meaning of the saying. But *the diaspora of the Gentiles* is to be examined, who they might be:[43] by *diaspora of the Gentiles* they were referring to the idolatrous nations,[44] because by such a name did they call the idolators at that time.[i]

i. Dionysius bar Salibi, *John*, 165, describes the Gentiles as *ḥnp'*, "pagans."

[7:37a] On the last day, the great [day] of the feast, Jesus stood, cried out, and said:

He indicates that on this day[i] the multitude of the crowds was even greater. And because the visitors to the feast were about to return to each one's own place, for their sake the Savior cried out in order to teach them before they scattered to their own places, so that he might impel their minds to the faith.[ii] Therefore he said:

i. In the Armenian lemma "great," *meci*, is declined but has no suffix to render the Greek *tē* (the article for *megalē*). If *mec* qualified "feast," *tawnin*, in initial position it would remain uninflected. Moše bar Kepha and Dionysius bar Salibi make the interpretation clear by rendering: "on the great, that is, last day of the feast." Step'annos of Siwnik', 136, indicates that the last day was the eighth, because they celebrated the feast for seven days; Cyril of Alexandria, *Comm. Jo.* 5.1, cites Lev 23:34–36 for the seven days, adding that the first and seventh day were holy and thus called "great." Tat'ewac'i, 338, says that the great day was the seventh or eighth.

---

42. **That,** *ayn*, MZ: om. N.
43. **Who they might be:** om. N.
44. **Nations:** sg. N.

ii. Išodad expands on the three main feasts of Judaism, and Dionysius bar Salibi, *John*, 165, gives a long discussion of the three feasts as shadows of Christian feasts: Passover corresponds to the passion; Pentecost to the descent of the Holy Spirit; Tabernacles to the transformation.

[7:37b] **If anyone is thirsty, let him come to me and drink.**

He did not indicate simply any water, that if anyone were thirsty he would be able to drink. But it was as if to say, if any of you will have in his mind a need for the faith by which he may wish to extinguish the heat of demonic error, **[172]** let him come to me and drink, because I shall give him as drink the water of life.[i] This the prophet Isaiah declared: *You who are thirsty, go to water.*[ii] See also what follows, indicating the same, what power he has in himself by saying:

    i. Tat'ewac'i, 339, quotes John Chrysostom for equating the water with faith.
    ii. Isa 55:1, also quoted by Tat'ewac'i, 340.

[7:38] **Whoever believes in me, as the scriptures say,[45] rivers of waters of life shall flow from his belly.**

Because the people were not united with each other[46]—since some said, *When the Christ will come, will he not perform more signs than this one does?*[47] while others said, *The Christ will come from the line of David and from the village of Bethlehem* (John 7:31, 42)—consequently the Savior contrived something else for their salvation.[48] After the signs and miracles at which they wondered and said, *When the Christ will come, will he not perform more than this one does?* he set down next the testimony of the scriptures and said, *Whoever believes in me, as the scriptures say,* in order to make firm those who said, *Do not the scriptures show that Christ will come from the line of David and from the village of Bethlehem?* Thereby he instructs them that the testimonies of the scriptures [spoken] by the prophets are about himself.

But what means: *Rivers will flow from his belly*? He did not wish to say, *from their bellies* but *from their hearts*, as David bears witness: *Your laws in my belly* (Ps 39:9).[i] He did not mean his stomach but his heart, the storehouse[ii] of

---

    45. Prov 18:4; Isa 58:11.
    46. **With each other:** om. N.
    47. **Than this one does:** om. N.
    48. **Salvation,** *p'rkut'iwn*, MV: "anger," *barkut'iwn*, N.

thoughts;[49] and he did not speak of rivers flowing from the belly[50] but of the faith. For just as the perpetual current of rivers indicates the inexhaustibility of nature, with such an example he proclaimed the flowing of faith from the mind proceeding incessantly by the grace of the Holy Spirit.[iii]

i. Moše bar Kepha and Dionysius bar Salibi (*John*, 168) both identify the belly with the heart, quoting this verse.

ii. The Armenian version of Basil of Caesarea, *Hex.* 5.6 (Muradyan, 148), also uses the term "storehouse," *štemaran*, of the heart.

iii. Tat'ewac'i, 340, quotes John Chrysostom on this perpetual motion.

[173] [7:39a] **This he said concerning the Spirit, which those who believed[51] in him would receive.**

See[52] how the evangelist revealed the meaning of this saying, teaching us clearly the Savior's words, so as to say that by *rivers* he indicated the grace of the Holy Spirit,[i] whereby faith, established in the storehouses of the hearts of the believers, causes propagation, bearing the example of the inexhaustibility of rivers.

i. Cyril of Alexandria, *Comm. Jo.* 5.1; and Dionysius bar Salibi, *John*, 168, also equate the rivers with grace.

[7:39b] **Since the Spirit had not yet been [given], because Jesus had not been[53] glorified.**

This saying is very much to be investigated. Since the disciples had often performed signs and miracles, how was the Spirit not yet [given]? Furthermore, the prophets prophesied through the Holy Spirit and performed signs and miracles, for which reason it is necessary to propose a solution. The disciples had received from the Savior authority to perform miracles, as he said to them: *Behold, I gave you authority* (John 10:19). And although the prophets prophesied by the grace of the Holy Spirit, yet that was not comparable to this, for then some[54] gifts and inspiration were received from the grace of the Holy

---

49. **Thoughts**: sg. N.

50. **Belly**: + "to the belly," N.

51. **Those who believed**, *or hawatayin*, NZ: "the believers," *k'awatac'ealk'n* [*sic*] for *hawatac'ealk'*, M.

52. **See**: "Did you see," M.

53. **Not been**, NZ: + "yet," M.

54. **Some**, *inč'*: om. N.

Spirit, but after the Savior rose from the dead the Holy Spirit descended to the upper room and rested on the apostles (Acts 2:1–13).[i] Not partially did it inspire them, but it filled them—and not only them but also the upper room in which they were sitting, and not only the upper room but also the whole world by shining out on the earth.

Now, what means: *Jesus had not been glorified*? He does not say that he acquired some glory that he did not previously possess, but he calls the cross glory (Gal 6:14).[ii] Why? Because on it the awesome signs and powers of his divine nature were revealed by heaven and[55] earth, and announced from heaven and from earth, and from then on suspicions of weakness were removed. Although the wicked nation of the Jews denied [him], all creatures glorified him, testifying[56] that he is the Son of God. If this were not so, why was the sun darkened, [174] and the moon hid its light, rocks were split, the veil was rent, and also the dead came out of their tombs and reproved the Jews (Matt 27:51–53)? Because of all that[57] he called the cross glory. Now why did the Spirit descend on the disciples not before the cross but after the cross, save that our Savior might first create peace in heaven and on earth *through the blood of his cross,[58] for which reason he said he sent him into the world, and that he might *crush* the enemy (Rom 16:20) and *destroy the partition of the wall* (Eph 2:14), and reconcile the Father with creatures according to Paul: *We were reconciled with God through the death of his Son* (Rom 5:10)? [Only] then would it be appropriate for the Spirit to descend to the world. For at first only the Father became known to creatures because of their thick-witted unbelief; later the Son was made known to the world; and afterward the Holy Spirit descended and was revealed to the world. In this way, gradually the Trinity became acknowledged to the thick-witted, who once through demons worshiped the images of idols.

i. Dionysius bar Salibi, *John*, 168; and Tat'ewac'i, 341, also contrast the effect of the Spirit on the prophets and on the apostles.

ii. John Chrysostom, *Hom. Jo.* 51.2; and Dionysius bar Salibi, *John*, 168, repeat the identification of cross and glory. Cyril of Alexandria, *Comm. Jo.* 5.2, states that the glory follows the resurrection.

[7:40–44] **Some of the people, when they heard these words, said: This is the true prophet. Others said: This is the Christ. While others said: Surely the**

---

55. **By heaven and:** om. N.

56. **Testifying:** om. N.

57. **All that,** N: "those things," M.

58. **Through … cross:** om. N.

Christ will not come from Galilee? Do not the scriptures say that the Christ will come from the seed of David, from the village of Bethlehem? And there was a division among the people concerning him. And some of them wished to arrest him, but[59] no one laid hands on him.

Did you see how they were reproached and rebuked by themselves? First they said: *When the Christ will come, we shall not know whence he is.* But then they said: *Do not the scriptures say that the Christ will come from the seed of David and from the village of Bethlehem?* So if we have testimony from the scriptures that Christ will come from the seed of David[60] and the village of Bethlehem, how do you deny it, [saying] that when the Christ will come no one will know whence he is? Furthermore, he says, they introduced another calumny that they did not know that[61] [175] Christ was born from the village of Bethlehem. Would they not also disavow what they said: *We know him to be the son of Joseph, and his brothers are James and John and Judas*[62] (Matt 13:55; Mark 6:3; John 6:42)? Did they not know at all that Joseph and Mary were from the house of David? But it was in order that their falsity and pride might be totally revealed.

Also when they heard him saying, *Whoever believes in me, as the scriptures say,* they should have examined what further[63] the scriptures say, for which reason you continuously apply the testimonies of the scriptures for yourself. But they paid no heed to that. Why? Lest he reprove and silence them by introducing the testimonies from the scriptures. But if they were to say, Why did he himself not reveal the testimonies?[64] because he knew that they would not receive them and be helped, therefore he refrained from expounding the testimonies.

[7:45–46] Then the servants came to the high priests and Pharisees, and they said to them: Why did you not bring him here? The servants replied: No man ever[65] spoke like that man.

Did you see how they were reproved by the servants as well, who were indeed Gentiles and did not know the law and the prophets, nor had they seen

---

59. **But,** MZ: "and," N.
60. **The seed of David:** om. N.
61. **They did not know that:** om. N.
62. **And Judas:** om. N.
63. **Further:** om. M.
64. **Testimonies:** sg. N.
65. **Ever,** MZ: "thus," N.

any signs [performed] by the Savior or ever heard [his] frequent teachings?ⁱ
They believed just a few words above and beyond men's confession of his
teachings. But the former had so assimilated the testimonies from the law and
from the prophets that they knew his line of descent and the village whence
the Christ would come. They had also seen a myriad signs and heard his sublime teachings, yet they paid no attention to the truth, but being stubborn
merely said to the servants: *Why did you not bring him here?*

    i. See above, commentary to v. 32, for the servants being soldiers.

[176] [7:47–49] **The Pharisees replied and said: Have you too not gone
astray? Did any of the princes believe in him, or of the Pharisees? But [only]
that vulgar crowd who do not know the law and are accursed.**

Why did they not ask about the words that they had spoken? But they
passed over that, lest perhaps the servants might describe something about
the Savior that would be against themselves and pleasing to the people. For
that reason they passed over that and replied, *Have you too not*ⁱ *gone astray?*
with further vague and unprofitable words.

    i. **Have you not:** for the sense of *mitē* in Armenian, see note to the commentary on
John 6:68, above.

[7:50–51] **Nicodemus, who had previously come to him by night and was
one of them, said to them: Do our laws judge a man unless they first⁶⁶ hear
something from him or know what he does?⁶⁷**

Why⁶⁸ does Nicodemus state that?ⁱ For when the Pharisees said, *Did any
of the princes believe in him? But [only] those who did not know the law and are
accursed,* therefore Nicodemus wisely declared what he said. Not only was he
from among the princes, but [he was] also a teacher of the Jews, and he did
not desire to say anything very harsh about Christ in opposition to them, or
to reveal the faith in Christ that he possessed in the depths of his heart (John
3:1–21). For that reason with a gentle word he calmed their wickedness by
introducing the judgments of the law: *Do our laws judge a man unless they first
hear something from him or know what he does?*⁶⁹ This was as if to say that you

---

66. **First,** MVZ: om. N.
67. **He does,** *gorcē,* MZ: editor prints *gorcen* (pl.) for *gorcēn* (sg. + suffix).
68. **Why:** + "does he teach," N.
69. **He does,** *gorcē,* MZ: editor prints *gorcen* (pl.); see note to the lemma.

must hold a tribunal, and investigate the man in front of all and hear from him about himself, and also know his deeds and not lay hand on him without some cause or charge. [177] By this he wished to frustrate their evil plans, because he knew that they would find no pretext[70] against him for condemning him to death.

 i. **Does Nicodemus state that**: *vardapetē* ["he teaches," om. M] *zayn dnē Nikodimos.* The grammar is confused. In John 3:10 Nicodemus is called *vardapet*, "teacher"; perhaps *vardapetn*, "the teacher," was introduced into the text and the scribe of N made it a verb.

[7:52] They replied to him[71] and said: Are you also a Galilean? Examine and see, because a prophet does not arise from Galilee.

Did you see how they disowned what Nicodemus had said, [that] the laws forbid judging anyone without investigation? They turned the argument[i] to a different pattern by saying, *A prophet does not arise from Galilee.* When, then, did he say he was a prophet or[72] from Galilee? Never[73] did they say this about him. So they introduced accusations and calumnies in accordance with their deceit and only attempted to invent and fabricate fictitious words, since they were planning to lay hands on him.[ii]

 i. **The argument**: *zbansn.* It is not clear whether Nonnus means that the Pharisees changed their own argument or that they distorted the words of Nicodemus.
 ii. Nonnus omits John 7:53–8:11, the Pericope of the Adultress. For the textual evidence, see Metzger 1975 (219–22). John Chrysostom, Cyril of Alexandria, Theodore of Mopsuestia, and Moše bar Kepha also omit the episode in their commentaries. Dionysius bar Salibi includes the pericope but places it after 8:20. Tat'ewac'i, 351, states: "Here is a supplement to the Gospel [*awelord awetarann*] about the adulterous woman, the commentary on which we shall put at the end of the Gospel." But in fact Tat'ewac'i did not complete his *Commentary on the Gospel of John*, which ends with comments on only a few verses of ch. 21.

---

70. **Pretext**: pl. N.
71. **To him**, MZ: om. N.
72. **A prophet or**: om. N.
73. **Never**: "indeed not," N.

[8:12] **Jesus spoke again with them and said: I am the light of the world. Whoever follows me will not walk through darkness but will receive the light of life.**

How would this be appropriate for their remarks, except because they were always repeating *Galilee* and that he was from there, because they despised Galilee[1] and counted it[2] as nothing? Just as Nathaniel had said, *Is it possible for anything good to come from Galilee?* here they said[3] the same: *A prophet does not arise from Galilee* (John 1:46; 7:52). Consequently he adds[4] something very important to the same, saying, *I am the light of the world.* It seems to me that in reproaching them he is introducing that prophecy that Isaiah spoke: *The land of Zabulon and the land of Nephtalim, Galilee of the Gentiles, a people who sat in darkness saw a great light,*[i] indicating that he was not a prophet from Galilee nor a light shining only on Israel, but on all [178] nations who believed in him. He also reveals something else by the sayings concerning Galilee, that by the *light* that he mentioned, when they recalled Galilee with contempt, he was speaking about that light from Galilee in order to demonstrate its being revealed there, which indeed did illuminate those sitting in the darkness of the ignorance of sin.

i. Isa 9:1–2, also quoted here by Theodore of Mopsuestia.

---

1. **Galilee:** "Galileans," M.
2. **It,** *na:* or "him."
3. **Said:** om. N.
4. **Adds,** *yarē,* MV: "arranges," *yardarē,* N.

[8:13] The Pharisees said: You bear witness about yourself, and your testimony is not true.

As if they were to say that you bear witness about yourself that you are the light of the world, and no one accepts it because it is not true when anyone bears witness about himself.[i]

i. Cyril of Alexandria, *Comm. Jo.* 5.2, notes that there is no law forbidding testimony by one's own self.

[8:14] Jesus replied and said to them: Although I testify concerning myself, my testimony is true, because I know whence I come and whither I go. But you do not know whence I come or whither I go.

What means, as a solution to their query: *My testimony is true, because I know whence I come and whither I go*? It is as if to say that I came in the flesh to the world from the Father, humbled for the salvation of the world. And what is: *My witness is true*? [It means] that I came from the Father and I am coessential and coglorious with him in every way,[i] and my testimonies[5] about myself are true because I am his Son. If you had so desired, you would have been able to receive my testimonies from the signs and[6] miracles that you have from the scriptures, which does not befit any other nature than the son of God.

i. Cyril of Alexandria, *Comm. Jo.* 5.2, refers here to Christ's divine nature made man, and Theodore of Mopsuestia to Christ's humanity and divinity. Dionysius bar Salibi, *John*, 172, notes the Son's equality of honor with the Father, while Išodad discusses the equality of the Trinity.

[8:15a] You judge according to the flesh.

Did you see how he clarifies the saying, as if to say that you do not believe or recognize or know me,[7] whence I come or whither I go, for the reason that you judge according to the flesh? You make such judgment concerning me in your minds, he says, as you see me[8] having put on a body and humbled to a state of weakness, [179] yet you pass over what through the signs you should notice with the eye of the spirit, or the testimonies that you should investigate

---

5. **Testimonies:** sg. N (but pl. verb).
6. **And:** om. N.
7. **Me,** *zis,* M: "whom," *zor,* N.
8. **Me:** om. N.

in your minds.[i] And you do not wish at all to question me truthfully who I might be, but only through deceit and testing.

i. Cyril of Alexandria, *Comm. Jo.* 5.2, states: "You see me clothed in your flesh, but you do not perceive the mystery of the *oikonomia* in the flesh."

[8:15b–16a] I do not judge anyone. Even if I judge someone,[9] my judgment is true.

Lest they were to say, Why do you not condemn us? Behold, according to your account we contradict you and despise and mock you, he interjects this distinction: *I do not judge anyone,* as if to say that this is not the time for condemnation, since I did not come into the world to judge but to give life; the time for revenge is different. But what means: *Although I judge, my judgment is true*? Because this does not follow from the previous, consequently it indicates that although now I do not judge, yet later I am to judge the judgment of the resurrection. And what is *true*? It means that the Father does not judge anyone, but *he gave all judgment to the Son* (John 5:22),[i] and he judges truly.

i. Dionysius bar Salibi, *John*, 172, stresses that the judgment of the Father and of the Son is one.

[8:16b] For I am not alone, but I and the Father who sent me.

He reveals the inseparability and undivided nature and unity of will of himself and the Father, in order to demonstrate that just as their essence and will are one,[i] so also their testimonies.[10] For not I alone testify about myself, but also my Father testifies to me likewise, just as he testified clearly in the ears of you all at [my] descent into the Jordan: *This is my beloved Son.*[ii]

i. For the technical terms, see the introduction, xxxv–xxxviii.
ii. Matt 3:17; see also at the transfiguration, Matt 17:5; Mark 9:6 (7).

---

9. **Someone**, MV: om. N.
10. **Testimonies**: sg. N.

[8:17–18] It is also written in your laws that the testimonies of two men are[11] **true. I am [the one] who bear witness about myself; the Father who sent me bears witness about me.**

Do not think that he set this down **[180]** in order to confirm the testimonies[12] of the Father and himself about himself, for if he had wished to confirm them he would also have cited John and[13] scripture, just as[14] he often did. But here it seems to me that he wished to awaken their minds to the faith, that I am God coequal with the Father. Whence is this clear? It was not appropriate for the Jews that he indicate himself and the Father as witnesses about himself, because whoever relates anything about himself, his own testimony about himself is consequently not acceptable, nor is it fitting for the witness to be a cowitness about himself. But because when he wished[15] to indicate the teachings that concerned his divine nature, therefore he said, *And the Father who sent me testifies about me*, indicating that no one else was sent from heaven, *nor did he ever call God Father.*[i] So by these sayings he reveals that in order to make his essence[ii] known he taught that it is no longer appropriate for a man to bear witness about himself, but only for the true God.

    i. **Nor … Father:** *ew oč' Hayr erbēk' zAstuac kočeac'.* As the text of M and N stands, the sense is unclear. A later hand in M added *ok'* ("anyone") between *z* (direct object marker) and *Astuac*; but that does not solve the crux: Nor did the Father ever call anyone God!

    ii. **Essence:** *ēut'iwn.* Here John Chrysostom, *Hom. Jo.* 52.3, refers to the Son and Father being of the same *ousia*, and Dionysius bar Salibi, *John*, 173, also notes their equality of *ousia*.

[8:19] They said to him: Where is your Father? Jesus replied and said to them:[16] **You do not know me or my**[17] **Father. If you knew me, perhaps you would know my Father.**

Did you see how the meaning of the passage was clearly indicated[18] and how he reproved them? It was as if to say: If you wished to know the Father, then you would investigate and understand what I am always teaching you

---

11. **Testimonies, are**, N: "testimony," "is," MZ.
12. **Testimonies:** sg. M.
13. **And:** "like," N.
14. **Just as:** om. N.
15. **He wished:** om. N.
16. **To them**, NZ: om. M.
17. **My**, MZ: "the," N.
18. **Was indicated**, N: "indicates," M (*sic*).

about me, *concerning the fact that I am his Son,[19] because knowledge of the Father is through the Son. For through my revelation even the invisible Father would be understood by you, if you wished to know [him]. For just as one comprehends the sun through its rays, [181] and the mind through its speech, and the tree from its fruit, likewise through the Son one may know the Father and his will.

[8:20] **This he spoke with them in the house of the treasury when he was teaching in the temple. And they did not seize[20] him, because his hour had not yet arrived.**

Why does the evangelist makes this[21] clear yet provide no indication of his teaching or signs? It was precisely in order to show us that they wished to seize him but were unable, especially because he was not where they expected because of the crowd, just as he indicates elsewhere. But while he was teaching openly in the temple and that wicked-minded nation[22] was nearby and very prepared to lay hands on him, yet they were unable to hold him, indicating that it was not possible for anyone to lay hands on him unless he himself wished.[i] And when they would be able to arrest him and bring him to the torments of the cross, it would be clear to all that he surrendered himself willingly to torments and death for the sake of the salvation of the world, just as he said: *I have power to lay down my life, and again I have power to take it up* (John 10:18).[ii]

    i. That Christ could only be arrested by his own will is stressed by Cyril of Alexandria, *Comm. Jo.* 5.3; and Dionysius bar Salibi, *John*, 173.
    ii. After v. 20 Dionysius bar Salibi inserts the Pericope of the Adulterous Woman; see above, note to commentary on John 7:52.

[8:21] **Again Jesus said to them: I go, and you shall seek me. And you will die in your sins, for where I go, you cannot come.**

Often he repeated to them the sayings[23] of his going. Why? In order thereby continually[24] to reprove their presumption in planning to kill him; and also to reveal his own foreknowledge of what they were going to do; and

---

19. **Concerning … Son:** om. N.
20. **They did not seize,** N: "no one seized," MZ.
21. **This:** om. N.
22. **Nation:** pl. M.
23. **Sayings:** sg. N.
24. **Continually:** om. N.

in order to show again that I am seized by you of my own free will, and you are quite unable to accomplish by force any of the things you are planning against me.

Now, what means: *You will die in your sins*? It is very obvious to all that it is as if to say: If after so many [182] teachings and signs, and even what you will see on the cross, you do not believe, consequently you will certainly[25] die in your sins; and thereby he taunts and nettles them. For what could be worse than to die in unbelief?

[8:22] The Jews said: Will he kill himself, *since he said that where I go you cannot come?[26]

Why did they say that, save because when they heard from him, *Where I go you cannot come*, they had such thoughts out of hatred and great wickedness: Will he then *do himself an injury and[27] commit suicide? And this they claimed as a boast for themselves, as if from fear of them he would do that.

[8:23] Jesus said to them: You are from below, I am from above. You are from this world, I am not from this world.

O sweetness and immeasurable pardon! Let us consider from his response to them and their insolence how gently he reproved them quite openly. For when they said such a thing, that perhaps he might kill himself, he then declared, *You are from below*, as if to say that what you say and think is nothing surprising, because you are thick-witted and malevolent, always dragged downward, and you have no thought for higher or heavenly things. Such wicked thoughts and intentions are appropriate for you to plan and carry out, for never do you eschew sin, but you wish to bring innocent blood upon yourselves.

What then is: *I am from above*? It is to indicate that never are such thoughts and intentions entertained by me, because such wicked thoughts are of earthly ones, but not of one who came from heaven. And what means: [183] *I am not from the world*? He does not reject taking the body[i] from us who are in the world, but it is to show that the wicked thoughts of the worldly that you entertain are never reflected in me.

i. **The body:** *zmarminn.* For the ambiguity of *marmin* as "body" or "flesh," see the introduction, xxxvii.

---

25. **Certainly:** om. N.
26. **Since … come:** om. M.
27. **Do himself … and:** om. N.

[8:24] But I said to you that you will die in your sins, because if you will not believe that I am, you will die in your sins.

Once more he reproves and taunts them that they will receive inevitable punishments by dying in their sins. As for their thinking that the Savior sins against himself by killing himself, he indicates that you are the ones who sin against your own selves and are to be surrendered to terrible torments, because you will kill your own selves through unbelief.

[8:25a] They said to him: Who are you?

O shameless impudence! After so much teaching and so many signs, as if not seeing or hearing, they asked: *Who are you?* What ingratitude or impiety could there be worse than that, when they not only did not believe but even showed themselves to be unacquainted with him, asking, *Who are you?*

[8:25b–26] Jesus said to them: *What at the beginning I also speak with you.[28] I have many things to say about you and to judge; but he who sent me is true, and what I heard from him, that I speak in the world.

These sayings seem unclear; therefore it is necessary to study the meaning of the passage.[29] First they asked, *Who are you?*; therefore he said, *What at the beginning I also speak with you.*[i] What does this mean? It is as if to say: Although I began to speak with you, yet you were not worthy, because my words concerning your not receiving [me][ii] are superfluous. For not because of believing or for advantage[30] **[184]** did you ask me who I am, but deceitfully you attempted to entrap me and to find some pretexts by trickery, for which reason it is not necessary to tell you who I might be. For I made known to you more than a few times through teachings and signs who I might be. But the more I multiplied these, even the more did you increase in deceit and evildoing.

But what means: *I have many things?* [He means] from your scriptures [with which] to reproach you.[iii] Now, *to judge* the following explains.[31] But

---

28. **What ... you:** For the ambiguities in the text, see Metzger 1975 (ad loc.). MNZ read literally: "At the beginning because also I speak indeed with you" (*tēn archēn hoti kai lalō hymin*).

29. **Of the passage,** *banin:* om. N.

30. **Or for advantage:** om. N.

31. **Explains,** *meknē,* N: "reveals," *yaytnē,* M.

the Father who sent me is true[32] is as if to say that I am now sent not to judge you but to give life to those who believe in the word of life. Why did he make worthy of this[33] those who would not listen and receive, save in order to make clear that nothing of their evil intentions was hidden from him, and in order to demonstrate his own ability, that not for that reason was he unable to condemn them, but because it was not the time for vengeance?

> i. For the literal sense, see the note to the lemma.
> ii. The verb "receive" has no object.
> iii. The text is phrased as a quotation: "I have many things from your scriptures to reproach you."

[8:27] **And they did not know that he was speaking to them about the Father.**

Here again the evangelist accuses them and says, *They did not know he spoke to them about the Father*, as if amazed at their folly and inflexible wickedness[34] that after so much instruction they did not realize that he was speaking to them about the Father.

[8:28–29a] **Jesus said to them: When you will raise up the son of man, then you will know that I am, and I do nothing by myself. But as the Father taught me, thus do I speak; and the Father who sent me is with me.**

Since[35] he had previously said, *I have many things to say about you and to judge, but the Father who sent me is true*, he made it clear that not now do I condemn and censure you, because the Father sent me not to judge but to give life to those who would believe. Again the evangelist testified, *They did not know that he spoke to them about the Father*, [185] therefore he said, *When you will raise up the son of man, then you will know that I am*, as if to say: Although you did not now understand that my words concern the Father, yet when you will raise up the son of man, that is, on the cross,[i] whom now you consider a mere man, then you will recall my sayings, that I came forth from God and am the Son of God, king of all creatures. How will this occur? When creatures hasten to preach this from heaven and earth.

And again after my being raised up into heaven, when I shall hand you over into the hands of enemies, and famines and slaughter and captivity and

---

32. **Is true:** om. N.
33. **Of this:** pl. M.
34. **And inflexible wickedness:** om. N.
35. **Since,** *vasn zi:* om. M.

expulsion[36] will hold sway over you, and your city will be destroyed, and the institutions of your laws will totally come to an end,[ii] then you will recall again my words that I am now speaking to you and [that] you do not receive and put out of your minds. And shaking and terrible fear will surround you, and you will call out and I shall not heed you. I shall omit to mention what you are to receive in the future judgment, the unending torments and unbearable punishments. And what will you have to say in excuse for opposing my words and signs for so long? Furthermore, then you will remember what I now said to you, but that will be of no help for you.

i. **On the cross:** Tat'ewac'i, 363, adds this after "raise up" in his lemma to v. 28.

ii. Cyril of Alexandria, *Comm. Jo.* 5.4, here refers to the war against the Romans and the disasters described by Josephus. Moše bar Kepha specifies the city as Jerusalem.

[8:29b] He did not leave me alone, because I continually do his pleasure.

He spoke very humble things about himself, not only showing that the Father did not leave him alone, which is itself a sign of humility, but also that *I continually do his pleasure*, as if for that reason *he did not leave me alone*. And let no one hasten to misinterpret this saying and reduce the rank of the Son to lower than the Father's, because the teaching is of service and economy[i] and not an indication of nature. And because they were always only saying that he was opposed to the Father, therefore he wished [186] to remove that excuse by saying: I continually do his will. For if I continually do his will, then I am not opposed to him, as you say. Furthermore, by this he removed the slander about the Sabbath, by saying: *My Father is with me, and I continually[37] do his pleasure.* By that he gives them the meaning of *The Father is with me, and I continually[38] do his pleasure.* So the healing I performed on the Sabbath, at which you were angry, was done by the pleasure and cooperation[39] of the Father.[ii] But *My Father is with me*, declares the indivisible and inseparable unity.[iii]

i. **Economy:** *tntesut'iwn*, which often renders the Greek *oikonomia*; see Lampe 1969 (s.v. *oikonomia*) for the use of this term regarding the incarnation. For the Armenian terms, see the introduction, xxxvi–xxxvii.

ii. **Cooperation:** *kamakc'ut'iwn*, the abstract noun from the adjective *kamakic'*, "of the same will," for which see the introduction, xxxvi.

iii. Christ's unity with the Father is here stressed by Cyril of Alexandria, *Comm. Jo.* 5.5.

---

36. **Captivity and expulsion:** "expulsion into captivity," M.

37. **Continually:** om. M.

38. **Continually:** om. M.

39. **And cooperation:** om. N.

[8:30] When he had said this, many believed in him.

Did you see *how much profit was worked by[40] very humble teaching? So then we said truly that in order to lessen their wickedness he spoke the most humble things about himself, in order to remove the suspicions concerning his being opposed to God. When they heard, *I continually do his pleasure*, they accepted his word and believed him not to be opposed to God, as the Pharisees slandered, but rather that he was very obedient and like-minded to God, and therefore he always did nothing other than his pleasure. See the [words] wisely spoken by the Savior: how appropriate it was in accordance with the humanity that they saw, and in accordance with the Jews' weak faith, that he thus tempered his speech. Furthermore, we[41] see very often the disciples speaking very humble things as long as they were still[42] very weak in the faith.

Then he introduced the highest matters through the signs and miracles so that, just as through the most humble things he might declare his bodily aspects and remove his being opposed to God, in the same way through the highest things [he might declare] the power of his divine nature and his being coessential with the Father. But let no one suppose the lowest things to pertain to his humanity, [187] and the highest things to his divinity. Far from it! But they both [pertain] to one person,[i] inseparable and indivisible by nature. And he only acts[43] for the profit of the listeners and onlookers in accordance with the appropriateness of the moment.

> i. **Person:** *eresk'*. For the terminology, see the introduction, xxxix.

[8:31–32] And Jesus said to the Jews who believed: If you will remain in my word, you are true disciples of mine; and you will know the truth, and the truth will make you free.

His all-seeing power realized that their faith in whom they believed had no foundation; therefore he said: *If you remain in my word, you are true disciples of mine.* That is, when I urge you to the most perfect and highest virtues[44] of the faith, you are very wearied and vexed; but if you will endure all that, then you will truly become my disciples. What does "truly" mean? It is not for one time to have faith in me because of the signs and miracles or the

---

40. **How much ... by,** M: "such," N.
41. **We:** "I," N.
42. **Still:** om. N.
43. **Acts,** *tnawrinē*, N: "arranges," *yawrinē*, M.
44. **Virtues:** sg. N.

teaching, then rapidly to deny, like those who ate the bread in the desert and so willingly followed me that they even wished to seize me and make me their king, but after a little they denied and fell behind. But what means: *The truth will make you free?* It is if you will believe in me, he says. Because he himself was the truth, he will free them from servitude to sin and from the law and the old religion, which did[45] not possess freedom but servitude.

[8:33] They replied to him and said: We are the seed of Abraham and have not ever[46] been in servitude to anyone. How do you say, You shall be free?

Did you see how they reckoned *to rejoice in the bodily and earthly life[47] more important than the freedom of the Spirit[48] and the inheritance of eternal life? Whence is this clear? The Savior **[188]** spoke to them on behalf of the Spirit, but they neglected that and turned it to bodies.[49] Therefore they did not wish to recognize the truth that he had spoken to them, because all that seemed wearisome to them. Angered at it, they said: *We are the seed of Abraham and have not ever been in servitude to anyone.* How were they never in servitude to anyone, when they were slaves of Pharoah in Egypt for so long; after that they were kept captive in servitude in Babylon; and then to the Romans as well?[i] But [they said it] in order to render their own falsity totally clear. For he said that the Spirit[50] was free from servitude to sin, whereas they, taking the saying to concern their bodies, spoke fancies.

i. John Chrysostom, *Hom. Jo.* 54.1, here refers to the Egyptians, Babylonians, and many others; Theodore of Mopsuestia refers to the Egyptians, Babylonians, and Romans, as does Išodad. Moše bar Kepha refers to the Egyptians, Babylonians, and other peoples in the time of the judges, as does Dionysius bar Salibi, *John*, 179, who notes 400 years to the Egyptians, 70 to the Babylonians. Dionysius, *Gospels*, 150, adds that glorying in Abraham and despising works of virtue was always a source of evil for the Jews. Tat'ewac'i, 367, also gives 400 years in Egypt, then 70 in Babylon, but adds "now under the Caesars." Cyril of Alexandria ascribes 430 years to the Egyptian servitude and refers to the Babylonians and Assyrians.

---

45. **Did:** "do," N.

46. **Ever,** MZ: om. N.

47. **To rejoice … life,** M: "bodily and earthly things," N.

48. **Of the Spirit,** *hogwoyn,* N: "of souls," *hogwoc'n,* M.

49. **Turned it to bodies:** "turned [causative, no object] to bodily things," N.

50. **Spirit,** *hogwoyn,* N: "souls," *hogwoc'n,* M.

[8:34] Jesus replied and said to them: Amen, amen, I say to you that everyone who commits sin is a servant to sin.

Did you see how he reproved the saying that they obscured?[51] Now, because he was speaking about souls being free from sin, and they applied the words[52] to bodies, therefore he explained it more clearly: [*Everyone*] *who commits sin is a servant to sin.* He indicates that those who love sin and those who commit sin are alien to divine service and are servants only to sin. Hereby he vexed them and set down next his remedy: *If you will know the truth, the truth*[53] *will set you free.* He was speaking about himself freeing them, because he himself was the truth and life.

[8:35a] And the servant does not remain in the house forever.[54]

He spoke most illuminating [words] and made things clear, for first he revealed the condition of servitude from which he promised to give them freedom [189] if they believed. And lest they were to say, Who are you, who are able to make [people] free from servitude? therefore by means of an allegorical expression he informed them that he himself was God and able [to carry out] the promises. For that reason he said, *The servant does not remain in the house forever,* as if to say that he does not remain in the house because of not having the authority, for servants are always in a rank of service and work.

[8:35b] But the Son remains forever.

That is, the royal heir is the possessor of the house and its ruler. And if this is sometimes so understood of those who rule temporally in the flesh, what must one understand with regard to me, because not only am I Son of God, but I always remain in my house, that is, in the world, before my descent and after my ascent to heaven? So then I am true in my saying, *The Son remains forever.*

---

51. **They obscured,** *cackēin,* N: "they were grieved," *płckēin,* M (*sic*).
52. **Words:** sg. N.
53. **The truth** (*bis*): "the true one," N.
54. M gives the full lemma of v. 35 here, repeating the second half in the commentary.

[8:36] So if the Son will free you, you will be truly free.

O great benevolence! How much effort he undertakes for their correction! What would the true freedom be? It is the freedom of the spirit,[55] which always remains free and secure—not that of the body[56] in which you boast, reckoning yourselves sons of Abraham though enslaved to sin and the Egyptians and the Babylonians.

[8:37] I know that you are the seed of Abraham. But you seek to kill me, because there is no place in you for my word.

Because they boasted in that and vaunted of being sons of Abraham, he confirmed their words: *I know that you are the seed of Abraham.* But you are [so] only according to the flesh; according to spiritual virtues you are totally illegitimate and foreign to Abraham. For as much as he loved God and performed noble deeds pleasing to the will of God, that much are you haters of God and [190] opponents of his will. Therefore the kinship with Abraham will be of no profit to you. And what means: *You seek to kill me*? Not only did he say, *You wish to kill me*, but unlawfully on account of envy and malice. Also, because it seems hard for you to follow the truth for love of the world, therefore you rather wish to kill me. And you arrogantly boast in Abraham, since my word finds[57] no place in you.

[8:38] What I have seen from my Father, I speak; and you do what you have heard[58] from your father.

Why did he so often repeat *from the Father*, which he says now: *What I have seen from my Father, I speak*? It was to remove their fanciful words in that they said he was opposed to God in order that[59] his unity of will with the Father might be[60] totally clear; as if to say that what you say is from the Father and not spoken specifically by me. But what means: *You do what you have heard from your father*? It is as if to say that what you wish to do, that is, to kill me, you have heard from your father. From whom, then? You have learned from Satan. In order to show them that as you are accomplices of Satan, he

---

55. **Spirit:** "souls," M.
56. **Body:** pl. N.
57. **Finds,** *gtaneloy,* N: "gives," *taloy,* M.
58. **Heard,** MNZ. For the variant "seen," see Metzger 1975 (ad loc.).
59. **In order that:** "because," N.
60. **Might be:** "is," N.

is closer to you in paternity than Abraham. But he does not yet mention the name, since they had not yet attempted the deed. But later he definitely indicates, as they said, that *you are from your father Satan* (John 8:44).

[8:39] **They answered him and said: Our father is Abraham. Jesus said to them: If you were sons of Abraham, you would do the works of Abraham.**

Did you see how again they grasp at Abraham but thereby turn on themselves their insolence and haughtiness? As for what the Savior said to them, [191] *You do what you have heard from your father*, he did not indicate to them: You are not sons of Abraham; consequently you do not walk according to his deeds. But they applied to Abraham his remark, *You do what you have heard from your father*, as if their own testimony confirmed what they wished to do.

[8:40–41a] **But now you seek to kill me, a man who has spoken to you the truth that I heard from my Father. That Abraham did not do. You do the works of your father.**

Once more he taunted them as if to indicate that, although when you boast in Abraham you adduce your kinship as being his sons, yet you seek to kill me. Why? For never do I follow your wishes, but what I have heard from the Father, that I relate to you, and continually I contemplate your salvation. But you in return wish to reciprocate[61] with torments and death. *That*, he said, *Abraham did not do*—that is, he always practiced hospitality, and he did not have rancor or envy for enemies. But you even wish to kill me after so many benefits; for I nourished [you] with bread in the desert, I healed your sick, and I continually instruct [you] to walk on the path of eternal life.

[8:41b] **They said to him: We are not born from fornication. We have one father, God.**

O shameless and impudent insolence! For when he separated them[62] from Abraham with such admonition, they then dared to draw themselves up to the highest level to say their father was God, being in no way scared or fearful of such awesome words. Therefore the Savior did not [192] respond in

---

61. **Reciprocate:** "reward me," N.
62. **Them:** om. N.

accordance with their audacity, but passing over it turned his words to profitable matters, which were very helpful to all the listeners.[i]

i. Cyril of Alexandria, *Comm. Jo.* 5.5, takes the reference to fornication in the lemma as an insult against the Virgin Mary. Tat'ewac'i, 373, equates it with idolatry.

[8:42] Jesus said to them: If God were your father, you would indeed love me, because I proceeded and came from God. And I did not come of myself, but he sent me.

You declared, he says, yourselves to be sons of God. Now if you were sons of God, you would need to love me, because *I came from God and not from my own self, but he sent me.* Yet you seek to kill me. Why are you so vexed and angry against me because of my calling God my Father? Behold, you said your father was God. Examine and comprehend my signs and miracles, and your own[63] weakness, and consider for which of us both it is most fitting to call God Father, for me or for you?

[8:43] Why do you not recognize my speech? For you cannot hear my words.

Not because of the fact that you do not receive my words as being not true or worthy of reception, but because of your frequent envy and hatred and wicked thoughts you are altogether[64] unable to hear the truth.

[8:44a] You are from [your] father Satan, and you wish to carry out the desire of your father; for he[65] was a murderer from the beginning and did not stay in the truth, since there is no truth in him.

Never do we see the Lord uttering such violent and angry words against them, but he always responded gently and mildly. Therefore one must inquire why he did this. When he divorced and separated them from the paternity of Abraham as not being kin to Abraham's works, then that shameless nation had the audacity to call his Father their own father, by saying: *Our father* [**193**] *is God.* Therefore, being so angered on behalf of the Father he indicated revenge with great wrath, which he never did for his own sake when they called him a Samaritan and possessed by a demon (John 8:48), so that he might teach us that when we suffer personal insults we are to endure them meekly. But when

63. **Own**: om. N.
64. **Altogether**: om. N.
65. **He**, *na*, NZ: om. M.

we hear any inappropriate things said by anyone about God, we are absolutely not to stand still, because not in the least did the Lord pardon that. As much as they thought themselves superior and said their father was the Creator of all, so much the more he showed [himself] humble[66] in opposition and said their father was Satan. Did you see the great incomparability with which he disdained them, in that he said that not some[67] man, but Satan, was their father?

These sayings have also another [meaning] to be known.[68] *You are from your father Satan*, and he indicates and makes clear their desire and vengeance and collaboration with Satan. How is that?[69] The latter, he said, slandered God with regard to the first-created Adam and Eve by saying that through envy and malice God prevented you from tasting of the fruit. *God knew that on the day you would eat of it, your eyes would be opened and you would become gods* (Gen 3:5),[i] *and for that reason he forbade you to taste.[70] And what does *From the beginning he was a murderer* mean? He was the origin and cause of human nature rebelling from God,[71] whereby he committed murder.

He did not remain in the truth, because truth is not in him. Not that Satan was conquered by evil or at the beginning such a thing had been created by God,[72] for that reason did he say, *There is no truth in him*, but rather he indicates his total separation from the truth by his autonomous will and his inclination to wickedness and his urging everyone to the same. To them he applied the example [194] that just as in the garden he killed the man through envy, without his being in any way responsible,[ii] likewise you out of envy wish to slay me, without finding any iniquity in me. So rightly he said that Satan was their father.

i. John Chrysostom, *Hom. Jo.* 54.3, explains that by the transgression he killed Adam and all future men. Step'annos of Siwnik', 136, adds a reference to Cain regarding Satan as murderer.

ii. **Without his being in any way responsible:** *očinč' patčar linelov* (lit. "not at all being the cause"). No subject is given, but since Satan is called "cause," *patčar*, of the rebellion, this phrase must refer to Adam.

---

66. **He showed [himself] humble**, *xonarh ec'oyc'*, M: "very humble," *xonarhagoyn*, N.

67. **Some:** om. N.

68. **To be known:** om. N.

69. **How is that?:** om. M.

70. **And for ... taste:** om. N.

71. **From God:** om. N.

72. **By God:** om. N.

[8:44b] When he will speak a lie, he speaks of his own, because he is a liar and its father.

He himself fabricated lying, therefore he is the origin of it; but he did not create something from some previously existing or created thing. What means: *and its father*? It is as if to say that he himself is the father and cause of lying, because he begat falsehood and passed it on to the human race, and caused it to stumble through various kinds of deceits.

[8:45–46] Now, I speak the truth. Which of you will reprove me for sin? If I speak the truth, why do you not believe me?

Because he first introduced falsehood with regard to Satan, whom he called their father,[i] and next said, *I speak the truth*, to that he also added: *Which of you will reprove me for sin?* As if to say: If you intend to say some falsehood about me, bring it up and introduce it, like your father Satan and yourselves. But if you are not able to produce it, and you know in yourselves that I speak the truth, although you pervert the truth, why do you not believe me?[73]

   i. Here Dionysius bar Salibi, *John*, 173–74, has a discussion of the names of Satan. For Satan's names in Armenian, see Thomson 2001 (notes to *Teaching* 278–79).

[8:47] Whoever is from God hears God's words. You, therefore, do not hear, for the reason that you are not from God.

Those who call God Father and are obedient to him do not receive this teaching, unless it be words from God. Also, if you were sons of God, as you claim, and obedient to his will, you would indeed receive my words and believe the truth. *But you do not hear, for the reason that you are not from God.* [195] Again he taunts them and applies his previous comment: *Therefore you do not hear, because you are from Satan, as I said before, and not from God.*

[8:48–49] The Jews replied and said to him: Did we not rightly say that you are a Samaritan and there is a demon in you? Jesus replied and said: In me there is no demon, but I honor my Father, and you dishonor me.

Let us be astonished at his ineffable benevolence and lack of malice. Why did he not bring down coals of fire from heaven as on the Sodomites and burn them up?[i] But he pardoned them and answered gently and ignored their

---

73. **Me:** om. M.

wicked words, and he made it clear that it was not for him to show revenge, as he demonstrated here. But he was as much the advocate of the Father as when angered[74] at the Jews when they said, *Our father is God,* and he did not simply pardon them but responded with a reproof: *Your father is Satan.*

Let us too, O beloved, resemble such mildness and lack of malice regarding vengeance for ourselves. But when we hear [such things] about God, let us not at all grant pardon but rather bear in ourselves God's vengeance[ii] and bear his matchless and incomparable beneficence toward all beings and his submission.[75]

   i. Gen 19:24, for the Sodomites; but "coals of fire," *kaycakuns hroy,* are not mentioned there; cf. Prov 25:22 and Rom 12:20.
   ii. Rom 12:19 and parallels in Deut 32.

[8:50] **I do not seek my own glory. There is one who seeks and judges.**

See how clearly he taught through these words: *I do not seek my own glory.* If I were to seek the glory of my own self, he says, I would certainly not pardon so much mockery; for you called me a Samaritan and possessed by a demon, but I did not put forward any rebuttal to you.[76] **[196]** Now, what means: *There is one who seeks and judges,* and who might he be? The Father[77] seeks that vengeance, he said, and he judges you. But I do not now judge, because I came into the world for the life and salvation of the world, not for the sake of judging anyone.

[8:51] **Amen, amen, I say to you that whoever will keep my word shall never see death.**

He previously said, *I speak the truth* with you, and set forth his word, saying, *Which of you will reprove me for sin?* showing that no one is able to reprimand [him] by adducing in him any cause of sin, so then what I teach is true. And if it is true, then whoever believes *will never see death.* What death? That of sin, he says; that is, just as I promised freedom, not of bodies, but of the souls of those who follow the faith, likewise do I say the immortality is of souls, not of bodies. Those who believe in the word of life and follow the deeds that are compatible with the faith, although after a little time they are to

---

74. **Angered:** pl. MN.
75. **And his submission:** om. N.
76. **To you:** om. N.
77. **Father:** + "who," M.

be awakened as if[78] from sleep (Rom 13:11) and inherit eternal life, yet they endure the sentence of death.

[8:52] The Jews said to him: Now we know that you are a Samaritan and[79] there is a devil in you. Abraham died and the prophets, yet you say that whoever will keep my word will never see[80] death.

Never do they cease from mocking and despising [him] with their cruel behavior. Here as if finding excuses for what he said, *Whoever will keep my word will not see death*, now they said, We have clearly realized what we once said about you, that there is a demon in you. For Abraham and the prophets died, yet you say: *Whoever will keep my word will not see death*.

[8:53] Are you someone greater than our father Abraham, who died, and the prophets have died? So whom do you make yourself?

[197] This was not an appropriate response: *Whom do you make yourself?* and Behold, *Abraham and the prophets died*. But they should have responded in accordance with his words: Who are those who will not die, as you say? And behold, Abraham and the prophets, who[81] kept the divine precepts, and others spoke and kept them, yet they all[82] died—would you be greater than God? But they did not say any such thing. Why? Because they did not reckon him worthy to be compared even with Abraham, let alone to be placed in equal honor with God, they did not wish to converse even with a brief word.

[8:54–55a] Jesus replied and said: If I glorify myself, my glory is nothing. There is a Father who glorifies me, of whom you say that he is our God, *yet you do not know him.[83]

Consequently he paid no heed to what they had said: *Abraham died and the prophets, yet you say that whoever will keep my word will not see death.* He was only concerned with what they asked: *Whom do you make yourself?* For that reason he gave them some indication to know that he was superior to Abraham, lest by always boasting in Abraham and pouring scorn on him

---

78. **As if:** om. N

79. **A Samaritan and,** N: om. MZ.

80. **See,** N: "taste," MZ.

81. **Who,** N: "some of whom," M.

82. **All:** "om." N.

83. **Yet … him:** om. M.

through their kinship they might despise his divine honor, as they did many times. To the same purpose he declared: *If I glorify myself, my glory is nothing*—not that to be glorified by himself was not more honorable, or that to those who believed in him that appeared in no way acceptable for the Jewish deniers, because those who did not believe in him, how would they reckon to be glorified by himself important? Therefore he said: *If I glorify myself, my glory is nothing, but there is a Father who glorifies me, of whom you say that he is our God, yet you do not know him.*

[**198**] And what means his saying, Because they called their own father God? What other than that would knowing be? Now, he so separated them from the condition of sonship as to say: *He is not your God.*[i] This what he meant by: *You do not know him.*

i. **He is not your God:** *oč' astuac jer ē*, or "You have no God."

[**8:55b**] **But I know him. And if I say that I do not know him, I would be a liar like you. But I know him,**[84] **and I keep his word.**

The *I know* is clear to everyone; for if he is coessential with the Father, he certainly knows him. But what is his saying *If I do not know him, I am a liar like you?* He indicates their falseness doubly: first because they said, *Our Father is God;*[85] second, because they did not know him, being stubborn in their unbelief.

[**8:56**] **Abraham your father desired to see my day. He saw [it] and was glad.**

How much need do we have to examine the divine scriptures and especially the divine sayings! For they have great profundities hidden in them, just as he said[86] earlier: *I shall open my mouth with parables*[87] (Matt 13:35; Ps 77:2). The Jews vaunted themselves, still declaring they were heirs of Abraham and had him as father. But here he does not separate or divorce them from Abraham, as he did elsewhere by saying, *If you were sons of Abraham, you would do the works of Abraham* (John 8:39). By that he greatly disparaged and reproved their works. But when again they mentioned Abraham with even greater bragging, saying, *Surely you are not greater than our father Abraham,* therefore he said: *Your father Abraham desired to see my day. He saw [it] and was glad.*

---

84. **Him,** MZ: om. N.
85. **God:** om. M.
86. **He said** (*asac'*, i.e., scripture), N: "we said," M.
87. **Parables,** NZ: sg. M.

By this he revealed the great incomparability and inequality, by showing that Abraham had desired to see my day. So then I am very superior to Abraham [199] and worthy of being received, the sight of whom your father Abraham desired. He also indicates their thinking, that he desired the sight of the latter, but we even seek to kill him. What impiety would be greater than that?

One must also examine the day that he said Abraham had the desire to see. It seems to me to be the day of the crucifixion, when the human race was saved from servitude to the Devil.[i] But what would *to see* be? *He saw and was glad*, in that[88] he brought his own son Isaac as a sacrifice to God, and Isaac was rescued by the giving of a ram in his place.[ii] In this fashion he saw the salvation of the world in the example, seeing Christ on the cross on behalf of the world, just as the ram was hung on the tree on behalf of Isaac. Abraham was indeed worthy of such a wonderful sight, he who for love of God laid hand on his son. For just as he offered his only and beloved[89] child willingly as a sacrifice to God, because of the love he had for God, likewise too the Father was to give his own only begotten and beloved Son as ransom[iii] for the world, because of the benevolent compassion that he had for his creatures.

i. **Devil:** *bansarku*, a literal rendering of *diabolos*. For the names given to the Devil in Armenian, see note to the commentary on vv. 45–46, above.

ii. John Chrysostom, *Hom. Jo.* 5.2, notes that Abraham desired to see the cross, prefigured by the sacrifice of Isaac; and Cyril of Alexandria, *Comm. Jo.* 6, indicates that the day Abraham desired to see was that of the death of Christ, of which Isaac's sacrifice was a *typos*. Theodore of Mopsuestia notes that the sacrifice of Isaac was an indication of future events, and Išodad refers to Isaac as a "type." Step'annos of Siwnik', 136, expands to claim that Abraham, Moses, and the prophets saw the incarnation and the mystery of the cross.

iii. **Ransom:** *p'rkans*; see 1 Tim 2:6.

[8:57–58] The Jews said to him. You are not yet fifty years old, and you have seen Abraham? Jesus said to them: Amen, amen,[90] I say to you, before Abraham existed, I am.

What means: *Before Abraham existed I am*? It was to inform the Jews about his having no beginning and his uncreatedness, and for the abolition of their evil words that they continually adduced as to the condition of his sonship from Joseph (Luke 4:22; John 6:42). Let Arius be ashamed, who said the Son was created; let the dyophysites also be silenced, who divide the one Son into two.[i] For he did not say, [200] Before Abraham existed, I was, so as to

---

88. **In that,** M: "when," N.
89. **And beloved:** om. N.
90. **Amen, amen,** NZ: "amen," M.

ascribe that to the divine nature, distinguishing it from this temporal nature that he put on from the Virgin, or, *That which is in me*[ii] *is prior to the existence of Abraham*. But with indistinguishable unity he spoke about himself: *Before Abraham existed, I am.*

What did they see except a perfect man? Therefore they said: *You are not yet fifty*[iii] *years old, and you have seen Abraham?* But he referred to the uncreated nature, which on being united with the temporal he counted as one. Let both sides be ashamed, perhaps of the Jews,[iv] since for those who divide the body from the Word, the same is appropriate to them: *You are not yet fifty years old, and you have seen Abraham?* But we confess the unity in orthodoxy and indubitably believe the nature of the flesh sharing and become one with the uncreated Word, who has no beginning, in the saying: *Before Abraham existed, I am.*

i. Arius is mentioned at the very beginning of the commentary, in the comments to John 1:1. For those who support two natures, see the commentary to John 5:18. The term "dyophysites," *erkabnakk'*, is only used here; cf. the introduction, xli.

ii. **That which is in me:** *or yiss ē* (i.e., the divine nature). Dionysius bar Salibi, *Gospels*, 64, indicates that the Word existed before Abraham, but the man after Mary.

iii. **Fifty:** "forty," in the lemma to John Chrysostom, *Hom. Jo.* 55.5. In the commentary Chrysostom notes that Christ was close to forty years old. According to Tat'ewac'i, 386, Jesus was thirty-three years old but looked older because of his labors and fasting.

iv. **Of the Jews:** *i* [om. N] *Hrēic'n*; the sense of the passage is unclear.

[8:59] The Jews took rocks to throw at him, and Jesus slipped away and departed from the temple.

The evangelist did not set that down accidentally: *Jesus*[91] *slipped away and went*[92] *from the temple*, in order to make clear that the *slipping away* was not an act of fear and terror and of fleeing from them, but in order to say that he was hidden from their eyes and departed from their midst. For when he would be handed over into their hands, they would know his willing submission, in accordance with what he had said, *I have power to lay down my life* (John 10:18), but not willingly to be betrayed into their hands.

---

91. **Jesus:** om. M.

92. **Went,** *gnac'*: "departed," *el gnac'*, MNZ (= lemma).

[9:1] **And while he was passing, he saw a man blind from birth.**

The Jews were very vexed at the Savior when they heard from him, *Before Abraham existed,* [201] *I am,* and they plotted to hasten to his[1] murder, as the evangelist makes clear: *They took up rocks to throw at him, and he slipped away*—he hid from their eyes so that they would not see him—*and departed.* Because he said, *Before Abraham existed, I am,* and the Jews thought the saying was much too elevated for him, he then described the life-giving encounter with the blind man. What sort of person might the blind man be? You should not frivolously think when you hear the story of the blind man, it was as if he were deprived only of light, or had acquired his disability only partially, as if by the deprivation of his eyeballs. But the matter was very fearful and awesome, and clear to everyone, and amazing to the Jews. He had the places of his eyes totally flat with his cheeks; no marks had ever appeared anywhere as the organs of the eye, but they were destitute of all formed vessels.[i] Therefore Christ arranged such a person to encounter him in connection with his saying, *Before Abraham existed, I am,* so that when he would heal him by his divine power he would show his existence not only before Abraham, as he said, but also before the first-created Adam, especially as he was the creator of Adam.

Why did he not perform the healing through a word and command, as for the paralytic? For then he said, *Take up your bed and go* (John 5:8), but here he spat on the ground and made clay and plastered the eyes of the blind man. In order to indicate that he himself was the creator of Adam, he fashioned what was lacking in his nature from the same matter from which he had created Adam.[ii] Rightly, then, he said, Before Adam existed, I am. See also another wonder. He shut their eyes and did not allow them to see[2] [202] when they wished to throw rocks at him, and he passed by and departed;

----

1. **His:** om. M.
2. **See:** + "just as," N.

and he illuminated the blindness of the one blind from birth, at which very cruel blindness the evangelist was amazed and said: *He saw a man blind from birth*. He indicates this one *from birth*, not in accordance with the example of others who had blindness by some[3] chance, but he revealed the complete lack of organs that hold the power of sight. By saying, *He saw a man blind from birth*, he also indicates the blind man did not request healing, but through his benevolence he condescended to him in order to form a testimony for his words: *Before Abraham existed, I am*.

i. A similar description of the blind man is found in Dionysius bar Salibi, *John*, 188.

ii. In v. 6 Jesus uses "clay," *kaw*; according to Gen 2:7 God used "dust," *hoł*. Different terms are also used in the Greek (Septuagint) and Syriac (Peshitta). In the commentary to v. 4 below, Nonnus says that Christ fashioned Adam with dust and that he uses the same here.

[9:2] His disciples asked him and said: Rabbi, whose fault was it, his own or his father's and mother's, that he would be blind from birth?

From the disciples' questioning it was clear that the Lord looked on the blind man with such a gaze that the disciples felt that he wished to heal him. Therefore they asked what they did. Furthermore, the questioning had a double meaning, as if to imply that should he say the cause of the blindness to be his own, they would say, How could it be his fault, as he would not have been able to sin before being born? But if he were to say it was his parents' [fault], then they would say, What fault of his is it that his parents sinned?[4] And why did they ask that about sin when they saw the blind man, save because when he healed the paralytic and afterward found him and said, *Behold, you have been cured; sin no more* (John 5:14),[i] the disciples supposed that sin would be the cause of this one's blindness as well?

i. Theodore of Mopsuestia has an extensive discussion of the question of blame, and Dionysius bar Salibi provides a number of different opinions, including those of Greek fathers. Step'annos of Siwnik', 137, refers to philosophers, outside the church, who explain such blemishes (blindness or ill health) as the result of souls sinning before their incarnations in bodies.

---

3. **Some:** om. N.

4. **Sinned,** M: "might sin," N.

[9:3] **Jesus replied: It is not his fault, nor that of his[5] father and mother, but in order that the works of God may be revealed in him.**

[**203**] Do not suppose that for the sake of making them sinless and holy he said that they never sinned. But because he was next going to perform this miracle, therefore he said, *In order that the works of God might be revealed in him*, that is, of power and ability, so that what he said might be confirmed, *Before Abraham existed, I am*, and that he is truly God, and not as the Jews and Pharisees slandered.

One must also investigate his saying, *It is not his fault, nor that of his father and mother*, not that he made them innocent of sin,[6] but in order to show that sin was not the cause of his blindness. In the same fashion, although he said, *But so that the works of God might be revealed in him*, the works of God being revealed in him was not the cause of his blindness, even though the foreseeing power of God knew in advance what would occur. But since he was going to reveal the power of the divine wonders in him, in order to indicate his uncreatedness that he said preceded the existence of Abraham, therefore he said, *For the sake of the glory of God*, that it might be revealed in him.

Do you wish that I should make these words more certain in some other way? See what David said: *Against you alone,[7] Lord, have I sinned and done evil before you, so that you might be righteous in your words and victorious[8] in your judging* (Ps 50:6).[i] Surely not for this reason did David sin and work evil, so that he might justify God in his judgment? But here he wished to speak about his foresight, as if to say that before my sinning you saw, and you knew before my working evil, but you pardoned me and did not punish or at all remove me from life. Why need I speak of a cause, save that you might be[9] righteous in your words and victorious in your judgment?

Many such instances are to be found from scripture, but this much[10] is sufficient for confirmation of the saying.[11] [**204**] Look at what the Lord said to the blind one in this way, for the sake of the glory of the Lord being revealed in him, not that that was the cause of the blindness, but by foresight he spoke about the marvelous signs that had not yet occurred.

---

5. **His,** *iwroy* ("his own"), NZ: "his," *dora* ("of that one"), M.

6. **Of sin,** M: "and sinless," N.

7. **Alone,** *miaynoy*, N: "only," *miayn*, MZ.

8. **Victorious,** NZ: "you may conquer," M.

9. **Might be,** N: "are," M.

10. **This much,** M: "this," N.

11. **Of the saying:** om. N.

i. Theodore of Mopsuestia gives the same quotation. Dionysius bar Salibi, *John*, 190, quotes the first part without mentioning David's name.

[9:4–5] I must carry out the work of the one who sent me while it is daytime. The evening comes, in which no one will be able to work. While I am in the world, I am the light of the world.

Because he first set down, *That the works of God might be revealed in him*, he added to the same: *I must carry out*[12] *the task of the one who sent me*; that is, *I am the one who works* (John 5:17), as I previously said, *that the works of God may be revealed in him*, but for me it is necessary to do the work of the one who sent me. He reveals his equality with the Father, that God sent me, and his work is to fashion bodies from dust, and that same I do.[i] From the same matter I complete what lack there is in him, so that you might know [I] have equal power with the Father and the lack of beginning that I mentioned: *Before Abraham existed, I am.*

Now, what means: *While it is daytime*? He called the time of his revelation on the world *daytime*; but *evening* is the time after his ascension to heaven.[ii] Whence is this clear? From what he said: *As long as I am in the world, I am the light of the world.* Just as the sun when it shines and fills the world with its rays, he said, guides mankind to their individual needful tasks, likewise too as long as I am in the world, I am the light of the world, and I guide everyone to good works and to walk on the path of life.[13]

Did you see what he said at the healing of the paralytic: *My Father works up to now, and I work*? Similarly to that he also spoke here: *It is necessary for me to do the work of the one who sent me.* O wonders! See how both sayings conjoined to both miracles have the same meaning! [205] Likewise from the signs something else may be seen: *He made clay and smeared the eyes of the blind one.* We said previously that he also fashioned Adam as an indication of himself. He brought him to completion from the same matter, [and] filled[14] the feebleness of his body. And not only[15] the lack of organs and vessels of light[16] did he fabricate from dust, he also established the power of vision[iii] in him, so that by the arrangement of the eyeballs and of the other vessels and organs he demonstrated the fashioning of Adam's body.

---

12. **Carry out**, *katarel*, N (= lemma): "do," *gorcel*, M.
13. **Of life**: om. N.
14. **Filled**: om. N.
15. **Only**: om. M.
16. **Of light**: om. N.

Now, by the theoretical he declares the existence[iv] of the soul; by the material, the dense fabric of the body; but by the insubstantial nature that is theoretical, the insubstantiality and invisible nature of the soul. In this way he accurately established the certainty of his own words: *Before Abraham existed, I am*. As for the Savior saying, *While it is still*[17] *daytime*, we have found it in some examples[v] again spoken differently, no less unworthy of respect than the previous. As if to say that he must perform the signs by which the human race is to believe and follow good works as long as they are alive, for that is the time for the human race to do what they wish. But when the day of judgment will arrive, which for the unbelievers is a darkness blacker than all nights, from then on there is no need of means for their salvation, because thereafter there is no time for faith and repentance and acceptance.[18] Furthermore, it is called night, which is the time after death, that is, the night when no one is able to work, that is, [to do] the deeds of virtue of the faith.

i. For dust, repeated later in the commentary to this lemma, see above, note to commentary on v. 1.

ii. John Chrysostom, *Hom. Jo.* 56.2–3, explains Rom 13:12 as having the same meaning: for Paul, night is the present time, because of those still sitting in darkness, but Christ called night the future time, when sin will be no more. Theodore of Mopsuestia also states that night is the time after the passion and death of Christ. Moše bar Kepha; Dionysius bar Salibi, *John*, 191; and Išodad note that "daytime" refers to the time of Christ's fleshly activity; night is the time after his ascension.

iii. **Power of vision:** *tesanołakan zawrut'iwn*. *Tesanołakan*, from the present stem of the verb "to see," is usually distinguished from *tesołakan*, which is derived from the aorist stem and renders the Greek *theōrētikos*. Here physical sight is implied, but just below the same adjective is used for the spiritual or intellectual aspect of a soul.

iv. **Existence:** *goyac'ut'iwn*; see the introduction for this and other technical terms. Tat'ewac'i, 394, states that the soul (*hogi*) is the seeing/theoretical part (*tesołn masn*).

v. **Examples:** *awrinaks*. See the introduction, xxviii–xxix, for Nonnus's references to other commentaries.

[9:6] When he had said this, he spat on the ground and made clay from the spittle and smeared the clay over the eyes of the blind one.

[**206**] We said earlier that in order to confirm the lack of beginning of his own essence, in that he indicated to them his being before Abraham existed, he arranged the encounter with the blind man born blind from birth. Since the Life-giver said, *I must perform the work of the one who sent me*, he did not command with a word and impose violently by his authoritative command,

---

17. **Still,** *der*, MN: om. Z.
18. **And acceptance,** *ew ĕndunelut'ean*: om. N.

as on the sea and it became calm (Mark 4:39), and on the paralytic and he lifted up his bed (John 5:9), and on Lazarus and he came forth (John 11:43); but *he spat on the ground and made clay and smeared it on the blind one's eyes,* showing that this creature that I am about to make is something new. *I must do the works of the one who sent me,* as if to say: I must complete what is lacking in the creation of the one who sent me. Whence? From the same matter.[i] And what means: *He smeared his eyes*? It was to complete all his organs as far as those of sight. But why did he not mix the dust with water but spit on the ground? Because he was intending to send him to Siloam, lest the Jews finding in that some means might be able to say that the power of the water granted him the miraculous healing, but not Christ.[ii] Therefore he omitted the power of the water[19] and spat on the ground, and with that smeared the eyes of the blind one.

i. See above, note to commentary on v. 1, for the equation of clay with dust. *Comm. Diat.* 16.28 notes that it was the same hand that had made creation in the beginning and that effected the cure. On the parallel with Gen 2:7, see also Mathews and Sanjian 1991 (152).

ii. John Chrysostom, *Hom. Jo.* 56.2, also stresses that Christ used spittle to show that he and not the pool of water effected the cure. This is echoed by Išodad.

[9:7] And he said to him: Go, wash in the pool of Siloam (which is translated "sent"). He went, washed, came, and saw.

Why did he send him to Siloam?[i] Was he not able to open his eyes himself? But just as not through a command according to custom did he perform this miracle, but arranged the matter beforehand, likewise in the sending to Siloam there is another mystery. What might that be? When in front of everyone he made clay and smeared[20] the eyes of the blind man and ordered him to go to Siloam, see how much astonishment gripped them as to what the conclusion of the act might be. **[207]** For that reason many followed the blind one in order to see what it might be that [Christ] had done. But others, remaining there, waited for whatever news they might hear. Now, when those who were in the city heard, they all, great and small, rushed to the sight, because the deed that he had done was so notable.

I also have something else to say. Siloam was a place of healing and miracles for the Jews, and they said that he opposed the law. So by sending him there he wished to remove that excuse.[ii] Also the blind man was

19. **The power of the water:** "the water," M.
20. **Made clay and smeared:** "smeared with clay," M.

more confirmed in the faith when he went with smeared eyes, with a twofold reflection, having both hope and doubt in his mind, followed by a multitude of people. Did you see how totally he operated his power for their profit and made the miracle and marvelous power visible to the world?

i. Nonnus does not comment on the etymology of Siloam in the lemma, for which see Edwards 2004 (99). Taťewac'i, 395, refers to John Chrysostom for the etymology "sent," aṙakʻeal; see Chrysostom, *Hom. Jo.* 57.1: *apestalmenos.* Cyril of Alexandria, *Comm. Jo.* 6, defines Siloam as an *eikōn* of baptism.

ii. Moše bar Kepha indicates that Jesus wished to stop the Jews' mouths.

[9:8–9] But the neighbors and those who had seen previously that he was a beggar said: Is not this the one who sat and begged? Some said: He is; others said: No, but he resembles him. And he himself said: I am he.

Did you see what we said, that he smeared the eyes of the blind man and sent him to Siloam so that the signs might be publicly seen and heard by the world?[i] But they continued to deny, and some said that it was not he but resembled him. What, indeed, did they not do in every way to sneer, that it was only by a word he had given him sight? But it seems to me that they were amazed as to how it would be possible that the eyes of a blind man, born blind from birth,[21] could be [cured]. Therefore they were unable to believe.

i. *Comm. Diat.* 16.3 emphasizes that by washing, the blind man did not doubt, and by walking and talking, he publicized Christ's power.

[9:10–11] They said to him: How were your eyes opened? He replied: The man whom they call Jesus [208] made clay and smeared my eyes, and said to me: Go and wash in Siloam. I went, washed, and I see.

O the frenzy and implacable[22] wickedness! Before their eyes he smeared the man's eyes, and in their ears he said: *Go to Siloam, wash.* What need was there to ask: *How were your eyes opened?* But they attempted in every way to fabricate suspicions and to contrive excuses, that perhaps they might be able to diminish the effect[23] of that very superior miracle. But what about the blind man? He said the same: *He made clay and smeared my eyes,* which you also saw, and said, *Go to Siloam and wash,* which you too heard. *I went, washed,* and the command of the man they call Jesus was accomplished, because behold, *I see.*

---

21. **Birth:** "[his] mother," N.

22. **Implacable,** *anhašt,* M: "continuous," *anhat,* N.

23. **Effect,** *gorc:* pl. N.

[9:12] They said to him: Where is he? He said to them: I do not know.

When he healed the blind man by sending him to Siloam, he did not stay and wait for his return, as for one having pride and glory in himself, in order that by his being absent the wonders of the miracles might be even more noised abroad than if he had been close by. Because of their wickedness the Pharisees still increased their opposition. And although they did not now abandon it, yet it was gentler than if he had been close by.

[9:13–15] They brought to the Pharisees the one who was once blind. And it was the Sabbath when Jesus had made clay and opened the eyes of the blind one. Once more the Pharisees questioned him: How do you see? And he said: He placed clay over my eyes, I washed, and I see.

Why did they bring him to the Pharisees? So that they might hear judgment from them and what should be done, because he had performed the healing on the Sabbath. Since they were more wicked than the others and prepared for opposition and deceitful, they brought the man to them [**209**] for investigation. But do you see the wisdom of the man, the one who was once blind, I mean? When he realized that the questioning was [the result] of envy and malice,[24] and they wished to find some cause against him, consequently he did not even mention his name but merely said: *He put clay over my eyes, and I washed and I see.* Nor did he declare, He ordered me to go to Siloam and wash, but, *I went, I washed, and I see.*[25] Did you see how [when] they wished to affirm the charge about the Sabbath, he did not at all give them the opportunity? So he had his benefit firmly in his mind.

[9:16] Some of the Pharisees said: That man is not from God, because he does not observe the Sabbaths.[26] Others said: How can a sinful man perform such miracles? And there were divisions among them.

Although the man who was once blind gave no excuses that they wished to find, yet they were unable to hide their wickedness, but said: *That man is not from God, because he does not observe the Sabbaths.* What is it that you said, O wicked ones and deniers? How can one who is not from God open the eyes of a blind man, born blind from birth? Are you, who once called God

---

24. **Malice,** *čaraknut'iwn*, N: "wickedness," *čarut'iwn*, M.
25. **And I see:** om. N.
26. **Sabbaths,** NZ: sg. M.

your father and said that you kept his commandment, the Sabbath, and what follows able to show such things in yourselves? But they only repeated words of wickedness.

[9:17a] They said again to the blind one: What do you say about him that opened your eyes?

It seems that they were divided into two, as the evangelist indicates by saying, *Some of them said*, as if not all.[27] Therefore the two sides wished to hear again from the man the circumstances of the events. Some hoped to find some cause. But those who said, *How can a sinful man perform such miracles?* they wished to hear something else opposed to the former [**210**] for the validation of the miracles. That is why a division occurred[28] between them.

[9:17b–19] He said: He is a prophet. But the Jews did not believe[29] about him that he had been blind and was healed, until they summoned the parents of the one healed,[30] questioned them, and said: Is this your son, of whom they said that he was born blind? So how does he see?

Because they were not helped by the healed one, since not only did he describe the miracles but also called him a prophet, consequently they ignored him, turned to other means, and summoned the parents. Hoping they would be able to find some causes from them whereby they could falsify his testimony, therefore they summoned the parents. Do not suppose that the evangelist said that *the Jews did not believe that*[31] *he was blind and had been cured* for the reason that they could summon the parents in order to confirm their not knowing, but he became an accuser against them, as if to say that they so plotted. And they indicated that if we do not know, we have need of testimonies from the parents. Whence is it clear that they knew? From their asking, *How do you see?* If he had never been blind, why would they have asked: *How do you see?* Unless Christ had healed [him], why did they ask,[32] *What do you say about him*, or why were[33] there *divisions among them?*

---

27. **All:** + "said," M.
28. **A division occurred:** "there were divisions," N.
29. **Believe:** impf. NZ, aor. M.
30. **Healed** (*bis*): lit. "opened," MNZ.
31. **The Jews did not believe that,** MV: om. N.
32. **Did they ask:** "do you ask," N.
33. **Were:** sg. verb N.

[9:20–21] **His parents replied and said: We know that he is our son, and that he was born blind. But how he now sees, we do not know, or who opened his eyes we do not know. Ask him. He is of age; he will speak for himself.**

Do you see their doubt and fear of the Jews?[i] They had admitted that *he is our son*, and that truly [**211**] *he was born blind.* But as for the miracles, they declined to testify from their fear, for which reason they directed their answer to the questions[34] to their son: *Ask him. He is of age; he will testify for himself,* so that they might verify by their wisdom the testimony of their son, that not only does he know what you ask but he is also worthy of trust, because he is of age and capable of testifying about himself. Did you see the willingness of the parents, how they were happy to testify but were unable to speak very clearly but only indicate the truth through a likeness?

i. The parents' fear of the Jews is stressed by Dionysius bar Salibi, *John*, 195; see also the following lemma.

[9:22–23] **Thus spoke his parents, because they feared the Jews, since the Jews had made a pact that if anyone were to confess him as Christ[35] he would be expelled from the synagogue. Therefore his parents said: He is of age; ask him.**

Did you see how the evangelist made clear what we said above, that for fear of the Jews the parents declined and said, *Ask him,* because of the pact? For they had so threatened that whoever might confess him as Christ, they would expel from the synagogue, which seemed a very great punishment to them. So they knew Christ and the circumstances of the miracles that had been accomplished for their son, but being reined in and silenced, they remained frightened of their scorn.

[9:24a] **Again a second time they summoned the man who had once been blind and said to him: Give glory to God.**

O betrayal and treachery! See what they said to him: *Give glory to God,* that is, separate yourself totally from him, give glory only to God, because your[36] healing was from God and not from him. Because they did not find any other means, [**212**] either with the man or his parents, whereby they might

---

34. **Questions:** sg. N.
35. **Christ,** NZ: "the Christ," M.
36. **Your:** "the," M.

fabricate an excuse, consequently they happily demonstrated this, teaching him: *Give glory to God*, do not neglect the great benefits, but separate from him. Since[37] they were unable to hide the power of the wonderful miracle, therefore they unwilling taught [him] to glorify.

[9:24b–25] We know that that man is a sinner. And he said: If he is a sinner, I do not know. But this I know, that I was blind and now I see.

What means: *We know*? It is as if to say that we who bear witness concerning sin against him are many; but you, one. And furthermore we speak with knowledge; but you are not comparable with us in knowledge, because you are simple[i] and lacking understanding. And because we know that he is a sinner, it is not right for you to call him a prophet. But that man responded with wisdom and great modesty toward them: *If he is a sinner*, as you say, *I do not know*. He was certainly not unaware that he was not a sinner, yet because of fear of them he was unable to contradict them. But despising them in his mind he uttered the words: You say he is a sinner because you deny the miracle performed on me. But I know the opposite to your words, and I have no need of testimony about him other than that he demonstrated in me this very powerful miracle.

i. **Simple:** *parzamit* (lit. "simple-minded," but it also has the nuance of "honest, straightforward").

[9:26] Again they said to him: What did he do to you? How did he open your eyes?

What need had they to ask again other than thereby to deceive him, [suggesting that] perhaps he had something else to declare other than what he had told them once already, something less or more, by which finding a cause for anger against him they might despise all the testimonies and **[213]** refute him:[i] Now you say one thing, then again you declare something different. They hoped to find something like that. But see the man's replies, how he cut short their questions.

i. Cyril of Alexandria, *Comm. Jo.* 6, suggests the same motivation.

---

37. **Since:** om. N.

[9:27] I have just now spoken to you, and you did not hear. Why do you wish to hear again? Do you too wish to be his disciples?

Because they so pressed the man, always inquiring into what had been asked once before, in order that they might be able to find some excuses and to disparage the power of the miracle, he did not reply to them save to declare a very bold response, as if to say: Why should your investigation be so persistent; *do you too wish to be his disciples?* Not that he was unaware that their investigations were carried out through wickedness or that they were asking inappropriate things about him; but [by saying], *Do you wish to be his*[38] *disciples?* he demonstrated to them his own enthusiastic discipleship of Christ, that is, for the faith.[39] So he cut short their questions, since he gave his response[40] as a rebuke and demonstrated his own faith.

[9:28–29] They reviled him and said: You become his disciple; we are disciples of Moses. We know that God spoke with Moses. As for this one, we do not know whence he is.

Did you see how they desisted from the investigation when they heard the man's response? Because they no longer hoped to extract from him words that might have pleased them, they then began to revile him, saying, *You become his disciple*; that is, since you said, *Do you too wish to become his disciples?* we comprehend your willingness [to become one]. *You become his disciple*, but we shall not, because *we are disciples of Moses.* And then they vaunted in themselves: *We know that God spoke with Moses*; [214] therefore we are his disciples.

See the unintelligent[41] words they spoke: We have not seen, they said, God speaking with Moses, or heard his words[42] with our ears, but *we know*, they said, that is, from the histories.[43] O most wicked ones! Whom we know from the histories,[i] his disciples we are; and of whose signs and miracles we are eyewitnesses and whose teachings we heard with our ears, him we deny. Furthermore, why are you disciples of Moses, yet behold, you deny such

---

38. **His:** om. N.

39. **That is, for the faith:** om. N.

40. **Response:** pl. M.

41. **Unintelligent,** *anmtut'ean*, M: "with unintelligence," *anmtut'eamb*, N.

42. **His words:** om. N.

43. **Histories:** "commandments," N.

amazing signs, and without testimony and investigation you seek to kill him,[44] which Moses forbade you?

    i. **Histories:** *patmut'iwnk'*. See 1 Esd 1:33 for "histories" as the books of the Kings of Israel.

[9:30] The man replied and said: This is indeed[45] amazing, that you do not know whence he is, yet he opened my eyes.

This means that for what you revile me, those things are worthy of wonder, because the man is very famous and renowned. Yet you say, *We do not know [him]*, although he showed such wonderful signs to me.

[9:31] We know that God does not heed sinners. But if anyone is a worshiper of God and does his will, to him he listens.

Why did he not say, I know, rather than, *we know*?[46] It was in order that he might bring them even unwillingly to testimony of the saying, as if to say: Not only I know *that God does not heed sinners*, but you also know, and everybody else, that God never heard a sinner. So then you[47] are not right in saying: *We know that that man is a sinner*. For if we know that God never heeds a sinner, then that man who performed such signs for me is not a sinner, as you claim.

[9:32–33] From eternity no one has heard that anyone opened the eyes of a blind one born blind from birth. Unless that man were from God, he would not have been able to do anything.

[215] After he had silenced them and removed the discussion about sin by saying, *We know that God does not heed sinners*, and they were unable to give any reply to that, he then proceeded to even more sublime words about Christ; for he knew that it was Christ who had healed him, although he never introduced his name for important reasons. Consequently he said, *From eternity no one has heard that anyone opened the eyes of a blind person born blind from birth*, in order to say that those who have blindness from accident, perhaps it is possible for them to receive healing from physicians.[i] But whoever is blind from birth has need not of treatment for ailments or renewal of his

---

44. **Him,** *zda*: om. N.
45. **Indeed,** *isk*, MZ: om. N.
46. **Rather than** we know: om. N.
47. **You:** "they," N.

former vision but of a new fashioning. Who, then, of mankind could do that, except the Son of God?

This is also clear from the following words: Since he is not a sinner, he is beloved of God. But he said, similarly to what Nicodemus said: *No one could perform these signs unless God were with him*[48] (John 3:2), as both possess the mark of the Son of God. Likewise, the blind one kept in his mind what he had heard, that the Son of God would announce[49] himself.[ii] Therefore, although he could not declare that openly, yet through an example he indicated the faith that he hid in his heart.

    i. For physicians, see also commentary to John 5:8.

    ii. **Would announce himself:** *k̇arozēr zink̇n* seems to be a reference to an OT prophecy, but the phrase as such does not occur in the Armenian biblical text.

[9:34] **They replied to him and said: You are born totally in sin, yet you would be our teacher? And they threw him out.**

Did you see what the evangelist previously said, that the Jews had made a pact that whoever confessed him as Christ[50] would be expelled from the synagogue (John 9:22)? Although the man had concealed his words through an allegory, yet these cunning ones understood the meaning of the remark. Therefore they cast him out. But see also elsewhere their falseness. They said: *You were born totally in sin.* And how is it possible to be born in sin [216] other than to come[51] into the world sinless, and then out of free will willingly commit sin? And why did they cast him out of the temple[i] and not find some falsehood in him? Because they themselves had never heard of the occurrence of such a miracle, they should have said: Why are you so astonished? Behold, we find other miracles similar to this one to have occurred at which you[52] would be amazed. But because he had silenced them and they were quite unable to respond, therefore[53] they cast him out, lest he relate even more truthful things for their reproof.

    i. Dionysius bar Salibi, *John*, 198, also specifies that the man was thrown out of the temple.

---

48. **No one … signs:** om. N.

49. **Would announce,** *k̇arozēr*, N: "announces," *k̇arozē*, M.

50. **Christ,** M: "the Christ," N; see note to the lemma of v. 22.

51. **Come,** *gal*, N: "be," *gol*, M.

52. **You:** sg. M (as just above), pl. N.

53. **Therefore:** om. N.

[9:35] Jesus heard that they had cast him out. And when he found him,[54] **he asked him: Do you believe in the Son of God?**

Because he had not been condemned by the Jews and was not afraid but remained firmly grateful for the blessings from the miracles, the Life-giver[i] then revealed himself by asking him, *Do you believe in the Son of God?* that is, as you said to the Jews, *Unless he were from God he could not perform such signs,* and *From eternity it has not been heard that the eyes of a blind one born blind from birth have been opened.* So do you believe in what you said? Furthermore, he did not say: Do you believe in the one who smeared your eyes with clay and sent [you] to Siloam? That he did not suggest, because he knew the secrets of his heart, that he was constant in opposition to the Jews, saying, *Unless he were from God,* he could not do this. So do you believe in what you said?

i. **Life-giver:** *kenarar,* rendering exactly the Greek *zōopoios,* more common as an adjective than a proper noun. It is used of God in the Psalms but not in the NT.

[9:36] He responded and said: Lord, who is he, so that I may believe in him?

Why did he ask, *Who is he?* except that before being healed he had not seen the Savior but had only heard his conversation when he said, *Go, wash in Siloam,* and only felt[55] the smearing of his eyes by the life-giving hands. Even when he was healed he had not then seen the Lord,[i] and for that reason asked: *Lord, who is he, that I may believe?* It indicates his zeal and [217] reveals: I still do not know the one who gave me light,[ii] and I have a great desire to see him.

i. Theodore of Mopsuestia also stresses that the blind man had not seen Christ.

ii. **The one who gave me light:** *lusaworič* (lit. "my illuminator"). The term is used here in a literal sense but is very common metaphorically, notably in the sense of baptism—hence the title *lusaworič* for Saint Gregory as "Illuminator" of Armenia.

[9:37–38] Jesus said to him: You have seen him, and he is the one who is speaking with you. And he said: I believe, lord. And he worshiped him.

See again what he said: *Lord,*[56] *who is he, that I may see and believe?* He awaited only the sight of him and had no need of investigation or instruction but merely indicated: To see him is alone necessary for me, and truly I believe

____

54. **Him,** MZ: om. N.
55. **Felt,** *gitēr* (lit. "knew"): om. N.
56. **Lord:** om. N.

in him. Therefore the Lord gave this response: *You have seen him, and he is the one who is speaking with you.* The one about whom you asked, *Who is he?* he says, is the one whom you have seen. Lest any of the onlookers suppose another, he then securely confirms him. *The one who speaks with you is he,* whom you seek to see, who indeed healed you. *And he said, I believe, lord, and worshiped him,* in order to show that just as I believed in his works, so also now in his words. And by saying, *I believe,* he revealed the confession of the firm[57] faith of his mind, while his worshiping was to show his gratitude for the benevolence of the one who gave him light.

[9:39] Jesus said: For judgment I came into this world, so that those who do not see might see, and those who do see might become blind.

Because the Jews made the decision to cast the man out of the temple because of the testimony he declared concerning Christ, Christ said, *For judgment I came into this world,* in order to declare that he thenceforth would be the judge of their impiety and to indicate that just as you expelled that man from the temple without any[58] culpability, likewise you will come forth from the temple, not without blame, but with great condemnation. [218] And their deeds turned out similarly to their words.

For judgment, he said, *I came into this world, so that those who do not see might see, and those who do see might become blind,* as if to say that just as you were given light through the eyes of the body, in the same fashion you were illuminated by the eye of your soul through your faith, and before this you were blind. In this way by the truth I shall illuminate the nations of the Gentiles who are blind in their unbelief, because they are to receive the word of life, since you became its[i] image and sign. But those who see will become blind, because they were the people of God but also a vineyard, just as he said: *The house of Israel is a vineyard of the Lord of hosts*[59] (Isa 5:7). This Moses and the other prophets dressed and dug, always urging[60] them to fruitfulness, that is, to faith in me. But after so many signs that they now saw in you, they did not believe yet wished to see the light; these will become blind.

 i. **Its:** *noc̕a*; the genitive is plural since "life," *keank̕*, is a plural form.

---

 57. **Firm,** MV: om. N.
 58. **Any:** om. N.
 59. **Of hosts,** MZ: om. N.
 60. **Urging:** "fashioning," M.

[9:40–41] Some of the Pharisees who were with him heard and said to him: Are we, too, blind? Jesus said to them: If you were blind, you would have no sin. But now you say, We see, and your sins are confirmed in you.

Because the Pharisees were so thick-witted and unconcerned with spiritual seeking, they reckoned that he spoke about blindness of the body, as on the occasion when they heard, *servitude* (John 8:34). Therefore the Lord said: *If you were blind, you would have no sin. But now you say, We see, and your sins are confirmed in you.* He declared very clearly to them: I did not say you were blind in the guise of the body, but through the willingness of the mind, you who never wish to look at the truth. For *if you were blind* in the body, you would have no blame. But not only are you not blind, you even claim to have the knowledge of God in you, yet you always wage war against the truth. [219] So then rightly he said: *Your sins are confirmed in you.* The sins that they possessed, he said, were envy and hatred. To be confirmed in them indicated their incorrigible wickedness, because they would not turn[i] from it and become profitable.

i. There is a play on words with the adjective "incorrigible," *andaṙnali*, and the verb "turn," *daṙnal.*

[10:1] **Amen, amen, I say to you: Whoever does not enter through the door into the sheepfold but ascends by another [way], he is a thief and a brigand.**

Because he responded to the Pharisees concerning their dispute with the blind man whom they had expelled from the temple, and they were the leaders and teachers[i] and instructors of the synagogue, consequently he reproved them as not rightly or worthily holding the authority to judge and the knowledge to teach, but they sinned in every way and worked no little harm; for they were continually teaching scandals and crookedness to people and were a cause of destruction rather than of life. Therefore through a parable[1] he added something about himself, showing himself to be judge and teacher.[ii] For that reason he called them blind, indicating that the blind one not only does not have the power of guiding others but [does] not even [have the power of guiding] himself, and he only creates error for himself and others because of his blindness. Such he informed them that they were.

To that he added also about himself: *Whoever does not enter through the door into the sheepfold but ascends by another [way], he is a thief and a brigand.* What would the door be? It is the path of God's commandments that the prophets transmitted to you,[iii] by following which you enter[2] the fold.[3] Which fold? The church of God, because that is the fold of rational sheep for which the noble[iv] shepherd came to the world in search of the lost sheep, [that is,] human nature.[v] By this he vexed them even more: You call yourselves teachers, and also authorities[vi] [220] concerning the commandment that leads your flock to enter this fold of salvation away from thieves and brigands, [that is,] evil teachings. Those who teach these ensnare the minds of the simple and sow tares (Matt 13:25), and like brigands they steal away the minds of the

---

1. **Through a parable**, *aṙakaw*, N: "more," *aṙawel*, M.
2. **Enter**, *linik' i* (lit. "you are in"), N: "they are in," M.
3. **Fold**: + "of Christ," M[corr].

weak and seduce mankind to destruction. What does[4] a thief or brigand do other than that?[vii]

i. **Teachers:** *vardapetk'*. For this office in the Armenian church, see note to commentary on John 1:29, above.

ii. Here Theodore of Mopsuestia indicates that Christ was more worthy of the title of teacher than the scribes.

iii. John Chrysostom, *Hom. Jo.* 59.2, indicates that the door is scripture, as do Moše bar Kepha and Dionysius bar Salibi. Išodad gives both scripture and the keeping of the commandments as explanations. But for Cyril of Alexandria, *Comm. Jo.* 6, the door is the Lord. Tat'ewac'i, 414, explains it as the "law," *awrēnk'*.

iv. **Noble:** *k'aj*; see note to commentary on v. 11, below.

v. Išodad and Dionysius bar Salibi (*John*, 201) explain the fold as lawful doctrine. Tat'ewac'i, 414, follows Nonnus.

vi. **Authorities:** *išxec'olk'*. The grammar of the following passage is unclear. If *išxec'olk'* is a predicate of "yourselves" (as is "teachers"), it should be in the accusative, not nominative, case.

vii. Theodore of Mopsuestia explains the "brigand" as one who does not keep the law.

[10:2–4] But whoever enters by the door is the shepherd of the sheep. To him the doorkeeper opens, and the sheep hear his voice. And he calls his own sheep by name and leads them. And when he leads his own, he goes in front of them, and the sheep follow him because they recognize his voice.

Whom, then, does he mean by *doorkeeper*? Moses.[i] Because through him were given the law and the book[ii] of the knowledge of God, therefore he was the steward of the divine law and commandments. So he said that he was the doorkeeper of the divine commandments that lead to the fold of salvation, as we said above, and he is the one who opens to those who wish in truth to go on that road. And those who go on that road he recognizes because they heard his voice, that is, the divine traditions that were given through him.

And he leads them. Where? To other sublime pastures, that is, to the meadows of gospel preaching, and he himself goes in front of them. Not Moses himself, but the commandment that he handed down to them,[5] being before their minds, always urges them to the preaching of the gospel,[iii] because that was an example and shadow of the truth of this gospel. *And the sheep follow him and heed[iv] his voice.* This indicates that those who follow [221] the preaching of the gospel, such people[6] always urge themselves on behind the faith and

---

4. **Does:** sg. M, pl. N.

5. **To them:** om. M.

6. **Such people:** om. N.

heed the voice of the commandments,[7] that is, whatever are the exhortations and counsels of virtues.

> i. Moses is the "doorkeeper," *dṙnapan*, according to John Chrysostom, *Hom. Jo.* 59.2; Moše bar Kepha; and Dionysius bar Salibi, *John*, 202. Cyril of Alexandria, *Comm. Jo.* 6, states that Christ is the doorkeeper.
>
> ii. **Book:** *gir*. Normally plural, *girk'*, for "book"; in the singular, "writing."
>
> iii. Preaching is also stressed by Cyril of Alexandria, and Dionysius bar Salibi, *John*, 203.
>
> iv. **Heed:** *lsen*. Nonnus combines two separate phrases from the lemma.

[10:5] They do not follow a stranger, but they flee from him, because they do not recognize the voice of strangers.

Again he turns his discourse to the Pharisees.[i] *They do not follow a stranger*, meaning the one who possesses leadership and stewardship and shepherdly care but who pays no heed[8] to the commandments of God and is not comparable to Moses in teaching—him[9] the sheep do not follow, because they do not recognize his voice, that is, your alien teaching.

> i. Moše bar Kepha also introduces the Pharisees here.

[10:6] This parable Jesus spoke to them, but they did not know what it was that he spoke with them.[10]

They did not understand, he says, that he was speaking the parable about themselves, because they were so thick-witted. Did you see[11] how he indicated their multifaceted impiety through an allegorical[i] saying? [He called them] *thieves and brigands* and *strangers* regarding judgment and teaching and leadership, which they exercised unjustly, and indicated that they never taught or judged according to Moses or the other prophets but always arrogantly robbed and oppressed. And as with regard to the blind man, after so many insults that they uttered, *You have been born in sin*, and they expelled him from the temple, here too they did not at all consider that he spoke about himself when he said, *Whoever enters through the door*, meaning through the law of Moses and the prophets. I fulfilled that not only through my coming

---

7. **Commandments:** sg. M.

8. **No heed,** *anp'oyt'*, N: "heed," *p'oyt'*, MV.

9. **Him:** "them," MN (*sic*).

10. **That he spoke with them,** NZ: om. M.

11. **Did you see,** *teser*, N: "see," *tes* (impv.), M.

but also by keeping the tradition, as if on a journey I entered through the door, opening [it] to all those who believe [222] in me and giving them habitation in the fold. After he had expounded this to them in a parable, then very clearly he instructed them, saying:

> i. **Allegorical**: *aṙakawor*, the adjective from *aṙak*, "parable, allegory."

[10:7–8] **Amen, amen, I say to you, I am the door for the sheep. All those who were before me were thieves and brigands, but the sheep did not hear them.**

Let no one here plead the contrary, as to how through an allegory[i] he spoke very unclear things, which afterward he wished to teach clearly. For when he instructed them and did nothing contradictory but multiplied signs and healings, they sometimes planned to lay hands on him and sometimes wished to pick up stones to throw at him. What cruel evils were produced when he clearly said they were *thieves and brigands*, and *strangers* to the prophetic [writings]. But first through the parable he informed a little and did not fully reprimand, lest they depart and turn their attention away from the teaching that he was later to expound. Therefore through the parable concerning the blind man whom they mocked and expelled, he compared himself with them regarding the keeping of the law of Moses and of the other prophets. And he revealed that for that reason he was able to become a shepherd for the flock, because he had not transgressed the commandment; but they, by not keeping it, were likened to *thieves and brigands*.

Therefore he enters through the door that they supposed their own, and with him introduces [the flock] by means of the preaching of the gospel into the fold,[12] in which he sets the flock in front of the Father. *But those who came before me were thieves and brigands*. He indicated Judas the Galilean and Theudas, and after them the Sadducees.[ii] But what means: *The sheep did not hear them?* [223] When they said of him that they would become what they all aimed for,[iii] they perished, and their associates were scattered and became nothing, and like the blind man he did not heed the Sadducees and did not follow their error; in the same way those who later would believe in him remained firm and were not scattered, nor did they perish like them.

> i. **Allegory**: *aṙakabanut'iwn*. This is the only instance of the compound from *aṙak* + *banut'iwn* (*parabolē* + *logia*) attested in *NBHL*.

---

12. **Fold**: pl. N.

ii. For the uprisings of Judas and Theudas, see Acts 5:36–37. John Chrysostom, *Hom. Jo.* 59.2, cites them along with antichrists, false Christs, and heretics; they are also mentioned here by Theodore of Mopsuestia, Moše bar Kepha, and Dionysius bar Salibi (*John*, 204). But they do not refer to the Sadducees; even Tat'ewac'i, 418 (ad loc.), who normally quotes Nonnus, omits reference to them. In the following verse Nonnus places the Pharisees, not the Sadducees, in connection with Judas and Theudas. More usually he changes Pharisees into Sadducees; see the introduction, xxvi.

iii. The meaning of this sentence is unclear; there is no significant difference between the MSS.

[10:9] I am the door. If anyone will enter through me, he will live. He shall enter, and go out and find pasture.

See how illuminating are the things he taught them clearly: *If anyone will enter, he will live*, that is, he who believes in me and enters[13] with me into the fold, where he will be in front of the Father through the grace of the font, he will live, not only in the spirit, but also he will not endure the destruction of the body like the followers of Judas and Theudas, or those followers of the Pharisees who were to endure famine and[14] sword and scattering into captivity and persecutions from the Romans; but they remain free of that. But what means: *He shall enter, and go out and find pasture*? He will enter with me into the fold, and go out and find pasture. Not that which fattens bodies for a short time, but that which provides the superior livelihood of eternal life, my[15] body and blood.[i]

i. Tat'ewac'i, 420, gives four interpretations of "pasture," *čarak*, of which "the saving body and blood" is the third.

[10:10a] A thief does not come except in order to steal and kill and destroy.

Just as the thief has such a plan, likewise they also. With deceitful teaching they plot nothing other than to kill and destroy: they tried to contradict the blind man who had been cured, in order to snatch him from the right faith by treacherous words and to destroy soul and body in the fire of Gehenna.

---

13. **He who believes, enters:** pl. N.
14. **Famine and:** om. N.
15. **My:** om. N.

[10:10b] I came that they might have life, and have it more abundantly.

When he showed them to be the cause of killing and destruction, **[224]** he then set out in the hearing of all that he was the cause of the opposite to that: *I came that they might have life*. From heaven, he said, I came incarnate[i] through the body. From the former death that was ruling over the race of mankind I wish to free those who follow me. *That they may have it more abundantly*[ii] does not mean by bestowing on me[iii] a life of many years but rather eternal life.

    i. **Incarnate:** *tnawrineal*. The verb is derived from a calque on the Greek *oikonomia*, for which in the context of the incarnation, see Lampe 1969 (s.v. *oikonomia*). For the Armenian terminology, see the introduction, xxxvi–xxxvii.
    ii. **Abundantly:** Išodad, 250, here refers to the grace of the Spirit through baptism.
    iii. **On me:** the dative *inj* is anomalous. One might expect a genitive, *im*, as subject of the verb *pargevelov* (i.e., "by my bestowing").

[10:11] I am the noble shepherd. The noble shepherd lays down his life for the sheep.

Noble in the translation of the Hagarene[i] tongue, from which we have rendered the entire text of this book, we found to mean "good."[ii] Therefore it seemed right to us not to alter the word into something else, lest the interpretations of the saying become different. Let no one speak unfitting things about the Savior when he hears the humblest things, like[16] the simple-minded. For unless he said such things, why would we confess his incarnation[iii] into our nature? And when we hear the most sublime things, let us ponder that they are the humblest [attributes?] of the same who condescended to our nature from the heights; he was not transformed, but by communication.[iv]

See here what he says. First he indicated about himself that the sheep enter through the door into the fold, not at all going astray on the path of the prophetic writings, from which they earlier preached. Then [he says] he is the door through which they enter with him into the fold. Into which fold? Into the church of God. And then he calls himself *the good shepherd. Shepherd*, because he leads the flocks and brings them into the fold, and gathers them in the pen, which he also called *fold*. And *good* because *shepherd* and *good* are appellations of their common divinity.[v] Hear the prophet who says:[17] *You who shepherds Israel, look down* (Ps 79:2). What means *Look down*? *You who shepherds Israel, look down* on us **[225]** by shepherding us, he means. But as

    16. **Like,** *ĕst*, N: "among," *i*, M.
    17. **Who says:** om. N.

for *good*, the Lord himself testified: *Why do you call me good? No one is good except one, God* (Luke 18:19). And what is: *He lays down his life for the sheep?* Again he accuses them, as if to say that they are killers of the sheep, but he lays down his life for them;[18] on behalf of them he was to lay down his life with torments of the cross and death for his rational flock.

He indicates also something else that is most sublime. He does not die for himself, paying his own debts just as all men pay the debts of death, as [scripture] said, *You were dust, and to dust you will return* (Gen 3:19), but he endured death for the sake of his flock. Why did he previously state that in allegorical words? It was so that when he would be forcibly taken to the death of the cross, they might be aware and consider what had once been said, that willingly and not by force the Lord[19] endured all that.

i. **Hagarene**: *hagarakan*, one of the terms used for Arabs in the Islamic period, found in Sebēos and later writers; it refers to the supposed ancestry of the Arabs from Hagar's son Ishmael (Gen 16:15). The earlier Armenian term for Arabs is *Tačik*.

ii. **Noble**: *k'aĵ*, as in the Armenian biblical text here and v. 14, and the commentary to v. 1 above. It renders the Greek *kalos*, which the translator interprets as *bari*. The Arabic original of the commentary is lost, but the modern Arabic version of the verse has the adjective *ṣāliḥ*, "good, right, virtuous." On the other hand, the text of the *Diatessaron* (Marmardji's edition) has *ḳayyir*, which has the sense of "generous, charitable, kind." *K'aĵ*, "valiant," plays an important role in Armenian and Sasanian royal imagery; see Garsoïan 1989 (534–35) and 1996.

iii. **Incarnation**: *t'ap'umn* (lit. "emptying"), the equivalent of the Greek *kenōsis*, for which see Lampe 1969 (s.v. *kenōsis*) and the introduction, xxxviii.

iv. Here M and N have different adverbs. The printed text reads *p'oxatrabar*, a calque on the Greek *metadotikōs*, rendered in Lampe 1969 (s.v. *metadotikōs*) as "by imparting, communication." M reads *p'oxarkabar*, which means "by transformation," the Greek *metabolē*. Lampe (1969, s.v. *metabolē*) notes that this term is specifically rejected as regards the incarnation. See further the introduction, xxxix.

v. **Of their common divinity**: *hasarakac' astuacut'eann*, "of the divinity of all," the meaning of which is unclear.

[10:12–13] **But the hireling who is not the shepherd, whose own the sheep are not, when he sees the wolf coming he abandons the sheep and flees. And**

---

18. Them, NM^corr: "his sheep," M.
19. The Lord: om. N.

the wolf carries them off and scatters[20] them; for he is hired, and he has no concern for the sheep.

When he said about his own oversight that it was not like that of the thieves and brigands who had come before him, he next set down something wonderful, recalling *the hireling, whose own the sheep are not*, meaning the prophets and righteous men. Although they were happy to save the flocks because of being hired,[i] so that being separated from the worship of idols they might save their souls from death, yet that oversight was not similar to mine. For although they often made efforts, yet they did not have as much zeal for the salvation of the flock[21] as I. Nor were they able, because those who endured death for divine love [**226**] gained for themselves the reward of their hire. But they did not die for the sake of the flock, because they were not yet thereby able to save them.[22]

Now, what means: *When he sees the wolf coming, he abandons the sheep and flees?* By *wolf* he wished to describe Satan.[ii] And *When he sees the wolf coming* means that on seeing the flock corrupted in wicked deeds, he would understand that [to be caused] by his coming; but he is unable to find means to chase him off but simply escapes merely to save himself, just as the prophets and righteous men only saved themselves and were of no help to the flock. Nor were they able to save them from bodily slaughter, because they were like servants, although they believed their hiring was from above. But despite delivering them from idols and preaching the coming of the true shepherd, they themselves possessed no more perfect power for the salvation of the flock.

i. Here the text adds: *aysink'n yayn edeals znosa astuacut'eann*, the meaning of which is unclear. If a scribe made an original *edeal* plural by attraction to the following plural *znosa*, then it could be interpreted: "that is, the Deity had set them to that [task]."

ii. Moše bar Kepha and Dionysius bar Salibi (*John*, 205) call the wolf "death"; but Dionysius, *John*, 206, gives the interpretation "Devil." John Chrysostom here alludes to 1 Pet 5:8: the "Devil" as a lion.

---

20. **Carries them off and scatters,** MZ: "scatters them and carries off," N.
21. **Of the flock:** om. N.
22. Them: om. N.

[10:14–15a] **I am the good**[23] **shepherd, and I know my own, and I am known by my own. Just as the Father knows me, I also know the Father.**

Because he taught without distinction of the sheep and did not separate[24] the others from the flocks, he then set down in another way the meaning of the saying *I know my own*, that is, I know those who love me and follow me. And lest they think that he only knows them like others from among mankind, he added, *As the Father knows me, I also know the Father*, showing that I have knowledge comparable to the Father's, that is, by seeing the thoughts of mankind. For not only do I look on the face,[i] but also into the heart, and not as you think you know anything in human fashion. He also shows something else, that not only does he have equality of knowledge with the Father but also of essence.[ii] [227] For *just as he knows me*, being his Son in essence, likewise *I also know him*, being of the nature of my Father. Now, if I am known [by] them in accordance with their faith in me and their good works, I also make myself known to them on the day of retribution by granting them great rewards and many gifts and glory that cannot be despoiled.[iii]

i. **Face:** *dēmk'*, the outer appearance; cf. Ezek 1:6. The word is also used for "person."

ii. The equality of Christ's nature, power, and will with the Father is stressed by Moše bar Kepha. Dionysius bar Salibi, *John*, 206, refers to their equality of nature, power, and divinity. Tat'ewac'i, 427, refers to their equality of "essence" (*ēut'iwn*) and their being one in "nature" (*bnut'iwn*) and "person" (*anjn*).

iii. Nonnus does not quote or comment on the second half of v. 15, but that theme is picked up in v. 17.

[10:16] **And I have other sheep that are not from this fold. These**[25] **too I must lead here, and they will hear my voice and become one flock and one shepherd.**

Since he first thus described the differences of the flocks, *I know my own, and I am known by my own*, distinguishing [them] from other flocks, he then added another mystery hidden from them. Because the Jews supposed that God did not have anywhere another people save only themselves, the Savior added: *I have other sheep that are not from this fold, whom I must lead.* He means the Gentiles,[i] because they had never entered the folds of the law and prophets; but since they were easily to believe in[26] the word of life, therefore

---

23. **Good**, *bari*, MN; *k'aj*, Z; see commentary to v. 11, above.

24. **Separate**, M: "indicate," N.

25. **These**, Z: sg. MN.

26. **Believe in:** "follow," M.

he indicated their easily following the shepherd by saying: *They will become one flock and one shepherd*. He revealed both nations that would become one through baptism, according to Paul's saying: *There is no distinction, neither of Jew nor Gentile, neither of male or female, because you are all one in Christ* (Gal 3:27–28).

i. **Gentiles**: *het'anoss*. The same identification is made by all commentators: John Chrysostom, *Hom. Jo.* 60.2; Cyril of Alexandria, *Comm. Jo.* 6; Theodore of Mopsuestia; Moše bar Kepha; Išodad; and Dionysius bar Salibi, *John*, 206.

[10:17–18a] **Therefore my Father loves me, because I lay down my life so that I may take it up again. No one takes it from me, but I lay it down by myself. I have authority to lay it down.**

Because he clearly set out in their hearing the account of his torments, by saying, [228] *I lay down my life for the flock*,[i] he then showed that this would occur by the will of the Father. That was very pleasing to the Father for the salvation of the world, since for that he had sent me into the world. In this way he showed their united will and reproved the harshness of their minds, and thereby he removed thoughts of opposition in saying: *Therefore the Father loves me*, because I do his will. He refers to the salvation of the world and thereby demonstrates the nature of the Father's unlimited benevolence.

But see how he reveals here the power of his own divine authority, although he veils the saying: *I lay down my life so that I may take it up again.* *Although the laying down reveals his willing [acceptance of] the torments, and the taking it up again predicts the resurrection after three days, yet notice for me something else: how he reprimands their weakness. He writes that[ii] he shows how all human nature endures a death different from his own. How would that be? *I lay down my life so that I may take it up again.*[27] Who from among human nature is able to cast from himself his soul[iii] with authority, and after a little time to take it again to himself? There is no way for that. For just as at the time of death no one has the power to hold back in himself his soul when it hastens to depart, likewise no one has the power of releasing it in time of health. But to take it again is to speak absurdly. Furthermore, we do not now know whether after our exit from the body[28] where we shall dwell, or how and in what way remain. But to return again to this corrupted body is to be understood only through faith and hope, that the Architect[iv] will refashion again the old body and link and unite its former soul [to it].

---

27. **Although the laying down … again**: om. N.
28. **Body**: pl. MN.

Now, Christ spoke about his own death very differently from this. *I lay down my life*, that is, willingly I dispatch my human soul, when expiring[v] happens to me on the cross, which indeed he demonstrated: *Jesus cried out and released his soul, *saying: Father, into your hands I commend my soul*[vi] (Matt 27:50).[29] *Then again I take it up*; by rising on the third day from the tomb he raised himself up again and united the soul and body with his indivisible and inseparable divinity. [229] Did you see how his death, which he endured for our salvation, was revealed to be with *authority* and willing?

Also the Jews and the unconvinced were wicked and perfidious. For if they had not been so, there would have been a different display of reproach of his sovereign and willing death, whereby they would have been able to know that many times they wished to lay hands on him and once to cast stones at him, but he without opposition prevented their action and was hidden from their sight, and passing through them emerged untested. And on the evening when they wished to arrest him and he said, *I am the one whom you seek, they stood back and were cast to the ground* (John 18:6). Even when he offered himself into their hands, he healed the servant's[30] ear *that had been cut off by Peter,[31] with *an authoritative command and by the power of his hand stretched out,[32] which was sufficient for them to experience his unlimited power (John 18:10).[vii]

i. **For the flock**: a reference to v. 15b, "I lay down my life for the sheep," which was omitted above.

ii. **He writes that**: *grē etē*. It can hardly be a mistake by the scribe of M (the passage being omitted in N) for *gretē*, "almost," since the totality of humankind is involved. That "he writes" refers to the evangelist is likely, since the same phrase occurs in the commentary to v. 19 just below.

iii. **Soul**: *hogi*, but *anjn* (lit. "self") in the lemma. Here John Chrysostom, *Hom. Jo.* 60.2, stresses the inability of men to put down their life.

iv. **Architect**: *čartarapet*. For God as *čartarapet*, see Wis 7:21; Heb 11:10, and Lampe 1969 (s.v. *technitēs*).

v. **Expiring**: *anšnčanal* (lit. being without *šunč'*, "breath").

vi. **Soul**: *hogi*. Here Dionysius bar Salibi, *Gospels*, 140, indicates the three senses of life: soul, mind, and spirit.

vii. Only John names Peter; the other evangelists merely say, "one of them."

---

29. **Saying ... soul**: om. N.
30. **Servant's**: om. M.
31. **That...Peter**: om. N.
32. **An authoritative ... out**: "authoritative power," N.

[10:18b] **This command I received from my Father.**

Since he made clear that with authority and willingly I endure the torments and death, he added to that also the Father, *This command I received from the Father*, in order to indicate that with the consent of the Father that would occur: *And I never do anything of myself,*[i] because through that he shows the unity[ii] of wills of himself and the Father in everything and makes it clear to those who continually said he was opposed to God. He did not say, *This command I received from the Father*, because of being less than the Father but merely attributed the cause to the fatherly name, as was appropriate indeed for the Son, so that he might render the unity of their wills more strong and confirm the unity of nature.

> i. John 5:19, and many subsequent references.
> ii. **Unity**: *anerkut'iwn*, N; *anerkewut'iwn*, M (lit. "not-two-ness"). *NBHL* notes that this word occurs only in Nonnus. Just below: "unity of wills," *kamac'n miut'iwn*; "unity of nature," *bnut'ean anerkewut'iwn*.

[10:19] **Again there was a split among the Jews concerning this saying.**

The evangelist continually wishes to demonstrate their unstable and unintelligent thoughts, [230] because he often writes showing that they were confused and squabbling, and there was never a united will among them.[i]

> i. Tat'ewac'i, 433, specifically refers back to ch. 7 for the divisions.

[10:20] **And many of them said: There is a demon in him, and he is mad. *Why do you listen to him at all?**[33]

This is the fourth[i] accusation of the evangelist concerning them of such shameless and indecent mocking of the Life-giver. For he demonstrates[34] not only their impudent derision but also his easily forgiving and modest pardon. He did not cast them into the abyss with a single nod, or bring down burning fire from heaven (cf. Ps 139:11), but he forgave them and responded so very gently in order to show us that he did not undertake any vengeance of his own but only that of the Father, as when he once made a whip and violently cast them out of the temple, and destroyed the tables,[35] saying: *Do not make the*

---

33. **Why … all?**: om. M.
34. **For he demonstrates**: "in order to demonstrate," N.
35. **Tables, MZ**: sg. N.

house of my Father a house of commerce (John 2:16). And as when they called the Father their God, saying, *We have one father, God*, at which he was angered and replied, *You are from [your] father Satan* (John 8:41, 44), in order to teach us not to become angry when we hear about ourselves, and not[36] to take any vengeance for our own sake; but when we hear anything unbecoming about God, absolutely not to forgive but to become defenders, as the Lord himself did and taught us.

i. **Fourth**: as John Chrysostom, *Hom. Jo.* 60.3, who cites three other occasions: John 7:20; 8:48; 10:38.

[10:21] Others said: Such words are not of one demon-possessed. Can a demon open the eyes of a blind one?

Who were[37] they who said this? The evangelist indicated that once more there were divisions among them, in order to show that some were so vexed as to call him *demon-possessed*, but others wished to hear [him] and were pleased with the signs. The latter said, *Such words are not of one demon-possessed*, for which they cited the miracle that was performed[38] for the blind one, **[231]** and thereby, as if reprimanding the former, [said]: You are not at all correct in what you say about the man, because in front of us he performed the great miracle. Hence it is clear that there is no way one *demon-possessed* can do such a thing.[i]

i. Here Moše bar Kepha ends Part 1 of his commentary, which is longer than the second part.

[10:22–23] At that time [the feast of] the dedication took place in Jerusalem, and it was winter. Jesus was walking in the temple, in the porch of Solomon.

What feast of dedication[i] would that be? It seems[39] not of Solomon's [temple] but of Zerubabel's, when they rebuilt the temple and made a dedication.[ii] The events were close: as every year came around, on the same day they carried out the dedication feast. Why on the feasts was the Lord walking in the temple and frequently doing that? On the festivals the Jews and dense throngs[40] used to gather in Jerusalem because of the feast; therefore the Life-

---

36. **And not**: "or," M.
37. **Were**: om. N.
38. **Was performed**: om. N.
39. **It seems**: om. N.
40. **Throngs**: sg. N.

giver would go up to Jerusalem on the days of the festivals in order to carry out his teaching and signs in front of the whole multitude of peoples. For that reason the evangelist indicated both the festival and the place, in order to show that he did nothing useless and unprofitable but only [taught] when the hearers and viewers were very numerous, so that nothing of what he did for the salvation of mankind would remain hidden.

i. **Feast of dedication:** *tawn nawakateac'*. The lemma has merely *nawakatik'* (Gk. *ta enkainia*), "dedication"; but the commentary adds "feast."

ii. John Chrysostom, *Hom. Jo.* 61.1, notes it was the feast for the dedication of the temple built after the Persian captivity. Cyril of Alexandria, *Comm. Jo.* 7, refers to the temples of Solomon and Zerubabel, as does Moše bar Kepha. Išodad notes that the temple was restored by the Maccabees after the overthrow of Antiochus, to which Theodore of Mopsuestia also makes reference. Dionysius bar Salibi, *Gospels*, 208, notes the overthrow of Antiochus, the victory of the Maccabees, and their restoration of the city and temple. Tat'ewac'i, 435, refers to the three temples of Solomon, of Zerubabel, and of Judas Maccabaeus.

[10:24] The Jews surrounded him and said: For how long will you wear us out? If you are the Christ, tell us openly.

Do not think that they asked the question in a search for the truth.[i] Whence is this clear? From the great miracles that they saw many times yet did not believe.[41] Likewise from the healing of the blind one and from the other signs, they should have confessed him[42] not only as Christ but more literally as God made man,[ii] for the proclamation[iii] of the blind one demonstrated that. *From eternity,* [232] he said, *no one has heard that the eyes were opened of a blind one born blind from birth* (John 9:32), meaning that such a thing had never been done by a man from eternity. And if it was not possible for a man to do this, then he is God and the Son of God. So it is obvious that they were not concerned with asking about the faith but were attempting to find excuses and to extract a statement from him. This is easy to understand from the responses of the Savior.

i. The deceptive nature of the inquiry is stressed by John Chrysostom, *Hom. Jo.* 61.1; Theodore of Mopsuestia; Moše bar Kepha; and Dionysius bar Salibi, *Gospels*, 209.

ii. **Made man:** *mardac'eal*; see the introduction, xxxvii, for the terminology.

iii. **Proclamation:** *bołok'* (lit. "protest").

---

41. **Yet did not believe:** om. N.
42. **Him:** om. N.

[10:25a] *Jesus replied and said:[43] I told you, and you do not believe me.

This means: Why do you ask me at all? I have spoken many times, and you do not believe. But you seek to kill me, for the reason that I say I am Son of God. They also said: *You bear witness about yourself, and your*[44] *testimony is not true* (John 8:13). Now if I am not true, why do you ask? So you wish[45] to extract some pretexts by deceit *in order to fulfill your wishes against me.[46]

[10:25b] The deeds that I do in the name of my[47] Father, those testify concerning me.

If you will not believe[48] in the task that I continually perform in the name of the Father, attributing the cause to the Father to make it easier for you to accept, when will you believe in the plain words? The deeds, then, are more persuasive for the faith than the words. So if you do not believe in the deeds, when will you believe in the words?

[10:26] But you do not believe, because you are not from my sheep.

Not because they are not worthy of credence do you not believe in the deeds, but because you do not wish to be of my sheep,[i] of which I previously said: *I know my own, and I am known by my own* (John 10:14). *You are not from my sheep*: not that there might be something preventing it—as if it were not possible to be of my sheep because they are not [233] from among them— but he reveals his foresight in order to show that you are never going to mingle with them. For that reason he said what had not yet occurred to be like things that had happened, according to the prophet who said:[49] *My eyes have seen your failings*[ii] (Ps 138:16). So then there is no need of your deceitful questions such as: *Tell us openly* who you are.

i. Here Tat'ewac'i, 438, defines the sheep as the disciples and believers.
ii. **Failings:** *angorcs* (lit. "nondeeds").

---

43. **Jesus…said**, N: om. M.
44. **Your**: om. N.
45. **You wish**: om. N.
46. **In order…me**: om. N.
47. **My**, MZ: om. N.
48. **Will not believe**: "did not believe," M.
49. **Who said**: om. M.

[10:27–28] My sheep hear my voice, and I know them, and they follow me. And I give them eternal life, and they will never perish, and no one shall snatch them from my hands.

My sheep, he says, who recognize me and *hear my voice, do not perish, and no one is able to snatch them from my hands, but I give them everlasting life.* By that[50] [the evangelist] writes that[i] he displeases them even more and urges them to the faith, because as those who know me *do not perish* nor are they *snatched from my hands,* you will endure the opposite to that. For after a little time you will *perish* by the sword by the Romans, and your wives and children will be *snatched away* into captivity,[ii] and instead of *eternal life* you will endure eternal and merciless torments.

i. [**The evangelist] writes that:** *gretē* (lit. "almost"). It is more likely that this should be read as *grē tē*; see note to commentary on vv. 17–18a, above. If Nonnus meant "almost," then *gretē* should come immediately before "even more."

ii. Tat'ewac'i, 439, does not refer to Nonnus here, although he is one of Tat'ewac'i's main sources and often is quoted as "the interpreter," *meknič'.* In one of his usual lists, he identifies the one who snatches as Satan, or as sin, or as (unnamed) tyrants.

[10:29–30] My Father, who gave me them, is greater than all. And no one is able to snatch them[51] from my Father's hands. I and my Father are one.

Did you see how in every way he promised the safekeeping of his flock, and thereby piqued them even more by calling the Father their guardian and protector? But see how he removes the grounds for doubt. For when they heard, *The Father, who gave me[52] them, is greater than all,* not only did the Jews consequently reckon him to be less, but even the believers. Therefore he added to the same, *I and the Father are one,* in order to show that by saying *one,* that had the indication of equality of nature and of power.[i] This is sufficient for a demonstration of the humility of his words, **[234]** that he always did that because of the harshness of the Jews, in order to remove their suspicions that he was opposed to the Father, as they continually claimed. So next he set down their equality, so that by that he might diminish their wickedness and thus correct their defective thoughts.

i. Here John Chrysostom, *Hom. Jo.* 61.2, stresses the equality of "power" and "essence," *dynamis* and *ousia,* of Father and Son. Išodad stresses the equality of their substance,

---

50. **By that:** om. N.
51. **Them:** om. MZ.
52. **Me, MZ:** om. N.

nature, and power, while Moše bar Kepha refers to their equality of nature, power, and will. Tat'ewac'i, 439–40, stresses the unity of nature and "essence," *ēut'iwn*, as opposed to the Arians, who said that there were three persons in the Trinity and three natures.

[10:31] The Jews took up rocks in order to stone[53] **him.**

Once more the evangelist makes clear that although they often wished to stone him or lay hands on him, yet they were unable, because with independent will he was to endure the torments and death, and not by force. Therefore when he himself wished, he suffered, and not when they wished.

[10:32–33] Jesus replied to them:[54] **Many good deeds have I shown you from my Father. For which of those deeds do you stone me? The Jews answered him: For good deeds we do not stone you, but for your blasphemy, because you are a man, yet you make yourself God.**

He reminded the obstinate[55] and ungrateful nation of the benevolent deeds that they were not intending to recognize, in accordance with the prediction of the Holy Spirit through the mouth of David: *A wicked and rebellious nation, a nation that did not correct its heart and did not establish its soul toward God* (Ps 77:8). But see how continually he ascribes the cause of his works to the Father, and thereby makes an effort for their correction and blocks the excuse that they alleged: We stone you for the reason that *you make yourself God*. So if in the name of the Father I have shown you good deeds, why do you stone me?[56] For if I am[57] not by nature God, why would my Father be coworker with me, a blasphemer? The good deeds[58] that they mentioned, that is, I healed your sick, gave sight to the blind, cleansed lepers, *fed the hungry in the desert, and at a command[59] raised the dead—all this I did in the name of my Father. [235] If I am a man, as you say, whence would come that power? And how would the Father be a coworker, or even pardon a creature calling his creator Father by nature[60] and saying he was equal to him in all respects?[61]

---

53. **To stone:** *k'arkocescen*, N; *k'arkoc arascen*, MZ.

54. **Them:** + "and said," M.

55. **Obstinate,** *anhawan*, N: "unbelieving," *anhawat*, M.

56. **Me:** om. N.

57. **I am:** "he were," M.

58. **Deeds:** sg. N.

59. **Fed ... command:** om. N.

60. **By nature:** om. N.

61. **In all respects:** om. N.

[10:34–38] **Jesus replied to them and said: Is it not written in your law: I said that you are gods?[62] Now, if he calls them gods to whom the word of God came, and it is not possible to destroy the scripture, then of the one whom the Father sanctified and sent into the world you say, You blaspheme, because I said that I am Son of God. *If I do not do the deeds of my Father, do not believe me. But if I do, if you do not believe me, at least believe the deeds, so that you may know and recognize that the Father is in me and I in the Father.[63]**

Pay attention for me here[64] to these lofty words,[i] how from the commandments themselves he sets out his rebuke. *Your law*, he says, and also the prophecy of David, which you testify to have been given by God, *calls them gods*. They only possessed the grace of words of prophecy, and you confess them to be your compatriots, yet you do not reject the title of divinity lest you contradict the scriptures. Now, as for *the one whom the Father sanctified and sent into the world*, why are you vexed and call him a blasphemer and seek to kill him for the very name? For you say:[65] *You are a man, yet you make yourself God*. Now if you do not believe in his words, at least you did believe in his deeds and recognized the immeasurable separation that exists between me and them in accordance with the great miracles, but also according to the testimony of the Father in the hearing of you all: *This is my beloved Son, in whom I am pleased* (Matt 3:17 par.).

But you, beloved, I know that you wish to know the circumstances of his sanctification. What means: *whom the Father sanctified and sent into the world*? I do not think that there is any sanctification of essence, [**236**] for how do the *light of glory* and of the power of God and *the image of the essence*[ii] receive sanctification? Or what is more holy than the *ray*, with the rest?[iii] And do not understand the body as brought from heaven because of its being sanctified there[66] and being sent. For if he has his body from there, why does he call David (Matt 22:45) and Abraham (John 8:58) prior to him? So then it is clear that by sanctification by the Father he wished to say that by putting on our body, through our [characteristics] he purified our bodies from the previous dark impurities caused by the smoke of demonic sacrifices and various evils, just as he attributes to the Father the other things by saying: *I have shown you many good deeds in the name of my Father*. He means the signs, as

---

62. Ps 82:6.

63. If I do not … Father: om. M.

64. Here: om. N.

65. For you say: om. N.

66. There: *and*, M; *ĕnd*, N.

this is similar to the Father's foresight and coworking of his will, for which reason he sent his Son for our purification, of which task he said he was the head and cause.

In this way he entrusts the whole world to the purification of the Father; through the purification of the holy font he offered to the Father what was once dyed black with sin. I wish to make it very pure, because he describes the Father's sending of the Son as the sanctification of our purity, as if to say that for this the Father established him.

Did you see[67] how later he set down very clearly the mystery of the saying with the very Father himself? He said: *I make myself holy for their sake, that they too might become purified through the truth* (John 17:19). Now, on coming[68] near to the cross, it is time to complete the purification of the world to which I have been sent. Paul too, steward[iv] of the mysteries of God, will testify to this saying: *The one who purifies and who is purified were all from one* (Heb 2:11). He did not reckon it shameful to call them brothers and to say: *I shall narrate your name to my brothers* (Ps 21:23). First he purifies, and then he calls them brothers. Did you see how the meaning of this saying came into the light?

    i. John Chrysostom, *Hom. Jo.* 61, omits vv. 33–38, and Cyril of Alexandria omits vv. 35–36.

    ii. **Light of glory, the image of the essence**: Heb 1:3.

    iii. This seems to be a reference to the description of God in Hab 3:3–4.

    iv. **Steward**: *hazarapet*; for "steward of the mysteries of God," see 1 Cor 4:1. *Hazarapet* is a calque on *chiliarchos* and is widely used in the secular sense of "chancellor, manager"; see Garsoïan 1989, 531–32.

[237] [10:39] Once more they wished[69] to seize him, and he escaped from their hands.

He verified here what had once been said to them, *I have authority to lay down my life, and I have authority to take it up again,*[70] so that perchance also at the time of the cross, when he first overturned them and then gave himself into their hands, they might reflect on the former and the latter, and might repent a little in themselves and realize what they were doing. He arranged all this, not unaware of their inflexibility, but he totally removed the excuse when they would encounter unendurable torments. *As he said to the disciples:[71]

----

67. **Did you see**: "see" (impv.), M.

68. **Coming**, *galov*, M: "being," *golov*, N.

69. **Wished**, N: "sought," MZ.

70. **Again**: om. N.

71. **As … disciples**: om. N.

Unless I had come and spoken[72] *there would have been*[73] *no sin, but now there is no excuse for their sins* (John 15:22).[i] And what after that would they have to say or to allege the causes of sin? He pardoned [them] so often and very frequently contrived their correction, yet they never were concerned.

    i. When this quotation is repeated in the "Exhortation" below, M gives the same text as N here.

[10:40–42] **And he went beyond the Jordan to the place where John was at first and baptized, and he stayed there. Many came to him and said: John did not perform any signs, but everything that John said about him was true. And many believed in him.**

Why did he go to that place, save that through the place in which John was continually baptizing he might remind them of the testimony of John that he testified concerning him,[i] *I am not worthy to loose the laces of his shoes* (John 1:27), and *He is from above* (3:31), and *He is the true Son of God* (1:34),[74] and thereby he might reprove their error, that the one whom you plan to stone, he is the one about whom your prophet John testified all this: how great he was and faithful in the eyes of you all? [238] And he acknowledged him to be so much higher than himself, who did not reckon himself worthy of loosing the laces of his shoe. But the one to whom he did not think himself worthy to render service, you still audaciously seek to stone.

    i. John Chrysostom, *Hom. Jo.* 61.3, and Moše bar Kepha also note that this was the purpose of going there.

[Exhortation][75]

O beloved, have you heard, then, what he said about the immeasurable *love of God, how to us was revealed[76] the providence of the Godhead, who so much desires our salvation that he said the Father sent the Son for the sanctification of our nature? The Savior came and first purified [us] and then called [us] brothers. Who indeed will testify to this saying? Paul the teacher

---

72. **Spoken:** + "with them," MZ.

73. **There would have been:** "they would have had," MZ.

74. **Of God:** om. N.

75. This section to p. 246 in the printed text is entitled *yordorak* by the editor; see the introduction, xxv. In this and later "Exhortation" sections, all notes are placed at the bottom of the page, not merely the variant readings in the MSS.

76. **Love … revealed:** om. N.

of the Gentiles (1 Tim 2:7): *He who sanctifies and those who are sanctified are all from one.*[77] For which reason he did not reckon it shameful to call them brothers and to say: *I shall relate your name to my brothers* (Ps 21:23)? First he purifies, and then he calls them brothers; afterward he also teaches the name of the Father, in order to teach those whom he made sons of God by the birth of the font also to call God Father through his brotherhood.

See the immeasurable benevolence that made us worthy of so much honor. When or how shall we pay him recompense? He does not even demand this from us but only that we retain our purity for the sake of our own salvation, and not for any profit to him, but that we assist him regarding our sanctification that he wrought. Let us not be found ungrateful and unthankful, and through our laziness make our splendor dark again. See how thereby we anger him and force [him] to punish us. For if he was so anxious for our purity that [he submitted] to the torments [239] of the cross and endured such contempt and mockery—he even endured death for us, and arising from the tomb made us luminous, whereas we are disgusted and indolent and trample on such benefits—of what pardon would we then be worthy; and especially when we transform ourselves[78] into our previous impure form, what do we have to allege as excuse?

If as regards the ungrateful nation of the Jews he thus sets out a review of their judgment by saying, *If I had not come and spoken there would have been no sin, but now there is no excuse for their sins* (John 15:22), what would we have to say, we whom did he not only instruct by word but also illuminate by deeds, and even loved so much as to give his own life as ransom for us (1 Tim 2:6)? The Lord himself testified: *Such love*, he said, *no one would have that he would lay down his life for his friends, as I lay down my life for you* (John 15:13; 10:15). He died for the sake of our purity, so let us preserve that purity in us.

Do you wish that we[79] persuade you with a small example from those outside [the church]? If anyone, receiving a gift from a king, even the royal purple, and in the morning soils it with nasty mud, and comes before the king in the palace with an insolent face, see how much punishment and chastisement he will consequently endure for scorning the royal robes. So then, does he not command the torturers to strip from him the royal garment that he despised and hand him over to the torments of punishment as one who despised the royal gift? Yet what will we be able to say when we darkly stain

---

77. Heb 2:11, also quoted in commentary to vv. 34–38, above. The translator uses the verb *srbel* for "to sanctify" and *mak'rel* for "to purify," and the corresponding nouns for "sanctification" and "purity."

78. **Transform ourselves**: "are transformed," N.

79. **We**: "I," N.

the luminous garment of the holy font with foul deeds, [240] especially the divine robe, because we who have been baptized in Christ have put on Christ[80] (Gal 3:27).

So let us go and stand before our king in the public court, in which are so many armies of holy angels and ranks of seraphim and cherubim, of powers and authorities, of thrones and principalities,[81] and of all the fiery watchers,[82] also crowds of the just, of prophets and apostles, martyrs and ascetics, and the entire race of mankind, gathered at the arena of judgment. The judge with fearful appearance sits on the throne of glory, and rivers of fire flow in torrents before him, and the fire waits to threaten the dark ones on the left-hand side. Of what pardon will we be worthy at that hour?[83] In accordance with the saying of the Gospel will he not order us to be cut in half (Matt 24:51; Luke 12:46), the glory of the font to be stripped from us, that luminous garment, and that we be placed with the unbelievers (Luke 12:46)? But perhaps someone of those listening may wish to hear details of the purity. The divine sayings will teach them through the prophet Isaiah:[84] *Make judgment for the orphan, and give justice to the widow. And if your sins are like soot, I shall make them as white as snow. And if they are red like scarlet, I shall make them as pure as wool.* Did you see how he obtains the victory? Not only does he keep pure those once sanctified, but he also transforms the purple redness of sin into the whiteness of snow. And the form of sin, scarlet red resembling[85] blood, he renders similar to wool-like purity. This is the work of his benevolence, so that he may teach us again means to preserve our purity.

Now, if you wish to learn the details of making judgment for the widow and orphan, [241] I shall not be slow to speak to that. Not only those tyrants outside [the church] who are deficient in making judgment but also those inside [the church] have within themselves conflict and injustice. And what I call conflict is always endured among the poor, who are continually hungry and afflicted by nakedness and homelessness; and being oppressed they do not have anyone to plead their case. Yet you are able to extinguish that familiar conflict, because when you fill the hungry and clothe the naked and take to your home the one without a roof, you demonstrate superior judgment and compassion in yourself for the care of orphans and widows, and consequently you render your luminous garment even more splendid and pure. So

---

80. **Christ:** + "said the Apostle," M.

81. **Of thrones and principalities:** om. N.

82. **Watchers:** *zart'unk'*, often used in the general sense of "angels."

83. **At that hour:** om. N.

84. **Isaiah:** om. N.

85. **Resembling,** *nmaneal,* M: *mnal,* N (*sic*); the editor prints *bnaw.*

let us urge ourselves on, brethren, to such good deeds, so that when we stand before our judge, Christ, in the universal tribunal, we may be able to enter the courts of light and receive the glorious crown and inherit unending life from our Lord Jesus Christ.[86] With whom to the Father and also the Holy Spirit [be] glory, honor, power,[87] and authority now and always and[88] forever and ever. Amen.[89]

Since through the gift[90] of the Holy Spirit we have finished and terminated the explanation of these divinely inspired[91] discourses, it is time now to make the luminous words of the Gospel resplendent for the holy catholic church, in accordance with the voice of the prophet, *Shine out, shine out, Jerusalem, for your light has arrived* (Isa 60:1), and also because[92] the commandment is entitled light, according to the seer:[93] *The commandments of the Lord are light and give light to the eyes.*[94] It seemed pleasing to us through a luminous [242] word to pronounce to the holy catholic church the gift[95] of the word of the Gospel. For if the one who once granted the precepts to the world through his servants called it light, how much clearer and purer and unclouded a light must we call the commandment of that light that John proclaimed, *He was the true light that illuminated every man who was to come into the world* (John 1:9), which the Savior himself took upon himself and testified for our instruction, saying: *I am light and truth and life* (John 8:12; 14:6).

Now, since in accordance with these shining and divine words of the inscrutable discourses we have frequently given light through a word, which now being assisted by heavenly grace in our explanation with logical defi-

---

86. **Jesus Christ**: "Christ God," M.

87. **Power**: om. N.

88. **Now and always and**: om. M.

89. Here a colophon in M notes, "This book ends," *awartecʿaw girkʿs ays*, which echoes the *awarteal glxaworecʿakʿ*, "we have finished and terminated [these divinely inspired discourses]" in the text. M continues, however, up to p. 245, line 17, of the printed text. Whether or not the passages marked "Exhortation" belong to Nonnus (but see the introduction, xxv, for evidence that at least parts are the responsibility of the translator), the rest of this section was clearly composed by an Armenian.

90. **Gift**: *jrikʿ*. The uninflected *jri* means "free, at no cost" and is used with "grace" in Rom 3:24.

91. **Divinely inspired**: "divine," M.

92. **Because**: om. N.

93. **The seer**: "the voice of the seer," M.

94. Ps 18:9 = Z.

95. **Gift**: *ĕncayaberutʿiwn* (lit. "the presentation of an offering").

nition[96] we have expounded very clearly the inscrutable meaning of the divine profundities, it seemed pleasing to us to eulogize a little the grace of the catholic church, although even that is not pompous and proud according to worth, but in accordance with the poverty of that widow has received the two mites into the treasury of Christ (Luke 21:2). Like her may you receive also the praises of my modest words from my poor mind, O bride of Christ and mother of believers, holy catholic church. Perhaps, my poverty being thus emboldened to this offering, we shall finish my account, O most favored and much blessed all-wondrous and flowering with felicity, mother and tutor of those who confess the triple-person[97] yet single Godhead.

In you[98] is summed up the boast of fullness of the right faith; in you all the youth of orthodoxy are instructed and confirmed in the faith. In you the Son of God is continually sacrificed, who once and for all was sacrificed for the salvation of the world; [243] in you are continually distributed the saving[99] body and blood for the propitiation and forgiveness of the race of mankind. In you the six-winged seraphim[100] always sing their triple *holy, holy, holy* to the Son of God invisibly.[101] In you the heavenly ones gathered with the earthly ones continually praise the essential God as at the birth (Luke 2:13).

Through you catechumens by rebirth are called sons of God by grace; through you the baptized, flying up from this lower habitat, are raised to the place of the fallen angels; through you the ranks of clerics are embellished and continually rejoice; through you bishops delight and are happy; through you priests are rendered splendid and are modest in honor; through you deacons are chaste, serving worthily. Through you ascetics endure and practice virtue; through you teachers authoritatively pronounce theology. Through you schismatics are subdued and crushed; through you Belial is dishonored and put to shame. Through you great sinners by repentance are freed from cruel[102] servitude to sin. Through you the souls of those departed from the world complete their memorials and acquire freedom.

------

96. **With logical definition**: *trmabanut'eamb taroroŝeal. Tramabanut'iwn* means either "logic" or "dialogue," but the latter seems inappropriate for this work.

97. **Triple-person**, *eṙanjean*: see the introduction, xxxix.

98. **In you**: M sets out the phrases of the following two paragraphs separately.

99. **Saving**: "of the Lord," N.

100. **Seraphim**: + "and many-eyed cherubim," M.

101. The six-winged seraphim sing this refrain in Isa 6:3; according to Rev 4:8 it was sung by four beasts with six wings and many eyes. The addition in M of cherubim with many eyes is based on Ezek 10:12, but there is no reference there to this refrain. For the application of the Trisagion to the Son, see the commentary to John 12:41.

102. **Cruel**: om. N.

So what is the cause of so many and such[103] myriad blessings, who is sufficient worthily to repay you a proper account? Receive now with pity the offering of my poverty, O church of all[104] Armenia. Not gold of solid matter from earth or sea, or shining[105] precious stones[106] like the tabernacle of Moses; not cypress wood from Lebanon, or ornamented garments, soft and noble but corruptible, like those of the temple of Solomon, but an offering incorruptible and inalienable, brimful with varied heavenly profit and splendid advantage. The armor of invincible believers,[107] [244] not a wall of bronze (Jer 1:18; 15:20) in accordance with the voice of[108] the prophet, is built around you, but you are guarded by a fiery and unapproachable wall. Not a column of iron in accordance with the seer (Jer 1:18) but a flaming sword in the hand[109] of a cherubim forms your defense (Gen 3:24). Not ignorant mortal soldiers but assembled cherubim, unblinking and immortal, are the barrier between your sheep and the wolves.

What, then, would be the bearer of such power, that our great weakness came to bring as a gift[110] for you, O holy church of the land of Armenia,[111] save the legacy of your bridegroom and of the Lord of all, which I did not bury and hide like the wicked and bad servant, but throwing it to the money changers of spiritual profit, I worked as best I could, fearful of the severe threats to the wicked and bad[112] servant (Matt 25:26–30)? For I have come to bring things allegorical and profound and filled with wonder, the clear and distinct teaching of the divine precepts, as a wonderful and splendid gift for your fulfillment, which having erected in your memory the youth[113] perpetually study. Strengthened thereby in the orthodox faith, they repel the errors of the schismatics' unorthodoxy and put to flight the ranks[114] of demons. They strip off the corruptible hide that they put on in the garden, and put on again the incorruptible and luminous robe of which they were stripped. The thirst of the fountain of Eden they quench with the blood of the Lord of Eden, and

---

103. **Such:** om. N.

104. **All:** om. N.

105. **Shining:** om. N.

106. **Stones:** *akans,* N; *k'arins,* M.

107. **Believers:** "your sons," M.

108. **The voice of:** om. M.

109. **In the hand:** om. N.

110. **As a gift:** om. N.

111. **Land of Armenia:** *hayastan ašxarh,* but *hayastaneayk'* just above.

112. **And bad** (*bis*): om. M.

113. **Youth,** *mankunk',* N: "your sons," M.

114. **Ranks:** "bands," M.

the hunger [they endured] in the garden they assuage by enjoying[115] the body of the Lord of the garden.

Furthermore, the unfading triple crown placed on the head of your sons[116] enriches them and links them with the heavenly mind of the hosts above. Therefore, falling before you, O church, [245] I shall speak with you as with one alone. Reward the labors of my vile inadequacy, converting [my] tongue from bastard words to divine speech by the grace of[117] your sons. Therefore hastening with restless speed in my course, from the inception of my challenge[118] I have finished and completed[119] the exposition of the divine sayings, on the day of the coming of your groom and the Life-giver of all to Bethany in order to resurrect Lazarus.[120] Hence casting supplications before you to request from the same Life-giver Christ that he renew with Lazarus my old mortality of sin; that he who commanded his bonds be loosed may also remove the fetters of the bonds of the chains of my sins, sending [me] to freedom of sin, so that on the morrow I too with the Hebrew youths may enter before him, not with olive branches and palms,[121] but rather that I may offer branches from heavenly shoots of most glorious writings with immortal fruits to the glory of the all-holy Trinity.

For I, the least of the studious, especially of translators,[122] through the divine love beg the patriarchs and priests, ascetics and teachers, and also the whole clergy of the holy church, when reading the explanation of these beautiful theological discourses, that you may remember me in the book of life. And may you who take up the commentary on these theological discourses in a written copy beseech the merciful God to save me from the fiery rivers of the fearsome day of just retribution, on which the unquenchable fire threatens

---

115. **Enjoying**: om. M.

116. **Sons**, M: om. N ("your head").

117. **The grace of**: om. M.

118. **From the inception of my challenge**: *I mtic' asparisi*, N; *I mtac' asparisi* ("in the challenge of my mind"), M. *Asparēs* means "race course," used in the sense of a fixed distance, *stadion*, or the physical race.

119. **Finished and completed**: see also the beginning of this section. This is the midpoint of the commentary, just as Mošе bar Kepha divided his own commentary into two parts at John 10:21. The phrase implies that it is the scribe who has completed his allotted task of copying the first part, rather than that the translator has finished the whole commentary; the phrase is common to both M and N. See further the introduction, xxii.

120. The day of the feast of Lazarus is Palm Sunday.

121. Here ends f. 179b in M; f. 180a begins with the lemma to John 11:1, in a different hand.

122. **Translators**: *t'argmanič'k'*. For the information in this colophon, see the introduction, xxi.

sinners like me. May they[123] write down next the memorial of these words for a memory of my most sinful person. [246] Now if anyone should despise and not heed this, may he give account with everyone at the judgment that [by omitting] these profitable memorials he has deprived my reprobate soul of eternal life.

May Smbat Bagratuni and Marem princess of Siwnikʻ, who commanded this holy book to be translated, request the same one to be remembered.

Glory to the unlacking, sublime, archetypal, equal hypostasis, without qualities, simple, immaterial and unjoined three persons, one nature....[124]

---

123. They: i.e., future copyists.
124. The editor does not complete the doxology in the manuscript.

[247] Of the Same Holy Nanay

Book II[1]

Chapter 11

[11:1] There was a certain sick Lazarus from Bethany, from the village of Mary and Martha her sister.

It is customary for those who have undertaken to expound a history of things that occurred earlier both to make clear the event and also to explain the place, so that from both of these the account may be better validated.[i] So the evangelist, being about to describe the great signs that were wondrously performed in Bethany, also reveals the place,[ii] *From the village of Mary and Martha her sister*, indicating that the divine miracle took place there. Furthermore, adding the names of the women to that of the place, he makes it even clearer. But one should investigate why he calls the place that of the women rather than of Lazarus. It was because although the place was of them all, especially of Lazarus rather than of his sisters, yet it was more appropriate to name the place of the living than of the dead one.[iii] Since at that time the Jews had gathered at their house for the purpose of consolation, therefore he set down their names and kept silent about the expired dead one.

i. For this idea, see Theodore of Mopsuestia (ad loc.), who states that the details confirm the account; and Cyril of Alexandria in note to commentary on John 1:28.

ii. Here Dionysius bar Salibi, *John*, 212, distinguishes the two Bethanys.

iii. Tat'ewac'i, 449, quotes John Chrysostom to the same effect; but in his exposition of this verse, at *Hom. Jo.* 62.1, Chrysostom does not refer to this reason. There are close parallels to Nonnus in the Armenian *Homilies on the Resurrection of Lazarus* attributed to Mambrē (for this passage, see Mambrē, 37).

---

1. The text is divided into two books in M and N.

[248] [11:2a] *This is that Mary who anointed the Lord's feet with oil and wiped them with her hair.[2]

To some it seemed that this one was the same as the one whom Matthew and Mark described, but they did not think rightly, for both of those were not like this one in modesty and good repute, but this one was different from them in her good and modest way of life.[i] Now, the anointing of the Lord's feet with oil was out of an excess of love for his incomparable beneficence;[3] and wiping [them] with her hair was because she possessed nothing more personally honorable than the hair of her head. Indeed the head is[4] the most honorable of all the [body's] members (1 Cor 11). Therefore humbling it, she served the life-giving feet of the Lord.[5] But why does the evangelist set this down first? Because the [other] three evangelists had previously described it, but this one later, therefore appropriately[6] he places the event first when he wishes to introduce the woman's righteousness.

i. John Chrysostom, *Hom. Jo.* 62.1, notes that the two Marys were different and that this one was an honest woman. See Matt 26; Mark 14. Moše bar Kepha and Dionysius bar Salibi (*John*, 212) also emphasize the distinction. Tat'ewac'i, 449, distinguishes six Mariams, including two (!) called Magdalene; he quotes Ignatios (i.e., Ignatios Sevleṙnc'i, *On Luke*) to the effect that Matthew, Mark, and John all refer to the same woman.

[11:2b–3] Whose brother Lazarus was ill. His sisters sent to him and said: Lord, behold, the one whom you loved has fallen ill.

Did you see the wisdom and intelligence of the women? Although they did not yet have perfect faith, yet through the recollection of his love they thought it best to summon him out of pity and compassion for their brother. *The one whom you loved, he has fallen ill.* Thereby they reckoned they would spur him urgently to the healing of the afflicted one.

---

2. **This … hair**, MN: "This was that Mary who anointed the Lord with oil and wiped his feet with her hair," Z.

3. **For his incomparable beneficence**: om. N.

4. **Is**: "was," M.

5. **Of the Lord**: om. N.

6. **Appropriately**, *ěst patšači*: "for the reason," *ěst patčaṙi*, M; see also variant to vv. 26b–27, below.

[11:4] **When Jesus heard, he said: This illness is not unto death but for the glory of God, so that the Son of God[7] may be glorified thereby.**

First he indicated that that illness was not able really to put him to death,[i] save for a little, [249] because he saw with his all-seeing power the approaching resurrection that he was going to bring about next. But what means: *For the glory of God*? It seems to me that he applies the expression to the Father in accordance with what he said in his prayers: *Father, I thank you that you heard me* (John 11:41). Let us also look at: *So that the Son of God may be glorified thereby*. First he applies the saying to the Father, and then he sets alongside it that by the divine command he was to summon with authority the one dead for four days. In this way he indicates and reveals the coglory and coworking of the Father and himself.[ii] Furthermore, he predicts the praise that was later to be given by old men and children, how when they saw him coming into Jerusalem they took branches of olive trees and palms, and going out in front cried out, *Blessed is he who comes in the name of the Lord*, with the rest (John 12:13), indicating that he is the very one who the previous day authoritatively summoned the one dead for four days and restored him to life.

i. See the parallel in Mambrē, 37. Here Tat'ewac'i, 451, adds a long discussion on illnesses and their causes.

ii. Here Moše bar Kepha emphasizes the identity of Father and Son as regards essence, power, and lordship.

[11:5] **And Jesus loved Mary and Martha her sister, and Lazarus.**

O blessed zeal that the evangelist inspires with regard to our[8] teaching by the grace of the Holy Spirit. *Jesus loved Mary and Martha and Lazarus*, for as they loved Christ, they were loved by him.[i] Therefore he raised up the brother dead for four days. If like them we too love Christ, like Lazarus he will summon us with his voice from the tombs, not from corruption to resurrection, but from a perpetually indissoluble life,[ii] and not to the judgment of the fearsome tribunal, but to the ineffable repayment of blessings.

i. Here Cyril of Alexandria, *Comm. Jo.* 7, notes that Martha represents those of the circumcision, and Mary those of the Gentiles.

ii. **A perpetually indissoluble life**: the ablative case, *i mišt anlucaneli kenac'*, in both M and N seems inappropriate. The phrase is common for eternal life, so one would expect an accusative: "to [eternal life]."

---

7. **Of God**, NZ: "of man," M.

8. **Our**: om. N.

[11:6] When he heard that he was ill, he stayed where he was for two days.

[250] May you not suffer such an affliction, to remain a reason for ignorance as to what would happen to the afflicted one, for with his all-seeing power he knew that he would die, as he later described: *Lazarus our friend has fallen asleep.* But in order to reprove the raving and ungrateful nation of the Jews he acquiesced in that, lest before the death of Lazarus was noised abroad and became known to the world they might be able to invent some excuse, working a cure for the illness, but not authoritatively summoning forth from a four-day death.[i] For that reason he let him expire and be for four days in the tomb, so that the wonders of the divine signs[9] might appear more splendid.

i. Moše bar Kepha offers a similar argument, not mentioning the Jews, but referring to "the people."

[11:7–8] Then after that he said to them:[10] Come, let us go again into Judea. The disciples said to him: Rabbi, now the Jews seek to stone[11] you, yet you will go again there?

The disciples said this not because of Christ but because of their own fear.[i] Whence it is clear that it was not always a custom for him to inform them about the places where he was intending to go. But here his first saying, *Come, let us go,* was to calm the fear from their hearts.

i. John Chrysostom, *Hom. Jo.* 62.1, and Moše bar Kepha also refer to the disciples' own fear.

[11:9–10] Jesus replied: Are there not twelve hours in the day? If anyone walks in the daytime, he does not stumble, because he sees the light of this world. But if he walks in the nighttime, he stumbles, because there is no light with him.

Do you see how with an allegorical saying he indicates to them the doubt that they had hidden in the storerooms of their hearts?[i] For if the one who walks in the daytime does not fear because of having the light of the sun with him, how much the more for you, being with me, who am the light of the world (John 8:12), [251] not only of bodies but also of souls. The shadows of

9. **Signs:** "grace," N.
10. **To them,** MZ: om. N.
11. **To stone:** k̔arkocel, N; k̔arkoc aṙnel, MZ.

the evil one[12] and his fellow workers will not come upon [you], like the darkness of the sun's light late in the day. So you have no need to fear. For behold, shortly I shall remove the yoke of the prince of this world, and through the rays of the divine light of faith I shall scatter the gloomy darkness in which he made the nations of mankind sit in the darkness of the ignorance of sin, according to the *prophetic voice: *A people who sat in the darkness of ignorance saw the great light*[13] (Isa 9:12; Matt 4:16).

Now, the twelve hours of the day indicate the whole course of hours of the revolving days. Likewise, through the twelve hours of the days,[ii] those Gentiles who went about in *the darkness of their idolatries, through the twelve disciples[14] were to be illuminated by the rebirth of the font with shining faith and to flower through their apostolic way of life.[15]

i. **Storerooms of their hearts:** *štemarank' srtic'*. This is a common phrase for the site of the mind; see note to commentary on John 7:38, above; references in *NBHL*; and Prov 20:27. See also the parallel in Mambrē, 42.

ii. Moše bar Kepha and Dionysius bar Salibi (*John*, 214) indicate that Christ is the day and the disciples are the twelve hours. According to Išodad the day indicates that Christ is the light of the world. *Comm. Diat.* 17.2, however, identifies the twelve hours with the twelve months of Jesus's ministry.

[11:11] When he had said this, afterward he said to them: Lazarus our friend has fallen asleep, but I am going to wake him up.

Here very clearly he indicates the reason for his going up to Bethany, for the release of the fear of their doubts that they entertained in themselves, indicating[16] not to Jerusalem, nor to Judea, of which you were worried, but to Bethany. And why? So that I may awaken my[17] friend Lazarus. By this he again shows his solicitude for Lazarus and predicts in advance his resurrection to the disciples, so that by being eyewitnesses of his resurrection they might be even more strengthened in faith, on remembering what had been said previously.

---

12. **Of the evil one:** om. M.

13. **Prophetic voice … light:** "prophecy," M.

14. **The darkness … disciples:** om. M.

15. **Life:** + "But he calls himself day," M.

16. **Indicating,** *c'uc'anelov*, M: "to indicate," *c'uc'anel*, N.

17. **My:** om. M.

[11:12–13] The disciples said to him: Lord, if he has fallen asleep, then he will recover; but Jesus was speaking about his death. [252] It seemed to them that he was speaking about his sleeping.

See how still being so thick-witted they did not understand the import of the saying. If he was speaking about sleeping, what need was there for the Lord to go to wake him up? He himself would have woken up in accordance with natural habit. But it seems to me that although they did not understand truly the meaning of the saying, they rather made this response because of the doubtful fear that they had in themselves, so that perhaps they might thereby find a way to prevent their teacher from going up there. *This they clearly fabricated with regard to Lazarus's life: *If he sleeps, then he will recover*, and there is no need to go there.[18]

[11:14–15] Then he said to them[19] clearly:[20] Lazarus our friend[21] has died. And I am happy for your sake so that you may believe me;[22] for I was not there. But now[23] come, let us go to him.[24]

You did not understand the meaning of the word, when I said: *He has fallen asleep, he has died.* So remove the doubts from your minds, and *come, let us go to him.* Not so that I may awaken him from sleep, as you supposed,[25] but that I may revive him from death. But what means: *I am happy for your sake?* Not by resurrecting him am I happy for myself, attracting boasts and praises to myself, but for the sake of the confirmation of your faith that will occur I am happy, so that you may take the measure of my power.[i] For just as, without my being there, I unerringly described his death, in the same way by summoning [him] with an authoritative voice from the tomb, you will recognize the capability of my divine power. Now, let us understand[26] *not being there* in the body, whereas in his divinity [he is] in all places, in accordance with the prophet's saying: *Our God in heaven and on earth, in the sea and in all deeps* (Ps 134:6).

---

18. **This … there:** om. M.
19. **To them,** N: "Jesus," M (Z: "Jesus said to them").
20. **Clearly:** *yaytnagoyn,* N; *yaytnapēs,* MZ.
21. **Our friend,** N: om. MZ.
22. **Me,** MZ: om. N.
23. **Now,** *ard,* MZ: om. N.
24. **To him,** MZ: "there," N.
25. **Supposed:** "suppose," M.
26. **Let us understand:** "we understand," N.

i. Another parallel in Mambrē, 41.

[11:16] Thomas, called the twin, said to his fellow disciples: Arise,[27] come, so that we too may die with him.

[253] Thomas[28] did not reply well, because he should have said something more helpful regarding the resurrection of Lazarus that he had heard from the Lord than to say: *Come, so that we too may die with him.* But he regarded the saying by the Lord with regard to the resurrection of Lazarus as of ambiguous meaning and doubtful. So with an unhelpful and unprofitable word he cited friendship for Lazarus by saying: *Come, so that we too may die with him.*[i]

i. Here John Chrysostom, *Hom. Jo.* 62.2, indicates that Thomas was the disciple most frightened of the Jews.

[11:17] Jesus came and found that he had been four days in the tomb.

This is the benevolence of his divinity, which the evangelists previously mentioned, that he stayed where he had heard [the news] for two days, and after two days journeyed to Bethany and found him four days in the tomb, so that the miracle of his resurrection might appear beyond all Jewish excuses and his amazing resurrection be more powerful and splendid, and profitable for the faith of the spectators.

[11:18] And Bethany was near to Jerusalem about fifteen stadia.

We rightly said that the distance of the journey was of two days. Therefore the evangelist puts down the number of the stadia,[i] so that after staying two days where he had heard [the news], and going on the journey for two more, on the fourth the miracle of the resurrection might take place, just as we said above.

i. **Stadia:** *asparēz.* John Chrysostom, *Hom. Jo.* 62.2, equates fifteen stadia with two miles (*milia dyo*), as do Theodore of Mopsuestia and Išodad. Tat'ewac'i, 460, equates eight *asparēz* with one *milay* or *młon* and notes that Bethany was not beyond the Jordan (i.e., the Bethany mentioned in John 1:28, also known as Bethabra; see commentary above).

---

27. **Arise:** *awn.* Tat'ewac'i, 457, discusses the meaning of this interjection and gives dialectical examples of its equivalent from Karin, Arčēš, and Xlat'.

28. **Thomas,** MV: "he," N.

[11:19] Many of the Jews had come to Mary and Martha in order to console them for their brother.

Although they had come according to custom for sympathy and their consolation,[i] yet that[29] should not be understood to be outside the divine oversight. **[254]** For such a crowd had gathered and were eyewitnesses of the divine miracles that no one would suppose the account of the wonderful signs to be pretended or falsified, but perhaps one of the onlookers or of those who heard would be helped in himself, and lest[30] the divine wonder-working would remain secret, if not many were present.

    i. Further parallels in Mambrē, 42.

[11:20] When Martha heard that Jesus was coming,[31] she went out to meet him. But Mary sat there at home.

It seems to me that Martha at that time alone heard, but not Mary.[i] Therefore the evangelist says: *She sat there at home.*

    i. Theodore of Mopsuestia stresses that Mary heard nothing.

[11:21–22] Martha said to Jesus: Lord, if you had been here,[32] my brother would not have died. Yet I[33] know that whatever you will seek[34] from God, God will give you.

The woman had faith, but not completely. Whence is that clear? From her saying, *If you had been here,* and *I know that whatever you will seek from God, God will give you.*[i] How was he not there in his divine nature, who also saw the death of her brother; or what need was there of seeking from God [for him] who with his voice authoritatively summoned him from the tomb and delivered him from death? So the woman had not yet experienced[ii] his divine power.

    i. Here the biblical text in N follows Z, not the lemma.
    ii. **Experienced:** *pʽorj areal ēr,* or "taken stock of" (lit. "tested").

---

29. **That:** "they," N.
30. **Lest:** om. N.
31. **Was coming,** *gay,* NZ; "going," *gnay,* M.
32. **Here,** NZ: om. M.
33. **I,** MZ: "we," N.
34. **Will seek,** MZ: "seek," N.

[11:23] Jesus said to her: Your brother will arise.

He said this in order to inform the woman's lack of faith, that not as you suppose is there need for pleading for his resurrection. And you suppose further to make requests, which you said God would grant to you, but your brother will arise without any doubt.

[11:24] Martha said to him: I know that he will arise at the resurrection on the last day.

[255] See the weak faith that the woman possessed. She possessed no hope of her brother's resurrection taking place immediately, save at[35] the general resurrection.[i]

   i. Here John Chrysostom asks how she knew about the general resurrection.

[11:25a] Jesus said to her: I am resurrection and life.

Because the woman did not understand the meaning of the saying, the Life-giver made it clear that there is no one else who resurrects at the resurrection save I who am speaking with you.[i] *I am resurrection and life*, he said, and if I am resurrection and life, who shall raise up everyone altogether, I am also able to raise up your brother now.

   i. This is also stressed by Theodore of Mopsuestia and Moše bar Kepha.

[11:25b–26a] Whoever believes in me, although he die, shall live. And everyone who is alive and believes in me shall never die.

Just as now[36] you are about to see this one dead for four days resurrected, so also those who believe in me, that *I am resurrection and life*, although they die, will live. For the resurrection of each one will be a resurrection as through a mirror in a image, seeing Lazarus coming out at my command, not striving against death, nor allowing the Devil to hold back his soul. The same voice will resurrect all from their tombs. And because he gave sublime instruction to the woman about himself:

---

35. **At:** om. N.
36. **Now:** om. M.

[11:26b–27] He said to her: Do you believe in this? She said: Yes, Lord, I have believed that you are the Christ, Son of God, who was to come into the world.

The woman did not reply appropriately,[37] because he asked, *Do you believe my being resurrection and life?* but she, passing over that, said, **[256]** *I have believed that you are Christ, Son of God,* and not that you are Son of God who are resurrection and life.[i] But by referring to *the*[38] Christ, she spoke in accordance with Jewish understanding, as they insisted that the Christ is to come. Hence the woman added: *Who was to come into the world.*

> i. John Chrysostom, *Hom. Jo.* 62.3, indicates that the woman did not reply to the question but answered another; so also Moše bar Kepha. Tat'ewac'i, 464, quotes Chrysostom but adds that other *vardapet*s say that the response was appropriate. Theodore of Mopsuestia notes that the elect and virtuous in the law were called anointed and prophets of God; while Išodad explains that in the scriptures elect and virtuous men were called Christs and Sons of God.

[11:28] When she had said this, she went and[39] summoned Mary, her sister, secretly.

Because she was astonished at what she heard from Christ, that he was resurrection and life, and although she still remained of uncertain mind, yet she had hope for its attainment. She summoned her sister secretly because she was cautious of the Jews gathered there, and she still did not wish that the saying be revealed until her sister also, by making the same request, might bring Christ to compassion regarding her brother. But we have found in some exemplars[i] that the Lord commanded Mary to be summoned,[ii] so that she too might participate in such luminous[40] teaching, and being instructed through [this] saying they might approach to see their brother's resurrection.

> i. **Exemplars:** *awrinaks*; see the introduction, xxvii. Here the reference must be to v. 28b, which is omitted in Nonnus's lemma.
>
> ii. **To be summoned:** *koč'el*; Z reads: "And she said, 'The teacher has come and summons you.'" Here the verb *koč'el*, "to summon/be summoned," echoes that in the commentary. Theodore of Mopsuestia and Moše bar Kepha note that it was not written in the

---

37. **Appropriately,** *ěst patšac'i*: "for a reason," *ěst patčaři*, M; see also variant to v. 2a, above.

38. **The:** om. N.

39. **And,** M: om. NZ.

40. **Luminous:** *lusawor*, N; *lusap'ayl*, M.

Gospel that the Lord commanded Mary to be summoned, because it was assumed. Dionysius bar Salibi, *John*, 218, states that Jesus said: "Go summon your sister."

[11:29] **When she heard that, she immediately arose and came.**

Well did we say that Mary had not yet heard, and it is indeed[41] clear from her rapidly arising after hearing [the news] and not heeding those who had come for sympathy. For she, like her sister, had hope, although not perfectly.

[11:30] **Jesus had not yet come but was in the place in which Martha had met him.**

Why did he hold himself back and not rapidly come to the tomb, save that when the report reached the crowd, first a gathering might be created, and the plan for the resurrection might fly to the ears of all, and everyone might rush to the carrying out of the miracles? But not rapidly did such a thing take place, nor publicly and in the hearing of all, for the profit and advantage of the crowds and the removal of suspicion and shadowy words.

[257]

[11:31] **Now,[42] the Jews who were with her in the house and were consoling her, when they saw that Mary had suddenly arisen, also went. They reckoned that she would go to the tomb in order to weep there.**

Because Martha had informed [her] secretly about the coming of the teacher, the Jews were unaware but reckoned that she had gone to the tomb according to the habit of those grieving. But they hastened to meet the Lord, although they were not at all pleased as to how they would consent to hear his teaching.[i]

i. Moše bar Kepha states that the Jews would not have accompanied Mary to the tomb if they had known that Jesus was there.

[11:32] **Then when Mary came to where Jesus was and saw him, she fell at his feet and said: Lord, if you had been here, my brother would not have died.**

Martha seems to me not to have done the same when she came to the Lord, because she did not heed the malevolence of the Jews and their hatred

---

41. **Indeed,** *isk*: om. N.
42. **Now,** *isk*, NZ: om. M.

of the teacher, but falling at the Lord's feet she revealed her firm and sincere love and hope, saying the same words about her brother's resurrection as her sister. It seems to me that both thought as one, so that the latter would say the same words and thereby bring Christ to greater compassion and sympathy. For which reason she also went down on her knees at the feet of the Lord.

[11:33–34] **When Jesus saw her weeping, and the Jews around her weeping, he was troubled in his soul. He was vexed and said:**[43] **Where did you place him? And they said to him: Come and see.**

What means *He was troubled in his soul,* because sadness could not really be active in him, like emotions overcome us?[44] But *he was troubled;* that is, he commanded sadness to come and tears to flow willingly, showing that [258] when he wished he condescended to these natural things, indicating the true willing condition of his humanity.[i] But unlike us he was not overcome by the conditions[ii] of the flesh. For although he took his body from us created beings, yet he never allowed the flesh to be moved to natural [sufferings]. But when he wished he condescended to food and drink and sleep; and when he wished he raised himself above those things that are in nature, because he himself was the fashioner of our nature.[iii]

Now his question *Where did you place him?* was not one of ignorance.[iv] For the Father too asked a question: *Where are you, Adam?* And to Cain: *Where is your brother?* And to Moses: *What is that in your hand?* And many other similar[45] [questions].[v] But it was providential management for them to show the tomb, so that the miracles might occur very quietly, and all would hasten to the tomb and the event of the resurrection. Also he himself, although far away, knew his death. How, then, being nearby, would he be ignorant of the tomb? But it was in order that those same ones might indicate and testify to the place of the dead one, so that the resurrection might be announced even more firmly and credibly by them.

i. Here John Chrysostom, *Hom. Jo.* 80.1, refers to Christ's human nature (*anthrōpinē physis*); and Cyril of Alexandria, *Comm. Jo.* 7, states that as Christ was both God and man *kata physin* ("according to nature"), here he endures *to anthrōpinon* ("the human [condition]"). Išodad says that Christ's emotion was a sign of his wrath against the Jews, as do

---

43. **And said,** NZ: om. M.

44. **Emotions overcome us,** N: "bodily emotions overcome us, because the divinity is passionless and ungrieving," M.

45. **And many other similar:** om. N.

Moše bar Kepha, and Dionysius bar Salibi, *John*, 209. Moše bar Kepha, however, says that Christ was above suffering.

ii. **Conditions**: *kirk'*; for the term, see the introduction, xxxviii.

iii. For a parallel to this paragraph, see Mambrē, 47.

iv. The editor notes a parallel here with Severian; see p. *le* (35) of his introduction, and the introduction above, xxx.

v. John Chrysostom and all other commentators indicate that God was not ignorant, giving the example of Gen 3:9. Moše bar Kepha also refers to the examples of Cain (Gen 4:9) and Moses (Exod 4:2); while Dionysius bar Salibi, *Gospels*, 49, adds that of Peter (John 21:17).

[11:35–37] **And Jesus wept. The Jews said: See how he loved him. Some of them said: Was he, who opened the eyes of the blind one, not able to act so that this one did not die?**

Why did he weep over Lazarus, whom he was about to bring to life? First, so that he might show his kinship for sympathy with us;[i] then, so that he might teach it as a limit and boundary for believers, who might have the hope of resurrection firmly in themselves, to weep as much as he did for Lazarus;[ii] again, by seeing the dead one, it was necessary to weep over the sins that from the beginning [259] bequeathed death to the human race. We found also in some exemplars[iii] that the tears are to be understood concerning the Jews, because on seeing that they would not believe in the divine signs, but would always remain in error, and they would make themselves heirs of Gehenna and not recognize the one who was going to buy them with his own incorruptible blood (Rev 5:9), he wept over them.

i. Cyril of Alexandria, *Comm. Jo.* 7; Moše bar Kepha; and Dionysius bar Salibi, *John*, 220, indicate that Jesus wept as a sign of sympathy. *Comm. Diat.* 17.4 states that Jesus wept in order to show his enemies that Lazarus was really dead.

ii. For a parallel to these lines, see Mambrē, 48.

iii. **Exemplars**: *awiranks*. Here commentators rather than variants to the biblical text (as in commentary to v. 28, above) are indicated. Indeed, Moše bar Kepha expands at length on this episode and explains the tears with reference to the Jews, as does Dionysius bar Salibi, *John*, 220. As usual, Tat'ewac'i, 468–69, lists his explanations, giving here six reasons for Jesus's tears, including those in Nonnus.

[11:38a] **Jesus again vexed in his mind came to the tomb.**

There *he troubled his soul*, summoned tears to himself, as we said above. Here, *vexed in his mind*, he bade his nature to refrain from the emotion of sadness, which having summoned he caused to erupt.

[11:38b–39a] **And it was a cave, and a stone had been placed over it.**[46] **And Jesus said: Remove that stone.**

What need had he to remove the stone, at whose command hell would vomit up the dead one, save because of the ungrateful nation of the Jews? For if they were to deny [the resurrection], their own hands that rolled away the stone would be their accusers.[i]

> i. John Chrysostom, Moše bar Kepha, Dionysius bar Salibi, Išodad, and the *Commentary on the Diatessaron* all offer the same argument: the Jews would not be able to deny the work of their own hands.

[11:39b] **Martha, the sister of the dead one, said to him:**[47] **Lord,**[48] **now he stinks, because it is four days.**

Once more the woman was weak in faith, not being able to comprehend the renewal of the dissolved and corrupted body.[i]

> i. Moše bar Kepha also stresses that Martha did not understand, but Mary believed that Jesus would raise Lazarus.

[11:40] **Jesus said to her: Did I not say to you, If you will believe, you shall see the glory of God?**

Did you see how he reproved her lack of faith and reminds [her] of what he had previously said, *I am resurrection and life,* and what he had asked the woman, *Do you believe in this?*

[11:41–42] **And when they had removed the stone, Jesus raised his eyes and said: Father, I thank you that you heard me. And I knew that at all times you hear me, but because of the people who surround me I do it,**[49] **so that they may believe that you sent me.**

[260] By saying this he placed in the minds of his listeners: You say I am opposed to the Father and a blasphemer, but now I am about to raise the dead.[i] So if I were opposed to the Father and a blasphemer, let him not be an accom-

------

46. N places the lemma of v. 38b immediately following that of v. 38a.

47. **To him,** NZ: om. M.

48. **Lord,** MZ: om. N.

49. **I do it,** *aŕnem,* MNZ. The Greek has "I said," *eipon*; the Syriac, "I said these things," *'mr 'n' hlyn.*

plice of me the blasphemer. But if he would be an accomplice, rightly receive the truth that is to be understood from his prayer: *I knew that at all times you hear me,* for he speaks of their will and power being one.[ii] *But because of the people, that they may know that you sent me,* as I said above, I summon you to cooperation, for the reprobation of these ones and the removal of erroneous thoughts and wicked envy, which they always work for the destruction of themselves.

i. The editor notes another parallel in Severian; see his introdution, pp. *le–lz* (35–36).

ii. Here John Chrysostom, *Hom. Jo.* 64.1, stresses that Christ is of the same *ousia* as the Father. Moše bar Kepha stresses the equivalence of will of the Father and Son, who have the same nature and *ousia*; and Dionysius bar Salibi, *John*, 222, also refers to Father and Son being one in will and nature.

[Interpolation from John Chrysostom][50]

Jesus raised his eyes and said, Father, I thank you that you heard me. But I know that at all times you hear me. However, because of the people, I shall speak.[51] Often he said this; and now I say[52] that God does not look so much to the honor of the glory of his own majesty as he does to the matter of our salvation. He does not consider what grand thing he might pronounce but what is able to bring us more easily into submission to himself. Therefore the elevated and great [expressions] are few and also hidden. But the humble and weak are many, and he incorporates them together[53] with the commandments. Now, since he fashioned them in this way, even more he was occupied with them and does not speak everything the same, lest[54] those who are to come after this be harmed. Nor again does he keep silent about them, lest those who live in the present time stumble, but that those who have attained full stature may also be able to see the whole of the sublime commandment from a single one. But who were at that time the most humble, [even] if they often heard them as if from God, were unable to grasp the faith.

---

50. The following section is found only in M (f. 182b) and V; a note in the margin of M correctly ascribes it to John Chrysostom (*Yova Oskeber*); it is a paraphrase of his *Hom. Jo.* 69.1. It is not taken from the Armenian translation of Chrysostom as found in the 1717 ed., itself a rendering from the Syriac version; see note to commentary on John 3:5, above. The editor Č'rak'ean prints the text of V; the variants from the text in M are here cited in the footnotes.

51. **I shall speak**, M: "I shall do," M[corr]. See lemma to v. 42.

52. **I say**, M: "he says," editor's correction.

53. **Incorporates them together**, M: om. V.

54. **Lest**, *zi mi*, M: "in order that," *zi*, V.

Did you see how not only were they unable to endure him but even stoned and persecuted and planned to slay [him]? And they called him blasphemer when he made himself equal to God. And once they said that he blasphemes, because he said: *Your sins will be forgiven you* (Matt 9:2, etc.). Again, they called him mad, when [he said] whoever will heed his word will be superior to death (John 8:51). Or when he would say, *I am in my Father, and the Father in me* (John 14:20), they abandoned him. And they were scandalized when he would say: *I have descended from heaven* (John 6:38). So then, if they were unable[55] to endure all this when he spoke moderately, how much the more, if the saying was superior in every way and he thus fashioned it, did they pay no attention to him. But when he said, *As the Father commanded me, thus I act; I speak nothing of myself* (John 8:28), many then believed in him. And the evangelist indicates that while he was saying this, his humble speech makes known[56] the faith and puts to flight that which is lofty.

So would it not be the ultimate folly not to understand the circumstances of the humble [words], that they were spoken for the sake of the hearers? For elsewhere[57] he wished to say something great but was silent. These circumstances he adduced and said: *But lest they be scandalized, cast and throw the fishhook into the sea* (Matt 17:27). In the same fashion here too. After saying, *I know that at all times you hear me,* he immediately added: *Because of the multitude of this people, I shall speak so that they may believe.*[58]

[261] [11:43] **When he had said this, he cried out in a loud voice and said: Lazarus, arise,[59] come forth.**

What need was there to cry out in a strong voice? Behold, the dead do not have any sensation regarding voices and the sounds of loud noises. But so that the divine command, propelled by means of a loud voice, might appear clear in the ears of all who were gathered there, at his command the one dead for four days came forth.[i] Furthermore, not by the name of anyone else did he summon the dead one from the tomb, like the prophets of old in the name of the Lord God, or later, the apostles in the name of Jesus Christ.[ii] But he commanded with his own powerfully authoritative voice: *Come forth* at my divine command.

---

55. **Were unable,** M: "would be unable," V.

56. **Makes known,** *canuc'anē,* M: "produces," *cnuc'anē,* V.

57. **Elsewhere,** *ayl urek',* V: *ayl uremn,* M.

58. At this point, the text of the *Commentary* by Nonnus resumes.

59. **Arise,** MZ: om. N.

It was also so that they might learn that souls are alive and have sensation, even if they are very far from the body.[iii] For which reason according to the custom of those alive, because they carry out a summons through a voice at a distance, in the same fashion he too acted through a familiar custom in accordance with their weakness. Wresting it from the hands of the Devil through his powerful voice, he brought up his soul, joining it to the body from which it had been loosed. The divine command renewed the corrupted body and raised it from the tomb totally alive.[iv]

i. Theodore of Mopsuestia and Moše bar Kepha indicate that Jesus summoned Lazarus from a distance and used a loud voice for the benefit of those standing by, as also John Chrysostom, *Hom. Jo.* 64.2. Cyril of Alexandria, *Comm. Jo.* 7, recalls the image of the loud trumpet when the judge shall come in the future. Dionysius bar Salibi, *John*, 223, notes that Lazarus alone was addressed, even though Christ had the power to raise many.

ii. E.g., 3 Kgdms 17:21–22; Acts 3:6; 4:10. The editor (in his introduction, p. *ld* [34]) notes a parallel with John Chrysostom (see *Hom. Jo.* 64).

iii. Dionysius bar Salibi, *John*, 224, notes that Lazarus's soul was not in the tomb with his body.

iv. For the tradition that Lazarus lived a long time and became a bishop, see note to commentary on John 12:1–2, below.

[11:44a] **And the dead one came forth with *feet bound, and hands in bandages,[60] and his face wrapped with a napkin.**

Again what wonders, not less than [262] the former, for the power of the divine command hastened on the fettered feet and the bound hands[i] with all his limbs and brought him out from the tomb up to where Jesus was standing. Amazed at this, the evangelist said: *And the dead one came forth with feet bound, and hands in bandages, and his face wrapped with a napkin.* Who has ever heard of such a transmigration,[ii] of feet bound and wrapped making their way from one place to another, save at the command of him whom all beings serve with awe, attending to his command with trepidation?

i. The terms are different, but the sense follows the lemma of the Armenian Bible rather than the Greek.

ii. **Transmigration**: *p'oxgnac'ut'iwn*, a calque on the Greek *metabasis*.

---

60. **Feet … bandages**: as MNZ, but the Armenian differs from the Greek.

[11:44b] And Jesus said to them: Loose him,[61] and let him go.

Why did he command them to loose the bindings of the feet, those who were unable to prevent the transmigration of the feet? He with his voice renewed the body that had been loosed for four days and reunited it with the separated soul. But as we said above, because they were shameless and were always attempting to subvert the truth and fabricate criticisms, therefore he made their hands and noses accusers and witnesses. For if they were to deny, their noses, which picked up the smell of the corpse's decay, would rebuke them; and their hands, which released the bindings of the feet and of the whole person, would reprove them.

[11:45–46] Many of the Jews who had come to Mary's, when they saw what he had done, believed in him. And some of them went to the Pharisees and told them what Jesus[62] had done.

Some believed through the wonderful signs of the miracles that it was not possible for a man to do such a thing but only for the Son of God, although in a little while they again hastened to the same unbelief. But others, although they were overcome by the amazing power that they had seen, yet they went astray as if driven by demons. [263] They rapidly went to the Sadducees[i] and described the awesome signs, which they were unable to hide. They became slanderers, rather antagonists according to their inclination, [saying]: Many people have believed in him, so hasten to do something to silence his signs and mighty deeds, lest perchance all the people follow him.[ii]

    i. Nonnus again changes Pharisees to Sadducees; cf. above, commentary to John 1:24 and 4:1–3.
    ii. See vv. 47–48, below.

[Exhortation][63]

But let us now, beloved, arouse your enthusiasm and turn our account to those same miraculous workings. O sickness, hope of life; sickness, sign of resurrection; sickness, adversary of death; sickness, enemy of the Devil;[64]

---

    61. **Him:** *zda*, NZ; *zna*, M.
    62. **Jesus**, MZ: "he," N.
    63. The following section is entitled *Yordorak*, "Exhortation," by the editor of N; there is no title in M. Tat'ewac'i, 479ff., refers to it as a *nerbołean*.
    64. **Sickness, enemy of the Devil:** om. N.

sickness, healing of woes; sickness, foundation of faith; sickness, reproof of the unbelieving! I delight in summoning, not sickness, but correction for sick minds; *not the sickness that causes death, but the cure of afflicted persons;[65] not sickness for mortal sleep, but restoration for those sleeping to death; not sickness, but the image of our resurrection. Let us be amazed at the unheard-of resurrection of Lazarus; let us glorify the divine activity; let us rejoice at the resurrection of Lazarus, confirming the same hope in ourselves. Let the souls of the saints also delight, for they shall again put on the bodies[66] that the Devil put to death. Let death mourn the destruction of its kingdom; let hell lament the overthrow of its power; let the first-created[67] exult at the coming of the Shepherd on his search for the lost sheep;[68] let the faithful clap their hands at the renewal of Lazarus, seeing their own restoration to life, and let them proclaim to those who dwell in tombs the hope of resurrection. Let death henceforth not terrify us, and [264] let the Devil, who put [us] to death, not frighten us:[69] we have found the tree of life. The cherub with the protection of the flaming sword has stood aside; the influence of the deadly tree has ceased; the leaf of the fig tree has been dishonored. For on this day of resurrection the token of incorruptibility has been indicated to us.

O the power of the divine voice[70] that shattered hell and drew forth the souls[71] seized by death. O power of the divine voice that renewed to immortal[72] life the loosened limbs. O power of the voice that brought together the separated soul with the loosened body as in the twinkling of an eye, working no less a remarkable miracle than the first creation. O power of the voice, raising up from the tomb the one dead for four days, and rapidly bringing the one with bound feet to the place where he was.

*Let us concentrate our minds,[73] beloved, on this voice with unsullied faith, and let us see[74] with the eyes of the mind the Life-giver Christ himself; and confessing the same as resurrection and life for us, let us not doubt the resurrection of all, for behold, this voice will also raise us from our tombs. Let

---

65. **Not the sickness … persons**: om. M.

66. **Bodies**: sg. N.

67. **First-created**: sg. N, pl. M.

68. For the lamentations of death and hell and the rescue of Adam, cf. the *Homily on the Passion of Christ* attributed to Ełišē (*Works*, 1859 [297ff.]) and the *Homilies on the Harrowing of Hell* (Der Nersessian 1954).

69. **Us**: om. M.

70. **Voice**: om. N (i.e., "divine power").

71. **Souls**: sg. N.

72. **Immortal**: om. N.

73. **Let us … minds**: "concentrate your mind," M (sg.; but "beloved" is pl. in M and N).

74. **Let us see**: "see" (sg. impv.), M.

us henceforth zealously store up deeds profitable for the coming resurrection, lest we go out to meet the groom with extinguished lamps, so that when we are summoned from the tombs we may find to hand the oil of mercy, with which our lamps will shine. For after this there will be no more gatherings of markets, and you will not be able to buy what you hope for. Now is the display of markets; here are the gatherings of the poor. Let us lay up treasures in them, and no moth will be able to approach. Let us entrust our treasures to them, and no thief will be able to dig [it out]. [265] Let us place it in their hands for security, so that we find it in the hands of the judge. Let us hasten to the dissolution of sins faster than deposing them at court; let us bribe the judge *before placing them at the throne. Let us not stand naked in the public tribunal. It is better now to speak with the judge;[75] it is easier here to absolve the blame, so that when the light will shine in the darkness and the glory of the just will be revealed, that is, the delayed groom, we shall be able to arrive before him with shining lamps, so that saved from judgment we may be worthy of entering the bridal chamber,[76] inheriting with those invited the unadulterated joys, the inexhaustible blessings in Christ Jesus our Lord, *with whom to the omnipotent Father and the Holy Spirit, glory, power, and honor, now and always, and forever and ever.[77] Amen.[78]

[11:47–48a] **The high priests and Pharisees gathered a council and said: What shall we do, because that man performs many signs? If we leave him thus, all will believe in him.**

See how the meaning of the saying became clear. For when the Pharisees heard from him about the sublime signs, and the slanders appeared pleasing, they then proceeded to conduct a council with the high priests and to relate most openly what they were hiding in their thoughts: *What are we to do, for that man performs many signs?* For through the resurrection of Lazarus they recalled what they had heard and the other things too. And once more they realized that perchance he might perform many other acts, and everyone would follow him, and our high priesthood would be despised and dishonored. After that they devised other deceits and tricks, whereby they might find means to turn the mind of the rabble to themselves.

---

75. **Before…judge**: om. M.

76. For the emphasis on the groom and bridal chamber, cf. the "Exhortation" following the commentary to John 2:11.

77. **With whom…ever**: "to whom glory forever," M.

78. At this point, the commentary resumes.

[266] [11:48b] And the Romans will come and remove our nation and place.[79]

By this they afflicted and angered the minds of the people;[i] for by the mention of nation and place[ii] they all hastened not only to prevent his signs and reject the teaching but also to lay hands on him, which indeed the high priest clearly related.

> i. John Chrysostom, *Hom. Jo.* 65.3, indicates that they wished to disturb the people.
> ii. **Nation and place:** Theodore of Mopsuestia and Moše bar Kepha follow the order of Nonnus's lemma and commentary. Dionysius bar Salibi, *John*, 225, refers only to "our place, as in the prophecy."

[11:49–50] One of them, whose name was Caiaphas, who was high priest for that year, said to them: You do not know anything, nor at all consider that it is better that one man die for the people, and the whole nation not perish.

The high priest gave these instructions for the sake of arousing them still more and urging them to killing. As he said, *You do not know* how to plan *anything*, that is, if you had any useful thoughts why do you let him teach so frequently, to perform signs and marvels and cause the people to rebel, but not rapidly remove him?

It must also be investigated what means *to be high priest for that year*. The evangelist wishes to indicate clearly that the ritual[i] of the Mosaic law had been destroyed and removed, because it was not possible to dismiss the high priest and create another one in his stead until his death. But here, when the divine grace had departed from them and the ritual of the law had been destroyed and perverted, and they had been subjected to the rule of the Romans, after that year by year they received from the Romans the honor of the priesthood for the price of silver.[ii]

Let us also see the meaning of *It is better that one man die for the people, and the whole nation not perish.* This he sets down in accordance with the previous treacherous words: *The Romans will come and remove our nation*; so then, it is better for only one to die rather than all[80] our nation, which was an indication [267] that it was better for Christ alone to die in the flesh for the sake of us fleshly ones, rather than the entire human race. This the following makes clear.

> i. **Ritual:** *kargk'* (lit. "order, arrangement"); cf. Heb 5:10.
> ii. All the Syriac commentaries refer to the buying and selling of the high priesthood: Theodore of Mopsuestia; Išodad; Moše bar Kepha; and Dionysius bar Salibi, *John*, 225.

---

79. **Our nation and place,** MNZ: "our place and nation" in Greek and Syriac.
80. **All:** om. N.

Tat'ewac'i, 483, explains the change from life tenure for the high priest to a yearly alternation by the avarice and love "of glory" of the Jews.

[11:51] This he did not say of himself; but because he was high priest for that year he prophesied that Christ would die for the nation.

That is, he did not know what he said, because the sayings were a prophecy that in that year Christ would die for the nation and save everyone. But first Christ was to die at the hands of the Jews, and not the nation of the Jews [at the hands] of the Romans.

[11:52] And not for the nation only, but so that he might gather into one[81] the scattered sons of Israel.[82]

The Lord died willingly and saved all his creatures and scattered ones whom the Devil had estranged from God through idolatry and various kinds of evil.[i] And those scattered over the face of the earth he gathered through the birth of the holy font, including them all in the adoption of the Father according to Paul's expression: *There is no distinction, not of Jew nor Gentile, not of slave nor free, not of male nor female, for you are all one in Christ Jesus* (Gal 3:27–28).

i. Dionysius bar Salibi, *John*, 227, also refers to the Devil estranging humankind through idolatry.

[11:53] Then on that day they took counsel, that they might kill him.

Although they had often planned to lay hands on him, yet here, when they heard about the signs he had performed regarding Lazarus and they feared everyone would believe in him, then they passed sentence of death against him.

[11:54] And Jesus thenceforth no longer went about openly among the Jews but went from there to a land that was near the desert, to a city whose name was Ephraim. And he was there with his disciples.

Not from fear does he indicate that he did not openly go about among them, but because when they passed sentence of death against him, he did not

---

81. **Into one,** NZ: om. M.
82. **Sons of Israel,** N ("of God," Z): om. M.

remain in [268] the place in which they plotted to seize him, [lest] by force[i] he come to the torments of the cross. But see what he carries out for correction. He did not go to Ephraim with the crowds according to custom but with his disciples only; and he was there alone with them up to the time of the cross, and then of his own free will he went up to Jerusalem, in order to show that he went willingly to the torments of the cross. But not in accordance with their plans was he unwillingly seized for torments and death.

i. **By force:** *akamay* (lit. "unwillingly," as just below). The willing death of Christ is stressed throughout the commentary.

[11:55] **And the Passover of the Jews was near, and many went up to Jerusalem from that province prior to the Passover in order to purify themselves.**

The Passover that he mentioned is the Pascha, which they celebrated in Egypt, in which he commanded a lamb to be sacrificed as a type of the true lamb of God, whose power may be seen in the type as in a mirror.[i] For those houses were preserved whose thresholds and windows[83] had been marked with the blood of the lamb, and the destroyer[ii] was not able to touch the first-born. Therefore on that same Pascha the true[84] lamb had to die for the salvation of the world, and with the same one's incorruptible blood the senses and hearts of mankind were to be sealed as protection against the various tricks of the Devil.

Furthermore, in that same month in which he fashioned creation, he came to the torments of the cross, indicating that the renewal of man would occur at the same time at which he had been fashioned. Hence on Friday *he arranged for it to occur, because then on Friday[85] he came out of paradise,[iii] and now on Friday in its place he brought the robber into paradise. Then on the sixth day death and corruption ruled over the first man, but here on the sixth day[86] life and incorruption were again granted through the torments of the cross.[iv]

As for many going up to Jerusalem before the feast, some [went] in order to purify themselves in preparation for the feast, and others to arrange and prepare the sacrifices prior to the feast.

i. **Passover:** *Zatik*; **Pascha:** *Pask'ay*; **type:** *awrinak*; see the introduction, xxxiii. For the

---

83. **Windows,** *patuhank'*, N: sg. M (not in Exod 12).
84. **True:** om. M.
85. **He arranged … Friday:** om. M.
86. **Day:** "age," M.

Passover as a *typos* of the death of Christ, see the extensive references in Lampe 1969 (s.v. *pascha*).

ii. **Destroyer**: *satakič'*, as in Exod 12:23.

iii. **Friday**: *urbat'*. Adam was created on a Friday and left paradise on a Friday. Mxit'ar Ayrivanec'i includes a discussion of these parallelisms in his *History*: see the section entitled *On the Six Days of God's Creation* (Patkanean, 8–11). The Syriac commentators do not refer to such ideas, at least at this point in their commentaries.

iv. The scribe of M here changes "day" to "age," *dar*. The six days as the six ages of the world is a common theme in Armenian writers, beginning with Agat'angełos; see Thomson 1976 (125–27). Step'annos of Siwnik', 127, correlates the six days of creation with the six jars of John 2:6.

[269] [11:56] They sought Jesus and said to each other while standing in the temple: How does it seem to you, will he not come to the feast?

As if to say that being really fearful of us because of what we threatened, he would prefer his own preservation to the commandment and would not come to the feast with the people. By this they again tried to fabricate criticism of him, that he never acted in accordance with the law but against it, in accordance with his own independent pleasure.

[11:57] The high priests and Pharisees had given a command, that whoever might know where he was, they were to inform about him so that they might arrest him.

He indicates that the high priests and Pharisees often had deliberations concerning him, but not including the crowds; for which reason they merely gave this command to the people.

[12:1–2] **Now, Jesus six days before[1] came to Bethany, where the dead Lazarus was, whom he had raised from the dead. *And they made a dinner for him, and Martha served, and Lazarus was one of those sitting with him.[2]**

Because the Life-giver was about to come to the cross, whereby the human race would be saved, he first came to Bethany.[i] And being near to Jerusalem he performed the miracle of Lazarus's resurrection, so that the report of his divine[3] miracles might be preached in Jerusalem, and beside the cross the wonderful power of the crucified one might be proclaimed by all. Also on going up to the feast, when he went to Ephraim, he did not act according to custom, going up to Jerusalem on foot *as he always did; for none of the people went up to Jerusalem[4] for the feast except on foot. But he entered Jerusalem sitting on a foal, so that by seeing him only in this fashion they might again recall the awesome wonder of the miracle, [270] that this was he who yesterday summoned the one [dead] for four days from the tomb with his authoritative voice. This also the evangelist presents, testifying that the people also bore witness that he summoned Lazarus and raised him from the tomb. For that reason the people went out to meet him, because they had heard that he had performed those signs.

Also, so that he might recall the prophetic [saying] that the high priests and scribes continually read: *Rejoice, daughter of Sion, for behold, your king comes to you sitting on a new foal* (John 12:15; Zech 9:9). From the signs and from his sitting on a foal, perhaps they might realize and confess that he is the Christ, the Son of God, for whom we were waiting in accordance with the

---

1. **Before**, MN: + "the Passover," Z.
2. **And they ... him**, NZ: om. M.
3. **Divine**: om. M.
4. **As ... Jerusalem**: om. M.

prognostication of the prophets, *and that the sayings by the prophets were about him.[5]

i. Išodad and Dionysius bar Salibi (*Gospels*, 61–62; *John*, 392) analyze the chronology of the different Gospels. Išodad, 255, refers to the tradition that Lazarus lived for many years and became a bishop; for the legend, see the entry "Lazarus" in *ODCC*. Nonnus does not explain the "six days," but Tat'ewac'i, 493, discusses the chronology in relation to the feasts of Gregory the Illuminator.

[12:3] Then Mary, taking a liter of oil of nard of fine quality and very expensive, anointed his feet; and with her hair she cleaned his feet. *And the house was filled with the odor.[6]

He demonstrates here that the woman had a different kind of faith in Christ than what she previously had. Also the forms of her love were frequently [expressed] and incomparable, like the resurrection of her brother, for which reason she also cleaned his feet with the hair of her head.[i] See the wisdom of the woman, so as to make clear that she had nothing else more precious to serve the divine feet than the hair of her head. Therefore, bending down her head, with her hair she served the life-giving feet.

i. Moše bar Kepha and Dionysius bar Salibi (*John*, 228) note that Jesus was anointed by women on three occasions (i.e., here; Matt 26:6–13; and Mark 14:3–9); Išodad only refers to Matt 26:7.

[12:4–5] One of the disciples said, Judas Iscariot, who was to betray him: Why was this oil not sold for three hundred dinars and given to the poor?

Here the evangelist mentions Iscariot, because since [the brother] of Jacob had the same name as him, he made a distinction between the Iscariot and Judas [brother] of Jacob.[i] And he described what was said by Judas concerning the matter of the oil, **[271]** so that those who love money might be aware and take guard for themselves. For love of money was the cause of Judas saying what he did, and being deceived by the Devil through the same desire, he was drawn to the thirty [pieces] of silver.[ii]

But one must investigate how it was possible for so little oil to be sold for *three hundred dinars*. Behold, never had such oil been seen that was sold at such a price of gold. Not in accordance with nature did any such oil exist; but because the awesome divine head was close by, consequently divine power

---

5. **And that … him:** om. M.
6. **And the house … odor,** NZ: om. M.

was active, and from the wonderful odor its quality smelled most gloriously in their nostrils, so that *the house was filled with the odor* of the oil. But he was astonished at such a sweet smell of the oil, and in accordance with his love of money he referred to a very great price: It would have been possible to sell [it] *for three hundred dinars*. This is not anything astonishing, that if the Creator of everything was to be sold for thirty [pieces] of silver, he thought the bottle of oil would provide much more, *three hundred dinars*, not for the sake of the poor but in accordance with his own mad desire for money.

i. Luke 6:16 distinguishes the two Judases; see also John 14:22.

ii. The "love of money" (*arcat'asirut'iwn*, as 1 Tim 6:10) is stressed by Moše bar Kepha and Dionysius bar Salibi. Cyril of Alexandria, *Comm. Jo.* 7, calls Judas *aischrokerdēs*. Tat'ewac'i, 496–97, states that when Judas was originally called, he was "good" (*bari*), but that he fell through avarice.

[12:6] He said this, not because he had any concern for the poor, but because he was a thief and he held the bag; and whatever was put in it he carried.

Did you see how the meaning of the saying was made clear? As we said above, *he had no concern for the poor* but [only] for his own miserly passion for theft. But be amazed at Christ's acquiescence and pardoning, who saw[7] so much earlier the evil machinations of his mind yet did not rebuke or chide him, and did not even deprive him of the honor to which he had appointed him, but still allowed him to remain in the same position and did not wish to evince any cause for hatred.

But it is necessary also to introduce the other disciples, because they too said the same about the oil, but not with his intentions.[i] For they, [272] in accordance with the Lord's words that they had heard about loving the poor, spoke with concern for the nourishing of the poor in order to show that they were more pleased with the teacher and the Lord than with what the woman did. But Judas was not of the same sort, but he acted through love of money and his mad and raving passion.

i. For the disciples' indignation, Nonnus is referring to the account in Matt 26:8–9 and Mark 14:4–5, not to the lemma in the Gospel of John.

---

7. **Saw:** om. M.

[12:7] **Jesus said: Let her be, so that she may keep this for the day of my shroud.**

He gives prior warning to them about his own burial and resurrection, so that by reflecting on the saying about his shroud the woman might understand the mystery of his burial; and in accordance with the custom of the Jews, on approaching for attendance at the tomb she might be present at the miracle of the resurrection by the recollection of the prediction. As indeed came about, when approaching for attendance at the tomb she encountered the news-bearing angel.[i]

i. Nonnus has confused two of the various Marys mentioned in the Gospels: here, Mary sister of Martha and Lazarus is intended; in the accounts in Matthew and Mark the woman who anointed Jesus is not named. In John 20 it is Mary Magdalene who encounters two angels at the tomb. But Nonnus's "news-bearing," *awetawor*, angel is the one in Matt 28:1–7, who gave the news to Mary Magdalene and "the other Mary," or the one in Mark 16:1–7, who spoke to Mary Magdalene and Mary the mother of James. Luke 24:10 refers to these two Marys but not to an angel.

[12:8] **The poor you have with you at all times; me you do not have with you at all times.**

He indicates nothing regarding the reply to Judas, knowing that he would not be helped. But leaving him aside, he turns his remark to the disciples: *Me you do not have with you at all times.*[8] Before this he had only prophesied regarding them that you will abandon me and flee[i] only at the time of the torments. After that, being in the tomb I shall not[9] be with you in the body, as now, but in my divinity [I shall be] at all times not only with you but also with all things, existent and nonexistent[10].[ii]

i. **Abandon me and flee:** Matt 26:56; Mark 14:50. For the prophecy, see John 16:32.
ii. **All things, existent and nonexistent:** *amenayn goyss ew angoyss.* For the terminology, see the introduction, xxxix at n. 90.

---

8. **At all times:** "continually," *hanapaz,* M (= Z, but not lemma).
9. **Not:** om. N.
10. **And nonexistent:** om. M.

[12:9] **When many people of the Jews knew that he was there, they came not only for the sake of Jesus but also so that they might see Lazarus, whom he had raised from the dead.**

Not from the Pharisees or the high priests [273] [were those] who he indicates hastened to meet Christ and to see Lazarus because of the wondrous miracle that they had heard, but from the rabble of the crowds; for they did not have any envy in themselves, nor like the Pharisees or high priests did they harbor any treachery to betray him.[i] But being astonished by what they had heard, they therefore wished to see the one who resurrected and the one who was resurrected. And they had gathered at the feast for the healing of each one's wounds and afflictions that they had.

i. Moše bar Kepha and Dionysius bar Salibi (*John*, 230) also stress that the mass of the people believed in Jesus, in contrast to their leaders.

[12:10–11] **The high priests took counsel that they might also kill Lazarus, because many of the Jews went and believed in Christ.[11]**

The evangelist set out his account concerning the high priests in a straightforward way, that they were the cause not only of their own destruction but also of the people's. They plotted to kill Lazarus too, because of the crowds who believed in his resurrection; and they were always trying to destroy themselves and the people.

[12:12–13] **In the morning many people who had come to the feast, when they heard that Jesus was coming to Jerusalem, took branches of palm trees and went out to meet him. They cried out and said: Hosanna, blessed are you who come in the name of the Lord, O king of Israel.**

Did you see how the rabble of the crowd bore in mind faith in the miracles of which they had heard and were trying to see him? Hence on hearing that he was coming to Jerusalem, they did not remain obedient to the command of the high priests and Pharisees but immediately *took branches of palm trees and went out to meet him*, crying out in accordance with the sublime miracle that they had heard, *Hosanna*, which is "salvation from the heights."[i] They said this in accordance with the resurrection of Lazarus, representing him as Savior and Life-giver. From the heights, that is, not from those of this world does he have such power, hence linking the prophetic saying to him: *Blessed*

---

11. **Christ**, MN: "Jesus," Z.

are you who come in the name of the Lord. This they said in accordance with [274] the prophecy of David (Ps 117:26).[ii] Although they did not know what they said, yet they prophesied what had once been prophesied, not only about the second coming, *blessed* [are you] *who are to come*, but that also after the torments *you are to come* from the tomb in order to confirm the faith.

Furthermore, [it was] for a testimony of the Lord's words that he continually taught, *The Father sent me*, and *I was sent by the Father*, and *I and the Father are one* (e.g., John 5:36; 10:30). He is also testified by those loudly confirming him: *Blessed [are you] who are to come in the name of the Lord*. And whom other than the Father did they recognize to be Lord, the one whom the high priests and Sadducees[iii] said was opposed to the Father? This vexed them even more, that not only did he cancel the Sabbaths but he called God his Father and made himself equal with God. Here they are reproved by the crowds themselves, merely by hearing loudly the same prediction from so many multitudes, especially as they reckoned David's saying to be appropriately revealed in accordance with the miracles and his entrance into Jerusalem. For by saying, *king of Israel*, they even more reproved them.[iv] I know, he said, what has been prophesied about my dwelling Jerusalem: *Rejoice, daughter of Sion, for behold, your king comes to you, sitting on a foal* (Zech 9:9).[v] Yesterday we saw[12] the glorious signs that were performed by him, which no one else could do save only the Son of God; but today we see the same one on a foal coming to Jerusalem. He, then, is the one we expected, for whom they pronounced their loud blessings.

    i. Dionysius bar Salibi, *John*, 230, notes that "Hosanna" means "Savior." Tat'ewac'i, 504, quotes Nonnus (whom he calls "the interpreter," *meknič'*) and adds that others state that in Hebrew "Hosanna" means "Save" (sg. impv.).

    ii. The text of Z gives the future: "Who are to come," *or galoc' es*, as in the commentary just below.

    iii. Sadducees are not mentioned in the Gospel of John, and in the previous paragraph the Pharisees were adduced. For this frequent change in Nonnus, see the introduction, xxvi.

    iv. Here Dionysius bar Salibi, *John*, 230, compares the entrance of a king into a city.

    v. See the next lemma.

[12:14–15] And Jesus, finding a foal, sat on it, as it is written: Do not fear, daughter of Sion. Behold, your king comes, sitting on a new foal.

[275] The evangelist demonstrates that for no other purpose did he sit on a foal than for the prophecies to be revealed[i] and the sayings by the prophet to be seen by eyewitnesses, and that through the signs he was worthy of that proph-

----

12. **We saw**, *tesak'*, N: "we learned," *usak'*, M.

ecy. He who yesterday authoritatively summoned the one dead for four days from the tomb, and today came to Jerusalem sitting on a foal, he then is the king of Israel, which the sequel to the prophecy also confirms, calling him *gentle*. [ii] That is, not proud and haughty king, like the kings who formerly dwelled among you, who afflicted you with a myriad evils and even handed you over to your enemies; but he, although being *gentle*, was to crush in rancor *the chariots from Ephraim and the cavalry from Jerusalem* (Zech 9:10).[iii] For in his own lack of vengeance, he saves those who believe in him not only from their visible enemies but also from their invisible ones. But the rebellious he hands over to the chastisement of the Gentiles, just as attacks and captivities were wrought by the Romans against the crucifiers, and after that unending torments.

i. Dionysius bar Salibi, *John*, 231, also refers to the fulfillment of prophecy.

ii. **Gentle:** *hez*, as Zech 9:9.

iii. Dionysius bar Salibi, *John*, 231, names Zechariah when quoting this verse, and Moše bar Kepha refers to the earlier kings as evildoers.

[12:16] That his disciples did not know at first; but when Jesus was glorified, then they[13] remembered that that was what had been written about him, and that they had done that to him.

At that time they did not truly understand the going out to meet him and the singing of the prophecies and the blessing to have been accomplished in accordance with the scripture concerning him but rather by happenstance and chance. For the disciples were not informed and aware of the prophecy but foolish and ignorant. But when he had risen from the tomb and they had been filled with the Holy Spirit, then they recognized what had happened earlier, and they realized through the teaching of the Holy Spirit that in accordance with the previously uttered prophecies they had gone out to meet him.

[276] Here the evangelist abbreviates the description of his coming. Why? Because he was never concerned to repeat again what had once been related by the three evangelists, but he described[14] what had been omitted by them concerning Christ's miracles, like the wedding at Cana of Galilee. However, as concerns his coming to Jerusalem he composed his narrative in a detailed manner down to the completion, which is the amazing story of Lazarus's resurrection and the enthusiasm of the crowds for meeting Christ with branches of palm trees and songs of blessing. *But when Jesus was glorified, then they*

---

13. **They,** NZ: "his disciples," M.

14. **Described:** "wrote down," M.

*remembered that that was what had been written about him, and that they had
done that to him.*

**[12:17–18] And the people who were with him testified that he had sum-
moned Lazarus from the tomb and raised him from the dead. Therefore the
people went to meet him, because they had heard that he had performed
those miracles.**[15]

He calls the cross "glory," because on the cross the glory of his divinity
was proclaimed by creatures: by the darkening of the sun, by the splitting of
rocks, by the tearing of the veil, by the dead coming out of their tombs, by the
prince of the world being cast out,[i] and being glorified by believers. Therefore,
after the resurrection, when they were filled with the Holy Spirit, they later
understood what had been said by the people concerning his coming, that is,
the prophecies concerning him: *Blessed [are you] who come in the name of the
Lord*, and *King of Israel*, according to the saying, *Rejoice, daughter of Sion.* This
the people did regarding him according to scripture.

    i. John 12:31, associated with Christ's death in v. 32.

[12:19] Then the Pharisees said to each other: See[16] **that we are not helped;
for behold, the whole world has followed him.**

The people, they said, will not accept deceit[17] from us regarding [our]
words about him. So see[i] how they go out all together with branches of palm
trees [277] and bless him. Unless we hasten to kill him, all the people will
believe in him.

    i. **See:** sg. impv.

---

    15. N omits the entire lemma. It is likely that Nonnus did not include these two verses,
because their insertion here in M breaks the continuity of the commentary explaining the
"glorified" of v. 16. Tat'ewac'i, 508–10, includes vv. 17–18 in his commentary, but he does
not refer to Nonnus and is primarily concerned with explicating vv. 15–16.

    16. **See:** *tesēk'* (2d pl. impf. or aor. indic.), NM; *tesanēk'* (pres. indic.), Z. Could be
interrogative.

    17. **Deceit:** om. N.

[12:20–21] **There were some of the Gentiles among those who had gone up there to worship at the feast. They approached Philip, who was from Bethsaida of Galilee, and requested him and said: Lord, we wish to see Jesus.**

These had been sent by King Abgar to Christ, when he heard that the Jews planned to kill him, and they were present at the feast.[i] But it is said somewhere also that the men had some inclination to Judaism, which the expression reveals: *for the sake of worshiping at the feast*. This is clear, that none of the Gentiles worshiped at Jerusalem. When these [men] heard what he had done for Lazarus, they were the more anxious to see him promptly, but they did not presume to go to him. Furthermore, Gentiles could not mingle with the Jews, as the Lord also[18] said to the disciples, *Do not enter the cities of the Gentiles* (Matt 10:5), and *I have been sent nowhere else save to the lost sheep of the house of Israel* (Matt 10:6), and *One must not take the bread of children and throw it to dogs* (Mark 7:27).

But see the willingness of the men and their great consideration for Christ. First they request Philip, and then they even call him *lord*. For if they called[19] his disciple *lord*, what would they think of the teacher? And if they requested him only to see [Jesus], what then would they be about to show when they were eyewitnesses of his signs and miracles?

i. There is no reference to Abgar in the Syrian commentators at this point. The Syrian version of the Abgar legend does not associate Abgar's envoys in Jerusalem with Philip (Labubna, ed. Phillips, 2), nor does the Armenian version (Ališan, 3). The connection with the episode in John 12:20–22, however, was made by the Armenian historian Movsēs Xorenac'i (*History*, 2.31) and thereafter became part of Armenian tradition. The account in Movsēs differs from the Abgar legend in that he quotes John 12:20 in connection with the visit of Abgar's (unnamed) envoys, when they brought the king's letter to Jesus; but according to the Abgar legend the letter was brought to Jerusalem by Hanan, after an earlier visit by the envoys to Jerusalem. The Abgar legend and the reference in Movsēs suggest not an inclination to Judaism on the part of the envoys, as the commentary suggests, but rather a curiosity to see Jesus, the fame of whose miracles had spread far and wide. The editor Č'rak'ean, in his introduction (p. *ib* [22]), thinks the reference to Abgar is more likely to be a comment by Nonnus from a Syriac source than an addition by the translator.

[12:22] **Philip came and told Andrew. Andrew and Philip told Jesus.**

Philip did not dare to inform Christ of the Gentiles' requests. For if he commanded us, he said, [278] *not to enter the cities of the Gentiles*, because

---

18. **Also:** om. N.
19. **Called:** "call," M.

he was not sent save only *to the lost sheep of the house of Israel,* how can we lead the Gentiles to him? Therefore he came to Andrew.[i] Since the latter had entered the discipleship of the Savior prior to Philip,[ii] he was bold enough to tell Christ. At this Philip was encouraged, and he too told what he had heard from the Gentiles.

> i. Cyril of Alexandria, *Comm. Jo.* 7, also quotes Matt 10:5 to explain Philip's fear.
> ii. John 1:40 for Andrew, 1:43 for Philip.

[12:23] And Jesus replied and said: The hour has come that the son of man should be glorified.

Not only does he mention next the setting up of the cross and the awesomeness[20] of the signs for proclamation from earth and heaven—not only that he is son of man but also Son of God—but also the calling of the Gentiles and the faith that was to occur. For the Gentiles, he says, hearing only the summoning of Lazarus from the tomb, were not eyewitnesses, like the Jews, and had not seen any other of the myriad signs performed by me, like the nation[21] of the Jews; yet now through this report alone they have such a desire to see me that they even called my disciple *lord,* which the Jews had never applied to me, but rather its opposite, a Samaritan, with the rest.[i] So by them I am to be frequently *glorified.* After the resurrection he expounds this most clearly in the ears of the disciples: *Baptize all Gentiles and teach them to observe everything, whatever I have commanded you* (Matt 28:19–20). That is, that they happily will receive the faith and observe everything, the laws and rituals of the faith.

But what means: *Now he has been glorified?*[ii] He refers to the promptness of the men to faith in him, being an image of the Gentiles who before knowing [him] evinced such a personal desire. And because the disciples did not realize [279] that what he said referred to the cross and the torments and the faith of[22] the Gentiles, he then added an example to make it easier for them to grasp it, and said:

> i. **With the rest:** *aylovk'n handerj,* the standard expression for "*et cetera.*"
> ii. **He has been glorified:** *p'araworec'aw.* This is the expression in John 13:31, not that of the lemma, *p'araworesc̄e.*

---

20. **Awesomeness:** "awesome," M (of the signs; *sic*).
21. **Nation:** om. M.
22. **The faith of:** om. M.

[12:24–25a] *Amen, amen, I say to you:[23] **Unless a piece of grain fall to the earth and die, it lives[24] alone. But if it dies, it creates much produce.**

By means of something familiar he teaches them that if the torments of the cross and death seem awful to you, and [you query] how the Gentiles will believe in me who[25] do not save myself from torments and death, take the truth from this example. Just as a piece of grain, unless it is buried in the heart of the earth, cannot produce anything for fruitfulness, but by being buried and dying it produces fruit and useful profit for the sower, likewise I, by enduring[26] death and being placed in the heart of the earth, offer to the Father all nations rendered fruitful through their true faith in me, by bringing back those lost and gathering those scattered by the deceits of the Devil.

[12:25b] **Whoever loves his life[27] shall lose it; and whoever hates his life in this world shall preserve it for eternal life.**

Like those who love the world, he says, if any of you loves his life in this age, he will be excluded from the future life. But he who hates his life, that is, by separating from bodily pleasures and following such suffering as I shall for your salvation and for teaching and to leave an example, will inherit his recompense in the eternal life, which death cannot again destroy, like the pleasures of the bodily life.

[12:26a] **If anyone would serve me, let him follow me.**

Whoever wishes to be a disciple of mine, *let him follow me* [280] in purity of deeds and teaching. For by conducting himself in the body in accordance with my thoughts and deeds, after that he will be able also to follow me with his soul to indestructible and unending life.

[12:26b] **And where I am, there also my servant shall be.**

Did you see how easily for their ears he set out the teaching of hope? After observing the [precepts] handed down by me[i] and[28] the preaching of the faith,

---

23. **Amen … you:** om. M.

24. **Lives,** *keay,* MN: "remains," *kay,* Z; cf. lemma to 12:34.

25. **Who:** om. M.

26. **By enduring,** *krelov,* N: "by baptizing," *mkrtelov,* M.

27. **His life,** NZ: "it," M.

28. **And:** om. N.

you will receive from me the recompense, being present in heaven[29] with me in ineffable blessings and illumination without shadow.[ii]

i. **Handed down by me:** *zawandealsn yinēn.* This phrase does not agree in case with "faith" or in number with "preaching."

ii. Dionysius bar Salibi, *John*, 233; and Tat'ewac'i, 516, equate the "where…there" of the lemma with heaven. But Cyril of Alexandria, *Comm. Jo.* 7, says that this verse refers not to a place but to a mode of virtue: *ou topon legei, alla tropon aretēs.*

[12:26c] **If anyone will serve me, my Father will honor him.**

Not only will you receive honor from me by being my true disciple but also from the Father. Thereby he awakes their minds and provides for them greater hope of eternal life. And he also indicates the unity of will of the Father and himself.

[12:27a] **But now my soul is troubled.**

These remarks were made concerning the torments and death that he was about to endure, and the disciples thought it insignificant;[30] namely, how could torments and death approach the one who by his voice had resurrected the one dead for four days? But although he endured it willingly, yet he could not bring about pains and afflictions resulting from sin,[i] for which reason he wished to remove that from their minds. Consequently he set down, *My soul is troubled*, in order to indicate his true humanity and trial of torments, that not falsely and apparently shall I endure all that for the salvation of the world, but truly. Therefore he demonstrates and reveals the kinship that he had with our weakness according to his bodily condition.[ii] This he also expressed close to the cross: *My soul is willing, but my body weak* (Matt 26:41; Mark 14:38). And since [281] what he said seemed awesome to the disciples, he added to it:

i. Christ was not subject to the results of sin; see the commentary to John 14:30b–31a. The infinitive *nergorcel*, "to effect, influence," here translated as "bring about," could be active or passive; here it governs two accusatives. One might have expected: "He could not be influenced by pains and afflictions resulting from sin."

ii. **Bodily condition:** *marmnaworut'iwn*, an abstract noun from the adjective *marmnawor*, "bodily."

---

29. **In heaven**, *yerkins*, N: "on earth," *yerkris*, M.
30. **Insignificant**, *t'et'ews*, M: "perhaps," *t'erews*, N.

[12:27b] **And what shall I say? Father, save me from this hour.**

It is most appropriate that my soul is sad because of the torments and death that I am about to endure. Let it not, then, seem good to you that [I] say:[i] Father, remove from me the torments of the cross. But you do not yet understand completely the salvation of the world.

> i. The subject of the infinite "to say" is not expressed.

[12:27c] **But for that reason I came to this hour.**

To the torments of the cross and death, he means, because thereby the salvation of the world is to take place. But the real torments that I am going to endure willingly, united with my body, I teach in advance for the strengthening of your faith; and it removes the suppositions of the schismatics who think that that will occur in appearance. But I do not desist from offering this request to the Father. Lest the salvation of the world be hindered, I go up to the cross without being forced by anyone, if there is need of entreaty, but willingly. For through the cross I shall condemn sin, and through burial I shall renew corruption into incorruption, and through death I shall destroy death, and through resurrection I shall bring up with me the souls to eternal life. In this way by enduring them in myself through their opposites I shall destroy the opponents who ruled over human nature, and I shall once more pour out life on mankind.

He also admonishes them for correction and their profit. For if I am to endure painful things for the sake of the world's salvation, and I do not flinch, because *for that reason I came to this hour*, how much the more when you will have occasion to endure [**282**] painful things must you not flinch and turn away. Because your [endurance] will be especially for the sake of the salvation of your own selves, and for the payment and compensation of the ineffable and unending blessings that await.

[12:28a] **Father, glorify your name.**[31]

Because first he expounded his torments and [that] I shall not flinch and turn away, begging the Father to prevent the cross, next he set down: *Father, glorify your name.* The time of my torments has come, he said. So through these awesome signs make known to the world that I am your Son, so that the

---

31. **Name**, MN: "Son," Z. The textual tradition of this verse offers both "name" and "Son"; see Metzger 1975, 237–38.

world may recognize me and glorify your name, confessing you as Father. For just as I made your name known to the world as Father to those who believe in you, and by always praising you in accordance with what I learned to say, *Our Father, who are in heaven, holy be your name* (Matt 6:9; Luke 11:2), glorify also your name, revealing me to be your Son, so that strengthened thereby in the faith they may remain unshaken in the glory of your paternal name.

[12:28b] **There came a voice from heaven:**[32] **I have glorified [it] and shall glorify it again.**

See the meaning of these sayings, from the *voice* coming *from heaven*. There is need of testimonies from above, he says, concerning your being seen to be a man. Just as at the birth I glorified [you] by the praising of angels and the appearance of the star and the worship of the magi; and at the baptism by the opening of heaven and the descent of the Holy Spirit and the voice from above: *You are my beloved Son* (Matt 3:17, etc.); and on the mountain of Tabor by the two prophets standing beside [you] and the sound of the voice for a testimony of [your] being my Son (Matt 17:5, etc.);[i] in the same fashion again I shall glorify [you] at the time of the cross with even more wonderful signs from heaven and earth—as indeed happened. For when he said, *Father, into your hands I commend my soul* (Luke 23:46), the sun was darkened, rocks were split, the veil of the temple was rent, the earth [283] moved, tombs opened and the dead arose and entered into the city, and thenceforth it was openly preached everywhere that he was the Son of God. The centurion, before his rising from the tomb, in amazement at the happenings at the time of the cross, said the same: *Truly this man is the Son of God* (Mark 15:39; cf. Matt 27:54).

Then after his rising from the dead he gave a command to his disciples: *Go, baptize the Gentiles in the name of the Father and of the Son and of the Holy Spirit* (Matt 28:19). And after this he was glorified by creatures: the Father was made known to the world by the Son; and the Son was testified by the Father; and the Holy Spirit was revealed at the descent into the Jordan at the sending of the Father, and then was preached by the Son to be of equal honor with himself and the Father, according to the power of the baptism by which the Jews and Gentiles were called to the glorification of the Holy Trinity.

i. Moše bar Kepha and Dionysius bar Salibi (*John*, 235) refer only to the baptism in the Jordan and the (unnamed) mountain. The site of the transfiguration is not named in the NT. In Agat'angełos, *History* 850, Tabor is named as the mountain on which Christ uttered

---

32. **From heaven**, MZ: om. N.

the Beatitudes and to which he withdrew in John 6:15; but when *Teaching* 703 refers to the transfiguration, the mountain is not named.

[12:29] And the people who were standing and heard said it was thunder. *Some said that an angel spoke with him.[33]

See their folly and darkened minds. Such a clear voice coming from above they attempted to change to something else, lest the people follow the testimonies that he was Son of God. But in accordance with their own thick-wittedness and weakness they invented some suitable excuse and said it was thunder. Because the voice was very close and obvious, yet these said it was thunder, some of the Jews were not pleased. Therefore the evangelist indicates that others said *an angel spoke*,[34] as if thus it would seem appropriate to please the minds of the people that it was not a voice, as you heard, nor thunder, as some said, but it was an angel and not the Father who spoke. For if they were to understand that the Father testified concerning the Son, they who said he was opposed to the Father would condemn themselves. But by attributing it to an angel, perchance they might find some small way **[284]** to prevent the faith of the people that it concerned the testimony of the Father.

[12:30] Jesus responded and said: This voice[35] **came not concerning me but concerning you.**

I had no need for testimony, he says, for *just as the Father knows me, I also know him* (John 10:5), and *I and the Father are one* (10:30); but for a reprimand of your errors. For if you did not believe[36] through the earlier testimonies at the birth and the baptism, perhaps you who said I am opposed to the Father, in terror will admonish yourselves by the awesome signs that will occur at the time of the cross.

[12:31a] Now is judgment of this world.[37]

After indicating that Satan is the cause of the destruction of mankind from the beginning, now came the testimony from the Father concerning me:

---

33. **Some … him**, NZ: om. M.
34. **An angel spoke:** "angels spoke," M.
35. **This voice:** *barbars ays*, MZ; *barbars*, N.
36. **Did not believe:** "will not believe," N.
37. **Of this world**, *ašxarhis aysorik*, MZ: "for this world," *ašxarhis aysmik*, N.

The time of the cross has arrived, *now is judgment of this world;*[38] for not in accordance with my divine power am I about to snatch the race of mankind from his hands, but through my human dispensation.[i] He once contrived[ii] against Adam but did not subject him; he will be tested by me but not subjected. I came to the world for the salvation of mankind, taking on the nature of mankind and enduring his condition, except for sin. Now with that same nature I am about to stand with him in the tribunal;[iii] in the form of human nature I shall endure dangers; willingly I shall suffer afflictions; I shall set up the wood of obedience in place of the wood of rebellion; I shall be raised up on it in return for his tricks [against] Adam when he raised his mind to desire the fruit. I shall nail my arms to it instead of his reaching his hands in yearning for the fruit; I shall taste the gall instead of his sweet tasting; I shall receive the wound of a rib in order to heal his ribmate Eve, and I shall fashion a new birth through the rib as a source for her offspring. Henceforth I shall remove the pains and the grief of her labor;[iv] [285] and by my stripping off my garments I shall clothe Adam again [in the robe] of which he was stripped.[v]

I shall be crowned with thorns, freeing my creation from the curse of thorns; through the cross I shall remove the protection of paradise by the cherubim; I shall introduce the robber into paradise instead of the first-created. By humbling my head I shall render all nations worshipers of the Father; by entrusting my soul into the Father's hands I shall put in the Father's hands all the souls of mankind. By being placed in the tomb I shall destroy the corruption of mankind; by my death I shall put death to death and grant life to my creation; on rising from the tomb I shall bring out with me their souls, in my human nature in the form of mankind. Through such obedience I shall squash the first rebellion of man. So then [this] is the *judgment of this world*, because in this way and to this extent will it come about at the time of my cross.

i. **Dispensation:** *tntesut'iwn*; for such terminology, see the introduction, xxxvi–xxxvii. Nonnus here refers to the second part of v. 31, which has a separate lemma below. All Syrian commentators identify the prince of this world with Satan.

ii. **Contrived:** *hnarec'aw*. This verb is not used in the Armenian version of Genesis. The following soliloquy in the first person is not found in Tat'ewac'i, who generally has some reference to Nonnus's commentary (acknowledged as the "interpreter," *meknič'*, or not) in his explanations.

iii. **Tribunal:** *atean*; i.e., not the future judgment, but the trial of human existence.

---

38. **Of this world,** *ašxarhis*, M: "of the world," *ašxarhi*, N. Without the accompanying demonstrative adjective, *ašxarhi(s)* could be genitive ("of the world") or dative ("for the world"); see note to the lemma.

iv. **Labor**: birth pangs.

v. For the theme of the robe, see the introduction, xlii.

[12:31b] Now the prince of this world will be cast out.

Things being just as I said above, he who once ruled over human nature and subjected it will be cast out; now he will be despised by those idols and sacrifices by which he was previously served with honors and sacrifices.[i]

i. Tat'ewac'i, 526, adds a reference to Satan being bound for a thousand years; see Rev 20:1. But the book of Revelation was little known in Armenia before the second translation by Nersēs of Lambron in 1179 (see the introduction to Thomson's edition of his *Commentary on Revelation*).

[12:32] And when I shall be raised up from the earth, I shall draw all to me.

He also indicates the time at which that will happen. On being raised up on the cross and through the awesome signs and miracles that will occur and when creatures will know me to be the Son of God, all will be drawn to me by faith as the prince of darkness[i] is cast out, whom once they worshiped, as I said above.

i. **Prince of darkness**: *išxan xawari*. This precise phrase does not occur in the Armenian Bible.

[12:33] This he said, indicating by what death he would die.

Because he spoke about the salvation and the faith that [**286**] would occur through his own torments and showed that he would truly die willingly through the torments of the cross, he rapidly said: I shall arise from the tomb.[i] For if he were not to rise from the dead, how would he draw this world to himself through faith, not being himself risen from the dead? Or how would *the prince of the world* be cast out, if he had not really raised himself from the tomb? Therefore the evangelist added this: *He said this, indicating by what death he would die.*

i. **I shall arise from the tomb**: not in the Armenian Gospels.

[12:34] The people responded and said: We have heard from the law that the Christ[39] lives[40] forever. So how do you say that the son of man must be raised up? Who is that son of man?

Did you see the trickery and veiled wickedness? We have heard, they said, that *the Christ lives forever*. And how[41] do you say that you will be tormented and die? You are not, then, the Christ. See again what they say: We know from the commandments that *the Christ lives forever*. Not thus did they know from the commandments concerning Christ, but its opposite, that Christ was to suffer torments, just as they continually read the prophecies concerning him: *He will remove our sins and suffer torments for us*, and *He was wounded for our sins and punished for our impiety*, and *The reproof of our peace is in him*, and *Through his wounds we shall be healed* (Isa 53:4–5), and *They gave gall as food to me, and in my thirst they gave me vinegar to drink* (Ps 68:22), and *They pierced my hands and feet, and shared my clothes among them, and for my robe they cast lots* (Ps 21:18–19).[i] Surely they could not say David endured this! Never! And many such things they knew from the prophets, but they did not wish to introduce them [287] in preference to what was totally opposed to the truth.

See also what they asked: *Who is the son of man* whom you say will be raised up? Did they not know that he was speaking about himself? Indeed, he often said that about himself, as: *You shall see the son of man ascending to where he was before* (John 6:63), and *Work not [for] perishable food but [for] that which the son of man will give you* (6:27), and *If he is the son of man, why are you astonished?* (5:27–28). But they never desired to come to correction and to learn the truth but continually to contradict him and destroy the truth.

i. John Chrysostom, *Hom. Jo.* 68.1, cites numerous proof texts, but not the same ones.

[12:35a] Jesus said to them: For a little time the light is with you. Walk while you have the light, lest darkness overtake you.

Because they only fabricated as an excuse, *The Christ lives forever*, and *How do you say he is tormented and dies?* he then indicated the short time to the torments and burial, revealing what he said was most certain and close. But not by his burial would he suffer dissolution and corruption, as you think, because like the sun, he said, although for a little time it is hidden from us, yet

---

39. **The Christ**, MZ: "Christ," N.
40. **Lives**, *keay*, MN: "remains," *kay*, Z; cf. lemma to 12:24.
41. **How**: om. M.

it is not spoiled and destroyed but rather rapidly shines out again according to rule with its rays and fills creation; in the same way I too, although hidden[42] for a short time in the tomb, will rapidly rise on the third day in accordance with the rule[i] I mentioned, and with divine rays I shall illuminate the minds of believers who now sit in the darkness of ignorance.[ii]

See also what he taught for their profit: *Walk while it is day, lest darkness overtake you.* Because with an allegorical phrase he said he was light, he bids them walk in the light, that is, in faith in him as long as he is in the world, that is, while it is day, lest after his teaching and [288] rising from the tomb and ascending to heaven indestructible darkness come upon you,[iii] overcoming you with the eternal torments that Satan and his accomplices have prepared.

i. **Rule:** *sahman,* or "definition."

ii. The parallel of the sun being hidden at night, but not extinguished, with Christ's death is also given by Theodore of Mopsuestia and Dionysius bar Salibi (*John,* 237).

iii. Moše bar Kepha and Dionysius bar Salibi (*John,* 237) make it explicit that light and darkness are the times before and after the cross.

[12:35b] **For whoever walks in darkness does not know whither he goes.**[43]

Although *whoever walks in darkness* does not stop walking, yet *he does not know whither he is going,* because he does not have the guiding light. Just as you, although you say you act by the law, yet you do not know what you do, because you do not have in your minds the light of true faith.

[12:36a] **While you have the light with you, believe in the light, so that you may become sons of light.**

By this he pains and distresses them, showing that the light would remain with them for a short time. Take care now, he said, and remain in the light, that is, in faith in me, so that through the rebirth of the font you may become sons of light and sons of the daytime.

[12:36b] **Jesus said this, and went away and was hidden from them.**

O the accurate account of this truthful evangelist! Despite expressing the most sublime things he does not pass over the least significant. Why does he also put this to use, save to become an accuser of their erring wickedness, that

---

42. **Hidden,** *cackelov,* N: "shining," *cagelov,* M.

43. The editor of N does not print this as a separate lemma.

after so many most sublime signs and teachings and efforts for their salvation, they wished to lay hands on him? Therefore *he went away and was hidden from them*, not forced to be seized by their hands or to come to the cross before the time he wished. Here he preserves himself without any opposition, and there he goes in person to the cross in order to show that when he wished, and how he wished, he delivered himself to the torments; but he was not seized in accordance with their plans.

For here the evangelist makes his narrative not like [**289**] on that [occasion] when they seized rocks in order to throw them at him. Or again when they wished to lay hands on him and he passed through their midst.[i] For there they indicated clearly that alone, but here they pondered in their minds. This the all-seeing power[44] observed and made himself clandestine until the time of the cross. Therefore the evangelist reveals this as *hiding himself*. But he holds back the cause, as we said above.

i. Moše bar Kepha refers to earlier occasions when they wished to throw rocks, unwilling to hear his words; cf. John 7:30; 8:59.

[12:37] **And he had performed so many signs in front of them, yet they did not believe in him.**

The evangelist reproves their evil, that from so many awesome signs and miracles of which they had been eyewitnesses they did not take fright and repent of their wicked plans, and convert and become useful, but always remained obstinately in the same denial.

[12:38] **So that the word of the prophet Isaiah might be fulfilled, who said: Lord, who believed in our report, and to whom has the arm of the Lord been revealed?**[45]

Here he recalls what had been prophesied about them, that they would not believe the testimonies from the prophets that they read[46] about him, nor would they accept the marvelous signs of which they were eyewitnesses.

---

44. **The all-seeing power,** *amenates zawrut'eann*, N: "the all-seeingness," *amenatesut'eann*, M.

45. Isa 5:1.

46. **They read,** *ĕnt'eṙnuin*, M: *ĕnt'eṙnloyn*, N.

[12:39–40] **Therefore they were unable to believe; for Isaiah said again: He blinded their eyes and made their hearts foolish, lest they see with their eyes and understand with their hearts and convert, and I heal them.**[47]

Let no one dispute this saying [on the grounds] that what fault was it of the Jews, since they could not believe because he had *blinded their eyes and made their hearts foolish*? And how did he blind their eyes concerning whom he said, *Nowhere was I sent save to the lost sheep of the house of Israel* (Matt 15:24), whom he perpetually urged to the faith with amazing signs and teaching? Yet despite his having so much zeal for that, they did not become useful. [**290**] Therefore he said: *If I had not come and spoken with them, they would have had no sin; but now there is no excuse for their sin* (John 15:22). That is, I had not been unconcerned with their salvation, but with signs and miracles and various teachings I had worked for their salvation, but they did not listen. So what do they have to excuse [themselves]?

So then, he himself is not the cause of their blindness and foolishness of heart. But the Holy Spirit saw in advance that they would deny and turn back, and would even be condemned to death by their own free will. Consequently he revealed their abandoning his care and not being drawn willingly to the faith and the truth, lest he remove their independent will. He makes this clear in saying, *Lest they be converted, and I heal them.* That is, their converting and not converting was [effected] by themselves. Do not be offended by his saying that they could not believe, because not being able indicates not wishing, in accordance with the saying *This world is unable to hate you* (John 7:7), as if to say: it does not wish to hate you because of your being like-minded with the world. *But it hates me*; that is, actions[i] were never found in me in accordance with their pleasure. Therefore, the Holy Spirit, seeing from afar the wicked thoughts of their unrepentant hearts, predicted in advance through his prophet the foolishness of their incurable denials.[ii]

 i. **Actions:** *šaržmunkʿ* (lit. "movements"), also used for emotions.
 ii. Moše bar Kepha emphasizes that prophets cannot lie. It was not prophecy that caused their unbelief but their own impudence.

[12:41] **Isaiah said this because he saw his glory and spoke many things about him.**

Namely, at the death of Uzziah, according to what the same prophet says: *In the year in which king Uzziah died I saw the Lord sitting on a high and*

---

47. Isa 6:10.

elevated throne (Isa 6:1).[i] He mentions *Lord* and *throne*, whereby it is clear that he indicates the single person[ii] and not three, as appeared to Daniel: *I saw that thrones were toppled* (Dan 7:9), which indicates the appearance of the three persons.[iii] [291] But here it is not the same, but *Lord* and *throne*; and the seraphim roundabout, covering their faces with their wings, were singing the Trisagion[iv] to the one sitting on the high throne. And I heard a voice that said: *Whom shall I send, and who will go to that people? And I said: I am here, send me. And he said: Go, and say to that people, Seeing, you will see but not see; and hearing you will hear and not understand. For the heart of this people has become hardened, and they have closed their eyes, lest they see with their eyes and hear with their ears, and they convert and I heal them* (Isa 6:8–10).

We find here what the holy evangelist John relates about the Son, [and] the blessed Paul says about the Holy Spirit: *The Holy Spirit spoke well through Isaiah the prophet to our fathers and said: Go to the people and say to them, Hearing you will hear and not understand, and seeing you will see and not know, because the heart of this people has become hardened, and with their ears they heard dully, and they closed their eyes, lest they see with their eyes and hear with their ears, and they convert and I heal them* (Acts 28:25–27).[v] Where, then, are the sick-minded and lovers of opposition, who contend against the truth and[48] that one must not posit the Trisagion concerning one person? At least let them be shamed by the evangelist John, because he related what the prophet had seen and heard concerning the Son.

Furthermore, Paul reproves them, because he indicates that what he saw and heard applies specifically to the Holy Spirit. He even more confirms the exposition of orthodoxy by showing to both sides that the Trisagion and praise of the three persons is one [and the same], in accordance with the single and equal nature and power and authority. So whoever praises the Son certainly praises [292] the Father as well; and whoever praises the Father, with him praises the Son and the Holy Spirit. For the glorification of the Father and the glorification of the Son and the glorification of the Holy Spirit are not[49] different, because although we saw the Son descending to human humility, yet he is God; with the same appellation as by the prophet the name of the one born is called God. And although he condescended to the rank of our weakness, yet he is mighty in accordance with the same prophet's prognostication: He is *mighty* (Isa 9:6). And although he endured death in his own body willingly, yet he is immortal according to the testimony of the same prophet: *Father of the world to come.* So the one who is Father of the world to come is eternal,

---

48. **And**: om. M.
49. **Not**: om. N.

and the eternal one is immortal. So then, we give praise, always offering the Trisagion with regard to the one who from such a height took on deprivation into our nature, so that he might raise us up to the habitations of the supernal praisers of his divinity.

So either let our opponents be persuaded and fittingly sing with us the Trisagion concerning the Savior, confessing him as "God, mighty, immortal," in accordance with the prophet's appellations, and also adding the boast of the cross in accordance with Paul's expression (Gal 6:14); for the "God," and the "mighty," and the "immortal," in these last times "was crucified for us."[vi] Or if they do not agree, let them send their dispute to John and Paul. But we shall remain orthodox in the faith and repeat the words before us.

i. Tat'ewac'i, 534, specifically refers to Isa 6.

ii. **Single person:** *mianjnut'iwn* (*mi*, "one"; *anjn*, "person"; -*ut'iwn*, abstract suffix). For *anjn*, see the introduction, xxxix.

iii. **Persons:** *anjnaworut'iwn*. Here the abstract noun is derived from the adjective *anjn-awor*. Dionysius bar Salibi, *John*, 239, refers to the three *qnwm'*.

iv. **Trisagion:** *erahiwsak srbasac'ut'iwn* (i.e., the triple "holy" of Isa 6:3). Cyril of Alexandria, *Comm. Jo.* 7, explains the triple singing of "holy" as a reference to the *mia theotēs en hypostasesi trisi* ("one Godhead in three hypostases"). Tat'ewac'i, 534–36, discusses the Trisagion in its Armenian form, with the addition of *xačec'ar*, "who was crucified for us"; for this, see just below.

v. This passage is also quoted by Thodore of Mopsuestia, and Moše bar Kepha notes that Paul spoke about the Spirit.

vi. For this form of the Trisagion, which became standard in Armenia, see Garitte 1952 (78–79) and Garsoïan 1999 (144 with n. 38). See also above, p. 243 of the printed text, in the "Exhortation" at the end of ch. 10, for the Armenian emphasis on the Son. For later Armenian evidence, see Mathews and Sanjian 1991 (30).

[12:42–43] Yet many of the rulers believed in him, but because of the Pharisees they did not reveal it, lest they be expelled from the synagogue. For they loved the glory of men more than the glory of God.

[293] Although they believed in him, he says, because of the signs that they frequently saw, nonetheless they preferred the vain and feeble glory of mankind to the permanent and stable [glory] from God. Therefore they did not wish to reveal their faith from doubts about the Pharisees, since they were more wicked and ready[50] to hinder the faith than everyone else.

---

50. **Ready,** *patrastk'*, N: "vainglorious," *patuasērk'*, M.

[12:44] And Jesus cried out and said: Whoever believes in me does not believe in me but believes[51] in the one who sent me.

This the Pharisees construed as a pretext for wickedness and hatred, that he was opposed to God and said he himself was God. Therefore in the ears of everyone he confronted their falseness and silenced the mouths of those who said he was opposed to the Father. He is so much of one will and one thought with the Father that he draws those who believe in him to the Father and says the faith to be in him. But see why he did not say that whoever believes in the Father believes in me, but puts himself first. For if he first spoke about the Father, perhaps they would say that we believe in the Father but not in you at all. Therefore he put himself first and thereby removed excuses for such responses, and he said: *Whoever believes in me does not believe in me but believes in the one who sent me.* Furthermore, he did not say something like, Whoever hears me, or Whoever receives me but *Whoever believes in me.* He revealed the sublime honor and equality that he has with the Father. And as I am coexistent and coglorious with the Father, so also faith in me is to be understood to be [faith] in the Father, because *I and my Father are one* (John 10:30).

[12:45] And whoever sees me sees the one who sent me.

Because first he taught that *whoever* **[294]** *believes in me believes in the one who sent me,* *after that he set down: *Whoever sees me sees the one who sent me.*[52] Just as the faith, he says, is understood equally in accordance with them being one nature, so also in accordance with the hierarchy of the person those who see me in faith will be understood to see the Father. By this he also confirms the saying, for if according to your supposition the Father is greater than me, how is the seeing of me comparable with that of the Father? For whoever sees the body could not at all say that he also saw the soul; nor whoever sees the servant could say he saw the king, because these are so superior to those. So then, from what has been said it is clear that he had a single and equal nature and authority with the Father.[i]

i. Here John Chrysostom, *Hom. Jo.* 69.1, refers to *to homoousion.*

---

51. **Believes**: om. M.
52. **After … me**: om. M.

[12:46] I came as light to the world, so that everyone who believes in me should not remain in darkness.

Although you see me in the world, he says, yet I am not from the world, but I came to the world, that is, from above. And although I am understood to you to be a mere man, yet I came as light to shine on this human nature, those who sit in the darkness of sin.[i] For just as the sun illuminates bodies, so too do I [illuminate] souls dwelling in bodies. And just as the sun allows itself to be visible not only to the eyes of bodies but also [to] all existing things, likewise I too make not only myself[53] visible to the eyes of those who believe in me but also the Father and the Holy Spirit. Truly, then, I said: *Whoever sees me also sees* my Father, and henceforth they shall *not remain in the darkness* of ignorance of sin.[54]

i. Moše bar Kepha compares the contrast between darkness and light to that between the Old and New Testaments.

[12:47] And if anyone will[55] hear my words and not keep them, I do not judge him, because I did not come that I might judge the world but that I might save the world.

He does not deny his being judge, for he himself will judge all nations on the day of judgment, as he said: *The Father does not judge anyone but gave all judgment to the Son* (John 5:22). But because **[295]** first he expounded in their ears the teaching of the faith, in accordance with *I came as light to the world,* and *Whoever believes in me will not remain in darkness* (John 12:46), and they did not then make any good response but plotted murder against him[56] in their hearts and thoughts, after that he set down the threats of reproof that were appropriate to their wicked thoughts.

It is not for now, he said, to judge them in accordance with their impiety; there is one who will judge you. Not now in the world, he said, because I came for the sake of your salvation to announce to you[57] the faith, whereby you are saved from torments. By that he demonstrates his pardoning and lack of vengeance and acquiescence that perchance[58] they might convert and become

---

53. **Myself:** om. M.
54. **Of sin:** om. M.
55. **If anyone will,** NZ: "whoever will not," M.
56. **Against him:** om. M.
57. **To you:** om. M.
58. **Perchance:** "and not," M.

useful. But by not heeding and not believing in this true teaching, although here I do not judge you, yet there is one who will judge you at the resurrection, at the time of judgment, when it will be the time not of teaching and faith but of judgment and retribution.

[12:48] **Whoever dishonors me and does not receive my words, there is one who will judge him. The word that I have spoken, that will judge him on the last day.**

See how simply he expounded the word in their ears and ascribed to himself the judgment and retribution, and also set forth the time when in the tribunal all nations will be gathered: *The word that I spoke with you will judge you*, because that alone do you frequently allege as cause that I am opposed to the Father. Now my word that I spoke often, *I did not come of my own but from the Father* (John 7:28; cf. 8:42), and *Whoever believes in me does not believe in me but in the one who sent me* (12:44), will be for a testimony and condemnation and rebuke of your denial on the day of retribution, you who always **[296]** merely fabricate excuses for your error, [alleging] that I am opposed to the Father and not of one will and thought [with him].

[12:49] **For I did not speak of my own self; but the Father who sent me, he gave a command, whatever I should say and[59] whatever I should speak.**

All the teaching that he performs he ascribes to the Father, since just as his coming to this world [was] not of himself but he was sent by the Father, likewise the teaching was not of himself but rather commanded by the Father. And he wishes to correct in every way their crooked thoughts and to make it secure on all sides from those who said he was opposed to the Father. Do not be surprised that he so often repeats the saying, because he was about to go to the cross, and after that he would no longer be teaching them. Here, as[60] often, he confirmed in their hearts the mystery of the single will of his nature and of his authority.

[12:50a] **And I know that that commandment is life everlasting.**

You do not know the power of the word that the Father commanded, but I know that it grants eternal life to those who receive and follow it with true

---

59. **And**, NZ: "or," M.
60. **As**: om. M.

faith. And no longer is death able to injure or seize them, because behold, in the future age[i] they will inherit indestructible life with inalienable joy.

i. The six ages of the world and the future age to come are common themes in early Armenian writers; see Thomson 2001 (40); *Teaching* 667–71.

[12:50b] **So what I speak, as the Father spoke to me, thus do I speak.**

Even if not by me, be put to shame at least by the Father, on hearing his words. For in no other way do I speak than what the Father commanded; for just as the salvation of the world is pleasing to the Father, it is also pleasing to me, because we both have one and the same will. [**297**] So cease from your vain suppositions, calling me opposed to the Father, and turn and save yourselves from infinite torments.

[Exhortation][61]

The wretched and miserable Jews are really worthy of lamentation, since he made so much effort to save and rescue them, and for their salvation he had such concern, even to estimating them above all [other] nations, as he said: *I was sent nowhere except to the lost*[62] *sheep of the house of Israel* (Matt 15:24). On its behalf he demonstrated myriad signs and miracles, yet they were perpetually stubborn and forced themselves to denial, and were always armed to oppose their own Savior, declaring him to be merely a man opposed to God, and also a deceiver and perverter of the people. Some of them even promised to become teachers in order to deceive and captivate the minds of the people. O impudent wickedness of those who thought to destroy the teaching of the true teacher and to create their own error. Let us see, in accordance with their habitual and familiar examples, how great is their effrontery, that those empty of good deeds through their transgressions should claim to illuminate others; or that one preoccupied with[63] bodily passions should promise to heal others; or one weighed down by loads of evil sin to lighten others' load of sin; or one devoid of sense to teach another; or one gone astray through impiety to provide guidance to others.

So most appropriate for their case is the following saying: *When a blind one leads a blind one,* [**298**] *they both stumble* (Matt 15:14; Luke 6:39). These

---

61. **Exhortation,** *Yordorak*: not in the text of N, but printed as a header; *Yk* in the margin of M.

62. **Lost:** *moloreals* (lit. "gone astray"), N; "destroyed," *koruseals*, MZ.

63. **Preoccupied with,** *graweal*: "captivated by," *gereal*, M.

ones have destroyed themselves and many [others] in inescapable abysses; for shutting the eyes of their minds to the rays of the knowledge of God, they have made themselves heirs of eternal darkness. For *they loved darkness more than light*, in accordance with the Lord's saying, *because their works were evil* (John 3:19). Therefore they will remain without a response on the day of the future judgment, when their works are finished and the truth reigns, in accordance with the Lord's saying to them: *Unless I had come and spoken, they would not have had any sin; but now there is no reason for their sin* (John 15:22).

But let us, beloved, preserve in ourselves the good tradition of the unsullied faith of the Holy Trinity; let us walk in the light of the divine rays that came to cast on earth the fire of the faith. Let us fan the spark of faith[64] through virtuous conduct; let us walk in its light before the arrival of darkness, lest the shadows of death overtake us in the night of sin. For if death seizes us in the middle of the night (Luke 12:20), then we shall be tormented in inescapable darkness; but if it arrives in the daytime, then we shall shine with permanent light. Consequently, let us take heed for ourselves, let us order our lives, let us create virtues, let us preserve purity, let us persist in fasting, let us spend time at prayer, let us be spurred to mercy, let us be inclined to modesty, let us be reconciled with enemies, let us love the hateful.

With love let us serve each other, let us lighten each other's load, let us purify our hearts from wicked thoughts, let us expunge rancor from our souls, let us turn laziness to zeal, let us cast out debauchery [299] and bring in love for the poor, so that we may pluck out the thorns of sin from the roots and make the flowers of virtue bud and sprout in our souls, so that we may separate ourselves from those who continually burn with unrepentant evils. Let us stand aside from breaking oaths and brigandage, let us totally kill fornication in the body, let us reprove all demonic error and never be found in the company of the impious; for there is no mingling of light with darkness, nor of righteousness with impiety. Likewise doves do not flock with crows, nor lambs with wolves, just as angels do not dwell with demons.

But let us make ourselves sober, let us vie with the virtuous, let us endure with the ascetics and also imprint all forms of virtue on ourselves, whereby our bodies are saved and our souls illuminated, and both inherit the title of heavenly adoption. For we must not only examine the evils committed specifically by us but also investigate our thoughts and reckon our vain words and review our unseemly reflections. Therefore while it is still day, let us bestir ourselves with good deeds, so that when standing before the fearsome tribunal we there shed the terrors of the awesome judgment; so that we may

---

64. **Of faith**: "of the word of faith," M.

flee public shame and save ourselves from the poisonous worms. Let us free ourselves from the gloomy and tangible darkness, and save ourselves from the evil-smelling cold of Tartaros, lest the flaming Gehenna consume us, the roar of the fiery rivers terrify us, and the perpetual burning of the furnace consume us. For we have no one there to help, no friends, no acquaintances, nor can the saints assist or the righteous provide salvation; neither do fathers have pity [300] or brothers mercy, because it is the day of retribution, not the day of acceptance (Rom 11:15).

So let us separate ourselves from those on the left-hand side; and joining the group on the right-hand side let us strip ourselves so that we may become worthy to see the desirable light of the Godhead, from whom the just will receive the unfading crowns and shadowless illumination and ineffable blessings. And with them may we also be worthy of such grace from Christ Jesus our Lord, with whom to the Father almighty and the renewing Spirit be glory, *honor, and authority, now and always and forever and ever.[65] Amen.

---

65. **Honor ... ever:** "now [and] forever," M.

[13:1a] **Before the Feast of the Passover, Jesus knew that his hour had arrived[1] that he might depart from this world[2] to the Father.**

The evangelist did not say that he knew now what he had not known previously, as if by some happenstance but not by foresight.[i] He had even known the death of Lazarus despite being absent and had often predicted about himself to the disciples. But he said this because of the feast being imminent at which he was to endure the torments of the cross, and death and resurrection and ascension. Therefore he mentioned his departure from the world to the Father, just as indeed happened after his resurrection and the strengthening of the disciples.

    i. This is the argument of Moše bar Kepha and Dionysius bar Salibi (*John*, 241).

[13:1b] **He loved his own who were in the world; he loved them to the end.**

He loved his own who were in the world in order to make clear that also among the dead were his friends, like Abraham, Isaac, Jacob, the prophets.[i] [301] But what does *He loved them to the end* mean? It indicates[3] that he always loved them, but that at the time when he was about to leave them, he loved them to the end, when he taught them so much and confirmed and consoled them, and promised the descent of the Holy Spirit, and said about himself: *Again you shall see [me], and your hearts shall rejoice, and no one will take your[4] joy from you* (John 16:22). See how these sayings are a demonstration of love. So truly he said: *He loved them to the end.*

    i. John Chrysostom, *Hom. Jo.* 70.1, here refers to Abraham, Isaac, Jacob, and those

---

1. **Had arrived**: *haseal ē*, NZ; *haseal*, M.
2. **From this world**: *yašxarhē ast*, M (*yašxarhē asti*, Z); "from the world," *yašxarhē*, N.
3. **It indicates**: om. M.
4. **Your**: om. M.

similar to them; Moše bar Kepha adds the righteous, while Dionysius bar Salibi, *John*, 241, refers to Abraham and the just. Dionysius makes it explicit that those in the world are the apostles, as also Taťewacʿi, 544.

[13:2] And when the supper took place, Satan had put into the heart of Judas [son] of Simon, Iscariot, to betray him.

By saying, *when supper took place*, he indicates another supper after the lamb.[i] Before he washed the feet of the disciples, *Satan had put* the plan of betrayal *into the heart of Judas*. The Lord was so compassionate and long-suffering that he came to table with him, and even washed his feet as well[5] with the other disciples, and in no way deprived him of honor,[ii] perhaps to cause him to relent from such wicked plans.

i. Moše bar Kepha says that this was the Pascha that Christ wished to eat, referring to Luke 22:15. Dionysius bar Salibi, *John*, 242, mentions Moše but notes that "others say this was after the Pascha."

ii. Moše bar Kepha notes that Judas was not ashamed to have his feet washed, despite his plot.

[13:3] Jesus knew that the Father had given everything into his hands and that he had come from God and would go to God.

Again here too we shall not say that he knew only then [knowledge] that he had not previously possessed. Nor: *The Father had given everything into his hands*, as if he acquired what he had not previously possessed; as he himself said: *Everything that the Father has is mine* (John 16:15), and *I and my[6] Father are one* (10:30), and again, *I came from the Father, and I shall go to the Father* (16:28). One must understand such coming and returning not as of bodily beings but as indivisibly and inseparably in accordance with their indivisible nature.[i] He endured this in accordance with what was pertinent to the body and the needs of the time.

i. John Chrysostom, *Hom. Jo.* 70.1, stresses that the coming and going are not to be interpreted in a human manner. Moše bar Kepha also refers to the single nature, will, and power of Christ and the Father; Dionysius bar Salibi, *John*, 242, refers to the single will and power.

---

5. **As well:** om. M.
6. **My,** M (= Z): "the," N.

[302] [13:4–5] He rose from the supper and set [aside] his garments, and taking up a towel put it on. And then, taking water he poured it into a basin, and began to wash the feet of the disciples and to clean[7] them with the towel with which he had girded himself.

He teaches them an example of love and humility[8] in many forms, with such service: first to set aside his garments[9] and to put on a towel. Then he himself poured the water into the basin and after washing even cleaned [their feet].[i] Not only does he teach multifaceted humility,[ii] but [he] also strengthens their heels against the original poison of the serpent who was always attending the heel of human nature (Gen 3:15b).[iii] Strengthened by this they will fearlessly *trample on snakes and scorpions* (Luke 10:19) in order to subdue the power of the enemy.

i. Tat'ewac'i, 546, discusses why Christ washed the disciples' feet and not any other limb.

ii. Humility is stressed by John Chrysostom, *Hom. Jo.* 70.2; and Dionysius bar Salibi, *John*, 243.

iii. Dionysius bar Salibi, *John*, 243, refers to trampling the head of the serpent (Gen 3:13a).

[13:6] He came to Simon Peter, and he said to him: Lord, will you wash my feet?

It seems to us that first he washed [the feet] of Judas, and next in order he came to him;[i] for this was an example of humility, that the greatest not be jealous of the honor of the least. As for Peter's saying, *Lord, will you wash my feet?* it means that you, who purified lepers and illuminated the blind and raised the dead, and [performed] innumerable other wonders, do you wash my feet?

i. John Chrysostom, *Hom. Jo.* 70.2, states that Jesus washed the feet of Judas first. Išodad and Dionysius bar Salibi (*John*, 243) indicate that this was in order to shame Judas.

[13:7–8a] Jesus answered him and said: Whatever I do, you do not now know; but you shall know later. Peter said to him: You shall not ever wash my feet.

He showed him that *now you do not know* at all the purpose I have in washing your feet, or the help that I provide you, whereby you learn [303] the

---

7. **To clean,** *srbel*, M: "cleaning," *srbeal*, N ("cleaned," *srbēr*, Z).

8. **An example of love and humility,** N: "humility and an example of love," M.

9. **Garments:** sg. M.

role of humility and love, which is the summit of the virtues and mother of blessings. When, indeed, would they know that or what [it is]? *Then will you know*: when I ascend to heaven, when the Holy Spirit descends on you and recalls to you what has happened and the things taught by me.[i]

i. Based on John 14:26.

[13:8b–9] Jesus replied to him and said: Unless I wash you, you will have no share with me. Simon Peter said to him: Not only my feet, but also my hands and my head.

For him the refusal to have his feet washed was a mark of respect for his teacher, and his agreement was a token of no small love. Beautifully did Peter come to both, to refusal and acceptance. In the first case he regarded himself as unworthy for his feet to be washed by those wonderful hands, and in the second he was afraid lest, having then refused, he might not have a share of love with him.[i]

i. Here John Chrysostom, *Hom. Jo.* 70.2, notes Peter's fear of being separated from the Lord, as do Moše bar Kepha and Dionysius bar Salibi (*John*, 244).

[13:10a] Jesus said to him: The one washed has no need save that he wash his feet, for he is clean in every way; and you are clean.

Because Peter said, *Not only my feet, but also my hands and head*, the Lord replied and said: *For the one washed there is no need to wash hands and head; and you are clean.* So if you are clean, you must understand my washing your feet, that is, the very least and most unworthy members of your bodies,[i] which is the most humble and lowliest of all [tasks], so that you too might have the same example for humility toward each other. He said also that they were *clean*, and in what way? Behold, not in accordance with the virtue of their lives were they yet purified, because the punishments of sin and of the curse had not yet been lifted before the cross, whereby he removed both. **[304]** But as a reason for their being clean he spoke about their reception of the word of the faith and their following him, indicating that now you are clean of the impurities of the Jews.[ii]

i. That the feet are the least honorable limbs is stated by John Chrysostom, *Hom. Jo.* 70.2.

ii. Dionysius bar Salibi, *John*, 245, refers to them being free of the errors of the Jews, the clean being those who received the word of Jesus and believed.

[13:10b–11] **But not all. Because he knew the one who would betray him, therefore he said: Not all.**

He informed them in advance what would occur and who was going to betray him, revealing his all-seeing power and also his immeasurable mildness regarding the one whose feet he had washed, whom he had brought to table, and whose name he had not uttered with reproach. Why, then, was this, save to prevent his creating a pretext for hatred and deception by expelling him from the disciples?

[13:12–14] **And when he had washed their feet, he took up his garments and reclined once more. And he said to them: Do you know what I have done for you? You call me Lord and teacher,[10] and you call [me that] well, because I indeed am. So then, if I, Lord and teacher, washed your feet, you too must wash each others' feet.**

When he had washed, then he explained the reason to them. But he did not say, I your Lord and teacher washed, as if thereby making some boast about himself, but *You call me Lord and teacher*, that is, what in accordance with the many signs and teaching you call [me], and it is true. But if I as Lord so humbled myself, and you are servants, I the teacher, you the pupils, then what humble love must you have toward each other,[i] on my example?[ii]

  i. Here Dionysius bar Salibi, *John*, 245, refers to Christ giving an "example," *twps'* (*typos*), of humility. For the interpretation of Christ's humility as an antidote to Adam's pride, see Mathews and Sanjian 1991 (156).
  ii. **On my example:** *awrinak inj linelov.* The grammar, with a dative *inj*, is unclear.

[13:15] **For I gave you an example, so that just as I did to you, likewise you also should do.**

As if to say that whoever is[11] the greatest among you [305] will be humble to the younger, so that whoever is the least perchance may do[i] the same, and there never be passion among you for pride or presumption. For just as pride begets hatred and enmity,[12] so too does humility [beget] love and unanimity, since that is the mother of all virtues.

---

10. **Lord and teacher**, MZ: "teacher and Lord," N.
11. **Is:** om. M.
12. **Hatred and enmity:** tr. M.

i. **May do**: the verb in MN is 2d pl., but the subject is sg.

[13:16] **Amen, amen, I say to you: A servant is not greater than his master, nor the one sent greater than the one who sent him.**

What then means what he said, save that he was strengthening them by indicating to them that *you call me lord and teacher*, and you are servants and disciples? So no more must you be presumptuous and refrain from the things I did, but [you must be] even more humble, like a servant compared to a master, and a pupil compared to a teacher.

[13:17] **If you knew this, you would be even more blessed if you were to do this.**

If you were to understand thus in accordance with the example, you would be productive toward each other and would receive the recompense of blessedness, because those who were instructed are not blessed, but those who have made their pupils fruitful.

[13:18] **I do not speak concerning you all, because I know whom I have chosen. But so that the scripture might be fulfilled: The one who ate bread with me created deceit for me.**[13]

Because he imparted instructions of humility and love to them all, he also noted through the prophecy the one who[i] would not obey him. Therefore he repeats it and recalls the prognostication of the prophet so they might know that nothing is unknown to him[14] of the things that will occur; [306] and also that they might understand that he who knew so far in advance his wicked plot in no way recompensed him as he deserved but even washed his feet,[ii] so that they might have the same long-suffering with regard to their enemies.

i. **The one who**: sg., but the following verb is pl.
ii. Here Moše bar Kepha explicitly names Judas.

---

13. Ps 40:10.
14. **Unknown to him**, N: "hidden," M.

[13:19] Consequently I say to you, that when it shall occur, you will believe that I am [he].

He indicates to them that it would not have been at all difficult for me to hide what would be done by the betrayer. But therefore I told you, so that *when it shall occur* you will recall that nothing was hidden[15] by me that would occur.

[13:20] Amen, amen, I say to you: Whoever receives whom I shall send receives me. And whoever receives me receives the one who sent me.

By this he strengthens and encourages them not to be saddened because of being called servants and pupils, for this will not be for you any contempt or dishonor, but because of it you will be revered so that they may obey you all the more. For whoever receives[16] you receives me, being my disciples; and whoever receives me through your preaching, through me also receives my Father.

[13:21] When Jesus had said this, he was troubled in his soul. He testified and said: Amen, amen, I say to you, one of you is to betray me.

When he said, They will obey[i] you,[17] *and those who receive you receive me and also through me the Father*, then Judas removed himself from such blessedness and great[18] honor. He had not repented through the washing of the feet, nor by his making him a participant[ii] in his body and blood. *He was troubled in his soul* and next related to his disciples the circumstances of the betrayal, which was then about to happen.

i. **They will obey:** *hnazandeloc' en.* There is no reference here in John's Gospel to obedience, but in his commentary to vv. 4–5 just above Nonnus refers to Luke 10:19, the commissioning of the seventy disciples. Here he may be referring to the following verse: "[the spirits] will obey you."

ii. **Nor by his making him a participant:** *ew oč' hałord arneloy zna.* No subject is given for the infinitive, though Jesus is implied, and it should be in the instrumental, not the genitive, case. The sense seems to be that Judas was unrepentant, even after having his feet washed and participating in the bread and wine; see the commentary to v. 26, below. The

15. **Hidden:** "not hidden" (double negative), M.
16. **Receives,** M: "will receive," N.
17. **You:** + "and will receive you," M.
18. **Great,** *mecagoyn,* N: "supreme," *cayragoyn,* M.

body and blood/bread and wine are not mentioned by John, but see Matt 26:26–27, and parallels in Mark and Luke.

[307] [13:22] The disciples looked at each other, confused about whom he might be speaking.

Because they believed the word of the Lord that he spoke, they consequently had no little doubt in themselves and grief.

[13:23] And there was one of the disciples[19] reclining beside Jesus, whom Jesus loved.

Who, then, would this be, if not the evangelist John himself?[i] Therefore he did not introduce his name in saying *whom Jesus loved*, lest he testify something so grandiose about himself. In the same fashion Paul spoke about himself: *I know a man snatched up to heaven and to paradise* (2 Cor 12:2–4).[ii] For it is appropriate for the saints to speak thus about themselves and never to boast about themselves or say anything too elevated.

i. This identification is found in all the commentators. Tat'ewac'i, 552, gives reasons why John was loved, including his relationship to Jesus as nephew (*k'uer ordi*); see the apocryphal *History of James and John* (*Ankanon Girk'*, III, 449–52), which informs us that James and John were sons of Salome, a daughter of Joseph and thus step-sister to Jesus. Nersēs of Lambron's *Commentary on the Dormition of John* also provides this information.

ii. John Chrysostom, *Hom. Jo.* 72.1, notes that the evangelist was writing about himself, as was Paul, but withheld his name so as not "to appear boastful" (*philokompein*).

[13:24–25] Simon Peter nodded to him to ask who it might be about whom he spoke. And the one lying on his breast said: Lord, who might it be?

He indicates that Peter made his request to John not through a word[20] but by nodding, because deeds were less susceptible to doubt. Therefore John, being closer, asked who it might be.

---

19. **Of the disciples**, NZ: om. M.
20. **A word**, N: "words," M.

[13:26a] **Jesus answered and said: It is the one for whom I shall dip a morsel and give it.**

He still does not provide a name but through a sign indicates the arrogance of his inflexibility. Neither by the washing did he feel ashamed, nor by receiving the bread from his hands, but [he] was stubbornly impassioned in his error.

[13:26b] **And dipping the morsel, he gave it to Judas Iscariot.**

He said this in order to indicate that the one to whom he said he would give the morsel was Judas Iscariot and not Judas brother of Jacob.

[308] [13:27a] **And after the morsel, then Satan entered into him.**

This was to predict that although he previously had that evil plan, yet after the morsel *[Satan] entered*, in order to say that he revealed the wickedness that once he concealed. Satan controlled him after he separated from the Lord, especially when he offered bread to him, that is, his own body, which great grace and honor he rejected.[i] From then onward he removed his support, and therefore Satan controlled him in accordance with Paul's saying: *Whoever eats unworthily eats judgment for himself* (1 Cor 11:29). Therefore illnesses and afflictions rule, but death also often occurs.

i. Išodad distinguishes the common bread on the table, given to Judas, from the bread of the mysteries; and Dionysius bar Salibi, *John*, 249, distinguishes the "bread," *lḥm'*, used for the morsel, from the unleavened bread. Tat'ewac'i, 553, states that the morsel was not from the Lord's body but from the bread on the table, which they later ate.

[13:27b] **Jesus said to him: Now, what you are about to do, do quickly.**

He indicates to him: Since you did not restrain yourself to come to correction, after my pardoning you so often for the wicked plans of which I had foreknowledge, so whatever you wish to do, *do quickly*; no one will prevent you against your wishes. This is a sure sign that he said to John that he would give the morsel to the one who would betray him. And why to John alone did he say that? Because after that the other disciples were not excusing him anymore, especially Peter, who in the midst of that great multitude wounded with a sword the high priest's servant on behalf of his teacher.[i] Was not then absolutely death planned for Judas? This the following makes clear.

i. John 18:10, where the servant is named Malchus. He is not named in the accounts of the other evangelists: Matt 26:51; Mark 14:47; Luke 22:50.

[13:28–30] This none of those at table understood, for what purpose he had spoken to him. For some reckoned because Judas kept the bag, he had told him: Buy something that might be[21] necessary [309] for us at the feast, or that he should give something to the poor. And he, taking the morsel, went out immediately; and it was night.

He refers to his going out to the Jews in order to betray the Lord. But he also adds: *It was night*. The evangelist wishes to indicate the immeasurable effrontery and shameless wickedness of Judas, who did not even allow the light to shine but hastened at night to carry out the plan of his wicked folly.[i]

i. Moše bar Kepha and Dionysius bar Salibi (*John*, 251) stress the betrayal as a work of darkness. Tat'ewac'i, 553, notes that darkness is a time of evil.

[13:31] And when Judas had gone out, Jesus said: Now has the son of man been glorified, and God glorified in him.

Note here his sublime service. For when Judas went out to betray him to the Jews, the hour of his torments was near, which he had predicted about himself. And why did he say, *son of man*?[i] The one whom they supposed to be only[22] a son of man, he hands himself over to torments, and because the disciples were grieving and doubtful, since they realized that he was about to leave them. So he began to give helpful commands and to remove from their hearts the doubt and fear they had. Jesus said, *Now has the son of man been glorified*; that is, at the time when they will reckon him handed over to torments and death and a myriad insults, now he is glorified. But you must not be sad and grieve, but rejoice and be glad, because the torments and death are indications of glory. Then, he says, the luminaries will be darkened, and the dead will arise, and all creatures will announce that I am Son of God,[ii] whereby many have believed him to be Son of God. And God is glorified in me, through my being made known to the world.

i. Dionysius bar Salibi, *John*, 251, defines "son of man" as the body in which Christ was the second Adam.

ii. These signs are also noted at this point by Theodore of Mopsuestia and Moše bar Kepha.

---

21. **Might be**, *icē*, MZ: "is," *ē*, N.
22. **Only**, *yatuk*: om. M.

[310] **[13:32a] For if God has been glorified in him, God will also glorify him in himself.**

For if God was glorified through his being made known to creatures, then God will glorify him through wonderful signs and miracles at the time of the cross, so that we might know that in their cooperative will they are one, and thus one in nature and glory.[i]

i. Moše bar Kepha and Dionysius bar Salibi (*John*, 252) here stress the identity of nature of Father and Son.

[13:32b] And immediately he will glorify him in himself.[23]

That is, before his rising from the dead, while still on the cross, or when they will suppose that their wickedness has been completed, and they have overcome him. Then fearful signs will occur, there will be darkness over the earth, tombs will be rent, the veil will be split, the dead will come out of their tombs.[i]

i. John Chrysostom, *Hom. Jo.* 72.2, refers to these signs while Christ is on the cross, echoed by Dionysius bar Salibi, *John*, 254. They are not mentioned by John, but see Matt 27:51; Mark 15:38; Luke 23:45.

[13:33] My children, for a little time I am with you,[24] **and as I said to the Jews: Where I go, you cannot come; and now I say it to you.**

Why does he here call them *children*?[i] It was to show them his excess of love, and so that they might have hope in him at the time when he was about to leave them.[ii] And since he also said, *As I said to the Jews, where I go you cannot come*, he indicates without a break the form of his love, by calling them *children*. But as for what he said to the Jews, why was he concerned for the disciples? It was for a recollection that after the events had occurred he had previously told everything.[25] Now, *You cannot come* means that the Jews, even if they were to follow me when they will be despoiled by the sword of the Romans, and their city is destroyed and their rituals uprooted, even then they cannot come to me.[iii] But you are not thus; for even if not now, yet when you will receive power from on high, **[311]** then for my name's sake you will be subjected to various torments and afflictions and imprisonment and death,

23. **In himself,** MN: om. Z.
24. **You:** + "you shall seek me," Z.
25. **Everything,** *zamenaynn*, N: "the Lord," *ztērn*, M (*sic*).

for which you will receive sublime and eternal recompense. For after my resurrection I shall be revealed again to you, before ascending to heaven.

i. Moše bar Kepha gives a number of reasons why the disciples were called "children,"
and he parallels of the use of "child." Dionysius bar Salibi, *John*, 254, among other reasons
suggests it was so that they would not think he made them equal to the Jews.

ii. Nonnus does not explain the "little time." Theodore of Mopsuestia indicates it
means the time up to the passion, and Moše bar Kepha the time up to the cross. Tat'ewac'i,
555, indicates that some say it was the time up to the cross, others say up to the ascension.

iii. Dionysius bar Salibi, *John*, 254–55, explains "where you cannot come" as Christ's
death.

**[13:34] A new commandment I give to you, that you love each other, just as
I have loved you.**

Because, when he informed them that he was about to leave them and
they could not follow him now, they were very sad, he then gave them the
commandment of love by which he renders them more steadfast by being of
one intention and will, to be encouraged and strengthened by mutual assistance when they were abandoned by their teacher. But what means: *I give you
a new commandment, that you love each other*? This commandment Moses
previously gave, but not in that way, for Moses commanded them to love their
companion[i] like themselves, which indicates kinship (Lev 19:18).[ii] But here
he told the disciples to love each other, *just as I*, he said, *loved you*. And what
means: *Just as I [loved] you*? He gave himself to death for us, as he said: *Greater
love than this no one will have, that he lay down his life for his friends* (John
15:13). And this is greatly superior to [the commandment of] Moses, which
commanded to love one's companion like oneself. But the latter lay down his
life for his friends, as he indicated to them in accordance with the same example, to lay down their lives for him in testimony of the word of life.

i. **Companion:** *ĕnker*, as Z.

ii. Theodore of Mopsuestia and Išodad state that the new commandment is to love
those of the household of faith. Moše bar Kepha does not quote Lev 19:18 but contrasts
the new commandment with the old one, "an eye for an eye and tooth for a tooth," as does
Dionysius bar Salibi, *John*, 255.

**[13:35] For in this everyone will know that you are my disciples, if you love
each other.**

Why does he give that as a marker of their being disciples, and not through
their acquiring **[312]** some astonishing miracles? But the bond of love was

the establisher of all virtues, as he said: *Do not rejoice at the fact that demons obey you but because your names are written in heaven* (Luke 10:20).[i] This he reckons their boast and glory, rather than the obedience of the demons. For he made the form of love an image for us, which he previously fashioned in accordance with his own image, because he is origin and cause and birth of all blessings.

i. Here John Chrysostom, *Hom. Jo.* 72.4, quotes the same verse.

[13:36a] **Simon Peter said to him: Lord, whither go you?**

Why, then, did Peter ask, *Whither go you?* except because he had heard the Lord say: *Where I go you cannot come*? Hence not in order to know the place did Peter ask but how he might find a way to follow[26] him, which one can appropriately learn from the responses.[i] Therefore he asked[27] Peter:

i. John Chrysostom, *Hom. Jo.* 73.1; Moše bar Kepha; and Dionysius bar Salibi, *John*, 256, all stress Peter's desire to follow Jesus.

[13:36b] **He responded to Peter: Where I go you cannot now follow me, but afterward you will follow me.**

That is, now you will deny [me], but later you will endure even the death of my cross for my sake.

[13:37] **Peter said to him: Why shall I not be able to follow you? Indeed I shall lay down my life for your sake.**

As if to say: Why did you say I cannot follow you? Surely not that I would not lay down my life for your sake with great zeal and happiness?

[13:38] **Jesus replied: Will you lay down your life for me? Amen, amen, I say to you: Before the cock crows, you will deny me three times.**

You have such an opinion of yourself, he said, confident only in the strength within you, and not from me will you look for assistance.[28] But you say you will die for my sake. *Before the cock crows you will deny me three times.*

---

26. **To follow,** *zkni gnal,* N: *ztełi gnal,* M.
27. **He asked,** *harcʿanēr,* M: *harcʿanel* (inf.), N.
28. **Assistance,** *jeṙntuutʿiwn,* N: *anjntuutʿiwn,* M (*sic*).

And not a few hours had passed [**313**] in the night when he said this: *Three times you will deny me*. And he shows that it would occur not once, as if by some chance, but three times in one hour,[i] so that his infallible foreknowledge of what would happen might be very clear.

i. John Chrysostom and Cyril of Alexandria do not mention the different account in Mark. Theodore of Mopsuestia refers to Mark 14:30 and 72, where the cock crows twice; he reconciles the two accounts by stating that the cock crowed a second time in case the first crowing was missed. Tat'ewac'i, 557, also tries to reconcile the two accounts by citing the confused crowing of groups of birds. "In one hour" does not appear in the Gospels.

[14:1] Let not your hearts be troubled, but believe in God, and believe in me.

When he said to Peter, who was the foremost[i] among them and who so loved the teacher, *You will deny me three times*, the disciples consequently suffered no little sadness and doubt. For if Peter will deny the teacher, will that not certainly happen also to us? They also thought: How will Peter deny, unless he suffer many torments and tribulations; and then will the same happen to us that we suffer similarly? Therefore he encouraged them with this: *Let not your hearts be troubled.* Then he added the example of encouragement: *Believe in God, and believe in me*, that is, in the same God, because by believing and grasping my support, you will never go astray.

i. **Foremost**: *glxaworagoyn.* The same term is applied to Peter as "head," *glux*, of the disciples in the commentary to John 20:2, 5 and 21:15a.

[14:2a] In the house of my Father there are many lodgings.

Just as he spoke to Peter after saying, *Now you are unable to follow me, but later you will come*, likewise also he bade farewell to the other disciples and said, *In the house of my Father there are many lodgings*, the safe harbor of life without sorrow, in order to say that although you are sad and in doubt, yet you cannot rapidly fly off but must participate in the contest of virtue. When I shall be raised to heaven and I send you as preachers through the whole world, after that **[314]** without doubt you will attain such lodgings.

[14:2b] Otherwise, I would have told you that I am going and preparing a place for you.

That is, the places are prepared for you, because from the beginning they were chosen[1] for the just and the holy.

[14:3a] And if I go and prepare a place for you, I shall come again and take you to me.

Those of the short-witted did not understand his words as in accordance with his previous statement. For first he said, *In the house of my Father there are many lodgings*, then, *Did I not tell you that I am going and preparing a place*[2] *for you, I shall come again and take you to me?*[3] But he indicates nothing different from that saying for those who have intelligence. So what did he mean by saying, *I go and prepare a place for you*? That is, the lodgings are prepared, but there is need of faith and works of virtue[4] before the departure from the world, so that you may be found worthy of that lodging. Furthermore, his saying, *I go and prepare a place for you*, removes their worry about torments and death that they suffered. As if to say, although I shall endure the cross and burial, yet I shall rise from the dead through my own[5] power and be raised to heaven, where your lodgings are prepared. *I shall come again and take you* indicates to them the descent of the Holy[6] Spirit, by whose coming they were perfectly illuminated with virtue and made worthy of the sorrowless and inseparable lodgings of heaven.

[14:3b–4b] For where I am, there you also will be;[7] and you will know the way.

[315] Why, then, did he repeat so much *the way*, save to confirm them in the previous teaching that he had spoken about the lodgings,[8] *And I shall come and take you to me*, so that the way might be even clearer for them that would lead them to the lodgings, by informing about the virtues and

---

1. **They were chosen**: sg. verb.
2. **A place**: om. M.
3. **To me**: om. N.
4. **Virtue**: pl. M.
5. **Own**, *ink'nakan*, N: "self-willed," *ink'nakam*, M.
6. **Holy**: om. N.
7. **The lemma omits v. 4a.
8. **Lodgings**: sg. M.

endurance according to his own saying: *How narrow and straight is the way that leads to life?*[i]

    i. Paraphrase of Matt 7:14.

[14:5] Thomas said to him: Lord, we do not know where you are going, so how shall we know the way?

Because the Lord merely said to them, *You will know the way*, therefore Thomas, thinking in accordance with straightforward understanding, responded: *As we do not know where you are going, how shall we be able to know the way?*

[14:6a] Jesus said to him: I am way and truth and life.

I am astonished at these lofty teachings, how perfectly he brings [them] to[9] correction in very few words: *I am [the] way*, indicating himself, through the faith that he taught; *way*,[i] leading them where he himself was to go[10] and to *illuminate every man who would come into the world* (John 1:9). As for *truth*, truthfully the gifts and lodgings have all been described to you and to all who believe in me. And *life*, although you will endure torments and death, yet I shall raise you up and grant immortal *life* in the lodgings that are in the house of my Father.

    i. Neither in the lemma nor in the commentary do the nouns "way," "truth," and "life" have a demonstrative suffix, the Armenian equivalent of the Greek definite article. Nor does the Syriac here indicate the presence or absence of a definite article.

[14:6b] No one comes to the Father except through me.

When he said, *I am way*, he showed them again another mystery of salvation and **[316]** life. Just as no one journeys, he said, from place to place except on a road, likewise no one comes to the Father, that is, knows the Father to be Father and Creator, *except through me*; *nor will you know to do his pleasure except through me.[11]

---

    9. **To:** om. N.

    10. **Go:** + "because through that he was to believe," M.

    11. **Nor … me:** om. M.

[14:7a] If you knew me, then you would also know my Father.

You do not perfectly know what you still need to know, since not under-standing me [to be] God of all and Creator, you [do not] confess very firmly without doubt in your most secret thoughts.[i] For if you knew this concerning me, certainly [you would know] also the Father, and thereby you would rec-ognize the equality of nature and the status of authority,[ii] and you would know me as *way* leading you to myself, just as the light of the sun shining from it inseparably allows viewers to see the whole sun with which it is united. And just as a word draws[12] those who hear it to the intention of the mind with which it is naturally united,[iii] likewise you by seeing through me would also recognize the Father, if you knew me perfectly as God by nature and Creator.

i. The grammar of this sentence is unclear. A negative with "confess" seems required.

ii. The equality of Father and Son is stressed by John Chrysostom, *Hom. Jo.* 73.2; and Cyril of Alexandria, *Comm. Jo.* 9, notes that the Son is of the *ousia* "of his begetter," *tou gennēsantos*. Dionysius bar Salibi, *John*, 257, refers to the equality of their nature, majesty, and honor.

iii. For a word being united with the mind, see the commentary to John 1:1.

[14:7b] From henceforth you will know him.

Because previously he had told them that you do not recognize the Father since you did not know me perfectly, he wished here to console them and to remove hesitation and doubt from them, and to reveal what would happen. So he said, *From henceforth you will know me*, in order to state that the hour has arrived in which you will be confirmed in the faith and you will know the Father, when the Holy Spirit will descend from above, when it will rest upon you to teach and recall everything. Then you will know the Father and see [him] with the eyes of the mind. But when Philip heard this, he did not at that moment understand the meaning of the saying, but he thought he would see the Father with the eye of the body.[i]

i. Here Moše bar Kepha contrasts the vision of the eye with the nonbodily eyes of understanding.

---

12. **A word draws,** *ban jgē*: "is high[er]," *barjr ē*, M.

[317]   [14:8] **Philip said to him: Show us the Father, and it is sufficient for us.**

By this the intention of the saying was made clear, in accordance with what we said above, because he thought such a thing. We have seen and known you, he said, but it still remains for us to see and know the Father. Therefore the Lord gave a response through which he informed him that you did not[13] know me perfectly. For if you had known the nature of my divinity, which is from the nature of the Father, how would you have asked to see the Father? Behold, *I and the Father are one* (John 10:30).

[14:9a] **Jesus said to him: Have I been with you for so long and you have not known me, Philip? Whoever has seen me has seen my Father.**

Regarding Philip's question, *Show us the Father*, it was not appropriate to say, *Whoever has seen me has seen the Father*, and not, Whoever has known me has known the Father. But lest Philip think something of the sort, although he had seen the Lord in the body, yet he knew him, and it was possible also to see the Father, he said to him: *For so long you have not known me*; for if you had known [me], you certainly would have known the Father too. It would not be possible to know or comprehend the character of the divine, uncreated, and incomprehensible nature, for that is not comprehensible even to the fiery ranks of the bodiless.[i] But it was as if to say: If you had known me as true Son, creator of creation, you would then have known the Father too, because through me, being Son by nature, the Father is known.[ii] Yet you, despite being with me for so long, did not know me.

See the testimony about himself, who knew himself and the Father, how he reveals the inseparability of their nature, being one in nature and power.[iii] Let the calumniator[iv] Arius be silent, diminishing the Son's uncreatedness to createdness. [318] Let Eunomius with his fellows be ashamed, who confess the Son to be created.[v] But let us, turning our discourse to orthodoxy, discuss the same. For we do not profess the incarnation[vi] to be in two natures, but we confess the natures became one after the ineffable union. That is clear from the Lord's saying to Philip, *Whoever has seen me has seen the Father*. So they saw the human nature, which Thomas touched after the resurrection (John 20:27). Now, if they were to say that was said about the divinity, as if to say, Whoever has known my divinity, not, Whoever has seen the humanity, to them we say as follows. Why did he not say, Whoever saw the divinity concealed in me,

---

13. **Not:** editor; om. MN.

that is, whoever believed? He was teaching them succinctly and clearly, especially because he was instructing the disciples who were still weak and ignorant, who had never been able to understand by themselves such a thing about
him,[vii] the invisible in him being greater than what they saw.

Likewise, for the Jews too it was no small reason to demonstrate[14] from
what they were saying they had envy concerning his invisible and incomprehensible divinity, and he said the visible and tangible nature was equal to the
Father.[viii] For if he had spoken something like this about himself to the Jews,
that I do not say this visible human nature, which I have taken from creatures,
is the Son of God, over which you stumble, but the divine invisible nature that
is concealed in it is the operator of signs and miracles, and for that [nature] it
is most fitting to be equal to the Father, but not the created and tangible nature
of this body—perhaps through that they would have come more easily to the
faith. So there was consequently no doubt for anyone that [319] there was one
nature[15] of Christ after the union from his two natures. The most elevated
and most humble were only accompanied by signs, but not according to any
particularity of nature.

i. *Comm. Diat.* 19.7 states that Philip expected to see the Father in the way that OT
figures saw angels and archangels.

ii. Here John Chrysostom, *Hom. Jo.* 74.1, distinguishes the *hypostaseis*, lest anyone
say he is Father, but he stresses the common *ousia*. Theodore of Mopsuestia refers to the
inseparable union and perfect communion of Father and Son, their common nature.

iii. **Power:** *zawrut'iwn*, which can also be used to mean *hypostasis*. See the introduction, xxxix, and Thomson 2001 (17).

iv. **Calumniator:** *c̆araxaws*, which often renders *diabolos*.

v. To Arius and Eunomius, Tat'ewac'i, 561, adds Sabelios and Aëtios.

vi. **Incarnation:** *tnawrēnut'iwn*, a calque of *oikonomia*. See the introduction, xxxvi-
xxxvii, for the terminology.

vii. Theodore of Mopsuestia stresses that Christ needed to teach his disciples about
his divinity.

viii. The grammar of this passage is unclear.

[14:9b] How do you say: Show us the Father?

For if *whoever has seen me has seen the Father,* because of [my] being
equal and one with the Father according to nature, how do you say: *Show us
the Father?* So you did not know me, despite my being with you for so long;
for if you had truly known this, you would not have asked me to show you the

14. **Demonstrate,** *c̆ucʻanel,* M: "diminish," *c̆acucʻanel,* N.
15. **One nature,** *mi bnut'iwn,* N: "unity," *miabanut'iwn,* M.

Father, because it would have been sufficient to know me. So I said well: *If you knew me, then you would have known my Father.*

[14:10] Do you not believe that I am in the Father and the Father is in me? The word that I speak with you I do not speak from myself, but the Father who dwells in me, he works the deeds.

What is this, save that he wishes Philip might say something positive, whereby he might come to perfect knowledge? Why do you ask [me] to show you the Father? This is sufficient as for one knowing, yet not knowing the Father through me, but also as not knowing me to be in the Father in equality with the Father by nature and power and cooperation,[i] and the Father in me according to his comparability. In the same fashion what I am saying *I do not say from myself,* nor is what I do of myself, because of my being in the Father and the Father in me. Hereby he confirms his inseparable unity of will with the Father. But he would not say he either spoke or did anything save only what the Father orders, because he is not understood to exist according to the condition of the body. Since the autonomous will belonged to the body, to speak and act according to the intention of his mind and will, how then was the Son not [320] able to speak or do anything of himself, being no less in his divine nature than the Father and enclosed in power? But because the Father was[16] in[17] him, it was thus the former who spoke and acted, and not the Son specifically. For just as they were inseparable by their nature,[18] so in will they were indivisible and equal.

i. Here Dionysius bar Salibi, *John,* 259, refers to the single *ousia* and notes that the Father and Son are comparable to the sun and its "radiance," ṣmḥ'.

[14:11] Do you believe me, that I am in the Father and the Father is in me? Otherwise, believe in me at least for the sake of the deeds.

When he had said to Philip, *I am in the Father, and the father is in me,* he then directed his words to them all and showed that, since you believe that I am truly Son of God, you must consequently believe all my sayings, that I and the Father have one nature and will; for the one who is Son by nature, is he not then by all means also equal in nature to his Begetter?[i] Now if these things seem to you difficult to understand, because of your still being weak, then test

---

16. **Was,** *elov,* N: "looking on," *hayelov,* M.

17. **In,** M: om. N.

18. **Nature:** pl. N.

the deeds, whereby you will comprehend the equality of power, and through
the equality of power you will be able then to understand the comparability of
nature. Then he indicated something else that was very wondrous, the honor
of the united power, which he mentioned next.

i. John Chrysostom, *Hom. Jo.* 74.2, refers here to the Father and Son being *homoou-sios*. Theodore of Mopsuestia notes that it is in his divine nature that the Son is similar to
the Father; in his humanity he could not be called similar to the Father. Moše bar Kepha
stresses the equality of nature, and Dionysius bar Salibi, *John*, 259, the equality of *ousia*.

[14:12a] **Amen, amen, I say to you, that whoever believes in me, he also will
do the works that I do and will do greater than these.**

He showed them that, because I said I would give such power and authority to you who believe in me to work in my name even superior signs and miracles than I, therefore that wonderful power and authority is of truly divine
force; as Peter (Acts 3:6) and Paul (Acts 19:12) not only through his name
healed the afflicted but also through napkins and handkerchieves worked no
less signs and miracles.

[321] [14:12b–13] **For I go to[19] the Father. And whatever you will ask in my
name, I shall do it, so that the Father may be glorified in the Son.**

As if to assure them about what I[i] earlier said, *Whoever believes in me will
also do the works that I do and even more than these*, he stated the time when
this would happen: When *I go to the Father*, when I am raised up from you,
and not as you suspect remain in the tomb like the others. For which reason at
that time you will work miracles in my name. Which indeed they did, saying,
In the name of Jesus of Nazareth arise and go,[ii] and many other such [miracles].
And when you will do all this, then you will recognize the measure of my
divine power, and consequently *the Father will be glorified in the Son*, confessing fully the single nature and power.

And whatever you will ask in my name, I shall do it. He repeats the saying,
it seems to me, because of his earlier saying *whatever you ask in my name*.[20]
Furthermore, he recalls the saying *whatever you will ask in my name, I shall do
for you*,[21] in order to make them firmer by repeating the saying, and in order

---

19. **To:** *aṙ*, NZ; *i*, M.
20. **In my name:** om. N.
21. **For you,** *jez*, N: "it," *zayn*, M.

that they might understand the previous modest and humble sayings to be for some reason but not weakness, nor that he spoke them being God.

    i. I: Nonnus frequently alternates between direct and indirect speech in his repetition of themes in the lemma.
    ii. Acts 3:36, also quoted by Dionysius bar Salibi, *John*, 260.

[14:15]²² **If you love me, you will keep²³ my commandments.**

Because he earlier said to them, *Whatever you will ask in my name, I shall do for you,*[i] lest they suppose that he would give them that grace without virtue of works, he clearly indicated to them the cause through which they would acquire the power of that grace, adding: *If you love me.* What, then, is the model of that love? The keeping of my commandment, because through that you will receive the promised gifts, but not through mere sayings or effortless virtues.²⁴

    i. **For you**: see the variant in the commentary to the previous verse.

[322] [14:16] **And I shall beg the Father, and he will give you another Consoler,²⁵ so that he may dwell with you forever.**

When you will keep my commandment, which is the sign of love for me, *I shall beg the Father* to send to you *another Consoler*, so that he may console you for the grief caused by my absence from you; but also through his power you will work even more [deeds] than those promised. Furthermore, because he said to them, *I go to the Father*, they consequently suffered no little grief and were in doubt. And since he also wished to tell them the various torments that they were to endure, he then encouraged them and therefore called the Holy Spirit *Consoler*, and was not content with the name Spirit.[i] He also indicated the particularity of the persons by saying: *I shall send you another Consoler, the Spirit of truth* (John 14:17). By saying, *another*, he distinguished the persons;[ii] but by calling him *Consoler*, because they were saddened by his absence, he made known *the equality also of the Holy Spirit, as he possessed the same power, by consoling[iii] the apostles for the grief they had because of the Lord.

---

22. Nonnus omits v. 14; see Metzger 1975, 244.
23. **You will keep**, *pahesjik'*: Dionysius bar Salibi, *John*, 260, gives an imperative form. For confusion in the Greek tradition, see Metzger 1975, 245.
24. **Sayings, virtues**: sg. M.
25. **Consoler**: *mxit'arič'*, NZ; *mxit'aričs* (pl.), M.

Now, in mentioning his begging the Father, perhaps by that he gave them greater confidence that he bore so much concern for them in himself that he would even pray, though he had no need of praying.[iv] Just as he said *When I go I shall send to you* and *As the Father sends the Holy Spirit*, but not he will come of himself, likewise he spoke about his praying, because it was still the time of service and he condescended to their weak understanding. But *He will dwell with you forever* was to show them that the Holy Spirit would not be removed from them in the same way as he had spoken about himself, nor was the Holy Spirit visibly with them as he had described *my dwelling with you.* While *forever* was [323] to indicate that the Holy Spirit remained unseparated even after their death, because He would remain always united with believers.

i. Step'annos of Siwnik', 138, quoting 1 John 2:1, indicates that the first consoler was Christ, the second was the Spirit.

ii. Dionysius bar Salibi, *John*, 260, refers to the distinction of the "persons," *qnwm'*, and notes that Our Lord was also reckoned as a "Paraclete," *p'rqlyt'*.

iii. **The equality…consoling:** The editor punctuates to give a slightly different order: "his equality, as he possessed the same power, as the Holy Spirit consoled the apostles…"

iv. **Praying:** *ałač'el*, or "beg, request," as in the lemma.

[14:17] **The Spirit of truth, whom this world cannot receive, because it does not see him or recognize him. But you know him, because he will dwell with you and be with you.**

The Consoler, whom I mentioned, is the Holy Spirit, who is *the Spirit of truth*, not like other spirits, which are not true but sometimes are.[i] And what again is the Holy *Spirit of truth*? He teaches the truth, the eternal truth, not some seeming and destructible teaching, but[26] the hidden mysteries that none of the worldly souls,[27] who are thick and fleshly, can see or recognize, since no one sees or recognizes him, but only those rarified in heart and mind and pure according to the Lord's saying: *Blessed are the pure in heart, because they will see God* (Matt 5:8). But you will recognize him, whom this world does not know, because their hearts are not pure for seeing, nor are their works worthy for recognizing. Therefore you will be found worthy of his indwelling. And lest you suppose that in some bodily appearance he will dwell with them, in his indwelling, he said, *Whom this world does not see*, in order to state that by his dwelling in you not even you will see him. And furthermore he informed

---

26. **But** (editor): "and," MN (*sic*).

27. **Souls,** *hogwoc'*, M: sg. N.

them, *He will dwell with you*, particularly with you alone, he means, not with the whole world,[ii] and *forever*, not some restricted time.

> i. Išodad here discusses spirits outside the Trinity.
> ii. Tat'ewac'i, 565, specifies: not with the wicked.

[14:18–19a] He will not leave you orphaned; I shall come to you. Yet a little more and this world will not see me; but you will see[28] me.

Because he sometimes called them children,[i] **[324]** therefore he said, *I shall not leave you orphaned*, that is, I shall not be unconcerned about your care. For although he had described to them the coming of the Spirit, they did not yet know whom they would meet[29] at the coming of the Holy Spirit. Therefore he expounded his concern for them even more firmly. Furthermore, he instructed them about another profitable advantage, indicating to them his providential power: Although I told you that I am going to the Father and shall send the Spirit to you, yet it is not the case that you will see me no more, but I shall come again soon to you, after my resurrection from the dead. And lest they suppose that his coming again would be as before the cross, his being always with them, he added, *This world[30] will not see me, but you will see*, in order to indicate: Although I shall come again, I shall appear only to you. So my coming is not to be understood like the previous coming, when going around with you I used to instruct all the people.

> i. E.g., John 13:33. Moše bar Kepha states that Jesus called them children here for the sake of consolation.

[14:19b] Because I am alive, you too will be alive.

He indicates his rapid rising from the tomb. After seeing that, he said, then you will believe without doubt regarding your own rising from the dead.[i]

> i. Here Moše bar Kepha and Dionysius bar Salibi (*John*, 262) discuss many different levels of life.

---

28. **You will see:** *tesanicĕk*, MZ; "you see," *tesanēk'*, N.
29. **They would meet:** "they met" (aor.), *handipec'an*, MN.
30. **This world**, N (= lemma): "the world," M.

[14:20] On that day you will know that I am in my Father, and you in me, and I in you.

For when I shall rise from the dead and you will see [me], not only through my being alive but also through signs and [my] appearance, then you will know me much better than you now know me, and you will be confirmed in the sayings *I [am] in the Father and the Father in me*, that I and the Father are one in nature, authority, and power.[i] Although by putting on a body I endured the conditions of human nature, even torments and death, yet I was not changed from the divine paternal [325] nature. As for saying, *And you in me*, not according to that model did he say *in himself*, like himself in the Father; but it meant: Just as I [am] in the Father in nature and authority, so also [are] you in me in faith and love.[ii] Therefore, in accordance with [my] putting on this body of kinship, I do not hesitate to call you brothers and limbs.

> i. Here Theodore of Mopsuestia and Dionysius bar Salibi (*John*, 262) stress the equality of nature.
> ii. Dionysius bar Salibi, *John*, 262, also stresses the indwelling through faith.

[14:21] Whoever has my commandments and keeps them, he it is who loves me. And whoever loves me[31] will be loved by my Father. And I shall love him and shall reveal myself to him.

When he spoke to them about the Holy Spirit, whom he said *the world did not see* but he dwelled in them, so that they would not therefore think no one would receive the grace of the Holy Spirit except them alone, he also added this: *Whoever has my commandments[32] and keeps them*, even if he were not from among you disciples, yet he loves me because of keeping my commandments; and because he loves me, *he will be loved by my Father*. And *I* too *will love him and reveal myself to him*, that is, I shall make myself known, even if he did not see me in the flesh like you because of my always being among you. And on the day of retribution, when death will no longer reign but there will be everlasting life, blessings for the righteous and torments for the sinners, then I shall compensate him for his love.

---

31. **And whoever loves me**, NZ: om. M.
32. **Commandments**: sg. M.

[14:22] **Judas said to him, not the Iscariot: Lord, why was it that you are to reveal yourself to us and[33] not to the world?**

The meaning of this saying was clear in accordance with what was said above. They did not understand what he said as applying to all who loved him, but he was thought to be speaking only about themselves.

[14:23] **Jesus replied and said: Whoever loves me will keep my word, and my Father will love him. And we shall come to him and make our lodging with him.**

Whoever loves me, he said, keeps my commandments. And my Father also loves him, and being with him we shall make him worthy[34] [**326**] of our lodging, even if such a person is not from among you and will not have seen the mystery of my dispensation in the flesh, so that thereby they may know the hope of the believers in Christ. Through them they will believe in the Son of God and thereby grasp the future hope even better. For if those who were after the believers were made worthy of that ineffable gift, what indeed will they then think regarding themselves about the sublime hope and ineffable rewards?

[14:24a] **And whoever does not love me does not keep my word.**

Just as the keeping of the commandment is[35] a sign of love for me, likewise the not-keeping of the commandment is [a sign] of not [having] love. But why does he not declare that I shall pay retribution to the one who does not keep my commandment, as to one who loves [me] and is loved by the Father, save that[36] you[37] may learn thereby the care of his limitless benevolence? And because he looks with zeal to the rewards of blessings, but by the torments he is condemned by us for his own unwilling benevolent will, to work the retributions of torments, because of being good by nature.[i]

    i. The sense of the final sentence is unclear.

---

33. **And,** MZ: om. N.
34. **Worthy:** pl. MN (*sic*).
35. **Is:** om. N.
36. **Save that,** *ayl zi: ayn zi,* N.
37. **You,** MN[corr]: "I," N.

[14:24b] **And my word that you hear is not mine but of the Father who sent me.**

Because he first said, *Whoever keeps my commandments*[38] *will be loved by my Father, and I and the Father shall come and make lodging with him,* and because he spoke of himself and of the Father, he added this: *The word that you hear,*[39] and *Whoever keeps my commandments*[40] *will be loved by my Father.* So not mine specifically is the commandment, but also the Father's. And I said, *I and the Father will come to him,* indicating that the commandment is one. For if this were not so, I would not have said to you, *What you hear*[41] *is not mine but of the Father who sent me,* and *What I say, I do not say of myself.* And because while he was teaching this, [327] the disciples had no little doubt in themselves for fear of the Jews, because of knowing that he was about to leave them, they had this supposition that they would not be able to receive all his sayings. So he said:

[14:25–26] **This I spoke with you while I was among you. But the Consoler, the Holy Spirit, whom the Father will send in my name, he will teach you everything, and he will remind you of everything that I said to you.**

See how gently he informs them of the circumstances of his leaving them: *This I spoke with you while I was among you,* in order to say that he was still to leave them. He repeats these things to show his foresight of what would later happen, and in order to render them hopeful through the descent of the Holy Spirit; also so that they might prepare themselves in advance to wait for the Holy Spirit and not be frightened at the unexpected strong blowing[i] at[42] the descent of the Spirit, but by being forewarned might grasp with rejoicing the ineffable grace that he had promised and that would occur after his ascension. He taught them actively [as] perfected and reminded them, lest they ever doubt what had been forgotten, [that] the Holy Spirit would not renew [them] again.[ii] But they had not yet rooted out from themselves their hesitation concerning fear of the Jews and were in no little apprehension about what he had said: *You will undergo torments.* After that he encouraged them, saying:

---

38. **Commandments:** sg. N.
39. **You hear,** N (= lemma): "you heard," M.
40. **Commandments:** sg. N.
41. **You hear:** "you love," M.
42. **At:** "of," M.

i. **Strong blowing**: *sastik hnč'umn*. See Acts 2:2: a "sound," *hnč'umn*, from heaven; a "mighty," *sastik*, wind.

ii. The sense of this sentence is unclear.

[14:27a] Peace I leave to you; my peace I give to you. Not as this world gives, do I give to you.

He stops them being so concerned and disconsolate in themselves about his leaving them and[43] being so frightened of their enemies. For my[44] peace that [**328**] I leave to you does not allow you to be alarmed as long as you hold firmly to faith and hope in me and in each other. Furthermore, by the command I gave, you will know each other in love, because my[45] peace is not to be understood in accordance with any peace of the world, which is close to turbulence.[i] My peace, however, is not mingled with turbulence, nor is it at all limited in time, but it permanently remains with those who love me, keeping them unshaken by all visible and invisible disturbances.

i. John Chrysostom, *Hom. Jo.* 75.5; Moše bar Kepha; and Dionysius bar Salibi, *John*, 265, give the same argument. Cyril of Alexandria, *Comm. Jo.* 10, states that the peace of Christ is the Spirit. Tat'ewac'i, 568, describes in some detail the turbulence and wickedness of this world.

[14:27b–28a] Let not your hearts be troubled or afraid. You[46] have heard that I told you that I go and shall come [again] to you.

Let not your hearts be troubled because of my leaving you for a little, since after my leaving you, in the times of your torments and death I shall rapidly bring about my return to you after the resurrection.

[14:28b] If you loved me, then you would rejoice that I go to the Father, because my Father is greater than I.

Because the disciples did not yet know him to be creator of all creatures, in that he taught them more humbly about himself and the Father in accordance with their understanding, therefore he meant that although you suppose that after the cross and burial you will not see me, [reckoning] my death to be like that of others, yet if you loved me you would have to rejoice because

---

43. **And:** + "not," N.

44. **My:** om. M.

45. **My:** om. M.

46. **You,** N (= Z): "we," M.

I said, *I go to my Father*, whom you reckon greater than I. I go so that after that you will be able to understand more sublimely about me, that I am going to one greater than I, in your opinion, who is in heaven, and after that you will have no fear or doubts about me. And so that this saying might be clear, **[329]** *My Father is greater than I*, he is not really greater than him,[i] but [only] in the suppositions of the disciples [regarding] the previous sayings by him, and also what he now said.

    i. Theodore of Mopsuestia attacks the heretics who take this remark to refer to the nature of the Son but not of the man assumed. Dionysius bar Salibi, *John*, 266, stresses the equality of the Son and Father, against the Arians.

[14:29] And now I have told you before it happened, so that when it will come about, you will believe.

    You must by all means believe in my sayings, by which I console and take care of you in order to remove the fear and doubt that you have concerning my leaving you. For it is I who am telling you about future events, one by one, about my torments and death; you are not informing me about myself. So then, unless I knew the joy without grief that you will encounter, I would not have previously told you about the sad things. But for that reason I explained in advance what would happen, so that when it will occur you will believe me to be God. For not only you but also those who through you will believe after[47] my ascension, for them also this will be no small indication by you of [my] teaching all these prognostications.

[14:30a] No longer shall I speak[48] much with you.

    Sufficient, he says, has been said. Therefore there is no need to add to it for encouragement.[i]

    i. Here in M there is a change of hand, in the middle of f. 198a, and an increase in the number of abbreviations.

---

    47. **After:** om. M.
    48. **Shall I speak,** *xawseċayċ*, editor (= Z): "I spoke," *xawseċay*, M; *xawseċa*, N.

[14:30b–31a] **The prince of this world comes and finds nothing in me. But so that the world may know that I love the Father, and as the Father commanded me, so I do.**

When he consoled them about his torments and burial with such teaching, he then related the circumstances from which all that would come. And so that they might know that not by force would he endure what he said, he remarked: *The prince of this world comes,*[i] who once ruled over them through unbelief and acts of wicked sin; and he will urge his accomplices[49] to rush me to the cross, to torments and death through the Jews, *but in me* [330] *he finds nothing.* He speaks about sin, through which in the beginning death ruled over human nature. Therefore not by right will death come upon me in accordance with the law of sin.[ii] And if this is so, then death does not really rule over me, but I suffer willingly; for he does not find a cause of sin in me whereby he condemns [me] to death.

Furthermore, the signs that were done by me previously, and those that will take place on the cross and afterward, indicate that not unwillingly do I[50] endure the torments of the cross, nor by force death, and not necessarily like other bodies and not by the power of the prince of the world, but for the sake of my love for creatures, since by my death they receive immortal life. And if my torments and death have this effect, that is my will and the will of my Father, it is that you too through my death may live, being renewed into [your] original glory.[51] So you must not be sad and fearful.

But what means: *the prince of this world?*[iii] He means someone not naturally and really having authority over this world, but he indicates the [authority] of that one who later *through deceit led them astray and ruled[52] over them by false thoughts and annulling the commandment.

    i. Here Dionysius bar Salibi (*John*, 267) and Tatʿewacʿi (570) specifically name Satan.

    ii. Dionysius bar Salibi, *John*, 267, stresses that the "nothing" of the lemma means that in Christ there is nothing of sin.

    iii. Išodad indicates that Satan was called "prince of this world" because of his rebellion. Cyril of Alexandria, *Comm. Jo.* 10, stresses that Satan is the cause of sin.

---

    49. **Accomplices**: sg. M.

    50. I: om. M.

    51. **Glory**: "life," N.

    52. **Through…ruled**: "through erring deceit ruled," M.

[14:31b] Up, arise,[53] let us go from here.

What means this? If such will be his death, as I described,[54] then we must not fear and cry alas,[55] or be indifferent, but rather be zealous and urge ourselves on to meet those who plan to kill us. I also said that the Lord consequently wished to give his disciples more commands concerning endurance in torments in accordance with the prolongation of sin. And the fear of the Jews that terrified the disciples he wished to remove from them for a while by saying: *Up, arise,[56] let us go from here* to somewhere else. And as they went, he said to them:

---

53. **Arise,** *arik'*, NZ: *ari* (sg.), M.
54. **I described:** "was described," M.
55. **Cry alas:** om. N.
56. **Arise,** pl.: sg. M; see lemma.

[331] CHAPTER 15

[15:1–2] I am the true vine, and my Father is the husbandman. Every branch that is in me and does not bear fruit he cuts off, and every one that bears fruit he trims so that it may become still[1] more fruitful.

After he had consoled and encouraged them concerning his torments and death, over which they were anxious, he also told them about his ascending to the Father and being glorified, and that he did not endure everything by brute force, nor was he guilty of death since he had not committed sin, because death ruled legally over other bodies. But because he loved the Father, whose wish was the salvation of the world through his death, he consequently instructed and advised them how they might render themselves even more worthy of his gifts. Therefore he said: *I am the true vine, and you the branch, and my Father is the husbandman.*[i] Just as the vine[2] by nature supports the upward[3] shooting of the branch, and also provides the potentiality of fruitfulness insofar as it is bound and united with it, but when it is pruned and cut [the branch] is separated from the vine and falls away,[ii] being no more useful save only for burning, in the same way, he said, you[4] too have been strengthened, as you are my bones and flesh[5] in accordance with the bodily kinship that [I] took from the Virgin.[iii]

As long as you remain firm in love for me, you will bear much fruit in virtue and in faith. But if you will not remain firm in me through faith and love, you will be separated from me and alienated.[iv] Who, then, will do this? *My Father*, he said, whose divinity and power you[6] have recognized. For he is

---

1. **Still,** *ews,* MZ: om. N.
2. **Vine:** "branch," M (*sic*).
3. **Upward:** the printed *zi ver* should be read as *z'i ver.*
4. **You:** "we," M.
5. **Flesh,** *marmin,* M: pl. N.
6. **You:** "we," M.

the husbandman who cares for his servants, the knower of their secrets and the remunerator of their[7] deeds.

    i. The quotation of the lemma incorporates v. 5a.

    ii. John Chrysostom, *Hom. Jo.* 76.1, explains the pruning as the tribulation that follows the death of Christ.

    iii. Theodore of Mopsuestia explains that believers, being the body of Christ, are thus joined to him.

    iv. Moše bar Kepha explains that without labor one cannot come to God.

[15:3] You, then,[8] are holy because of the word that I spoke with you.

When he said, *Every branch that is in me and* **[332]** *does not bear fruit he cuts off,* lest they suppose that he said that of themselves and they would be troubled and disturbed, and consequently being thrown into doubt would not reckon the power of his word[9] to be consolation and encouragement for them, he also added this: *You are holy,* he said,[10] *because of the word that I spoke with you,* that is, because of having the word of faith that I taught you.

[15:4] Remain in me, and I in you. Just as the branch is not able to bear fruit of itself unless it is firm in the vine, likewise neither [can] you unless you are firm in me.

Because he first told them, *You are holy,* lest for that reason they become lazy and unconcerned for the virtues of the law, he added this: *Just as the branch cannot bear fruit of itself, unless it is firm in the vine,* likewise you must[11] not be slothful for virtue because of being told that you are holy. For just as the branch without being firm in the vine does not bear fruit, likewise you too without my example in endurance of torments and persecution cannot be fruitful with regard to virtue for the better.

---

7. Their: om. N.

8. Then: *ardēn isk,* NZ; *ardēn,* M.

9. **Of his word:** om. N.

10. **You are holy, he said,** *asē, surb ēk',* N: "you say," *asēk',* M (*sic*).

11. **Must:** om. M.

[15:5] I am the vine, and you the branch. Whoever is firm in me and I in him, he bears much fruit, because without me you cannot do anything.

To say *[you] cannot do anything* was not that they would not be able to commit any[12] sin from then on but meant that you can do nothing good without my assistance. For if in their thick minds it was interpreted that they could not do anything except through him, why did he exhort and arouse their minds to good things for so long, and then behold, they could not do anything? Such frequent teachings would then have been superfluous. [333] Nor, just as no one can do good save through him, can he likewise do evil except through him; for the evil is opposed to the good, and the good is pleasing to God, while the evil[13] is not pleasing. Our obedience to God is good, but our rebellion evil. So through him we do not do what does not please him, as that makes us rebels from him; but we do it against his will.

What example should we give to confirm this saying? Light, without which it is impossible to see creation, *not because of its being impossible to see creation without it[14] are we unwillingly obliged to take from anyone his vision of it. For there is in us the possibility of sometimes preventing the eyes from looking at it. And again,[15] just as there is no means for us to see anything except through it, so we do not see[16] except through it. Not for that reason do we not see, because we see through it. Furthermore, since[17] as when there is no light we are unable to see anything among beings, in the same way unless [we had] vision, whereby we see the light, the light could not show us anything of beings. Likewise, although we are not able to do anything of good save through God, yet unless there was in us independent will it would not be possible for us to do anything[18] that we do except through him. And it would not be possible, although he is our God, [for him] to do anything through us, unless he had established in us independent will, whereby he leads us to action, but only if he were to change totally the form, which he would not be incapable of doing. But he does not do what is not fitting for his divinity, although he is not at all incapable [of doing] what he wills.[i]

---

12. **Any**: om. M.

13. **The evil**, M: "evil things," N.

14. **Not because ... it**: om. M.

15. **Again**: + "not," N.

16. **See**: + "it," M.

17. **Since**: om. N.

18. **Anything**: om. N.

i. The argument concerning light in this tortuous passage is unclear; the numerous variants indicate that the scribes also had difficulty in comprehending it.

[15:6] If anyone is not established in me, he goes out like the branch[19] and becomes dry. And they gather [it] and cast into the fire, and it burns.

[**334**] See, after so much consolation, how he afflicts them with threats. Likewise, he gives a small indication and demonstration of the many tribulations and destruction that were to befall the Jews, although the saying was addressed not to them but to his disciples.[i]

i. Moše bar Kepha and Dionysius bar Salibi (*John*, 271) indicate that this saying applies to the Jews, and that the fire is Gehenna.

[15:7] If you remain in me, and my words remain in you, you will ask whatever you wish, and it will be done for you.

Observe here how rapidly he introduces his consolation and then adds, *If you remain in me* according to the example that I gave, like a branch in the vine, and grasp very firmly the love and commandment that I gave, not only will you not be cast out, but as you are my disciples, whatever you request, everything will be granted[20] you: the miracles and healings that they performed in his name after his ascension to heaven.

[15:8] Then my Father will be glorified, so that you may bear much fruit and become my disciples.

This means that through your good works that I taught you many times and that you will do by being firm in me, *then the Father also will be glorified in you according to the saying:[21] Then they will see your good works and glorify your Father, who is in heaven.[i]* And that will be no small reason for great rewards to you from the Father. And in every way he will encourage and strengthen them to remain unbending in the keeping of the commandment.

i. Matt 5:16, also quoted here by Dionysius bar Salibi, *John*, 271.

---

19. **Like the branch**, NZ: om. M.
20. **Will be granted:** "he will grant," M.
21. **Then … saying:** om. M.

[15:9a] **Just as the Father loved me, I too have loved you.**

For if my Father will be glorified in you because of your good works, and I loved you as much as the Father [loved] me, then there is no need for you to withdraw and be fearful of the Jews. For if in my carrying out the will of my Father, who sent me, I endure so many torments and death for the sake of the salvation of the world, being the Son of the Father, [335] how much the more you, being disciples and servants, not only for the sake of my love for you but also for the salvation of your own selves and of the world who will believe through you, must you patiently endure tribulations and troubles.

[15:9b–10a] **Remain firm in my love. If you will keep my commandment,[22] you will remain in my love.**

For if I so loved you[23] that I laid down my life for you, then you must likewise stand firm in my love according to the example that I gave you. And what would be the sign of that love? The keeping of my commandment.

[15:10b] **Just as I have kept the commandments of my Father, and I remain in his love.**

Again in a different way he exhorts them to firmness of love. *Just as I kept the commandments of my Father*, similarly he summons them to keep the commandment, just as I kept the Father's. Why, then? Perhaps he condescends to them, because they did not yet think about him as was appropriate, although they were his disciples. Therefore he condescended to them,[i] to speak always more highly about the Father than about himself. But when he had ascended into heaven and the Spirit had come, then they recognized perfectly the status of his equality,[24] and the power of his intimacy[ii] and nature.

i. Moše bar Kepha and Dionysius bar Salibi (*John*, 272) here refer to Christ's condescending to the hearers' ability.

ii. **Intimacy:** *mtermut'iwn.* See the introduction, xxxvi, for the technical terms.

---

22. **My commandment:** *zpatuirans*, MN, which could also mean "the commandments," but "my commandment" in the commentary. "My commandments" in Z, Greek, and Syriac.

23. **You:** om. M.

24. **Status of his equality,** *zhawasarut'ean payman*, M: "his equality, status," *zhawasarut'iwnn*, *zpayman*, N.

[15:11] This I spoke with you, so that my joy might be in you, and your joy might be full.

He then revealed the reason for the teaching that he was imparting to them at that moment. It was, he said, to encourage you and to describe in advance what would come about, and to confirm you in my love and works, whereby *the Father is glorified* in you, so that through all that you might become my disciples, whereby my joy remains in you, and you might receive the gifts of your reward, **[336]** through which your joy remains full and complete for unending ages.

[15:12] This is[25] my[26] commandment, that you love each other, as I loved you.

He does not lay down the commandment as something new, although he fashions his remarks in that way. But see the meaning of the saying. The law also commanded the same, but not in the same way. For there it commanded to love one's neighbor as oneself, but here even to lay down one's life for the loved one, which he himself did.[i] Therefore he said: *Just as I loved you.* And if there is such a distinction between me, who am lord and teacher, and you, who are disciples and servants, yet I laid down my life for you, what must you endure, not only for me but also for yourselves and the faithful?[ii]

> i. Here Moše bar Kepha refers to Matt 7:12; 22:40; Rom 13:10.
> ii. *Comm. Diat.* 19.13 has the disciples say: "How can we, being equals, love each other just as you as master loved us, your servants?"

[15:13] Greater love than this has no one, that he lay down his life for his friends.

When he commanded them concerning loving each other as he loved them, then he revealed the form of his love, and that he was about to lay down his life for them so that they might act according to his example and also might understand that he would endure death for the sake of the love that he had for them, and that he was not forcibly condemned to the torments of the cross.

---

25. **Is**, NZ: om. M.
26. **My**, NZ: "the," M.

[15:14] **You are my friends, if you will do what I command you.**

The commandment that I imposed on you, if you perform it, that it is that makes you my friends. For although I explained to you the cause that makes you and all believers in me firm in me, yet there is nothing more honorable than loving each other according to the example that I gave you, by laying down my life for you.

[15:15] **I shall not call[27] you servants, because the servant does not know what his master does. But I shall call you friends, because I shall make known to you what I heard from my Father.**

[337] When he revealed that his love for them was so great that he would no longer call them servants but friends, he gave another even[28] higher sign that was superior to the others: *What I heard from the Father*, I told you, and I revealed what you are able to comprehend but not what you are unable to comprehend up to the time of your death. Just as he said above, *I have much to speak to you, but you are not able to endure it now, but when the Holy Spirit will come he will teach everything* (John 16:12–13), likewise he said concerning the servant: *The servant does not know what his lord does.* *He is not ignorant of the deeds, he said, that his lord does,[29] but he means even if he were to know, yet he knows in his understanding only, not by participation and equality like friends and dear ones.[i] Thus he shows and reveals to them the power of the grace that they were to receive, being coworkers through signs and miracles in his name.

i. Theodore of Mopsuestia and Išodad state that servants do learn something, but not equally with friends.

[15:16a] **You did not choose me, but I chose you.**

He gives them this third token of love for them in order to show them: *I chose* and loved you, and made [you] worthy of such sublime[30] honor and authority. *You did not choose me* and through your request become worthy of such superior grace, so that having understood they might comprehend the benefits of his love and of the limitless gifts they were to receive.

---

27. **I shall call**, *kočec'ic'*, N: "I called," *kočec'i*, M; "I call," *kočem*, Z.

28. **Even**: om. M.

29. **He is not … does**: om. N.

30. **Sublime**: om. N.

[15:16b] And I imposed on you that you should go and become fruitful, and your fruit should remain. And whatever you will ask from my Father in my name, he will give you.

For as I told you, I implanted you in me like the branch in the vine, so that **[338]** you might be always fruitful, which will not occur in your own time[i] like the pattern of other fruits.[31] But you will be always fruitful through the preaching of the gospel, whereby you will be made worthy by the Father of the fulfillment of all the requests that you may make in my name. They did indeed receive the power of the grace for the working of miracles and signs that they performed in his name.

> i. **In your own time:** i.e., at only a given time in the year's cycle.

[15:17] This I command, that you love each other.

When he had revealed to them his love for them and that he would even[32] lay down his life for them, and had made them worthy of his mysteries that they had heard from the Father, and that he had so chosen them that he had established them in himself like the branch in the vine in order to make them always fruitful, whereby they became worthy of such powers as they afterward received from on high, he then added to the same the commandment about loving each other:[33] *This I command you, that you love each other.* This was in order to state that making you worthy of such grace is not for the sake of requesting[34] that you receive praise as a reward,[i] or of any other such things, but rather so that in accordance with this example you too might love each other, which is the fulfillment of the entire commandment.

> i. The grammar of this part of the sentence is unclear.

[15:18] If the world hates you, know that[35] previously it hated me.

When with so many examples he often spoke to them about his love for them, laying down his life for them and making them worthy of so much

---

31. **Fruits:** om. N.

32. **Even:** om. M.

33. **Commandment about loving each other,** *zsiroyn zmimeans patuirn,* N: "the details of the love," *zsiroyn hangamans,* M.

34. **Of requesting:** om. N.

35. **That:** *zi,* NZ; *etē,* M.

honor and grace, he then described the tribulations and troubles they would later endure, with the remembrance of his love. He described this so that they would know he would not be unconcerned for them during such times, when they would endure those things from all nations.[i] [339] Furthermore, that would be not for their detriment but for their great advantage and profit. For if it would be at all to their detriment, he would not allow those things to fall[36] upon them in accordance with his measureless love that he had mentioned. Also it would be no small boast for them in imitation of the Lord, that the world would hate them. They were not only consoled by this but also realized the great hope of reward in being equal with him in tribulations.

i. Here John Chrysostom, *Hom. Jo.* 77.2, refers to the persecution of Christ's followers, which is echoed in Dionysius bar Salibi, *John*, 274.

[15:19] **If you were of the world, the world would indeed love its own.[37] But because you are not of the world, therefore this world[38] hates you.**

Consequently, he said, you must not be sad and sorrowful because of the world hating you; but rejoice and be glad since through your good works you are[39] no longer of the world, whose works are very evil.[i] Therefore you should be sad rather for this, that it loved you with its wicked works,[40] but not because of its hating and persecuting you, in order to show that you are in no way their accomplices, but for you to exhibit behavior and deeds in accordance with the future age, being heavenly rather than worldly.

i. Dionysius bar Salibi, *Gospels*, 400, notes that scripture habitually refers to those who live in sin as "the world."

[15:20a] **Remember the word that I spoke to you: The servant is not greater than his lord. If they have persecuted me, then they will persecute you also.**

*The time[41] has come, he said, in which it is necessary to remember what I said: *The servant is not greater than his lord.*[42] And you must not be sorrowful and grieve over your persecutions and tribulations, because being my servants

---

36. **To fall:** om. M.
37. **Its own,** pl. NZ: sg. M.
38. **This world,** *ašxarhs*, N: "the world," *ašxarh*, MZ.
39. **You are:** om. M.
40. **Works:** sg. N.
41. **Time,** *žamanak*, N: "hour," *žam*, M.
42. **The time … lord,** MV: om. N (see editor's note).

you must not be vexed and separated from what I shall endure, but rather rejoice because of sharing with me, since you are not greater than me but very humble and small.

[15:20b] **If they will keep**[43] **my word, then they will also keep yours.**

[**340**] As they did not receive my[44] word, he means, neither will they receive yours.

[15:21] **But they will do the same to you for my name's sake, because they do not know**[45] **the one who sent me.**

When he encouraged them to endure the tribulation and troubles, and gave this reason, *You are not of the world*, and that it was sufficient for their consolation as servants to be equal with their lord, he also provided them with further consolation and hope: *This they will do to you for my name's sake, because they did not recognize*[i] *the one who sent me*. By that he informed them of the punishment of the Jews from above by the Father. For if they had recognized him and were obedient, they would not do all this to you. So you will encounter no small reward, not only from me but also from the Father; therefore they hated you. Then he turned his remarks to those who hated them.

    i. **They did not recognize:** see note to the lemma.

[15:22] **If I had not come and spoken with them, they would not have had any sin. But now there is no excuse**[46] **for their sins.**

They always made this calumny against me, that I am opposed to God. So unless I had come and through many examples and words and acts made [myself] known to them as not being opposed to God, but as Son of God and God, they would have had no sin.[i] But now henceforth they cannot make any[47] excuses or speak about denial, and especially about the torments and persecutions that they will inflict on you, but first on me when they set up the cross, reckoning me guilty of death.

---

43. **Will keep,** *pahesc'en*, MN: "kept," *pahec'an*, VZ (see editor's note).
44. **My:** om. M.
45. **They do not know,** *oč' giten*, MN: "they did not recognize," *oč' canean*, Z.
46. **Excuse,** N: pl. MZ.
47. **Any:** om. N.

i. Cyril of Alexandria, *Comm. Jo.* 10, notes that this verse could be interpreted *dichē*: as applying to everyone, or to the Jews only. Step'annos of Siwnik', 138, states that this verse was said only to the Jews, not to all those to whom Christ had not been announced.

[15:23] Whoever hates me, he[48] also hates my Father.

Not because of this did they hate[49] me, as they deceitfully pretended I was opposed to God and made myself equal to God, but their hatred was even greater and involved the Father, [despite] so many [341] signs that they had seen and heard, when I said: *Father, I know that at all times you hear me, but for the sake of these people who stand around me I do them, so that they may believe* (John 11:42). But they were not profited, nor did they pay heed to the Father's testimony in his saying: *This is my beloved Son* (Matt 3:17 par.). Rightly did he say that they had no excuse to say anything, after so many revelations and testimonies.

[15:24–25] If I had not done among them the works that no one else did, they would have had no sin. But now they have seen and hated me and my Father. But so that the saying may be fulfilled that is written in their law: They hated me without cause.[50]

Unless I had[51] justified my words in order to remove their supposition that I was opposed to God, by which they sought a pretext to torment and kill me, they would have had sin. But if I fulfilled the laws of Moses, and in addition performed no insignificant signs in order to persuade them, which no one else had done—as they said regarding the healing of the blind one: *From ages no one has heard of the opening of the eyes of a blind one, born blind from birth*[i]—perhaps they would have had occasion to contrive excuses and to suppose that I am opposed to God, and then they would not have had sin. But now, after acts and signs performed by me, they testify *without cause* that they hate me and my Father. And a token of their hatred is what David prophesied concerning them through the Holy Spirit: *Without cause they hate me* and my Father. So then you must not be sad and fearful concerning the persecutions and torments that will happen to you,[52] because this will be no small consola-

---

48. **He**, *na*, N: om. MZ.

49. **Did they hate**: sg. M.

50. **Without cause**, *tarapartuc'*, NZ: *i tarapartuc'*, MZ at Ps 68:5.

51. I **had**, *ēi*, M: "he had," *ēr*, N.

52. **To you**: om. M.

tion for you, that those who hate me and the Father will hate you even more in our name, as you will be preachers and evangelists.

i. John 9:32, also quoted here by Moše bar Kepha.

[15:26–27] **But when the Consoler will come, whom I shall send to you from the Father, the Spirit of consolation who [342] proceeds from the Father, he will testify concerning me. And you testify that from the beginning you were**[53] **with me.**

Since he first said, Now there is no excuse for the Jews because of the deeds and signs that no one else had done among them, yet they did not believe but *hated me and my Father* all the more *without cause*, lest the disciples be disturbed in their minds as to why he gives us over to evils as opposed to them—yet behold, they did not accept the signs and miracles [performed] by him but hated him and are still to be tormented; are not, then, totally superfluous our evangelizing and preaching?[54] For that reason he next set down the following: *When the Spirit, the Consoler, will come,* whom previously I announced to you, *he will remind you of everything that from henceforth you will do in my name through signs and miracles.* Through him *you will testify that you were with me from the beginning,* and that from me you heard what you should speak, just as they later said, *We ate and drank with him after the resurrection* (Acts 10:41).

Let us also examine this: *The Spirit of truth, who proceeds from the Father,*[i] to distinguish the Holy Spirit from the angelic powers. For they too are said to be spirits, and by others that they are created spirits. And he said: *The Spirit of truth.* Because *he proceeds from the Father,* therefore he is certainly true, because he knows totally the Father and his wishes, being with him and proceeding from him. *When the Spirit will come,* he said, you will know more securely what I told you: *They hated me and my Father without cause.* So then, this will be no small consolation to you for their hating you. But you will understand the details of the reward that you are to receive on the day of recompense.

i. Tatʿewacʿi, 574, emphasizes the "procession," *blxumn,* of the Spirit from the Father and not from the Son. But by his time the controversy over the Filioque had reached Armenia.

---

53. **You were,** *ēikʿ,* N: "you are," *ēkʿ,* MZ.
54. **And preaching:** om. M.

[343] Chapter 16

[16:1] **This I have spoken with you, lest you be offended.**

For that reason, he said, I previously made known to you what would happen, so that when troubles and tribulations befall you, you would not think it to be some unexpected occurrence and stumble, not being forewarned; but being made aware in advance, you might prepare yourselves with fine acquiescence to endure it all, whereby you[1] will receive no small compensation.

[16:2] **They shall cast you out of their synagogues. But the time will come that everyone who kills you will think he is offering service to God.**

Not only will they expel you from their synagogues, as haters and despisers, but they will reckon[2] your killing to be offering a sacrifice[i] to God. By this he wished to reveal to them in advance their deeds of immeasurable wickedness[ii] and to show them that by being forewarned they might prepare themselves for patience and endurance.

    i. **A sacrifice:** *patarag;* "service," *paštawn,* in the lemma, as Z.

    ii. Here Theodore of Mopsuestia refers to the sect of Simon Magus, called Borborites, citing Eusebius, *Hist. eccl.* 5.1. Išodad also mentions the crimes of the Borborites. Dionysius bar Salibi, *John,* 276, notes that not only the Jews but also the Gentiles will afflict believers.

[16:3] **And that they will do to you,[3] because they did not recognize the Father or me.**

As I said, although so many tribulations and great troubles will befall you, yet this will be sufficient to you for[4] consolation,[i] that they will do all this to

---

    1. **You,** *ēkʼ,* N: "he" (?), *ē,* M.

    2. **They will reckon:** "they reckon," M.

    3. **You:** + "for the sake of my name," M.

    4. **For:** om. M ("this will be sufficient consolation to you").

you because of not knowing the Father and me,[5] and as a consequence you will receive no small rewards. So then, you should rejoice and be glad that because of not knowing me and the Father they will inflict such condemnation on you.

i. John Chrysostom, *Hom. Jo.* 80.1, stresses the theme of consolation.

[16:4] But this I told you;[6] the time will come, you will remember that I told you.[7]

After he had told them that he was speaking in advance to them, lest they be fearful or disturbed when the tribulations came unexpectedly upon you,[i] **[344]** but being forewarned and acquiescent they would happily accept it all, after that he gave them further encouragement: When all this has befallen you, remember that I spoke to you previously to this effect and about the rewards that I had promised you, to prepare lodgings for you in the house of my Father. Have no doubt, but stand even more firmly in the hope that I promised you.

i. As noted before, Nonnus frequently alternates in midsentence between the first, second, and third person.

[16:5a][8] At the beginning I did not say this to you, because I was with you.

That I did not mention all this up to the present was not for the reason that I was unaware of it, but *I was* still *with you*. There was no need [to mention] these things until the time when they would all occur. Furthermore, as long as I was with you, my enemies hated me and plotted torments and death for me, but not for you. Previous to this he had also spoken to them and indicated what they would suffer, saying: *I send you out as lambs among wolves* (Luke 10:3). But perhaps in that way he had not been teaching them as clearly as he now was speaking: *When they will kill you, they will reckon they are offering a service to God.* And they were not so cast into worry and doubt[9] as when they heard this.

---

5. **The Father and me:** "me and the Father," M.
6. **You:** om. MN; + "that when," Z.
7. **You,** Z: om. MN.
8. This is v. 4b in the Greek and KJV.
9. **And doubt:** om. N.

[16:5b–6] **But I go to the one who sent me. And let none of you ask me: Whither do you go? But since I spoke all this with you, sadness has filled your hearts.**

Before this, he said, when you were hearing from me that I would leave you, you were continually questioning to know where I was going, as Peter queried, *Lord, where are you going?* (John 13:36),[i] and *How shall we be able to know the way?*[ii] But now that sadness has filled your hearts, you will not question in the same way. Thereby he again revealed to them the grief of their hearts that they were veiling in their worry when they heard it.

    i. John Chrysostom, *Hom. Jo.* 80.1, and Moše bar Kepha also quote this verse.
    ii. John 14:5; but there Thomas asks the question.

[345] [16:7a] But I tell you the truth. It is better for you that I go.

Although great sadness gripped you on account of my leaving you, he said, and you had so many doubts, yet I tell you the truth, that sadness, which is the product of joy, is better than joy that brings[10] sadness; and also, so that you may have greater perfection and firmness through the cross and torments that I am to suffer, because I shall endure all that for you and all who believe in me.

[16:7b] **For if I do not go, the Consoler[11] will not come to you. But if I go, I shall send him to you.**

So long as there is still sin in the world, and the kingdom of Satan has not yet been destroyed, *and the curse has not yet been removed,[12] and humankind is still under the first condemnation, the Consoler will not come,[i] which is to say he will not rest over you;[ii] nor will you encounter the perfect gifts that will come about through the descent of the Holy Spirit. For all that will occur when my dispensation[iii] will attain completion, when the enmity between God and humankind is removed and the wall of the fence is broken (Eph 2:14), and no longer do the cherubim with flaming sword guard the way to the tree of life (Gen 3:24), but the garden, your first habitation, is opened again. So when will this occur? When I shall go up to the cross, when I shall send the thief to paradise, when I shall endure the torments, when even death I shall

---

    10. **Brings:** "will bring," N.
    11. **Consoler,** NZ: + "the Spirit," M.
    12. **And the curse ... removed:** om. N.

willingly accept, and you will see awesome signs from heaven and earth, when having been raised up to heaven I shall send the Spirit to you.

i. Dionysius bar Salibi, *John*, 278, also notes that until the curse has been removed and sin destroyed, the Consoler will not come.

ii. **Rest over you**: as John 1:32, 33, of the Spirit at Jesus's baptism.

iii. **Dispensation**: *tnawrinakank'n*, rendering the Greek *oikonomia* in the sense of "incarnation"; see the introduction, xxxvi, for such terms.

[16:8] And when he has come, he will reprimand this world for sin, [346] and for righteousness, and for judgment.

By saying, *world*,[i] he meant particularly the Jews. Although he mentioned all nations, in that Satan ruled over all through love of the world, they had followed love for it and denied the truth. Since he mentioned these three and profound examples, they regarded them as not insignificant. He then explained to them that they were most important for their knowledge; therefore he said:

i. **World**: *ašxarh*, but *ašxarhs*, "this world," in the lemma. Dionysius bar Salibi, *John*, 278, notes that there will be no forgiveness for the Jews.

[16:9–11] For sin, because they did not believe in me; for righteousness, because I go to my Father and you see me no more; for judgment, because the prince of this world is condemned.

When the Holy Spirit will come and fill you and all who believe in me with great grace, through whom you will perform signs and miracles superior to those done by me, and all this will be in my name, then you will understand and know that I am alive and death in no way reigns over me, as supposed the Jews who condemned me to be killed, thinking to put me to death completely. *And he will teach you everything* (John 14:26). Not, he says, in accordance with the former ones; for although some were rendered worthy of a certain grace, yet not of the most superior, because of their not being capable of bearing in themselves the total grace before my descent to earth, but they were worthy of only partial grace. However, he will teach[13] you perfectly, you who once were weak and impotent and unlearned and ignorant in the world, in order to reprimand the denial of the Jews, *who hated light and loved darkness more, for their works were evil* (John 3:19), for which reason they called me Nazarene,[i] and son of a carpenter (Matt 13:55; Mark 6:3), among other things.[ii]

---

13. **Will teach**: "teaches," M.

Then they will not be able [347] to find or propose any excuses but will be reprehended by the great miracles that will be done through you in my name, whereby they will become aware of and understand my teachings and deeds, and that I am truly Son of God. In accordance with their calumniating me as being opposed to God, [they will understand] that I truly ascended to the Father, and they no longer see me, because I am beside him and with him as I always was, although I was made incarnate[iii] and humbled to the world for the sake of the salvation of those who will believe. But those who will deny will be unable to respond at the judgment, as I said previously, *If I had not come and spoken with them*[14] *they would have had*[15] *no sin* (John 15:22), but from then on they have nothing to say or make excuses.

Furthermore, he will reprove the world when through you he will cast out demons from their habitation wherever they will happen to dwell. And all this you will do in my name. And you will despise all ease,[iv] which is the cause of evil deeds for the race of humankind. All of this I earlier showed by examples, by removing the races of humankind from the hands of Satan by judgment and law and truth, which I brought about through the cross and the torments and death. Thereby his authority was stopped, when he knew the details of the resurrection, of which once he was ignorant and had no worries in himself, because death was still reigning, who from the various sins begat wicked deeds. Then he will know that I am not a Samaritan or possessed by a demon, as his accomplices called [me] (John 8:48), but God and true Son of God.

And when he mentioned the reproof of the world to them, which was to occur through the coming of the Holy Spirit, he next set down another teaching, by which [348] he made known the power of his divinity, that convinced them what he was going to do. Therefore he said:

i. **Nazarene**: passim.

ii. **Among other things**: *aylovk'n handerj* (lit. "*et cetera*").

iii. **I was made incarnate**: *marmnac'ay*, from *marmin*, "flesh." For the terminology, see the introduction, xxxvii.

iv. **Ease**: *heštut'iwn*, "pleasure, voluptuousness."

---

14. **With them**: om. N.

15. **They would have had**: "there would have been," N.

[16:12–13a] I have many more things to tell you, but you are not able to endure them now. But when the Spirit of truth will come, he will lead you with all truth.

Although many will know me and believe in my name, yet even more at the coming of the Holy Spirit, when he will come and dwell among you and be with you, then you will truly know my divinity and power. So when I truthfully told you, *It is better for you that I go* (John 16:7), I spoke to you about the coming of the Spirit. And what mean: My going is better for you, and the coming of the Spirit? Whatever is now hidden from you, what you have heard from me, from then on you will know totally, and you will recognize the power of my sayings, because he will remind you of everything, and by dwelling with you and among you will fill you with all knowledge and truth. The details of my divinity and power I have not explained to you because of your still being weak and unlearned, lest you think that I have myself testified about myself.[i] But when the Holy Spirit will come, he will testify and teach you everything and reveal it to you (John 14:26; 15:26).

So these modest things spoken by the Lord[16] about himself are sufficient for us against those who divide him into two natures, not understanding the humbler things spoken by the Lord [to be] for the sake of the imperfect and weak audience, not in order to divide him into two. But when the Holy Spirit came and taught the apostles the more perfect things, no more thenceforth were there such weak utterances, **[349]** but they openly proclaimed him to be totally Son of God, and totally God.

i. An allusion to John 5:31; 8:13. Here Theodore of Mopsuestia discusses the nature of the Father and Son and their mutual relationship.

[16:13b] For he shall not say anything of himself, but what he will hear he shall speak.[17]

After he had told them about the divinity and power of the Holy Spirit and his teaching them the truth, whereby they would have better knowledge and power than they possessed previously *while they were still going around with the Lord[18]—especially because he clearly stated to them: *It is better for you that I go, because unless I go the Comforter will not come*—lest the disciples think that through all this the Holy Spirit was greater than him and

---

16. **By the Lord:** om. N.
17. **He shall speak,** MZ (and editor): "he speaks," N.
18. **While … Lord:** om. N.

they turn to some other form of schism,[19] he set down the following: *He will not say anything of himself, but what he will hear*, showing them the nature of united authority and power. *He will not say anything of himself, but what he will hear*—from the Father who sent him, he means; and he will not say [anything] outside mine, **because he takes from mine and will relate*[20] [them].[i]

He fully reveals the equality of their nature and independent will,[ii] in order to state: *The Son cannot do anything of himself unless he see the Father doing it*, and likewise the Holy Spirit *will not say anything save what the Father will speak*. So then, their authority and nature are one. And just as no one knows the man except the spirit that dwells in him, likewise [no one knows] God except the Holy Spirit who dwells in him (1 Cor 2:11). So then, there is no distinction of divisions regarding their nature, but they are separate only in person,[iii] and united by nature.

i. Nonnus anticipates, combining vv. 14b and 15b with their different tenses. Here "mine" is plural, *imoc'*, but it is singular in 14b and 15, *immē*.

ii. **Independent will:** *anjnišxanut'iwn* (lit. "self-authority"), often stressed regarding Christ, men, or Satan. Here John Chrysostom, *Hom. Jo.* 88.3, discusses at length the nature of the Trinity and their unity of will. Išodad refers to the conjunction and equality of Father, Son, and Spirit. Moše bar Kepha stresses the equality of the Trinity in nature and honor, while Dionysius bar Salibi, *John*, 280, notes the equality of the *ousia* and power of the three "persons," *qnwm'*.

iii. **Person:** *anjnaworut'iwn*. For the terminology, see the introduction, xxxix.

[16:13c] **And what is to come he will relate.**

[350] When he said to them, *He will not say anything of himself, but what he will hear*, lest they suppose that he is then not God because he does not teach of himself but will relate[21] what he will hear from someone else, he gave them a sign that is not fitting save for his divinity: *And*[22] *what is to come he will relate to you*. Because it is for God alone to know the future, but not created nature, he said, *What is to come he will relate to you*, that is, the future. And because the Lord himself, despite being for so long a time with them, had given them no power to know the future, nor such authority and power as they would receive at the coming of the Holy Spirit, lest they be mistaken[23] again to suppose the Holy Spirit greater than himself [he said]:

19. **Schism:** pl. N.

20. **Because … relate:** om. N.

21. **Will relate:** "relates," M.

22. **And:** om. M.

23. **Be mistaken,** *aylgunak axtasc'en*, M: *axtasc'en*, N.

[16:14a] **He will glorify me.**

That is, as for the gifts and the power you will receive at his coming, although it is he who grants them to you, yet all this will be for my glory, because you will perform all the wonders and miracles in my name.

[16:14b] **For he will take[24] from mine and will relate[25] to you.**

That is, he will remind you of my teachings and will teach you nothing else alien and unknown. So then, as their teaching is one because of their will being one, likewise their nature is one. Therefore he did not say *He will take* from me but *from mine.* Not what I now command when I send [him], but what I once told you; because all things are clear to him, since they are one in nature and power.

[16:15] **Everything that the Father has is mine. Therefore I told you that he will take from mine and relate to you.**

For if everything that the Father has is mine, and he relates [to] you what he hears from the Father, then what has been said by me is true, that he will take from mine and will remind you.

[351] [16:16] **A little and you shall see me no more. And a while and you shall see me. And I go to the Father.**

When he told them about the coming of the Spirit and his power, and of the advantages for them from that and the help they would have, the condemnation of the prince of this world, that is, his being cast out through the preaching of the gospel, and because he had also previously mentioned, *It is better for you that I go,* because then I shall send the Holy Spirit,[i] and *it is better for you that I go,* revealing to them the signs and powers that they would receive by the coming of the Holy Spirit, by which he lessened for them the sadness they bore in themselves[ii]—therefore he also informed them about himself, his torments and death, and the tribulation and troubles that the disciples themselves would endure.

In addition he recalled his saying concerning the torments, so that he might bestir them all the more to patience and long-suffering. Therefore he

---

24. **He will take,** NZ: "he takes," M.
25. **Will relate,** NZ: "will teach," M.

added this: *A little and you do not see me.* The short time seems to mean his burial. *And a while and you shall see [me],* that is, after my resurrection and when I shall ascend to my Father in heaven, doing that in front of you, of which you will be eyewitnesses.[iii] And lest they should think the sayings not to be appropriate, on the grounds that by his going it is not possible to see [him], and by his not going not to see [him], therefore the evangelist says:

i. Here Theodore of Mopsuestia recalls v. 7 above.
ii. Moše bar Kepha explains this verse as consolation.
iii. Here Tat'ewac'i, 580, specifically mentions the forty days from resurrection to ascension.

[16:17] **Some**[26] **of the disciples said among each other, What is this that he is saying to us: A little you do not see me, and a while and you will see me, and I go to the Father?**

As if they were understanding his saying as something like this: If he will go, we do not see [him], and if he will not go, we do see [him].[i]

i. Dionysius bar Salibi, *John*, 281, phrases his comments similarly, but in the second person: "If we see you … if you go."

[16:18] **And they said: What is still a little more? We do not know what he**[27] **is saying.**

[352] As we said earlier, they were doubtful regarding these sayings: by going, to be visible, and by not going, to be invisible, because they did not understand the meaning of the saying.

[16:19–20] **Jesus knew that they wished to ask him,**[28] **and said to them: Why do you query among yourselves that I said to you, A little and**[29] **you shall not see me any more, and a while and you shall see? Amen, amen, I say to you**

---

26. **Some**, NZ: om. M.
27. **He:** *sa*, N; om. MZ.
28. **Him**, MZ: om. N.
29. **And**, MZ: om. N.

that you will weep and lament, and this world will rejoice and you shall be sad. But your grief will turn into[30] joy.

When he told them all this *and they were unable to comprehend, because he spoke to them about his burial,[31] by which he would be absent from them for a short time and they did not realize it, he then taught them clearly as a warning to them to prepare themselves to be strong when all this would occur to make them sad: when they would see him nailed to the cross, and they would suffer so much sadness and worry, and on all sides enemies would attack and be boastful.[i] Therefore he moderated all this and spoke to them more simply: *Your grief will turn into joy.* Which indeed happened when they saw him risen from the tomb, and at the coming of the Holy Spirit when they became recipients of so much ineffable grace. Therefore he gave them a more recognizable example, by which example they might be able to comprehend the details of the truth.

i. John Chrysostom, *Hom. Jo.* 79.1, explains the weeping and lamenting as caused by seeing Jesus on the cross, in which he is followed by the other commentators. Tat῾ewac῾i, 580, identifies "this world" as the Jews.

[16:21–22] When a woman gives birth, she has grief because her hour has arrived. But when she will have delivered the child, she no longer remembers the travail for her joy, because she has born a man into the world. And you now have grief, [353] but I shall see you again and your hearts will be glad, and no one will take your joy away from you.

Let not my sayings seem astonishing to you: *Your grief will turn into joy,* for just as a woman, although she will give birth with tribulation and much *grief,* *yet when she will have given birth[32] and has returned to a time of health, she forgets *the grief and travail* that she endured, which has passed from her, and *she has born a man into the world;*[i] in the same way you also will grieve and endure many[33] travails at the time of the cross and my torments. But when you will see me risen from the tomb and ascended from the dead, then no more will my torments or death bring back the grief that you experienced at the time of the cross. *It will turn into joy,* because from then on the former doubts and fear will be gone. *And no one will take your joy away from*

---

30. **Turn into,** *darjc῾i,* N: "become," *ełic῾i,* MZ.
31. **And … burial:** om. M.
32. **Yet … birth:** om. M.
33. **Many:** om. M.

you, because of my being always alive and with you forever.[34] For although you will suffer tribulations and grief from them, yet you will receive so much power and faith when the Holy Spirit comes to you that those tribulations will not be able to remove from you the hope of joy and faith. But you will rejoice all the more and happily accept all that.

Furthermore, just as the tribulations and grief of the mother are forgotten when they depart from her, because of her begetting a man into the world, likewise fear of death and grief will depart and be forgotten by my resurrection.[ii] And just as there is rejoicing at the new birth that came into the world, so too those who believe in me, by doing good works in the world, give birth in the future to the reward of great gifts. Its joy remains forever and does not permit the recollection of the tribulations of virtue [**354**] that they endured here for the sake of the eternal blessings that they will inherit.

i. Moše bar Kepha notes that the prophets often used the imagery of giving birth; and Tat'ewac'i, 581, calls this a "familiar example," *ĕndelakan awrinak.*

ii. Here John Chrysostom, *Hom. Jo.* 79.1, stresses Christ's resurrection, as do Moše bar Kepha and Dionysius bar Salibi (*John*, 282).

[16:23] **And on that day you shall not ask me anything. Amen, amen, I say to you: Whatever you will ask from my Father in my name, he will give you.**

This means that after such completion and joy have been accomplished, there will be no need for you to ask me,[i] but only by the recollection of my name *whatever you will ask from my Father in my name* will be done for you. This indeed they did when the Jews came upon them and threatened them not to teach anything in the name of Jesus, and they prayed and said: *So, Lord, look upon their threats, and allow your servants to speak your name with all boldness, to stretch out your hand for healings and signs and miracles to occur in the name of your Son Jesus. And while they were at prayer, the place moved in which they were gathered, and they were all filled with the Holy Spirit and spoke the word of God with boldness* (Acts 4:29–31).

i. Išodad specifies that prayer will no longer be necessary.

---

34. **Forever:** + "and no one will take your joy away from you," M.

[16:24] **Up to now you have asked nothing in my name. *Ask and you will receive, so that your joy may be full.**[35]

Up to this point, he said, you[36] have not known me truly to be Son of God, whereby had you asked from the Father in my name, he would have granted you your requests. *Ask and you will receive, so that your joy may be full.* When all this will occur and the time that I told you will arrive, *ask,* so that you may *receive* everything that you wish *in my name, *so that your joy may be* complete through the gifts that *you will receive in my name,*[37] when you see me risen from the dead.

[16:25] **This I spoke with you in parables. The time will come [355] when I shall not speak with you in parables but I shall tell you clearly about the Father.**

Up until now I spoke hidden matters with you, not revealing the most sublime things on account of your being still weak and unlearned, but I managed as much as you are able to take; *for when the Holy Spirit will come, he will teach you everything truly.*[i] Consequently, he promises another time in which he will explain everything to them clearly. What time might that be? After his resurrection from the tomb,[ii] at which time they will know and understand his omnipotent power and will regard him as worthy of his sayings about himself and all that he had said to them previously as true. Therefore he then told them more about the Father and the future life, and that he was his Father truly and not supposedly, as they had earlier considered, which he also wrote in the Catholic Epistles: *He showed himself* to us *alive after his torments; in many signs during forty days he appeared to them and spoke about the kingdom of God* (Acts 1:3).[iii]

    i. Cf. v. 13, conflated with 14:26.

    ii. This is stressed by John Chrysostom, *Hom. Jo.* 79.2, followed by Moše bar Kepha.

    iii. The reference to the Catholic Epistles and the injection of *to us* perhaps reflect 1 John 1:1. Moše bar Kepha and Dionysius bar Salibi (*John,* 283) also refer to the instruction between the resurrection and ascension.

---

    35. **Ask…full:** om. M.

    36. **You:** "we," M (*sic*).

    37. **So that your … name:** om. M.

[16:26] **On that day you will ask in my name. And I do not say to you that I shall ask the Father for you.**

On that day you will truly understand the most complete things about my authority and power; whereby you will be capable of receiving what you may ask in my name only. And there will be no need for me to administer to you the humble things again in accordance with your ignorance, as I said earlier: *I shall beg the Father for you, that he send you the Consoler* (John 14:16). For after that you will be so perfect as to accept ministration of the most sublime things. It is clear from these sayings that all the most humble things about himself were [spoken] on account of the ignorance [356] of the listeners. Since they did not yet know him completely, therefore they often stumbled at him, just as once some of the disciples turned back and did not go around with him, when he taught about his body and blood (John 6:53–67). And the Jews continually were offended and for that reason always tried to invent some excuses concerning him.

[16:27] **For the Father himself loves you, because you loved me and believed that I came forth from God.**

You [will have] faith in me[38] at that time and recognize me not to be a man, as you now think, but coming forth from God, being his Son and truly equal. And through that love of yours for me and strong faith, there will be no need henceforth for you to ask the Father, because the Father himself loves you on account of your loving me and having faith, and he will grant you everything that you request in my name.

[16:28] **I came forth from the Father and came into the world. Once more I leave the world and go to the Father.**

When he had said, *You believed in me that I came forth from the Father*, he then described an example of his coming forth, to be clearly visible and tangible through the flesh [yet] not separated from the Father at all according to his divinity.[i] In the same way his ascending from the world to the Father [means] that he remains invisible[39] to the world according to the flesh, but not that he is separated in his divinity, of which all creation is full.

---

38. **In me:** om. M.

39. **He remains invisible,** *zanerewoyt' mnal,* N: "[he] remains visible," *zna erewoyt' mnal,* M.

i. Moše bar Kepha stresses that the Son did not leave the Father's bosom. Tat'ewac'i, 581, states that the Son did not leave the Father, and he uses the simile of a word proceeding from the mind through a voice but not being divided from it. For that argument, see note to the commentary on John 1:1.

[16:29–30] His disciples said to him: Behold, now[40] you speak clearly and say not a single proverb. Now[41] we know that you know everything, and there is no need that anyone ask of you. In this we believe that you came forth from God.

When he said to them, Now *I have spoken with you*[42] *in parables*, [357] after that he taught them[43] a little more clearly. Thereby he consoled them and cheered [them] from their doubts and fear by saying: *The Father loves you because of your believing in me, that I came forth from God.* Let us also look at what the disciples said: *Now we know that you know everything.* We have often stated that as they were incomplete and weak they did not know him perfectly, for which reason the Lord condescended to them, speaking in humble terms about himself so far as they were able to receive it, and not as was appropriate for his divinity. Because by believing in him, that *I came forth*[44] from God, the Father would love them and grant them powers in his name after his resurrection from the dead, at the coming of the Holy Spirit, when they were perfected through the vestiture of heavenly power.

He had not yet revealed to them that you did not truly understand these sayings, lest being in doubt they be troubled in some other way to their stumbling. Consequently he turned them to a different teaching by which they might understand that they had not rightly comprehended the earlier things but that they were still weak and ignorant. Therefore he did not yet speak about the most sublime [aspects of the] faith but only what would console them for his leaving them and that *I shall always be with you*,[i] even if in the flesh I shall be[45] invisible to you.

i. Cf. Matt 28:20; not a direct quotation.

---

40. **Now**, *ard*, MZ: om. N.
41. **Now**: *ayžmik*, MZ; *ayžm*, N.
42. **With you**: om. N.
43. **Them**: om. M.
44. **I came forth**, *eli*, M (= lemma): "he came forth," *el*, N.
45. **I shall be**: "I am," N.

[16:31–32a] **Jesus replied to them and said: Now will you believe?**[46] **Behold, the time will come, and indeed has come, that you will be scattered to each one's place and will leave me alone.**

What, then, means what he said, save that he was reprimanding them in accordance with their weak thoughts[47] and making clear to them that if you had truly believed and were firm in what I have taught[i] you, that *I came forth from* God and *am going to* God, **[358]** you would not have been fearful when you saw the Jews gathered against me? Nor would you have stumbled over my torments and death and, *being scattered, would you have left me alone*. But now there still remains weakness in you, which I shall explain to you before those events.

    i. **I have taught:** *vardapetec'in*. The *-n* is the demonstrative ending after the relative pronoun, but the scribe of M erased it, thinking it reflected the 3d pl. ending.

[16:32b] **And I am not alone, but the Father is with me.**

Lest they stumble, thinking he would be alone in his torments, he added, *I am not alone, my Father is with me*, in order to indicate that although you will abandon me, yet my Father is with me. So then, no harm will come upon me, as you suppose, as I am with the Father.

[16:33a] **This I spoke with you, so that with me you might have peace.**

Not as you supposed did I teach you, because you will not now have faith, but so that you may recall when I shall leave, and know that I previously told you everything that would occur, whereby you may move away from the thoughts that you now have and may hope in me, that I shall not leave the promised gifts, which I often promised, incomplete for you.

[16:33b] **In this world you will have tribulation, but be encouraged, because I have conquered the world.**

The peace that I promised to leave you will come about through me,[i] he said, not from the world; for with this world[48] you will have to endure tribulations and troubles. But do not be fearful on that account, because it was for

---

46. **Will you believe,** N: "did you believe," M ("do you believe," Z).
47. Thoughts: sg. M.
48. **This world,** *ašxarhis*, MN: the editor prints, "me," *is*.

that reason I was incarnate and carried through all my dispensation,[ii] even enduring the cross and torments so that I might conquer the world for you. What then is *conquering the world*? It is to stop the evil deeds that occur in the world and to destroy the works of its overseer,[iii] Satan, and make a way for you by which you may despise [359] all his afflictions but store up in yourselves through patience the profit and advantage that will come about. This is what I handed down to you: *My peace I leave to you* (John 14:27).

    i. See also John 14:27.

    ii. **I was incarnate**: *marmnac'ay*; **dispensation**: *tnawrineal*. For the technical terms, see the introduction, xxxvii.

    iii. **Overseer**: *verakac'u*, a term often used for bishops. For a variety of names applied to Satan, see Thomson 2001 (notes to *Teaching* 278–79).

[17:1a] When Jesus had said this, he raised his eyes to heaven and said:

Why, then, did he need to raise his eyes to heaven, he who was equal in nature and authority and power, save on account of the disciples? [He acted] in this fashion in order thoroughly to instruct and admonish them and to give them this example,[i] that when sadness and tribulations would come upon them to raise their eyes and minds to heaven and take refuge in God, and to place there their hope of salvation and help, and always to remain there in the time of trials with the eyes of the body[1] and the mind.

i. Moše bar Kepha indicates that Jesus raised his eyes to heaven as a lesson to us to raise our hearts to God. He notes that this was a habit of men in prayer and refers to other such actions of Christ.

[17:1b] Father, the hour has arrived. Glorify your Son, so that your Son may glorify you.

The hour of cross and torments has arrived,[i] he said. *Glorify your Son*, at this time when[2] demons will be disturbed and Jews agitated in their wicked plans, and they will think their wickedness has been fulfilled. For at this very hour they will boast and reckon they have won the victory through his torments and death. Now *glorify your Son*; he means by revealing the divine signs and miracles for testimony that I am your Son and for a reproach to them, so that the power of his divinity may be clear whereby the Father will be glorified. For just as the Son was hidden, so also they did not yet completely recognize the Father, because [only] after that did they recognize the Father and the Son. Likewise Israel did not know the Father, as God said to the prophet Isaiah: *My people did not recognize me, and Israel[ii] did not comprehend me* (Isa 1:3).

---

1. **Body:** pl. M.
2. **When:** "in which," N.

But that the Son did not say, Glorify me, [**360**] as if he had some need of glory and sought as a gift what he once did not possess, this the following makes clear: *So that your Son may glorify you.* For if the Son were less than the Father and lacking in glory and power, why did he say: *And so that your Son may glorify you*? For it is much more appropriate for the greater to glorify the one who is subordinate; but how can the lesser glorify the greater? So then, it is clear from these sayings that to glorify refers to the divine miracles, by which he was known to creatures to be Son of God, and by which the Father also was known and glorified by creatures.ⁱⁱⁱ

    i. Dionysius bar Salibi, *John*, 285, stresses that the hour refers to the cross. And Moše bar Kepha defines the cross as glory, as expounded in the second part of the verse; see also Išodad, 272.

    ii. **My people, Israel**: tr. Z. Isa 1:3 is also quoted here by Moše bar Kepha.

    iii. Moše bar Kepha notes that the Son is not greater than the Father to glorify him, but they are mutually equal. Here he refers to the wonders at the time of the cross with OT parallels and discusses at length the hypostases of the Father and Son, attacking both the Arians and the Nestorians.

[17:2a] **Just as you gave him authority over all flesh.**

Your glorifying him on the cross through marvelous signs [indicates] he has authority not only over Israel in particular but also over all flesh, that is, all nations, just as he handed down to the disciples the power of his authority: *Go, teach all Gentiles, baptize them in the name of the Father and of the Son and of the Holy Spirit,*ⁱ by which is fulfilled the glorifying of the Son by the Father and of the Father by the Son, and also of the Holy Spirit, through baptism and faith.³

    i. Matt 28:19, quoted here also by John Chrysostom, *Hom. Jo.* 80.1.

[17:2b] **So that to everyone whom you gave him he might give life everlasting.**

He describes the details of his authority, not only by ruling over them, but through their faith he will bring them from darkness to light and from death to eternal life, where from then on death will no longer reign.

---

3. **Baptism and faith**: "faith and worship," M.

[17:3] **This is eternal life, that they may know you only as true God, and Jesus Christ whom you sent.**

This is eternal life, that two great peoples may know you, who are scattered [**361**] over the face of the earth—he means the Jews and the Gentiles—and may believe in the words of the gospel; and that the Gentiles may know you alone as true God in order to destroy the multitude of gods[4] whom they serve, fabricated out of various materials and handcrafted in various forms;[i] and that the Jews, who had accepted to recognize you as true God, might recognize Jesus Christ, whom you sent, as God and your Son. For it is necessary to distinguish the polytheistic tradition of the Gentiles from his single divine nature.

But why did he not say: Your coexistent[ii] Son, whom you sent? It was to prevent his disciples, who were still ignorant and weak, from being scandalized, and especially the audience. For the Holy Spirit had not yet descended on the apostles, nor were they complete in knowledge and faith whereby they would have been able to grasp such sublime teaching. Not in this way did he speak about himself, but he put himself in the same honor by saying: *So that they might know you alone as God, and Jesus Christ whom you sent.* Now that which seemed impossible concerning his incarnation to those who heard him call himself equal to the Father, he left for a while until the coming of the Spirit. Not that he placed any division between the Father and the Son by saying, *Whom you sent,* but [he treated them] equally, although he somewhat obscured the saying. See also what he said to the women: *Go, tell my disciples and Peter* (Mark 16:7). Was, then, Peter not one of the disciples? But because it was appropriate for the time, he spoke thus, as here too can be seen.

i. False gods: cf. Cyril of Alexandria, *Comm. Jo.* 11. Tat'ewac'i, 583, explains that they are not really gods but demons and the works of men's hands. The term "nongod," *č̣astuac,* in M just above is common in Armenian; see *NBHL,* s.v. *č̣astuac.*

ii. **Coexistent:** *ēakic';* for such terminology, see the introduction, xxxvi.

[17:4a] **And I glorified you on earth.**

I revealed your name on earth, and I manifested your glory. But in heaven you are continually glorified, that is, recognized by the angels who continuously and unceasingly glorify you.[i]

i. John Chrysostom, *Hom. Jo.* 80.2, also refers here to the praises of the angels.

---

4. **Gods,** *astuacoc',* N: "nongods," *č̣astuacoc',* M.

[362] [17:4b] I have completed the works that you gave me to do.

He calls *work* what he accomplished in his incarnation[i] through words and actions, whereby he illuminated through faith the nations of mankind. But *I have completed* means the cross and torments that he next fulfilled, whereby the plan of his incarnation[ii] received completion and he was victorious over death and corruption, and made incorruption and immortality flourish again.

i. Išodad gives the same explanation.
ii. **Plan of his incarnation:** *tnawrinakan xorhurdk'.* For *tnawrinakan,* see the introduction, xxxvi; *xorhurdk'* (pl.), "plan," could also mean "mystery."

[17:5] And now glorify me, Father, with the glory that I had from you before the world came into being.

What means *the glory*[5] *that he once had from the Father* and now again requests? He had not fallen away from that former glory, but rather he speaks very advantageously in accordance with their weakness. They think me to be a mere man in my incarnate form,[i] but not to many am I known as Son before ages. *Glorify me, Father;* he means, reveal [me] to creatures, to set down such knowledge about me as I had from you before the creation of the world, [namely], the equality and glory. For if *I glorified you* by revealing and making you known to the world, I am indeed happy to be glorified by you, to be revealed to the world.

See the truth of the saying, *A voice came from heaven: I have made glorious, and shall again make glorious* (John 12:28). So for our sake the voice came for a testimony, but there was no need for it to occur. Likewise, the unprecedented signs at the hour of the cross from heaven and earth announced and testified[6] the same, in order to reveal his *glory* and power *that he had before the world came into being,* and that he was not merely a man, as the onlookers thought, having taken the beginning of his existence from creatures.

i. John Chrysostom, *Hom. Jo.* 80.2, also refers here to the incarnation.

5. **The glory:** "with the glory," N.
6. **Testified:** "testify," N.

[17:6a] **I revealed your name to the men whom you gave to me from the world. They were yours, and you gave them to me.**

After he had described his glory with the Father, [363] which we mentioned above, then he provided something else for the assistance of the disciples, turning the saying to them, whereby they might understand the troubles and tribulations and security of faith they were going to endure. Thereby he brought them in advance to agreement and long-suffering. For that reason he said: *I have made known your name to men.* He means not to the Jews alone, for although they recognize you as true God because of the many signs that you showed them in Egypt and the law that you imposed, yet I revealed the most powerful and most secret name. He means that of fatherhood, which no one previously had heard, nor had Israel recognized that you are truly Father, I being Son from the same paternal nature.[i] But those who knew the paternal name of grace, through which you always care for and serve them like a father, were not worthy of that.

After that he added: *Whom you gave to me from the world, they were yours.* What does that mean? Although I revealed your name to everyone, yet not everyone received it and believed; but those who loved [you] followed and received it. So those who loved [you] and willingly believed, these were found[7] worthy to be and to be called yours, rather than the others of mankind who did not at all believe, nor did they follow the commandment by which they might have known you.

i. Moše bar Kepha also refers here to the equality of nature of Father and Son.

[17:6b] **And they kept your word.**

That is, they did not at all follow the wishes of the Jews[i] but my teachings, by which they recognized[8] you. Furthermore, he indicates something else by saying, *They were yours and you gave them[9] to me,* in order to strengthen the minds of the disciples and to entrust them to the Father's providence. When they heard that they were the Father's, thereby they would grasp more firmly the faith and hope; they would be encouraged because of their present fear and doubts. But those who are opposed[10] and understand the sayings in a literal manner [364] are much harmed, as after the Son gave them they are

---

7. **Were found**: "are found," N.
8. **Recognized**: "recognize," M.
9. **Them**: om. M.
10. **Are opposed**: "were opposed," M.

not the Father's after that; just as they are not the Son's before the Father gave them. Even more inappropriately, as long as they were the Father's they had not followed the truth but were very weak and ignorant. Whereas when they became the Son's, then they were strengthened and became wise and recognized the truth.

i. John Chrysostom, *Hom. Jo.* 81.1, offers the same explanation. But Moše bar Kepha states that this was said about the Jews.

[17:7–8] Now they knew that everything that you gave to me, I gave to them.[11] And they received [them] and recognized truly that I proceeded from you. And they believed that you sent me.

See how he arranges the saying and exhorts them to the faith. *They knew that everything that you gave to me, I gave to them*, the promised powers that he previously mentioned: *When the Holy Spirit will come*, such will you also receive, the signs that I continually performed in front of you, as indeed they did after his ascension. Why did he turn the saying to the Father, *What you gave to me, I gave to them*, for he had previously[12] said: *They were yours, and you gave them to me*? By this he confirmed them even more in the faith, when the disciples continually heard that he proceeded from God and would go to him and was his Son, and from him distributed grace and always entrusted them to him.[13]

The Lord did not only know that at that hour did they receive and recognize the word, but he set it down for usefulness and convenience. This he also said to Abraham: *Now I have known that you are fearful of God* (Gen 22:12).[i] Not that before this he did not know, but because when he revealed the mystery of his love by drawing his own son to the sacrifice, he revealed that he was so fearful of God that he did not even[14] spare his only begotten Son. So then, such sayings were for convenience and assistance both there and here, but not out of ignorance of the future.

i. This verse is quoted also by Theodore of Mopsuestia.

---

11. MNZ omit: "Because the words that you gave to me I gave to them."
12. **Previously,** *nax*, M: "he," *na*, N.
13. **To him,** *nma*, N: "he gives," *tay*, M.
14. **Even,** *angam*, N: "once," *miangam*, M.

[17:9] And for them I pray; and I do not pray for the world but for those whom you gave to me, because they are yours.

[**365**] Here the meaning of the saying is clear, as we said above, for the strengthening and encouragement of the disciples through all this, so that they might be more encouraged when they would see that he was so solicitous and caring for them that he would even pray to the Father for them. And if not thus, how would it be? Surely the Father was not ignorant that he prayed for them but not for the world? But he needed that someone make it known to him. So then the meaning of this saying is clear.

[17:10a] And whatever is mine, that is yours; and whatever is yours, that is mine.

See how he arranges the saying. First he said: *They were yours, and you gave them to me.* And lest they think that once they were not his before his giving, or that afterward they were not Father's when they became the Son's, he added to the same such profitable words whereby he made clear their equality and single authority.[i] For if he had been less than the Father, it would have been appropriate that what was his should become the Father's because of the Father being greater than himself. But it would not have been appropriate that what was once the Father's should also be the Son's, because of his being less than the Father. So then it is clear that in every way he revealed their united authority[ii] and equality.[iii]

i. Here Dionysius bar Salibi, *John*, 289, stresses the equality of honor and glory of Father and Son.

ii. **Authority:** *petut'iwn*, not the usual *išxanut'iwn*; in the NT *petut'iwn* generally renders *archē*.

iii. John Chrysostom, *Hom. Jo.* 81.1, emphasizes their *isotimia* and *isotēs* ("equal honour and equality"); Moše bar Kepha refers to their equal honor.

[17:10b] And I am glorified in them.

Let us see what he said: *I am glorified in them.* For although they are mine, just as they are yours, yet as you are glorified by them, so also am I. How would this be? Just as in your name they will perform signs and miracles, likewise too in my name; and just as for your sake they will endure torments, likewise for my sake; and just as they will preach you to the world, likewise also me. See how he gently[i] showed to them the equality and single divinity.

i. **Gently:** *mełmov*, which can also mean "carefully."

[17:11a] **And I am no more in the world. But they are in the world, and I come to you.**

[366] These [words] contain very profound [meaning] for the disciples. Once more he fashions the saying for advantage, as much as they were able to be receptive and understanding. For if we look straightforwardly at the meaning of the saying, as if he were not in the world, yet behold, is still in the world, he teaches all this[15] in their hearing. Although he ascends to heaven, by no means is he not in the world in his divinity,[i] since all creatures exist through him, just as the evangelist said: *He was in the world, and the world came into being through him* (John 1:3). Likewise, he also said to the disciples: *I am with you all the days until the end of the world* (Matt 28:20). But just as he said, *I pray for them but not for the world*, so also he set down here. He was about to leave [them] and described future events that were coming next as if they had happened, in order to indicate to them the immeasurable solicitude of his love that he bore for the sake of their salvation. For by that they were no little consoled and confirmed in the faith.

i. John Chrysostom, *Hom. Jo.* 81.1, here notes that Christ is present in the Spirit.

[17:11b] **Holy Father, keep them in your name, in which you gave [them] to me, so that they may become one, as we are one.**

Keep them in your name, he says. Make them worthy and let them call you Father, whereby they become worthy of protection by you, and united thenceforth through faith in us and linked with each other by love, just as we are one in nature.[i]

i. Dionysius bar Salibi, *Gospels*, 134, stresses that Christ is in the Father by equality of nature, and he is in us by taking a human body.

[17:12a] **While I was in the world with them,[16] I kept them in your name, in which you gave [them] to me.**

In accordance with the previous sayings this is understood as a mystery of service and oversight for their profit, indicating the providence of his love. Otherwise, what would it be? It would not have been appropriate, while he was in the world, for him to keep [367] them without the Father, as he said: *I*

---

15. **This:** "that," N.
16. **With them,** NZ: om. M.

kept them in your name. So then [it was] for a demonstration to the disciples of the care that he had for them. It indicates his asking their supervision from the Father when he was still about to leave them, so that by hoping in the Father they might remain firm in hope when he would be absent from them for a short time. If this were not so, how would he later have said, *Behold, I am with you all the days until the end of the world* (Matt 28:20)? But in this way he arranged the saying for their advantage.

Paul also once spoke likewise[17] about the Holy Spirit: *The Holy Spirit intercedes for us in silent groanings* (Rom 8:26). Not because the Holy Spirit needed anything, for behold, he is coequal in glory and nature, but for an indication to us and for hope of providence being provided to us always from the Holy Spirit.

[17:12b] And I kept[18] [them]; and none of them was lost, save only[19] the son of perdition, so that the scripture might be fulfilled.

By *son of perdition* he means Judas.[i] But what means: *So that the scripture might be fulfilled*? Not that scripture was in any way[20] the cause of his perdition,[ii] which the prophets had mentioned;[iii] but what he in later times through his independent will would do, previously the Holy Spirit had predicted through the prophets. So then, *that the scripture might be fulfilled*, not that he caused it to be done[21] by force for the fulfillment of the scripture, but his infallible knowledge [of] what would occur called it fulfillment, completing it at that time.

i. Theodore of Mopsuestia; Išodad; and Dionysius bar Salibi, *John*, 290, all identify Judas with the "son of perdition."

ii. John Chrysostom, *Hom. Jo.* 81.2, notes that it is scripture's mode of expression to set down an *aitiologia* of events; this is echoed by Moše bar Kepha.

iii. "The scripture" is generally identified as Ps 41:9, or 109:8 (Arm. 40:10; 108:8).

[17:13] But now I come to you. And this I say in the world, so that they may have my joy completely in themselves.

I say this, for the reason that I am about to leave them in the world, and I wish that they remain firm in [368] faith in us and have no fear of troubles

---

17. **Likewise:** "the same," N.

18. **I kept,** *pahec'i*, NZ: "they kept," *pahec'in*, M.

19. **Only:** om. MZ.

20. **In any way,** *inč'*: om. M.

21. **Caused it to be done:** *zayn gorcel ta*[*y*], M; *gorceloy zayn*, N.

and tribulations when they come upon them. But when they will announce to the world the word of life, bringing mankind to faith, then *they will have*[i] *my joy completely in themselves*, being perfected for the preaching of the gospel throughout the whole world.

i. **They will have:** *unic'in*, the same form as "[so that] they may have" in the lemma.

[17:14a] I gave them your word, and the world hated them.

I taught them about the faith, he means, and about knowing you.[i] But the lovers of the world, who did not wish to follow the truth, therefore hated them. So they are worthy of protection from you, because of which[22] *they are hated by the world.*

i. Tat'ewac'i, 584, expands this to indicate that Christ taught first the faith, then eternal life, and thirdly the name Father.

[17:14b] For they are not from the world, just as I am not from the world.

Although they are from the world by nature, yet by works they are not from the world,[i] since the lovers of the world do not perform the virtues that I revealed and taught them. But those who followed the future life had no concern for the world. Truly, then, *the world hated them.*

i. Theodore of Mopsuestia explains that they are not from the world because of regeneration, and Išodad specifies through baptism.

[17:15] Not that you should remove them from the world, but that you may keep them from evil.

The Father was not ignorant regarding the requests, but [he so prayed] as a demonstration for the disciples, since they did not understand such unlimited care as his. He revealed it in accordance with their weakness, so that they might be confirmed and strengthened in their minds when the world would hate them, and would in no way be deceived and lose hope but, always keeping that in their minds, might stand more firmly in the faith.[i]

i. Nonnus omits the following v. 16, which repeats the theme of v. 14b. Nor is it cited in Tat'ewac'i; but his commentary is very abbreviated after ch. 16.

---

22. **Of which:** "of you," M.

[17:17] Make them holy through your truth, because your word is truth.

[**369**] Sanctify them, render them pure through knowledge of the faith in you, which is the truth; as I said earlier: *You are holy because of the word that I spoke with you* (John 15:3). Just as through virtue they created solidity of the faith, likewise through evil works they become bestial and filthy. *Make them holy through your truth.* Strengthen them, and make them firm in faith, so that they may preach your word in the world. Furthermore, they do not understand now in accordance with the previous sayings, since those were examples[23] and signals, but these are perfect and true.[i]

    i. Moše bar Kepha notes that God's word is no *typos* but the truth of the matter.

[17:18] Just as you sent me into the world, I too have sent them into the world.

*Just as I came into the world for the salvation of the world, likewise I send them into the world.[24] Therefore *make them holy through truth.*

[17:19] And for them I make myself holy, so that they too might be sancti-fied through the truth.

He was speaking about the cross and the torments and the death, which he[25] would endure for their sake.[i] He called that *holy* on account of its being the purity of the world, because the earlier sacrifices that were offered had that name, so that they too in accordance with the same example might prepare themselves for torments and death, offering themselves as a sacrifice to God,[26] according to Paul's saying,[ii] and might be called truly *holy.*

    i. Theodore of Mopsuestia here refers to the passion.
    ii. Rom 12:1, quoted also by John Chrysostom, *Hom. Jo.* 82.1, and Moše bar Kepha. Moše refers specifically to the paschal lamb as an "example," *typos*, and an offering for the sins of the people.

---

23. **Examples:** sg. M.
24. **Just … world:** om. M.
25. **He,** N[corr]: "I," MN. But see note to 16:4 above.
26. **To God:** om. M.

[17:20] But not for them alone do I pray but also for all believers in me through their word.

What I request for their sake, he says, not for their sake only do I ask, because many will believe in me through their preaching; so all [370] of them are worthy of care from you. And through that perhaps he brought them even more to faith and to hope.

[17:21a] That they all may be one. As you, Father, [are] in me and I in you, so that they too may be[27] in us.

My prayer is for them and for those who through them believe in me firmly, that they may become one in the faith and in love, just as I and you are one by nature.[i] And this particularly, for although he said, *Be compassionate, just as your Father in heaven is compassionate* (Luke 6:36), [their] ability for compassion compared to the Father is not as great, for the former are extremely sluggish and, as far as sin is concerned, very feeble. But as much as the ability is in us, to bear[28] the example of compassion.[ii]

    i. Here Moše bar Kepha refers to the Trinity.
    ii. The last phrase seems incomplete.

[17:21b] So that the world may believe that you sent me.

This is not separate from what was said before. By this[29] they would know that you are my disciples, so that you may love each other, imitating me. Furthermore, he said: *A new commandment I give you, that you love each other* (John 13:34). In this way he seals the fulfillment of the saying through the recollection of love, showing it to be the cause of all blessings.

[17:22] And the glory that you gave to me I gave to them, so that they might be one, just as we are one.

What glory does he mean? The power and the authority whereby they will perform great[30] miracles;[i] he also indicates the perfect knowledge that they

---

27. MNZ omit "one," found here in some Greek MSS; see Metzger 1975 (ad loc.).
28. **In us, to bear:** "to bear in us," M.
29. **By this,** *yaysmanē:* "in this, he says," *yaysm asē,* N.
30. **Great,** *mec:* "very great," *mecamec,* M.

received after his resurrection. And what is: *That they might be one?* Their ability through love and unity of will as regards the word of life.[ii]

 i. John Chrysostom, *Hom. Jo.* 82.2, here refers to the signs and teaching. Moše bar Kepha also explains "glory" as the signs and wonders.
 ii. This last phrase is unclear.

[17:23] I in them, and you in me, so that they may be perfect in one; and that the world may know that you sent me. And I loved them as you loved me.[31]

Many times we have said that all such things **[371]** that he once repeated in their ears he did for their confirmation and encouragement, and as an indication of his love for them. *I in them*, in accordance with what he previously said: *The glory that you gave me I gave to them.* I have made them sharers of my power; I fashioned thus the word in their ears: *The glory that you gave to me*, receiving not any acquired gift but what by nature and essence I possessed given by you. The *by you* I mentioned for their profit, and thereby confirmed in them the forms of the love by which the world, seeing so many amazing miracles and signs, may believe that you sent me.

Furthermore, as the greatest indication of my love for them I am about to indicate the torments of the cross and death for their sake and that of all those who will believe in me through them, so that on seeing all this when rebukes and afflictions[32] come upon them they may not be fearful but may become pure, even sacrificing themselves for me. When he had thus instructed them, he sealed in another greater way the mystery of the saying of the eminent gifts that he had promised them, as a demonstration for them. Therefore he said:

[17:24a] Father,[33] those you gave me, I wish that where I am they too may be[34] with me.

He indicated to them the thrones at the future judgment, which he had once described to them: *You also will sit on twelve thrones to judge the twelve tribes of Israel.*[i] Not that he had any need to request that from the Father; but as he was always requesting gifts for them from the Father and the Father provided them for their confirmation, since they received it happily, in the same way here too he set down an example, when he referred to the future events.

---

 31. **Me:** + "Father," M (see the lemma to v. 24).
 32. **Afflictions:** sg. N.
 33. **Father:** + "holy," M.
 34. **May be**, NZ: om. M.

i. Matt 19:28, to which John Chrysostom, *Hom. Jo.* 82.2, also refers. Moše bar Kepha mentions the thrones but not the tribes.

[17:24b] So that they may see my glory that you gave me, because you loved me before the creation of the world.

[372] These also are teachings of support: *The glory that you gave me*; for when he heard what he had previously said, *Father, I wish that where I am they too may be*, then he provided the further example by which they were to be raised up on the last day in the general resurrection, according to Paul's saying: *We shall be snatched up in clouds to meet the Lord in the air, and thus we shall be continuously with the Lord.*[i] At that time you shall see clearly the glory of my divinity, he says, being always with me and glorifying.

i. 1 Thess 4:17, also quoted here by Cyril of Alexandria, *Comm. Jo.* 11, and Theodore of Mopsuestia. John Chrysostom, *Hom. Jo.* 82.3, quotes 2 Cor 3:18.

[17:25a] Just Father, the world did not know you, but I knew you.

When he said, *I wish that what you gave me, that where I am they too may be*, he means those who knew and believed,[35] not the others. Although they already also saw his glory in the world, the divine signs, they did not believe and did not follow my words and did not know you, as they were always making [them] known to them and preaching, whereby they too were worthy of the gift with the latter.[i] But[36] because they promised to recognize you in themselves, yet they do not. Since they did not know me and did not believe in my word, they have no excuse to make. And behold, as for everything that I once did in the world, I attributed to you the most sublime reasons and the commandments, and that you sent me and loved me and glorified [me], but they were not profited, since they did not wish to listen.

i. The grammar of second part of this sentence is unclear, as is the sense.

[17:25b–26a] And they knew that you sent me. And I made your name known to them and shall make it known.

He turns his words to the disciples. They knew that I came forth from you, and I am not opposed to you according to the calumny of the Jews. *And I*

---

35. **And believed:** om. M.
36. **But:** om. M.

made known your name: the name of fatherhood, he means; *and I shall make it known*, after my resurrection from the dead, when once more [373] I shall teach them even higher things, and *to baptize in your name*, Father, *all nations* (cf. Matt 28:19). But at the coming of the Spirit, when he will remind you[37] of all my sayings, and since[38] these [things] are to occur in this way, and you [are] true and just, for their sake I request from you that they be with me where I shall be, so that they may also see my glory and rejoice at receiving the reward of their labors.

[17:26b] **So that the love [with] which you loved me may be in them, and I also in them.**

So that when they believe in my words and know you truly, I shall justly ask that your love be in them as in me; so that when this will occur—your love in them—I also thereafter may be in them through love because of your being in them. Likewise, all these sayings concern them: *I wish that where I am they too may be, so that they may see my glory*, and that one concerning the occurrence of true judgment and compensation (John 8:16). For the world did not know, but only they knew and believed that you sent me. Therefore this also I ask, that you love them, because I am with them forever.

Now when the evangelist John had related all this and revealed how great was his care and concern for the disciples, encouraging[39] them with many examples, entrusting them to the Father and promising the promised rewards, and revealing it before the cross and torments, and had rendered them firm in the faith and handed on the details of their long-suffering,[i] after this he begins [his account] of the torments and the cross.[ii]

i. **Of their long-suffering**: *žužkaluteann*; the demonstrative suffix could mean "their" or "his."

ii. Theodore of Mopsuestia also indicates that here the Lord ends his words to the disciples, and the evangelist proceeds to the passion. Moše bar Kepha does not break his commentary in this way.

---

37. **You**: "them," N.
38. **Since**, *zi*: om. M.
39. **Encouraging**: "to encourage," N.

[18:1–2] **When Jesus had said this, he went out with the disciples to the other side of the valley of Kedron, where the garden**[1] **was where he and his disciples entered. Judas, who was to betray him, also knew the place, for** [374] **Jesus had often gathered there with the disciples.**

Be amazed at the wisdom of the evangelist. Why did he state that *Judas also knew the place*, except to show that the Lord did not go to that place in order to be hidden from the Jews, as he said earlier that he went and hid from them (John 12:36); for if he had wished that, why did he linger in that spot? He also indicates the wall and fence[2] of the place, that it would not have been appropriate if anyone wished to flee there, for he said that it was a garden.[i] But it was to show that he willingly endured and not by force—I mean, the cross and burial. Now, saying that he often gathered there with the disciples means that [he went there] when he engaged in private[ii] instruction to them, which he did not teach to many openly, but for their personal instruction[iii] that he did for their aid. And he chose the place[3] for being apart from the crowd, so that their attention would not be disturbed by other conversation or action, so they would be unable to pay attention and be helped by the teaching.

i. Cyril of Alexandria, *Comm. Jo.* 11, draws a parallel here with paradise.
ii. **Private:** Dionysius bar Salibi, *John*, 294, here refers to "secret words," *ml' gnizt'*.
iii. **Personal instruction:** as John Chrysostom, *Hom. Jo.* 83.1.

---

1. **The garden**, MN: "a garden," Z.
2. **Fence:** pl. N.
3. **Place:** pl. M.

[18:3] And Judas, taking the band with him and the attendants from the high priests and Pharisees, came there[4] with torches and lanterns and weapons.

The band and the high priest[5] and the Pharisees, as they planned to come with Judas, are obvious. But what means *attendants*? He means those of the Romans who were from Pilate's militia,[i] for whom it was appropriate to bear weapons lest anyone oppose them, because many believed in him from among the crowds. The torches and lanterns were simply because of it being night, so that without mistake they might recognize him and lay hands on him.

i. John Chrysostom, *Hom. Jo.* 83.1, refers to "soldiers," *stratiōtai.*

[18:4] But Jesus, since he saw everything coming upon him, went out and said: Whom do you seek?

[375] He demonstrates here his foreknowledge[i] and that he went out beforehand to them from the garden in order to meet them. Saying, *Whom do you seek?* was to show that he delivered himself up willingly and not by force.[ii] But he did not do that before putting many reasons and trouble to them, in order to remove their responsibility at the future judgment.

i. **Foreknowledge:** implies a lemma similar to the Greek *eidōn*, "knowing," not the variant *idōn*, "seeing," the Armenian "he saw," *etes*, in MNZ.
ii. Christ's willingness to suffer is stressed throughout the commentary; cf. *Comm. Diat.* 20.13; Išodad; and Dionysius bar Salibi, *John*, 294.

[18:5] They replied to him: Jesus of Nazareth. He said to them: I am he. Judas, who betrayed him, was also with them.

Notice here what he said. If they had torches and lanterns yet even by speaking to the Lord they did not recognize him, what more certain sign than this [was there] that he did not wish to hand himself up? They certainly did not recognize him. So how much the more were they unable to seize him by force.

---

4. **There,** NZ: om. M.
5. **Band, high priest:** pl. M.

[18:6] And when he said, I am he, they went backward and fell to the ground.

Why did the Lord do that, save to show them that you are unable to lay hands on me by tricks or your power? Furthermore, he did those signs and miracles close by,[6] in order to confirm even more their inflexible wicked character[7] and invariable envy, that they were not fearful of that or turned away from their evil plans.

[18:7–8a] Again he asked them: Whom do you seek? And they said: Jesus of Nazareth. Jesus replied to them:[8] I am he.

Why did he repeat: *I said that I am he?*[i] It was to show that by saying once, *I am he*, you went back and fell to the ground, but you did not understand, nor were you helped, being reproved by his power.

i. The commentary gives the phrase "I said that," which MN omit in the lemma.

[18:8b–9] Now, if you seek me, let these ones go. So that the saying might be fulfilled that he said: Of those whom you gave me I shall not lose[9] any.

[376] He wishes merely to indicate their frenzy and error, in that they wished also to arrest the disciples. *Now, if you seek me*, as you say, *let these ones go.* As for what the evangelist said, *That the saying might be fulfilled that he said: Of those whom you gave me I shall lose not a single one,*[i] he wished to speak about his foreknowledge.[ii] He did not do that in order to abandon them, but he arranged to leave them for a time, for which reason he calmly said: *Let these ones go.*

i. **A single one**: *ew oč' mi*. The commentary changes the lemma, *ew oč' zok'*, in MNZ.
ii. Theodore of Mopsuestia here explains that Christ knew what would happen and so predicted it. He indicates that scripture uses this way of speaking to express what was certain to happen. See further n. ii to the commentary on John 17:12b, above.

---

6. **Close by**: om. M.
7. **Wicked character**, *čarabarut'iwn*, N: "wickedness," *čarut'iwn*, M.
8. **Them**: + "I told you that," Z. See commentary below.
9. **I shall not lose**: MNZ, as John 6:39; "I have not lost" in the Greek.

[18:10a] But Simon Peter, because he had a sword, drew it and struck the high priest's servant, and took off his right ear.

Examine this too. Why did Peter carry a sword with him? Behold, he well knew the gentleness of his teaching, who had even given the command: *Whoever strikes your cheek, offer him the other one.*[i] A sword is[10] also the cause of killing, as the evangelist[ii] [said]: *He struck the servant's ear.* But he did not do it for his own sake, but he tried more than everyone to save his teacher, especially on seeing that they had cast hands on him in vain and uselessly. Now, he had prepared to have a sword with him when they sacrificed[11] the Passover lamb.[iii] And when he understood what they were plotting against his teacher, he carried it with him in order to effect something, just as he also showed his vengeance.

i. Luke 6:29; the parallel in Matt 5:39 specifically refers to the right cheek. Cyril of Alexandria, *Comm. Jo.* 11, refers to the *typos* of the Jews not having a right ear to hear (*akoēs hōsper erēmous tēs dexias*).

ii. **Evangelist:** John, also Luke 22:50.

iii. John Chrysostom interprets the sword as a table knife from the Passover; see Mathews and Sanjian 1991 (110). Moše bar Kepha states that perhaps Peter had a sword out of fear, or a knife in order to kill the lamb for the evening meal; he also refers to Peter's vengeance for his Lord. Edwards (2004, 166) quotes the explanation attributed to Theophylact: Peter acquired the sword for the sacrifice of the lamb.

[18:10b] And the name of the servant was Malchus.

Why did he show such benevolence for the healing of such an immoral servant who laid hands on him before the many others, except to reveal not only his gentleness and immeasurable patience but also the divine power? He set back in place the ear that had been cut off and removed,[i] he who up to that hour still demonstrated signs in order to help [377] and reprove them, but they were not helped. That same servant after his healing was the very one who struck him,[ii] lest they might leave an excuse for pardoning themselves at the [day of] retribution.

i. John does not mention the healing. Theodore of Mopsuestia refers to Luke (i.e., Luke 22:51); he notes that the evangelists did not consult each other in writing their accounts, but each wrote as seemed good to him—hence the omissions and mixed order of events in

---

10. **Is:** "was," M.
11. **They sacrificed:** om. N.

the Gospels. Moše bar Kepha and Dionysius bar Salibi (*John*, 295) refer to the healing but give no source.

ii. See v. 22. *Comm. Diat.* 20.13 notes that Christ's love was repaid by hate on the part of Malchus.

[18:11] Jesus said to him: Return your sword to its sheath. The cup that the Father gave me, shall I not drink it?

That is, I have no need of what you are doing in attempting to help me, because not by force but willingly I shall endure the torments and death. Why did he say: *The cup that the Father gave me, shall I not drink?* It shows that even more willingly I accept death than those who will drink the cup with joy. For those will be the salvation of the world,[i] which to the Father also is not a little pleasing.

i. For an extensive discussion of the cup of joy of the Spirit contrasted with the cup of anger for the wicked, and the apostles as bearers of the cup to the world, see *Teaching* 507–16. Moše bar Kepha; Dionysius bar Salibi, *John*, 296; and Tat'ewac'i, 591, all stress again Christ's free will in accepting the torments and crucifixion.

[18:12–13a] Then the band and the chiliarch and the attendants of the Jews seized Jesus and bound him. And they brought him first to Anna.

Why does he set down only this except to show their poisonous fury, that they had not at all[12] desisted from the anger they possessed? Behold, at first he cast a veil over their eyes so they would not know him. And when he again said, *I am he, they went backward and fell on the ground.* And furthermore, he restored the servant's ear to its original state in the twinkling of an eye, while his anger against Peter shows that I have no need of assistance. But of all this they were unaware and comprehended nothing but seized and bound him.

[18:13b] Who was the father-in-law of Caiaphas, who was high priest for that year.

Why does he mention Caiaphas, except to indicate that the Jews reckoned him to be a great adornment and[13] boast for themselves, for which reason [378] they promoted him to high priest? And what would *for that year* be, except that they did not hold the high priesthood in accordance with the ear-

---

12. **At all:** om. M.
13. **And:** "even," N.

lier rules, which did not change save only by death? But now the regulations had been destroyed and corrupted by the Romans through bribes,[i] and they received year by year the honor of the high priesthood, which was usurped by those who were able to give more money to acquire the high priesthood.

i. **Bribes:** *kašark'*. Tat'ewac'i, 592, notes that the high priesthood was acquired annually by "payments," *varjk'*.

[18:14] **This was that Caiaphas who had advised the Jews: It is better that one man die for the people.**

Why does he mention Caiaphas again? It was so that the evangelist could make it clear that this Caiaphas himself prophesied about the Savior. How did he prophesy? He previously stated, *It is better for one man to die for the people* (John 11:50–51), which death indeed the Lord suffered willingly for the people so that he might save not one nation alone but all the nations of mankind, although he did not know what he said.

[18:15–16a] **Simon Peter and the[14] other disciple followed Jesus. And that disciple, because he was known to the high priest, entered with Jesus into the court of the high priest. *And Peter stood by the door outside.[15]**

The evangelist speaks of himself as the other disciple but does not introduce his name. Why, then? Lest he draw any pretext of praise to himself, indicating that when the disciples left him, I remained with him.[i] As for the fact that he was known to the high priest, he set down also his entering after Jesus, but not Peter with him. Not that I show any superiority of love for Christ than Peter, nor any audacity of courage, nor putting myself above [379] Peter, but because of being known to the high priest he did that, so that thereby he might better remove from himself any excuse of praise, and furthermore, through entering into the court he might show that he would be an eyewitness of all the events that he related.

i. John Chrysostom, *Hom. Jo.* 83.2, notes that the other disciple is the author of the Gospel, who gives priority to Peter. Cyril of Alexandria, *Comm. Jo.* 11, states that John avoided glory (*philokompia*). Moše bar Kepha indicates that John the evangelist does not identify himself here, or in the references to the one who leaned on Jesus's breast (John 13:25; 21:20), in order to put Peter in first place. Dionysius bar Salibi, *Gospels*, 96; and

---

14. **The,** *-n*: MNZ, not Greek.
15. **And Peter … outside:** om. M.

Tat'ewac'i, 591, state that John wished to avoid glory. Tat'ewac'i, 592, mentions various interpretations of why John was known to the high priest.

[18:16b] The other disciple, who was known to the high priest, went out and spoke to the doorkeeper and brought in Peter.

Again he speaks about himself. And he indicates and reveals that the reason why Peter did not enter with them into the court was fear or hesitation, but not permission to enter.[i]

i. Moše bar Kepha suggests that Peter was afraid because all the other disciples had fled. Tat'ewac'i, 593, says that Peter was concerned that he might be recognized as the one who cut off the servant's ear.

[18:17] The girl who was the doorkeeper said to Peter: Are you also not from among the disciples of that man? And he said: I am not.

It was indicated now very clearly that the evangelist was known to be a disciple of Christ, as the girl asked Peter: *Are you too not one of his disciples?* The evangelist indicates: I[16] know this one to be his disciple, so are you too not his companion?

[18:18–19] There were standing there servants and attendants; they had made a fire because it was cold, and they were warming themselves. Peter also stood with them and warmed himself. And the high priest asked Jesus about his disciples and about[17] his teaching.

Why did the high priest interrogate them, save because he did not find any case against him? He then attempted by deceit to interrogate [him] about his disciples and about his teaching in order to be able to find some words of praise, so that[18] he could slander him to Peter.

[18:20–21] Jesus answered him and said: I [380] openly spoke in the world.[19] At all times I taught in the synagogue and in the temple where all the Jews

---

16. I: "we," N.

17. **About** (*bis*), MZ: om. N.

18. **So that:** "whereby," N.

19. **In the world,** *yašxarhi*, NZ: "to the world," *ašxarhi*, M.

were gathered, and I spoke nothing in secret. Why do you ask me? Ask those who listened as to what I spoke with them. Behold, they know what I said.

See again[20] how to their faces he gives only gentle responses to the question: *I never spoke anything with them in secret*, if it is necessary for you to ask these things from me, but openly in my teaching. Ask the Jews who hate and insult me, so that they may relate to you what I was continually teaching and instructing with signs.

[18:22] **When he had said this, one of the attendants who was standing there struck Jesus and said: Do you thus respond to the high priest?**

Surely the Lord did not so respond to the high priest as to be worthy of being struck,[i] but it was so that they might make completely clear their own fury and error[21] and show their pointless hatred.

    i. Dionysius bar Salibi, *Gospels*, 96, indicates that John Chrysostom says that the attendant was the one whose ear the Lord had healed; but at *Hom. Jo.* 83.3, Chrysostom does not explicitly make that identification.

[18:23] **And Jesus said to him: If I have spoken something evil, testify concerning the evil. But if good, why do you strike me?**

Once again, gently to harshness, he reproved their wickedness.[22] If I gave any harsh answer, indicate it to me, and he added the appropriate retribution. But if you did not hear anything of that sort, *why do you strike me?* He did not say this in vexation, on the grounds that you[23] struck me pointlessly or suchlike, but this only: *If I said [something] good, why did you strike?* revealing his limitless patience and long-suffering. He also taught us to be similarly gentle and not to bear a grudge, and not even to seek an excuse for contrariety.[i]

    i. Here Step'annos of Siwnik', 139, adduces Isa 50:6. Tat'ewac'i, 593, quotes Christ's injunction to turn the other cheek (Luke 6:29).

---

20. **Again:** om. M.
21. **Error:** pl. N.
22. **Wickedness:** pl. N.
23. **You:** "they," N.

[381] [18:24] And Anna sent him bound to Caiaphas the high priest.

Why, then, did he send him, except that because he found no cause in him he had him sent to Caiaphas? This is the one about whom the evangelist earlier had said that he asked Jesus about his disciples and teaching (John 18:18–19). There was also a kinship between them both, for which reason he had him taken to him, attracting some advantage to himself and by further investigation[24] to find some words worthy of death.

[18:25–27] And Simon Peter was standing and warming himself. They said to him: Are you not also from among his disciples? He denied it and said: I am not.[25] And one of the high priest's servants, a relative of the one whose ear Peter had cut off, said: Did I not see you in the garden with him? Again Peter denied it, and immediately the cock crowed.

Why did the evangelist set this down, except in order to make very clear that when Peter denied, the cock crowed, just as the Lord had previously said. He gave a firm indication, saying: *Before the cock crows, you will deny me three times* (Matt 26:34, 75; Mark 14:30, 72).[i] The evangelist wishes to pass over in secret nothing of what Peter did. And not to calumniate Peter in any way did the evangelist set this down, but to demonstrate the unerring predictions by the Lord, and also [to indicate] his healing again of his denial and receiving repentance, so that thereby he might teach no little consolation to those who turn to him. Through this he advises us not to take refuge in one's own power and be deprived of his assistance, boasting to act without his help, lest in that way we also stumble. Furthermore, the evangelist indicates his own truthfulness by not passing over Peter and hiding his denial.

i. Theodore of Mopsuestia and Dionysius bar Salibi (*John*, 297) note the evangelists differ in their Gospel accounts of these events; Dionysius adds that they all described the one passion.

[382] [18:28a] And they brought Jesus from the lodging of Caiaphas to the palace of the judge, and it was dawn.

See again how they act madly and move him from place to place, and do not stop in one place but [go] from judge to judge until they stood him[26]

---

24. **Investigation**: pl. N.
25. **I am not**: *tĕ čem*, NZ; *oč' em*, M.
26. **Him**, *zna*, M: "even," *ews*, N.

before Pilate the Roman. Why did they bring him to Pilate? It seems that they thought something like the following: Unless we bring him before him and bear witness to things that please him, in order to kill him, perhaps he will not consent for us to do what we wish against his will. But because he was judge and prince over them, therefore in every way they tried to influence him, in order to make him an accomplice in their own wicked plan.

[18:28b] **And they did not enter the palace, lest they be defiled; but so that they might eat the Passover.**

By saying, *Passover*, he means the sixth day, on which they ate unleavened bread, for which reason *they did not enter the palace*, lest they defile the Passover.[i] For the prince whom he mentions was a Roman, and it was not possible to mingle with them. Therefore they abhorred entering the palace, on account of the Passover.

i. **Passover:** *zatik.* Moše bar Kepha states that by "Pascha" John means either the whole feast or the moment when they prepared the Pascha. Dionysius bar Salibi, *John*, 298, counts the days from Jesus's going to Bethany (six days before the Passover, John 12:1) and notes the discrepancies in the evangelists' accounts. Išodad says that John refers not to a single day of the Passover but to the whole week. He notes that "some say" Jesus ate the unleavened bread on the previous day.

[18:29] **Pilate went out to them and said: What accusation do you offer against this man?**

When they did not enter the palace for the reason we stated above, Pilate came out to them in order to ask why they accused him, so that he might verify the cause.

[18:30] **They answered**[27] **and said: Unless that**[28] **man were an evildoer, we would not have delivered him to you.**

This was clear, that they found no cause against him, save only that they demonstrated their wicked envy by an unclear accusation. [383] But we can understand at this point that although the empire of the Romans ruled over them, yet they were not yet completely triumphant, because they had not yet separated them from their own rituals.[i]

---

27. **Answered:** + "him," M ("said" + "him," Z).
28. **That,** MZ: "the," N.

i. **Rituals:** *krawnkʻ*, sometimes translated as "religion." It has the particular overtone of "customs, rituals"; see, e.g., Acts 26:3, referring to Judaism, or *Buzandaran*, 6.2, referring to the "regulations" (Garsoïan's translation) of the apostolic church. The term *awrēnkʻ* (in the following lemma, translated as "laws") is more embracing, meaning "traditions," and is basic to Ełišēʻs understanding of the Armenian church and people. See Thomson 1975; and more broadly, Mahé 2000.

[18:31–32] **Pilate said to them: Take him to you, and judge [him] according to your laws. The Jews said to him, It is not right for us to put anyone to death, that the saying of Jesus might be fulfilled that he uttered, indicating by what death he would die.**[29]

See how they distorted the intention[30] of their wicked plan by saying: *It is not allowed*[31] *to us to put anyone to death.* Perhaps they would have alleged the feast, that it is not allowed to us to put to death on the feast, but they would have said that not truthfully but by trickery and deceit. But because they wished to kill him with a more cruel death, that is, to hang him on a cross, perhaps[i] the death of malefactors, it was not possible for them to do so, and as confirmation of the saying, to stone Stephen after the ascension.[ii] The evangelist's declaring, *That the saying that Jesus uttered might be fulfilled*, the Jews carried out by delivering him into the hands of Pontius Pilate.[iii] Also [they said], *It is not allowed to us to put anyone to death*, because they did not find cause against him by which according to their customary laws[iv] it would have possible to put him to death. But it is allowed to you, that is, if he says he is king of Israel; and this is very opposed to Caesar, so you must be zealous about it.

i. **Perhaps:** *tʻerews*, a curious hesitation on the part of Nonnus. Tatʻewacʻi, 595, states that the Jews wished to put Jesus to death in a more derisory (*jałeli*) way.

ii. Acts 6–7. John Chrysostom, *Hom. Jo.* 83.4, adduces the case of Stephen as proof that the Jews were allowed to put people to death. Dionysius bar Salibi, *Gospels*, 105, states that the Jews could put people to death *except* by crucifixion. Here the infinitive "to stone" presumably also depends on "it was not possible."

iii. **Pontius:** *pontacʻi*, with the place-name suffix *-acʻi*, as if Pilate came from the province of Pontus. Movsēs Xorenacʻi, *History*, 2.15, states that the father of Pontius Pilate lived in Pontus.

iv. **Laws:** *awrēnkʻ*. See note to commentary on v. 30, just above.

---

29. **Would die,** *meranelocʻ icē*, NZ: "will die," *meranelocʻ ē*, M.

30. **Intention,** *mtacutʻiwnsn* (pl.), MV: "extent," *taracutʻiwnsn* (pl.), N.

31. **Allowed,** *part*: "right," *aržan*, in the lemma.

[18:33–34] **Pilate entered the palace again, summoned Jesus, and said to him: Are you the king of the Jews? Jesus replied: Do you say that of yourself, or did others tell[32] you about me?**

Why did he ask that, for he had heard only from them: *It is not allowed to us to put to death*? So, understand that [**384**] they wished to say something like:[i] He is king of the Jews and opposed to Caesar, so you must put him to death. Therefore he asked him: *Are you the king of the Jews? Jesus replied: Do you say it of yourself, or did others tell you?* And why did the Lord say that, save to show him that what you ask, if it is from you and you spoke of yourself, you ask rightly; and it would be necessary for me to tell you concerning what you asked? But if others told you, that is the Jews, make them appear before you, so that you may hear what they accuse me of.

> i. The following *etē* could either mean "that," introducing the reported speech, or "if," i.e., "If he is king … then you must."

[18:35] **Pilate replied: Am I a Jew? Your people and the high priests[33] delivered you up. What have you done?**

When he heard from the Lord, *Do you say this of yourself?* he replied: I am not from among the Jews that I might calumniate you, because they accused you, making you guilty, about which I asked, namely, your people and the high priests.[34] He did not reply in accordance with his words, because Pilate wished to mediate between the two parties, especially to hear from the Lord an account concerning the deeds that he mentioned: *What have you done?* that is, very wicked deeds, just as they accuse you, against Caesar or their laws.

---

32. **Tell**, NZ: "teach," M.
33. **People, high priests:** "peoples," "high priest," M.
34. **High priests:** sg. M.

[18:36] **Jesus replied: My kingdom is not of this world. If my kingdom were of this world, my servants would indeed fight against you[35] so that I not be delivered to you.[36] But now my kingdom is not from here.**

What sort of statement did the Lord make to Pilate? Mark the lofty meaning of this saying. You examine me because they[37] said: *I am king of the Jews.* I am a king, but not from this world [**385**] did I acquire my kingdom, that can be dissolved and destroyed, but [it is] a heavenly one, permanent and eternal. For I am not[38] earthly but heavenly. So the Jews have no cause of which to accuse me, nor are you permitted to act with partiality, joining in their wickedness, supposing that like some king you exact some vengeance from me, as I am the opposite to what they say. For if I were such, *my servants would fight against the Jews[i] to prevent me [from] being delivered to you.* Also I would need crowds and weapons and treasure. If I am such a person, examine that. But because I am heavenly, I have no need of those things.

See also what he said: Not that *my kingdom* is not over the world, but it *is not of the world,* in order to indicate that unlike that of mankind it is not perishable and destructible and temporary. So, if it is[39] of heaven, then not only is it unending and over heaven, but I am also king over heaven and of earth.

i. **Against the Jews**: cf. the lemma of Z.

[18:37a] **Pilate said to him: If this were[40] so, you are some king. Jesus replied and said: You say that I am a king.**

With what intention, then, did Pilate say this, save to show that by your saying that your kingdom is not of this world you revealed that you are truly a king? But here the Lord made no other response but only repeated the same as the first comment: *You said.*

---

35. **Against you,** N: om. MZ.
36. **You,** MN: "the Jews," Z.
37. **They:** "I," M.
38. **Not:** om. M.
39. **It is:** om. N.
40. **Were,** NZ: "is," M.

[18:37b] But for this I was born, and for the same have I come[41] **into the world, *that I may testify to the truth.**[42]

He showed clearly that he possessed his kingdom by essence,[i] in order to state that he did not receive it as something acquired, like a gift from someone else. For just as being born from the Father before all time I remain inseparably, likewise my kingdom is without beginning **[386]** and timeless. But Pilate did not understand the meaning of this remark, as we did later. His saying, *To this I was born,* is not to be understood as *all authority was given me in heaven and on earth* (Matt 28:18), because those [words] belonged to his providential dispensation in accordance with his teaching at the time the still weak minds of the disciples, just as again he said about the Father, *Also to the Son he gave to possess life in himself* (John 5:26), and what resembles these [sayings].

So where are those foolish ones, especially if they denied only Christ, saying that if *authority was given* to him, as he said after the resurrection, Christ is a mere man? But if you truly believe these sayings by the Savior: *I was born* to a kingdom; and you posit that of his heavenly nature, and later by what *was given* he meant the authority of his human nature, that he was born king from Mary; let us say this to them: How is it understood in this way? Behold, he said: *For this I was born, and for the same I came into the world.*[43] He shows that I am not *of the world,* for which reason he said, *I came into the world,* because the one who is of the world does not naturally say, I came into the world, and behold, he has from this the being born and growing up.

Furthermore, he[44] said: *All authority was given to me in heaven and on earth,* after the resurrection. For after the resurrection he said: *It was given to me.* But if that were so, he was not born king from Mary, but it was as if he was to receive the kingdom through some suitable way or by chance, but not as someone saying, *Born for*[45] *the kingdom,* and *Coming into the world for the same.* And what means: *I*[46] *may testify to the truth?* It means what he said about knowing the Father and his uncreated kingdom that has no beginning or end. For that was[47] the truth, to know him to be the Son of the Father by nature, and through his torments to be freed from our debts.

---

41. **Have I come,** *ekeal em,* MZ: *ekeal,* N.
42. **That … truth:** om. M.
43. **The world,** N (= lemma): "this world," M.
44. **He:** "you," M.
45. **For,** M: "in," N.
46. **I:** "he," M.
47. **Was:** om. M.

i. **Essence:** *ēut'iwn.* For the terminology, see the introduction, xxxix.

[387] [18:37c] Everyone who is[48] of the truth hears my voice.

He indicates that those who have a mind of truth easily hear my voice; but those who still have thoughts of envy and evil never hear my voice. For which reason very willingly he wished to hear him, hence Pilate asked:

[18:38a] What is the[49] truth? And having said this, he again went out to the Jews.

When Pilate asked, *What is the[50] truth?* and wished to learn, first he went out to the Jews, so that perhaps he might find a way to extricate him from their hands and then to examine the[51] truth from him through a complete account of his teaching at an appropriate time. For that reason the evangelist set down that he went out to them, showing his going out for a second time, because they did not enter the palace, lest they be defiled.

[18:38b–40] He said to them: I do not find a single cause in him. But it is your custom that I release to you someone on the Passover. So do you wish that I release to you the king of the Jews? They all cried out and said: Not that one, but Barabba. And that Barabba was a brigand.

Because Pilate was able to release him, he tried thereby to extricate him from their hands, saying: *I do[52] not find any fault[53] in him.*[i] But seeing that he was not profited, he tried another method, which he thought would much please them. *It is a custom,* he said, *to release someone to you on the feast. So whom do you wish? Shall I release to you the king of the Jews?* Perhaps by mentioning the gift[ii] of the Passover[iii] they would be pleased, and they would agree through their natural disposition. If not as a just person, as least as a guilty one they would allow him to release him on the feast. But he did not calm their fury and rage.

i. The text of this quotation in N is from John 19:4, not the lemma.

---

48. **Is,** NZ: om. M.
49. **The,** NZ: om. M.
50. **The:** om. M.
51. **The:** om. M.
52. **Do,** N (= Z): "did," M.
53. **Fault:** "cause," M.

ii. **Gift:** *ĕncay*, or "offering."
iii. **Passover:** *zatik*, as in the lemma; just above, Nonnus refers to the "feast," *tawn*.

[388] CHAPTER 19

[19:1] **Then Pilate took Jesus and scourged him.**

When he saw that he was not helped at all in what he had aimed at, *he took and scourged him*, perhaps in order to be able thereby to calm them and save him from death and to win him over.[i]

i. Tat'ewac'i, 596–98, refers to the accounts of these events in the other Gospels.

[19:2–3] **And the soldiers, having made a crown from thorns, placed it on his head. And they clothed him in a purple robe and came to him and said: Greetings, king of the Jews. And they smote him.**

The soldiers did this, ridiculing[1] him as king of the Jews, mocking and deriding him.[i] And at the pleasure of the Jews they increased their insults on him, so that the attendants even received a present from the Jews, since that activity seemed very pleasing to them. Now, the evangelist describes the soldiers doing all this in order to inform us that they did not do all this at the command of Pilate but that they wished to kill him and were striking him and insulting him with insatiable wickedness.

i. Dionysius bar Salibi, *Gospels*, 112–13; and Tat'ewac'i, 596, here discuss the significance of the purple robe.

[19:4] **Pilate came out again and said to them: Behold, I bring him out to you, so that you may know that I[2] find no fault in him.**

What means *I bring him out*, save to show that he has no fault [worthy] of death, therefore it is not possible for me to put him to death? But since I have presented him to you, do what you wish, that is, if unjustly and wrongly

---

1. **Ridiculing**, *nšawakelov*, N: "indicating," *nšanakelov*, M.
2. I, *es*, NZ: om. M.

-389-

you even wish to kill him. By this it became more obvious that he was only attempting to extricate him from their hands and to expose their lawlessness.

[19:5–6] **Jesus came out, and he had a crown of thorns and a purple robe. [389] And he said to them:[3] Behold, your man for you. When[4] the high priests and attendants saw [him][5] they raised a cry and said: Crucify him. Pilate said to them: Take him for yourselves, and crucify him yourselves, for I find no fault in him.**

Why [did he say], *Take him for yourselves and crucify him yourselves, for I find no fault in him*, except once more to show to them and reveal his innocence, and that they only wished to crucify him? Therefore Pilate made many attempts, not only with words but also by scourging, that he might be able to soften their minds and in this way to please them and extricate him from their hands. But because they were filled with mad rage, he was totally unsuccessful.

[19:7] **The Jews replied and said: We have laws, and according to our laws he must die, because he made himself Son of God.**

Since they were unable to give any response to Pilate about Christ when he said to them, *I have found not a single fault in him*, they introduced another accusation. For first they said that he calls himself king, but now that he made himself Son of God. Hence they mentioned the laws, according to which he must die. Behold, previously when Pilate delivered him into their hands, they rejected him and said: *It is not lawful for us to put anyone to death*. Be amazed[6] at their madness, how they reshaped their falsehood in every way. First they calumniated him as calling himself king in opposition to Caesar, later as Son of God: first, *It is not lawful for us to put anyone to death*; later, *According to our laws he must die.*

[19:8] **When Pilate heard these words, he was even more afraid.**

[390] What does it mean: *He was even more afraid*, when he heard this? Previously Pilate often had heard[7] about the signs and powerful acts[8] and

---

3. **To them**, NZ: om. M.

4. **When**, NZ: om. M.

5. **Him**, Z: om. MN.

6. **Be amazed**, M: "he was amazed," N.

7. **Had heard**, *lueal ēr*, N: *lueal ē*, M.

8. **And powerful acts**, *ew zawrut'eanc'n*: om. M.

miracles that Jesus was performing; and when he heard from the Jews that he made himself Son of God, he was disturbed in himself at the great danger and tried to release him.

[19:9] **He entered the palace again and said to Jesus: Whence are you? And Jesus did not give him any response.**

Why, then, did he not give him a response? Since Pilate was afraid, therefore he wished to question him, especially because in the previous interrogation he had heard from the Lord about his kingdom, *For this I was born and came into the world*, and *My kingdom is not of this world*. Through this alone he could have believed in the truth and extricated him from the hands of the Jews. But he did not do anything of the sort; therefore the Lord from then on gave no response, indicating that he was not aided thereby nor was it useful.[i] Furthermore, it was no longer a time for instruction but for torments, because Satan had inspired them all. Therefore by his silence he demonstrated more clearly the state of his endurance for the torments that he would suffer for us.[9]

i. John Chrysostom, *Hom. Jo.* 84.2, indicates that Jesus's silence was the fulfillment of Isa 53:7–8. Tat'ewac'i refers to Isa 53:7 and also to Ps 37:15.

[19:10] **Pilate said to him: Do you not speak to me? Do you not know that I have authority to crucify you, and I have authority to release you?**

For that reason the Lord even more refrained from giving him a response, because he had *the authority to release* him and did not release him but complied with their wishes. He tried to release him; but being cowardly and feeble he was not possessed of authority, as he had said: *[I] have authority to crucify you and possess authority to release [you].*

[19:11a] **Jesus replied and said: You would not have [391] authority over me at all, unless it had been given to you from above.**

Why did the Lord say that, except because Pilate had spoken very loftily and boastfully about the authority that he possessed? Therefore he informed him that not in accordance with your supposition and authoritative ability do you judge me but *from above*, that is, from the Father, indicating that it was his will that through these torments he would be reconciled with his creation, for which very reason *I came into the world.*

---

9. **For us:** om. M.

[19:11b] Therefore he who delivered me to you, his is the greater sin.

Let us consider the meaning of this saying, what sort of statement he made. He had earlier said, *You would not have authority over me, unless it had been given to you from above*, that is, from the Father for the salvation of the world. But you do not remain innocent[10] of your evil deeds, because you do not act thus in order to carry out the will of the Father but because of the will of the Jews and fear. Therefore *he who delivered me has the greater sin.* These [words] he set down next, indicating that they did not do this to me because of the Father's will but following Satan's will to become his accomplices. They did[11] this through envy and hatred, carrying out the wickedness of their own will, but not being supporters of the Father. So then, the greatest sin is his who through such plans delivered me to you.

[19:12a] And from then Pilate sought to release him.

Therefore when Jesus said, *[He] who delivered me up has the greater sin*, he felt remorse, but he did not completely come to the truth.

[392] [19:12b] And the Jews cried out and said: If you release this one, you are not a friend of Caesar's. Everyone who calls himself a king is opposed to Caesar.

When first they referred to their laws, *We have laws and according to the laws*[12] *he must die*, and gained no advantage from Pilate, they turned to other means, by which they frightened Pilate, saying, *Everyone who calls himself*[13] *a king is opposed to Caesar; so if you release this one, you are not a friend of Caesar's.* Did you see their multifarious calumnies and ruses full of falseness, how in every way they treacherously sought means how they might be able to kill him?

[19:13–14] Now when Pilate heard these words, he took Jesus outside and sat on the bench in the place that is called "stone pavement," and in Hebrew,

---

10. **Innocent,** *anpart:* "guilty," *part,* M.
11. **Did:** "do," N.
12. **The laws:** "them," N.
13. **Calls himself:** "is called," N.

kappat'a. It was the eve of the Passover, *and was about the sixth hour,[14] and he said to the Jews: Behold, your king for you.

Not even here does Pilate understand the truth. For sitting in the place called *stone pavement*,[i] where he always made judgment between them,[ii] he should have made an investigation and had the accusation[15] presented and very thoroughly examined what they were saying about him, that *he was opposed to Caesar*. But he did not grasp the truth but delivered him into their hands. It seems to me that by this he wished to save him from death and calm them a little from their fury, by saying: *Behold, your king for you*.

    i. **Stone pavement**: *k'arayatak* (lit. "stone floor"). Moše bar Kepha explains this as the Hebrew equivalent of *gpypt'*, the meaning of the Syriac being "convex, hollow."
    ii. Dionysius bar Salibi, *John*, 305, notes that this was the place of judgment.

[19:15a] And they cried out: Remove [him] from us, remove [him] from us, and crucify him.

Why, then, did they cry out thus, save because he had delivered him into their hands, they themselves did not wish to kill him in a different fashion but *You crucify him*? Why did they insist on crucifixion? It was lest **[393]** by killing him in a different way many, who had seen his miracles, might believe that he endured a death of the just at their hands; but by hanging him on wood they might remind the people what Moses had said, *Cursed is everyone who will hang on wood* (Deut 21:23), and thereby perhaps move the hearts of them all[16] to denial and hatred. But they did not comprehend what Moses had also written: *You will see your lives hanging on wood, and you will not believe in your lives* (Deut 28:66).

[19:15b] Pilate said to them: Shall I crucify your king?

Why did Pilate repeat the name king? It was so that perhaps by this name he might shame[17] them, and there would be a way to extricate him from their hands, by calling him their king.[i]

    i. John Chrysostom, *Hom. Jo.* 84.2, offers the same argument.

---

14. **And was … hour**, NZ: om. M.
15. **Accusation**: pl. M.
16. **The hearts of them all**: "every heart," M.
17. **He might shame**: "he shames," M.

[19:15c–16a] **The high priests responded: We have no king except Caesar. Then he gave him into their hands, so that he might be crucified.**

Did you see at what hour, or after how many words Pilate handed him over? First he heard, *I am a king not of this world, but for this I was born and came into the world*, revealing the uncreated and indissoluble[18] kingdom; then also[19] what he heard from the Jews: *He calls himself the Son of God*; and after releasing him [he heard] his wife, as Matthew narrated: *Have nothing to do with that just man* (Matt 27:19). Rightly, then, when Pilate was questioning, *Who are you?* he gave no response, knowing that it would be of no help, as we said above.

[19:16b–17a] **And they took him and led him away. And he carried his own wooden cross.**

Why, then, did he carry his own[20] wooden cross? By doing that as an indication to him that he is guilty of death and wood, legally do we do this to him. And furthermore, because they were in the Passover, [**394**] it was not possible for them to carry the wood themselves.[i] But they were unaware and did not understand that it would be merely the fulfillment of the law, Isaac himself carrying the wood when he approached the altar on which he was to be offered as a sacrifice to God (Gen 22:6).[ii] That foretold Christ's offering himself as a sacrifice to propitiate the Father, not for himself but for the salvation of the whole[21] world.

    i. Theodore of Mopsuestia's account of the passion engages with the versions of the other evangelists, and here he refers to Simon of Cyrene carrying the cross: Matt 27:32; Mark 15:21; Luke 23:26. Tat'ewac'i, 598, also mentions Simon.

    ii. Dionysius bar Salibi, *John*, 306, also makes the same comparison.

[19:17b–18a] **And he went out to *a place that is called "the skull,"[22] and in Hebrew, Gołgot'a, where they crucified him.**

Why *was the place named Gołgot'a?*[i] We have found from the tradition of the ancients, from the Hebrew nation, that there they buried the protofather

---

18. **Indissoluble**, *anlucaneloy*: "indestructible," *anełcaneloy*, M.
19. **Also**: om. M.
20. **His own**: om. M.
21. **Whole**: om. M.
22. **A place … "the skull"**: "the place that was named of a skull," Z.

Adam.[ii] Rightly there did he set up the cross, for which reason he came in search of the original man, so that where the victory of death occurred, there death might be defeated; and where corruption arrogantly ruled, there incorruption might flourish again; and especially that where our human nature had been subdued, conquered by sin, there he might raise up the original freedom; because he who in the beginning fashioned man, for him it was fitting also to renew him.

i. Here the text of the commentary is close to the text of the lemma in Z, not that of MN. Č'rak'ean, editor of the printed text, notes that the section from v. 17 to v. 35 is found separately in a thirteenth-century *čarĕntir* (no. 13 in the Venice collection) under the name of Chrysostom.

ii. John Chrysostom, *Hom. Jo.* 85.1, states that "some say," *tines phasin*, that Adam was buried there, but he does not expand on its significance; Cyril of Alexandria does not mention the tradition. Moše bar Kepha indicates that Adam's skull was buried there, and he gives the tale of Noah taking Adam's bones into the ark and their division among his three sons. Moše also refers to the wood of the tree on which was found the ram when Abraham was about to sacrifice Isaac. Dionysius bar Salibi, *John*, 306, notes that Adam's skull was buried at Golgotha by Shem, who received it when Noah divided Adam's bones. Tat'ewac'i does not here refer to Adam or his skull.

[19:18b] **And with him two others on either side, and in the middle Jesus.**

Why did they do this? It was to confirm totally his being guilty of death; therefore they crucified him between the brigands. And this was in no way a support to their fury, because thereby they merely gave shape to what Isaiah had prophesied about him: *He shall be reckoned among evildoers* (Isa 53:12).[i] See how all their wickedness worked as a reproach and censure of themselves.

i. This is quoted by John Chrysostom, *Hom. Jo.* 85.1; Moše bar Kepha; Dionysius bar Salibi, *John*, 307; and Tat'ewac'i. Tat'ewac'i adds information about the brigands: Demnos the believer, and Kestos, who did not believe.

[395] [19:19] **And Pilate wrote a notice and placed it on the cross. And it was written: Jesus of Nazareth, king of the Jews.**

Why did he write the notice[i] except[23] to show to all passers-by the reason why they crucified him? The sign caused the Jews much reprehension and mockery, for if Pilate wrote *king of the Jews* about him, showing that for that reason he had been crucified, then what the Jews had only feigned, crucifying

---

23. **Except:** om. M.

him with evildoers, was true, so that in every way their wicked[24] and malign plan might be obvious, and there might be no means to turn it to their advantage, but everything was for their reproof.[ii]

> i. **Notice:** *taxtak* (lit. "board, plank").
> ii. This is the argument of John Chrysostom (*Hom. Jo.* 85.1) and Moše bar Kepha.

[19:20] This notice many of the Jews read, because the place where Jesus was crucified was close to the city; and it was written in Hebrew and Greek and Latin writing.

It seems to me that Pilate did not inscribe these [words] in various languages[i] save to demonstrate to all nations—because they had gathered from all nations at the feast[ii]—that not as the Jews condemned him to be put to death with evildoers did he have any fault but that they only crucified their kings out of envy.

> i. In Armenian "Latin" is rendered by *dałmaterēn*, "Dalmatian." For an explanation of the term, see Pisani 1966, and the note to Agat'angełos, *History* 874, in Thomson 2010.
> ii. Moše bar Kepha also makes this observation. Dionysius bar Salibi, *John*, 308, states that the title was in three languages so that it might be known to those far and near.

[19:21–22] The chief priests of the Jews said to Pilate: Do not write king of the Jews, but that he said I am king of the Jews. Pilate replied and said: What I have written, I have written.

Why did they ask this from Pilate, save to remove from themselves at least a little the mockery that Pilate had written, *king of the Jews*? Hence they tried [to change it to]: *He said* [396] *I am king of the Jews.* They were totally divorced from the truth and desired to indicate that he had said about himself, *I am king of the Jews*, as someone saying what he did not truly possess. Rightly did Pilate merely give this response: *What I have written, I have written*; for although Pilate did not understand what he had said, that he was king of the Jews, yet this was a matter of prophecy, as we later realized.[i]

> i. Moše bar Kepha and Dionysius bar Salibi (*John*, 308) here quote the angel to Mary (Luke 1:33): "And he shall reign ... and of his kingdom there shall be no end."

[19:23–24] Then the soldiers, when they had crucified Jesus, took his garment and made four parts, one part for each soldier. As for the robe, because

---

24. **Wicked:** "wickedness," M.

it was without a seam, being totally woven from above down, they said to each other: Let us not tear this, but let us cast lots for it, to whom it shall go. So that the scripture might be fulfilled that said: They divided my garment among themselves, and for my robe they cast lots. This the soldiers did.

Why did the evangelist enumerate all these [actions][25] of the soldiers one by one? It was to show that not by chance or confusedly did the soldiers do this but in accordance with the prediction of the prophet;[i] therefore unfailingly these things were accomplished in later times according to the earlier sayings as an indication of their truth. But let us not pass over the robe in our review, because he says, *It was woven without a seam from above*, and also that it was not divided into parts. Let us note what he says. First he sets down the prophecy and then repeats all this about the robe. Now, the Palestinians did not wear such a thing, for which reason the evangelist uses the expression *woven without a seam from above*, in order to indicate how [397] the robe was [fashioned], unlike other robes but *from above without a seam*; he means in the weaving.[ii]

In the same fashion too his divinity, which was in the body in which he had put on this *robe*, was[26] *from above*, that is from heaven; but [he was] not a mere man in accordance with the errors of the Jews. And just as the robe was *without a seam*,[iii] likewise in him the body is not to be understood as something created, corruptible, or contaminated, separate and distinct.[27] Just as the robe did not take its existence from two, that is, *without a seam*, likewise his human nature is not from a father and mother but from one alone, that is, from the Theotokos[iv] and ever-pure virgin. And just as the robe was not torn into parts and divided among them but [remained] single according to the chance of the lot, likewise too when believers communicate in[v] the saving body, individuals do not receive it partially, but each one bears completely in himself its power, although many may be gathered to taste it, just as did those here for the division by lot.

Furthermore, just as there it was not split and divided into four, nor in the tomb like our bodies was it corrupted and turned into its individual elements,[vi] but it remained always incorruptible and indissoluble, united with the divine Word, who was pleased to become flesh, in accordance with the Gospel saying (John 1:14), for the salvation of mankind.

i. Ps 21:19, as in the lemma.

---

25. **Actions,** *gorc*: om. MN; added by the editor.
26. **Was:** "is," M.
27. **Distinct,** *oriš*: "other," *uriš*, M.

ii. John Chrysostom, *Hom. Jo.* 85.2, notes that there were in Palestine two kinds of "tunic," *rakē*: that woven from above was the humbler. Theodore of Mopsuestia, 241, notes that the tunic was different from *today*'s style. Dionysius bar Salibi, *Gospels*, 119, explains that there were two kinds of cloak used in Palestine, of one or two pieces. Christ's tunic was his body, not from heaven but from Mary.

iii. John Chrysostom, *Hom. Jo.* 85.1, explains that the seamless robe represents the indivisible union of God and man in Christ. According to *Comm. Diat.* 20.27, the robe without a seam represents Christ's undivided divinity. Išodad quotes Mar Ephrem: the tunic not rent is a mystery of his divinity, which is not divided; and the division into four parts is an image of the gospel being spread to the four ends of the earth (see Ephrem, *Sermo VI in Hebdomadem sanctam* [Lamy, 1:507–10]), as also in the *Commentary on the Diatessaron*, and Cyril of Alexandria, *Comm. Jo.* 12. Moše bar Kepha interprets the seamless robe as meaning that after the union Christ was indivisible. Dionysius bar Salibi, *Gospels*, 119, indicates that after the union Christ cannot be divided into two natures; and in *John*, 308, he equates the four parts of the tunic with the four elements of the body. For the robe as an image of the incarnation, see Brock 1982; Lampe 1969 (s.v. *chitōn*). For the death of Christ in Armenian theology, see the discussion in Mathews and Sanjian 1991 (158–63).

iv. Theotokos: *astuacacin*, "begetter of God," a literal calque and the standard Armenian term.

v. **Communicate in:** *hałordin*; the verb means literally "to share."

vi. **Elements:** *seṙ* (lit. "kind, genus"). The usual Armenian term for the four "elements" is *taṙr*.

[19:25–27] And there stood by the cross of Jesus his mother, and his mother's sister, Mary of Kłēopas, and Mary Magdalene. When Jesus saw his mother, and the disciple whom he loved standing nearby, he said to his mother: Woman, behold your son. Then he said to the disciple: Behold your mother. And from then on that disciple took Mary to his [house].

[**398**] Why did he not indicate this previously at an opportune time about his mother and the disciple, but leave it to the time[28] of the torments, except to teach us that in the same way[29] we must always take care of our parents, and at a time of torments not neglect them, so that it might be an example for us, not for any cause to abandon care for our parents, even though afflictions or various bodily troubles may come upon us?[i] But let us respect them, for it is no minor observance and fulfillment of the commandment.

i. John Chrysostom, *Hom. Jo.* 85.2, expands on our duty to mothers, as does Cyril of Alexandria, *Comm. Jo.* 12. Moše bar Kepha and Dionysius bar Salibi (*Gospels*, 130) also refer to our duty to parents. Dionysius, *Gospels*, 128–29, has a long discussion giving different theories as to the identity and number of the women.

---

28. **Time:** "hour," M.

29. **In the same way,** *ayspēs*: "as," *orpēs*, M.

[19:28] After this Jesus knew that behold, everything had been accomplished. He said: I thirst.

The evangelist shows again that it was he himself who managed the torments of his body and death, and [they occurred] not by any force. But what means:[30] *Everything had been accomplished*? Not in any fear of the torments did he say that as something doubtful, but that the redemptive torments, which he had to endure for the salvation of the world, were completed. Therefore he also indicates his thirst, for the fulfillment of the prophecy spoken through David: *In my thirst they gave me vinegar to drink.*[i]

   i. Ps 68:22b, also quoted by Cyril of Alexandria, *Comm. Jo.* 12, and Moše bar Kepha. The latter part of John Chrysostom's *Homilies on John* is briefer in its coverage, and he does not here quote David.

[19:29] And there was there a vessel full of vinegar. And they filled a sponge with vinegar and gall, [put][31] thereon hyssop, and offered it to his mouth.

Notice here the raging fury of the men and the harshness of their merciless behavior, how in their unbearable wickedness they contrived to prepare this too for him in his thirst! Not to give him some wine in a vessel or water but vinegar.[i] Nor were they content with that, but they even mixed in gall, so that **[399]** they might fully reveal their implacable[32] rancor and insatiable wickedness,[33] which David had earlier prophesied against them: *They gave me gall as food, and in my thirst they gave me vinegar to drink.*[ii]

   i. Moše bar Kepha states that it was a custom to have water to hand and a sponge in order to pass it to the one crucified.
   ii. Ps 68:22, partially quoted in the previous section.

[19:30a] When Jesus had taken the vinegar with the gall, he said: Everything has been completed.

We mentioned those [words] earlier, which now we repeat. *Completed* referred to the mystery of the incarnation[i] but now also refers to the fulfillment of the prophetic saying regarding the tasting of gall and vinegar.

---

   30. **Means:** + "behold," M (= lemma).
   31. **Put,** *edeal,* Z: om. MN.
   32. **Implacable,** *anhašt:* "indivisible," *anhat,* M.
   33. **Wickedness:** pl. N.

i. **Mystery of the incarnation**: *tnawrinakan xorhurdk'*; for the terminology, see the introduction, xxxvi. Theodore of Mopsuestia refers to the *oikonomia* (of which *tnawrinakan* is a calque) and the passion willingly accepted.

[19:30b] **And lowering his head, he gave up his**[34] **soul.**

Once more he indicates and reveals his willing death. First *he cried out* (Matt 27:50), and then *he lowered [his head]*, revealing that just as the crying out was with authority, likewise the lowering is as Lord. See also the secret mystery that he foretells here, since the Lord came for the salvation of the world in order to liberate the human race from servitude to demons and make himself known as Creator. Matthew and Luke say, *He cried out in a loud voice: Into your hands I entrust my soul* (Matt 27:50; Luke 23:46; see also Mark 15:37);[i] and here[35] he says, *Having lowered his head, he gave up his soul.* They both make clear his death with authority and as Lord: the former by crying out, the latter by lowering his head, since both are superior to our nature—the crying out and the lowering. For we at the hour of death close our mouths and are speechless, whereas he cried out with a loud voice. At that hour madness and extreme folly take hold of us; but he lowered his head with great sobriety and power.[ii]

So what was the presage of the hidden mystery that we mentioned above, save [**400**] that by crying out and lowering his head he might indicate something like this? By crying out, *Father, into your hands I commend my soul,* [he indicated] that by entrusting human souls to the hands of the Father he demonstrates the souls of the whole human race to be removed from the hands of demons and entrusted to the Father's hands. And by lowering his head, [he indicates] all human bodies to be separated from the worship of idols and recast as worshipers of the Trinity alone through the preaching of the gospel, which he foretold would occur later.

i. For Armenian exegesis of the "crying out," see Mathews and Sanjian 1991 (162).

ii. John Chrysostom, *Hom. Jo.* 85.3, explains that lowering one's head is a sign of acquiescence. Moše bar Kepha and Dionysius bar Salibi (*Gospels*, 139–40) state that normally one gives up the ghost and then lowers one's head. Jesus did the opposite to show that he gave up his soul freely.

---

34. **His,** *iwr,* MN: om. Z.
35. **Here,** *ast:* "he," *sa,* M.

[19:31a] But the Jews, because it was the eve, lest the bodies remain on the cross until the Sabbath, because it was a high day of that Sabbath.

They feigned that it was not right to leave the bodies on the cross[i] because it was the Sabbath of the Passover, hence they called it great. Also it was indicated that on that same night they ate the Passover, for thus the Lord had arranged to make the Passover a little earlier, so that he might be crucified on the eve. Why, then, on the eve? Because on the eve Adam broke the commandment, and on that same day he left paradise, rightly he was crucified on the eve, so that on that very[36] same day he might bring renewal.[ii]

See again the truth of the matter. On that eve Adam stretched out his hand to the tree to take the fruit, which he should not have approached; on this eve the Lord nailed his undefiled arms to the cross. On that eve Adam tasted the sweet fruit, which became the mother of death for the race of mankind; on this eve the Lord tasted gall, whereby he healed that mortal taste. On that eve Adam was deceived by the one born from [his] rib, whereby their offspring were born to corruption; on this eve the Lord received the wound in his ribs, whence he fashioned a spiritual bath for the renewal of incorruption for the human race. On that eve Adam raised his head to look at the fruit, which he should have renounced; on this eve [401] the Lord lowered his head on the cross instead. On that eve Adam was expelled at the ninth hour from paradise on account of the transgression of the wood; on this eve through the cross the brigand entered paradise at the ninth hour. On that eve on account of his transgression of the commandment Adam is defined as mortal; on this eve the dead[iii] Christ receives burial in the garden. Then all this was done on the eve through the protofather; here everything was done on the eve through Christ.

i. See Deut 21:22–23. Here N reads *p'ayt* (lit. "wood"), but M has *xač'* (lit. "cross"), as in the lemma. The two words are often used interchangeably for Christ's cross.

ii. The parallels in the days of the week between Adam's transgression and Christ's passion are popular themes in Armenian. See Stone 1996, esp. 109–13 and the discussion of *urbat'*, "eve," the day before the Sabbath.

iii. **Dead:** *anšnč'ac'eal* (lit. "not breathing, inanimate"); the verb is often used, meaning "to die."

[19:31b–34] They begged Pilate that they might break their legs and remove them. The soldiers came and broke the legs of the first one, likewise also of the other one who had been crucified with him. But when they came to

---

36. **Very,** *isk:* om. M.

Jesus and saw that he was dead, they did not break his legs. But one of the soldiers pierced his ribs, and immediately there came forth blood and water.

Why did they break [their legs]? It was to hasten their death, so that before the Sabbath they might bring down the bodies. And because the brigands were not yet dead, they broke theirs. Christ's, however, they did not break, because he had died from the torments and had given up his soul. But someone wounded him with a lance, so that thereby they might complete their wickedness rather than breaking [his legs].[i] For the attendant knew that would be very pleasing to the Jews.[ii]

    i. Nonnus does not here comment on the significance of the blood and water; see below, commentary to v. 37.
    ii. Dionysius bar Salibi, *Gospels*, 145, states that "some say" the soldiers broke their legs to see if they were dead; but "we say" that it was to please the Jews and to fulfill the scripture of Zech 12:10. See further Nonnus's commentary to v. 37, below.

[19:35a] **And the one who saw it bore witness, and his witness is true.**

The evangelist speaks about himself but does not introduce himself. And he said *his witness was true* in order to show that not from hearsay do we form our narrative, nor in any other way than by being an eyewitness of all this. Furthermore, by saying, *true*, he demonstrates something like this, that what I am saying is not very sublime by adding some boasting to it but very humble and modest and sad in that he was vilely tortured. [402] For if I delivered any eulogy or praise, may it not seem anything other than the truth to those who love opposition. But if my account is about ridicule and dishonor, then what I say is very true, for these are not helpful for belief in him.

[19:35b–36] **And he knows that his witness is true, so that you also may believe. This occurred so that the scripture[37] might be fulfilled: A bone of his shall not be shattered.**

When he declared, *He knows that his witness is true*, and *So that you also may believe*, he added to it what was said about the lamb of old; for it was an example of the true lamb, the Son of God, who was also called lamb by John.[i] If it were not an example, what need would there have been for such a command and ritual, according to which he commanded to eat the lamb in

____

37. The scripture, NZ: om. M.

manifold examples,[ii] because they were not appropriate or adapted for the divine legislation?

Now, as for the evangelist saying, *So that it might be fulfilled: A bone of his shall not be shattered*,[iii] not because of that did the soldiers avoid [breaking his legs], for behold, they had already shamelessly committed all evils, but he reveals the unerring prophecies and laws: that first the Holy Spirit gave a model of the future, and then the events were fulfilled unerringly one by one, so that knowing everything in this way, you might understand and believe.

    i. **John**: i.e., the Baptist, John 1:29. Step'annos of Siwnik' adduces Exod 12:10, concerning the lamb, the model of Christ.

    ii. Cf. Heb 1:1, of the OT prophecies.

    iii. Exod 12:46; Num 9:12, of the Passover lamb.

[19:37] And again another scripture says: They shall look on whom they wounded.[38]

He introduces another testimony to provide confirmation of the events that happened, namely, *they wounded*[39] [him] in order that the prophecy of Zachariah might be fulfilled.[i] Now, if the prophecies testified to these things in advance and [**403**] indicated them to us, we must with faith totally accept the wounding and its results. Why, then, these? Just as Thomas's touching the wound was for him a cause for being strengthened in the faith, so it was for others also after the resurrection. Furthermore, by this the predictions of the prophets are fulfilled. Such means also what I am saying: just as when God cast drowsiness on Adam, he took his rib and from it fashioned Eve, as Adam testified saying,[40] *She is now bone from [my] bones and flesh from my flesh* (Gen 2:23)—not that God was unable in any other way to make Eve except by casting drowsiness over Adam[41] and taking a rib from him, with which he created Eve[ii]—in the same way must one understand concerning the death of the Lord. For he would have been able, without becoming incarnate and being tormented and dying, in some other way to make us sons of God and his members, according to Paul's saying (Rom 8; 1 Cor 12). But because he was pleased to purchase us with his own blood [and] because we were baptized into his death (Acts 20:28; Rom 6:3), for that reason the water has the token

---

38. **They wounded**, NZ: "they shall wound," M.

39. **They wounded**, *xoc̕ec̕in*: "I shall wound," *xoc̕ec̕ic̕*, M.

40. **Saying**: om. M.

41. **Adam**: om. M.

of baptism, and the blood that of the cup of life.[iii] So through the two we are saved from the original curse, and we receive again our first freedom.

i. Zech 12:10, which Step'annos of Siwnik', 139, quotes in both the Septuagint version and that of Theodotion; see also Exod 12:46; Num 9:12.

ii. M omits what follows down to p. 408, line 20, of the printed text.

iii. The blood and water of v. 34 are extensively interpreted by the commentators; for Armenia, see also Mathews and Sanjian 1991 (163). *Comm. Diat.* 21.11 gives several interpretations and notes that blood is life (Lev. 17:11). John Chrysostom, *Hom. Jo.* 85.3, interprets the water as baptism and notes that the *mystagōgoumenoi* ("initiated," i.e., newly baptized) are reborn by water and fed by blood and flesh. Theodore of Mopsuestia interprets the water as baptism and the blood as the Eucharist, as does Išodad. Moše bar Kepha refers to water as a *typos* of baptism; he has no reference there to the blood, but the text lacks some lines. Dionysius bar Salibi, *Gospels*, 145, refers to the blood and water as a mystery of *our* faith, which is not like that of the Armenians, who use only wine (i.e., in the eucharistic cup, for which see Garitte 1952, 243–44). Tat'ewac'i, 608–9, discusses the use of water and wine in the liturgy, but Nonnus and his translator make no reference to the Armenian tradition. For a contemporary attack on the Armenian use of unleavened bread and wine not mixed with water, see Lamoreaux 1992.

[Exhortation][42]

When various theaters[43] of error appear installed in the streets of cities, then one can see the press of people in throngs urging themselves to the spectacle that is harmful to souls, so happy and puerile as if they thought the vain shows were a cure to their eyes. Many, despising their business, [404] go and linger there; others, neglecting their trades and handicrafts, sit the whole day in idleness to listen to the harmful sounds that work the corruption of souls. But when the time comes to hear some divine and profitable stories, in disgust they depart. Lazily and listlessly they turn their ears away, lest perchance it arouse and waken their minds to the consideration of the sublime divine mysteries. Therefore I beg [you] all willingly to pay attention, and to store up with horror in the storehouses of your thoughts[44] the impudence of the miserable and wretched nation of the Jews, which the divine accounts have related to us, and to rejoice and be glad at the divine workings of salvation, delighting in our salvation and lamenting the misery of the Jews.

---

42. Č'rak'ean notes that the following passage (to p. 408, line 24) appears elsewhere under the name of Cyril of Jerusalem; see the *čarĕntir*, Jer. 961, and the Miscellany, Jer. 299.

43. There were no theaters in the classical sense in Armenia after the Arsacid period, but for a rhetorical attack on them see *Homily* 17 of those attributed to Yovhannēs Mandakuni. See also the Armenian version of Basil of Caesarea, *Hex.* 4.

44. "Storehouse," *štemaran*, is commonly used of the receptacle of the mind.

O awesome events full of disquiet, O ungrateful people quick to forget! Well did the Holy Spirit prophesy about you in saying, *A people wicked and rebellious, a people that did not set its heart aright and whose soul did not trust in God* (Ps 77:8). The first prophet[45] foretold clearly the impudence of that nation: *You shall see your lives hanging on wood, and you shall not believe in your lives* (Deut 28:66). Truly they wished to hang on wood the one who came to give life to the race of mankind. He as an example through the blood of the lamb in Egypt saved the firstborn from slaughter; now they, by pledging the blood of the true lamb on their own and their sons' heads (Matt 27:25), have made themselves guilty of eternal torments.

[405] He who with a pillar of fire and light led them from Egypt,[46] [for him] now they set up the wood of torments and death, and in return for feeding them with heavenly manna, the bitter taste of gall. In return for making water gush from a rock, they forced him to drink vinegar on a sponge; and in return for hiding them with a cloud from the face of Pharaoh, they arranged a tomb. At least be ashamed in fear of lifeless elements, for the sun cast a shadow as veil over the nakedness of the one from whom they[47] intended to strip the robe. The curtain was split and torn, and you wounded his rib with a lance. The rocks were split from the echoes, and you dare to nail his arms. The earth shook with tremors, and you in mockery dressed him in purple. Hell in terror vomited up its long-dead, and you arrange a tomb.

O miserable and unfortunate one! I still see you joyful and your haughty enthusiasm for a vain plan. But when you seal the security of the tomb with a rock, then you will see the ranks of the heavenly hosts shining from heaven. When you will reckon him to be lifeless, then you will see him on the third day coming forth from the tomb with authority. When you reckon your wickedness has been consummated, then you will see him going again to heaven.

Let us then glorify the one dishonored by the Jews, and praise the one denied by them, and worship the one crucified by them. Let us confess the one placed by them in the tomb as our resurrection, since he died in order that he might give us life. He was dishonored so that he might render us glorious.

[406] Gentiles, clap your hands, for you have been invited to the status of adoption. Instead of those *who turned back* (John 18:6) you have been named the new Israel. For the hands that made heaven were today nailed on the cross for our salvation. He who adorned the earth with various flowers

---

45. The term *naxamargarē*, "first prophet," is also used for Moses by Movsēs Xorenac'i, *History*, 3.37.

46. The text reads, "to Egypt"! See Exod 13:21. I have indicated only the direct quotations in what follows, most of the biblical allusions being quite obvious.

47. **They**: sg. in the text.

and the heavens with stars, today was crowned with thorns. He who clothed the heavens with clouds was stripped of his robe; [he] whom the six-winged seraphim veiled with their wings, to him they sing the Trisagion (Isa 6:1–3).[48] Now he is struck by impure attendants; and he before whom stand groups of fiery ones with awe in service is condemned before Pilate. Now let us repeat words of poetry to the wood of the cross, the instrument of our salvation; for in that fashion lifeless creatures served him, trembling at the power of the all-glorious cross that received God.

The hard rock was split from the top, producing the flow of twelve streams;[49] the sea, dividing the depths, opened its bed to form paths for the people; the Jordan, restrained in its flooding boundaries, piled back on itself for the passage of Israel. The angel, seeing on the thresholds the bloody sign of the lamb, in terror passed over the firstborn. Amalek by the spreading of Moses's arms was delivered to defeat. King Constantine through the starry inscription[50] in the sky acquired the victory. O most glorious power of the divine sign! In place of the first wood of Adam, which was the cause of rebellion and death, you became the wood of reconciliation and obedience. And in place of the subjection to death of the first man through the wood in paradise, you [became] the restorer and rod of stability, as by prophetic grace [407] David cried out to the Savior in thanks, as if in the person of the original ancestor: *May your staff and rod comfort me* (Ps 22:4).

Therefore, extending our discourse a little on this subject, briefly in accordance with our feeble-minded speech, let us praise this saving, divine, and holy sign, although we shall not be able competently to bring our discourse to its full measure. For just as the first plant through the virgin born from Adam was the cause of corruption and death for human nature, Christ, born from a virgin, being raised over you as a lamb[51] was the source for mankind of incorruption and immortality. For through his cross he reopened paradise to us; through his cross he gave us the tree of life; through his cross demons were put to flight; through his cross angels spread out from heaven to earth; through his cross temples were destroyed; through his cross churches were

---

48. See further commentary to John 12:41.

49. Exod 17:6; Num 20:11, but there is no reference to twelve streams. Numerous other OT references to twelve were interpreted as references to the apostles.

50. **Starry inscription:** *astełatesak nkaragrut'iwn* (lit. "inscription appearing like stars"). The wording is reminiscent of the description of Constantine's vision in the Armenian *Life of Silvester*, p. 715 in the Armenian text of Socrates' *History*, long and short versions.

51. **As a lamb:** *garnačašak*, otherwise unattested (lit. "tasting of lamb"); a reference to the Passover.

founded; through his cross the catholic church was glorified; through his cross the altar of faith was set up; through his cross the holy sacrifice was blessed; through his cross baptism was sealed; through his cross the anointing of the holy priesthood was established; through his cross priests were granted grace; through his grace the apostles acquired fame; through his cross the prophets rejoiced; through his cross martyrs were crowned; through his cross angels were united with mankind; through his cross orthodox kingdoms were rendered pious; through his cross soldiers gained the victory; through his cross those in danger were saved; through his cross those in affliction were consoled; through his cross the fortunate rejoiced; through his cross the rich became temperate; through his cross the poor gained subsistence; through his cross the insolent became discreet; through his cross virgins became illustrious; through his cross the married were sealed; through his cross youths were protected; through his cross children were instructed; through his cross the old gathered together; through his cross ascetics persevered; through his cross hermits were preserved; through his cross the sick were healed; through his cross sinners found forgiveness; [408] through his cross the dead encounter hope of resurrection according to the Lord's word: *And then the sign of the son of man will appear in heaven* (Matt 24:30).

Who would be competent to give a thorough account of you who were the cause of so many and such myriad blessings? For you are the crown of the church; you are the boast of the holy apostles; you are the fortitude of the martyrs; you are the sharp sword held in the hand of patriarchs; you are the invincible weapon of priests; you are the trophy of kings; you are help to those in danger; you strike fear in demons; you are healing for the afflicted; you are expiation for sinners; you are guard of the innocent; you are the seal of the married; you are the adornment of virgins; you are strength for youths; you are a haven for the aged; you are consolation for those suffering; you are at once wall and defense and shade and seal for humankind.

Therefore, setting aside impure passion of earthbound thoughts, bending our necks let us all worship the holy cross of the Lord that bore God, as we now see on it the Son of God with outstretched arms, praising him with the Father and Holy Spirit, now and always and forever and ever. Amen.

[19:38a] **After that Joseph, who was from Arimatheia, a disciple of Jesus in secret for fear of the Jews, requested Pilate that he might remove the body of Jesus.**

This Joseph was noble and distinguished in the nation of the Jews but also a follower of good works. He himself had been a disciple of Jesus and later was reckoned in the number of the seventy.[i]

i. John Chrysostom, *Hom. Jo.* 85.3, notes that he was "perhaps," *isōs*, one of the seventy. Moše bar Kepha states that he was not one of the Twelve and gives his titles from Matthew, Mark, and Luke. According to Dionysius bar Salibi, *Gospels*, 145, Joseph was one of the seventy-two; and in *John*, 311, he indicates that Joseph was not one of the Twelve, although John here calls him a disciple.

[19:38b–39a] **And Pilate gave permission. They came and removed him. Nicodemus also came, who had come to Jesus the first time by night.**

[409] Nicodemus also among the Jews was not from some lesser and insignificant [origins] but from the most honorable. Therefore, avoiding the Jews, he had come by night to Jesus. It was he who had said to the Lord previously, *Teacher, I know that you proceeded*[52] *from God* (John 3:2),[i] and from then on he had the form of love and willingness for the faith, although he did not yet openly hasten to the faith for fear of the Jews.

i. Note the significant change to the biblical text in N.

[19:39b–40] **And he brought myrrh mixed with aloes, about a hundred liters. They took the body of Jesus and wrapped it in linen with the spices, as it was customary for the Jews to wrap.**[53]

He shows at this point that they conducted the burial not according to the accusation of the Jews, who had pronounced him to be guilty of death, but in accordance with the model that the Jews were accustomed to do for the greatest and honorable and true.[i] Accordingly, they dressed him in linen and myrrh with the aloes, because they had that custom.

i. This is the argument of John Chrysostom, *Hom. Jo.* 85.3; Moše bar Kepha; and Dionysius bar Salibi, *John*, 311.

[19:41] **And there was in the place in which he was crucified a garden, and in the garden a new tomb, in which no one had yet been placed. There, because of the eve of the Jews, since the tomb was nearby, they laid Jesus.**

He indicates the burial was there, toward evening and the day being late. It also has another symbol, placing him in a tomb in which no one had ever been laid. Why? Lest even in that regard the Jews might find means and pretexts to say that someone else rose from the dead.[i] And furthermore, because

---

52. **You proceeded,** *eler*, N: "you have come," *ekeal es*, MZ.
53. **For the Jews to wrap,** NZ: om. M.

no one before him had risen from the dead to incorruption and immortality, it was necessary that his tomb was new. Also because just as he matched this eve to that eve, and the wood of the cross of obedience [410] to the wood of rebellion, and the taste of bitterness to the taste of sweetness, and the others in the same way, whereby our guilt was to be annulled, likewise he matched the garden to paradise. For just as the first father was made corruptible and mortal by the former, so from the garden, which was the tomb, he raised our kindred body to incorruption and immortality. Therefore the grieving women indicate the women bringing the news in place of Eve.[ii]

i. This suggestion is found in John Chrysostom, *Hom. Jo.* 85.4; Moše bar Kepha; Dionysius bar Salibi, *John*, 312; and Taťewac'i, 610.

ii. The grammar of this last sentence is quite unclear: there is no noun in the pl. nom. for the 3d pl. verb, "indicate." The "women bringing the news" (*awetawors*; i.e., news of the resurrection, a reference to those of Matt 28:1 and Luke 24:10) are in the direct acc. case, but the "grieving women" are in the gen./dat. case.

[410] Chapter 20

[20:1] **And on the first day of the week Mary Magdalene came in the morning at daybreak to the tomb and saw the stone had been removed from the entrance of the tomb.**

This first coming to the tomb is understood of Mary, when she saw the angel as he rolled away the stone from the entrance of the tomb after the Lord's rising from the tomb, according to the account of Matthew (Matt 28:2).[i] So the angel did not roll away the stone in order that the Lord might rise[ii] but to convince the women, for they would not yet have really believed in the account of the resurrection were the stone to be over [the entrance]. For the same purpose it was said: *Come and see* (Matt 28:6).[iii]

i. Išodad discusses the different modes of reckoning the daytime, some from the morning, as the Armenians hold. Theodore of Mopsuestia begins his comments to this passage with a comparison of the four Gospel accounts of the resurrection and tries to reconcile them. Moše bar Kepha also notes the times of the women going to the tomb as described by the different Gospels.
ii. This is also the argument of Išodad.
iii. Here in the singular, but plural in Matthew.

[20:2] **Then she ran and came to Simon Peter and the other disciple whom Jesus loved, and she said to them: They have removed my[1] Lord from the tomb, and I do not know where they have placed him.**

For when she saw the tomb empty she thought that perhaps they had opened the tomb in order to remove the body, because they still had weak faith concerning the resurrection of Jesus. Therefore she ran rapidly to Peter as the chief[1] and most prudent one, and to John as to[2] a friend, because he was

---

1. **My**, N: om. MZ.
2. **To**: om. M.

loved, saying: *They have removed the Lord from the tomb, and I do not know where they have placed him.*[3]

    i. **Chief:** *glxaworagoyn*, as elsewhere (e.g., commentary to John 14:1 and 21:15a).

[411] [20:3–4] Peter went out and the other disciple, and they came to the tomb. They both ran together, and the other disciple ran in front faster than Peter and came first to the tomb.

How should we understand the other disciple coming first and preceding[4] Peter? Not only because Peter was weaker in strength in his old age, and the other more powerful in his youthful years,[i] but because[5] Peter, it seems to me, fell back out of doubts and fear, having hesitation in his mind from his denial. But the [other] disciple, with all his heart out of the full love that he had,[ii] was running faster.

    i. Moše bar Kepha also notes that Peter was older than John.
    ii. This is one of the four reasons given by Išodad for Peter's slowness.

[20:5] And bending down he saw that the linens were lying there. But he did not enter.

Why did he not enter? Although he had arrived first at the tomb, he did not enter, as he was waiting for Peter, who was[6] the chief;[i] he saw from the teacher that he was more worthy of honor than his fellow disciples[7] and yielded to him.

    i. **Chief:** *glxaworagoyn* (lit. "most pre-eminent"). Nonnus notes several times that Peter was the "chief," *glux* or *glxawor*, of the apostles; see just above.

[20:6–8] Simon Peter came, who was following him, and entered the tomb. And he saw the linens lying there; and the napkin that was on his head was not lying with the other[8] linens but was wrapped separately on one side.

---

    3. **Him:** om. M.
    4. **Preceding:** "before," M.
    5. **Because:** om. M.
    6. **Was:** "is," M.
    7. **Fellow disciples:** sg. M.
    8. **Other, MZ:** om. N.

Then the other disciple, who had come first to the tomb, also entered; he saw and believed.

He indicates that when Peter entered the tomb and saw the linens lying and the napkin wrapped separately to one side, distant from the linens, he realized that this was no work of thieves or body snatchers.[i] For what need had the one who stole his body or removed it,[9] first to detach the linen from it and wrap the napkin separately, especially because by lingering he would have had greater need of care to unwrap the body that was sewn up and[10] covered with myrrh that adhered to the wrappings, [412] and without tearing them to release it, though it was attached and so many liters of myrrh adhered to it? So it was not a sign of stealing. He also considered the anger of the Jews; perhaps those who did it had spilled[11] their rage on them while lingering in the tomb. And if this were so, then it is the work of his divine power. So he has risen from the tomb in accordance with his prediction, as he said to us: *After three days I shall arise* (Matt 27:63; Mark 8:31).

But let us not pass over the hidden mystery that he prophesied for us as an example by leaving the linens in the tomb. What might this be, save to show us that we have no need of garments after the resurrection? Propriety requires such things for facing the present life, or to hide the shame of our nakedness; but no other pleasures or troubles arise with us, as of adoption or other such things, as there in the garden for Adam and Eve. For at first they were naked of clothing, having no need to hide, because they did not see their nakedness. But when they were overcome by pleasure by which they were vanquished, they had need of clothing in order to hide their shame with leaves of the fig tree, being stripped of glory (Gen 3:7).[ii] But the desires of the saints, I mean of the prophets and apostles and martyrs in the kingdom of heaven, are opposed to the earlier pleasures. And therefore spiritual and bodily ones have no other desire in themselves than the wish for the beauty of divine love, by which they receive the inalienable glory of which Adam was stripped. Rightly they have no need thereafter of garments, which the Lord indicated at his resurrection by leaving the linens in the tomb.[iii]

One must also inquire why [413] the linens were not rolled up like the napkin, but the napkin on his head only [was rolled up]. Since the linens were wrapped only around the body—and they did not remove or steal the body—the rolled napkin not only indicates that the body had not been stolen

---

9. **Stole, removed:** tr. M.
10. **Sewn up and:** om. N.
11. **Had spilled:** "would spill," N.

but also has another sign of sublimity. For just as the head is the most honorable and prime [part] in a person, because it contains the sensations by which a man operates all his limbs, in the same way the napkin too contains an indication of the divine nature.[iv] Therefore it was rolled up by the angels in order to show us that the divine nature remained ungraspable and incomprehensible to our minds.

Now as regards the incarnate body, although human minds cannot fully comprehend the why and how, yet understanding a little, they described the economy of his dispensation.[v] Therefore the Baptist says, *I am not worthy even to loose the lachets of his shoes* (Mark 1:7; John 1:27), meaning that I cannot understand even a part of his incarnation. But they did not hesitate to say, *The Word became flesh*[vi] (John 1:14), that is, man, although by the descent of the Spirit, outside the common constitution of the body.

i. All commentators note that the position of the linen shows that the body had not been stolen by a thief.

ii. For the theme of Adam losing the glory with which he was robed, see Lampe 1969 (s.v. *doxa*, F 10a).

iii. Theodore of Mopsuestia explains that Christ had no need of human clothes, because he had put on the garment of immortality.

iv. This is the argument of Dionysius bar Salibi, *John*, 314.

v. **Incarnate:** *tnawrinakan;* **dispensation:** *tnawrēnut'iwn.* For the vocabulary, see the introduction, xxxvi.

vi. **Flesh:** *marmin*, or "body." Armenian makes no distinction between the Greek terms *sarx* and *sōma.*

[20:9–10] For they did not yet know the scripture, that it is necessary for him to rise from the dead. The disciples went back to their own [places].

He indicates again what we said above, that by seeing they believed through the linens and napkin that the deed was not one of theft; but they did not perhaps know the prophecies[i] and thus confirm the report of the resurrection. And by *the disciples going back to their own*, he means the upper room, because they went there to consider what they had seen.

i. Here Tat'ewac'i, 612, quotes Hos 6:3.

[20:11–12] **But Mary stood outside the tomb [414] and wept.**[12] **And while she wept, she bent down into the tomb and saw two angels in white sitting, one at the head and one at the feet, where the body of Jesus had lain.**

It seems to me that the two disciples had not informed the woman about what they had seen and believed, or that the body had not been stolen as you supposed but had risen indeed. This is yet another aspect of the Lord's dispensation; for just as the cause of giving us life was arranged appropriately to our guilt and faults, in the same way he decreed to the angels[13] that they should announce the news of the resurrection to the woman first. The woman was to be the first to bring the news of the resurrection of the man, but not a man to the woman. For just as the snake poured the mortal poison into the ear of the woman first, thereby defeating her, and Adam tasted the fruit through her and became the cause of the destruction of the race of mankind and announced the sad news of death to the world, in the same way to a woman was first announced by the angel the good news of the resurrection and the gospel of immortality and incorruption.

Furthermore, the shining appearance of the angels that she saw, and their sitting where she said,[14] was no little sign of the Lord's resurrection. For the shining form of the angel was a sign of joy and good news. Now *the sitting of one*[15] *at the head and one at the feet where the body* of the Lord[16] *had lain* reveals its immeasurable greatness and superiority. For if he was really in the tomb, how would they have been able to sit, who were not allowed[i] to sit in the place where the body had been, but at the head and feet, not approaching the spot in which the holy body had lain? And the angel provides yet another sign, in order to show the woman that if, as you think, the body had been removed or stolen, we would not have been revealed in such glorious and shining forms, but rather the opposite.

i. **Were not allowed**: *oč' išxēin* (i.e., did not have the authority); cf. the frequent use of *išxanut'iwn*, "authority," in Christ's own remarks (e.g., John 10:18: "I have authority to lay down my life").

12. **And wept**, MZ and editor: om. N.
13. **To the angels**: "the angel" (nom.), M.
14. **She said**, *asac'*: or "he [the evangelist] said."
15. **Of one**: om. M.
16. **Of the Lord**: "of Jesus," M (= lemma).

[**415**] [20:13a] **And they said to her: Woman, why do you weep?**

As if to say that by seeing us in such glorious forms dressed in light, sitting in the place where the body had lain, we present the proof of a time of joy and good news but not of grief and sadness. *Why do you weep?*

[20:13b–14] **She said to them: They have removed my Lord from the tomb, and I do not know where they have placed him. When she had said that she turned backward *and saw Jesus standing and did not know that it was Jesus.**[17]

Why, then, did she turn backward? She was still speaking with the angels, still questioning them, and she had not yet heard any response to her query from them. It was because the angels, seeing the Lord behind the woman and being afraid, suddenly rose up in great awe. At which the woman turned her gaze to the look on their faces and turned backward. But the Lord was not visible to the woman in the same way as to the angels, for which reason she did not recognize him.[i]

i. John Chrysostom, *Hom. Jo.* 86.1, indicates that the angels, on recognizing Jesus, showed it in their eyes and movement. Išodad offers numerous explanations.

[20:15a] **Jesus said to her: Woman, why do you weep? Whom do you seek?**

Because the Lord showed himself in this manner to the woman and not some awesome form, before she recognized him, [he spoke] in very gentle and calm words in order to lessen the woman's doubts and fear in accordance with her weakness, and also so that after her remaining without hope about the resurrection, the truly bodily proof of the resurrection might be for her even more sublime and worthy of honor.

[20:15b] **It seemed to her that he was the gardener. She said to him: Lord, if you have removed him, tell me where you have put him, so that I may take him away.**

Why did she suppose that he might be the gardener? She had such a thought that for fear of the Jews he had removed him from the tomb, [**416**] for the sake of protecting the garden, thinking it not inappropriate to let him [do so], because they were confused and troubled.

---

17. **And saw ... Jesus**, NZ: om. M.

[20:16] Jesus said to her: Mary. And she turned and said to him in Hebrew: Rabuni (which means "teacher").

Why does he introduce her name at this point, save because the woman did not recognize him despite seeing [him]? He also added his voice by calling her by name in order to remove her doubts. Turning backward in the face of the angels, who while they were speaking with her suddenly stood up in unexpected alarm as if terrified at his appearance, with them the woman turned her gaze. But she did not see such as she had expected, because the Lord did not reveal himself to her as something awesome, as to the angels. Hence it seemed to the woman that he was the gardener. Therefore he added her name, to make himself known to her gently in accordance with the weak woman's nature, as we said above.[i]

i. John Chrysostom, *Hom. Jo.* 86.1, and Moše bar Kepha state that Mary recognized Jesus by his voice.

[20:17a] Jesus said to her: Do not approach me, because I have not yet ascended to my Father.

What the meaning of his saying, *Do not approach me, because I have not yet ascended to my*[18] *Father*, might be requires investigation, for it contains profound words hard to understand.[i] We have found from accurate examples[ii] that the woman was still thinking in human terms about him, and that is clear from her calling him *Rabbi*, but not Lord, or Son of God, or God. By approaching with the great joy that she had, although she did not fully understand about him, she was about to ask such questions as about the torments that he had endured, and about the cross and his death, [417] and about his rising from the dead, how or in what way these were experienced by you. The woman was not yet competent to be receptive to all this, because they were ineffable and most sublime, and it also required a pure mind to be able to understand it. But she was not yet strong enough to bear the greatest mysteries, for which reason he forbade her, saying, *Do not approach me*, because of such a mystery.

This too we should investigate, what he also said: *I have not yet ascended to my*[19] *Father*. He expressed this to the woman as a reason, and very appropriately as we have related. Since she wished to ask such questions about inconceivable mysteries, he responded, *I have not yet ascended to my Father*, whereby the Holy Spirit is sent to you, the consoler who fills and confirms you

---

18. **My:** om. M.
19. **My:** om. M.

in the truth, and recalls to you all my sayings.[iii] And at that time you will not
be unable to examine what I am now saying symbolically.[iv]

i. *Comm. Diat.* 21.26 offers a range of explanations, none identical with that of
Nonnus, but at 21.27 it does refer to Mary's doubt. Dionysius bar Salibi, *John*, 317, also
gives a range of unnamed sources for various views about Jesus saying, "Do not approach
me." John Chrysostom, *Hom. Jo.* 86.2, states that it was a warning by Jesus that they cannot
now enjoy the same familiarity as before his death.

ii. **Examples**: see the introduction, xxviii–xxix, for references to other texts used by
Nonnus.

iii. Cyril of Alexandria, *Comm. Jo.* 12, also explains that "I have not yet ascended"
means "I have not yet sent the Holy Spirit."

iv. **I am saying symbolically**: *xorhrdacem. Xorhurd* means "mystery, symbol."

**[20:17b] But[20] go to my brothers and say to them: I ascend to my Father and[21]
to your Father, my God and your God.**

Why did he write that he said to them: *I ascend to my Father*? It was
because when the woman announced to the disciples his resurrection and
she also related what he said, *I ascend to my Father*, they were even more convinced of the account of his resurrection by his rising up to heaven in accordance with his prognostication *I go to my Father* (John 14:12), which here too
he recalled to them. Why, then, did he call them *brothers* at this point? Let us
not pass over it, for at the time of the crucifixion they all abandoned him and
scattered, and one of them even denied him. By this name he wished to expel
their doubts and remove their fear.

Furthermore, this saying contains another significance. His calling [them]
brothers was [418] in order to indicate that in the same body, related[i] by
nature, which I took from your nature, in the same I arose from the tomb,
and[22] not some other sort. Furthermore, by that same name by which he called
them brothers he also indicates that you too are to rise from your tombs in
accordance with[23] this example, bearing with you bodies of incorruption and
immortality and having no need of any garments or other comforts. And lest
they might think themselves in all ways equal with and comparable to him by
his calling them brothers, he introduces a distinction: *I ascend to my Father and
to your Father*, and by that he excludes their thoughts of equality. For he did not
say, to our Father and our God, so that thereby he might distinguish between

20. **But**, NZ: om. M.
21. **And**, NZ: om. M.
22. **And**: om. M.
23. **In accordance with**: "in," N.

being son and being servant, and to show that although he called them brothers for his own sake, being their brother through the putting on of the body, his Father, through his being brother of the servants, was named his God.[ii]

Now, just as by nature the son of the Father was called son of man, in accordance with the [saying], *He is the son of man; why are you astonished at that?* (John 5:28), in the same way too the sons of men by nature were named sons of God by grace, in accordance with the [saying], *Those who received him, to them he gave the authority to become sons of God* (John 1:12). And just as through his being brother his Father by nature was called our Father, likewise too through us being called his brothers, our God by creation was called his God.[iii] But let not the dim-witted understand the saying of paternity and divinity between us and Christ to be equivalent and equal, because he is his Father by nature but ours by grace; likewise he is our God by creation and providence, and his by equality and incarnation, since for that reason he took on the form of a servant so that we might receive that of freedom.

[419] By being dishonored he glorified [us], and through his torments he freed us from the original debt, and through his death he gave us life, and through the resurrection he raised us from eternal death, and by ascending he brought us with him to the supernal dwellings. Just as [although] sons of men, through grace we were called sons of God without being changed from our nature, likewise the Son of God, [despite being] called son of man, was not changed from his essential nature.

i. **Related**: *hamazgi*. Tat'ewac'i, 613, refers to Christ being *nmanakic'*, "similar," to human nature.

ii. Moše bar Kepha has a long discussion of Christ as our brother through the incarnation, but not our brother in his divinity.

iii. Dionysius bar Salibi, *John*, 318, refers to our being brothers through baptism.

[20:18] **Mary Magdalene came and told the disciples that she had seen the Lord**[24] **and he had said this to her.**

She then announced what she had seen and heard, especially the sublime words that she had heard, telling them about the ascending to heaven, to confirm the predictions, *I go to my Father*, which she indicates here that *I have not yet ascended to my Father*. She reminded them that his teaching was true in all respects. The woman also stated that these were a boast for herself, indicating that she had been worthy of such sublime words before them.

---

24. **She had seen the Lord**, NZ: "the Lord had seen her," M.

[20:19] And it was[25] evening on the first day of the week. And the doors being shut where the disciples were gathered for fear of the Jews, Jesus came, stood in their midst, and said to them: Greetings to you.

The evangelist relates the hour and the day on which all this happened in order to confirm the account of the resurrection, that it was on the same day on which he had risen from the dead. But why, then, does he delay his meeting the disciples until the evening? Perhaps he consented for the following reason: lest by entering among them in a wonderful appearance he astonish[i] them, when they were only just gathered together; or again, as they were more terrified of the Jews at that hour than during the daytime, they might at least be encouraged by the fact that they saw him entering when the doors were closed;[ii] [420] or again, because he wished to show his entering among them to be miraculous, as we said above, he allowed them to engage in inquiry about his resurrection, for by seeing him inside when the doors were closed, they would have no need of many words about his resurrection, as that was no small miracle.

But nowhere in the holy scriptures before this do we find him giving them a greeting.[iii] Why? Perhaps he calms the fear in their minds because of his unexpectedly entering with the doors closed, and thereby he removes the fear of the Jews from them, and because he reminds them again of what he previously had said to them: *My peace I give to you, my peace I leave to you* (John 14:27). Let us examine this further. Why did he not give them a greeting before this? Because men were enemies of God by their denial and idolatry, but at the time of the cross he slew the Enemy and *made peace* in heaven and earth, and *broke down the partition wall* (Eph 2:14), and the Father was reconciled[26] with creatures through the death of his Son, as Paul states, *We were[27] reconciled with God by the death of his Son* (Rom 5:10), rightly here he gives a greeting to his disciples.

i. Here there is no verb, but an adverb: *sk'ančelapēs*, "astonishingly."

ii. Dionysius bar Salibi, *Gospels*, 85, draws a parallel between the closed doors here and Christ's birth, which left the Virgin intact. Tat'ewac'i, 614, also says that just as the doors were closed, so was Christ born from the Virgin.

iii. **Greeting:** *ołjoyn*; it does not literally mean "peace," *eirēnē* in the Greek. The word occurs several times in the Gospels (except Mark), but in John only in 20:20, 19, 21, 26, as a greeting from Jesus to the disciples. Dionysius bar Salibi, *John*, 321, notes that Jesus gives the greeting *šlm'* (lit. "peace") only after the resurrection.

---

25. **It was**, Z: om. MN.

26. **Reconciled**, *haštec'aw*, M: "pleased," *hačec'aw*, N.

27. **We were:** "I was," M.

[20:20a] **When[28] he had said this, he showed them his hands and feet.**

Why does he show them? First through giving a greeting he removed fear from them; and then he showed them his hands and feet, lest they suppose his appearance to be a phantom, but so that through the places of the nails and the wound of the spear they might truly believe in the resurrection and also that they might understand that he had risen from the tomb with the very[29] same body in which he was crucified and tormented.[i]

i. Tat'ewac'i, 615, also emphasizes that it was the same body that was crucified and arose. Išodad, 285, states that the wounds were not in the body that rose from the dead, and for that reason "he coerced the nature of the facts."

[20:20b] **And the disciples rejoiced when they saw the Lord.**

He shows again that by seeing the Lord they did not remain in their former sadness [**421**] but rejoiced and were freed from the fear they earlier had of the Jews. Also so that he might confirm his earlier promises to them, *You will see me again, and your hearts will rejoice, and no one will take your joy away from you* (John 16:22), which indeed was fulfilled after his resurrection from the dead.

[20:21] **He said again to them: Greetings to you. As the Father sent me, I also send you.**

Why, then, did he again[30] give the greeting that he had given once before? Through the greeting he calmed their fear and removed their doubts [caused] by his entering unexpectedly. Furthermore, since he was also[31] to send them to the ends of the world, he repeated the greeting in their ears in order to make them firmer, in that they always carried his greeting and peace with them, because they were confirmed in the account of his resurrection and understood the miracles [of] his divine power by his entering with the doors closed.

But let us look at what further he said: *As the Father sent me, I also send you.* It seems to me that he indicates what he endured for the salvation of the world, the cross and burial, and for the following reason shows his being sent by the Father: Perhaps you, having been sent by me, will have the same long-

---

28. **When,** NZ: "And when," M.

29. **Very,** *isk:* om. M.

30. **Again,** M and editor: om. N.

31. **Also:** om. M.

suffering[i] and will proclaim the same preaching for the salvation of the world, and so that you may gain for yourselves, and for those who will believe in me through you, no small reward when you arrive at the place of retribution.

i. Theodore of Mopsuestia also refers to Christ teaching the disciples to have long-suffering in their labors and tribulations.

[20:22] When he had said this, he breathed on them and said: Receive the Holy Spirit.

Since previously he had only said, *As the Father sent me, I also send you*, they [now] became aware and realized the meaning of the saying, that he indicates we too will endure the same as he himself endured. [422] But after this they suffered no little doubt, knowing their own weakness and that at the time of the cross they had not been courageous but had all abandoned him and scattered, and one had even denied him. So they would not be able to receive the Holy Spirit when he descended on them and reminded them of all the earlier sayings by the Lord. Therefore *he breathed on them*, showing them that strengthened through this breath they would be able to endure the things of which they now despaired because of their weakness.[i]

But why did he not say, Receive the Holy Spirit, but first *breathed on them and* then *said: Receive the Holy Spirit*? It was to indicate to them that he is the same who breathed on Adam and placed in him the spirit of life. And just as he was still made from earth, being immobile and inactive and lifeless, and through the divine breath became so very honorable and the highest of all creatures, as is related in the books of Moses,[ii] likewise you too being renewed through the divine breath will become the most powerful and able in everything. As indeed they acquired after such endurance and long-suffering, and he renewed their former incorruption and immortality.

i. Dionysius bar Salibi, *Gospels*, 304, here refers to the three grades of gift through the Holy Spirit: that given to the prophets, that given to John the Baptist, and that given to the apostles here.

ii. Gen 2:7, to which Theodore of Mopsuestia also refers.

[20:23] If you will remit for anyone his sins, they will be remitted for them; and if you retain anyone's, they will be retained.

Mark here for me the meaning of this saying, as to why he gave them the Spirit while he was still with them. Previously he said: *Unless I go, the Comforter will not come to you* (John 16:7). What he did seems to be different from what he said, so for what reason? Now, we explained once above the meaning of this saying, and yet he indicates something else by saying: *If you will remit for anyone his sins, they will be remitted, and if you retain anyone's,*[32] *[they will be] retained.* Because the gifts of the Holy Spirit are numerous and numberless, here he does not give them all [423] but only one, which he defines through the saying: the remitting or retaining of sins. But the complete powers of the gifts, whereby they would be able to raise the dead,[i] heal the afflicted, move mountains, and preach to the world the beautiful message of the gospel with fearless joy and happy rejoicing, he left to be operated at the coming of the Holy Spirit, which was indeed fulfilled at the coming of the Spirit[33] in the upper room, when divided into fiery tongues he sat upon them. Under the influence of the Spirit they began to speak in foreign tongues, and there made a beginning of signs and miracles, and preached boldly that Christ is Son of God (Acts 2).

i. John Chrysostom, *Hom. Jo.* 87.3, indicates that the powers given here by Christ do not include the raising of the dead. Dionysius bar Salibi, *John*, 322, notes that the gifts of the Spirit are many, but only one was given here; after a few days he gave them the power to raise the dead and work miracles.

[20:24–25] **But Thomas, one of the Twelve, called twin, was not with them when Jesus came. The other disciples said to him: We have seen the Lord. And he said to them: Unless I see the mark**[34] **of the nails on his hands,** *and I put my fingers into the place of the nails,**[35] **and I thrust my hands into his ribs,**[36] **I shall not believe.**

Let us then examine why Thomas did not believe the testimony of the ten apostles that they had stated. He surely did not attempt to suppress the account of the resurrection. Far from it! Yet he carried a certain doubt in himself that perhaps it had occurred as an illusion and a phantom and not in reality and truly, which the following makes clear by his saying: *Unless I put my fingers into the places of the nails and thrust my hands into his ribs, I shall not believe.* He clearly revealed his doubts: Perhaps the sight only of him will be for me too a phantom or an appearance, but through touching the place of the nails and by touching [that] of the spear that he endured on the cross, I shall

32. **Anyone's,** *zuruk'*, N (= lemma): "any one," *zok' ok'*, M.
33. **Of the Spirit:** om. N.
34. **Mark,** NZ: pl. M.
35. **And I put ... nails,** NZ: om. M.
36. **Ribs,** NZ: sg. M.

be confirmed[37] in the faith. Why so? Because they were still very weak and did not fully understand the divine resurrection.

[424] [20:26a] **And after eight days the disciples were again inside, and Thomas with them.**

He means the second first day of the week, which is the day after the resurrection. And the disciples were gathered in the upper room because of fear of the Jews, *and Thomas [was] with them.*

[20:26b] **Jesus came, the doors being closed. He stood in their midst and said: Greetings to you.**

It seems to me that his coming the second time and being inside when the doors were closed not only confirmed the first appearance to the disciples but also [occurred] because of Thomas being with them, and it indicates what he said to Thomas.

[20:27] **Put out your hand,[38] and thrust it into my ribs. And do not be disbelieving, but believing.**

Let us examine what he said to Thomas: *Put out your hand, and thrust it into my ribs;*[i] and he did not hold back a little so that Thomas might entreat and request that for himself. So he revealed to him his omniscient power, that nothing[39] is hidden from his all-seeing eye: I have seen the declaration of your unbelief. But what means: *Do not be unbelieving, but believing?* Especially as he first said, *Put out your hand and thrust it into my ribs,* and then later added that, showing him that it is not for persons who love the truth to believe through sight and touch but through hearing and hope, in accordance with the Apostle's saying: *What someone sees, why does he still hope for it?* (Rom 8:24). But you by seeing and touching have been confirmed in the faith. Never again admit that, when there will be times for faith and hope and preaching, to those who have never seen me.

i. The lemma and commentary omit the first part of v. 27.

---

37. **I shall be confirmed:** "they were confirmed," M.
38. **Hand,** NZ: pl. M.
39. **Nothing,** *oč' inč',* M: "not," *oč',* N.

[20:28] Thomas replied and said: My Lord and my God.

Let us see what theological profession the holy[40] apostle expressed, for he saw the human body of the divinity and touched **[425]** the hurt and painful [parts], the wounds of the nails, I mean, and the place of the lance,[i] and pronounced the name God. Yet, as I said above, he did not see as amazing or sublime things the details of the torments. And why did he call him Lord and God? He confessed whom he had seen and touched to be one in union with the Word, as was indeed appropriate. God made man and body made divine; and not God in his individual divine nature, and man separate in accordance with the individuality of the body.

So where are the hordes of schismatics[ii] who divide the one Christ into two natures? They have been reproved by the apostle who called the visible and tangible *my Lord and my God*, confessing his lordship and divinity with indivisible unity. He did not proclaim distinctions of difference in accordance with the thoughts of those who divide [the natures], one wounded and another glorified; but he pronounced one Lord and God descended from heaven, assuming a garment from the Virgin, and being tormented and wounded, with an inseparable and indistinguishable unity.

Furthermore, he expounded something else very amazing and sublime by appearing to Thomas, so that not only would he be confirmed in the faith, but also it would be a sign of future events that would take place in later time. What, then, am I saying? Just as those who did not believe in the preaching of the true gospel also did not [believe] in the earlier law and prophecies[41] about Christ, likewise neither did Thomas believe in the testimonies of the disciples about the Lord's resurrection, nor did he recall the words spoken earlier by the Lord: *After three days I shall arise* (Matt 27:63; Mark 8:31). In accordance with this example he left his second coming to the disciples until the eighth day, because that number contains a mystery.

On the eighth day, when **[426]** the disciples were gathered in the upper room, some confessed him as Lord and God, but another was enveloped in doubt regarding the prediction of his second coming on the first day of the week at the beginning of the eighth age, according to the saying of the wise one[iii],[42] on which all nations will be brought together, believers and nonbelievers. And just as Thomas opposed the disciples by not believing their true testimonies, nor by recalling the predicted testimonies was he confirmed in

---

40. **Holy**: om. M.
41. **Prophecies**: "prophets," M.
42. **Saying of the wise one**: "wise saying," M.

the faith, but he asked to see and to touch in order to be confirmed in the faith; likewise too the unbelievers by opposing the believers do not accept the prophecies and the examples that previously occurred and spoke about Christ. And just as Thomas on the eighth day believed in the resurrection of the Lord through seeing and touching and professed, *My Lord and God*, in the same way too at the beginning of the eighth age on the first day of the week at his coming, through seeing him truly according to the prophecy,[43] *They shall look on the one whom they wounded* (John 19:37; cf. Zech 12:10), everyone will recognize and confess him to be God. And just as he said to Thomas:

i. **Lance:** *gełard.* The centurion's weapon is called *tēg,* "spear," at John 19:34, but the usual expression (for the relic, etc.) is *gełard,* which is not used in the Armenian NT.

ii. **Schismatics:** *herjuacołk'.* For Nonnus's references to heretics and schismatics, see the introduction, xl.

iii. **The wise one:** i.e., the Preacher. See Eccl 11:2, quoted here by Moše bar Kepha as he refers to the eighth age, which is mentioned also by Tat'ewac'i, 616. For the important theme in Armenian theology of seven, or eight, ages, see *Teaching* 667–71 (Thomson 2001, with further references in n. 500 [p. 215]); also the introduction above, xxxii.

[20:29] **Since you have seen me you also believed. Blessed are those who will not have seen yet[44] will believe.**

According to the same pattern he will also say to them: Now, *because you have seen* and *believed,* you are not profited regarding the faith[i] at the time when everything will receive its completion, because the time has passed for faith and good works, and it is only the time of judgment and retribution. Now you believe, but you are not profited. But *blessed are those who have not seen yet believed,* that is, he reveals the believers who followed the preaching of the gospel.

i. **Faith:** preceded by *yetin,* "last," which seems to be misplaced from the following phrase, *i žamanaki,* "at the time" (i.e., in the last time).

[427] [20:30] **Many other signs did Jesus do in front of his[45] disciples, which are not written in this book.**

He indicates that not only what we have written but also many other miracles were performed by the Lord for the disciples after his resurrection from

---

43. **Prophecy:** "prophet," M.
44. **Yet,** *ew,* NZ: om. M.
45. **His,** *iwroc',* NZ: om. M.

the dead in order to confirm them, which neither I nor the other evangelists have described completely.

[20:31] **But this much has been written, so that you might believe that Jesus Christ is Son of God, and that you might believe and receive eternal life in his name.**

Such is what he said: These few words that we have recorded in brief,[i] we have not written down by including any eulogies or praises; for[46] if we had been concerned with that we would not have described the Lord's activities partially but would have [set down] his entire amazing and sublime acts and the myriad things worthy of wonder. *But this much we have written so that they may believe that Jesus Christ is Son of God*, which means that those who will not believe in him will not be profited by these many writings. But those who believe that he is Son of God will receive perpetual and unending life through faith in his name.

i. John Chrysostom, *Hom. Jo.* 87.1, notes that this evangelist deliberately recorded less than the others.

---

46. **For:** om. M.

[21:1–2] **After this Jesus again revealed himself to his disciples, by the lake of Tiberias. And he revealed himself thus: There were together Peter, and Thomas called the twin, and Nathaniel who[1] [was] from Cana of Galilee, and the sons of Zebedee, and two others from among the[2] disciples.**

What, then, perhaps does this show: *He again revealed himself to his disciples?*[i] For after the resurrection he was not all the time among them and with them, as before the cross. It is clear from the saying *He again revealed himself* that it means [428] that after entering among them when the doors were closed, nowhere else did he reveal [himself] until in this place. He makes the further observation that there were not such bodily passions[ii] in him as before the cross, because after that there was no need of passions or sufferings, but only to confirm the disciples in faith in the resurrection. Why before that were the apostles not visible anywhere going around boldly, save because they were still terrified of the Jews and were sitting shaking in the upper room? But when they saw the Lord and were confirmed in the faith, openly they scattered from the upper room, in which they had been sitting hidden, through the ends of the earth.

i. Dionysius bar Salibi, *John*, 325, notes that the two unnamed disciples were Andrew and Philip.
ii. **Passions:** *kirk'*, the incidents and emotions of the human condition, equivalent to the Greek *pathē*; see the introduction, xxxviii.

[21:3–4] **Simon Peter said to them: I shall go fishing. They said to him: We also will go with you. *They went and entered a ship,[3] and that night they**

---

1. **Who,** MZ: om. N.
2. **The,** NZ: "his," M.
3. **They went ... ship,** NZ: om. M.

caught nothing. When it was morning Jesus was standing at the edge of the lake, but the disciples did not recognize that it was Jesus.

What means: *They did not recognize him*? He first wished to show the signs and miracles, and then to make himself known,[4] for that was the most useful and profitable for them regarding the faith.

[21:5] He[5] said to them: Children, have you anything to eat? They replied and said: No.

Why did he call[6] them *children*, yet behold, some of them were already very old? When he first summoned them to the rank of apostleship he had merely told them to give up fishing, so that they might become fishers of men (Matt 4:19; Mark 1:17). Here he sets down the recollection of those earlier words that he had spoken, that by fishing you still have the minds of children and not of mature persons.[i] For if I said you would become fishers of men, how do you have the childish mind still to fish?

i. Išodad explains that like children, being defective in complete knowledge, they had returned to their former craft. Dionysius bar Salibi, *John*, 325–26, elaborates on the various senses of "children," *ṭly*, including the lack of complete knowledge.

[21:6a] He said to them: Throw your nets to the right side of the ship, and you will find.

[429] [This was] in order to reveal that not by chance on the right side of the ship were the fish caught, which they had not found despite laboring all night, but that it was the result of his divine commands.

[21:6b–7a] They threw and were unable to pull it in from the multitude of the fish. That disciple whom Jesus loved said:[7] It is[8] the Lord.

From the signs that had occurred he said to Peter, *It is the Lord*, in order to say that in no other way than by his command was this done, but not through seeing anything did he recognize the Lord.

---

4. **Make himself known:** "show himself," M.
5. **He,** MN: "Jesus," Z and editor.
6. **Did he call:** om. M.
7. **Said,** MN: + "to Peter," Z and editor.
8. **Is,** NZ: om. M.

[21:7b] When Simon Peter heard that it was the Lord, he threw around himself his loincloth, because he was naked, and threw himself into the lake.

When he heard from John that it was the Lord, which he had said because of the sign, then he did not continue to be concerned with what he was doing but rapidly went off, revealing the warm love he had.

[21:8] But the other disciples came in the ship, for they were not far from the land but about two hundred cubits. They were dragging the tackle with the fish.

This further reveals Peter's fervent love, that although the ship was so close, he could not wait even a brief time to reach the Lord in the ship but threw himself into the lake, not at all afraid of the depth of the waters.

[21:9] When they came to land, they saw a brazier of coals, and a fish on it,[9] and bread.

Why *fish and bread*? Since he had previously said, *Children, do you have anything to eat*, this was lest they think that because of having some need for food[10] he had said that to them. But since bread and fish were to hand, they might understand perhaps thereby that not out of a desire for food did he say that, but he was pointing to something different by it. Why previously had he not [430] revealed to the people in the desert similar bread and fish that had been created by some command but had increased what they had? Because perhaps that was a time of instruction and oversight, while this particularly [a time] of revealing the divine things.

Furthermore, the wonders revealed at this point were greater by his demonstration of a single miracle: first, the multitude of fish caught in the net at the command; second, they were all very large and not mixed with small ones, such as the lake contained; third, at which the evangelist too was astonished, how many they were, yet the tackle was not broken; fourth, the brazier of coals and the fish and bread, since this had taken place and[11] been done by his command.

---

9. It, M: om. NZ.

10. **Food,** *kerakroc'*, N: "eating," *kerakreloy*, M.

11. **Taken place and:** om. M.

[21:10] Jesus said: Bring of the fish that you have now caught.

First he showed them the fish and bread and revealed that not for there being any need of food did I say, *Do you have anything to eat?* and you recognized the extent of my power. So *now bring also from the fish that you caught.* By this he reveals their honor, which after the wonderful signs had descended to them and made them worthy to have distributed to them bread and fish from the Lord's hands.

[21:11] Simon Peter entered [the ship] and pulled the tackle to land, full of very large fish, 153. There were so many, yet the tackle was not broken.

Again he indicates the same as we once said: there was such a large multitude of fish *yet the tackle was not broken*, which is a sign of the divine command and[12] power.[i]

i. For the interpretation of the number 153, see the commentary to vv. 13–14, below.

[21:12] Jesus said to them: Come, dine. And none of them dared to ask, Who are you? because they knew it was[13] the Lord.

[431] *What, then, does what he said reveal: *They did not dare to ask, Who are you?*[14] For if they knew he was the Lord, why did they wish to ask, *Who are you?* But we found from examples[i] that here they saw something most glorious and fearful in appearance; and although they recognized him to be the Lord, yet they did not dare to ask how or what sort of appearance this might be.[ii]

i. **Examples:** *awrinakkʿ*; for other commentaries seen by Nonnus, see the introduction, xxviii–xxix.
ii. John Chrysostom, *Hom. Jo.* 87, indicates that awe had trapped their tongues.

---

12. **Command and:** om. M.
13. **It was, NZ:** om. M.
14. **What … you:** om. N.

[21:13–14] **Jesus came and took the bread and gave to them, likewise also the fish. This [is the] third time Jesus appeared to them after rising from the dead.**

Why did he distribute the bread and fish to them save in order to remove from them the doubts that the appearance was seeming and a phantom?[i] Although the evangelist John did not say that the Lord himself tasted, yet the other disciple stated: *[We] who ate and drank with him after the resurrection* (Acts 10:41). However, we have not explained the straightforward action of events that occurred at the lake of Tiberias according to their profundity. So let us now set forth the unrecognized appearance at the shore of the lake a little more, as much as our minds comprehend it; for it contains no insignificant profound paradigms.

The unrecognized appearance to his disciples, after their laboring all night and catching nothing, patterns in a hidden fashion the prophets who sometimes labored so much yet were unable to draw any of mankind to the truth of the faith. They were submerged in sin like the fish of the lake, plunged in the mire of wicked deeds, and always remaining in the gloom of darkness and the *shadows of death* (Ps 22:4) through their dark sins, according to the scripture: *A people who sat in darkness saw a great light* (Isa 9:2). The Lord came, rising like the morning after [432] hiding in shadow the nature of the varied sins of mankind. *For he indeed was the light of the world, who illuminated every man who was to come into the world* (John 1:9); and through his disciples at his divine command and by his glorious resurrection he caught the nations[15] of mankind in the net of the gospel, drawing them to himself in the true faith.[ii]

Since he will place the righteous at his right hand on the day of retribution, and the sinners to the left, he commanded them to make preparations for fishing on the right side of the ship, as David had predicted by saying: *A princess will stand on your right, adorned and splendid[16] in garments woven with gold* (Ps 44:10). Since by the net of the gospel he was to catch a multitude of nations for the true faith, in the same way in the paradigm were predicted the multitudes of large fish seized in the tackle. And since *among those who have believed in Christ there is no distinction, neither of Jew nor[17] Gentile, neither of slave nor free, neither of male nor female, but all are one in Christ through the birth of the font,*[iii] *those who have drawn near to the mountain of Sion and to the city of the living God, to Jerusalem in heaven, and to the myriad hosts of*

---

15. **Nations:** sg. M.
16. **Adorned and splendid,** NZ: om. M.
17. **Nor:** "and," M.

angels and to the churches of the firstborn inscribed in heaven (Heb 12:22–23);
in the same way the equal and uniform multitude of the catch were large, not
having any distinction. And just as the gathering of the net of the gospel was
to take place through baptism in the name of the Holy Trinity—Father, Son,
and Holy Spirit—likewise too the number of the catch of the net was a mystical one hundred and fifty-three individuals.

What, then, do the fifties or the three individual numbers augur? It seems
not at all incomprehensible for those who wish to understand fully. The three
fifties predicted the extinguishing of the multitude of sins that would occur by
the grace of the font; but the individual three [433] indicated specifically the
confession of the three persons of the Holy Trinity whereby freedom in baptism is granted to us.[iv] And just as the net of the gospel remains indestructible
until the end, according to the Lord's saying, *I am with you until the end of
the world* (Matt 28:20), likewise the net was not torn despite containing such
a multitude of great fish. And just as we have been summoned to Christ and
invited to his kingdom, likewise the net with its catch was dragged to encounter the Lord himself. And just as those who were called to the faith through
the gospel believed, not through the understanding of their own minds or the
sight of their eyes but through the divinely wondrous acts, that the one crucified was God, likewise too the disciples believed, not through his appearance
and voice but through the amazing sign that occurred. And just as through
the gospel we sinners are transformed into the state of childlike innocence by
the grace of baptism, likewise they, according to the grace of transformation
that they were to receive, were called *children*.

Just as the coming of the Lord at the last time was near to fulfillment,
likewise too the disciples, by being at the lake, had come close to the Lord.
And just as among those who became disciples of the gospel, some encountered it stripped of bodily comforts, while others had bodily occupations yet
were found pleasing to the Lord, likewise too the disciples came to him, some
stripped, and others clothed. And just as those who became disciples of the
gospel were invited to the kingdom of heaven and to the prepared blessings,
likewise these too found the food prepared, the bread and fish, I mean. Just
as those who believed in the gospel will receive the reward of their virtue at
which they labored, likewise too these encountered those things in which[18]
they had been instructed and fed. [434] And just as those who believed in the
gospel recognized their creator, although the nature of his divinity remains
incomprehensible, likewise the disciples, when they saw the Lord, were unable
to ask: *Who are you?*

---

18. **In which,** *yors*, M: "by which," *yoroc'*, N.

i. Nonnus does not elaborate on the significance of the "third." Išodad quotes Gregory the Theologian (Gregory of Nazianzus) that "three" represents the threefold grace given to the disciples.

ii. The simile of catching (*orsal*, lit. "hunting"; here by fishing) is common in Armenian; see Thomson 2010 (§81, with further references in the notes).

iii. Gal 3:27–28 (not exact).

iv. Išodad refers to Origen in explaining the number 153: the three fifties symbolize the psalms, and three the Trinity. Moše bar Kepha also identifies the three with the Trinity, but for him the hundred represents the Gentiles, and the fifty the Jews; Dionysius bar Salibi, *John*, 328, offers a similar explanation. This has a parallel in Cyril of Alexandria, *Comm. Jo.* 12: the three represents the Trinity, the hundred equals ten decades, a *plērestatos* number; also Christ had a hundred sheep (Matt 18:12); fifty is imperfect, being half of one hundred, and is a reference to the Jews. For a more mathematical interpretation, see Ełišē, *A Homily on the Passion of Christ* (Thomson, 334–35).

[21:15a] And when they had dined, Jesus said to Simon Peter: Simon [son] of Yovnan, do you love me more than these?

Why did he ask only Peter this specific question and not anyone else of the disciples? It was because he was more eminent[i] than his fellow disciples. In bodily age he was fitted for the rank of teacher, but he also loved his teacher more than all [the others]. For that reason he entrusted the flock to him. Furthermore, it was in order to reveal to Peter that he bore no grudge because of his doubting, at his denial at the time of the cross. By that he showed him even more his forgivingness and gave him confidence by saying, *Do you love me*,[ii] just as once you said you would lay down your life for me; so *pasture my sheep*.[iii]

i. **More eminent:** *glxaworagoyn*, "chief," the usual epithet for Peter in Nonnus.

ii. Here John Chrysostom, *Hom. Jo.* 88.1, explains the difference between the two verbs used in Greek, Jesus saying *agapas*, and Peter replying, *philō*. The Armenian Gospel uses the verb *sirel* in both cases.

iii. **Pasture my sheep:** from v. 16, which is omitted below.

[21:15b] He said to him: Yes, Lord. And you know that I love you. He said to him: Pasture my lambs.

Peter did not say, I love you, but, *You know that I love you*. Why would this be? Peter introduced doubts into his mind, that perhaps now I shall not know as in the former manner, because I said, *Even if it comes to dying for you, I shall not abandon*[19] *you* (Matt 26:35; cf. John 11:37), and you accurately described

---

19. **Abandon**, MN: "deny," Z.

the future. So perhaps now too regarding what you asked, something other will occur than what I am saying. But you know the truth. Therefore he said: *You know that I love you.*

[21:17a] **He said to him the third time: Simon [son] of Yovnan, do you love me? Peter was saddened that he had said to him [435] three times: Do you love me? And he said: Lord, you know everything and you recognize everything, also that I love you.**

Why, then, was Peter saddened, save that he was in great doubt by such a mode of questioning whether this was just as previously, perhaps the future is hidden from me but clear to the Lord, as was prophesied about him. Therefore he said: *Lord, you know everything and recognize*; that is, my secrets[20] and my future actions are clear to your all-seeing power, for *you examine the hearts and reins of mankind* (Jer 11:20; 20:12; cf. Ps 7:10). For that reason Peter remained troubled by the triple question, remembering his earlier denials[21] that he had made by contradicting three times. Hence he said: *You are aware that I love you*; that is, the thoughts of my mind are better known to you than to me. Perhaps now by contradicting I shall fall again, but you have no need of examination, since you know whether I love you or whether I shall weaken again. But lest we pass over why the Lord asked three times, it was so that through these three confessions he might purify and heal the three denials.[i]

i. This is the argument of John Chrysostom, *Hom. Jo.* 88.1; Theodore of Mopsuestia; Išodad; and Dionysius bar Salibi, *John*, 330. But Nonnus confuses the issue by omitting v. 16 and therefore including only two confessions of love for Jesus by Peter.

[21:17b] **He said to him: Pasture my sheep.**

He shows here that nothing was more honorable and pleasing to him[22] than the oversight of the believers and their guidance to correction, just as he himself was an example by laying down his life for the flock, as he declared: *The noble shepherd lays down his life for his sheep* (John 10:11).[i] Something similar he indicated to him in the superabundance of his love, to whom he said, *You are a rock, and on this rock I shall build*[23] *my church*, and *I shall give you the keys of the kingdom of heaven* (Matt 16:18–19), with the rest.

---

20. **Secrets:** sg. M.

21. **Denials:** sg. M.

22. **Him:** "God," M.

23. **I shall build,** *šinec'ic'*: "I built," *šinec'i*, M.

i. See note to the commentary on John 10:11 for the translation of *kʾaǰ*, "noble." Theodore of Mopsuestia distinguishes various categories of people intended by the triple reference to "lambs" and "sheep." Moše bar Kepha indicates that the lambs are the apostles, and the sheep the rich and noble.

[21:18a] Amen, amen, I say to you, that while you were young, [436] you placed a girdle around you yourself and went wherever you wished.

What means what he said, save that because he repeated the saying about his love, he predicted to him here what would happen? For Peter had been seized by no little doubt from now on regarding himself: What I said does not seem at all reliable to him.[24] Therefore the Lord said: *While you were young, you placed a girdle around you yourself and went wherever you wished.* That is, what you previously said, you would lay down your life for me, you said yourself with force and willingness, like one girdled, or as those who wish to hasten to their work adjust themselves; likewise you too, but you have not grasped my omnipotent power.

[21:18b] But when you will grow old, you will hold up your hands, and others will gird you and lead you where you do not wish.

When the previous actions by Peter, the three denials, he had healed through the three confessions, and Peter had confessed his own weakness,[25] *You know everything and recognize that I love you*, he here removed Peter's doubts that something similar might be done by him again, and he predicted to him the death that he was still to endure for his sake, and that he would be crucified.[i] According to custom, the one whom they crucify, they bind firmly his middle. Therefore by saying, *When you grow old, you will hold up your hands, and other will gird you*, he informed him of the torments that he would endure through the cross.

And they will lead you where you do not wish. He did not mean that his crucifixion would be unwilling. Of your own will at that hour[26] you will lay down your life for me as testimony. But he predicted the future weakness of his body at the hour of his death, in order to indicate that [437] your body will not remain without sadness at the time of the separation of the soul, when they will lead you to the cross. As I too bore witness to the weakness of human

---

24. **To him,** *nma*, N: "he remains," *mna*[*y*], M.
25. **Weakness:** pl. M.
26. **At that hour:** om. M.

bodies at the hour of torments by saying, *My soul is willing, but my body is weak* (Matt 26:41; Mark 14:38).

i. Theodore of Mopsuestia and Išodad describe Peter's crucifixion upside down; cf. Eusebius, *Hist. eccl.* 3.1.2ff. Cyril of Alexandria, *Comm. Jo.* 12; Moše bar Kepha; and Dionysius bar Salibi, *John*, 330, merely refer to Peter's crucifixion.

[21:19a] **He said this, indicating by what death he would glorify God.**

When he had removed the suspicious doubts from Peter's mind, he showed him the manner of the death that he would endure. *To glorify God*, because he said he would be glorified through the testimonies of his saints, as he himself through the divine ineffable gifts glorifies those who became his fellows in torments and death, according to Paul's saying (2 Tim 2:11–12), who will also reign at the second coming.

[21:19b] **And when he had said this, he said to him: Follow me.**

This was not a little indication and demonstration of love, to summon him alone to follow him.

[21:20–21] **Peter turned and saw the disciple whom Jesus loved following, the one who fell on his breast, and said: Lord, who is it that will betray you? When Peter saw him, he said to Jesus: Lord, what about this one?**

Why did the evangelist talk so much about himself by saying, *whom Jesus loved, who fell on his breast*, and was bold enough to ask the Lord about the betrayer, *Who might he be?* unless he did not desire to reveal his own importance and honor but rather the abundance of Peter's love for the Lord. After his denial he showed his love so forgivingly that that disciple who was so loved by the Lord, who had also fallen on his breast and had dared to ask from what the others had refrained, about this same one Peter [438] loudly spoke to the Lord, saying, *What about this one?*; that is, Why did you not also tell him to follow you?

[21:22] **He said to him: If I wish that he stay until I come, what concern is it to you? You follow me.**

Since what Peter said about the disciple was a demonstration of his love, and he wanted John not to leave, therefore he asked this briefly: *What about this one?* But the Lord showed that the abundance of his own love for that disciple was greater than for Peter, as he supposed. Also it was lest he inquire about what he did not know the cause. But because Peter desired that the sending of himself and of that disciple be equal, he indicated: *If I wish that he stay until I come, what concern is it to you? You follow me.*[27] That is, I am not going to send you to preach the gospel equally, but you are going to leave each other, because the gospel of the kingdom must be preached to the whole world.

[21:23] **And this saying went out among the brethren, and they reckoned that that disciple would not die. But Jesus did not say, He will not die, but, I wish that he stay until I come.**

He indicated that not as the disciples had understood did the Lord say what he did about the disciple but because of Peter's words, as we said above.[i]

i. Moše bar Kepha glosses "brethren" as the apostles.

[21:24a] **This is the disciple who testifies about these things, who also wrote these things.**

Why does the evangelist here introduce himself, save to show again that Peter's conversation with the Lord was about him, the very one who at the supper had fallen on the Lord's breast and asked what he did? It is the same *who testifies about these things, who also wrote them down*, having been an eyewitness of all these things and testifying truly about these words.[i]

i. Here Theodore of Mopsuestia, Išodad, and Dionysius bar Salibi (*John*, 331) indicate that John lived for 73 years after the ascension and died a natural death after all the apostles.

[**439**] [21:24b] **And we know that his testimony is true.**

The evangelist also said this in another place, when blood and water flowed from his ribs: *He saw and testified, and we know that his testimony is true* (John 19:34–35). He puts down the same again. Why, then, save to show *both the true testimony and the details of the events,*[28] that the testimony he wrote is not confused, for those who wish such things compose eulogies and praises? If I had had any zeal for the like, I would not have passed over the multitude of wonders [performed] by him, but I would have written down in

---

27. **Me:** om. M.

28. **Both … events,** M: "the details of both the true testimony and of the events," N. Events, *irac'n*, N: "scripture," *groyn*, M.

detail his miracles, which I only undertook to write down for those who wish to believe that Christ is Son of God. But this also I have frequently testified in writing in order not to conceal the Jews striking and mocking him, not only the tormenting and suffering, but also the insulting and despising, the calling him *a Samaritan* (John 8:48) and *son of a carpenter* (Matt 13:55; Mark 6:3), and also *demon-possessed* (John 10:20), in order to show that that does not at all prevent the strengthening of the faith but rather confirms the patience and service that he endured for our salvation. And it was written down for our instruction.

[21:25] But there is much else that Jesus did, which if they were written one by one, I think even this world would not be[29] sufficient to contain the books that might be written.

Since he previously said, *We know that his witness is true,* he added to that through a brief statement the wonders of the infinite and innumerable signs and miracles that he did on earth, indicating that the divine and wondrous powers[30] and signs and miracles were so many that *this world would not be sufficient to contain* [440] all the accounts of the divine powers performed, especially for the historians to produce an account of the multitude of events that occurred.

[Exhortation]

When the unpleasant harshness of wintertime arrives, it holds all forms of living things in melancholy. But at the change to the pleasant and lively season of spring, the living species take delight. As they split the air above our heads the swallows sing pleasing refrains in our ears. Likewise too the diverse types of birds trill their music at the change to the glorious time of pleasing and delightfully sweet air. The sun joins in, spreading over us the splendor of its ever milder and temperate rays. The earth provides the shoots of its various plants and flowers, while the leafy trees give beautiful shade.

Shepherds and herdsmen bring out [their flocks] from where they had sheltered in idleness from the harshness of the bitter winter winds.[31] Sailors, seeing the extent of the raging sea without its surging billows, immediately trust themselves to it rather than to land. The vine grower, having sharpened

---

29. **Would not be,** NZ: "is," M.
30. **Powers:** "acts," M.
31. **Winds:** sg. M.

his pruning knife, comes and cuts the unproductive part of the vine. Also all pots necessary for us are changed from emptiness to each one's use. And for us now the heavenly spring, Christ, rising from the tomb, renders glorious not only the temporary bodily and volatile delights but those spiritual ones that cannot be stolen or lost. [441] *Now no irrational birds sing,[32] but the holy angels descend to earth and chant with mankind the song of praise inspired to David: *Your rod and staff will console me* (Ps 22:4). For now the grieving of our mortality has fled, because the news of the resurrection through the wood of the cross has shone upon us, and from cruel death a sweet fountain has flowed forth for us.

O mystery of this good day of the sacrifice of the lamb. The first father has been redeemed, and not only the first father but all his offspring. Now let us rejoice[33] at our wonderful resurrection; let us celebrate with spiritual joy, delighting in our souls, but not to support the pleasures of the stomach. With the shining angel let us too shine with the faith, rejoicing in the resurrection of our hope. Let us well contemplate the great mystery of our resurrection; let us hasten thoughtfully to enter the tomb, becoming fellow disciples. Let us serve with the women; let us encounter the resurrection; let us come to Christ; let us proclaim the story of his resurrection to the pure-minded; let us instruct ourselves and worthily celebrate the divine resurrection.

Worthily let us taste the body and blood of the Lord, and let us store up for ourselves the eternal viaticum for everlasting life. [Let us don] purple robes, but not dyed red with anything other than the blood of Christ, so that on approaching the ranks to the right-hand side we may be rendered worthy to offer glory to the Father and Son and Holy Spirit, now and always and forever and ever.[34] Amen.

[442] Colophon [in N]

The letters of the divine books, which by the largesse of the Spirit were transmitted as a gift to the human race, are sublime and inscrutable. But more especially superior to the faculties of understanding and hearing are the activities of the divine dispensation[35] proclaiming Christ. They flow and spread like the shining rays of the sun in the ears of us rational ones through the quadruple currents of the rivers that flow from the boundless sea, through

---

32. **Now ... sing**, M and editor: om. N.

33. **Let us rejoice**, editor: "we have rejoiced," MN.

34. **And ever**: om. M.

35. **Dispensation**: *tnawrēnut'iwn*. For the terminology, see the introduction, xxxvi.

four of the initiated and inspired chosen men before the creation of the upper and lower beings.

Of these, like trumpets announcing the gospel to the universe,[36] the first to write was the great and blessed evangelist Matthew, rendered worthy of two sublime ranks and grace: of apostleship with the eleven, and of evangelist with the three. As beginning he set down the ancestral patriarchs and the line of the Virgin and begetter of her Creator, [443] namely, the Book of the Birth of Jesus Christ, son of David, son of Abraham. Likewise, following in order, Mark [set down] the coming to baptism, the forerunning of John the Baptist, and the selection of disciples.

His sublime successor as vessel of election, who attained the third heaven (Acts 9:15; 2 Cor 12:2), Luke, [set down] the annunciation of Gabriel to Mary, proclaiming her joy and rejoicing, and also the greeting of Elisabeth and the loosing of Zachariah's tongue. While the one beloved by the Lord and pure of all downward-bearing passions, the son of thunder (Mark 3:17), loftier than all, proclaimed the uncreated essence of the Son, declaring in inspired words, *In the beginning was the Word* (John 1:1), and revealing the equality of substance and eternity of the Son and Spirit with the Father.

Now the unbounded and ineffable gifts of the Holy Spirit that he pours out on each one according to merit, and which when distributed remain without being consumed or exhausted, moved the mind and thoughts of a just man called Nanay, of the language of the Syrians, by the election and grace of the Word without beginning, to ponder and expound this supreme and incomprehensible Gospel of John, illuminating its meaning and spirit for all believers in Him. This I the sinful and most worthless Kirakos desired, and I was imbued with a triple flame of love for this [444] divinely inspired book. But no copy was to be found anywhere.

Then I heard that it could be found in Amida. And summoning up great zeal and regarding as naught my own weakness, I traversed many places, and by the providence of God what I had begun was completed through the grace of the same. But by the circumstances of the time in which this book was completed, deep winter and severe wind and the foreign places, I suffered much affliction from the cold. For my hands remained without sensation like frozen iron, and my whole body stayed numb for forty days as if in the snow, and there was no attendant or acquaintance.

Yet because of my great desire, for love of it I disregarded my afflictions and weakness, and also [my] inelegant and untrained writing, taking refuge

---

36. The apostles as trumpets is a popular theme in Armenian theological writing; see *Teaching* 638, with further references in Thomson 2001 (note ad loc.).

in the forgiveness of my readers, since I worked for love. So I beg not to be blamed for the roughness of my writing and its defectiveness, because of the severity of the weather. No other copy could be found anywhere, and the owner of the copy, an uncivil and boorish man, reckoned that I was stealing what belonged to him. And only after much effort in seeking to finish the book was it rendered into many *seṙs*.[37]

In the era of the Armenians and the year of the Armenian calendar 604 [= 1155], in the patriarchate of Gregory Catholicos of Armenia,[38] and in the anarchy of Armenia, while the pious and great prince of the Christians T'oros shone out,[39] when he attacked Aleppo and captured and destroyed many places and castles, [445] and very victoriously returned to his own land—this divine and spiritual book was written by my hand, that of the miserable and unworthy monk Kirakos, a great transgressor before the Lord, in memory of my own sinful person and of my parents. Now, you who read or take notice of it, request forgiveness for my sinful soul from the provider of all gifts. And may God have mercy on you who remember, and on those remembered. Amen.

---

37. The meaning is unclear. *Seṙ* means "type, gender."
38. Gregory III, Catholicos 1113–66.
39. T'oros II, prince 1143–69.

Bibliography

Primary Sources

Abū Ra'ita. G. Graf, ed. 1951. "Refutation of the Melchites." In *Die Schriften des Jaco-biten Ḥabib ibn Ḥidma Abū Ra'ita.* CSCO 130 (pp. 65–72), 131 (pp. 82–90), Scriptores Arabici 14, 15. Leuven: Peeters.

Agat'angełos. *History.* G. Tēr-Mkrtč'ean and S. Kanayeanc', eds. (1909) 1980. *Patmut'iwn Hayoc'.* Reprint, Delmar, N.Y.: Caravan.

———. *History.* R. W. Thomson, trans. 2010. *The Lives of Saint Gregory: The Armenian, Greek, Arabic, and Syriac Versions of the "History" attributed to Agathangelos.* Ann Arbor, Mich.: Caravan.

Ankanon Girk'. Vol 3. K'. Č'rak'ean ed. 1904. Venice: San Lazzaro.

Athanasius. *De incarnatione.* R. W. Thomson, ed. and trans. 1971. *Contra Gentes and De Incarnatione.* OECT. Oxford: Clarendon.

Basil of Caesarea. *Hexaemeron.* E. Amand de Mendieta and S. Y. Rudberg, eds. 1997. *Homilien zum Hexaemeron.* GCS N.F. 2. Berlin: Akademie.

———. *Hexaemeron.* S. Giet, trans. 1968. *Basile de Césarée: Homélies sur l'Hexaéméron.* SC 26 bis. Paris: Cerf.

———. *Hexaemeron.* K. Muradyan, ed. 1984. *Barseł Kesarac'i: Yałags vec'awreay ararč'ut'ean.* Erevan: Haykakan SSH GA Hratarakč'ut'yun.

———. *Hexaemeron.* R. W. Thomson, ed. 1995. *The Syriac Version of the "Hexaemeron" by Basil of Caesarea.* CSCO 550, 551, Scriptores Syri 222, 223. Leuven: Peeters.

———. *Hexaemeron.* R. W. Thomson, trans. 2012. *Saint Basil of Caesarea and Armenian Cosmology.* CSCO 646, Subsidia 130. Leuven: Peeters.

Book of Letters. Y. Izmireanc', ed. 1901. *Girk' T'łt'oc'.* Tiflis [Tbilisi?]: Tparan T. Rōtineanc'. 2d ed. 1994. N. Połarean, ed. Jerusalem: Tparan Srboc' Yakobeanc'.

Buzandaran. N. G. Garsoïan, trans. 1989. *The Epic Histories attributed to P'awstos Buzand (Buzandaran Patmut'iwnk').* HATS 8. Cambridge: Harvard University Press.

———. K'. Patkanean, ed. (1883) 1984. *P'awstosi Buzandac'woy Patmut'iwn Hayoc'.* Reprint, Delmar, N.Y.: Caravan.

Commentary on the Diatessaron. L. Leloir, ed. and trans. 1963. *Saint Éphrem: Commentaire de l'Évangile concordant; Texte Syriaque (Manuscrit Chester Beatty 709).* Chester Beatty Monographs 8. Dublin: Hodges Figgis & Co.

———. L. Leloir, ed. and trans. 1966. *Éphrem de Nisibe: Commentaire de l'Évangile concordant ou Diatessaron, traduit du syriaque et de l'arménien.* SC 121. Paris: Cerf.

———. L. Leloir, ed. and trans. 1990. *Saint Éphrem: Commentaire de l'Évangile concordant; Texte Syriaque (Manuscrit Chester Beatty 709); Folios Additionels*. Chester Beatty Monographs 8. Leuven: Peeters.

Cyril of Alexandria. *Commentary on the Gospel of John*. P. E. Pusey, ed. (1872) 1965. *Cyrilli archiepiscopi Alexandrini in D. Ioannis evangelium*. 3 vols. Reprint, Brussels: Culture et civilisation.

Diatessaron. A. Marmadji, ed. and trans. 1935. *Diatessaron de Tatien, texte arabe établi, traduit en français*. Beirut: Imprimerie catholique.

Dionysius bar Salibi. *Commentary on John*. R. Lejoly, ed. 1975. *Dionysii bar Salibi enarratio in Ioannem*. 4 vols. Dison: Éditions Concile.

———. *Commentary on the Gospels*. I. Sedlácek and I.-B. Chabot, eds. 1906–22. *Dionysii bar Salibi commentarii in evangelia I*. CSCO 15, 16, 77, 85, Scriptores Syri 15, 16, 33, 40. Leuven: Peeters.

———. *Commentary on the Gospels*. A. Vaschalde, ed. 1931–40. *Dionysii bar Salibi commentarii in evangelia II*. CSCO 95, 98, 113, 114, Scriptores Syri 47, 49, 60, 61. Leuven: Peeters.

Dionysius the Areopagite. See Pseudo-Dionysius.

Ełišē. *History of Vardan*. E. Ter-Minasyan, ed. 1957. *Ełišēi vasn Vardanay ew Hayocʻ Paterazmin*. Erevan: Haykakan SSH GA Hratarakčʻutʻyun.

———. *History of Vardan*. R. W. Thomson, trans. 1982. *Elishē: History of Vardan and the Armenian War*. HATS 5. Cambridge: Harvard University Press.

———. *Works*. 1859. *Srboy Hōrn meroy Ełišē vardapeti Matenagrutʻiwnkʻ*.Venice: San Lazzaro.

———. *Homily*. R. W. Thomson, trans. 2000. *A Homily on the Passion of Christ attributed to Elishe*. ECTT 5. Leuven: Peeters.

Ephrem. *Commentary on Genesis*. E. G. Mathews Jr., ed. 1998. *The Armenian Commentary on Genesis attributed to Ephrem the Syrian*. CSCO 572, 573, Scriptores Armeniaci 23, 24. Leuven: Peeters.

———. *Sermo VI in Hebdomadem sanctam*. Th. J. Lamy, ed. 1882–1902. *S. Ephraemi syri hymni et sermones*. 4 vols. Malines: Dessain.

Epiphanius. *De gemmis*. R. P. Blake and H. De Vis, eds. 1934. *Epiphanius: De gemmis*. SD 2. London: Christophers.

Eusebius of Caesarea. *Historia ecclesiastica*. K. Lake and J. E. L. Oulton, trans. 1926–32. *Eusebius: The Ecclesiastical History*. 2 vols. Loeb Classical Library. Cambridge: Harvard University Press.

Eznik of Kołb. *On God*. L. Mariès and Ch. Mercier, ed. and trans. 1959. *Eznik de Kołb: De Deo*. PO 28.3–4. Paris: Firmin-Didot.

Hamam. *Commentary on the Book of Proverbs*. R. W. Thomson, ed. and trans. 2005. *Hamam: Commentary on the Book of Proverbs*. HUAS 5. Leuven: Peeters.

Ignatios Sevleṙncʻi. *On Luke*. 1824. *Meknutʻiwn srboy Awetaranin or ēst Łukasu*. Constantinople: Tparan Abraham Terzean.

Išodad of Merv. *Commentary on the Gospels*. M. D. Gibson, ed. and trans. 1911. *The Commentaries of Isho'dad of Merv*. Horae Semiticae 6. Vols. 1–3. Cambridge: Cambridge University Press.

John Chrysostom. *Commentary on John*. 1717. *Meknut'iwn srboy Awetaranin or ĕst Yohannu*. 2 vols. Constantinople: Tparan Grigor Marzvanec'i.

———. *Commentary on John*. J.-P. Migne, ed. *In Iohannem homiliae*. PG 59.

Kirakos Ganjakec'i. *History*. K. Melik'-Ōhanjanyan, ed. 1961. *Patmut'iwn Hayoc'*. Erevan: Haykakan SSH GA Hratarakč'ut'yun.

Labubna. *Teaching of Addai*. Ł. Ališan, ed. 1868. *Labubneay diwanagir dpri Edesioy T'ułt' Abgaru*. Venice: San Lazzaro.

———. *Teaching of Addai*. A. Desreumaux, trans. 1993. *Histoire du roi Abgar et de Jésus*. Turnhout: Brepols.

———. *Teaching of Addai*. G. Phillips, ed. 1876. *The Doctrine of Addai the Apostle*. London: Trubner.

Łazar P'arpec'i. *History*. G. Tēr-Mkrtč'ean and S. Malxasean, eds. (1904) 1985. *Patmut'iwn Hayoc' ew T'ułt' aṙ Vahan Mamikonean*. Reprint, Delmar, N.Y.: Caravan.

———. *History*. R. W. Thomson, trans. 1991. *The History of Łazar P'arpec'i*. Columbia University, Suren D. Fesjian Academic Publications 4. Atlanta: Scholars Press.

Mambrē. *Homilies on the Resurrection of Lazarus*. 1894. *Mambrēi Vercanołi Čaṙk'*. Venice: San Lazzaro.

———. *Homilies on the Resurrection of Lazarus*. R. W. Thomson, trans. 2005–7. Mambrē and His Homilies. *REArm* 30:99–168.

Michael the Syrian. *Chronicle*. 1871. *Teaṙn Mixaēli Patriark'i Asorwoc' Žamanakagrut'iwn*. Jerusalem: Tparan Srboc' Yakobeanc'.

Mošē bar Kepha. *Commentary on John*. L. Schlimme, ed. and trans. 1978–81. *Der Johanneskommentar des Moses bar Kepha*. Göttinger Orientforschungen, Reihe Syriaca 18. 4 vols. Wiesbaden: Harrassowitz.

Movsēs Dasxuranc'i. *History of Albania*. V. Arak'elyan, ed. 1983. *Movsēs Kałankatuac'i: Patmut'iwn Ałuanic'*. Erevan: Haykakan SSH GA Hratarakč'ut'yun.

———. *History of Albania*. C. J. F. Dowsett, trans. 1961. *The History of the Caucasian Albanians by Movses Dašxuranci*. LOS 8. London: Oxford University Press.

Movsēs Xorenac'i. *History*. M. Abełean and S. Yarut'iwnean, eds. (1913) 1981. *Patmut'iwn Hayoc'*. Reprint, Delmar, N.Y.: Caravan.

———. *History*. R. W. Thomson, trans. 2006. *Moses Khorenatsi, History of the Armenians*. Rev. ed. Ann Arbor, Mich.: Caravan.

Mxit'ar Ayrivanec'i. *History*. M. F. Brosset, trans. 1869. *Histoire Chronologique par Mkhithar d'Aïrivank, XIII s*. Mémoires de l'Académie impériale des Sciences de St. Petersburg, ser. VII, 13.5. St. Petersburg: l'Académie impériale des Sciences.

———. *History*. K'. Patkanean, ed. 1867. *Patmut'iwn žamanakakargakan*. St. Petersburg: Kayserakan čem. Gitout'eanc'.

Mxit'ar Goš. *Lawcode*. R. W. Thomson, trans. 2000. *The Lawcode [Datastanagirk'] of Mxit'ar Goš*. DSALL 6. Amsterdam: Rodopi.

———. *Lawcode*. X. T'orosyan, ed. 1975. *Girk' Datastani*. Erevan: Haykakan SSH GA Hratarakč'ut'yun.

Nersēs of Lambron. *Commentary on Revelation*. R. W. Thomson, ed. and trans. 2007. *Nerses of Lambron: Commentary on the Revelation of Saint John*. HUAS 9. Leuven: Peeters.

Nersēs Šnorhali. *Letters.* 1871. *Endhanrakan Tʻułtʻkʻ.* Jerusalem: Tparan Srbocʻ Yako-
beancʻ.

Nonnus/Nanay. *Commentary on John.* Kʻ. Čʻrakʻean, ed. 1920. *Nanayi Asorwoy
vardapeti: Meknutʻiwn Yovhannu awetaranin.* Tʻangaran haykakan hin ew nor
Dprutʻeancʻ 7. Venice: San Lazzaro.

Origen. *Commentary on John.* C. Blanc, ed. 1966–82. *Origène: Commentaire sur Saint
Jean.* SC 120, 157, 222, 290. Paris: Cerf.

Philoxenus of Mabbug. *Commentary on the Johannine Prologue.* A. de Halleux, ed.
1977. *Philoxène de Mabbog: Commentaire du Prologue johannique.* CSCO 380,
381, Scriptores Syri 165, 166. Leuven: Peeters.

Pseudo-Dionysius the Areopagite. R. W. Thomson, ed. 1987. *The Armenian Version
of the Works attributed to Dionysius the Areopagite.* CSCO 488, 489, Scriptores
Armeniaci 17, 18. Leuven: Peeters.

Sargis Kund. *Commentary on the Gospel of John.* 1177. Unpublished.

Severian of Gabala. *Homilies.* M. Awgerean, ed. and trans. 1827. *Seberianosi kam Sew-
erianosi Emesacʻwoy Gabałacʻwoy episkoposi Čaṙkʻ.* Venice: San Lazzaro.

Socrates Scholasticos. Armenian versions of the *Ecclesiastical History. Sokratay
Skʻolastikosi Ekełecʻakan Patmutʻiwn ew Patmutʻiwn varucʻ srboyn Silbestrosi epis-
koposin.* M. Tēr-Movsēsean, ed. 1897. Vałaršapat: Tparan surb Eǰmiacni.

Stepʻannos of Siwnikʻ. *Commentary on the Four Evangelists.* G. Yovsepʻean, ed. 1994.
Meknutʻiwn Čʻoricʻ Awetarančʻacʻn. Athens: Nor Ašxarh.

———. *Commentary on the Four Evangelists.* M. B. Papazian, trans. 2014. New York:
Armenian Apostolic Church of America.

Stepʻannos Orbelean. *History of Siwnikʻ.* 1910. *Patmutʻiwn nahangin Sisakan.* Tiflis:
Ałanean.

———. *History of Siwnikʻ.* M. Brosset, trans. 1864–66. *Histoire de la Siounie par
Stéphannos Orbélian.* 2 vols. St. Petersburg: Académie Impériale des Sciences.

Tatʻewacʻi, Grigor. *Commentary on John.* Ł. Zakʻaryan, ed. 2005. *Surb Grigor Tatʻewacʻi:
Meknutʻiwn Yovhannu Awetarani.* NKGM 12. Surb Ēǰmiacin: Mayr Atʻoṙ.

Teaching of Saint Gregory. R. W. Thomson, trans. 2001. *The Teaching of Saint Gregory.*
Rev. ed. AVANT 1. New Rochelle, N.Y.: St. Nersess Armenian Seminary.

Theodore of Mopsuestia. *Commentary on John.* I.-M. Vosté, ed. 1940. *Theodori Mop-
suesteni commentarius in Evangelium Iohannis Apostoli.* CSCO 115, 116, Scriptores Syri 62, 63. Leuven: Peeters.

Timotheos. *Disputation with Caliph Al-Mahdī* . M. Heimgartner, ed. 2010. *Timotheos
I, Ostsyrische Patriarch: Disputation mit dem Kalifen Al-Mahdi.* CSCO 631, 632,
Scriptores Syri 244, 245. Leuven: Peeters.

Tʻovma Arcruni. *History of the Arcrunikʻ.* Kʻ. Patkanean, ed. (1887) 1917. *Tʻovmayi
vardapeti Arcrunwoy Patmutʻiwn Tann Arcruneacʻ.* Reprint, Tiflis: Ałanean.

———. *History of the Arcrunikʻ.* R. W. Thomson, trans. 1985. *Thomas Artsruni: History
of the House of the Artsrunikʻ.* Detroit: Wayne State University Press.

Vardan Arewelcʻi. *Historical Compilation.* Ł. Ališan, ed. (1862) 1991. *Hawakʻumn
Patmutʻean Hayocʻ.* Reprint, Delmar, N.Y.: Caravan.

———. *Historical Compilation.* R. W. Thomson, trans. 1989. The Historical Compilation of Vardan Arewelcʻi. *DOP* 43:125–226.

Xosrov Anjewac'i. *Commentary on the Liturgy.* S. P. Cowe, ed. and trans. 1991. *Commentary on the Divine Liturgy by Xosrov Anjewac'i.* New York: St. Vartan.

Yovhannēs Drasxanakertc'i. *History.* M. Emin, ed. (1853) 1980. *Patmut'iwn Hayoc'.* Reprint, Delmar, N.Y.: Caravan.

———. *History.* K. Maksoudian, trans. 1987. *Yovhannēs Drasxanakertc'i: History of Armenia.* Atlanta: Scholars Press.

Yovhannēs Mandakuni. *Homilies.* 1860. *Čaṙk'.* Venice: San Lazzaro.

Secondary Sources

Accad, M. 1998. Did the Later Syriac Fathers Take into Consideration Their Islamic Context When Reinterpreting the New Testament? *ParOr* 23:13–32.

Akinean, N. 1922. Tēodor Apukuṙa ew Nana Asori Hayastani mēǰ. *HA* 36:193–205, 357–68, 417–24.

———. 1952. Timotēos vardapet ew ir Meknut'iwn Araracoc' groc'. *HA* 66:1–17.

Ananean, P. 1995. *Zak'aria Kat'ołikos Jagec'i, Čaṙk'.* Venice: San Lazzaro.

Baronian, S., and F. C. Conybeare. 1918. *Catalogue of the Armenian Manuscripts in the Bodleian Library.* Oxford: Clarendon.

Boisson-Chenorhokian, P. 2005–7. Notes sur Kirakos Ganjakec'i. *REArm* 30:237–48.

Brock, S. P. 1982. Clothing Metaphors as a Means of Theological Expression in Syriac Tradition. Pages 11–40 in *Typus, Symbol, Allegorie bei den östlichen Vätern und ihren Parallelen im Mittelalter.* Edited by M. Schmidt. Regensburg: Pustet.

Bundy, D. D. 1982. The Commentary of Nonnus of Nisibis on the Prologue of John. Pages 123–33 in *Actes du premier congrès internationale d'études arabes chrétiennes.* Edited by K. Samir. OCA 218. Rome: Pontificium Institutum Orientalium Studiorum.

Č'amč'ean, M. 1784–86. *Patmut'iwn Hayoc'.* 3 vols. Venice: San Lazzaro.

Canard, M. 1980. See Laurent, J.

Čemčemean, S. 1998. *Mayr C'uc'ak Hayerēn Jeṙagrac' Matenadaranin Mxitareanc' i Venetik.* Vol. 8. Venice: San Lazzaro.

Cox, C. 1984. Introduction to *Astuacašunč' Matean hin ew nor Ktakaranac'.* Edited by Y. Zōhrapean. Delmar, N.Y.: Caravan.

de Halleux, A. 1963. *Philoxène de Mabbog: Sa vie, ses écrits, sa théologie.* Leuven: Orientaliste.

Der Nersessian, S. 1954. An Armenian Version of the *Homilies on the Harrowing of Hell. DOP* 8:203–24.

———. 1963. A Homily on the Raising of Lazarus and the Harrowing of Hell. Pages 219–34 in *Biblical and Patristic Studies in Memory of Robert Pierce Casey.* Edited by J. N. Birdsall and R. W. Thomson. Freiburg: Herder.

Dorfmann-Lazarev, I. 2004. *Arméniens et Byzantins à l'époque de Photius: Deux débats théologiques après le Triomphe de l'Orthodoxie.* CSCO 609, Subsidia 117. Leuven: Peeters.

Edwards, M. 2004. *John.* Blackwell Bible Commentaries. Oxford: Blackwell.

Eganyan, Ō., A. Jeyt'unyan, and F. Ant'abyan. 1970. *C'uc'ak Jeṙagrac' Maštoc'i anvan Matenadarani*. Vol. 2. Erevan: Haykakan SSṘ Gitut'yunneri Akademiayi Hratarakč'ut'yun.

Garitte, G. 1952. *La Narratio de Rebus Armeniae*. CSCO 132, Subsidia 4. Leuven: Imprimerie Orientaliste.

Garsoïan, N. G. 1989. *The Epic Histories attributed to P'awstos Buzand (Buzandaran Patmut'iwnk')*. HATS 8. Cambridge: Harvard University Press.

———. 1996. The Two Voices of Armenian Mediaeval Historiography: The Iranian Index. *Studia Iranica* 25:7–43.

———. 1999. *L'église arménienne et le grand schisme d'Orient*. CSCO 574, Subsidia 100. Leuven: Peeters.

———. 2003–4. L'*Histoire* attribuée à Movsēs Xorenac'i: Que reste-t-il à en dire? *REArm* 29:29–48.

———. 2010. *Studies in the Formation of Christian Armenia*. Variorum Collected Studies 959. Burlington, Vt.: Ashgate.

———. 2012. *Interregnum: Introduction to a Study on the Formation of Armenian Identity (ca 600–750)*. CSCO 640, Subsidia 127. Leuven: Peeters.

Greenwood, T. 2006. Failure of a Mission? Photius and the Armenian Church. *Mus* 119:123–67.

Griffith, S. H. 1980. Ḥabīb ibn Ḥidmah Abū Rā'iṭah, a Christian *mutakallim* of the First Abbasid Century. *OrChr* 64:161–201.

———. 1991. The Apologetic Treatise of Nonnus of Nisibis. *Aram* 3:115–38.

———. 2001. "Melkites," "Jacobites," and the Christological Controversies in Arabic in Third/Ninth-Century Syria. Pages 9–55 in *Syrian Christians under Islam: The First Thousand Years*. Edited by D. Thomas. Leiden: Brill.

———. 2008. *The Church in the Shadow of the Mosque: Christians and Muslims in the World of Islam*. Princeton, N.J.: Princeton University Press.

Hovannisian, R. G., ed. 1997. *The Armenian People from Ancient to Modern Times*. 2 vols. New York: St. Martin's.

Hübschmann, H. 1897. *Armenische Grammatik*. Leipzig: Von Breitkopf & Härtel.

Lamoreaux, J. C. 1992. An Unedited Tract against the Armenians by Theodore Abū Qurrah. *Mus* 105:327–41.

———. 2005. *Theodore Abū Qurrah*. LCE 1. Provo, Utah: Brigham Young University Press.

Lampe, G. W. H. 1969. *A Patristic Greek Lexicon*. Oxford: Oxford University Press.

Laurent, J. 1980. *L'Arménie entre Byzance et l'Islam depuis la conquête arabe jusqu'en 886*. Rev. ed. M. Canard. Lisbon: Bertrand.

Lehmann, H. J. 1975. *Per Piscatores: Studies in the Armenian Version of a Collection of Homilies by Eusebius of Emesa and Severian of Gabala*. Åarhus: Odder.

Mahé, A., and J.-P. Mahé. 2012. *Histoire de l'Arménie: Des origins à nos jours*. Paris: Perrin.

Mahé, J.-P. 1993. L'église arménienne de 611 à 1066. Pages 457–547 in vol. 4 of *Histoire du Christianisme*. Edited by J. M. Mayeur, Ch. Pietri, A. Vauchez, and M. Venard. Paris: Desclée.

———. 2000. Norme écrite et droit coutûmier en Arménie du Ve au XIIIe siècle. *TM* 13:683–705.

Maksoudian, K. 1988–89. The Chalcedonian Issue and the Early Bagratids: The Council of Širakavan. *REArm* 21:333–44.

Mariès, L. 1920–21. Un commentaire sur l'évangile de saint Jean rédigé en arabe (circa 840) par Nonnos (Nana) de Nisibe conservé dans un traduction arménienne (circa 856). *REArm* 1:273–96.

Mathews, E. G., Jr. 1998. *The Armenian Commentary on Genesis attributed to Ephrem the Syrian.* CSCO 572, 573, Scriptores Armeniaci 23, 24. Leuven: Peeters.

———. 2010. Syriac into Armenian: The Translations and Their Translators. *JCSSS* 10:20–44.

Mathews, T. F., and A. K. Sanjian. 1991. *Armenian Gospel Iconography: The Tradition of the Glajor Gospel.* DOS 29. Washington, D.C.: Dumbarton Oaks.

Metzger, B. M. 1975. *A Textual Commentary on the Greek New Testament.* London: United Bible Societies.

Muradyan, G. 2012. *Grecisms in Ancient Armenian.* HUAS 13. Leuven: Peeters.

Ortiz de Urbina, I. 1965. *Patrologia Syriaca.* Rome: Pontificium Institutum Orientalium Studiorum.

Outtier, B. 1996. À propos des traductions de l'arabe en arménien et en géorgien. *ParOr* 21:57–63.

Petrosyan, E., and A. Ter-Step'anyan. 2002. *S. Grk'i Hayeren Meknut'yunneri Matenagrut'yun.* Erevan: Hayastani Astvacašnč'ayin Ěnkerut'yun.

Pisani, V. 1966. Armenische Miszellen. *Die Sprache* 12:227–36.

Pogossian, Z. 2012. The Foundation of the Monastery of Sevan: A Case Study on Monasteries, Economy and Political Power in IX–X Century Armenia. Pages 181–215 in *Le Valli dei Monaci: Atti del Convegno internazionale di studio, Roma-Subiaco, 17–19 maggio 2010.* Edited by L. E. Pani. Spoleto: Fondazione Centro italiano di studi sull'alto Medioevo.

Pummer, R. 2002. *Early Christian Authors on Samaritans and Samaritanism.* Tübingen: Mohr Siebeck.

Sanjian, A. K. 1966. *Crazatik* Erroneous Easter—A Source of Greco-Armenian Religious Controversy. *StCauc* 2:26–47.

Sargisean, B. 1897. *Dei Tesori patristici e biblici conservati nella letterature armena: Memoria.* Venice: San Lazzaro.

Stone, M. E. 1989. An Armenian Epitome of Epiphanius's *De Gemmis. Harvard Theological Review* 82:467–76.

———. *Armenian Apocrypha relating to Adam and Eve.* Leiden: Brill.

Swanson, M. N. 2007. Apologetics, Catechesis, and the Question of Audience in "On the Triune Nature of God" (Sinai Arabic 154) and Three Treatises of Theodore Abū Qurrah. Pages 113–34 in *Christians and Muslims in Dialogue in the Islamic Orient of the Middle Ages.* Edited by M. Tamcke. Beiruter Texte und Studien 117. Beirut: Orient-Institut.

Ter-Ghewondyan, A. 1976. *The Arab Emirates in Bagratid Armenia.* Translated by N. G. Garsoïan. Lisbon: Calouste Gulbenkian Foundation.

Terian, A. 2008a. *The Armenian Gospel of the Infancy.* Oxford: Oxford University Press.

———. 2008b. *Macarius of Jerusalem: Letter to the Armenians, AD 335.* AVANT 4. Crestwood, N.Y.: St. Vladimir's Seminary Press.

Thomson, R. W. 1962. *Vardapet* in the Early Armenian Church. *Mus* 75:367–84.

———. 1965. The Transformation of Athanasius in Armenian Theology. *Mus* 78:47–69.

———. 1975. The Maccabees in Early Armenian Historiography. *JTS* 26:329–41.

———. 1976. Number Symbolism and Patristic Exegesis in Some Early Armenian Writers. *HA* 90:117–38.

———. 1986. Muhammad and the Origin of Islam in Armenian Literary Tradition. Pages 829–58 in *Armenian Studies in Memoriam Haïg Berbérian.* Edited by D. Kouymjian. Lisbon: Calouste Gulbenkian Foundation.

———. 1987. *The Armenian Version of the Works attributed to Dionysius the Areopagite.* CSCO 488, 489, Scriptores Armeniaci 17, 18. Leuven: Peeters.

———. 1994. *Studies in Armenian Literature and Christianity.* Variorum Collected Studies 451. Aldershot: Variorum.

———. 1997. *Indices to the Armenian Version of Pseudo-Dionysius the Areopagite: Greek-Armenian and Armenian-Greek.* DSALL 5. Amsterdam: Rodopi.

———. 2000. *The Lawcode [Datastanagirk'] of Mxit'ar Goš.* DSALL 6. Amsterdam: Rodopi.

———. 2001. *The Teaching of Saint Gregory.* Rev. ed. AVANT 1. New Rochelle, N.Y.: St. Nersess Armenian Seminary.

———. 2006. Is There an Armenian Tradition of Exegesis? *SP* 41:97–113.

———. 2010. *The Lives of Saint Gregory: The Armenian, Greek, Arabic, and Syriac Versions of the "History" attributed to Agathangelos.* Ann Arbor, Mich.: Caravan.

———. 2012. *Saint Basil of Caesarea and Armenian Cosmology.* CSCO 646, Subsidia 130. Leuven: Peeters.

———. Forthcoming. Arabic in Armenia. *TM.*

———. Forthcoming. Armenian Traditions concerning the Writing of the Gospels. *St. Nersess Theological Review.*

Toumanoff, C. 1990. *Les dynasties de la Caucasie chrétienne.* Rome: Grafimex Italia - Padova.

van Roey, A. 1949. *Nonnus de Nisibe: Traité apologétique; Étude, texte et traduction* Bibliothèque du Muséon 21. Leuven: Bureaux du Muséon.

Index of Biblical Citations and Allusions

Biblical books are listed here in the standard English order, not that of the Armenian Bible. However, the numbering of the Armenian text has been followed; where this differs from standard English (especially in the Psalms), the English number is given in parentheses. A reference to a note may refer to the notes following each section of the commentary or to the notes at the foot of each page. Page numbers are not given for the individual lemmata.

John (cont.)

General Index

Names that introduce biblical quotations or are mentioned within them are not listed. Entries are in English alphabetical order, disregarding diacritical marks.

Aaron 54
Abgar, king 275
Abram, Abraham 16, 32, 74n, 77, 80, 85, 163, 185n, 187–89, 193–199, 232, 297, 362, 395n, 442
Abū Qurrah. *See* Theodore Abū Qurrah
Abū Ra'ita xviii, xlv
Adam xxix, xxxiv, xlii, 10, 29, 37, 50, 54, 61, 66, 102, 106, 146, 190, 197, 200–201, 261n, 282, 301, 401, 403, 406, 413, 414n, 415, 422; skull of at Golgotha, 395
Aētios 316n
Agadron 127n
Agat'angełos xviv, 280
Amida [Diyarbekir] xxi, xxiv, 442
Al-Mahdi, caliph xliii
Al-Mutawwakil, caliph xliv
Amalek 21, 406
Anania of Širak 19n
Andrew 31n, 32, 125, 276, 429n
angels passim in commentary
Antioch xxx
Antiochus 47n, 228n
Apostles passim in commentary; "the Twelve," 152, 154–56, 408n
Arabs 221n
Arčēš 249n
Architect [i.e., God] 224
Arians, Arius xl, 9, 195, 315, 326n, 358n
Armenia, Armenians passim in introduction, 239, 340n, 404n, 411n

Ašot Bagratuni, prince of Taron xviii, xliii–xlv,
Assyrians 185n
Athanasius 18n
Ayrivank' xxiv

Babylon xxxi, 47n, 185
Babylonians xxxi, 185n, 187
Bagrat Bagratuni xix–xxi, xli, xliv, 3,
Basil of Caesarea 11n, 12n, 404n
Bedhezda [*Propatikē* pool] 97
Belial 238
Bet'abra xxvii, 26, 249n
Bet'ania, Bethany xxvii, 26, 240, 243, 247, 249, 267, 382n
Bethel 81n
Bethlehem 33, 34, 172
Borborites 341n
Buzandaran 383n
Byzantium, Byzantines xvii

Caesar 383, 384, 390, 392, 393
Caesarea [in Anatolia] xxiii, xxiv
Caiaphas 377, 378, 381
Cain 190n, 255n
Č'amčean, Mik'ayēl xlv
Cana xxvii, xxvi, xxxiii, 6, 30, 42n, 158, 273
Capernaum xxviii, 43, 92, 101, 128
catholic church 237, 238, 407
Chalcedon, council of xvii, xviii, xliv
Chalcedonians 105

CPSIA information can be obtained at www.ICGtesting.com
Printed in the USA
BVOW07s0411040914

364597BV00011B/7/P